THE
NEW
SETTLEMENT
COOKBOOK

THE
NEW
SETTLEMENT
COOKBOOK

Edited by
Charles Pierce

SMITHMARK

This edition published in 1997 by
SMITHMARK Publishers
a division of US Media Holdings, Inc.
16 East 32nd Street,
New York, NY 10016

SMITHMARK books are available for bulk purchase for sales,
promotion, and premium use. For details, write or call
the manager of special sales, SMITHMARK Publishers
16 East 32nd Street, New York, NY 10016; (212) 532-6600

This book is printed under special agreement with
Simon & Schuster
1230 Avenue of the Americas
New York, NY 10020

ISBN: 0-7651-9310-8

Printed in the United States of America

10 9 8 7 6 5 4 3 2 1

THE HEIRLOOM

Heirloom recipes are cherished treasures from old traditions that salute the heritage of *The Settlement Cookbook*. Some have been adapted to reflect a trend toward lighter, healthier eating. Others have been left intact and are, in fact, timeless.

THE FOOD PROCESSOR

The food processor can be used to save time and energy. This symbol indicates that it is particularly practical at this point in the recipe. We suggest using the food processor judiciously even though it is one of the most important kitchen appliances for today's modern home. There are times when a simple grater or a good, sharp knife can be just as effective as the processor, for example.

THE MICROWAVE

The microwave is an increasingly important part of the kitchen. This symbol is used to inspire the reader to make the most of its timesaving and efficient means of food preparation. Become familiar with your particular appliance to ensure best results.

CONTENTS

ACKNOWLEDGMENTS

My sincere thanks to the women of the board of the Settlement Cookbook Company in Milwaukee, who have carried a glorious heritage one step further. Also I extend my heartfelt appreciation and thanks to Kerri Conan. Her vision, persistance, humor, and gentle nudging guided me deftly through the entire process of this revision. Also, a special word of gratitude goes out to the following few folks who walked down this path with me: Carole Lalli, who got the ball rolling before rolling away; Jan Newberry, whose assitance was invaluable; Karen Holden, for all of her help; Paul Rankin, Fran Lanier, and Tina Ujlaki, who tasted, helped, advised, and held my hand. Most importantly, to Eligal, without whom this work would not be possible, and WFA, who makes it all worthwhile.

—C.P., 1991

GENERAL INTRODUCTION

The Settlement Cookbook is an American classic. Its unique heritage tells the story of our country's woven tapestry rich in immigration and cultural adaptation.

The latter part of the nineteenth century saw a large number of immigrants migrating to many parts of the American Midwest. Milwaukee received its share of newcomers, mostly from eastern Europe. To help them learn about American life and American ways, a committee of community-active ladies established classes in English, a Keep Klean Mission, sewing instruction, and cooking lessons. Among the committee members, Mrs. Simon Kander was in charge of cooking classes. She worked diligently to provide the large group of students with information about American foods, proper nutrition, sanitation in cooking, and economy of meal preparation.

Most of the pupils were of high school age, working in after-school hours. The children spent much of their valuable time copying the simple recipes devised for them. The committee in charge felt that printed lessons would help solve this problem. Also, there was often opposition from the students' parents to the "new ways." Having the recipes in print might add dignity and importance to the endeavor in the eyes of the immigrant parents.

By this time all the activities had been coordinated within an organization called The Settlement. Mrs. Kander's committee directed a request for eighteen dollars to print the recipes. The gentlemen of the Board turned it down as an "unnecessary expense."

The women decided to have the recipes printed themselves. With the help of a friendly printer and solicited advertising to help defray expenses, the financial crisis was solved. Treasured recipes of some of the committee members and foreign dishes contributed by families of the students were collected and put into a cohesive manuscript.

In 1901, a cookbook was born. It consisted of 174 pages including the advertisements, and was divided into two sections. One contained simple recipes for the classes, the other included the heirloom recipes which were generally more elaborate. The first printing was 1,000 copies. Some were given to the students, some were saved for future use, and a Milwaukee merchant volunteered to sell the rest at fifty cents each. To everyone's astonishment, the supply was soon exhausted. In 1903, the ladies published a second and enlarged edition. This time 1,500 copies were printed. So began the growth of this book which has to date sold more than two million copies.

When the gentlemen of the board turned down the request for eighteen dollars to cover the printing expenses in 1901, they did nevertheless give the project their blessing and laughingly added that The Settlement would "be happy to share in any profits."

As it turned out, the benefits to The Settlement were immediate. The proceeds of the first two editions enabled the committee to purchase the site for the new Settlement House. The Settlement Cook Book Company was soon established and funds were generated to provide useful educational and recreational projects for the city of Milwaukee. Scholarships, nursery schools, and day-care centers, as well as English classes and other philanthropic activities have long been provided by the monies realized from these auspicious beginnings.

The New Edition

Revising a cookbook of this magnitude has been a happy challenge. The goal has been to retain the charm while making the book a more useful tool for modern homemakers. Information and recipes that no longer serve the reader have been deleted. Additions that have been made do not directly replace this information but introduce methods and ingredients relevant to today's household management. Heirloom recipes have been especially valued. Many appear in this edition and have been noted.

The emphasis in this revision is centered on basic techniques. Roasting, broiling, frying, and baking are executed by a series of easy-to-learn rules. Once the concept has been mastered, the more creative process of expanding into variations comes naturally. A classic roast chicken can be enhanced by the addition of any combination of ingredients to provide texture and extra flavor, for example. This formula has been followed throughout the new edition in keeping with the origins of *The Settlement Cookbook*. Cooking classes needed the guidelines provided by the printed page. We find this method of technique and variation as viable today as when Mrs. Kander put together the first few pages in 1901.

New appliances and kitchen machinery have had a tremendous impact on today's kitchen life. Food processors, microwave ovens, blenders, pasta-making machines, mixers with dough hooks, as well as electric fryers, ice-cream machines, and instant bread cookers are becoming standard equipment in many new homes. We've done our best to include references to and suggestions of ways to use this equipment sensibly. We try not to encourage depending on machines to do many tasks that are more logically performed by hand. Gadgets often give only the illusion of saving time and energy.

The food processor especially has had a huge impact on modern cooking. We've incorporated the use of this handy tool wherever it might be most useful. We urge its use and have made frequent references to the machine both in the text of recipes and by including its symbol as explained in the legend at the front of the book.

The microwave oven has probably made more of an impact than any cooking utensil introduced in this century. Its use is widespread and will continue to become so in years to come. How to address this phenomenon *vis à vis* the project at hand has been tricky. We've included instructions on how to cook fish, meat, and poultry using the most up-to-date information possible. Because the power of machines varies, the reader will find that we have had to refer them to manufacturer's instructions for capacity setting and timing. We've hardly mentioned the microwave in baking, candy making, or many desserts, nor in the making of breads, muffins, or quick breads. These foods require very exact details for best results. We find the process of adapting classic recipes to the microwave oven outside the jurisdiction of this revision. Instead, we've made an attempt to use the microwave where applicable, if only in a very general way. For melting butter, chocolate, or shortening, it can be a timesaver. For quick reheats or for softening hard butter, boiling small amounts of water, milk, or stock in a hurry, or for defrosting, mention is made of and encouraged both in text and by using the microwave symbol described in the legend at the front of the book. We urge readers who rely heavily on the microwave oven to purchase one of the many fine publications available devoted entirely to this subject.

Emphasis on healthy eating has been a consideration when new recipes have been added. Some of the heirloom recipes have been revised to omit the unnecessary enrichments of eggs, cream, and butter. Charts and dietary guidelines have been updated to reflect new information supplied by trained nutritionists and government agencies. Stick-to-your-ribs fare has been the foundation of this book. We cannot adapt this kind of old-fashioned goodness into a diet book. However, we can urge all of our readers to use common sense. This includes making good use of information at hand proving that certain life-styles promise a longer, healthier, and happier life. While experts may disagree on details, most authorities advocate lowering our intake of fat and sugar, regular exercise, and stopping smoking to be keys to an improved quality of life.

For readers who would like to lower their cholesterol, calorie intake, or both, some easy substitutions are available:

- For heavy cream (as an ingredient, not for thinning), use equal amounts of undiluted evaporated milk.
- For light cream, use equal amounts of undiluted evaporated skim milk.
- For butter, use equal amounts of corn oil or safflower margarine. This type of margarine has the same number of calories but the amount of cholesterol is nil.
- For butter, use olive or canola oil. Again, these oils have the same number of calories but no cholesterol.
- Yogurt can be substituted for sour cream. However, yogurt will separate at high temperatures. Make this substitution with only cold preparations.
- Use Yogurt Cheese (page 104) in place of cream cheese.
- Frozen concentrate of apple juice can be used in place of sugar.

A few specifics about the revision are worth mentioning here.

- We've simply called for "butter" in the ingredient lists in the book. Many cooks prefer to use unsalted butter. We leave the choice up to the discretion of the reader. Some authorities say that unsalted butter is of better quality and has less water, which is desirable for baking. This is debatable. Industry spokespeople dispute this claim and encourage the interchangeability of the two. Most of the new recipes here were developed using unsalted butter. Be sure to take this into account when seasoning if salted butter is used.

- Yields have been a challenge in the present revision. Many of the heirloom recipes have been handed down over generations without a thought to how many people a particular dish might feed. Part of the charm of this book is that the traditional heirloom recipes have been tested in homes by non-professionals under loving but perhaps inexact conditions. The first recipes were developed in home economics classes by eager students. The yields for these recipes were for four people. This is the norm that we've assumed throughout the book. In all new recipes the yields are also for four people. In most cases, an accurate estimate has been easy to provide. Use good judgment in instances where yields do not fall into this category.

- We encourage the use of fresh herbs. They are plentiful these days. Gardeners are discovering the ease and beauty of growing them at home. Many entrepreneurial farmers are providing market places with plenty of fresh thyme, rosemary, oregano, and bay leaves to name a few. However, dried herbs are often a convenient and perfectly acceptable alternative. The usual ration for substituting is 1 tablespoon of dried herb for every 2 tablespoons of fresh. (Dried herbs become more concentrated in flavor as moisture evaporates.) Most recipes in the book give the option of dried or fresh herbs.

- Rapid-rise yeast is often used in place of traditional leavening in modern kitchens. The heirloom recipes are not adapted for the rapid-rise variety. Substitution is quite easy if this fast-action yeast is desirable. Simply follow manufacturer's instructions for best results.

- Fresh tomatoes can be found year-round today. Quality is assured only during the local growing season. Middle to late summer is the time for ripe tomatoes, depending on geographical regions and type of variety grown. Canned tomatoes are a perfectly valid choice during the remainder of the year and for cooking are a superior choice over the greenish, cotton-like texture of out-of-season ones.

  However, we discourage the use of canned vegetables, other than for tomatoes. We urge the reader to seek out sources of fresh produce where possible. When prepackaged fruits or vegetables are necessary, we find that the texture and flavor of frozen products are of better quality than canned fruits or vegetables.

- The canning section of *The Settlement Cook Book* does not appear in this revision. There have been so many changes in home processing that we could not provide accurate information in a small, condensed section. Books are available today that deal specifically with new products and pieces of equipment, as well as how to handle foods safely. A comprehensive explanation necessitates more space than we can allot to guarantee perfect results. We urge readers who wish to pursue this endeavor to seek out information in publications that deal with risk-free processing. The U.S.D.A. as well as state or county extension services provide detailed instructions and a wide array of basic recipes for the true enthusiast.

The goal of this new edition is to strike a happy balance of old and new. Working within the framework of such a fine tradition has made the task a pleasure.

BEVERAGES

A *beverage includes all drinkable liquids from a glass of water to coffee and tea, from milk to a festive punch, from an aperitif to blazing Café Brûlot. Hot or cold, sweet or sour, fluids are a necessary and important part of daily life.*

You will find recipes that have been a part of the Settlement since its inception. At first glance some do not seem well suited for today's entertaining and surely some sound old-fashioned. After all, times are changing. Coffee consumption is giving way to herbal teas; chilled white wine or champagne (sometimes with a splash of intense fruit syrup) is more commonplace than a strong cocktail; punches are rare and fruit drinks are seldom served to a crowd. There is something to be said for keeping parts of the heritage alive if only as a source for a nostalgic beverage consumed long ago in the foggy memory of someone nurtured on The Settlement Cookbook.

It is impossible to talk about today's beverages without mentioning bottled water. Ten years ago, ordering a favorite brand of bottled water instead of wine, beer, or a drink would have been unconventional for most party goers or bar patrons. From expensive mineral waters to plain club soda, with gas or without, flavored or unadulterated . . . the range is vast. For almost any social function these days, it is a good idea to have cold bottled water on hand.

Milk, coffee, tea, chocolate, and fruit drink suggestions follow. Descriptions of these beverages have been adjusted to suit the tastes of modern Settlement Cookbook readers, since the way we drink today is as different from the past as the way we eat. Lighter, less-alcoholic, and less-caloric libations are replacing traditional habits of a less-complicated yesteryear.

Milk

Milk is one of the most important foods. It contains a well-balanced protein, carbohydrate, fat, and mineral content as well as most essential vitamins.

By law, virtually all milk on the market is pasteurized today. Some desirable nutrients are lost in the process but many harmful bacteria are destroyed.

Homogenized Milk is pasteurized milk with the fat globules broken and dispersed so that they remain stable. In homogenized milk, the cream cannot rise to the top of the bottle.

Skim, Nonfat, and Lowfat Milk all contain less milk fat than whole milk, which has at least 3.25% milk fat. Examples of *skimmed* or *lowfat* milk are 1% or 2% milk. (The percentages refer to the balance of fat reserved to keep flavor and texture similar to those of whole milk.) *Nonfat* milk is guaranteed to contain no more than 0.1% milk fat.

Evaporated Milk is pure, whole milk with much of the water taken out and nothing added. It is homogenized and may or may not be enriched with Vitamin D. Evaporated milk mixed with an equal amount of water can be used in any recipe calling for milk.

Nonfat Dry Milk and Whole Dry Milk are made from skim and whole milk respectively, with just the water removed. When water is added according to the package directions, the liquid can be used in any recipes calling for milk.

Fortified Milk is pure, fresh milk to which essential vitamins and minerals have been added.

Buttermilk is the liquid that remains when butter has been churned. Cultured buttermilk is made by introducing a culture of lactic acid bacteria into skimmed or partially skimmed milk.

Cream is the fat that rises to the top of milk.

Half-and-Half is a mixture of milk and cream, about 10% milk fat.

Light Cream contains about 20% fat.

Heavy Cream (Whipping Cream) contains not less than 36% fat.

To boil milk: Bring to the boiling point. Remove from heat and cool as quickly as possible.

To scald milk: Heat milk over very low heat, or over simmering water in double boiler, until small bubbles form around the edge of the pan.

Crème Fraîche is heavy cream to which a lactic bacteria culture has been added. This gives a sharp flavor without souring the cream. Crème fraîche can take higher temperatures in cooking than sour cream, which breaks down fairly easily. Almost always imported, a substitute can be made by adding 2 tablespoons cultured buttermilk to a cup of heavy cream. Heat to 85° F and let stand in a warm spot until thickened, 12 or more hours. Refrigerate until ready to use.

Sour Cream is light cream to which a bacterial culture has been added.

Coffee

COFFEE BEANS AND THEIR CHARACTERISTICS

Choosing coffee depends on both personal preferences and on what type of preparation is used. The modern consumer is blessed with a wide array of blends and roasts that range from mild to strong. All sorts of coffeemakers abound. The following examples of beans and their characteristics might be helpful when purchasing a special coffee. Flavor is determined by the quality of the chosen coffee bean. How coffee is grown, picked, and processed makes a difference in the end product. Some of these procedures are described below.

In response to consumer demands, decaffeinated coffee is available in virtually every form from the whole bean to the freeze-dried crystal. Due to a process that uses water rather than harsh chemicals to eliminate caffeine in the bean, a purer product is increasingly available. New methods can provide the same full flavor without the potential harms associated with caffeine.

Lighter blends are best for general purposes and darker ones preferred for demitasse and espresso-type drinks. Many specialty food stores have their own special blend of beans and roasts that offer good quality for the price. Store coffee in a dry, cool area. Both whole beans and ground coffee will keep indefinitely in the freezer. Whole beans ground at the last minute is the best way to ensure fresh flavor.

Brazilian: Much of Brazilian coffee is of low quality. Grown and processed under crude methods, the beans are often used in making blends. The best bean grown there is called Santos. Stick to this one for good results.

Colombian: Beans from Colombia make a rich, full-bodied cup of coffee. Colombian coffee beans have a good balance of acidity, mellow body, and excellent flavor.

Costa Rican: These beans make a strong, aromatic, and robust cup of coffee. Often of top quality, Costa Rican coffee is favored by Europeans.

Haitian: Coffee from Haiti can be rich and mildly sweet. Musty and poor in the lowlands, full-bodied and flavorful in the higher hills, Haitian coffees vary a great deal.

Jamaican Blue Mountain: Subtle and exquisite, the genuine beans from the jungles of the Blue Mountain area can be among the finest in the world. Widely sought after for its delicacy, it is expensive due to limited production.

Java: Java includes almost all Indonesian coffee. Sharp but with low acidity, good-quality Java coffee is difficult to find.

Kenya: Good Kenyan beans grown in the highlands make excellent coffee. Lower-quality Kenyan coffee can be acid with a piercing flavor. Look for Kenya AA, a designation that guarantees it to be from the highlands.

ROASTS AND THEIR CHARACTERISTICS

Green coffee beans are roasted after picking and fermentation. The process used has a direct effect on taste. Some of the more common roasts and their characteristics follow. Try experimenting with a few to find a roast that is pleasant and full of character for your purposes.

Light: This roast enhances acidity in coffee and produces a thin-flavored brew.

Medium-High: A bit darker than Light but not as dark as City roast.

City or Regular: This is the most popular roasting style in the country. It makes coffee richer than Light but the taste of coffee roasted this way may be slightly flat.

Full City: Slightly darker than City, it produces a deep, hearty brew.

Brazilian: This roast is a bit darker than Full City with a hint of dark-roasted flavor.

Vienna: This type is roasted midway between Full City and French. It is rich, spicy, and full-bodied.

French or Dark: This makes a slightly oily bean and has a burnt umber color. Its flavor is sweet and smooth.

Spanish or Cuban: Darker than French with a taste approaching Espresso without the bite.

Italian or Espresso: Black and oily, this roast has a bitter, caramelized flavor.

Turkish: Darkest of all roasts with little acidity and a strong flavor.

COFFEE PREPARATION

Coffeemakers come in a variety of models. Along with the traditional drip, percolated, and vacuum-style examples come a staggering array of new electric machines that can perform various functions. Some can be programed the night before to start at a certain time the next morning. Some can replicate the intensity of that found in European cafés. Others make as little as one cup and some make enough for large crowds. Each machine comes with its own set of instructions that should be followed carefully.

BASIC PROPORTIONS TO MAKE COFFEE

For One Serving (5½ ounces)

¾ cup water (6 ounces)   2 level tablespoons coffee

For Four Servings

3 cups water   8 level tablespoons coffee

For Eight Servings

6 cups water   16 level tablespoons coffee

Notes: Plastic coffee measures equal 2 level tablespoons. If using unusually large or small cups, check the liquid content and adjust the above proportions accordingly.

Drip Coffee

Scald coffeepot with very hot water. Place fine grind coffee in filter cup of coffeepot. Add boiling water gradually and allow it to filter or drip.

Percolated Coffee

When using a percolator, put freshly boiled or cold water in bottom and regular grind coffee in top compartment. Cover coffeepot. Place over heat (or plug in) and perk 5 to 10 minutes, counting from the time that the water begins to bubble up in the glass top. The percolator should never be less than half full.

Vacuum-Style Coffee

Measure fresh cold water into lower bowl. Put on heat. Put filter in upper bowl and fill with extra-fine grind coffee. When water boils, reduce heat and insert upper bowl with slight twist. Let most of the water rise to upper bowl. Stir thoroughly; let stand until brew returns to lower bowl.

Espresso

Espresso is made by using steam to extract a powerful, concentrated coffee from a fine grind. Machines vary from sophisticated European espresso makers to small, simple contraptions suited for home use. Follow manufacturer's instructions for best results.

Basic Grinds	*Use In*
Regular	Percolator
Fine (Drip)	Drip Maker
Extra Fine (Espresso)	Espresso Machine or Vacuum Maker

TO MAKE COFFEE

CAFÈ ESPRESSO

Brew coffee double strength or in a machine made expressly for this type of coffee. Serve in demitasse cups or 4-ounce glasses, with sugar and a twist of lemon peel. Serve after dinner.

CAPPUCCINO

Brew coffee double strength or in a machine made expressly for this type of coffee. Serve in cups with an equal volume of hot, but not boiled, milk. (Follow manufacturers' instructions for heating milk in an espresso coffeemaker.) Top with whipped cream, grated orange rind, or a dusting of cocoa. Serve with pastries.

VIENNESE COFFEE

Pour hot, freshly brewed regular coffee and hot but not boiled milk into a cup simultaneously, so that the mixture froths. Serve at breakfast.

ICED COFFEE

 1

Prepare regular coffee and add sugar to taste. Chill. When ready to serve, add to each quart of coffee ½ cup of cream and pour into pitcher. Serve in tall glasses.

2

Prepare regular coffee, add sugar, and chill. Have ready a bowl of sweetened whipped cream or vanilla ice cream, and serve coffee in tall glasses, placing 1 rounded tablespoon of either on top of each glass.

3

Pour freshly made strong coffee into tall glasses filled with ice cubes made of coffee. Serve with cream and sugar.

Tea

BASIC TYPES OF TEA

As consumption of coffee is decreasing, thirst for a lighter, healthier beverage like tea is increasing. With the rising interest comes a marketing blitz that provides the consumer with as wide an array of teas as there are coffee beans and roasts.

Tea made from the tea plant contains caffeine. Herbal teas are good substitutes for those who wish to avoid caffeine but enjoy the flavor of a brewed, hot beverage.

There are three types of caffeinated teas:

Black tea is fermented and accounts for the vast majority of teas consumed in the United States.

Green tea is best known in the East and among Muslims who are prohibited from drinking fermented tea.

Oolong tea is made from semifermented leaves and is graded according to quality, which varies from season to season.

Here are the basic tea families and their categories.

BLACK TEAS

Darjeeling comes from India and is considered the finest of teas. Quality varies according to growths and seasonal attributes. The purest of leaves can be quite expensive. Some Darjeeling is blended with lesser-quality leaves to increase sales. Generally fruity, the flavor can vary according to soil, season, and weather.

Assam is strong and full of character. The leaves are large and well formed.

Ceylon is intensely flavored and flowery.

Lapsang Souchong is smoky and strong. It is usually blended with other varieties to round out its sharp-edged quality.

GREEN TEAS

Gunpowder is bitter and has a yellowish hue. It should steep for only a minute or two.

Bancha is a common Japanese tea that is characteristically thin flavored.

OOLONG TEAS

Black Dragon usually refers to any semifermented teas that have a taste of half black tea and half green tea. It has a refined, sophisticated taste of a somewhat exotic nature.

Jasmine is a scented tea usually blended with a stronger selection of hearty leaves from another variety.

BLENDS

Many of the better-known blends like English Breakfast and Earl Grey are good choices for all-purpose uses. These are mixtures of mostly black teas that are generally reliable for the average shopper.

Herbal teas have been brewed from herbs, roots, vines, twigs, flowers, and even bark for centuries. Infusions, tisanes, and teas have been used as stimulants and restoratives that have been known to cure afflictions from impotency to constipation. Long considered savage and particular to uncivilized tribes from remote corners of the world, herbal teas have recently found their place in today's health-conscious society. Anise, chamomile, mint, fennel, linden blossom, and verbena are a few examples of the range of plants used to make some of the soothing concoctions often known for their medicinal as well as their pleasurable attributes.

Commercial herbal teas are readily available and are usually of exceptional quality. Dried herbs used for seasoning in the kitchen can be made into tea as well. The rule of thumb is to use 1 teaspoon of strong herbs like thyme, sage, or rosemary per cup of water. For milder herbs like chamomile or verbena, use twice as much. Steep for 5 to 10 minutes and strain into warmed cups.

TO MAKE TEA

Heat an earthen or china teapot by rinsing it with boiling water. Then put in one teaspoon tea or one tea bag for each cup of water. Pour freshly boiled water directly on the tea leaves or tea bags and steep 3 to 5 minutes. Pour into warmed cups or mugs, straining if necessary. Serve with sugar, milk, or lemon if desired.

With Lemon or Orange

Serve tea hot with a slice of lemon or orange for each cup. Add a few whole cloves if desired.

With Preserved Fruit or Rum

Serve tea hot, allowing 1 teaspoon of rum, preserved fruit, or strawberry, raspberry, cherry, or pineapple preserves to each cup.

With Flavored Sugar

Cubes of sugar may be flavored with lemon or orange and packed and stored in jars to be used later to flavor and sweeten tea. Wash rind of lemon or orange and wipe dry. Then rub over all sides of sugar.

ICED TEA   *Makes 1 cup.*

Pour ¾ cup of boiling water over 1 teaspoon of tea or 1 tea bag. Let stand 3 minutes. Strain into a glass ¾ full of cracked ice. Serve with lemon and sugar. Or make tea usual strength using 1 cup water for each glass, steep, strain into a pitcher, and chill. Serve with ice, lemon, and sugar.

Chocolate

Nothing soothes the sensual soul like chocolate. Warm, rich, and sweet, chocolate drinks from the earliest editions of Settlement have survived changing times intact. Try reducing sugar and using lowfat milk in some of the following recipes for a healthy alternative.

CHOCOLATE SYRUP FOR DRINKS

2 cups sugar
1 quart water
4 ounces unsweetened chocolate
½ teaspoon salt

2 tablespoons cornstarch
2 tablespoons cold water
2 teaspoons vanilla

   1. Boil sugar and water 5 minutes. Add chocolate, salt, and the cornstarch dissolved in cold water. Stir until smooth. Cook over high heat for 3 minutes. Remove from heat and cool.

   2. Add the vanilla to the cooled mixture. Store in a jar in the refrigerator. Use 2 tablespoons to a glass of milk when ready to serve. Serve with or without sweetened whipped cream or ice cream.

CHOCOLATE

3 cups milk
1½ ounces unsweetened chocolate
4 tablespoons sugar

few grains of salt
1 cup boiling water
1 teaspoon vanilla

   1. Scald milk and set aside.

   2. In a small saucepan over hot water, melt the chocolate. Add the sugar, salt, and stir in boiling water gradually. Boil 5 minutes.

   3. Pour the scalded milk into the chocolate mixture. Add the vanilla. Beat with egg beater or a whisk and serve hot. Can be chilled and served with ice.

Note: If sweet chocolate is used, omit the sugar.

RUSSIAN CHOCOLATE

Follow recipe above using ½ cup milk and ½ cup cream in place of milk. Then add 2 cups hot, strong coffee just before serving. Beat well with rotary beater or a wire whisk.

RUSSIAN CHOCOLATE WITH COFFEE

chocolate syrup
chilled strong coffee
coffee ice cubes

vanilla ice cream
whipped cream

Put 2 or 3 tablespoons chocolate syrup in a glass. Fill glass with coffee and coffee cubes. Add a scoop of ice cream and top with whipped cream.

COCOA   *Makes 2 cups.*

1 cup milk   1 cup boiling water
2 teaspoons cocoa   ½ teaspoon vanilla
2 scant teaspoons sugar

    1. Scald the milk.

    2. In a saucepan, combine the cocoa, sugar, and boiling water. Bring to a boil and cook for 1 to 2 minutes. Add to the scalded milk along with vanilla.

    3. Taste and add more sugar if desired.

COCOA PASTE

½ cup cocoa   few grains of salt
2 cups boiling water   ¼ teaspoon vanilla

    1. Place the cocoa in a saucepan and gradually pour on the boiling water. Stir until cocoa is thoroughly dissolved. Boil until thick, about 3 minutes, stirring constantly. Add the salt and vanilla.

    2. Cover the mixture and keep refrigerated. For hot chocolate, add 1 cup hot milk (or milk and water combined) to 1 teaspoon of the paste. Stir until dissolved and add sugar to taste. Keeps indefinitely.

Fruit Syrups

The original Settlement book called for the following recipes to be used for making "an endless variety of drinks using fruit syrup and juices." This comes from a frugal heritage of making good use of seasonal fruits and bountiful ingredients. Sugar is a natural preservative, so why not make a sweet syrup with some of the lemons, oranges, or berries that were seasonal bumper crops? The same holds true for imported ginger and spices usually bought in bulk. The amount of sugar often sounds excessive by today's standards. Try adjusting the proportions to obtain a palatable degree of sweetness for your tastes. Keep in mind that the less sugar you use, the shorter the syrup's shelf life will be. Use nonreactive bowls, pots, and pans to prevent discoloration.

GINGER SYRUP

Pour 1 quart of water over ½ cup of grated gingerroot. Let stand undisturbed for 48 hours. Carefully pour off water into a nonreactive pan, leaving sediment undisturbed. Measure the flavored water and add an equal amount of sugar. Boil for 10 minutes. Pour into hot sterilized jars and seal. Use as a flavoring with fruit juices.

LEMON SYRUP

grated rind of 6 lemons
juice of 12 lemons

2 quarts boiling water
1 pound sugar

Add grated rind of lemons to juice and let stand overnight. Pour water over sugar and stir until sugar is dissolved. Boil for 5 minutes. Cool, then add lemon mixture. Pour into hot sterilized jars and seal. Serve with equal amount of water.

ORANGE SYRUP

Follow directions for making Lemon Syrup, above. Substitute orange juice and rind, adding a little lemon for tartness.

RASPBERRY SYRUP

2 quarts raspberries
2 pounds sugar

2 cups water

Wash berries, mash and strain through a jelly bag. Boil sugar and water to soft-ball stage, 234° F. Slowly add fruit juice and boil again. Skim, then pour into hot sterilized jars and seal.

Variation: Strawberries, black raspberries, blackberries, currants, cherries, or loganberries can be substituted.

Fruit Drinks and Punches

Cold fruit juices provide welcome relief in hot weather. Punches are good for entertaining large crowds. The following drinks can be garnished with slices of fresh fruit, sprigs of mint, or simply topped with fresh berries for a festive touch.

ADES

FRESH FRUIT LEMONADE   *Makes 1 drink*

4 tablespoons sugar   2 cups water
juice of 1 lemon

Add the sugar to lemon juice and water. Stir until dissolved. Add crushed ice if desired.

PICNIC LEMONADE   *Makes 4½ quarts*

Sweeten juice of 12 lemons with 1 pound of sugar. Add grated rind of 2 lemons, put in quart jar, and seal. When ready to serve, add 4 quarts of ice water.

LEMONADE FOR 150 PEOPLE

The original Settlement book says that "The rule is 1 pound of sugar to every dozen of fruit." For a more tart lemonade that is refreshing and not so cloyingly sweet, try using half the amount of sugar.

5 dozen lemons, squeezed   1 fresh pineapple, peeled, cored,
6 pounds sugar   and chopped
1 dozen oranges, sliced   6 gallons water
                                     cracked ice

1. In a nonreactive pot, combine the lemon juice and sugar. Bring to a boil and let stand to cool.
2. Combine the lemon-and-sugar syrup with the orange slices and pineapple. Pour in the water and a generous amount of cracked ice.

ORANGEADE   *Makes 1 drink.*

4 tablespoons sugar   juice of ½ lemon
juice of 2 oranges   1½ cups water

Add sugar to liquid. Stir until dissolved. Chill and serve over cracked ice.

LIMEADE   *Makes 1 drink.*

½ glass cracked ice   1 tablespoon sugar
juice of 3 limes   ice water

In glass with cracked ice, place lime juice and sugar. Fill with ice water, stir, and garnish with thin slices of lime if desired.

LEMON SODA   *Makes 1 drink.*

2 tablespoons sugar   ice water
juice of 1 lemon   ¼ teaspoon soda

Mix sugar and lemon juice. Add cold water and fill glass ¾ full. Briskly stir in the soda and serve at once.

RASPBERRYADE

1 pint Raspberry Syrup (page 25)   4 pints water

Place ice in pitcher or bowl. Add syrup and water. Stir until well mixed and serve. Will make 20 punch servings.

FRUIT PUNCHES

FOUNDATION FOR PUNCH

1 cup sugar   1 cup orange juice
1 quart water   grated rind of ½ orange
½ cup lemon juice   grated rind of 1 lemon

Cook sugar and water for 5 minutes. Cool completely. Add fruit juices and grated rinds. Chill until ready to use and add any of the following combinations:

Ginger Punch

1 quart ginger ale   ¼ cup preserved ginger, cut into
                                     fine slivers

Pineapple Punch

1 cup grated pineapple   1 quart carbonated water

Raspberry Punch

1 pint raspberry juice   1 quart carbonated water

Grape/Ginger Punch

1 quart grape juice   1 quart carbonated water
1 quart ginger ale

Grapefruit Punch

1 quart grapefruit juice and pulp   1 quart ginger ale

Berry Punch

strained, sweetened juice of 1 quart   1 quart raspberries
  strawberries

Cider/Grape Punch

1 quart cider   1 quart ginger ale
1 quart grape juice

FRUIT PUNCH FOR 50 PEOPLE

1 cup water   juice of 5 oranges
2 cups sugar   1 cup grated pineapple
1 cup strong tea   1 quart chilled club soda or bottled
2 cups strawberry syrup (see   seltzer
  Raspberry Syrup, page 25)   1 cup maraschino cherries (optional)
juice of 5 lemons

1. Combine water and sugar in a saucepan. Bring to a boil over high heat. When sugar is dissolved, cook for 10 minutes. Remove from heat.

2. In a large serving bowl, combine the sugar syrup with the tea, strawberry syrup, lemon juice, orange juice, and pineapple. Let stand for ½ hour.

3. Strain and add the chilled club soda or seltzer and enough cold water to make 2 gallons. Stir in cherries if desired.

TEA PUNCH

1 tablespoon tea leaves   juice of 1 orange
2 cups boiling water   1 quart club soda or bottled seltzer,
2 cups sugar   chilled
juice of 1 lemon   fresh mint for garnish (optional)

Place tea in a large, nonreactive, heat-proof pitcher. Pour on the boiling water. Cover well and let steep for 5 minutes. Strain. Add the sugar and fruit juices. Cool and serve, adding ice and chilled carbonated water. Garnish with sprigs of fresh mint if desired.

CRANBERRY PUNCH

1 quart cranberries
4 cups water
2 cups sugar

juice of 2 lemons
juice of 2 oranges
2 quarts bottled seltzer or club soda, chilled

Cook cranberries in water until soft. Strain through a jelly bag. Add sugar and bring to boiling point. Remove from heat. Add the lemon and orange juice. Place in a punch bowl with ice. Pour in the club soda or seltzer and serve.

WISCONSIN PUNCH

2 cups sugar
1 quart water
3 quarts grape juice
juice of 12 lemons

juice of 3 oranges
32 ounces pineapple juice, bottled or canned
3 quarts club soda or bottled seltzer, chilled

In a large, nonreactive saucepan, combine the sugar and water. Bring to a boil. Cook over high heat until sugar is dissolved and consistency is syrupy. Cool. Add the fruit juices and place in a large punch bowl over a large block of ice. Pour in the carbonated water and serve.

WINE PUNCHES

WASHINGTON PUNCH FOR 12 PEOPLE

1 cup sugar
2 pineapples, peeled, cored, and sliced
½ bottle Moselle wine
2 bottles Rhine wine

1 bottle claret (hearty dry red wine)
large block of ice
1 quart champagne

Sprinkle the sugar over one of the pineapples. Add the half bottle of Moselle wine and let stand for 24 hours. Strain. Add the Rhine wine, the claret, and the remaining pineapple. Place over ice in a punch bowl and just before serving add the champagne.

CHAMPAGNE PUNCH

1 quart Lemon Ice (see page 644)
1 quart champagne, chilled

1 pint club soda or bottled seltzer, chilled

Place Lemon Ice in punch bowl. Stir in the champagne and the carbonated water. Serve when ice is melted.

CLARET CUP

3 pints claret (dry red wine)
½ cup Curaçao
juice and rind of 3 lemons
½ cup sugar
1 bunch fresh mint sprigs

1 orange, thinly sliced
12 strawberries
1 small pineapple, peeled, cored, and sliced
1 pint club soda or bottled seltzer, chilled

Mix all ingredients except carbonated water. Chill and just before serving pour in the chilled soda.

EGGNOGS

VIRGINIA EGGNOG

6 eggs, separated
1¼ cups sugar
1½ quarts cream

1 pint rye whiskey
1 jigger of rum
nutmeg

Beat yolks with 1 cup sugar. Add cream and whiskey and rum alternately. Season with ground nutmeg. Beat the whites of the eggs stiff adding ¼ cup sugar. Drop this on top of mixture in bowl. Dust top with nutmeg. Chill.

KENTUCKY EGGNOG   *Yields 80 servings.*

3 dozen eggs, separated
3 cups sugar
1 pint whiskey
1 gallon heavy cream

1 pint rum
1 pint gin
1 pint brandy

1.   Beat yolks of eggs until very light. Beat the whites stiff. Add 1 cup of sugar to the whites and beat well to mix.

2. Add the remaining sugar to the yolks and beat until thick and lemon colored. Combine the mixtures lightly. Slowly add the whiskey.

3. Whip the cream and add it to the above mixture alternately with the rum, gin, and brandy. If mixture is too thick, thin to desired consistency with rich milk. Beating makes it smooth and prevents separating.

EGGNOG WITH COOKED EGGS   *Makes about 2 quarts.*

Uncooked eggs are a questionable ingredient these days (see page 86). For a holiday nog with cooked eggs, try the following recipe.

1 quart milk	1 teaspoon vanilla
6 eggs	1 cup heavy cream, whipped
¼ teaspoon salt	ground nutmeg for garnish
½ cup sugar	

1. Heat milk in a large saucepan until hot but not boiling.

2. In a large bowl, beat together eggs and salt. Stir in the sugar. Gradually pour in the hot milk. Transfer the mixture back to the large saucepan and cook on medium heat until the mixture thickens and coats a spoon (thermometer should reach 160° F). Stir in the vanilla. Cool completely. Cover and refrigerate until thoroughly chilled, several hours or overnight.

3. Pour into a large serving bowl. Fold in the whipped cream and garnish with a dusting of freshly ground nutmeg.

Wine

Wine can make the simplest meal a memorable one. The experience of others has taught us certain facts about the relationship between wine and food from which we can benefit. Choosing wine is very personal, however, and you should always serve and drink the wine that most pleases you and your guests.

There are some guidelines for choosing the right wine go to with a planned menu. Champagne can be served any time. It makes an excellent drink before or after a meal. It can be served with fish, chicken, veal, or some pork just like a dry white wine. Dry fortified wines like Madeira, port, and some sherries have an appetizing quality that makes them especially good at the beginning of the meal. Sweet fortified wines can be served either before or after a meal, depending on preference. Fish, seafood, and light meats are best accompanied by a white, dry wine or a young, chilled red wine. Hearty red meats strong in flavor like beef and lamb need heavy-bodied red wines to bring out their best character. Sweet wines are reserved for use with ripe fruit or desserts. If more than one wine is to be served during a meal, the rule is to proceed from the lightest, driest wine to the richest and heaviest.

Champagne, sweet wines, and white wines should be served chilled. Lighter red wines like Beaujolais, California gamay, simple French country wines like the red wine from the Touraine, and even some light wines made from Pinot Noir are actually best when served slightly chilled. Hearty red wine should be served at cool room temperature (about 60° F) for greater aroma and flavor.

An all-purpose wine glass can take the place of the different sizes and shapes once thought necessary. It should be tulip-shaped, and have a capacity of 8 ounces. Wine glasses should be no more than half filled, leaving an air space where the bouquet can be concentrated.

Store wine in a wooden or metal rack that holds the bottles at a slant. This keeps the cork from drying out and shrinking, which would admit air to the bottle and spoil the wine. Keep wine stored in a dry, cool area. The custom of having the host first pour a little wine into his own glass to taste before serving others should be observed. It can prevent the embarrassment of offering a "corky" wine to guests.

WINES WITH FOODS

While not as rigid as yesteryear, there are some rules for choosing wine that are useful. The following suggestions are not strict edicts, just recommendations. Choose a wine that you like in a price range to suit your pocketbook.

Appetizers

Entre-Deux-Mers, Muscadet, Aligoté; most standard white Italian wines; California Chenin Blanc and French Colombard; Portuguese Vinho Verde.

Fish

Chardonnays, Riesling, Gerwürztraminer, Pinot Gris, Sancerre, Pouilly Fumé, Graves; white Rhône wines like Hermitage Blanc and Condrieu; some superior-quality Italian white wines like Frascati, Soave Classico, and Pinot Grigio; white Rioja from Spain.

Poultry, Veal, and Pork

Most of the wines suggested for fish (above) can go well with white meats. A rounder, more mature white wine will go best with most sautéed, roasted, or broiled poultry, veal, or pork. Choose a lighter, younger, and more acidic white that will cut the richness of creamy dishes. Slightly chilled light red wines like young burgundy and Bordeaux, Beaujolais (Gamay) and young Rhône wines can be served as well.

Beef and Lamb

Choose full-flavored, powerful reds for most beef and lamb dishes. Château or estate-bottled Bordeaux and Burgundy of exceptional vintage are reliable. Older Rhône Valley wines like Hermitage and Châteauneuf-du-Pape are robust enough to match up to some red meat. Italian Barolo and Barabresco, Brunello di Montalcino, Amarone from Valpolicella are good choices, too. California reds like Zinfandel and Cabernet Sauvignon and some Merlot are big wines suitable for most beef and lamb.

Cheese

For stronger cheeses select one of the hearty red wines suggested for beef and lamb. For milder, creamier cheese choose dry white wines suggested for fish or one of the light red wines like Beaujolais, California Gamay, light Merlot, or young Rhône wines. A good-quality rosé wine can be excellent with a hard, cooked cheese like Swiss or a mild cheddar.

Fruit and Desserts

Sauternes, Barsac, Montbazillac, and some of the sweet Muscat wines like Beaume-de-Venise are excellent with fruit, cakes, and some pastries. German Beerenausleses and Trockenbeerenausleses are outstanding sweet wines for most desserts. California sweet Muscat and Semillion wines go well with most desserts.

"KIRS" AND THE SPRITZER

"Kir" is a chilled, dry, white wine served with a splash of crème de cassis. This makes an excellent drink for aperitifs. The same black currant liqueur is mixed with champagne and called a "Kir Royale" for a more festive touch. A ligher aperitif known as a spritzer is chilled white wine mixed with a carbonated water and usually garnished with a slice of lemon or lime.

Beer

Beer is brewed from barley malts and hops. It can be light and frothy or dark and bitter, depending on the process used in fermentation. Many Americans prefer golden, clear beer to the amber, heavier dark brews popular in Northern Europe.

Beer goes well with many foods. It's great with hamburgers and hot dogs, wonderful with sandwiches, a natural accompaniment for pizza and a whole array of snacks.

As the world grows smaller, Americans are introduced to ethnic cuisines from every corner of the world. Beer is often the choice for some of the foods we've come to embrace. Indian curries, Chinese food, Mexican cuisine, hot Thai dishes, and even Caribbean fare are enhanced when cold beer is the beverage served alongside.

Lower calorie beer, nonalcoholic beer, dark beers and ales—imported and domestic—are now available throughout the country.

APPETIZERS

Appetizers are small portions of well seasoned foods to be served with drinks before dinner or as part of a buffet for cocktail parties. They may also function as a first course of a larger meal or the main course of a small luncheon. Some are small meals preceding the main one as suggested in the Crudité and Antipasti features on pages 54 and 56. In addition to foods prepared specifically as appetizers, many other dishes are appealing to serve as snacks, "pickups," or first courses.

Appetizers can be simple or intricate but they must always be tasty. Often they can be prepared in advance to be served either hot or cold. Not all are designed for passing around. Cold appetizers may be put at each place just before guests are seated to simplify serving. Hot hors d'oeuvres can be done in advance and reheated quickly either conventionally or in a microwave oven.

Parties have succeeded with just two great appetizers, one hot and one cold, augmented with nuts, chips, and olives. If you offer a wider variety, include some contrasting flavors and textures; try serving something crunchy and something smooth, some bland dishes and others sharp. Use leftover meats, vegetables, and even seafood. Combined with a spicy sauce or condiment, they can be perfect to serve with drinks. Serve plated appetizers in small portions that will not be too filling when a meal is to follow.

Hors d'oeuvres, canapés, finger foods, savory pastries, dips, and spreads all fall under the heading of appetizers. The following recipes will be helpful when planning your next dinner or cocktail party, or any time when a snack is in order.

Hors d'Oeuvres

An hors d'oeuvre is, by definition, "in addition to" the meal. It should stimulate the appetite and act as a harbinger of good things to come. Here they are divided into hot and cold varieties. We suggest that hot hors d'oeuvres either be passed around on a tray, served as a first course of a large meal, or become the main course of a luncheon. Cold dishes are perfect for buffets, picnics, and snacks as well.

COLD HORS D'OEUVRES

Seafood

Any cold, cooked seafood may be served as an hors d'oeuvre. Try serving crab, lobster, or shrimp with one of the cocktail sauces below or one of the mayonnaises found on page 130.

COCKTAIL SAUCE FOR SEAFOOD

½ cup tomato catsup
2 teaspoons prepared mustard
3 tablespoons lemon juice
½ cup chopped fresh parsley

1 clove garlic, finely minced (optional)
a few drops of hot pepper sauce (optional)
salt and freshly ground black pepper to taste

In a nonreactive bowl, combine all of the ingredients above. Chill well for several hours. Serve with any cooked, iced seafood.

OYSTER COCKTAIL

Place 5 or 6 small shucked oysters in each glass and top with Cocktail Sauce, above. Garnish with chopped fresh parsley.

CRABMEAT COCKTAIL

Pick through lump crabmeat to remove bones and then shred it. Mix with enough Cocktail Sauce, above, to moisten, and chill. Serve in glass dishes with fresh herbs for garnish.
   Note: Lobster can be substituted for the crab.

Charcuterie

Serving pork or offal as part of an array of cold hors d'oeuvres has long been a European tradition. Try serving terrines, pâtés, pickled meats, sliced hams, or sausages when planning your next party. We particularly like the following recipe for pâté. This is simple, flavorful, and easy to do in advance. Serve it with gherkins or pickled onions and a good, hearty bread.

EASY COUNTRY PÂTÉ   *Serves 10 to 12.*

2 whole chicken breasts, skinned
   and boned, sliced into thin strips
¼ cup fresh lemon juice
½ pound fatback or salt pork, rind
   removed and cut into cubes
2 pounds ground pork

2 eggs, lightly beaten
½ teaspoon ground nutmeg
½ teaspoon ground allspice
1 teaspoon salt
½ teaspoon freshly ground black
   pepper
1 pound thinly sliced bacon

   1.   Toss chicken breasts with lemon juice. Salt and pepper to taste. Cover and refrigerate for at least 4 hours but not more than 6 or the meat will start to disintegrate.

   2.   Preheat oven to 425° F and chill all utensils.

   3.   In the workbowl of a food processor, briefly process the fatback or salt pork to chop. Add the ground pork and process just to mix. Do not overwork the mixture or it will be tough. Add the eggs and seasonings and process just until mixed.

   4.   Line bottom and sides of a loaf pan with as much of the sliced bacon as is needed to completely cover. Leave ends to overlap. Add ⅓ of the pork mixture and top with half of the marinated chicken slices. Continue layering the pork and chicken ending with a layer of pork. Fold the overlapping ends of the bacon over the top layer of pork so that it is completely enrobed, add additional sliced bacon if necessary to cover top.

   5.   Cover with foil and bake in a water bath for 1 hour.

   6.   Remove from oven and set the loaf pan on a cooling rack. Cut a piece of cardboard to fit the inside of the loaf pan and cover it with foil. Set the board on top of the pâté and place two or three weights on it. (Weights can be heavy cans, full bottles, or any utensil that fits well.) Let cool, then refrigerate overnight, still weighted. Remove the weights but keep refrigerated until ready to serve. The pâté will be easier to slice when well chilled. Will keep for up to 5 days.

Vegetables

The best cold vegetable hors d'oeuvre for a party is a nicely done crudité as described on page 54. The following ideas are some simpler tidbits to have with drinks before dinner or as part of a cocktail party spread.

CUCUMBER APPETIZER

 Peel a large, firm cucumber. Cut into 1-inch slices and scoop out a well in each center. Put each piece on a thick slice of tomato and fill center with riced yolk of hard-cooked eggs and caviar, moistened with Mayonnaise (page 130).

STUFFED CELERY STALKS

With Cheese

Wash tender stalks of celery in cold water to crisp. Peel if desired. Cut into 2-inch pieces. Mix Roquefort cheese with a little butter. Spread mixture in grooves of celery. Or, stuff 1-inch pieces of celery stalks with cottage cheese, insert thin half slices of red radishes, red edge up, at equal distances.

With Crabmeat

Pick over 6 ounces of lump crabmeat and gently flake it apart with your fingers. Add 1 tablespoon lemon juice and 3 tablespoons Mayonnaise (page 130). Fill grooves of celery.

ARTICHOKE LEAVES AND SHRIMP

 Place chilled, boiled shrimp (page 216) on separated artichoke leaves (page 366). Top with Mayonnaise (page 130).

STUFFED CHERRY TOMATOES

Cut off the tops of cherry tomatoes, scoop out the seeds with a small melon baller, and fill. These are good with any number of fillings: chicken salad, tuna salad, fish, crab, salmon, chopped ham, or cream cheese with herbs. Garnish with chopped hard-boiled eggs or chopped parsley.

ENDIVE TIPS WITH BLUE CHEESE AND WALNUTS

Separate and wash the leaves of several heads of endive. On the thin, tip end of each leaf, place a teaspoonful of blue cheese creamed with a small amount of butter. Top with coarsely chopped walnuts. Arrange attractively on a platter and serve chilled.

Eggs

Eggs make excellent appetizers. The following are heirloom recipes that are valuable ideas for modern entertaining. Some of the best hors d'oeuvres are Deviled Eggs, found on page 88.

EGG AND TOMATO APPETIZER

2 or 3 eggs	3 large, firm, ripe tomatoes
¼ teaspoon salt	lettuce leaves
¼ teaspoon paprika	mayonnaise
onion juice	

1. Cook fresh eggs in boiling water for 12 to 15 minutes. Remove shells and, while warm, pass through ricer or food grinder. Add salt, paprika, and onion juice.
2. Pack tightly into small buttered molds or straight-sided glasses and refrigerate for 4 to 5 hours. Unmold and cut into ½-inch slices. Cut tomatoes into thick slices. Place on a lettuce leaf, top with a slice of molded egg, and cover with bottled mayonnaise.

HAM AND EGG APPETIZER

5 hard-cooked eggs	paprika
1 teaspoon chives, chopped	mayonnaise
salt	½ pound ham

Separate the yolks and whites of the eggs. Mash the yolks, add the chives, salt, and paprika and mix to a smooth paste with mayonnaise, ground ham, and egg whites. Form into balls the size of a walnut. Serve with mayonnaise.

HOT HORS D'OEUVRES

As mentioned earlier, hot hors d'oeuvres can either be passed around on a tray or served on small plates as a first course. If passed around, be sure to provide plenty of napkins and toothpicks or skewers because eating standing up can be a messy affair. We also suggest adapting other dishes like Fish Cakes (page 203), made very small and served with toothpicks; Oysters Rockefeller (page 209); and Sautéed Shrimp (page 217), for example.

SPINACH CHEESE TURNOVERS   *Makes 30 to 35 turnovers.*

2 tablespoons olive oil
1 onion, peeled and chopped
1 pound fresh spinach, washed, stemmed, and chopped, or 1 10-ounce package frozen spinach
½ pound feta cheese
3 egg yolks, beaten
¼ cup toasted pine nuts

1 tablespoon fresh chopped oregano or 1 teaspoon dried
salt and freshly ground black pepper to taste
1 pound phyllo dough, thawed if bought frozen
melted butter for brushing

1.   In a heavy skillet, heat the oil, add the onions, and cook slowly until the onions are soft but not browned. Add the spinach and cook until wilted. Let cool.

2.   In a large bowl, crumble the cheese. Add the beaten egg yolks, the cooled spinach mixture, and the nuts. Mix well.

3.   Season with oregano and add salt and pepper to taste.

4.   Preheat oven to 400° F.

5.   Gently unfold the sheets of phyllo. Using a pair of scissors, cut the sheets in half lengthwise, cutting through the entire stack at once. Keep the sheets moist by wrapping them in a damp towel. Remove one sheet of dough at a time and lay it on a large work surface. Fold the two long sides together to make a strip 2 inches wide and 12 inches long. Using a pastry brush, lightly moisten all four borders of the dough with melted butter. Place a heaping teaspoon of the spinach mixture at the bottom right-hand corner of the strip. Pick up the corner with the filling and fold it over so that it forms a right-angle triangle. Brush the dough lightly with butter again. Continue folding over from side to side into neat triangles until you reach the end of the strip, as you would fold a flag. Place on ungreased baking sheet, about 1 inch apart. Repeat for each sheet of dough. (Reserve any leftover sheets for another use.)

6.   Bake for 12 to 15 minutes, or until plump and golden. Do not turn the triangles over while baking. Serve warm.

SPICY CHICKEN LIVERS

This is a simple recipe for quick entertaining. The livers can be served with toothpicks on a tray and passed around or as a first course on individual plates. If there are any leftovers, the livers can be pureed in the food processor with a tablespoon of brandy or cognac for a tasty liver spread to go on toast points or crackers.

2 tablespoons butter
1 pound chicken livers, cut in half
salt and freshly ground black pepper
    to taste

¼ cup red wine
¼ cup chicken stock (page 59)
1 tablespoon tomato paste
1 teaspoon crushed red pepper
    flakes

1. In a medium-size skillet melt the butter. Add the chicken livers and season with salt and pepper. Sauté until the livers are light brown.

2. Remove livers from pan and keep warm. Pour wine into the skillet and deglaze the pan. Add chicken stock and over high heat reduce by half. Stir in tomato paste and pepper flakes. Return livers to the pan. Toss or stir to evenly coat and heat through. Serve warm.

SHRIMP AND PORK WONTON

1 tablespoon peanut oil
1 medium onion, peeled and
    chopped
2 ribs of celery, peeled and finely
    chopped
1 teaspoon finely chopped fresh
    ginger
½ pound ground pork
½ pound shrimp, peeled, deveined,
    and coarsely chopped

¼ cup toasted peanuts, coarsely
    chopped
2 tablespoons chopped cilantro
salt and freshly ground black pepper
    to taste
1 package wonton skins, 3 inches
    square
oil for deep-frying

1. In a heavy skillet heat the peanut oil and sauté the onion and celery until soft but not browned. Add the ginger and pork. Continue cooking over moderately high heat until pork begins to brown, stirring occasionally. Add shrimp and cook until pink and firm.

2. Remove from heat and stir in peanuts and cilantro. Salt and pepper to taste.

3. Place 1 teaspoon filling just below the center at a corner of each wonton skin. Fold corner over filling and roll toward center, leaving an inch of the opposite corner unrolled. Brush the end of the rolled skin with water. Pull the two rolled ends toward each other until the ends are connected and overlap. The finished wonton should look like a nurse's cap. Repeat until all the wontons are made.

4. Deep-fry in hot vegetable or peanut oil until crisp and brown. Drain on paper towels and serve hot.

Canapés

A canapé refers to small shapes and sizes of bread or crackers topped with a burst of flavor. They are served attractively presented on trays with drinks before a larger meal. Canapés can be fun for a party of 6 to 8 as well as for entertaining a crowd.

SMOKED SALMON WITH DILL CANAPÉS

Cut rounds from fresh white bread with a cookie cutter. Spread with softened cream cheese or butter. Top with thin slices of smoked salmon. Garnish with tiny sprigs of dill.

LOBSTER OR CRABMEAT CANAPÉS

 Chop lobster or crabmeat, add salt, cayenne, and a few drops of lemon juice, and moisten with Thick White Sauce (page 400). Spread rounds of toasted bread with this mixture. Sprinkle with Parmeasan cheese and brown in the oven.

CHICKEN LIVER AND MUSHROOM CANAPÉS

 Cook chicken livers slowly in hot chicken fat for a few minutes. Drain and pass through a sieve. Finely chop fresh mushrooms and sauté. Mix with the liver, add lemon juice, onion juice, and salt and pepper to taste. Spread on pieces of buttered toast.

CAVIAR WITH ONIONS

 To 1 part caviar add ¼ part Mayonnaise (page 130). Mix and spread on buttered toast; sprinkle with finely chopped onion.

TOMATO, CHEESE, AND ANCHOVY CANAPÉS

 Spread rounds of toasted bread with butter, then anchovy paste. Place thin slice of tomato on top, sprinkle with grated cheddar or mozzarella cheese; place under broiler until cheese is melted. Serve hot, garnished with sprigs of parsley or a coiled anchovy.

CHUTNEY AND CHEESE CANAPÉS

 Toast rounds of bread on one side, cover the other side with English Chutney (page 704), and sprinkle with grated cheddar cheese. Broil a few minutes until the cheese is melted and serve at once.

SALMON ROE

On crackers or toast rounds, place a heaping teaspoon of fresh salmon roe. Top with half a teaspoon of chilled sour cream. Garnish with finely chopped chives.

CHICKEN WITH ROASTED GARLIC

Roast whole cloves of unpeeled garlic in the oven until soft. Cool and peel. Using a fork, mash the garlic into a smooth paste and spread on rounds of toast or crackers. Top with small pieces of cooked chicken. Garnish with sprigs of fresh chervil or flat leaf parsley.

Spreads

CAMEMBERT-ROQUEFORT SPREAD

1 garlic clove	¼ pound butter
½ pound Camembert cheese	paprika
¼ pound Roquefort cheese	chopped parsley

 Rub a garlic clove along the inside of a bowl and discard. Place cheeses and butter into the bowl and blend well. Mold and chill. Unmold and sprinkle with paprika and chopped parsley.

CHEDDAR CHEESE SPREAD

Mix together ¼ pound grated cheddar cheese, ¼ teaspoon salt, a little paprika, and ½ teaspoon mustard. Add 1 tablespoon each of butter and cream and stir until smooth.

WATERCRESS CREAM CHEESE

1 3-ounce package cream cheese
½ teaspoon salt

1 tablespoon heavy cream
1 tablespoon finely chopped watercress

Mash cream cheese, season with salt, add cream and watercress. Stir until smooth.

LIVER PASTE

½ pound cooked liver (chicken or goose)
2 hard-cooked eggs
½ onion, grated

½ teaspoon salt
¼ teaspoon pepper
½ cup poultry fat

In a meat grinder, combine the liver, eggs, onion, salt and pepper. Grind several times until very fine. Alternatively, process in a food processor fitted with a metal blade until very smooth. Add the fat and mix well. Serve with toast rounds.

SMOKED FISH SPREAD

1½ pounds smoked fish, skin and bones removed
2 teaspoons minced onion
2 teaspoons finely chopped celery
1 clove garlic, minced
2 tablespoons finely chopped sweet pickle

1¼ cups bottled mayonnaise
1 tablespoon mustard
2 tablespoons chopped parsley
dash of Worcestershire sauce

Gently flake the fish apart with your hands. Mix all ingredients together and chill 1 hour before serving.

GOAT CHEESE SPREAD

 Add freshly chopped herbs to softened fresh goat cheese. Spread on crackers or small toasts. Garnish with sprigs of fresh herbs.

SHRIMP SPREAD

1 pound medium shrimp, peeled
  and deveined
1 cup butter, softened
1 small onion, finely chopped

2 teaspoons lemon juice
2 tablespoons chopped chives
salt and freshly ground black pepper
  to taste

1. Plunge shrimp into a large pot of boiling, salted water. Bring back to a boil and cook for 1 to 2 minutes. Drain shrimp and pat dry with paper towels. Cool.

2. In the bowl of a food processor fitted with the metal blade, place the shrimp. Pulse 2 to 3 times to coarsely chop. Add the butter and process until mixture is smooth and spreadable.

3. Empty into a large mixing bowl. Add the onion, lemon juice, and chives. Beat to combine with a wooden spoon. Season to taste with salt and pepper.

4. Pack the mixture into a bowl and refrigerate for 2 to 4 hours or overnight. Use to spread on toasts or crackers.

TAPENADE

1 cup pitted black olives, oil cured
6 anchovy fillets, coarsely chopped
2 tablespoons capers, coarsely
  chopped
1 clove garlic, chopped
1 tablespoon Dijon mustard

2 dried figs, quartered
juice of 1 lemon
¼ cup olive oil
freshly ground black pepper
2 tablespoons chopped fresh basil

 Place all of the ingredients, except the basil, in a food procesor fitted with the metal blade. Process until smooth. Pour into a mixing bowl and correct the seasoning to taste. Add oil to thin out if mixture is too thick. Refrigerate until ready to serve. Add fresh basil at the last moment. Serve on crackers, toasts, or fresh vegetables, like carrot or celery sticks.

Snacks

Snacks and finger foods should be small enough to swallow in one or two bites, and they must leave the fingers reasonably clean. Messier morsels should be simply pierced with toothpicks or spears. They are usually spicy and stimulating to the appetite. Try augmenting the following recipes with bowls of chips, nuts, or vegetables with dips.

STUFFED OLIVES

 Fill large pitted olives with Basic Cream Cheese Spread (page 138). Serve on toothpicks.

ASPARAGUS AND PROSCIUTTO

Spread softened butter on thin slices of prosciutto. Place blanched tips of asparagus on each one and roll tightly. Secure with toothpicks if necessary.

SMOKED SALMON AND CAVIAR CORNUCOPIA

 Roll thin slices of smoked salmon into cornucopia shape. Rice hard-cooked egg and mix with caviar. Season with lemon or onion juice and fill each cornucopia.

SNACKS IN BACON BLANKETS

With Shad Roe

Cut parboiled roe into small pieces and wrap each piece with a thin slice of bacon. Broil until crisp.

With Shrimp

 Wrap shelled and deveined shrimp in a thin slice of bacon. Broil slowly until bacon is crisp and shrimp are bright pink and firm.

With Chicken Livers

Sauté chicken livers briefly in butter. Wrap each one with a thin slice of bacon and broil until crisp.

With Prunes

 Wrap pitted prunes with a thin slice of bacon and broil until crisp.

SPICY GLAZED NUTS

½ cup pecan halves
½ cup raw cashews
¼ cup raw almonds, whole with
 skins intact
1 cup raw peanuts
½ teaspoon ground cumin

½ teaspoon ground cloves
½ teaspoon ground ginger
½ teaspoon cayenne
1 tablespoon sugar
¼ teaspoon salt
2 tablespoons peanut oil

1. Preheat oven to 250° F. On a large straight-sided baking sheet, toss nuts with the spices, sugar, salt, and oil until well coated. Spread nuts evenly across the sheet.

2. Bake until nuts are toasted through, stirring every 10 or 15 minutes. Test for doneness after 30 minutes.

3. Remove from oven. Place nuts on paper towels to cool. Sprinkle with additional salt if desired.

Dips

Dips are easy to prepare, simple to serve, and can be made in an endless variety of flavors and combinations. Use attractive trays or baskets to arrange crackers and chips. Arrange crisp vegetables or shrimp on a flat bowl or in a large bowl of ice.

Foods To Be Dipped

Crackers, potato or corn chips, bread sticks. Raw vegetables such as celery, carrot, or cucumber sticks, sliced mushrooms, radishes, cherry tomatoes in season. See page 54 for other hints. Blanched and crisped florets of cauliflower or broccoli, or strips of zucchini. Boiled shrimp, fried oysters or clams.

Base for Dips

Sour cream, cream cheese, ricotta cheese, bottled mayonnaise, or yogurt—either separately or combined—all make great bases for dips. For fragile chips that break easily make dips a thinner consistency than for vegetables or sturdy crackers.

Easy Dip Combinations

Mix a base with any combination of the following:

Cheese
Cheddar, grated
Parmesan, grated

Seafood
Boiled shrimp, peeled and chopped
Raw clams, minced
Smoked salmon, minced
Caviar or salmon roe
Crabmeat

Meat
Ham, chopped
Tongue, minced
Bacon, fried and crumbled

Relishes
Chopped olives
Pepper relish

Herbs and Other Seasonings
Scallions, thinly sliced
Garlic, roasted and peeled
Lemon, lime, or orange zest
Finely chopped thyme, rosemary, chives, chervil, parsley are good choices

SALSA CRUDA

There are excellent brands of bottled salsas on the market these days. None can match the appeal of this homemade version, full of fresh tomatoes and tender loving care. It will keep for a week or so in the refrigerator. Let it come to room temperature before serving.

2 pounds tomatoes, peeled, seeded, and coarsely chopped
1 medium red onion, diced
2 jalapeño peppers, seeded and finely chopped
1 teaspoon lime zest
1 tablespoon fresh lime juice
2 tablespoons olive oil
½ teaspoon salt
2 tablespoons coarsely chopped cilantro

In a medium bowl, combine tomatoes, onion, and jalapeños. Add zest, lime juice, olive oil, salt, and cilantro. Toss gently until thoroughly mixed. Set aside to rest and allow the flavors to blend. Serve at room temperature. The salsa can be made in advance but do not add the cilantro until just before serving.

ANCHO CHILI DIP

Ancho chilies are available in specialty food markets. They have an almost nutty flavor that mixes well with nuts and sour cream. Serve with lightly salted tortilla chips.

1 ancho chili pepper, seeded and deveined
¼ cup toasted almonds, finely ground
1 cup sour cream
1 teaspoon tomato paste

2 tablespoons coarsely chopped cilantro
salt and freshly ground black pepper to taste

 In a small bowl, cover the ancho chili with boiling water. Let soak for 30 minutes. Drain, and peel the chili. Combine all ingredients in the workbowl of a food processor fitted with a metal blade until smooth. Correct seasonings if necessary and serve.

HOT BLACK BEAN DIP

2 cups cooked black beans (page 179)
¼ cup olive oil
¼ cup lime juice
1 jalapeño, seeded, deveined, and finely chopped
2 tablespoons cilantro, coarsely chopped

1 clove garlic, peeled and finely chopped
2 scallions, white part only, thinly sliced
½ teaspoon salt

 In the workbowl of a food processor fitted with the metal blade, puree the black beans. With the motor running pour in the oil and lime juice. Scrape beans into a small mixing bowl and fold in remaining ingredients. Serve in a chafing dish over a low flame. If the dip becomes too thick, thin with tablespoonfuls of hot water as needed.

GUACAMOLE

For a smoother taste and a more authentic chunky texture, put away your food processor and make this dip by hand.

3 ripe avocados
3 tablespoons fresh lime juice
½ teaspoon salt
1 small red onion, finely chopped
1 small tomato, peeled, seeded, and finely chopped

1 clove garlic, peeled and finely chopped
1 small jalapeño, seeded, deveined, and finely chopped
1 teaspoon finely chopped cilantro

Peel and mash the avocados. Mix in the lime juice and salt. Combine with the remaining ingredients and mix well. Taste and adjust the seasoning. To store, place one of the avocado pits in the guacamole, press plastic wrap against the surface of the dip to keep it from discoloring, and refrigerate.

EGGPLANT CAVIAR

2 roasted eggplants, peeled and finely chopped
¼ cup plus 2 tablespoons olive oil
1 onion, peeled and finely chopped
1 tomato, peeled, seeded, and finely chopped

1 clove garlic, peeled and finely chopped
1 tablespoon fresh parsley, finely chopped
salt and freshly ground black pepper to taste

1. Preheat oven to 375° F.
2. Cut eggplants in half and make several gashes in the flesh with the tip of a sharp-bladed knife. Place cut side up in a large baking pan and drizzle over ¼ cup of the olive oil.
3. Cook in preheated oven until flesh is softened, about 30 minutes. Scoop out flesh and finely chop. Discard skins.
4. In a mixing bowl, evenly combine the eggplant, onion, tomato, and garlic. Slowly pour in the remaining 2 tablespoons oil and whisk continuously as if making mayonnaise. Add parsley and season with salt and pepper to taste. Store in the refrigerator.

HUMMUS

2 cups cooked chick peas (page 179)
½ cup tahini
¼ cup olive oil
½ cup lemon juice

2 cloves garlic, peeled and finely chopped
2 tablespoons finely chopped parsley

 In the workbowl of a food processor fitted with the metal blade, puree the chick peas and tahini to a rough paste. With the motor running, pour in the olive oil and lemon juice. Scrape into a mixing bowl, add garlic and parsley, and season to taste.

HERB DIP

Try this recipe with plain lowfat yogurt to save calories. Do not add herbs until just before serving.

1 cup sour cream
2 tablespoons finely chopped mixed herbs (parsley, thyme, rosemary, and chervil)

1 clove garlic, peeled and finely chopped
salt and freshly ground black pepper to taste

 In a mixing bowl, combine all ingredients until well mixed. Chill and serve.

Cocktail Pastries

CHEDDAR CHEESE STICKS   *Makes about 24 sticks.*

2 tablespoons butter
⅔ cup flour
1 cup fresh breadcrumbs
1 cup grated cheddar cheese

¼ teaspoon salt
⅛ teaspoon white pepper
pinch of cayenne pepper
2 tablespoons milk

1. Preheat oven to 325° F.
2. Cream butter, add flour, crumbs, cheese, and seasonings. Mix thoroughly, then add milk. Roll and cut in strips ¼ inch wide and 6 inches long.
3. Bake until brown, about 10 minutes.

GOUGÈRES   *Makes about 15 pieces.*

¾ cup water
¼ cup milk
¼ teaspoon salt
½ cup butter
1¼ cups sifted unbleached flour

4 eggs
1 cup grated Swiss cheese
pinch of cayenne pepper
freshly ground black pepper to taste

1.   Preheat oven to 400° F.

2.   In a medium saucepan, bring water, milk, salt, and butter to a rolling boil. Pour in all the flour at once and stir vigorously over medium heat until the mixture no longer sticks to the side of the pan.

3.   Remove from heat; cool slightly; add eggs one at a time, beating well after each addition. After all the eggs are incorporated into the batter, stir in the cheese and the seasonings.

4.   Fill a pastry bag with the dough. Press out mounds of dough about 2 inches in diameter—equal to about a tablespoonful—onto a large baking sheet lined with parchment paper or foil.

5.   Bake in the preheated oven. After 10 minutes reduce the heat to 375° F and cook until the dough is puffed and lightly browned, about 15 more minutes. The puffs will be crisp when done. Remove from baking sheet to cool.

POTATO CHEESE PUFFS   *Makes 20 to 25*

1 cup Gougères dough (see above)
1 cup mashed potatoes

salt and freshly ground black pepper
  to taste
vegetable oil for deep-frying

1.   Combine dough with mashed potatoes and season with salt and pepper.

2.   Fill a large skillet with about 1 inch of vegetable oil and heat until the oil begins to smoke. Using 2 tablespoons dipped in hot water, shape ovals of the dough and potato mixture and drop them into the hot oil. Fry until well browned, 3 to 5 minutes on each side. Drain on paper towels and serve hot.

PUFF PASTRY

Good-quality puff pastry can be bought frozen for making quick, easy, and elegant cocktail tidbits. Making your own isn't as overwhelming as it first appears. Mastering the art of preparing this versatile dough takes some practice but will be infinitely useful for all sorts of sweet and savory pastries. See page 523 for complete instructions. The following three recipes can be made up, frozen, and popped in the oven just before serving.

MATCHSTICKS   *Makes 64 1-inch pieces*

½ recipe Puff Paste (page 523)
¼ cup Dijon mustard

10 anchovy fillets, drained, patted
    dry, and trimmed into thin strips
1 egg, beaten with 1 teaspoon water

1.   Cut pastry in half. Roll out each piece to a 12-by-10-inch rectangle and cut each rectangle into 4 equal pieces. Working with 1 piece of dough at a time, roll the pastry to a rectangle ⅛ inch thick. With a ruler and a pastry wheel or sharp knife, trim the rectangle to a precise size and shape, a 4-by-8-inch rectangle.
2.   Set the dough on the work surface so that the long edge of dough is facing you. Spread 1 tablespoon of the mustard evenly over the bottom half of the pastry and place the thin strips of anchovies in an even line across the mustard.
3.   Brush edges of the pastry with egg water and fold top over to meet the bottom edge of the pastry. Gently crimp the edges with the back of a knife to seal. Repeat with the remaining quarters of pastry.
4.   With a pastry wheel or knife, cut the pastry into 8 1-inch-wide strips. Lift the matchsticks from the work surface with a spatula and place on a baking sheet, close together but not quite touching. Lightly brush with the egg water. Repeat with the remaining dough. Cover and refrigerate for 45 minutes before baking. Preheat the oven to 400° F.
5.   Bake until golden brown and completely cooked. Remove to cool on a rack. The matchsticks may be frozen before baking and go directly in the oven.

CHEESE TWISTS   *Makes 75 to 100 pieces.*

½ recipe Puff Paste (page 523)
1 egg beaten with 1 teaspoon water

1 cup grated Parmesan cheese
cayenne pepper

1.   Preheat oven to 400° F.
2.   Cut dough into 4 equal parts. Working with 1 piece at a time, roll out to a 13-by-5-inch rectangle about ⅛ inch thick.
3.   Brush the surface with a small amount of egg water. Sprinkle each quarter of dough with ¼ cup of the grated cheese. Dust with cayenne pepper.
4.   Cut into ½-inch strips. Pick up each strip and gently twist. Place each twist on an unbuttered baking sheet, pushing on the ends to adhere. Place close together without touching. Repeat with the remaining quarters of pastry.
5.   Bake until golden brown and cooked through, about 15 minutes. Watch closely as they burn quickly. Remove to cool on racks.

CHEESE "ELEPHANT EARS"   *Makes 75 to 100 pieces.*

½ recipe Puff Paste (page 523)   cayenne pepper
1 cup grated Parmesan cheese

1.   Cut dough into 4 equal pieces. Working with one piece at a time, roll out into a 12-by-10-inch rectangle. Brush the surface with water and sprinkle with 2 tablespoons of the cheese and the cayenne pepper.

2.   Fold the long edges of the dough to meet in the center. Brush again with water and sprinkle with 2 more tablespoons of the cheese. Fold in half to meet in the center. (You should have a rectangular roll that is about 2 inches in diameter.) Repeat with the remaining quarters of pastry.

3.   Cut rolls into ½-inch-wide pieces. Place cut side up on unbuttered baking sheets, about 1 inch apart. Refrigerate for 45 minutes. Preheat oven to 425° F. Bake until golden brown and cooked through, 20 to 25 minutes. Watch carefully as they burn quickly.

CRUDITÉ

Crudité, from the French word for raw, refers generally to vegetables thinly sliced, grated, or cut into small pieces and served as hors d'oeuvres.

A well-done offering of fresh vegetables is the epitome of cold hors d'oeuvres. This means more than just assembling an arrangement of raw vegetables. Take the time and trouble to select the freshest possible ingredients. Be sure to cut and trim the vegetables into a variety of suitable sizes, to blanch those that need it, and to serve a proper sauce that will enhance the flavors of these good things from the earth. Preparation can be done in advance but be careful if the platter is refrigerated. A successful crudité is served at the right temperature. The vegetables should be cool and crisp but not ice cold. Neither should they be overwarm and limp. It is the attention paid to such detail that will guarantee satisfying results.

Use your imagination to create a lavish display. Garnish large trays with exotic lettuces and leafy herbs. Hollow out a cabbage and fit in a small bowl or ramekin to hold the sauce. Fill a basket with lettuces that will support the prepared vegetables. Use hard-boiled eggs and tomatoes for garnish. Choose contrasting textures and colors for visual effect. Crudité can be served on individual plates as a first course, too. These can be done in advance, held in the refrigerator, and pulled out a half hour before serving. This makes a wonderfully light and healthful beginning to a large meal.

Use the following list to help plan the preparation for a crudité platter or first-course plate.

Asparagus: Use only when fresh ones are in season. Trim off tough ends with a vegetable peeler, leaving the tip intact. Plunge into rapidly boiling water for just a minute or two. Drain and refresh under cold running water and pat dry. Do not overcook or the spears will be limp for dipping.

Avocados: Difficult to pick up and dip, this should be included with other vegetables to be served as a first course.

Beets: Should always be fully cooked, but not mushy. Cut into thick rounds for dipping. Be careful when arranging vegetables with beets. They will bleed their color. Arrange next to other colorful vegetables like carrots or squash, away from white ones like cauliflower or green cabbage.

Boiled Potatoes: Choose very small ones (preferably red skins) and boil whole. Either cut into rounds and serve on plates with other vegetables for a first course or include, whole, in a large crudité arrangement for a party.

Broccoli: Trim into tiny florets. Peel away tough skin from stem ends. Can be quickly blanched for easier digestion. Be sure to drain well; the porous ends can hold a lot of water.

Brussels Sprouts: Choose small ones, only when very fresh. Blanch until soft but not mushy. Drain and refresh under cold running water. Serve whole or cut in half if very large.

Carrots: Trim and peel whole small ones with greens left on tops if possible. Tiny baby ones are increasingly available and a particularly good choice for dipping.

Cauliflower: Trim a whole head into tiny florets just large enough to be dipped. Can be blanched for 3 to 5 minutes, drained, and completely dried if desired.

Celery: Peel stalks of tough fiber. Cut into thin sticks.

Celery Root: Peel and trim, cut into thin julienne strips, and toss with mayonnaise. This should be served only when offered as part of a plate of crudité for a first course.

Cucumbers: Peel, cut in half lengthwise, and remove seeds. Trim into long, thick sticks.

Endive Leaves: Separate the leaves from each bulb carefully. Wash and drain dry. Arrange on platter with pointed end out for maximum effect.

Green Beans: Choose very thin, long ones in season. Trim and blanch for a minute. Drain and refresh under cold running water. Pat dry.

Mushrooms: Gently clean and pat dry. Cut large ones into halves or quarters. Toss with a small amount of lemon juice to prevent discoloration.

Radishes: Choose small ones. Scrub clean and trim ends. Keep 2 or 3 inches of the stems intact for easy dipping.

Red Cabbage or Green Cabbage: Shred by hand and toss with mayonnaise and lemon juice. Serve on a plate with other vegetables for a first course. Alternatively, hollow out a large one and use it to hold a bowl full of sauce.

Scallions: Choose thin ones if possible. Trim off all but 2 or 3 inches of the greens and the sandy root ends. Cut large ones in half lengthwise.

Snow Peas: Trim ends and blanch for just a minute. Drain and refresh under running water. Pat dry and chill before including with other vegetables. Remove string membrane.

Sweet Peppers: Choose red, yellow, or green peppers with no blemishes. Cut in half, remove seeds and membranes. Cut into large, thick strips for dipping.

Tomatoes: Cut into wedges for dipping or sliced on a plate with other vegetables for a first course. Can be peeled if desired.

Zucchini and Yellow Squash: Trim but do not peel. Cut into thick rounds or lengthwise into sticks. Can be blanched for easier digestion but do not overcook. Refresh under running water and pat dry when done.

Sauces for Crudité Plate or Platter

Try one of the following sauces to go with a selection of vegetables. Offer two or three different ones for variety. This is especially useful when a large array is presented. A vinaigrette sauce is the favorite for a plate of crudité.

Anchovy Sauce (page 407)
Hot Black Bean Dip (page 49)
Eggplant Caviar (page 50)
Guacamole (page 50)
Yogurt and Herb Dressing (page 132)
Hummus (page 51)
Tapenade (page 45)
Tarragon Flavored Vinaigrette Sauce (add 2 tablespoons chopped fresh tarragon to Vinaigrette Sauce found on page 129)

ANTIPASTI

Literally translated, antipasto means "before the meal." This can be a platter of a colorful assortment of starters to be served with drinks or it can be a first course of an elaborate meal. The following items are foods that can make a great antipasto for your next gathering.

Marinated or Pickled Vegetables
Cooked Seafood with Lemon
Olives
Slices of Salamis, Dried Sausages, and Hams
Vegetable Salads
Cubes of Sharp Cheese
Tomato Slices
Anchovies
Cold Ratatouille (page 396)
Hard-Boiled Eggs
Artichoke Hearts
Roasted Red or Yellow Peppers (page 385)

GRAVLAX

This raw, salt-and-sugar-cured salmon is easy to do and quite elegant when the glistening pink slices are presented with a spicy golden yellow mustard sauce. Choose the freshest salmon possible and have the scales removed but keep the skin intact. Also, scoring the skin side in two or three places will help the salt/sugar mixture to penetrate.

2 pounds centercut of fresh
   Atlantic, sockeye, coho, or
   chinook salmon
¼ cup salt

½ cup sugar
2 teaspoons crushed peppercorns
1 bunch fresh dill, coarsely chopped

1. Remove all small bones from the salmon. Cut the fish into two pieces along the line of the backbone. Pat dry cut flesh with paper towels.

2. Mix salt, sugar, and peppercorns in a spice mill. Rub the fish with some of the mixture. Dust part of the mixture and some of the dill in a nonreactive dish. Place one piece of the salmon, skin side down, in the dish and sprinkle generously with dill and salt mixture. Cover with the second piece of salmon, skin side up.

3. Sprinkle the salmon with remaining salt mixture. Cover with a sheet of aluminum foil and a weight such as a heavy can atop a small cutting board. The fish will give off juices in about 4 to 5 hours. Check periodically and pour off liquid. Keep the gravlax refrigerated for not less than 48 hours, turning the fish from time to time. It keeps for about a week if properly chilled.

4. To serve, cut into thin slices free from the skin. Garnish with sliced cucumbers, dill, and lemon wedges. Serve with Gravlax Sauce.

GRAVLAX SAUCE

3 tablespoons olive oil
1 tablespoon red wine
   vinegar
¼ teaspoon salt

pinch of pepper
2½ tablespoons prepared Dijon
   mustard
2 to 3 tablespoons fresh chopped
   dill

Combine oil and vinegar in a small bowl. Add salt and pepper. Stir to dissolve. Blend in mustard. Add dill just before serving.

SOUPS

Soup is an offering of warmth and comfort. A clear broth, hearty chowder, gutsy gumbo, or a satisfying cream soup is a welcome part of any meal. Soup provides an economical way to round out a light meal or to serve as a meal itself.

Many of the following soup recipes have been in The Settlement Cookbook *since the beginning. The frugal heritage of the book emphasizes good use of seasonal ingredients, an important item for the best soups. We've added a few recipes, too, with the purpose in mind of continuing the thrifty manners of our forebears.*

The base for a successful soup is good stock. In this day of hurried convenience, it is tempting to turn to canned stock to use in making soup. While quite acceptable and certainly understandable, nothing can take the place of a carefully prepared mixture of blending flavors characteristic of homemade stock.

The Beef and Chicken Stocks are for general use in soup making. Clear Soups, Hearty Soups, Cream Soups, Fish Soups, Chowders, and Fruit Soups follow. Garnishes include toasts, wafers, dumplings, and noodles. These can be used to add substance and decoration to even the most simple soup.

Keep soups well covered or tightly sealed in the refrigerator. Stock-based soups will keep easily for 4 to 5 days. Cream soups should be consumed fairly quickly, 3 to 4 days at the most. Clear soups freeze better than cream-based ones or chowders. Careful, slow reheating is necessary to prevent separation. The microwave is useful for quick defrosting. Follow manufacturer's instructions.

Clear Soups

The following recipes serve as the basis for almost any soup. For chicken stock, use feet, backs, necks, wings, or cut-whole chickens. For beef, use brisket, plate, round, or skirt. Bones will give a gelatinous quality to stock. Trim any chicken or meat of as much fat as is possible before beginning.

To clear stock, add the white of 1 egg mixed with 1 teaspoon water. Add the crushed eggshell. Boil for 2 minutes, stirring constantly. Add 1 tablespoon ice water and then let stand to settle. Strain through cheesecloth placed in strainer or colander.

Bring simmered stocks to room temperature and then chill in the refrigerator. The fat will rise to the top and form a firm layer that is easily removed. When there is no time for chilling, skim fat with a spoon or paper towel.

Stock will keep for several days if refrigerated. The cake of fat that forms on top will exclude air and should not be removed until the stock is used. If desired, save all remnants of meat, bones, trimmings, gristle, marrow bone, fat, and gravies to add in making soup stock. Onions, celery, celery root, parsley, and carrots may also be added to enrich the flavor of all stocks.

Stock freezes well. A convenient way to keep it is to pour the stock into ice-cube trays. When frozen, remove the amount desired and return the rest to the freezer.

CHICKEN STOCK

5 pounds chicken parts (backs, necks, feet, wings, or thighs)
3 medium onions, peeled and quartered
3 carrots, peeled and cut into 1-inch pieces
2 stalks celery, cut into 1-inch pieces
1 bay leaf, crumpled
10 to 15 peppercorns
½ teaspoon salt

1.   Trim chicken parts of all excess fat. Place in a stockpot with the onions, carrots, celery, bay leaf, and peppercorns. Pour in enough cold water to cover. Add the salt.

2.   Bring to a boil, skimming off any foam that comes to the top. Reduce heat to a simmer and cook gently, uncovered, for 3 to 4 hours. Watch carefully, regulating heat to maintain a slow bubbling. Do not boil. Skim frequently to remove foam that rises to the surface.

3.   Strain stock through a large sieve set inside a heat-proof bowl, discarding bones and vegetables. Allow to come to room temperature. Refrigerate overnight. When ready to use, remove congealed fat from surface.

BEEF STOCK

5 pounds meaty beef bones (chuck, flank, or shank), trimmed of excess fat
5 carrots, peeled and trimmed into small pieces
2 large onions, peeled and cut into quarters
2 ribs celery, trimmed into small pieces
1 bay leaf, crumpled
10 peppercorns
parsley stems (optional)
salt

1.   Place bones in a large stockpot and cover with cold water. Bring quickly to a boil then drain. This will help to remove impurities resulting in a clear stock.

(*continued*)

2. Add the carrots, onions, celery, bay leaf, peppercorns, parsley stems, if using, and salt. Cover with cold water. Bring slowly to a simmer, skimming any foam that might rise to the surface.

3. Adjust heat to maintain a steady simmer. Cook slowly, uncovered, for 5 to 6 hours. Skim any foam that rises to the top.

4. Strain the stock through a large sieve set inside a heat-proof bowl. Discard bones and vegetables. Allow strained stock to come to room temperature. Refrigerate overnight. When ready to use remove layer of congealed fat that covers the chilled stock.

FISH STOCK

Use only lean fish for making stock. Bass, flounder, halibut, whiting, and sole are good choices. Avoid strong, oily fish like mackerel, salmon, sardines, or bluefish. Be sure that fish are well rinsed, trimmed, and free of scales before proceeding.

2 pounds fish bones (including heads and tails if available)	several sprigs fresh parsley
2 tablespoons butter	1 bay leaf, crumpled
1 small onion, finely chopped	several sprigs fresh thyme
	salt and freshly ground black pepper

1. Coarsely cut the fish parts into pieces large enough to fit into a 4- to 6-quart stockpot. Rinse under cold, running water for several minutes to remove any impurities.

2. Melt butter in stockpot. Add the onion and cook over medium heat until softened but not browned, stirring occasionally.

3. Add the fish parts and pour in enough cold water to cover. Add the parsley, bay leaf, and thyme. Season lightly with salt and pepper. Bring to a boil, skimming off any debris that rises to the top. Reduce heat to a simmer and cook gently, uncovered, for 20 minutes, skimming from time to time.

4. Pass the stock through a strainer lined with cheesecloth. Let come to room temperature then refrigerate until needed. Will keep for 1 to 2 days, well chilled.

VEGETABLE BROTH

2 onions, peeled and quartered
2 carrots, peeled and cut into 1-inch
    thick slices
2 ribs celery, coarsely chopped
2 leeks, white parts only, cleaned
    and split in half
1 turnip, peeled and quartered

1 bay leaf, crumpled
several sprigs fresh thyme
5 to 10 peppercorns
salt
2 medium potatoes, peeled and
    diced

1. Place all of the vegetables except the potatoes in a large stockpot or soup pot with the bay leaf, thyme, peppercorns, and salt.

2. Cover with water. Bring to a simmer over moderately high heat, reduce heat, and let cook just below a simmer, uncovered, for 2 to 3 hours. Add the potatoes during the last hour of cooking.

3. Remove from heat and strain if desired. If not to be strained, remove the bay leaf, thyme, and peppercorns with a slotted spoon before serving.

CONSOMMÉ

2 pounds chicken
1 pound veal bone
1 pound marrow bone
1 beef knuckle
1 pound lean beef (round)
1½ teaspoon salt

¼ teaspoon freshly ground black
    pepper
¼ teaspoon nutmeg, grated
⅓ cup each, onion, celery, and
    carrots, diced
1 tablespoon fat

1. Clean chicken if necessary. Separate it at the joints and place in soup pot with the soup bones. Cut beef into small pieces and brown in hot skillet with the marrow from the marrow bones. Add to soup pot. Cover with cold water and seasonings.

2. Heat quickly to the boiling point. Skim if a clear soup is desired. Cover, reduce heat, and simmer slowly for 5 hours, adding more cold water as necessary. Fry the vegetables in the fat for 5 minutes. Add to the soup and let boil 1 hour longer. Strain and season to taste. When cool, remove fat. Serve hot in cups with any soup garnish.

Note: The chicken should be removed as soon as tender. It can be served with any well-flavored sauce or used for salads or croquettes.

Hearty Soups

Hearty soups often include the meat and vegetables from which they are made. They can be served in small portions as a first course or in larger portions as the main course for a light lunch or supper. Good bread, a salad, and dessert will round out the meal. Hearty soups are an excellent way of making good use of leftover meat, chicken, or vegetables.

BORSCHT

The following recipe calls for citric acid, also known as sour salt. Formerly found in pharmacies, it was added to foods of low acidity to bring out flavor. The soup can be made without this rather obscure ingredient. We're including it as an optional component in case it is still available in your community.

½ of a 5-pound chicken
3 quarts boiling water
½ cup cooked lima beans
2 cups strained tomatoes
5 or 6 large beets, peeled and cut in strips
2 onions, sliced
2 apples, peeled, cored, and sliced

2 potatoes, peeled and cut in cubes
1 small celery root, diced
1 teaspoon salt
⅛ teaspoon freshly ground black pepper
2 tablespoons sugar
½ teaspoon citric acid (optional)
3 egg yolks, well beaten

1. Cut chicken at joints and place in a large, nonreactive pot. Cover with the water. Add lima beans, tomatoes, beets, onions, apples, potatoes, and celery root. Season with salt and pepper. Bring to a boil, reduce heat, and cook slowly for 2 to 3 hours, covered.

2. Add sugar and citric acid, if using, and boil for 3 minutes.

3. Remove from heat and gradually stir about 1 pint of this soup into the yolks so it will not curdle. Return tempered yolks to soup and mix all together. Boiling water may be added if mixture is too thick.

CABBAGE BORSCHT

2 pounds cabbage, shredded
  coarsely
½ cup Kosher salt
½ teaspoon pepper
1 medium onion, chopped
1½ quarts water
1½ pounds beef chuck, cubed

1 large soup bone
1 28-ounce can tomato puree
1 large potato, cubed
2 teaspoons sour salt (or to taste)
1 cup sugar
2 cloves garlic, minced

  1. Combine cabbage, salt, pepper, onion, and 1½ quarts water in a large kettle. Cover and bring to a boil.

  2. Add beef, soup bone, and tomato puree. Cover and simmer for 1 hour.

  3. Add the potato and simmer for 40 minutes, covered. Add sour salt and sugar. Simmer for 15 minutes.

  4. Add garlic and simmer for 5 minutes. This soup freezes well.

Vegetable Soups

Vegetable soups are good for making use of seasonal bounty and leftovers. Any fresh, seasonal vegetables can be used. Let the marketplace or home garden be your guide. Remember that most vegetables do best when cooked quickly. Do not overcook. Blanch in lots of boiling, salted water and drain. Rinse under cold running water and add to soup just before heating up or steam or microwave vegetables before adding to soup. When reheating soup, take out just what you need for the number of people being served. Do not reheat the whole pot or vegetables will be limp and without character due to several reheatings. The following suggestions for additions to vegetable soups might be helpful:

- broccoli or cauliflower cut into small florets
- green beans, trimmed and blanched
- winter root vegetables like turnips, rutabagas, parsnips, or potatoes, peeled and cut into small uniform-sized cubes
- asparagus spears cut in half and blanched, rinsed under running water
- dried beans, lentils, or peas cooked and added before heating up soup for serving
- okra, sliced and blanched
- fresh corn scraped off the cob, rice, barley, or small shaped pastas added to stretch and give character to the soup
- chopped fresh herbs added just before serving to insure best flavor
- leeks, spring onions, and/or garlic added to the onions, carrots, and celery that serve as a soup base
- green, red, or yellow peppers cut into thin strips or uniform dice, to add a colorful touch

HAMBURGER-VEGETABLE SOUP

½ pound ground beef
2 tablespoons fat
1 cup tomatoes, peeled, seeded, and
    chopped
1 small onion, chopped
1 small carrot, peeled and diced
1 rib celery, diced
¼ cup chopped parsley

½ teaspoon freshly ground black
    pepper
2 or 3 medium potatoes, peeled and
    diced
1½ cups water or beef or chicken
    stock (page 59)
1 teaspoon salt

1. In a soup pot, brown ground beef in fat.
2. Add remaining ingredients and simmer until vegetables are tender.

MULLIGATAWNY SOUP

3 pounds uncooked chicken
2 sour apples, sliced
¼ cup sliced onion
¼ cup thinly sliced celery
¼ cup peeled and chopped carrot
1 cup tomatoes, peeled, seeded, and
    chopped
½ green pepper, finely chopped
¼ cup butter

1 tablespoon flour
1 teaspoon curry powder
2 cloves
⅛ teaspoon mace
1 teaspoon chopped parsley
1 teaspoon sugar (optional)
4 quarts cold water
salt and freshly ground black pepper
    to taste

1. In a large soup pot, brown the chicken, apples, and vegetables in butter over high heat. Add the flour, curry powder, cloves, mace, parsley, and sugar if desired.
2. Cover with the cold water and stir to blend. Bring to a boil, reduce heat, and cook slowly, covered, until chicken is tender, 45 minutes to 1 hour.
3. Remove the chicken bones and cut the meat into small pieces. Strain soup and rub vegetables through a sieve. Add cut-up chicken to strained soup. Season with salt and pepper and serve hot with Boiled Rice, page 171.

DRIED PEA SOUP

1 pound split peas
2 tablespoons oil
2 medium onions, chopped
2 ribs celery, thinly sliced
1 ham hock, small piece of smoked
    bacon, or ham bone

2 bay leaves
8 cups chicken stock (page 59),
    water, or a combination of the
    two
salt and freshly ground black pepper
    to taste

1.   Wash peas in cold water until the water runs clear. Cover with plenty of cold water and let sit overnight. Rinse and change water several times. As a shortcut, pour boiling water over the washed peas and let sit for 1 hour.

2.   In a soup pot, heat the oil. Add the onion and celery. Cook over moderately high heat until onions are translucent. Drain the peas and add them along with the ham or bacon and bay leaves.

3.   Pour in the stock or water. Bring almost to a boil, reduce heat, and simmer gently until peas are cooked, about 30 minutes. (Time will vary according to the peas used. If they have been on the shelf for a long time, they will need more cooking than younger peas. The peas must be quite soft before proceeding or the soup will be gritty.)

4.   Remove the ham or bacon and, working in batches, puree cooked peas in a food processor until very smooth. Cut any lean pieces of pork into small pieces and add to the soup, if desired. Return to heat and season to taste with salt and pepper. The soup can be thinned out with additional stock or water if desired. Working the soup through a sieve will give it an even silkier texture. Serve hot with Baked Croutons (page 77) or thin toasts.

Variation:

Lentil Soup   Substitute 1 pound green or red lentils for the peas above. Wash several times and soak as for above. The pureeing of the soup is optional; lentils can be left whole.

WHITE BEAN SOUP WITH TOMATO AND THYME

1 pound white beans, preferably Great Northern	4 or 5 parsley stems
2 tablespoons oil	2 bay leaves
2 onions, chopped	2 cloves garlic, crushed
3 or 4 fresh tomatoes, peeled, seeded, and chopped (or 1 cup drained canned tomatoes)	8 cups water, chicken stock (page 59), or combination of the two
several sprigs fresh thyme (or 1 teaspoon dried thyme)	salt and freshly ground black pepper to taste

1.   Wash and rinse the beans several times in cold, running water. Cover with cold water and let soak overnight, rinsing and changing the water often. As a shortcut, pour boiling water over the washed beans and let sit for 1 hour.

2.   Heat the oil in a soup pot. Add the onions. Cook over moderately high heat until translucent.

3.   Add the tomatoes, thyme, parsley stems, bay leaves, and garlic. Stir to blend. Drain the beans and add to the vegetables. Pour in the water and/or stock

and bring almost to a boil. Reduce heat and simmer until beans are very soft. (Time will vary according to the beans used. If they have been on the shelf for a long time, they will need more cooking than younger beans. The beans must be quite soft or the soup will be gritty.)

 4. When done, remove bay leaves and, working in batches, puree soup in a food processor until very smooth. Return to heat, season to taste with salt and pepper. Thin out with additional stock or water if desired. The soup can be worked through a strainer for an even silkier texture. Serve very hot garnished with dropped fresh herbs.

BLACK BEAN SOUP

2 cups black beans
2 quarts cold water
2 tablespoons chopped onion
2 ribs celery or celery root, chopped
2 teaspoons salt

⅛ teaspoon freshly ground black
  pepper
2 tablespoons butter
2 tablespoons flour
1 lemon, thinly sliced
2 hard-boiled eggs, chopped

1. Rinse beans and soak overnight. Drain and rinse thoroughly. (As a short-cut, pour boiling water over rinsed beans and let sit 1 hour.)

2. In a large soup pot, add the beans. Cover with the 2 quarts cold water. Add the onion and celery or celery root. Bring to a boil over moderately high heat. Reduce heat and cook, covered, until beans are tender, 3 to 4 hours. Add more water if necessary to keep the beans covered during cooking.

 3. Working in batches, puree the beans in a food processor fitted with the metal blade. Mash the puree through a strainer or sieve. Return to the pot and season with salt and pepper.

4. Heat the butter in a large separate saucepan. Add the flour and blend. Add about 1 cup of the bean soup and cook until thickened. Pour in the remaining soup gradually until soup is of desired consistency. Thin out with hot water if too thick. Correct seasoning.

5. Serve the soup in heated bowls. Garnish with lemon slices and hard-boiled eggs.

POTATO SOUP

2 tablespoons butter
1 small onion, finely chopped
½ rib celery, peeled and thinly
   sliced
3 potatoes, peeled and cut into
   small dice

1 quart boiling water
1 tablespoon flour
salt to taste
⅛ teaspoon white pepper
1 teaspoon caraway seed
2 teaspoons chopped parsley

1. In a large saucepan, melt 1 tablespoon of the butter. Add the onion and celery. Cook over moderate heat until onions are translucent and celery is softened, about 10 minutes. Add the potatoes, cover and cook for 2 more minutes. Add the water and cook over moderately high heat until potatoes are soft, 45 minutes to 1 hour.

2. In a separate pan, melt the remaining tablespoon butter. Add the flour and cook until lightly browned. Add about a cup of the potato cooking liquid. Bring to a boil, stirring. When thickened, return to the soup. Stir to blend. Heat until thickened and season with salt, pepper, caraway seed, and parsley. Serve hot with Baked Croutons (page 77).

Note: Any cooked leftover vegetable can be added before serving if desired.

ONION SOUP

6 large onions, about 1½ pounds
3 tablespoons butter
1 quart beef stock (page 59)
salt and freshly ground black pepper
   to taste

4 to 6 slices rye, pumpernickel, or
   french bread, toasted
freshly grated Swiss or Parmesan
   cheese

1. Peel onions and cut into ⅛-inch slices. Cook slowly in butter until tender and slightly browned, stirring constantly. Add stock, heat to boiling point, and boil for 2 to 3 minutes. Season to taste with salt and pepper.

2. Pour the hot soup into cups or soup plates. Float the toast on top and cover with 1 tablespoon cheese. Serve with additional cheese if desired.

TOMATO SOUP

1 pound ripe tomatoes, quartered
2 cups of water or chicken stock
  (page 59)
4 cloves
1 small onion, sliced

2 teaspoons sugar (optional)
1 teaspoon salt
2 tablespoons butter
2 tablespoons flour
freshly ground black pepper to taste

1. In a nonreactive soup pot, combine the tomatoes, water or stock, cloves, onion, sugar (if tomatoes are very acid), and salt. Bring to a boil, reduce heat, and simmer, covered, until onions are soft and tomatoes have been cooked through, about 20 minutes.

2. Strain, pressing hard on the vegetables to extract as much flavor as possible. Reheat.

3. In a separate saucepan, heat the butter. Add the flour and blend. Add to the strained tomatoes and stir. Cook over moderate heat until thickened. Season with pepper to taste.

CHICKEN GUMBO SOUP

Chicken feet are gelatinous, adding a wonderfully velvety texture and good flavor to stock. If unable to find, try substituting chicken necks, wings, or backs. Remember that the more fat that is trimmed from the chicken parts before beginning, the lighter and healthier the soup will be.

3 to 4 pounds chicken
10 chicken feet, scalded and
  skinned, nails removed
3 to 4 quarts cold water
1 tablespoon salt
2 ribs celery or ¼ cup celery root,
  diced
1 onion, peeled and thinly sliced

¼ cup rice
1 cup okra, sliced and blanched
1 tomato, peeled, seeded, and
  chopped (optional)
⅛ teaspoon nutmeg
¼ teaspoon freshly ground black
  pepper

1. Cut chicken at the joint and place in a soup pot along with chicken feet. Cover with the cold water and add the salt. Bring to a boil, reduce heat, and cook until chicken is tender, 45 minutes to an hour. Remove chicken pieces and cut meat into chunks.

2. Strain the chicken stock and discard the feet. Add the celery or celery root, onion, and rice to the strained stock and cook until they are tender, about 30 minutes. Add the chunks of chicken, the okra, and tomatoes if desired. Heat through and season with nutmeg and pepper. Serve hot.

Cream Soups

Cream soups are rich. They should be served in small portions only as part of a light meal. Season these soups well. Milk and cream can be bland when not livened with additional salt and pepper.

CREAM OF TOMATO SOUP

1 quart milk	1 teaspoon salt
1 small onion, thickly sliced	¼ teaspoon white pepper
1 bay leaf, crumpled	2 cups tomatoes, peeled, seeded,
2 tablespoons butter	and chopped
2 tablespoons flour	2 teaspoons sugar (optional)

1. Scald the milk with the onion and bay leaf. Cover and let infuse for 10 to 15 minutes. Remove and discard the onion and bay leaf.

2. In a nonreactive saucepan, melt the butter. Stir in the flour and cook over moderately high heat until lightly colored. Pour in about 1 cup of the infused milk and stir until thickened. Gradually add the rest of the milk. Season with salt and pepper.

3. Cook the tomatoes over medium heat in a separate saucepan until they begin to give off liquid. Neutralize with sugar if tomatoes are acid. Work through a strainer.

4. Add strained tomatoes gradually to the thickened milk. Correct seasoning to taste. Serve hot with toasts or Baked Croutons (page 77).

Note: This soup can be made with canned tomatoes although it is best when made at the height of the short summer tomato season when fresh ones are most flavorful. Substitute a large can of tomatoes for the 2 cups called for here. Strain canned tomatoes of packing liquid before using in this soup.

CREAM OF ASPARAGUS SOUP

1 pound green asparagus
6 cups chicken stock (page 59)
3 tablespoons butter
3 tablespoons flour

½ cup milk or cream
½ teaspoon salt
½ cup whipping cream, whipped
(optional)

1.   Wash and drain asparagus. Cut off tips 1½ inches from the top. Bring the stock to a boil in a large soup pot. Cook the asparagus tips in the boiling stock until tender, about 5 minutes. Remove with a slotted spoon, drain well, and set aside.

2.   Dice the remaining stalks and boil in the stock until very soft, about 15 minutes. Press stalks and some of the stock through a strainer or coarse sieve. Return puree to the pot.

3.   In a separate saucepan, melt the butter. Add the flour and cook over moderately high heat until lightly browned. Add about 1 cup of the hot soup. Cook until smooth. Add this to the remaining stock. Stir to blend.

4.   Add the milk or cream and salt, and heat through. Garnish with reserved asparagus tips and whipped cream, if desired.

CREAM OF CORN SOUP

1½ cups fresh corn, scraped from
   the ear
2 cups water
3 cups milk
1 small onion, thinly sliced

2 tablespoons butter
2 tablespoons flour
1 teaspoon salt
⅛ teaspoon white pepper
Popcorn (optional)

1.   In a saucepan, combine the corn with the water. Bring to a boil, reduce heat, and simmer until softened, about 10 minutes. Drain and set aside.

2.   Scald the milk with the onion. Leave to infuse for 10 to 15 minutes. Strain and discard the onion.

3.   In a separate saucepan, melt the butter. Add the flour and stir to blend. Cook until lightly colored. Pour in about 1 cup of the milk. Cook over moderate-high heat until thickened. Add the rest of the milk and blend. Bring to a boil, reduce heat, and simmer uncovered until soup is of desired consistency.

4.   Just before serving, add the corn to the soup. Season with salt and pepper and heat through for 1 to 3 minutes. Garnish with popcorn, if desired.

CREAM OF SPINACH SOUP

1 pound spinach, cleaned, large
   stems removed
1 quart chicken stock (page 59)
2 cups Thin White Sauce (page 399)

salt and freshly ground black pepper
   to taste
grated nutmeg (optional)

1. Put the spinach in a large, nonreactive soup pot. Cover and cook over moderately low heat until wilted, about 5 minutes. Stir constantly to prevent scorching. Let cool, squeeze out liquid. Rub through a sieve or puree in the food processor.

2. Return the spinach along with the stock to the pot. Bring to a simmer. Add the white sauce and blend. Season with salt and pepper. Serve hot with a pinch of grated nutmeg, if desired.

Note: Two heads lettuce finely chopped or 1 bunch watercress may be substituted for spinach. Be sure to remove tough, bitter stems from watercress before cooking.

CREAM OF MUSHROOM SOUP

This is a traditional favorite of the Settlement book. For a more exotic soup, try substituting different varieties of mushrooms. Oyster mushrooms, shiitake, chanterelle, and cepes can all be used in place of the mushrooms called for here. Substitute milk for cream if a less rich soup is desired.

4 tablespoons butter
½ pound mushrooms, cleaned and
   thinly sliced
salt and pepper to taste

1 quart chicken stock (page 59)
2 tablespoons flour
1 cup heavy cream
paprika for garnish, if desired

1. In a soup pot, melt 2 tablespoons of the butter. Add the mushrooms; season to taste with salt and pepper. Cover and let cook over moderately high heat for 5 minutes.

2. Pour in the chicken stock. Bring to a simmer and let cook for 5 to 10 minutes.

3. In a medium saucepan, melt the remaining 2 tablespoons butter. Add the flour and stir to blend. Cook over moderately high heat until lightly colored. Pour in about 1 cup of the stock with mushrooms. Blend until thickened, stirring constantly. Return to the rest of the stock and mix well. Season to taste with more salt and pepper.

4. Just before serving, add the cream. Bring to a simmer but do not boil. Serve in warm soup bowls and garnish with a pinch of paprika, if desired.

VICHYSSOISE

2 tablespoons butter
4 to 5 medium leeks, trimmed of
 green parts, cleaned, and thinly
 sliced
4 medium potatoes, peeled and
 thinly sliced

1 quart chicken stock (page 59)
1 rib celery, thinly sliced
several sprigs parsley, chopped
2 cups heavy cream
salt and white pepper to taste
chopped chives for garnish

1. In a soup pot, melt the butter. Add the leeks and cook over low heat until softened, about 5 minutes. Add the potatoes and cook for 5 more minutes.
2. Pour in the stock. Add the celery and parsley. Bring to a boil, reduce heat, and cook for 30 minutes. Strain, pressing down to extract as much liquid as possible, and let come to room temperature.
3. Add the cream and season to taste with salt and white pepper. Refrigerate for several hours or overnight. Serve very cold in chilled bowls. Garnish with chopped chives.

Seafood Soups and Chowders

FISH SOUP

1 medium onion, chopped
2 tablespoons olive oil
3 medium potatoes, peeled and
 thinly sliced
4 cups fish stock (page 60)
1 pound lean, firm-fleshed white
 fish fillets (scrod, sole, flounder,
 whiting, or perch)

½ pound medium shrimp, peeled
 and deveined
salt and freshly ground black pepper
 to taste
chopped parsley for garnish

1. In a soup pot, combine the onions and the olive oil. Cook over moderately high heat until onions are translucent. Add the potatoes, reduce the heat, cover, and cook slowly until potatoes are heated through, about 5 minutes. Stir if necessary to prevent scorching. Pour the stock into the pot, bring to a simmer, and cook gently for 10 minutes.
2. Cut the fish into large chunks and add to the pot along with the shrimp. Season with salt and pepper. Cook until potatoes are very soft and fish is cooked through, about 10 more minutes.
 3. In a food processor, working in batches if necessary, puree the soup. Scrape down sides and pulse until very smooth. Reheat gently, correct seasoning, and serve at once with parsley and Baked Croutons (page 77) or thin toast.

OYSTER STEW *Serves 2.*

1 pint shucked oysters and their
   liquor
2 tablespoons butter
2 cups scalded milk, cream, or
   cream and boiling water mixed

½ teaspoon salt
paprika

Put oysters in a strainer over a saucepan to catch the liquid. Keep the oyster liquor, remove any bits of shell, then add oysters to strained liquor. Put butter and oysters with liquor in a large skillet, cook slowly until edges of oysters curl, 3 to 5 minutes. Add milk or cream and cook for 1 more minute. Sprinkle with salt and paprika. Serve at once with crisped crackers.

LOBSTER BISQUE

2 pounds lobster, boiled
2 cups water, chicken stock (page
   59), or fish stock (page 60)
3 tablespoons butter

3 tablespoons flour
salt to taste
cayenne pepper to taste
2 cups milk
1 cup cream, scalded

1. Remove the meat from the lobster shell and dice. Set aside.
2. Chop the empty shell of the lobster into small pieces. Place in a soup pot and pour over water or stock. Bring slowly to the boiling point. Reduce heat and simmer for 20 to 25 minutes. Strain, reserve the liquid, and discard the shell.
3. In a saucepan, melt the butter over moderately high heat. Add the flour and blend. Add the lobster liquid and stir until smooth. Season with salt and cayenne pepper.
4. Scald the milk and stir in gradually. Add the reserved lobster meat and cook slowly for 5 minutes. Add the cream and heat through but do not boil. Serve at once.

CRAB SOUP

2 cups milk
1 small onion, sliced
2 bay leaves
3 tablespoons butter
3 tablespoons flour
1 cup fish stock (page 60) or water
2 tablespoons dry sherry

1 pound lump crabmeat, picked
  over to remove any shells and
  cartilage, and flaked
salt and freshly ground black pepper
  to taste
grated nutmeg for garnish

1. Scald milk with the onion and bay leaves. Cover and let infuse for 10 to 15 minutes.

2. In a large saucepan, melt the butter. Add the flour and cook over low heat until well mixed and raw edge of flour is cooked off, about 5 minutes. Stir often.

3. Strain infused milk over the butter and flour. Discard the onion and bay leaves. Pour in the stock or water. Bring to a boil, whisking constantly, until mixture is thickened.

4. Add the sherry and the flaked crabmeat. Season with salt and pepper. Serve hot with a small grating of fresh nutmeg as garnish.

CLAM CHOWDER

1 quart shucked clams and their
  liquor
2-inch piece fat salt pork
1 medium onion, sliced
5 to 6 medium potatoes, peeled and
  diced

4 cups milk
1 tablespoon butter
salt and freshly ground black pepper
  to taste
8 soda crackers

1. Drain the clams in a strainer set over a bowl and remove any pieces of shells. Retain the liquor.

2. Cut the pork into fine pieces and fry slowly until crisp. Add the onion and cook until softened, about 5 minutes. Add the potatoes, clam liquor, and enough water to cover. Cook until nearly tender. Drain and empty potato mixture into a nonreactive saucepan.

3. Pour milk into saucepan. Add butter and season with salt and pepper. When the potatoes are done, add the clams and the crackers. Cook 3 minutes longer.

MANHATTAN FISH CHOWDER

6 large potatoes, peeled and diced
6 large tomatoes, peeled, seeded, and chopped
2 large onions, peeled and thinly sliced
6 cups water, or water and fish stock (page 60) mixed

salt and freshly ground black pepper
1½ pounds raw halibut, flaked
2 tablespoons butter
1 cup heavy cream

1. In a soup pot, combine potatoes, tomatoes, and onions. Pour in water and/or stock, season with salt and pepper, and bring to a boil. Reduce heat and simmer until potatoes are cooked, about 45 minutes.

2. Add the fish and cook until white and tender, about 15 minutes.

3. Just before serving, stir in the butter and cream. Heat through and serve in warmed bowls.

NEW ENGLAND FISH CHOWDER

4 pounds cod or haddock
4 cups water
1½-inch cube of salt pork, chopped
1 medium onion, thinly sliced
6 to 7 medium potatoes, cut into ¼-inch slices or cubes

3 tablespoons butter
4 cups scalded milk
8 soda crackers
salt and freshly ground black pepper to taste

1. Skin and bone the fish. Cut the fish meat into 2-inch pieces and set aside. Place the head and backbone in a saucepan. Cover with 2 cups of the water and bring to a boil. Reduce heat and simmer for 20 minutes. Strain and reserve liquid.

2. In a soup pot, cook the salt pork until all fat is rendered. Add the onion and cook until softened. Add the potatoes and cover with the remaining 2 cups of water. Bring to a boil. Reduce heat and cook over moderately low heat for 5 minutes. Add the fish pieces and the strained liquid. Cover and simmer for 10 more minutes.

3. Just before serving, add the butter, milk, crackers, and salt and pepper. Heat through and serve in warmed bowls.

Wine and Fruit Soups

APRICOT AND ORANGE SOUP WITH GINGER

1 cup dried apricots (about ½ pound)
2 cups orange juice
1 teaspoon ground ginger

1 cup hot water
1 tablespoon lemon juice
2 tablespoons chopped candied ginger, for garnish

1. In a nonreactive saucepan, combine the apricots with one cup of the orange juice. Cook over moderately high heat until most of the juice is absorbed, about 10 minutes. Stir often.

2. Remove the plumped apricots to the bowl of a food processor along with the ground ginger and any accumulated juices. With the blade in motion, add the remaining cup of orange juice and the cup of hot water. Pulse on and off. Scrape down sides and puree until very smooth. Remove to a bowl. Stir in the lemon juice. Let soup come to room temperature.

3. Cover and refrigerate for at least 4 hours before serving. Serve in chilled, small, shallow soup bowls. Garnish with a bit of candied ginger. Serve with butter cookies or pound cake for dessert.

RED FRUIT SOUP WITH WINE

4 cups strawberries (about 1 to 1½ pounds)
2 cups raspberries (about 8 ounces)
2 cups red wine

½ cup sugar
thin julienne strips of lemon peel for garnish, if desired

1. Rinse and wash half of the strawberries and raspberries. Reserve the remaining berries.

2. In a nonreactive saucepan, combine the washed berries with the wine and the sugar. Bring to a boil. Cook vigorously until wine is slightly syrupy and berries are quite soft, about 10 minutes.

3. Remove to the bowl of a food processor. Puree until smooth. Strain and let come to room temperature. Chill for several hours.

4. Wash and rinse the remaining berries. Cut strawberries in halves or quarters. Pour about ½ cup of the soup into chilled, shallow soup bowls. Arrange the fruit attractively in the center. Garnish with thin strips of lemon peel, if desired. Serve with Gingerbread (page 558) or Lebkuchen (page 493).

Note: Frozen berries may be substituted for fresh, but be sure to drain off excess liquid or syrup before proceeding.

MELON SOUP

Use only very ripe honeydew, cantaloupe, or watermelon for this soup. Beaumes-de-Venise is a popular French sweet wine made from the muscat grape. If not available, substitute any fortified wine like port, Madeira, or sherry. Serve as an appetizing first course on a warm evening or for dessert with butter cookies or pound cake.

4 cups peeled, ripe melon cut into
   1-inch pieces
½ cup Beaumes–de–Venise wine

2 tablespoons lemon or lime juice
mint leaves for garnish

 Puree melon in a food processor. Pour on the wine and lemon or lime juice with the blades in motion. Chill for several hours or overnight. Serve in chilled bowls garnished with mint leaves.

Soup Garnishes

Soups can be garnished in a number of ways. In addition to the preparations here, soups can be more simply embellished with a julienne of vegetables, chopped fresh herbs, thin slices of lemon or lime, a dusting of paprika or nutmeg, or a dollop of whipped cream or sour cream.

BREAD, TOAST, AND WAFERS FOR SOUP GARNISH

BAKED CROUTONS

 Cut dry bread into cubes, spread flat on a baking sheet, and brown in a 300° F oven. The bread can be buttered before browning for better flavor.

FRIED CROUTONS

 In a skillet cook cubes of dry bread in a mixture of butter and vegetable oil over moderately high heat. Drain well on paper towels before serving.

PLAIN WAFERS

1 cup flour
1 teaspoon salt
1 tablespoon butter, chilled and cut
  into small pieces

milk

In the bowl of a food processor fitted with the metal blade, combine the flour and the salt. Add the butter and pulse on and off a few times until butter is cut into the flour. Add just enough milk to make a very stiff dough. Turn out onto a work surface and knead until smooth. Form the dough into small balls and roll each one into a thin wafer. Place in shallow greased and floured pans. Bake in a 400° F oven until puffed.

CARAWAY POTATO WAFERS

¼ pound boiled potatoes, riced
  while warm
½ cup butter, softened
1⅛ cups flour
1 tablespoon caraway seeds, plus
  more for sprinkling

1 egg, slightly beaten with 1
  teaspoon milk
salt

    1. Combine the potatoes, butter, flour, and caraway seeds in a large bowl. Work quickly with a fork to form a smooth dough. Cover and chill in the refrigerator for ½ hour.

    2. Preheat oven to 350° F. Working with half the dough at a time, roll out to ⅛-inch thickness on a board dusted with flour. Place on a baking sheet and brush top with egg and milk mixture. Sprinkle with salt and additional caraway seeds. Cut with a hot knife into narrow strips 1 inch by 3 inches. Place in the preheated oven. Increase heat to 400° F. Bake until crisp and delicately browned, about 15 minutes. Serve with soup or salad.

DUMPLINGS FOR SOUP

ALMOND DUMPLINGS (MANDEL KLOESE)

2 eggs, separated
salt and freshly ground black pepper
½ teaspoon chopped parsley

6 almonds, blanched, dried, and
  grated
½ teaspoon baking powder
flour

    1. Beat yolks until very light. Season with salt and pepper to taste. Add the parsley, almonds, baking powder, and enough flour to make a stiff batter. Beat the egg whites until stiff and add to the batter.

2. Test a teaspoonful in boiling water and if it boils apart, add more flour. Drop one by one from a teaspoon into boiling soup 10 minutes before serving.

SPATZEN (EGG DUMPLINGS)

1 egg	¾ cup flour
½ teaspoon salt	⅓ cup water

Beat egg well. Add the salt, flour, and water. Stir to make a stiff, smooth batter. Drop by teaspoonfuls into boiling soup 10 minutes before serving.

MATZO BALLS

1 cup boiling water	1 teaspoon salt
1 cup matzo meal	freshly ground black pepper and
2 tablespoons chicken fat	nutmeg to taste
1 egg, slightly beaten	½ teaspoon chopped parsley

1. Pour boiling water over matzo meal. Stir until water is absorbed. Add fat, egg, salt, pepper, nutmeg, and parsley. Mix well. Chill thoroughly.

2. Roll dough into balls the size of a walnut. If sticky, grease palms of hands or moisten with cold water occasionally. Drop into boiling soup 15 minutes before serving. Boil gently, uncovered.

MATZO KLOESE (MATZO DUMPLINGS)

2 matzos	⅛ teaspoon freshly ground black
2 tablespoons fat	pepper
¼ onion, finely chopped	¼ teaspoon ground ginger
1 teaspoon chopped parsley	⅛ teaspoon nutmeg
1 teaspoon salt	2 eggs
	about ¼ cup matzo meal

1. Soak the matzos a few minutes in cold water. Drain and squeeze dry.

2. Heat the fat in a skillet and add the onion. Fry to a golden brown. Add the soaked matzos, stir until mixture leaves the skillet clean. Off the heat add parsley, salt, pepper, ginger, nutmeg, and eggs. Mix well. Add just enough matzo meal to make a soft dough. Let stand several hours to swell.

3. Shape into balls the size of marbles. Test one by dropping into boiling water or soup. If it boils apart, add more meal. Boil dumplings for 15 minutes.

MATZO ALMOND DUMPLINGS

3 eggs, separated
⅛ teaspoon nutmeg
⅛ teaspoon salt
½ teaspoon sugar
½ cup grated almonds

1 tablespoon butter or poultry fat
matzo or cracker meal
oil for deep-frying

Beat the yolks until very light. Add nutmeg, salt, sugar, almonds, butter or fat, and enough matzo or cracker meal to make a stiff batter. Beat the whites stiff and fold them into the batter. Drop by teaspoonfuls into deep hot oil. Fry until light brown. Try one. If it does not hold together, add more meal. Place in oven to keep warm and put in soup just before serving.

PARSLEY SPONGE DUMPLINGS

3 eggs, separated
1 cup chicken or vegetable broth
   (page 59 or 61)

½ teaspoon chopped parsley
¼ teaspoon salt

1. In a mixing bowl, beat the yolks until lemon colored. Add the stock, parsley, and salt. Beat the egg whites until stiff and fold them into the batter.
2. Pour into a buttered cup and place in a covered pan of simmering water. Steam until firm. Cool, remove from the cup, and cut into small dumplings with a teaspoon or melon baller.

Variation: Preheat the oven to 350° F. Follow the instructions in step 1 and then bake in small frying pan until brown. When cool, cut into small triangles. Add to boiling soup.

NOODLES FOR SOUP

EGG NOODLES FOR SOUP

1 egg
¼ teaspoon salt

about ⅔ cup flour

1. Beat egg slightly. Add salt and enough flour to make a stiff dough. Knead well. Let stand, covered, ½ hour. On a lightly floured breadboard, roll out very thin and spread on a cloth to dry. The dough must not be the least bit sticky, though it should not be so dry that it will break or be brittle.
2. First cut into 3-inch strips, then place the strips all together, one on top of another. Now cut these long strips crosswise into very fine strips or threads.

For broad noodles, cut ⅓ to ½ inch wide. Toss them lightly with your fingers to separate well. Spread them on the board to dry. When thoroughly dry, put in covered jars for future use. Drop by handfuls into boiling soup 5 minutes before serving.

Variation: Prepare and roll dough as for Egg Noodles above. Let stand until almost dry, fold dough in half and cut through this double thickness with a small floured cutter or thimble. Press well so that edges stick together. Fry in deep hot fat until brown. They should be puffed like little balls. Place in tureen or put a few in each bouillon cup and pour the hot broth over them.

PANCAKE GARNISH

⅛ teaspoon salt
2 eggs

2 tablespoons matzo meal or ¼ cup potato flour

 Add salt to eggs. Beat slightly and stir in matzo meal or potato flour. Heat a little fat in skillet. Pour in egg mixture. When cooked on one side, turn on the other. Roll pancake and cut into noodles ⅛ inch wide. Drop into boiling soup before serving.

NOODLE PFARVEL

 Take scraps of rolled noodle or pasta dough that are too brittle or use leftover broken noodles. Crush on breadboard with rolling pin into small bits but not to a powder. Shake a little at a time through colander into mixing bowl, forming even grains. To 2 cupfuls add 1 egg, slightly beaten. Mix thoroughly, press through colander again. Let stand until thoroughly dry. Store well covered. Cook until tender in boiling soup.

MATZO PFARVEL

 With a rolling pin, crush broken pieces of matzos into crumbs. Heat 1 tablespoon fat in skillet. Add 2 eggs, slightly beaten, and the matzos crumbs. Stir well until the crumbs are well separated. Let stand for several hours until thoroughly dry. Serve in boiling soup.

ADDITIONAL SOUP GARNISHES

CHINESE EGG DROPS

Beat 1 egg well and gradually pour into boiling soup just before serving.

EINLAUF

1 egg
⅛ teaspoon salt
3 tablespoons flour

¼ cup water
1 teaspoon chopped parsley

Beat egg, add the salt, flour, and water. Stir until smooth. Pour slowly from end of spoon into boiling soup. Cook 2 to 3 minutes and add the chopped parsley just before serving the soup.

EGG FLUFF

Beat the whites of three eggs until stiff. Place in a tureen and pour over 2 quarts clear boiling soup. Sprinkle with paprika. Serve a portion of fluff with the soup.

Quick Soup Ideas

It is possible to make soup on the spur of the moment with what's on hand. Light, quick, and relatively easy to do, the following ideas depend on fresh seasonal ingredients. All of them call for water as the base. For an added dimension, homemade stock can be substituted if desired. Season the soups well, especially the ones to be served chilled. Be creative with garnishes, too. Small touches can make the most humble of soups visually alluring.

These soups serve 4 as a first course and 2 as the main part of a lunch or supper.

CARROT SOUP WITH CUMIN

1½ pounds carrots, trimmed,
   peeled, and cut into ½-inch slices
1 medium onion, chopped
2 tablespoons oil
1 teaspoon ground cumin

½ teaspoon salt
2 cups water
white pepper to taste
lemon twists, lime twists, or
   chopped fresh parsley for garnish
   (optional)

1. Rinse carrots and set aside. In a saucepan, combine the onions and the oil. Cook over moderately high heat until onions are translucent.

2. Add carrots, cumin, and salt. Stir to blend. Pour in the water and bring to a boil. Reduce heat and cook until carrots are tender, about 15 minutes.

 3. Puree in a food processor or blender. Season to taste with more salt and pepper if desired. Garnish with twists of lemon, lime, or chopped fresh parsley if desired.

ARTICHOKE SOUP WITH LEMON

4 artichokes, ¾ to 1 pound each
1 lemon cut in half, zest removed
   and julienned
1 medium onion, chopped
2 ribs celery, thinly sliced

2 tablespoons oil
2 cups water
salt and freshly ground black pepper
   to taste

1. Snap off the stem of the artichoke and discard. Use a stainless-steel knife to cut leaves from the choke. Remove the fibrous center of the choke with a small spoon. Trim the artichoke bottom of any green parts. Immediately rub with a lemon half to prevent discoloration.

2. In a saucepan, combine the onion, celery, and oil. Cook over moderately high heat until vegetables are translucent.

3. Slice the artichoke bottoms as thinly as possible. Immediately add to the onions and celery. Add two teaspoons of fresh squeezed lemon juice. Stir to blend.

 4. Pour in the water. Add salt and pepper. Bring to a boil, reduce heat, and simmer until artichokes are tender, about 15 minutes. Puree in a food processor or blender. Correct seasonings to taste with additional lemon juice, salt, and pepper. Serve immediately garnished with thin julienne slices of lemon zest.

Note: This soup tends to lose color and becomes bitter if not consumed relatively quickly after pureeing.

CUCUMBER AND YOGURT SOUP WITH MINT

2 medium cucumbers (about 12 ounces), peeled and seeded
2 cups plain yogurt

¼ cup chopped fresh mint
salt and white pepper to taste
mint leaves for garnish (optional)

1. Cut cucumbers lengthwise into quarters and coarsely grate. Squeeze out excess moisture with hands.

2. In a mixing bowl, combine cucumbers and yogurt. Cover and refrigerate for at least an hour and at most overnight. Add mint just before serving. Season with salt and pepper. Serve in chilled bowls and garnish with whole leaves of mint, if desired.

AVOCADO AND TOMATO SOUP

2 ripe avocados, peeled and seeded
2 tablespoons red wine vinegar
3 to 4 medium tomatoes, peeled, seeded, and chopped
½ cup plain yogurt
2 tablespoons chopped fresh cilantro

salt and freshly ground black pepper to taste
chopped fresh tomato for garnish (optional)
several sprigs of cilantro for garnish (optional)

1. Cut avocado into quarters. Place in the bowl of a food processor fitted with the metal blade. Add the vinegar. Pulse on and off several times to puree. Scrape down sides and pulse again until very smooth.

2. Add the tomatoes and continue processing until blended. (This may have to be done in 2 batches if processor bowl is too small.) Turn out into a mixing bowl.

3. Thin with the yogurt. Season with cilantro, salt, and pepper to taste. Refrigerate until ready to serve. Serve in chilled bowls and garnish with chopped, fresh tomatoes and small leaves of cilantro, if desired.

Note: For a smoother, silkier soup, the puree can be put through a strainer.

GAZPACHO

1 medium onion, chopped
6 tomatoes, peeled, seeded, and
  chopped
½ cup red wine
1 tablespoon olive oil
1 tablespoon paprika
1 clove garlic, minced

1 cucumber, peeled, seeded, and
  thinly sliced
3 to 4 oil-cured black olives, pitted
  and sliced (optional)
salt and freshly ground black pepper
  to taste
chopped fresh parsley, for garnish

 1. In the bowl of a food processor or blender, combine the onion and tomatoes. Puree, scraping down the sides and repeating until smooth.

2. In a nonreactive saucepan, combine the puree with the wine, oil, paprika, and garlic. Simmer for 10 minutes. Let come to room temperature then chill thoroughly in the refrigerator.

3. Just before serving, add the cucumber and the olives, if desired. Season with salt and pepper. Garnish with the chopped parsley.

WINTER SQUASH AND LEEK SOUP

4 tablespoons butter
1 small onion, finely chopped
2 medium leeks, trimmed, washed,
  and thinly sliced
2 acorn squash, peeled and cut into
  1-inch chunks (butternut squash
  or pumpkin may be substituted)

4 cups water
salt and freshly ground black pepper
  to taste

1. In the bottom of a large saucepan, melt the butter. Spread the onions and the leeks in an even layer over the bottom of the pan and cover with a sheet of parchment or waxed paper. Sweat the onion and leeks over very low heat until soft and translucent, 15 to 20 minutes.

2. Remove the waxed paper. Add the squash and water. Bring to a boil, lower to a simmer, cover and cook until the squash is very soft and can be mashed with the back of a spoon.

 3. Remove from heat. In the workbowl of a food processor, puree the soup in small batches until very smooth. Or press through a fine-meshed sieve.

4. Reheat the soup and season with salt and freshly ground black pepper to taste. Serve hot.

EGG AND CHEESE DISHES

Eggs

Eggs fall under that soothing term of "comfort food" that evokes a familiarity during times of stress, illness, or melancholy. Many Americans look for eggs on big hotel menus when traveling to far corners of the world, for example. A simply prepared egg is traditionally thought of as soft, digestible, and soothing to lost souls. There is trouble in paradise.

Eggs are increasingly becoming a challenge for today's cook. Eggs were once considered the epitome of healthy eating. Now a bacteria called Salmonella enteritidis is wreaking havoc within the egg production industry. Illness (and in extreme cases even deaths) from eating contaminated eggs "has increased more than sixfold in the northeastern part of the U.S. since 1976," according to Robert Tauxe, M.D., from the Center for Disease Control. This phenomenon has spread from New England to the mid-Atlantic states and has now become a problem in the south Atlantic states as well.

The current problem is different from past outbreaks. Investigations have shown that the infection is coming from the inside of the egg rather than from the outside. Washing and sanitizing shells of commercial eggs does not rid them of the virus as it has done in the past. Scientists suspect that the egg yolk becomes infected before the shell forms. Steps are being taken to prevent transmission and spread of the disease within the flocks. Until strides are made to ensure the safety of all eggs, the modern consumer is best served by following some simple procedures outlined below (see page 96).

There are recipes included here from the early edition of the book that call for cooking times that do not coincide with some of the safety tips provided by the F.D.A. Most of us find that softly cooked eggs taste better than overcooked, rubbery ones. Individuals must weigh the risk of indulging in undercooked eggs against the potential hazards. We suggest such consumption only if the quality of the product can be guaranteed.

From the original edition comes the following advice: "A stale egg rises in water; fresh eggs are heavy, and sink to the bottom. Eggs should be well covered and kept in a cool place (this means in the refrigerator for today's cook). Wash eggs just before using. Eggs should never be boiled, as that renders them tough. They should be cooked just under the boiling point."

SOFT-COOKED EGGS

Some of the following instructions for cooking eggs are given with a certain amount of trepidation. While absolutely the best way to eat eggs, we suggest that attention be given to the dangers of Salmonella contamination mentioned in the introduction of this chapter.

Soft-Cook Method

 Have enough boiling water in saucepan to cover eggs. Drop in slowly with tablespoon and place where they will simmer but not boil, from 3 to 5 minutes, according to the desired consistency.

CODDLED EGGS

 Take eggs from refrigerator to remove chill. Have water boiling in both top and bottom of double boiler, then remove from fire. Drop eggs gently with tablespoon into upper half of double boiler, letting stand 4 to 8 minutes over lower half. Do not return to fire.

HARD-COOKED EGGS

Hard-Cook Method

Slip the eggs into boiling water, place over low heat where they will simmer, not boil, and let cook 12 to 15 minutes. Plunge in cold water to keep yolks from discoloring. Remove shells, serve whole or cut into quarters lengthwise and pour browned butter over them. Serve hot.

GOLDENROD TOAST

 4 hard-cooked eggs, peeled   6 to 8 slices toast
2 cups Medium White Sauce (page   parsley
    399)

Separate the egg yolks and whites. Chop the whites. Add the whites to the sauce. Heat thoroughly and pour the mixture over the toast. Sprinkle with riced egg yolks and garnish with toast points and parsley.

CURRIED EGGS   *Serves 4 to 6.*

1 small onion, chopped
2 tablespoons butter
2 tablespoons flour
¼ teaspoon curry powder, or more
  to taste

⅛ teaspoon freshly ground black
  pepper, or to taste
¼ teaspoon salt, or to taste
1 cup hot milk
6 hard-cooked eggs, peeled

Sauté onion in butter until softened but not browned. Add the flour, curry, pepper, and salt. Pour in the hot milk and stir to blend. Simmer over low heat, stirring constantly, until thickened. Slice the eggs and reheat in the sauce. Serve on rice or garnish with fingers of fresh toast.

EGGS À LA TARCAT   *Serves 4 to 6.*

6 hard-cooked eggs, peeled
¼ pound chopped ham
1 tablespoon chopped onion
¼ teaspoon prepared mustard

1 teaspoon salt
dash of cayenne pepper
lettuce leaves
bottled mayonnaise

Cut the eggs in half lengthwise. Remove the yolks. Mash the yolks with the rest of the ingredients and refill the whites with this mixture. Serve cold on lettuce leaves with mayonnaise.

DEVILED EGGS

4 hard-cooked eggs, peeled
¼ teaspoon salt
½ teaspoon dry mustard
¼ teaspoon cayenne pepper

1 teaspoon vinegar
1 tablespoon melted butter
lettuce leaves

1. Cut each egg in half lengthwise. Remove yolks and set whites aside.

2. In the bowl of a food processor fitted with the metal blade, combine egg yolks with the remaining ingredients. Pulse several times to mix well. Scrape sides after each pulse.

3. Roll the yolk mixture into balls the size of the original yolk. Place a ball in each egg white half. Serve on a platter with lettuce leaves.

Variation: To the yolk mixture, add four anchovies, pounded and strained. Or add ¼ cup of chopped chicken, veal, ham, or tongue.

POACHED EGGS

Poaching Method

To 1 quart of boiling water, add 1 tablespoon vinegar and 1 teaspoon salt. Pour into shallow pan. Remove from stove. Break eggs carefully, one at a time, into a saucer, then slip them into the hot water. Cover the pan, set over slow fire where they will keep hot, but not boil, about 5 minutes, or until the whites are set and a film has formed over the yolks. Remove from pan with a skimmer, drain, and serve on hot butered toast; or use buttered egg poacher and proceed as above.

For an added effect, stir the water with a wooden spoon to form a deep vortex in the center. Carefully slip in the egg. The swirling water will keep the egg shape. Do one egg at a time and remove to warm water until wanted.

POACHED EGGS AND CHEESE   *Serves 4 to 6.*

6 eggs	6 teaspoons butter
½ teaspoon salt	6 tablespoons grated cheddar cheese
¼ teaspoon paprika	

Butter 6 ramekins and crack a whole egg into each. For each, add salt, paprika, 1 teaspoon butter, and cover with 1 tablespoon of the cheese. Place ramekins in a pan of hot water about ½ inch deep. Bake until eggs are set. Place under broiler and brown quickly.

POACHED EGGS MORNAY

Cut toast rounds and put a poached egg on each. Sprinkle with cheese. Pour Medium White Sauce (page 399) over each egg. Garnish with parsley.

EGGS BENEDICT   *Serves 2.*

2 English muffins	Hollandaise Sauce (page 404)
4 slices boiled ham or Canadian bacon	green or black olives, pitted and sliced
4 poached eggs	small dill pickles, halved and thinly sliced

Split and toast the English muffins. Fry rounds of ham and place on buttered muffins. Slip poached egg on ham. Cover with Hollandaise Sauce. Garnish with olive and pickles.

SHIRRED EGGS

Shirring Method

Butter an egg shirrer or small vegetable dish; cover bottom and side with fine breadcrumbs. Add an egg very carefully, cover with seasoned breadcrumbs. Bake in slow oven (300° F) until white is firm and crumbs are browned.

EGGS IN A NEST

 Separate whites from yolks, beat whites until almost dry. Butter a small baking dish in which eggs are to be served. Sprinkle fine breadcrumbs in bottom. Place beaten whites in dish, make hollows and slip in the yolks. Season with salt and pepper. Set dish over boiling water, cover, and cook until whites are firm.

BAKED EGGS A LA COLUMBUS

 Select green peppers of uniform size. Cut around the stem and remove the seeds and veins. Parboil for 5 minutes. Drain. Set the peppers in small muffin pans. Break a fresh egg into each. Add salt and pepper. Bake in a moderate oven for about 15 minutes or until egg is set. Serve on hot buttered toast. Cover with Basic Tomato Sauce (page 405).

FRIED EGGS

Frying Method

Break eggs carefully, one at a time, and slide gently into enough hot fat to cover bottom of frying pan. Let fry slowly, take up fat with spoon and pour over egg until yolk has a thin white covering. If fat is too hot, a hard, indigestible crust is formed. Or, if desired, turn egg to brown top.

BACON AND EGGS

Lay thin strips of bacon close together in cold skillet. Place over low heat, fry slowly until bacon is crisp and brown. Pour off fat as it accumulates. To keep edges from curling, press occasionally with spatula. Remove bacon from skillet, drain, and keep warm on hot platter. Fry eggs in bacon fat, serve with bacon.

HAM AND EGGS

Slice ham ¼ inch thick. Grease skillet very lightly. Brown ham quickly on both sides. If cooked too long, it will become hard and dry. Remove ham from skillet and keep hot. Fry eggs in same pan, adding more fat if necessary.

SCRAMBLED EGGS

BASIC SCRAMBLED EGGS   *Serves 2.*

3 eggs	speck of freshly ground black
½ teaspoon salt	pepper
⅓ cup milk or water	1 teaspoon butter

1

Beat the eggs slightly, add the milk and seasoning. Cook in a hot, buttered frying pan over slow fire, stirring constantly until thick; or let cook until white is partially set, then stir.

2

Beat eggs slightly, add the milk and seasoning. Place in hot buttered frying pan. Let cook until bottom layer becomes set, then with fork or spatula lift up the layer around the edge of the pan, allowing the uncooked egg on top to run underneath. Continue this cooking and lifting process until the whole mixture is set and jelly like.

3

Mix ingredients and pour into cold, greased frying pan or in the top of a double boiler. Stir constantly with fork until fluffy.

SCRAMBLED EGGS AND CORN   *Serves 2.*

4 to 6 ears of cooked corn (or 1 can corn)	⅛ teaspoon freshly ground black pepper
1 tablespoon butter	4 eggs, beaten
1 teaspoon salt	

   1. Cut corn from cob. Melt butter in a skillet, add the corn and seasonings.

   2. When well heated, add the beaten eggs, stir and scrape carefully from bottom of pan and cook gently until eggs are set. Serve at once.

EGGS AND SAUSAGE   *Serves 2.*

1 pound sausage, boiled   3 eggs, beaten lightly
2 tablespoons fat

Skin and slice sausage into half-inch pieces. Place in frying pan with hot fat. Brown on both sides a few minutes. Just before serving, add the eggs. Mix and cook until the eggs are set and serve immediately.

SCRAMBLED EGGS WITH TOMATO SAUCE

5 eggs   ½ cup milk or water
½ teaspoon salt   2 tablespoons butter
⅛ teaspoon freshly ground black   1 cup Basic Tomato Sauce (page
  pepper   405), heated

Beat eggs slightly with a fork. Add the salt, pepper, and milk. Heat skillet, put in butter and, when melted, turn in mixture. Cook until of creamy consistency, stirring and scraping carefully from bottom of pan. Stir in Tomato Sauce. Serve hot on toast or crackers.

Variation: Add several sliced mushrooms and 1 tablespoon of capers to the tomato sauce while heating it.

SCRAMBLED EGGS WITH MATZO

6 matzos   4 tablespoons goose fat or oil
2 cups boiling water   4 tablespoons sugar
3 eggs

   1.   Break matzos in small pieces in a colander. Pour boiling water through them, drain quickly. They should be moist but not soggy. Beat eggs well. Fold the matzos in lightly.

   2.   Heat the fat in a skillet. Add the egg mixture, scrape and scramble carefully with spoon from the bottom of the pan. While scrambling, sprinkle the sugar over the mixture and cook gently until eggs are set. Serve at once.

OMELETTES

An ideal omelette is moist and tender all the way through. This is difficult to achieve when the cooking time required to kill any harmful bacteria is longer than the thirty or so seconds needed for a perfect omelette. We're including a traditional recipe but we once again remind the reader that there are risks involved.

For best results, an omelette pan should not be used for other purposes. Keep omelette pan well greased and wipe with paper towel after each use. Do not overbeat the eggs.

Omelette Method

Heat butter in pan. Add the beaten egg mixture and use a fork or spatula to pull in edges as egg sets, allowing the uncooked portion to run underneath. Shake pan as egg sets to prevent sticking. When set, fold and roll onto platter and serve immediately.

To fill a cooked omelette, put a few spoonfuls of cooked filling on half of the omelette, fold part over it and roll onto a platter. Or put the filling near the edge and roll the omelette around it. Serve at once; omelettes begin to shrink when they are removed from the heat.

CREAMY OMELETTE AND VARIATIONS   *Serves 2.*

4 eggs
4 tablespoons milk or water
½ teaspoon salt

⅛ teaspoon freshly ground black pepper
1 tablespoon butter

1. Beat eggs slightly to combine yolks and whites. Add liquid and seasonings.

2. Melt butter in a hot 8- or 9-inch skillet over moderate heat. Add egg mixture.

3. As mixture cooks, draw edges to center to allow uncooked portion to run underneath. Omelette is done when it is just set.

4. To brown the bottom, hold over heat briefly, shaking pan to prevent sticking. As soon as set and browned, tip the pan and fold one side of omelette. Roll onto a hot platter and serve at once.

Variations:

Cheese Omelette: Follow directions for Creamy Omelette. Add ½ cup grated cheddar cheese to the beaten egg. Sprinkle finished omelette with grated cheese.

Herb Omelette: Follow directions for Creamy Omelette. Add 1 generous tablespoon chopped fresh herbs like parsley, chives, thyme, tarragon, or any desired combination.

Asparagus Omelette: Follow directions for Creamy Omelette. Fill with cooked asparagus (about 1 pound for a 4-egg omelette). Spoon 1 cup hot Medium White Sauce (page 399) on top. Fold omelette over and serve at once.

Chicken or Sweetbread Omelette: Mix 1½ cups diced cooked chicken or diced cooked sweetbreads with 1 cup hot Medium White Sauce (page 399). Follow recipe for Creamy Omelette above. Use half of the mixture to fill the cooked omelette and the other half to pour over after folding onto a serving platter. This will serve four.

SOUFFLÉ OMELETTE   *Serves 1.*

3 eggs, separated	3 tablespoons hot water
½ teaspoon salt	1 tablespoon butter
dash of freshly ground black pepper	

1.   Beat the yolks until thick. Add salt, pepper, and water. Beat the whites stiff and fold into yolk mixture.
2.   Preheat the oven to 350° F.
3.   Melt butter in an 8- or 9-inch skillet with oven proof handles. Add egg mixture. Cook over moderate heat without stirring until bottom sets. Test by lifting with a spatula. Transfer pan to the highest oven shelf and bake until top is golden. Fill as desired and fold.

CORN OMELETTE   *Serves 1.*

1 egg, separated	freshly ground black pepper to taste
½ cup corn scraped from cob	2 tablespoons cream
¼ teaspoon salt	2 tablespoons fat or butter

Beat the egg yolk well. Beat the egg white until stiff. Chop corn very fine. Add to the yolk. Season with salt and pepper. Pour in the cream and fold in the egg white. Heat a small skillet and add fat or butter. Pour in the egg mixture and cook until set and well browned underneath. Fold and serve at once.

ORANGE OMELETTE   *Serves 1.*

1 egg, separated	1 tablespoon orange juice
rind of ½ orange, grated	2 tablespoons powdered sugar

Beat the yolk of the egg and add the orange rind and juice. Add the sugar. Fold in the egg white, beaten until stiff, and turn into a heated buttered pan. Cook until set. Garnish with powdered sugar.

CHINESE PANCAKES (EGG FOO YUNG)   *Serves 2.*

Sauce	*Pancakes*
1 tablespoon cornstarch	1 cup cooked pork or chicken
2 teaspoons cold water	1 cup bamboo shoots
1 cup hot soup or chicken stock	¾ cup water chestnuts
(page 59)	6 eggs
1 tablespoon soy sauce	1 tablespoon salt
	½ cup oil for frying

1. To make the sauce, dissolve cornstarch in cold water. Add soup or stock and soy sauce. Cook until clear and thickened.

2. To prepare the pancakes, cut meat into small strips. Slice bamboo shoots finely and then into strips 2 inches long. Peel chestnuts, slice finely, and cut into strips 2 inches long. Squeeze the ingredients dry.

3. Place meat, bamboo shoots, and water chestnuts in a mixing bowl. Add the eggs and salt and beat together lightly.

4. Drop egg mixture into hot oil from tablespoon to make individual pancakes. Brown on both sides and remove to a hot platter to keep warm. Pour on hot sauce and serve.

Variations: Use other vegetables to replace the bamboo shoots and/or water chestnuts. Try bean sprouts, chopped green pepper, or onion.

ALMOND OMELETTE   *Serves 2.*

½ cup sweet almonds	4 tablespoons cream
4 eggs	1 tablespoon butter
pinch of salt	powdered sugar

Blanch, chop, and pound almonds until relatively smooth. Beat eggs slightly and add the salt and cream. Melt butter in a small skillet and pour in the egg mixture. Let cook gently, tilting pan back and forth until nearly set. Sprinkle most of the almonds over top, turn edge on one side, and roll. Serve at once on hot platter. Sprinkle with powdered sugar and remaining chopped nuts.

SAFETY TIPS FOR EGGS

The following tips for handling eggs come from the April 1990 edition of the *FDA Consumer*.

Handling Eggs

- Wash hands with hot, soapy water and wash and sanitize utensils, equipment (such as blenders), and work areas before and after they come in contact with eggs and uncooked egg-rich foods.
- Use only Grade A or higher eggs. Avoid eggs that are cracked or leaking.
- Discard the egg if any shell falls into the eggs.
- Leave eggs in their original carton and store them in the main section of the refrigerator—not the egg section in the door, as the temperature in the door is higher.
- Never leave eggs or foods containing egg at room temperature for more than two hours, including preparation and serving (but not cooking) times.
- When refrigerating a large amount of a hot egg dish or leftovers, divide it into several small shallow containers so the eggs will cool quickly.
- Cook scrambled eggs in batches no larger than three quarts. Serve at 140° F or hotter.

Cooking Eggs

The elderly, patients already weakened by serious illness, and people with weakened immune systems area at risk for death or serious illness from *Salmonella enteritidis*. Nursing homes, hospitals, and other food institutions serving those in high-risk groups should strictly follow these safe egg guidelines. The precautions also apply to home preparation.

You can't tell a good egg from a bad egg by the way it smells, tastes, or looks. But these precautions can help minimize risks:

- Review recipes, and consider using pasteurized eggs instead of whole eggs whenever possible.
- Avoid serving raw eggs and foods containing raw eggs. Caesar Salad, Hollandaise Sauce, homemade ice cream, homemade eggnog, and homemade mayonnaise are possible vehicles for *Salmonella enteritidis*.
- Lightly cooked foods containing eggs, such as soft custards and French toast, may be risky.

- Cook eggs thoroughly until both the yolk and white are firm, not runny. These cooking times are now recommended by researchers at Cornell University:

Scrambled—1 minute at 250° F

Poached—5 minutes in boiling water

Sunnyside—7 minutes at 250° F or cook covered 4 minutes at 250° F

Fried, over easy—3 minutes at 250° F on one side, then turn the egg and fry for another minute on the other side

Boiled—7 minutes in boiling water

EGGS AND THE MICROWAVE

Microwave ovens vary in power and added features. Follow manufacturer's instructions for your particular model. While difficult to generalize, there are some basics about cooking eggs in the microwave that can be applied to poaching, hard-cooking, and scrambling.

Poached Eggs: Place 2 tablespoons water with several drops of distilled vinegar in individual ramekins. Boil on high power. Break eggs into boiling liquid. Arrange in a circle with a 1-inch space between them. Cook on medium power for 3 to 4 minutes. Cover and let stand for 2 more minutes. Watch carefully. Some eggs will cook faster than others. Position and reposition as eggs cook to distribute energy. Puncturing the yolk will help prevent it from bursting as steam builds up.

Hard-Cooked Eggs: Never cook eggs in their shells as the steam will build up and the contents will burst. Break into ramekins as for poached eggs. Make a hole in the yolk and cover tightly. Cook on medium power for 6 to 8 minutes. Position and reposition as eggs cook to distribute energy. Let stand for 2 minutes after removing from oven.

Scrambled Eggs: Use a buttered dish large enough to hold the beaten eggs in an even, thick layer. Additional liquid like water or milk will give a creamier texture. Beat eggs well with salt and pepper. Cook on high, uncovered, for 1½ minutes. Stir and cook for 1 more minute. Remove, stir, and cover tightly. Let stand for 1 more minute before serving.

Cheese Dishes

Cheese is a concentrated food, rich in protein, fat, minerals, and vitamins. It is considered a meat substitute and valued for the flavor it lends to other foods. When eaten in moderate quantities, it is easily digested.

Unripened Soft Cheeses such as cottage cheese and cream cheese are very perishable and should be kept in the refrigerator and used within a few days.

Ripe Cheeses of all kinds keep well in the refrigerator, wrapped in foil or plastic over the original wrappings if possible. However, these continue to ripen, even in the refrigerator, and should be used before they become too strong.

Hard Cheeses such as Parmesan and Romano are best when freshly grated, but they can be grated in advance and stored in the refrigerator, in a tightly covered jar, until wanted for garnishing or flavoring cooked dishes. Dry ends of other cheeses, such as swiss and cheddar, may be grated (by hand or in an electric blender or food processor) and used the same way.

COLD CHEESE DISHES

COTTAGE CHEESE

Heat some milk or buttermilk slowly until the whey rises to the top; pour off whey, put curd in a perforated bag, and let drip 6 hours without squeezing it. Place curd in a bowl and break it fine. Season with salt. Refrigerate. It tastes best when fresh.

KOCH KAESE (BOILED CHEESE)

1 quart cottage cheese	1 tablespoon butter
1 teaspoon salt	1½ cups water
1 teaspoon caraway seeds	1 egg yolk, beaten

1. Press cottage cheese until dry. Add salt and caraway seeds to taste.
2. Put in earthen dish, cover well, set in a warm place. Stir with a fork every day for a week or until very ripe.
3. Place butter and water in a skillet. When warm, add cheese and boil slowly for 20 minutes, stirring constantly.
4. Remove from heat, add egg yolk and beat until glossy. Pour into bowl or cups that have been rinsed with cold water. Refrigerate. Serve when cold.

COLD CHEESE MIXTURES ON CRACKERS

Pimento

Mash a cream cheese, season with salt and a tablespoon finely chopped pimento, and stir with a little cream until smooth and creamy. Pile a small mound very lightly on top of an unsweetened wafer cracker and garnish with deviled olive.

American Cheese

 In the bowl of a food processor fitted with the metal blade, grind ¼ pound American cheese. Season with ¼ teaspoon salt, a little paprika, and ½ teaspoon mustard and a tablespoon each of butter and cream. Spread lightly on crackers.

Watercress

Follow Pimento Cheese recipe, above, adding 1 tablespoon cream and 1 tablespoon finely chopped watercress.

Camembert

Thoroughly beat a well-ripened Camembert cheese with 2 tablespoons butter, ½ teaspoon paprika, 3 or 4 dashes of Tabasco, and 3 drops of Worcestershire sauce. Beat until smooth. Serve with hot toasted crackers, or in a dish surrounded with chopped ice, or shape into tiny balls rolled into paprika.

Roquefort

⅛ pound Roquefort cheese	1 tablespoon lemon juice
¼ pound cream cheese	1 teaspoon salt
1 tablespoon butter	½ teaspoon chives, finely chopped

Mash the cheeses, stir with other ingredients until smooth. Serve on hot buttered rye crackers or toast.

HOT CHEESE DISHES

BAKED CHEESE FONDUE

2 cups soft breadcrumbs	1 teaspoon salt
1 cup milk	4 eggs, separated
¾ cup grated cheddar or Swiss cheese	1 loaf French bread, cut into bite-size chunks
4 tablespoons butter	

   1. In a saucepan, heat the breadcrumbs, milk, cheese, and butter until melted. Stir in salt. Remove and cool slightly.

   2. Preheat the oven to 350° F.

   3. Beat the yolks slightly and the whites until stiff. Add the beaten yolks then fold in the whites. Pour into a buttered baking dish. Bake until firm, about 20 minutes. Serve from the dish in which it was baked, or transfer to a fondue dish. Each guest dips a bit of bread into the fondue.

SWISS FONDUE

1 clove garlic	salt, freshly ground black pepper,
2 cups dry white wine	nutmeg to taste
1 pound cubed Swiss cheese	2 tablespoons kirsch
1 tablespoon flour	1 loaf French bread

1. Rub a heat-proof casserole with garlic clove. Set on a rack of a chafing dish, over low heat, add wine, heat till first bubbles rise.

2. Toss cheese with flour. Add to heating wine gradually; stir until melted. Repeat until all cheese is added and mixture is smooth. Season to taste. Add kirsch.

3. Break or cut French bread into bite-size chunks, each with a bit of crust. Each guest spears a bit of bread with a long-handled fork and dips into the fondue.

CHEESE SOUFFLÉ

2 tablespoons flour	½ cup grated cheddar or Swiss
2 tablespoons butter	cheese
2 cups milk	4 eggs, separated
½ teaspoon salt	

1. Preheat oven to 350° F.

2. Rub butter and flour together in a heavy-bottomed skillet over moderate heat. When it bubbles, gradually add hot milk. Season. Add cheese. When melted, remove from fire. Cool.

3. Lightly beat yolks and beat egg whites until stiff. When cheese mixture is lukewarm, add beaten yolks, then fold in beaten whites. Pour into buttered baking dish. Set in a pan of hot water.

4. Bake until a knife comes out clean, 45 minutes to 1 hour. Heat may be increased during last 15 minutes. Serve at once.

WELSH RAREBIT

1 tablespoon butter
½ pound cheddar cheese
⅛ teaspoon salt
freshly ground black pepper

⅛ teaspoon mustard
pinch of cayenne (optional)
1 egg
¼ cup milk

Melt the butter. Break the cheese into small pieces and add to the butter. Season with salt, pepper, mustard, and a pinch of cayenne pepper if desired. Beat together the egg and milk and add when cheese is melted. Cook one minute. Serve at once on toast or wafers.

RINKTUM-DITY

1 8-ounce can tomatoes, drained
  and chopped
1 cup grated cheese
½ cup grated onion
1 green pepper, chopped

1 teaspoon salt
2 tablespoons butter
2 eggs, slightly beaten

Mix tomatoes, cheese, onion, and the pepper and salt. Melt the butter in a double boiler. Add the cheese mixture. When heated, add the eggs. Cook until creamy, stirring constantly. Serve on toast.

HOT CHEESE ON TOAST

Prepare grated cheese, moisten with cream seasoned with salt and cayenne pepper. Butter and cover toast or cracker with the mixture and put in hot oven. Serve when cheese is melted.

NATURAL CHEESES

(Courtesy of U.S. Dept. of Agriculture)

Soft, Unripened Varieties

Cottage Cheese: Mild, acid flavor. Soft curd particles of varying size. White to creamy white in color. Use in salads, with fruits, vegetables, sandwiches, dips, cheesecake.

Cream Cheese: Mild, acid flavor. Soft and smooth texture. White. Use in salads, dips, sandwiches, snacks, cheesecake, and desserts.

Neufchâtel: Mild and acid in flavor. Soft, smooth, similar to cream cheese but lower in milk fat. White. Use in salads, dips, sandwiches, snacks, cheesecake, and desserts.

Ricotta: Sweet, nut-like flavor. Soft, moist, or dry. White. Used for appetizers, salads, snacks, lasagne, ravioli, noodles, and other cooked dishes, grating, and for desserts.

Firm, Unripened Varieties

Gjetost: Sweetish, caramel flavor with a firm buttery consistency. Golden brown in color. Used in snacks, desserts, served with dark breads, crackers, biscuits, or muffins.

Feta: Firm and salty but mild-flavored Greek cheese made from ewe's or goat's milk. Used in salads and for cooking casseroles or gratins.

Mysost (also called Primost):   Sweetish, caramel flavor with a firm buttery consistency. Light brown in color. Used in snacks, desserts, served with dark breads.

Mozzarella: Delicate and mild flavored. Slightly firm, plastic texture. Creamy white in color. Used in snacks, toasted sandwiches, cheeseburgers, for cooking as in meat loaf, or topping for lasagne, pizza, and casseroles.

Soft, Ripened Varieties

Bel Paese: Mild to moderately robust in flavor. Soft to medium firm, creamy texture. Creamy yellow interior, slightly gray or brownish surface sometimes covered with yellow wax coating. Use for appetizers; good with crackers, snacks, on sandwiches, and for dessert.

Brick: Mild to moderately sharp flavor. Semisoft to medium firm, elastic texture with numerous small openings. Creamy yellow in color. Use for appetizers, sandwiches, snacks, and dessert.

Brie: Mild to pungent flavor. Soft, smooth when ripened. Creamy yellow interior; edible thin brown and white crust. Used in appetizers, sandwiches, snacks; good with crackers and fruit, and for dessert.

Camembert: Mild to pungent flavor. Smooth, very soft when fully ripened. Creamy yellow interior; edible thin white or gray-white crust. Use for making sandwiches, snacks. Good with crackers and fruit like pears and apples for dessert.

Limburger: Highly pungent, soft cheese. Smooth and very soft when fully ripened. Creamy yellow interior with a reddish-yellow surface. Use for appetizers, snacks; good with crackers, rye or other dark breads, and for dessert.

Muenster: Mild to mellow in flavor. Semisoft cheese with numerous small openings. Contains more moisture than brick. Creamy white interior with yellow tan surface. Used for appetizers, sandwiches, snacks, and dessert.

Port du Salut: Mellow to robust in flavor. Semisoft, smooth, buttery cheese with small openings. Creamy yellow color. Used for appetizers, snacks; served with raw fruit for dessert.

Firm, Ripened Varieties

Cheddar: Mild to very sharp in flavor. Firm, smooth, some small openings. White to medium yellow-orange in color. Use for appetizers, sauces, sandwiches, grating, cheeseburgers, or dessert.

Colby: Mild to mellow flavor. Softer and more openings than cheddar. White to medium yellow-orange in color. Use for making sandwiches, snacks, or cheeseburgers.

Edam or Gouda: Mellow, nut-like flavor. Semisoft to firm; smooth with small irregularly shaped or round holes. Gouda is higher in milk fat than Edam. Both have a creamy yellow or medium yellow-orange interior; may or may not have red wax coating. Used for appetizers, snacks, salads, sandwiches, seafood sauce, or dessert.

Provolone: Mellow to sharply smoky, salty flavor. Firm, smooth texture. Light creamy interior; light brown or golden yellow surface. Use for appetizers, sandwiches, snacks; in soufflés, macaroni and spaghetti dishes; on pizza. Suitable for grating when fully cured and dried.

Swiss: Sweet, nut-like flavor. Firm, smooth with large round eyes. Light yellow in color. Used for making sandwiches, snacks, fondue, cheeseburgers.

Very Hard, Ripened Varieties

Parmesan: Sharp, piquant flavor. Very hard, granular texture; lower moisture and milk fat than Romano. Creamy white. Used for seasoning in soups, vegetables, pastas, breads, popcorn; used extensively for pizza and lasagne.

Romano: Sharp, piquant flavor. Very hard, granular texture. Yellowish-white interior, greenish-black surface. Used in seasoning soups, casseroles, pastas, breads; suitable for grating when cured for about one year.

Blue-Veined, Mold-Ripened Varieties

Blue: Tangy, peppery flavor. Semisoft, pasty, sometimes crumbly texture. White interior, marbled or streaked with blue veins of mold. Used for appetizers, salads, dips, salad dressing, sandwich spreads; good with crackers, dessert.

Gorgonzola: Tangy, peppery flavor. Semisoft, pasty, sometimes crumbly, lower in moisture than Blue cheese. Creamy white interior, mottled or streaked with blue-green veins of mold. Clay-colored surface. Used for appetizers, salads, dips, salad dressing, sandwich spreads, good with crackers, dessert.

Roquefort: Sharp, peppery taste. Semisoft, pasty, sometimes crumbly. White or creamy white interior, marbled or streaked with blue veins of mold. Used for appetizers, salads, dips, salad dressing, sandwich spreads, good with crackers, dessert.

Stilton: Piquant, milder than Gorgonzola or Roquefort. Semisoft, flaky, slightly more crumbly than Blue. Creamy white interior, marbled or streaked with blue-green veins of mold. Used for appetizers, salads, dips, salad dressing, sandwich spreads, good with crackers, dessert.

Goat Cheese

A fairly new cheese in America, this now-popular variety is imported and made domestically. Because of its versatility, personal preferences are easy to oblige. Goat cheeses come in varying forms ranging from long logs to triangular blocks. Aging is one of the most important considerations when selecting goat cheese. Fresh ones are mild in flavor and creamy textured. As they age, goat cheeses lose moisture and take on a stronger taste. Choose according to desired degree of tanginess. Low in fat, easy to digest, and full of flavor, goat cheese is used in dips, spread on toasts to go with salads, and often served as a course in itself as part of a formal meal. This cheese easily takes to flavoring. Firmer ones can be kept in olive oil with fragrant herbs, peppers, or garlic for preserving. Try covering younger, softer ones with herbs, cracked black pepper, or paprika before serving.

Yogurt Cheese

Using lowfat or nonfat yogurt, a homemade cheese can be made with little effort. The result can be used like cream cheese for dipping, spreading, or for making sandwiches. Try mixing the cheese with fresh herbs and garlic. Season with salt and pepper and serve with crackers. The same cheese can be blended with sugar and flavorings like vanilla or lemon rind to be served with fresh berries. Low in fat, easy to digest, and versatile for general kitchen use, this is a healthy alternative for cheese lovers who are watching their diet.

Empty lowfat yogurt into a colander lined with a triple layer of cheesecloth set over a bowl. Allow yogurt to drain for a few minutes. Pull up corners of the cheesecloth and tie them together. Hang the bag from the kitchen faucet and let whey drain off for 12 to 24 hours. Remove the "cheese" from the bag and refrigerate.

There are kits available that are made specifically for draining yogurt to make this type of cheese. Follow package directions carefully for perfect results.

SALADS

Salads are increasingly popular additions to modern meals. Whether a mixture of simple greens or an elaborate combination of contrasting tastes and textures, a perfect salad requires careful preparation.

Green salads—or greens with other vegetables—included as a part of a meal can add a fresh, satisfying touch that is in line with today's trend toward lighter eating. Whether served as a first course, between courses, or as a side dish with a main course, a crisp salad of quality, healthful ingredients is always well received.

Composed salads may be served as a first course or as part of a main course. These concoctions are usually of more substance than green salads and include diverse elements like meat, eggs, poultry, fish, or shellfish as well as lettuces and/or other vegetables. Tossed with a simple dressing or a complex mixture of exotic flavored oils and vinegars, these salads provide dishes of great character.

Green Salads

An increasing number of salad greens that are available throughout the year makes it easy to add extra interest and appeal to salad bowls.

Choose a mixture of salad greens with an eye to contrast and harmony of texture and flavor; mix buttery leaves and crisp, sweet leaves with sharp and biting varieties.

SOME KINDS OF SALAD GREENS

Crisphead   is the correct name of the solid compact head lettuce usually called *Iceberg* or *Simpson* or *head lettuce*. Since it transports well, is usually available all year round, and is reasonably priced, this has long been the most widely used lettuce in America. Increasingly popular are varied, tastier kinds of lettuce now available throughout the country.

Leaf Lettuce,   a loose head of long, frilly leaves, is mild and sweet in flavor, decorative in appearance. This variety is the lettuce most often grown in home gardens. Modern methods of cultivation make it more and more available throughout the year. *Oak Leaf* lettuce is a colorful member of this family.

Boston is the best-known variety of *Butterhead* lettuce. The head is round but soft, loose and light for its size. The leaves have a smooth, buttery texture and a mild, sweet flavor.

Bibb lettuce is an excellent salad green. The head is smallish, the color is dark green shading toward pale green, the flavor sweet and nutty.

Romaine or **Cos** lettuce has long, stiff leaves, crisp texture, and a distinctive rich flavor. Romaine is widely available and inexpensive during the local growing seasons. Avoid the tough, outer dark green leaves and look for the younger, lighter colored heads of this sturdy lettuce. Romaine is the lettuce used for the famous Caesar Salad.

Escarole has flat, lightly curled leaves that are darker green on the outside than the yellow-white ones in the middle. Search for the younger, more tender heads that have a pleasantly biting flavor. The older ones can be very bitter. Use your discretion when using this lettuce. You might want to mix it with more mellow varieties to add contrast rather than using it as the main component in your salad. Escarole is also often prepared cooked.

Chicory (sometimes called **Curly Endive**) comes in large heads of decorative curly-edged leaves. Like escarole, the leaves may be too bitter to use in large quantities.

Endive (sometimes called **Witloof** and known as **Chicory** in England) is a very small head of tightly packed, smooth, rather thick leaves shaped like an elongated oval. Endive is sometimes cut into rings, sometimes served with the spear-shaped leaves separated from the head. The flavor is slightly bitter but with a pleasant, nutty taste. The leaves are pale green to white.

Watercress has a sharp, lemony bite and tiny, rich green leaves that make it a most attractive garnish for the salad bowl. Avoid bunches that have large leaves and thick, tough stems.

Radicchio is a member of the endive family. Of Italian origin, it is increasingly grown year-round in all parts of the world. It is a red lettuce with white veins and a small center. Its bitter, spicy taste adds color and zip to any tossed salad.

Arugula, a peppery, small-leafed salad green, has a distinctive nutty taste. Once found mostly during the summer months, many varieties of this popular lettuce are being cultivated all year long. Many people find its strong flavor needs to be mixed with another, less aggressive green for a balanced salad.

Spinach has young, tender leaves that make a welcome addition to the salad category. Avoid tough, older leaves and be sure to wash well.

Dandelion, a perennial flowering plant, has greens that are ideal for salads when picked young, especially in the spring. Cultivated leaves are less vibrant in flavor but edible throughout the year. This hearty green goes well with a combination of forceful vinegars and oils as well as condiments like bacon pieces and hard-boiled eggs. Dandelion is also served cooked.

Mâche or **Lamb's Lettuce** is a delicate, round-leafed lettuce that is found mostly during the winter months but increasingly cultivated throughout the year as demand rises. It has a sweet, mellow taste that calls for a light hand when dressing. This salad is best when simply dressed with a splash of good olive oil and red wine vinegar.

PREPARING SALAD GREENS

Discard any withered or darkened leaves before cleaning. Gently hold the head or bunch of greens with one hand and twist or cut away the core to separate the leaves from each other. Use only the young, tender parts.

Biting into salad that has even the slightest trace of sand or grit is an unpleasant experience that can be avoided by proper cleaning. Wash in several changes of cold, clear water. Spread out a clean kitchen towel and place paper towels on top. Or use a salad spinner—a device made for this purpose—and carefully remove the washed salad to the paper towels. Continue cleaning the leaves, working in small amounts, laying out to dry on the toweling. Top with additional paper towels to absorb more moisture. Loosely roll up, carefully working the greens between the paper towels to soak up any liquid that might remain.

When dry, place the washed greens in plastic bags that close with a zipper seal or a container with a lid that forms a tight seal when closed. Keep in the bottom of the refrigerator until ready to serve.

Salad greens will wilt as soon as they are tossed with a dressing. This should, therefore, be done seconds before serving. Try pouring your dressing in the bottom of a large bowl. Pile the greens on top without tossing. Bring to the table with utensils that are long enough to reach deep into the bowl. At tableside, carefully turn the salad to coat the leaves. Then serve.

Vegetable Salads

BASIC VEGETABLE SALAD METHOD

Any desired combination of raw or cooked vegetables may be used in a salad, or cooked vegetables may be added to a tossed green salad. For an attractive appetizer salad, cook whole green beans, asparagus, leeks or your favorite vegetable until just tender, cover with a good vinaigrette sauce while vegetables are still warm, and serve chilled. For best flavor, cook the different kinds of vegetables for a mixed salad separately, until tender but still crisp. Drain well, cover with dressing, and marinate in the refrigerator until chilled. A few rings of onion, hard-boiled eggs, or chopped fresh herbs may be added to any cooked vegetable salad before seasoning. Vegetable salads are ideal for large crowds.

The microwave is sometimes useful for preparing vegetables for salads. Follow instructions for your particular make and model. We've noted some vegetables we find particularly well suited for microwave cooking.

Note: Vegetable salads are especially suitable to serve at picnics or outdoor barbecues. Extra dressing may be added just before serving, if necessary.

MIXED BEAN SALAD

Long an American favorite, this recipe is often done by mixing canned beans with bottled salad dressing. Try making the real thing with the following. We find it best when served at room temperature.

1 cup cooked kidney beans (page 179)
1 cup cooked chick peas (page 179)
1 cup green beans, blanched and refreshed under cold running water and cut into 1-inch pieces
½ cup chopped red onion
2 tablespoons vinegar

¼ cup salad or olive oil
salt and freshly ground black pepper to taste
¼ cup (loosely packed) chopped fresh parsley, for garnish
lettuce leaves, for garnish

Combine all the ingredients except the parsley and lettuce leaves in a large bowl. Stir in the parsley just before serving. Garnish the bowl with lettuce leaves and sprinkle on some extra parsley if desired.

CHICK PEA SALAD WITH BLACK OLIVES AND ONIONS

This Mediterranean-inspired recipe is a good accompaniment to grilled fish or chicken. It is also an excellent idea for a large, cold buffet. Use first-quality olives as they are the predominant flavor.

2 cups cooked chick peas (page 179)
1 small red onion, sliced into rings
½ cup pitted black olives (preferably oil-cured)
2 tablespoons vinegar

¼ cup olive oil
salt and freshly ground black pepper to taste
¼ cup (loosely packed) chopped, fresh parsley

Mix together the chick peas, onion, and olives in a large bowl. Pour over the vinegar and the oil. Mix well. Season with salt and pepper. Stir in fresh parsley just before serving.

BLACK BEAN SALAD

2 cups cooked black beans (page 179)
½ cup (about 6 ounces) tomato, peeled, seeded, and chopped
½ cup (about 4 ounces) red onion, chopped
½ cup canned or cooked corn

2 tablespoons lime juice
¼ cup olive oil
¼ cup (loosely packed) fresh cilantro, chopped
salt and freshly ground black pepper to taste
lettuce leaves, for garnish

Combine all of the ingredients except the lettuce in a large bowl. Refrigerate and serve in a bowl with lettuce leaves for garnish.

LENTIL SALAD

2 cups cooked lentils (page 179)
1 cup boiled ham, cut into small cubes
¾ cup Vinaigrette Sauce (page 129)
¼ cup (loosely packed) chopped fresh parsley

salt and freshly ground black pepper to taste
2 hard-boiled eggs, quartered, for garnish (optional)

Combine the lentils and ham in a large bowl. Pour over Vinaigrette Sauce and mix well. Stir in parsley just before serving. Season with salt and pepper to taste. Garnish with quartered hard-boiled eggs if desired.

BLACK-EYED PEA SALAD

2 cups cooked black-eyed peas
(page 179)
½ pound shrimp, boiled, peeled,
and deveined then cut into ¼-inch
pieces

4 slices crisp cooked bacon,
crumbled
⅓ cup diced yellow onion
½ cup Vinaigrette Sauce (page 129)
¼ cup chopped fresh parsley

Combine the peas, shrimp, bacon, and onion in a large bowl. Pour the Vinaigrette Sauce over all and toss to blend. Add parsley just before serving and mix well. Serve chilled.

ENDIVE, BEETS, AND WALNUTS

4 or 5 heads endive (about 1
pound), washed, rinsed, and cut
into ¼-inch rounds
3 to 4 medium beets (about ½
pound), cooked, peeled, and cut
into small cubes

½ cup walnuts, toasted and broken
into small pieces
½ cup Vinaigrette Sauce (page 129)

Combine all of the ingredients. Toss just before serving. Season with freshly ground pepper if desired.

CELERY SALAD

2 small celery roots (celeriac)
2 cups stalk celery, diced
½ cup vinegar
¼ teaspoon freshly ground black
pepper

1 teaspoon salt
¼ pound almonds, blanched and
slivered
½ cup thick, sour cream

Scrub celery root well. Cook in salted water until tender. Peel and slice, then measure out 2 cups and add stalk celery. Mix with the rest of the ingredients, adding the sour cream last. Place in salad bowl and chill thoroughly. Serve cold.

Note: Try substituting lowfat plain yogurt for the sour cream to save a few calories if desired.

COLE SLAW

1 teaspoon salt
4 cups shredded cabbage
½ cup green pepper, chopped
½ cup green onion, chopped
1 teaspoon celery seed

½ cup salad oil
½ cup lemon juice
2 tablespoons sugar
salt and pepper to taste

In a large bowl, sprinkle salt over cabbage. Let stand for 1 hour. Squeeze out liquid. Add green pepper, onion, celery seed, salad oil, lemon juice, and sugar. Toss well. Season to taste with salt and pepper.

CABBAGE ROSE SALAD

1 medium white cabbage
about 2 cups diced celery or 2 cups
    boiled potatoes, sliced

½ cup Hot Salad Dressing (page 131)
1 red pepper, very thinly sliced

Remove the outside leaves of the cabbage and cut off stalk close to leaves. Cut out center leaves with sharp knife so that a shell remains. Place "Cabbage Bowl" in ice cold water for one hour, then drain as dry as possible. Meanwhile, shred remaining cabbage, mix with equal parts of celery or potato. Moisten with Hot Salad Dressing and refill cabbage. Turn back outer leaves of cabbage to resemble open rose. Lay the finely sliced red peppers over the top of leaves, and serve cold.

CUCUMBER SALAD

1

Choose firm, slim cucumbers, about 6 inches long or longer. Keep in a cool, dry place until ready to use. Peel rather thick, lengthwise, cut off ends, slice crosswise in ⅛-inch slices, drop into ice cold water. Let stand from ½ to 3 hours until wanted. Drain thoroughly. Pour on Vinaigrette Sauce (page 129) to cover and chill.

2

2 cups diced cucumbers
¾ cup bottled mayonnaise
1 teaspoon chopped capers

1 teaspoon parsley, chopped
½ teaspoon anchovy paste
2 tablespoons vinegar

Chill the cucumber. Mix mayonnaise thoroughly with the rest of the ingredients. Add to the cucumber.

CUCUMBER AND MINT SALAD

2 cucumbers (about 1 pound) peeled, halved, seeded, and very thinly sliced
1 cup plain yogurt (preferably lowfat)

2 tablespoons chopped fresh mint
salt and freshly ground black pepper to taste

Combine sliced cucumbers and yogurt in a bowl. Add mint and mix well. Season to taste with salt and pepper. Serve well chilled.

CUCUMBER SALAD WITH SOUR CREAM

3 firm cucumbers, peeled
½ cup sour cream
2 tablespoons lemon juice
2 tablespoons white vinegar

2 tablespoons sugar
¼ teaspoon salt
2 tablespoons freshly chopped dill, optional

1. Slice the cucumbers very thin by hand or in a food processor. Drop in salted ice water for 1 hour. Drain well.

2. Mix together sour cream, lemon juice, vinegar, sugar, and salt. Add to cucumbers and stir to blend. Add dill, if desired. Serve chilled.

FENNEL SALAD

¼ teaspoon salt
1 medium fennel bulb (about ½ pound), peeled and cut into thin julienne strips
1 medium red pepper (about ½ pound), rinsed, dried, seeded, and very thinly sliced

½ cup Vinaigrette Sauce (page 129)
freshly ground black pepper

1. In a small saucepan, bring water to a boil and add the salt. Plunge in the strips of fennel and bring back to a boil. Cook over high heat until fennel is soft but not mushy, about 3 minutes. Refresh under cold running water and drain well.

2. Combine the blanched fennel with the red pepper slices. Just before serving, toss with the Vinaigrette Sauce and season with black pepper to taste.

GRILLED PEPPER SALAD

1 red pepper (about ½ pound)
1 yellow pepper (about ½ pound)
1 tablespoon lemon juice

1 clove garlic, finely chopped
½ to 1 cup olive oil
freshly ground black pepper to taste

Roast, peel, and seed the peppers (page 385). Lay flat in a small, nonreactive baking dish. Sprinkle over lemon juice and garlic. Cover with olive oil. Season with pepper. Let marinate for 1 to 2 hours. Serve at room temperature.

Note: This is delicious served as a first course or as an accompaniment to grilled meats or fish. If being held for longer than 1 or 2 hours, omit lemon juice. It tends to give the peppers a soft, flabby texture. Sprinkle it on an hour or two before serving and turn the peppers often.

POTATO SALAD

1

4 cups boiled potatoes (1 to 1½ pounds), peeled and sliced while hot
salt and freshly ground black pepper
1 medium-size onion, finely chopped

1 cup Hot Salad Dressing (page 131)
chopped parsley or chives, for garnish
sour cream (optional)

Toss the hot potato slices with salt and pepper, then add the onions and mix with the Hot Salad Dressing. Garnish with parsley or chives. Serve warm. A little sour cream may be added, if desired.

2

6 cold, boiled potatoes, peeled
2 hard-boiled eggs
1 teaspoon onion juice
1 teaspoon mustard
1 teaspoon salt
speck of freshly ground black pepper

2 tablespoons vinegar
1 cup milk (or cream, if desired)
½ grated onion
1 cup Hot Salad Dressing, page 131 (optional)

Cut potatoes into small cubes. Separate whites from yolks of cooked eggs. Coarsely chop the egg whites. Mash yolks with onion juice, mustard, salt, and pepper, then add vinegar and mix well. Bring milk or cream to a boil and pour over yolk mixture. Add potatoes, egg whites, and grated onion, and mix well. Correct seasonings. Serve with Hot Salad Dressing, if desired.

HOT GERMAN POTATO SALAD

1 to 1½ pounds all-purpose potatoes	½ cup vinegar
1 teaspoon salt	¼ pound bacon or fat smoked beef,
⅛ teaspoon pepper	sliced and finely chopped, or 2
½ teaspoon sugar	tablespoons poultry fat
½ teaspoon flour	1 medium onion, finely chopped
½ cup water	1 teaspoon prepared mustard

1. Scrub potatoes and cook in boiling salted water until tender. Drain and, while hot, skin and cut into ¼-inch slices. You should have about 4 cups. Sprinkle with the salt, pepper, sugar, and flour. Set aside.

2. Add water to vinegar and heat thoroughly.

3. Place bacon or beef in a skillet and fry until light brown. Add onion and let brown slightly, then add potato slices and pour the hot vinegar mixture over all. Let heat through to absorb the vinegar and water.

4. Stir in mustard. Place in serving dish and serve warm.

Note: The bits of bacon or beef may be omitted. If the salad is too dry, add a little hot water. It should have a glassy look, without being lumpy or greasy.

SPINACH SALAD

Wash young, tender leaves of spinach very carefully in several changes of cold water. Drain well then refrigerate in a closed plastic bag until crisp. Mix with Vinaigrette Sauce (page 129). Add finely chopped crisp bacon and chopped hard-boiled egg if desired.

Main Dish Salads

Main dish—or composed—salads are made by varying flavors, textures, and colors. Contrasting but complementary elements like chicken and nuts or celery and apples or an assortment of cheeses and meats are combined to provide either the first course of a meal or a one-dish meal in itself.

Use your imagination when putting together a composed salad. Leftover meats, vegetables, and even seafood can be creatively combined and bound with a good salad dressing. The following recipes are some of the better known composed salads that have been in *The Settlement Cookbook* for years as well as other new ideas. Remember that some of the greatest dishes in the world have been conceived when some odd ingredients were put together just because they happened to be on hand.

VEGETABLE COMPOSED SALADS

CAESAR SALAD

1 clove garlic
2 heads romaine lettuce, washed, dried, and chilled
¼ teaspoon dry mustard
¼ teaspoon freshly ground black pepper
½ teaspoon salt

4 ounces Parmesan or blue cheese
6 to 8 anchovy fillets
6 tablespoons olive oil
juice of 2 medium lemons
2 eggs
2 cups Baked or Fried Croutons (page 77)

1. Rub a large wooden bowl with garlic. Add the chilled romaine, torn into bite-size pieces. Season with mustard, pepper, and salt. Add the grated or crumbled cheese, the anchovies, olive oil, and lemon juice.

2. Boil the eggs for 1 minute and break them over the greens. Toss contents thoroughly but carefully. Add croutons, tossing just enough to mix. Serve at once.

CHEF'S SALAD

Use a mixture of lettuces (Boston, endive, romaine, leaf, and/or watercress). Wash, crisp, and tear the leaves into pieces. Add cucumbers, celery, or radishes, cut in pieces. Chill. To serve, place in salad bowl. Add 6 to 8 anchovies, drained and chopped. Arrange strips of Swiss cheese, cooked turkey, ham, tongue, or chicken in heaps on the mixtures of greens. Garnish with hard-boiled eggs and tomato wedges. Toss the salad at the table with Vinaigrette Sauce (page 129). The dressing may be seasoned with crumbled Roquefort or blue cheese if desired.

WALDORF SALAD

2 cups celery, trimmed, peeled, and sliced into crescents
2 cups apples, peeled, sliced, and diced
1 cup pecans and walnuts, broken in pieces

½ to 1 cup bottled mayonnaise
lettuce leaves, for garnish
additional apple and celery, sliced, for garnish
2 fresh figs, sliced, for garnish (optional)

Mix the celery, apples, and ¼ cup of the nuts with enough mayonnaise to hold together. Arrange the mixture on a platter in a mound with lettuce around the edge. Cover with additional mayonnaise and the remaining nuts. Garnish with thin rings or crescents of red-skinned apple and celery tips. Add figs if desired.

SALAD NIÇOISE

Use a mixture of lettuces (Boston, endive, romaine, leaf, and/or watercress). Wash, crisp, and tear the leaves into pieces. Place in a large salad bowl. Add a cucumber, peeled, seeded, and sliced, 2 quartered tomatoes, and 1 cup of artichoke hearts cut into small pieces. Drain a small can of tuna and add to the bowl with some anchovy fillets and small rings of raw onion. Add about a cup of pitted black olives (preferably oil-cured) and some chopped, fresh basil. Toss the salad with Vinaigrette Sauce (page 129) and serve at once. Garnish with garlic croutons if desired.

FISH AND SHELLFISH COMPOSED SALADS

HERRING SALAD

Early editions of the Settlement had several recipes for Herring Salad. This popular European delicacy was surely a staple at the turn of the century. We've included just one of the original recipes, because herring is increasingly hard to obtain.

4 hard-boiled eggs, separated	¼ cup chopped cooked veal
¼ cup vinegar	1 pickle
3 herring, cleaned and picked in pieces	a small onion
	freshly ground black pepper
3 apples	¼ cup sugar
3 boiled potatoes	a few capers
½ cup mixed nuts	

Mash the yolks of the eggs and mix with vinegar. Finely chop the remaining ingredients and mix all together. Serve with rye rounds or toasts.

SHAD ROE AND CUCUMBER SALAD

1 shad roe	½ cup Vinaigrette Sauce (page 129)
1 slice onion	2 fresh cucumbers
1 bay leaf	½ cup bottled mayonnaise
1 tablespoon vinegar	lettuce leaves

1. Let shad roe simmer 20 minutes in salted water with the onion, bay leaf, and vinegar. Cool, cut in slices and cubes. Cover with Vinaigrette Sauce.

2. Peel and cube one of the cucumbers. Add to the roe and moisten with mayonnaise.

3. Place salad on a bed of crisp lettuce leaves. Slice the other cucumber and use for garnish.

OYSTER SALAD

1 pint oysters, shucked
2 cups celery, peeled and thinly sliced
1 scant teaspoon Worcestershire sauce

½ cup Vinaigrette Sauce (page 129)
lettuce leaves
lemon sliced
parsley sprigs

Wash and drain oysters. Place in a saucepan with a little water and cook until oysters are plump and edges begin to curl. If oysters are large, cut into quarters. Let cool. Add celery to oysters. Add Worcestershire to the Vinaigrette Sauce and pour on top. Serve on lettuce leaves and decorate with lemon slices and sprigs of parsley.

LOBSTER SALAD

Cut cold boiled lobster into small pieces. Marinate with enough Vinaigrette Sauce (page 129) to moisten. Place on lettuce leaves. Cover with Mayonnaise (page 130) and garnish with lobster claws, olives, hard-boiled eggs, and capers.

CRABMEAT SALAD

We've eliminated the 2 cups of heavy cream that was listed among the ingredients for the salad below. We find it quite rich with just the mayonnaise. By all means add the cream (stiffly whipped) if desired. Gently fold it in just before serving.

1 pound crabmeat, picked over to remove shells and cartilage
4 hard-boiled eggs, separated
½ cup slivered almonds, toasted

1 cup Boiled Mayonnaise Dressing (page 131)
salt and paprika
lettuce leaves
1 green or red pepper, sliced

1. Cut the crabmeat into large pieces. Cut the whites of the eggs into cubes. Combine the crab, egg whites, and almonds.

2. Fold in the Boiled Mayonnaise. Add salt and paprika. Serve on salad plates on crisp lettuce. Garnish with green or red pepper slices and top with riced egg yolk and almonds.

TUNA SALAD

Tuna Salad can be varied and embellished according to one's time and the ingredients on hand. A simple version follows. Try adding chopped nuts, leftover cooked vegetables, capers, or hard-boiled eggs. Increase the amount of dressing as is necessary to coat the ingredients thoroughly.

1 6½-ounce can tuna fish
2 stalks chopped celery
1 chopped green pepper

½ cup Boiled Mayonnaise Dressing
(page 131)

Have everything ice cold. Break tuna into ½-inch pieces. Add the celery and pepper. Arrange on lettuce leaves and cover with Boiled Mayonnaise Dressing.

SEAFOOD SALAD

This is not an easy recipe to throw together at the last minute. It requires some special time and trouble but with results well worth the efforts. It can be done with any number of seafoods. Choose what looks best at your market. For example, mussels could be added or substituted, a less expensive fish could be used instead of salmon, slightly poached oysters or flaked crab would be a welcome addition. Monk fish, fresh tuna, or swordfish are wonderful for salads, too. Use first-quality seafood and be careful not to overcook it. Dress it lightly and serve well chilled.

1 leek, white part only, trimmed
and cleaned
1 carrot, peeled and coarsely
chopped
1 stalk celery, trimmed, cleaned,
and coarsely chopped
several sprigs of fresh parsley
1 quart water
½ teaspoon salt
1 lemon, quartered
½ pound white-fleshed fish
(flounder, sole, cod, or snapper)
fillets, cut into 1-inch pieces

½ pound shrimp, peeled and
deveined
½ pound sea scallops
4 to 6 ounces fresh salmon, cut into
1-inch pieces
assorted lettuce leaves
¼ cup lemon juice
½ cup olive oil
lettuce and fresh chervil or
coriander for garnish
salt and freshly ground pepper to
taste

1. In a large, nonreactive saucepan, combine the leek, carrot, celery, and parsley. Pour the water in and add the salt. Add the lemon quarters to the mixture squeezing the juice from each piece. Bring to a boil. Reduce heat and let simmer for 30 minutes. Strain through a fine mesh sieve, reserving the liquid,

rinse out the pan, and return the poaching liquid to the pot. Keep at a slow simmer over moderately low heat.

2. Add the pieces of white fish to the pot. Cook until no longer opaque and slightly firm to the touch. Remove with a slotted spoon to paper towels to drain. Continue this process with the shrimp, scallops, and end with the salmon. Keep the liquid at an even, poaching simmer. Handle carefully to keep the pieces of seafood from breaking up. Do not overcook. Drain the pieces very well or they will exude too much liquid into your salad. Let come to room temperature, cover, and refrigerate for at least 2 hours before assembling the salad.

3. Arrange lettuce leaves attractively on individual salad plates or on a large serving platter. Place the cooked fish in the middle and surround with the shellfish. Mix the lemon juice with the olive oil in a small bowl. Pour over the seafood salad and garnish with fresh chervil or fresh coriander. Season lightly with salt and freshly ground black pepper. Serve at once.

CHICKEN, MEAT, AND EGG SALADS

CHICKEN SALAD

2 cups cooked chicken, diced
1 cup celery, diced
½ cup Vinaigrette Sauce (page 129)

about 1 cup bottled mayonnaise
green olives, for garnish
hard-boiled egg slices, for garnish

Mix chicken and celery. Marinate with Vinaigrette Sauce. Chill for several hours. Drain. Before serving, mix well with mayonnaise. Serve on crisp lettuce. Garnish with olives and slices of hard-boiled eggs.

CURRIED CHICKEN SALAD

2 cups cooked chicken, diced
⅓ cup toasted coconut
⅓ cup currants, plumped in hot
    water for 1 hour then drained
2 tablespoons slivered almonds,
    toasted
½ cup bottled mayonnaise

1 teaspoon curry powder, or to
    taste
½ teaspoon chopped fresh ginger
    (optional)
½ teaspoon lemon juice
lettuce leaves

1. In a large mixing bowl, combine the chicken, coconut, currants, and almonds.

2. In a separate bowl, stir together the mayonnaise, curry powder, ginger, if desired, and lemon juice. Add to the chicken mixture and blend well. Chill.

(continued)

Serve on individual salad plates or a large platter surrounded with lettuce leaves.

Note: Instead of mayonnaise use lowfat yogurt for a healthful alternative. If currants are not available, subsitute halved plain or golden raisins. Fresh ginger lends an exotic touch. Serve the salad with some good chutney on the side if desired.

TONGUE SALAD   *Serves 12.*

Substitute boiled ham in the following recipe if desired. This salad is a good choice for a large buffet of assorted cold foods.

2 pounds cold boiled tongue, finely
  chopped
½ teaspoon paprika

about 1 cup bottled mayonnaise
dill pickle, chopped (optional)
grated horseradish to taste
  (optional)

Sprinkle chopped tongue with paprika and mix with mayonnaise to moisten. Form into loaf, score top. Chopped dill pickle or grated horseradish may be added. Serve with radishes and potato chips.

EGG SALAD

4 hard-boiled eggs
½ cup chopped celery
1 teaspoon prepared mustard
¼ cup bottled mayonnaise

salt and freshly ground black pepper
  to taste
parsley, chopped (optional)

In a large bowl, combine all the ingredients and chill thoroughly.

For readers who would like to lower their cholesterol, calorie intake, or both, some easy substitutions are available:

* For heavy cream (as an ingredient, not for thinning), use equal amounts of undiluted evaporated milk.
* For light cream, use equal amounts of undiluted evaporated skim milk.
* For butter, use equal amounts of corn oil or safflower margarine. This type of margarine has the same number of calories but the amount of cholesterol is nil.
* For butter, use olive or canola oil. Again, these oils have the same number of calories but no cholesterol.
* Yogurt can be substituted for sour cream. However, yogurt will separate at high temperatures. Make this substitution with only cold preparations.
* Use Yogurt Cheese (page 104) in place of cream cheese.
* Frozen concentrate of apple juice can be used in place of sugar.

BEEF SALAD

Cold roast or boiled beef makes a wonderful salad. Try the following recipe using good-quality, leftover steak or roast.

½ pound cooked beef, thinly sliced
2 to 4 small potatoes, boiled, skins on
¼ cup chopped capers
½ cup Hot Salad Dressing (page 131)
assorted salad greens

½ pound cherry tomatoes, halved
¼ cup chopped fresh herbs (cilantro, chervil, thyme, parsley, or dill) or 2 tablespoons dried herbs

1. Combine the beef, potatoes, and capers in a small bowl. Pour over enough of the Hot Salad Dressing to coat and let marinate for 15 to 20 minutes.

2. Trim, wash, and crisp enough lettuce greens to fill a large salad bowl. Arrange the beef, potatoes, and capers attractively in the middle. Surround with the tomatoes. Pour over additional Hot Salad Dressing and top with the herbs. Toss just before serving, with more dressing on the side, if desired.

LAMB SALAD WITH MINT

The following recipe is a good way to use leftover lamb. The best results come from using thin slices of medium-rare lamb from the leg. However, any large, lean piece of lamb will do. The salad can be done several hours in advance but do not add the chopped mint until the very last minute.

½ pound lean, cooked lamb, cut in thin slices
1 medium red pepper, roasted, peeled, and seeded (page 385)
1 small onion or 2 small shallots, finely chopped

¼ cup olive oil
2 tablespoons vinegar
salt and freshly ground black pepper to taste
2 tablespoons chopped fresh mint
black oil-cured olives (optional)

1. Lay thin slices of lamb flat on a serving platter. Cut the red peppers into thin strips and arrange attractively over the meat.

2. Sprinkle with the chopped onion or shallot. Combine the oil and the vinegar and pour on top. Season with salt and pepper. Chill.

3. Just before serving, sprinkle the salad liberally with the chopped mint. Garnish with black olives if desired and serve at once.

Rice, Pasta, and Grain Salads

Rice Salads

RICE SALAD

2 cups boiled, long-grain white rice (page 171)
½ cup cucumber, diced
½ cup green peas or sugar snap peas cut into ¼-inch pieces, blanched
⅓ cup scallions, thinly sliced
½ cup cooked carrots, diced
¼ cup (loosely packed) chopped, fresh parsley
½ cup Vinaigrette Sauce (page 129)
salt and freshly ground black pepper to taste

In a large mixing bowl, combine the rice, cucumber, peas, scallions, and carrots. Add the parsley and Vinaigrette Sauce. Blend well. Season to taste with salt and pepper. Cover and refrigerate until ready to serve. Garnish with lettuce leaves.

WILD RICE SALAD

2 cups cooked wild rice (page 174)
4 to 5 medium mushrooms, cleaned, trimmed, and thinly sliced
2 tablespoons butter
⅓ cup golden raisins
⅓ cup fresh orange juice
⅓ cup toasted pecans, coarsely chopped
½ cup scallions, thinly sliced
2 teaspoons grated orange rind
2 teaspoons fresh thyme (1 teaspoon dried)
½ cup Vinaigrette Sauce (page 129)
salt and freshly ground black pepper to taste
additional sprigs of thyme or fresh parsley

1. Have the rice at room temperature. In a medium skillet or sauté pan, cook the mushrooms in the butter. Drain on paper towels. Reserve until ready to assemble the salad.

2. In a small saucepan, combine the raisins and orange juice. Bring to a boil, cover, and remove from heat. Let steep for 30 minutes.

3. In a large mixing bowl, combine the rice, mushrooms, raisins, and any accumulated juices, pecans, scallions, orange rind, and thyme. Pour the Vinaigrette Sauce over all. Mix well. Season with salt and pepper. Serve on individual salad plates or on a large platter. Garnish with sprigs of fresh thyme or parsley.

Pasta Salads

Whether served as a main course for a luncheon or a light supper, or as part of a cold buffet or picnic, pasta salads are very satisfying. The following recipes showcase the universally loved pasta that we've recently come to know so well. These are meant to be guides, not pat formulas. Use your imagination. Any shaped pasta will do nicely; shells, ziti, macaroni, penne, or wheels are good salad pastas. Try using some of the ingredients found in the recipes in the Pasta section for making your own creations. Many of the hot pasta combinations served at room temperature or chilled make nice salads, too.

PASTA SALAD WITH CHERRY TOMATOES, PROSCIUTTO, AND GOAT CHEESE

2 cups cooked pasta, drained
12 to 14 cherry tomatoes, halved or quartered
¼ pound prosciutto, cubed
2 ounces fresh goat cheese, cubed

½ to 1 cup Vinaigrette Sauce (page 129)
¼ cup (loosely packed) coarsely chopped fresh parsley
freshly ground black pepper

Combine the pasta, tomatoes, prosciutto, and cheese in a large bowl. Pour over enough sauce to lightly bind. Stir well and chill until ready to serve. Stir often to prevent drying. Add the parsley just before serving. Season with freshly ground black pepper to taste.

PASTA SALAD WITH BLACK BEANS, TUNA, AND TOMATO

2 cups cooked pasta, drained
1 cup cooked black beans (page 179)
½ cup peeled, seeded, and chopped tomatoes
1 can (6½ ounces) tuna, drained

½ cup Vinaigrette Sauce (page 129)
¼ cup (loosely packed) chopped cilantro
salt and freshly ground black pepper to taste

Combine pasta, beans, tomatoes, and tuna in a large bowl. Pour over Vinaigrette Sauce. Add cilantro just before serving and toss well. Season with salt and pepper to taste.

Note: Try adding ¼ cup of your favorite bottled salsa sauce. Use canned tomatoes if good, ripe ones aren't available.

Grain Salad

TABBOULI (CRACKED WHEAT SALAD)   *Serves 6 to 8.*

2 cups medium cracked wheat,
    bulgur, or couscous
2 medium tomatoes, peeled, seeded,
    and chopped
4 to 5 small scallions, trimmed and
    thinly sliced
1 small cucumber, peeled, seeded,
    and diced
¼ cup lemon juice

¼ cup Vinaigrette Sauce (page 129)
salt and freshly ground black pepper
    to taste
¼ cup (loosely packed) chopped
    fresh mint
¼ cup (loosely packed) chopped
    fresh parsley
lettuce leaves

1.   Rinse the wheat under cold, running water until water runs clear. Place in a large bowl and cover with cold water. Leave to soak for 20 minutes. Drain off any excess liquid.

2.   Toss the grains with the tomatoes, scallions, and cucumber. Add the lemon juice and Vinaigrette Sauce. Season with salt and pepper. Let rest at room temperature for 1 hour or in the refrigerator for up to 24 hours.

3.   Just before serving, add the freshly chopped herbs. Heap on a large platter and garnish with crisp lettuce leaves.

Fruit Salads

The days of the congealed salad with chunky bits of fruit are over. Today's cook has an array of fresh fruits that need only modest embellishment. We propose fruit salads made of quality ingredients with only a simple sauce to set them off.

Fruit salads can be sweet or savory. Savory salads should be a balanced combination of sweet and salty flavors. These are suitable for serving as a first course or a side dish. They can make an excellent main course for a light luncheon or supper, too. Fruit salads make superb desserts. As we develop healthier attitudes about the food we eat, we find that fruits can be a satisfying alternative to rich desserts full of sugar, cream, and egg yolks. Whatever your preference, remember that any fruit salad is going to be only as good as the fruit you use. Be selective when choosing the components of the following recipes.

FRESH FRUIT SALAD

Select good-quality, seasonal fruits that are ripe but not too soft. In the summer, peaches, plums, berries, apricots, nectarines, and melons are good choices. Apples are good for the fall. In the winter, citrus fruits are plentiful, economical, and flavorful ingredients for fruit salads. Try adding fresh cherries and strawberries in the spring. Use your imagination and always make the best use of what is to be found in the market. Prepare all fruits simply and carefully. Be sure that they are well chilled. Slice them in different shapes and sizes and arrange attractively in large glass bowls. Serve with one of the fruit salad dressings found on pages 133–135, if desired, or top with yogurt, fresh whipped cream, or lemon wedges on the side.

EXOTIC FRUIT SALAD

Fancy fruits are being shipped into our markets from all over the world. Wonderful salads can be made with a variety of rich and novel tastes that can be pulled together with the right dressing. Try this dish with plain butter cookies or cake for a new and different dessert treat.

In a glass bowl, mix together attractive slices and chunks of papaya, kiwi fruit, avocado, passion fruit, mango, pineapple, coconut, banana, kumquats, and any other available tropical fruit. Toss with fresh lime juice. Serve well chilled. Top or side with any of the fruit salad dressings found on pages 133–135, if desired.

ORANGE AND GRAPEFRUIT SALAD WITH ZESTS

Cut several inch-long pieces of zest from oranges and grapefruit. (Avoid the white pith as it is bitter.) Cut into thin julienne strips and blanch several times in boiling water, refreshing under cold running water each time. Working over a mixing bowl to catch the juices, cut the oranges and grapefruit into whole sections discarding the tough membranes as you work. Arrange on individual serving plates. Squeeze the pulp to extract any juices. Mix the juices with honey (1 tablespoon per ½ cup juice) and mix well. Strew the zests over and pour on the sweetened juices. Serve very cold, with a scoop of sherbet if desired.

TANGERINE SALAD

12 tangerines
1 red pepper, finely chopped
½ cup grapefruit juice
lettuce leaves
¼ cup pecans, chopped

¼ cup strawberries, halved or
quartered
¼ cup chopped fresh pineapple
(optional)

Peel tangerines, remove pulp in unbroken sections, free from membrane. Mix with pepper. Sprinkle with fruit juice and chill for 1 hour. Serve each person a portion on a lettuce leaf. Top with the nuts and garnish with strawberries and pineapple if desired. Serve with Fruit Salad Dressing (page 133).

PEAR SALAD WITH BLUE CHEESE

2 large pears
1 tablespoon lemon juice
½ cup crumbled blue cheese
(preferably Roquefort)

½ cup Vinaigrette Sauce (page 129)
thinly shredded lettuce leaves for
garnish

1. Carefully peel the pears. Cut in half and remove the core with the seeds. Cut into very thin slices. Sprinkle with lemon juice as you work so that the pears do not turn brown.

2. Arrange the pear slices fanned out on individual salad plates. Sprinkle about a tablespoon of the cheese on each one. Drizzle on a bit of Vinaigrette Sauce. Garnish with thinly shredded lettuce leaves. Serve right away.

Note: If the salad is to be held for more than a half hour or so, sprinkle the pears with additional lemon juice.

Salad Dressing

Mayonnaise and Vinaigrette Sauce are the two basic kinds of dressings for savory salads. Much can be done to add variety and invention to these two classics. Ingredients can be incorporated, oils and vinegars can be flavored, and consistency can be altered. There are some fundamental guidelines to insure success.

Homemade mayonnaise poses a problem for the modern cook. The use of raw eggs in this day of Salmonella contamination is a risky proposition. It is impossible to talk about salads without mentioning the virtues of mayonnaise; for so long it has been used to bind all sorts of ingredients. We make an effort in the section on salads to use dressings without it or to use the cooked mayonnaise when possible. We call for bottled mayonnaise to avoid risks. We are including recipes for mayonnaise with all the variations but with a certain amount of trepidation. The only way to insure a healthy product is to know where your eggs are coming from. Buy only from a producer whose reputation you can count on. Otherwise, stick to the store-bought kind.

The classic Vinaigrette Sauce is our favorite for today's salads. The recipe that follows can be made to be almost as rich and emulsified as a mayonnaise. Although it might not be able to stand up to the binding properties of a thick mayonnaise, it can be used successfully to add flavor and finesse instead of the egg-based original.

The quality of the oils and vinegars used is the key to a successful salad dressing. There are many kinds of oils on the market today. First-pressed, virgin olive oil is preferred by many. Lesser quality olive oils and vegetable oils can be adequate substitutions, but for truly great salads, use the good stuff. Nut oils are good used sparingly, especially with more delicate green salads. Hazelnut, walnut, and even pecan oils are available in specialty food stores. A word of caution: these oils, unlike olive oils that can stay on the shelf for a long period of time, can quickly go rancid. Keep them refrigerated and check before using to insure that this isn't the case. Vegetable oils such as canola and safflower are fine for salads. Because they are generally lighter, they might lack the character of some of the finer oils but they will make a perfectly acceptable dressing. Try cutting some of the finer oils with a bit of vegetable oil to make the good stuff go further. By the same token, a portion of a strongly flavored oil will impart character to a vegetable oil.

Vinegars vary greatly in quality, too. The range goes from the precious Balsamic variety that is held for years in special woods to the chemically based white kind that has never seen a day of real fermentation. Again, your salad will only be as good as the choices you make. While the subject of vinegars is worthy of a book itself, we will limit our focus to a few rules of thumb. Use good-quality red wine vinegar for general purposes. It has enough character to stand up to hearty salads and enough subtlety not to overpower more delicate foods. Store it in a cool, dry spot and keep it well sealed. Buy small quantities if you use it infrequently. Cloudy, sediment-filled vinegars that have been left on the shelf for too long can be bitter.

Flavored oils and vinegars can be fun additions to your salads. See the box (below) for some ideas. Sweet and sour, tart and mellow, or fragrant mixtures from these simple preparations make different and interesting dressings.

Fruit salad dressings are meant to complement, not overpower, the delicacy of the produce used. Most of those included below can be made ahead. Try adding flavored sugars, citrus zests, cocoa, chopped mint, or liquors where appropriate.

INFUSED OILS AND VINEGARS

Infused oils and vinegars are simple to make at home. Use your imagination and take advantage of the wide variety of herbs, spices, fruits, and vegetables to create your own flavor combinations. These delicious condiments are an easy way to add extra flavor to your food. Remember that cholesterol-free oils are a healthy alternative to butter-rich sauces.

Flavoring Oils Cold-pressed, extra virgin olive oil is the best vehicle for most herb and vegetable flavorants. Use grapeseed oil for fruit infusions and corn or peanut oil for infusions that are heated.

Use fresh herbs at the peak of the season when they have the most flavor. Basil, garlic, bay, thyme, lavender, marjoram, and rosemary make wonderful oils. Using garlic requires additional care. An acidic ingredient like lemon peel or juice must be added to prevent harmful bacteria from forming. Make sure the herbs are clean and thoroughly dry before you put them in the oil. First bruise the herbs and fill a clean quart bottle with them. The more herbs you use the stronger the infusion will be. Pour olive oil over the herbs, seal the bottle, and put it in a cool, dark place. After two to three weeks, strain the oil through a cheesecloth and discard the herbs. Pour the oil into a smaller bottle and add one small fresh sprig or leaf. Refrigerate.

To make fruit oils, slice the fruit thinly and lay the slices flat in a shallow container, then cover them with oil. Stacking the slices in an upright container will force the juices out of the fruit and it will not blend well with the oil. Store in a cool, dark place for 2 to 3 weeks, then strain carefully through a sieve lined with cheesecloth. Bottle and store in the refrigerator. Lemons, oranges, peaches, and berries all make delicious oils.

Cinnamon, cloves, anise, vanilla, pepper, hot chilies, and juniper berries are good choices for spice oils. Choose an oil that does not have too strong a flavor, like corn or peanut oil. Heat the oil with the spice but be careful not to let it burn. Cover the pan and remove it from the heat and let it sit until the oil has cooled. Strain and store in the refrigerator.

Vegetable juices and purees can be suspended in oil to create intensely flavored, heavy-bodied oils. Simply beat a slow stream of oil into the juice or puree as if you were making a mayonnaise. Tomatoes, roasted peppers, turnips, and horseradish are all delicious choices.

Oils are no longer sterile once they have been infused so they cannot be stored indefinitely. When tightly covered and stored in the refrigerator infused oils should keep for several months. Smell oil before using to check freshness.

Flavoring Vinegars To make herb vinegars use a good-quality white wine vinegar. Red wine vinegar is too strong for most herbs; however it does go well with garlic.

Again, choose fresh herbs at the peak of the season when they are most aromatic. Make sure the herbs are clean and thoroughly dried. Fill large, clean jars with the herb you have chosen and cover with vinegar. Seal the jars and set them aside to steep for three to four weeks, then strain the vinegar and discard the herbs. Pour the vinegar into smaller bottles and add a fresh sprig of the herb, if desired. Keep the vinegars away from direct sunlight and use them within a year.

Fruit vinegars combine the acidity of vinegar with the sweetness of fruit to make a very special addition to sauces and foods. Raspberries make a wonderful vinegar but don't overlook blueberries, peaches, figs, or pears. In a nonreactive pan, combine one part vinegar to two parts fruit and bring to a simmer. Remove from heat and let come to room temperature. Pour into a crock or jar, cover and steep for ten to twenty days. Strain through cheesecloth, bottle, and store in a cool dark place or refrigerate.

SAVORY DRESSINGS

VINAIGRETTE SAUCE   *Makes about 1 cup.*

The following recipe makes an emulsified dressing that is just thin enough to coat lettuce leaves, thick enough to serve as a sauce for cold salads and sturdy enough to lightly bind. Here the olive oil is cut with the addition of some vegetable oil.

½ tablespoon Dijon mustard
½ teaspoon salt
⅛ teaspoon freshly ground black pepper

¼ cup red wine vinegar
¼ cup vegetable oil
½ cup olive oil

1. In a mixing bowl, combine the mustard, salt, and pepper. Add the vinegar and stir with a wire whisk until well mixed and the salt is dissolved.

2. Slowly pour in the vegetable oil beginning with a drop or two at a time. Whisk constantly, making sure all of the oil is incorporated before adding more. The mixture should start to lightly thicken. After adding all of the vegetable oil, continue with the olive oil, adding drops slowly, until sauce is completely emulsified.

Variations:

- Add 2 tablespoons freshly chopped herbs after blending. Mix well and serve at once.
- Finely chop 1 small shallot or 1 small clove of garlic and add after the oil is incorporated.
- Add ¼ cup freshly grated Parmesan cheese. Mix well, breaking up any lumps that might form.
- Add 1 finely chopped hard-boiled egg.
- Substitute any of the flavored oils or vinegars found in the box on page 128.
- Add 1 tablespoon heavy cream for a richer sauce.
- Add one teaspoon finely grated lemon, lime, or orange rind and add just before serving.

MAYONNAISE   *Makes about 2¼ cups.*

Here is the original Settlement recipe for mayonnaise, just slightly altered. We find that Dijon mustard gives a flavor superior to the "ballpark" kind called for in the original. We've also eliminated the small amount of sugar that was included. Try substituting olive oil for part of the vegetable oil for an added dimension. Please see page 96 for notes on how to handle raw eggs.

1 teaspoon Dijon mustard	2 egg yolks
½ teaspoon salt	1½ to 2 cups vegetable oil
⅛ teaspoon freshly ground black pepper	1 tablespoon lemon juice
	3 tablespoons good-quality vinegar
dash of cayenne pepper	

1. In a small mixing bowl, combine the mustard, salt, peppers, and egg yolks. Beat with a wire whisk until blended and lemon colored.

2. Beating constantly, add the first ¼ cup of the oil in drops, incorporating after each addition. Carefully whisk in the rest of the oil, slowly, in a steady stream. Stop and beat thoroughly from time to time to insure a proper emulsification. When thick and creamy, thin with the lemon juice and vinegar to desired thickness. Season with more salt and pepper if desired. Stir and keep very cold until ready to serve. Mayonnaise will keep in the refrigerator for up to three days.

Note: This mayonnaise may be made in a blender. Follow the same instructions, being careful not to overwork the sauce. We find that using the food processor is difficult because of the small amounts involved. However, if you are making mayonnaise in volume, by all means follow manufacturer's instructions using the preparation above.

Variations:

Russian Dressing: To 1 cup mayonnaise add 1 tablespoon more mustard, 3 tablespoons grated horseradish, and 3 tablespoons prepared chili sauce.

Thousand Island: To 1 cup mayonnaise add 2 tablespoons finely chopped green peppers, 2 tablespoons finely chopped red pepper, 1 tablespoon chopped onion, 1 chopped hard-boiled egg, 1 teaspoon Worcestershire sauce, and salt and pepper to taste. Fold in ½ cup whipped, heavy cream. Serve very cold.

Green Mayonnaise: Blanch 1 cup (firmly packed) fresh green herbs such as parsley, dill, cilantro, rosemary, or chervil with 2 tablespoons chopped fresh spinach or watercress for 1 minute. Drain and eliminate moisture by placing in a piece of cheesecloth and squeezing to extract all liquid. Chop with 2 hard-cooked egg yolks and work through a sieve. Combine this mixture with 1 cup mayonnaise. Season with salt and pepper to taste.

Red Mayonnaise: Roast, peel, and seed a red pepper (page 385). Chop coarsely. In the bowl of a food processor fitted with the metal blade, combine the pepper with 2 hard-boiled egg yolks, 1 teaspoon tomato concentrate, and 1 small clove garlic. Process until smooth. Add to 1 cup mayonnaise and pass through a strainer. Season to taste with salt and pepper.

Curry Mayonnaise: Combine 1 cup mayonnaise with 1 to 2 tablespoons good-quality curry powder. Season with several drops of additional lemon juice and freshly ground black pepper to taste.

Lincoln House Special Dressing: To 2 cups mayonnaise add ¾ cup Pepper Relish (page 705). Seal well and chill.

BOILED MAYONNAISE DRESSING *Makes about 2¼ cups.*

2 tablespoons flour
1 cup plus 2 tablespoons oil
⅛ cup vinegar
⅛ cup lemon juice
1 cup boiling water

2 egg yolks
½ teaspoon mustard
½ teaspoon salt
cayenne pepper

1. Mix flour, 2 tablespoons oil, vinegar, and lemon juice in a small, nonreactive saucepan. Add the boiling water and boil for 5 minutes, stirring constantly.

2. Beat the yolks in a heat-proof bowl until light and lemon colored. Pour in the hot mixture, stirring constantly. Add seasonings and cool. When cool, but not cold, gradually beat in the remaining cup of oil.

HOT SALAD DRESSING *Makes about ½ cup.*

2 teaspoons sugar
½ teaspoon salt
½ teaspoon dry mustard
⅛ teaspoon freshly ground black
   pepper
¼ cup vinegar

¼ cup water
1 tablespoon butter, at room
   temperature
1 teaspoon flour
1 egg or egg yolk

1. Place the sugar, salt, mustard, pepper, vinegar, and water in a small, nonreactive saucepan. Bring to a boil.

2. Blend the butter and flour and gradually add to the boiling liquid bit by bit. Cook for 5 minutes.

3. In a heat-proof bowl, beat the egg or egg yolk until light and lemon-colored. Gradually beat in the boiling liquid. Blend until smooth. Use immediately.

ROQUEFORT DRESSING   *Makes about 1 cup.*

¾ pound Roquefort cheese, at room
   temperature
4 tablespoons heavy cream
4 tablespoons olive oil

salt to taste
¼ teaspoon paprika
3 tablespoons lemon juice

1. Rub the cheese through a fine-meshed strainer or sieve. Gradually mix in the cream and olive oil. Season to taste with salt and paprika.

2. Add the lemon juice in drops until well blended. Chill until ready to serve.

YOGURT AND HERB DRESSING   *Makes 1¼ cups*

The following is a good low-calorie alternative to creamy, rich salad dressing.

1 cup plain yogurt (preferably
   lowfat)
2 tablespoons chopped fresh herbs
1 clove garlic, finely chopped

1 teaspoon fresh lemon juice
freshly ground black pepper to taste

In a small mixing bowl, combine the yogurt, herbs, garlic, and lemon juice. Season to taste with pepper. Serve well chilled but soon after preparing.

Note: Do not keep this dressing for too long before serving. The herbs and the garlic tend to become strong and overpowering when held for more than an hour or so.

Variation: Fold in ½ cup peeled, seeded, and chopped tomatoes when they are at their seasonal best.

HOT BACON DRESSING   *Makes about ¼ cup.*

3 slices bacon
¼ cup vinegar

½ teaspoon salt
freshly ground black pepper to taste

Cut bacon into small pieces. Cook slowly until crisp. Stir in vinegar and seasonings. Reheat and pour at once over lettuce, spinach, or any hearty salad greens.

SOUR CREAM SALAD DRESSING *Makes 1¼ cups.*

This is one of the three original Sour Cream Dressings found in the earlier editions of The Settlement Cookbook. While a bit heavy for today's salads, we still think that it can be a delicious accompaniment for cooked vegetables, pastas, and cold meats.

1 cup sour cream	1 teaspoon salt
2 tablespoons lemon juice	¼ teaspoon freshly ground black
2 tablespoons vinegar	pepper
1 tablespoon sugar	1 teaspoon dry mustard

1. Beat the cream until smooth, thick, and light.
2. Mix together the lemon juice, vinegar, sugar, salt, pepper, and mustard. Gradually add to the cream, beating constantly. Serve chilled.

FRUIT SALAD DRESSINGS

The following recipes are all original recipes from the early editions of the book. Simple blendings of quality ingredients are truly timeless. Even in today's world of trends and fads, these are still excellent ideas for good, basic food.

FRUIT SALAD DRESSING

1 *Makes about 1 cup.*

½ cup sugar	2 tablespoons lemon juice
⅓ cup white grape juice	

Mix all ingredients together and serve ice cold over any fruit salad.

2 *Makes ½ cup.*

¼ cup olive oil	¼ teaspoon paprika
2 tablespoons grapefruit or orange juice	½ teaspoon powdered sugar
½ teaspoon salt	2 tablespoons lemon juice

Mix together in order given. Chill and shake or stir well just before serving.

FRUIT SALAD DRESSINGS WITH CREAM

 With Lemon   *Makes about 1½ cups.*

⅓ cup sugar

½ teaspoon dry mustard

½ teaspoon salt

⅛ teaspoon paprika

2 eggs or 4 yolks, beaten

2 tablespoons lemon juice

⅓ cup water

1 cup whipping cream

Mix dry ingredients, add eggs, lemon juice, and water. Cook over boiling water, stirring constantly until thick. Cool. When ready to use whip the cream stiffly and add.

With Orange   *Makes about 1½ cups.*

1 tablespoon butter

½ cup granulated sugar

juice of ½ lemon

juice of 1 large orange

3 egg yolks

1 cup whipped cream

Cook butter, sugar, lemon and orange juice, and egg yolks in double boiler until smooth. Let cool and fold in the whipped cream. Serve alongside fruit salad.

With Maple Syrup   *Makes about 1 cup.*

1 egg yolk

¼ cup maple syrup

¾ cup cream, whipped

juice of half a lemon

Beat yolk well in top of double boiler. Add maple syrup and cook for a minute until thick. Cool, fold in cream, and add the lemon juice. Serve alongside fruit salad.

With Honey   *Makes about 2 cups.*

3 egg yolks

½ cup strained honey

4 tablespoons oil

½ teaspoon salt

¼ teaspoon paprika

1 cup cream, whipped

juice of 1 lemon

Beat yolks until creamy. Heat honey in a saucepan, pour in yolks. Beat over fire one minute, then beat off heat for five minutes until thick. Add oil, salt, and paprika. Chill. When cold, add lemon juice and then fold in the whipped cream. Or, add lemon juice to the fruit instead of to the dressing. Serve with peach, cherry, or pineapple salad.

With Cheese   *Makes about ¾ cup.*

Mash 4 ounces of cream cheese. Mix and thin with a little heavy cream. Add enough raspberry or strawberry jam to color. Chill to ice cold. Pour over fresh peaches or pears.

BANANA FRUIT SALAD DRESSING   *Makes about ⅔ cup.*

2 ripe bananas, peeled and cut into
   thick slices
2 teaspoons lemon juice

2 tablespoons heavy cream
   (substitute yogurt, if desired)
1 tablespoon honey

In the bowl of a food processor fitted with the metal blade, combine the banana, lemon juice, and cream (or yogurt). Dribble in the honey. Process until smooth, scraping down the sides of the bowl as necessary. Chill for at least an hour before serving.

RICOTTA CHEESE AND
CINNAMON FRUIT SALAD DRESSING   *Makes about 1 cup.*

1 cup ricotta cheese
½ teaspoon cinnamon
1 tablespoon honey

½ grated lemon or orange rind
   (optional)

In the bowl of a food processor fitted with the metal blade, combine the ricotta, cinnamon, honey, and rind if using. Process until smooth and creamy. Refrigerate until ready to serve.

Note: Use either whole or skim milk ricotta for this recipe. It is thick and may be spooned on rather than poured over fresh fruit. If a more liquid sauce is desired, thin out the mixture with tablespoons of milk or cream. Stir after each spoonful until desired consistency is obtained.

SANDWICHES

Sandwiches can be plain, simple, and humble—or fanciful, festive, and exotic. Serve them for meals, or just snacks, and they're perfect for parties or picnics. Sandwiches go well with soups, salads, chips, pickles, and relishes. In short, a sandwich can be just about anything you want it to be. It's easy to create surprising sandwiches from ingredients on hand.

The secrets of a successful sandwich are the quality of the bread used and of the ingredients used in the filling. Homemade bread makes the best sandwiches, of course, but other types of store-bought can be used with good results. (See the Bread chapter, page 451, for recipes). Day-old bread is good for toasting but should be kept moist by spreading with a layer of softened butter or cream cheese before filling.

Sandwiches may be assembled ahead. When making large quantities, stack the sandwiches between sheets of waxed paper, on platters or a cookie sheet, cover with a damp cloth, and store in refrigerator until wanted. Cover with plastic wrap if desired and change cloth from time to time to keep in moisture. Add dressings just before serving. Likewise, sandwiches can be frozen. Wrap individually in foil, freezer bags, or freezer wraps and label. Avoid freezing fillings that contain mayonnaise, fresh salad vegetables, cream cheese, or hard-cooked eggs. None of these freeze well.

Butter Sandwich Spreads

Use butter that is softened or creamed but not oily. Spread butter thin. This will keep the base from becoming soggy and provide subtle flavor to the butter that may be used to fill dainty party sandwiches or as bases for canapés. The food processor will be helpful if making a large quantity of butter spreads. Try spreading fillings on an array of dark and white breads. Pumpernickel, white loaf bread, and thinly sliced whole wheat can provide contrast for a festive touch. Use cookie cutters to make interesting shapes and sizes. For added crunch, butter spreads can be put on toast and crackers too.

ANCHOVY BUTTER

 Mix anchovy paste with an equal amount of softened butter. Add a few drops of lemon juice and freshly ground black pepper.

HERB BUTTER

 Combine ½ cup butter with ¼ cup mixed fresh herbs (parsley, thyme, rosemary, marjoram, oregano, chives, or sage) in the bowl of a food processor fitted with the metal blade. Add a few drops of lemon juice and blend until smooth. Season to taste with salt and pepper.

PEPPER BUTTER

 Remove the seeds and white portion of 3 or 4 green, red, or yellow peppers. Cook peppers in boiling water until soft. Drain well. Pat dry with paper towels. Finely chop, drain again, and rub through a sieve. Add pulp to ½ cup of softened butter.

OLIVE BUTTER

 Grind ripe olives, preferably oil-cured, and mix with an equal amount of softened butter.

ONION BUTTER

 Mix ½ cup of finely minced young onions with ½ cup softened butter.

PIMIENTO BUTTER

 Drain 3 large pimientos and rub through a sieve. Work the pulp into ½ cup softened butter. Season to taste with salt and pepper.

SHRIMP BUTTER

 Clean and finely chop 1 pound of peeled and deveined, cooked shrimp. Blend with 1 cup of softened butter. Season to taste with lemon juice, salt, and pepper.

SMOKED SALMON BUTTER

 Combine ¼ pound smoked salmon, finely chopped, and 1 cup of slightly softened butter. If desired, blend in the bowl of a food processor fitted with the metal blade. Add a few drops of lemon juice and white pepper to taste. Mix well but do not overwork. Butter should be firm and not oily.

SARDINE BUTTER

Remove bones and skins of sardines or use boneless and skinless variety. Chop very fine and combine with an equal amount of slightly softened butter and one tablespoon of finely chopped onion. Add lemon juice to taste.

 Alternatively, combine sardines with butter in the bowl of a food processor fitted with the metal blade. Proceed as for above and process until smooth.

HORSERADISH BUTTER

Cream ¼ cup butter with ¼ cup grated horseradish, 1 teaspoon lemon juice, and a little salt and sugar.

Cream Cheese Spreads

To soften cream cheese, let stand at room temperature for 30 minutes. For a quicker solution, use the microwave oven following manufacturer's instructions. Fresh goat cheese can be substituted for cream cheese when preparing these spreads.

BASIC CREAM CHEESE SPREAD

 Blend softened cream cheese with milk, cream, or mayonnaise. Add small amounts to reach desired consistency. Beat well.

WITH PEPPER RELISH

Soften ½ cup cream cheese with ¼ cup drained Pepper Relish (page 705). Mix until smooth.

WITH PINEAPPLE

Mix until smooth ½ cup cream cheese and ¼ cup crushed pineapple.

WITH OLIVES

 Blend ½ cup cream cheese with ¼ cup chopped green or black olives.

WITH WATERCRESS AND NUTS

Chop ¼ cup favorite nuts, mix with finely minced watercress and ½ cup softened cream cheese until smooth.

WITH PRUNES

Chop and drain ½ pound Stewed Prunes (page 413). Add 2 tablespoons creamed butter to 6 ounces cream cheese. Mix with ¼ cup chopped walnuts and prunes.

WITH MINCED CLAMS

Mix 4 to 6 ounces minced clams, drained, with 3 ounces cream cheese. Season with salt and pepper, a pinch of dry mustard, and finely chopped onion. Blend well.

WITH FINES HERBES

Combine ½ cup softened cream cheese with ¼ cup chopped fresh herbs. Add ¼ teaspoon grated lemon rind and season to taste with salt and pepper.

WITH RED OR YELLOW PEPPERS

 Roast a red or yellow pepper (page 385). Peel and chop it and add to 8 ounces cream cheese. Blend in the bowl of a food processor fitted with the metal blade. Puree until smooth. Season to taste with salt and pepper.

Cheese and Seafood Fillings

COTTAGE CHEESE FILLINGS

½ cup cottage cheese, riced
cream or milk

¼ cup green or black olives,
chopped
salt and freshly ground black pepper

Mix cheese to a smooth paste with a little cream or milk. Stir in olives. Blend and season to taste with salt and pepper.

CHEESE FILLING

¼ pound Swiss or cheddar cheese
¼ pound walnuts

¼ cup butter, softened
salt and freshly ground black pepper
to taste

Grate the cheese and finely chop the nuts. Blend in the butter, season with salt and pepper to taste. Or combine the cheese and nuts in the bowl of a food processor. Pulse until blended. Add the butter and process until smooth. Season to taste.

CAVIAR SANDWICHES

To ¼ pound of caviar add 2 tablespoons lemon juice, a little paprika, and 3 tablespoons olive oil. Blend. Spread on thin, small round slices of white or whole wheat bread.

CRABMEAT SANDWICHES

2 hard-cooked egg yolks
1 tablespoon butter, melted

1 tablespoon lemon juice
½ pound lump crabmeat, finely
chopped

Mash the yolks to a smooth paste with the butter. Add the lemon juice and the crab. Mix well and spread between thin slices of buttered brown bread.

LOBSTER SANDWICHES

 Remove cooked lobster meat from shell and chop. Season with salt, pepper, prepared mustard, and lemon juice. Spread on thin slices of buttered bread.

Meat and Poultry Sandwiches

Appetizing sandwiches can be made with plain slices of cooked meat, cold cuts, or cooked poultry. Use thin-sliced meat or poultry when possible. Several thin slices of meat are easier to eat than a single thick slice. Spread the bread with butter or mayonnaise. Lettuce greens, tomatoes, relish, and peppers can be added for embellishment, if desired.

GOOSE LIVER SANDWICHES

  Sauté goose liver in goose fat until soft. Cool. Place the liver in the bowl of a food processor with three hard-cooked eggs, salt and pepper, paprika, and chopped onion. Process in several quick pulses. Scrape down sides and repeat until smooth but not oily. Spread on thin slices of toast.

SWEETBREAD SANDWICHES

 Follow recipe for Boiled Sweetbreads (page 329). Let cool then chop finely. Mix with mayonnaise, chopped celery, and nut meats. Spread on thin slices of brown bread.

TONGUE SANDWICHES

Take thin slices of boiled, smoked, or pickled tongue. Slice or mince. Place between bread, spread with mayonnaise, mustard, or butter.

CHICKEN OR VEAL SANDWICHES

 Cut cold boiled, or roasted chicken or veal into thin slices. Place between slices of buttered bread. Or chop chicken or veal and moisten with mayonnaise. Sprinkle with finely minced celery or sweet green peppers.

CLUB SANDWICHES

For each sandwich, butter 3 slices of fresh toast. On 1 slice place cold, sliced chicken and thin slices of fried bacon. On second slice spread mayonnaise and top with lettuce with sliced tomato. Cover with third slice. Cut in fourths diagonally and decorate plate with pickles, red radishes, and olives.

Fruit and Vegetable Sandwiches

AVOCADO OR ALLIGATOR PEAR SANDWICHES

Peel a ripe avocado and mash with a fork. Sprinkle with salt and pepper. Season with lemon or lime juice. Vinaigrette Sauce (page 129) or mayonnaise may be added if desired. Serve on thin slices of bread.

FRUIT AND NUT FILLING

1 pound raisins or figs
1 pound dates or prunes
juice of 2 oranges
juice of 2 lemons

½ pound shelled pecans, finely chopped
½ pound shelled English walnuts, finely chopped

 Remove stems and stones of fruit. Finely chop or grind. Moisten with fruit juices. Add nuts. Filling keeps well in refrigerator in airtight jars.

ONION SANDWICHES

Cut Bermuda onions in thin slices, sprinkle with salt and a few grains of sugar. Place between slices of rye bread that have been buttered or spread with goose fat. Or fry the onions in fat until tender. Add salt and pepper and spread on top of a slice of fresh or toasted rye bread.

Fancy Sandwiches

RINGS

WITH TOMATO

With large biscuit cutter, cut slices of wheat bread into rounds. With smaller cutter remove inside of half of these, thus forming rings. Spread large rounds with creamed butter. Cover with lettuce and mayonnaise. Place ring over lettuce and fill center with slice of tomato cut with smaller biscuit cutter so it exactly fits. The small remaining rounds may be spread with any desired sandwich filling.

WITH WATERCRESS

Cut bread into rounds and rings as directed above. Wash, drain, and chop about 1 cup of watercress and mix with softened cream cheese. Spread on rounds of bread topped with rings.

WITH CUCUMBER

Cut bread into rounds and rings as directed above. Pare and chop medium cucumber, season with grated onion, and mix with mayonnaise. If desired, add and mix in 4 hard-cooked eggs, finely chopped. Spread on large rounds topped with rings.

CHECKERBOARD SANDWICHES

 Cut 3 lengthwise slices each of white and dark bread ½ inch thick. Spread each slice well with creamed butter and any desired sandwich filling. Put together alternated slices of dark and white bread. Press slices together well, put in refrigerator, and place plate on top of pile. When filling is firm, cut off crusts. Then cut each pile crosswise into ½-inch slices. Spread cut sides thickly with creamed, butter and sandwich filling. Put together so that the brown and the white slices alternate each other. Place in refrigerator again and lightly weight down. When butter is firm, cut crosswise into thin slices. Arrange on platter to show checks.

RIBBON SANDWICHES

1 medium cucumber, peeled, chopped	mayonnaise
1 loaf firm dark bread, unsliced	Pimiento Butter (page 137)
½ cup butter, softened	2 hard-cooked eggs, riced
Pepper Butter (page 137)	salt and pepper to taste

Salt the cucumber and set aside in a colander to drain. Remove crust from bread. Cut bread lengthwise into 5 slices ¼ inch thick. Butter the top and bottom slice on one side only, the middle slices on both sides. On the bottom slice spread the pepper butter filling. Mix the cucumber with mayonnaise and spread on the next slice. Spread Pimiento Butter filling on the third slice. Then mix the eggs with mayonnaise and seasoning and spread on the fourth slice. Cover with the last slice of bread, buttered side down. Wrap in plastic wrap and chill until firm. Cut crosswise into thin slices. Any desired spreads in contrasting colors may be used.

PINWHEEL SANDWICHES

Remove crust from unsliced fresh bread. Cut lengthwise into slices as thin as possible. Spread evenly with creamed butter and any well-seasoned sandwich filling. Roll each slice tightly, wrap in damp cloth with outer edge down. Chill until firm. When ready to serve, cut into thin slices crosswise.

Hot Sandwiches

MILWAUKEE SANDWICH

1

Butter 2 slices of white bread. Trim off crusts. Place a slice of white chicken meat on 1 piece of bread. Sprinkle with Roquefort cheese. Season with paprika. Cover with the other slice, toast on both sides. Garnish with parsley. Serve hot.

2

Place sliced white chicken between 2 slices of toast. Moisten insides with Cheese Sauce (page 400). Put into individual casserole and cover with more Cheese Sauce. Season as desired. Heat thoroughly and serve in casserole.

FRENCH TOASTED SANDWICHES

½ pound cold boiled ham	2 eggs
prepared English mustard	¾ cup milk
8 thin slices day-old bread	2 tablespoons butter

 Chop or grind the ham very fine and moisten throughly with the prepared mustard. Spread a layer of this mixture between thin slices of bread and press firmly together. Beat the eggs slightly, add milk and beat again. Dip sandwich in this egg mixture and sauté in butter until golden brown on both sides. Cut the sandwiches diagonally.

HOT CHEESE SANDWICHES

Butter thin slices of bread very lightly, sprinkle generously with grated Swiss or cheddar cheese. Season with paprika. Press 2 slices firmly together, cut in half and toast on both sides under broiler. Serve at once.

HOT MUSHROOM SANDWICHES

Chop one recipe Sautéed Mushrooms (page 379) very fine and bind with ¾ cup Medium White Sauce (page 399). Spread between thin slices of bread. Press firmly together, cut in half crosswise or in finger-shaped pieces, and toast under broiler until each side is slightly browned.

OPEN-FACED SANDWICHES

HOT BACON AND PEANUT BUTTER SANDWICHES

Cut wheat bread lengthwise into ¼-inch slices. Toast on one side. Spread untoasted side with a thick layer of peanut butter. Sprinkle top with crumbled crisp bacon. Before serving put under broiler to heat thoroughly. Cut into strips and serve.

CHEESE, TOMATO, AND BACON SANDWICHES

Slice white bread and toast on one side. Cover untoasted side with sliced cheddar cheese. On top of this, place ¼-inch slice of tomato and 2 slices of thinly sliced partly cooked bacon, placed crisscross on tomato. Broil until bacon is crisp and brown.

HOT HAM AND ASPARAGUS SANDWICH WITH CHEESE SAUCE

Cover buttered slice of toast with a slice of boiled ham. On this place cooked asparagus spears. Cover with hot Cheese Sauce (page 400).

GRILLED SANDWICHES

FILLINGS FOR GRILLED SANDWICHES

For best results, use the oven broiler for grilling sandwiches. Have broiling pan about 4 inches from the heat source and always preheat. Alternatively, melt butter or oil in a skillet and toast over moderately high heat. Turn often.

Brick Cheese and Ham

Slice of brick cheese, covered with thinly sliced sweet/sour pickles, covered with slice of ham.

Brick Cheese and Tomatoes

Slice of brick cheese covered with slices of tomato, sprinkled with chopped green pepper.

Sweetbread and Cheddar Cheese

Slices of cooked sweetbread between slices of cheddar cheese.

Chicken and Mushrooms

Sautéed slices of fresh mushrooms between slices of cooked chicken.

Anchovy Paste and Sardines

Sardines and sliced hard-cooked eggs between slices of bread lined with anchovy paste.

Sardine Paste and Cream Cheese

Spread one slice of bread with paste, top another slice with cream cheese and put together.

Peanut Butter and Tomato or Pineapple

Put slices of tomato or pineapple between slices of bread lined with peanut butter.

IMAGINATIVE SANDWICHES

Sandwiches are best when put together spontaneously with ingredients on hand. Consider leftover meat, vegetables, seafood, chicken, or cheese. Use contrasting tastes, textures, and colors to create memorable sandwiches made from humble beginnings. Try black breads, pita bread, fresh French or Italian bread, or homemade loaves for variety. The following ideas are suggestions for some combinations that might inspire you to make the most of the odds and ends that seem to be part of any busy kitchen.

ROAST BEEF AND EGGPLANT SANDWICH
WITH TOMATO/GARLIC SAUCE

Peel, seed, and chop two ripe tomatoes. Gently fry 1 clove chopped garlic for 10 to 15 seconds in a teaspoonful of olive oil. Add the tomatoes, season with salt and pepper. Add a pinch of sugar if tomatoes are acidic. Increase heat and cook over high heat until mixture is thick and spreadable. Stir often. Cut an eggplant into ½-inch slices. Sauté in olive oil until tender and golden brown, adding more oil as is needed to prevent pan from drying out. Season well with salt and pepper. Drain on paper towels. Cut roast beef into thin slices. Spread tomato mixture on both sides of hearty black bread and alternate with layers of eggplant and roast beef. Put sides together, cut in half, and serve immediately. The bread quickly becomes soggy after tomato is spread.

LAMB AND MÂCHE SANDWICH WITH MINT SAUCE

Spread slices of French bread with a small amount of mayonnaise. Slice cooked lamb roast very thin and place on top of every other slice. Add two tablespoons of freshly chopped mint to Vinaigrette Sauce (page 129) and lightly drizzle over lamb. Top each with cleaned and stemmed mâche and other bread slice.

GRILLED RED PEPPER AND BERMUDA ONION SANDWICH
WITH ANCHOVIES

Soak anchovy fillets in a little milk for 10 minutes. Pat dry. Roast and peel peppers (page 385) and cut into strips. Slice French bread lengthwise and spread softened butter on each slice. Top half with pepper strips, rings of Bermuda onion, and anchovy fillets. Cover with the plain buttered halves and cut sandwiches in half before serving.

CHICKEN, BACON, GOAT CHEESE, AND FRESH HERB SANDWICH

Spread each slice of dark bread with softened, fresh goat cheese. Top one side with crisp bacon and thin slices of cooked chicken. Sprinkle with chopped fresh herbs (thyme, rosemary, sage, chives, parsley, oregano, or marjoram). Cover with the other piece of bread and serve immediately.

BEET, WATERCRESS, AND CREAM CHEESE SANDWICH

Slice cooked beets about ¼ inch thick. Spread each slice of dark bread with softened cream cheese. Season with freshly ground black pepper. Just before serving top half with beets and garnish with cleaned and stemmed watercress. Cover with the remaining bread halves.

PASTA

Rich in complex carbohydrates, and low in fats, pasta is a healthful product. The flour used is often enriched with iron and B vitamins. The best is made with durum flour, a hard-grain wheat that produces a large amount of gluten—which is desirable for pasta—when worked into a dough. Rolled thin and then cut into a variety of shapes and sizes, dried or fresh, pasta is one of our most versatile foods.

Recipes for classic Macaroni and Cheese, Scalloped Noodles, and Spaghetti with Meatballs are included below, although we've also added some recipes that reflect today's lighter, simpler treatment of pasta.

Commercial pasta is available in all sizes and may be used in any of the following recipes. The shelf life of dried pasta is practically indefinite, making it a convenient food to have on hand for last-minute occasions. Elbow macaroni and spaghetti used to be the only kinds found in local supermarkets, but now there are many domestic and imported varieties available. Since pasta has become so popular, the marketplace now provides the modern cook with a wide selection to choose from.

Dried pasta gains approximately 50 percent bulk in cooking; one-half pound (8 ounces) of dry pasta yields about 4 ½ cups of boiled noodles. Follow instructions on package for cooking.

Most pasta enthusiasts prefer a slight firmness to their cooked noodles ("al dente"). Doughy, limp, and swollen with tasteless flaccidity, overcooked pasta lacks character. Timing is everything. The surest way to find desired texture is to remove and cool a strand of pasta, and then bite into it. There should be a slight resistance, but the dough should be cooked through. Drain immediately and serve as soon as possible.

Fresh pasta is not always necessarily better than dried pasta. It is simply different. Some cooks actually prefer the somewhat chewy texture of dried pasta to the softer lightness of fresh. Good-quality fresh pasta is available in specialty shops and grocery stores across the country. A pound of fresh pasta yields about 6 cups.

Making your own is time consuming but the result is worth the extra effort. Now there are machines that make this process easy. The most sophisticated extrusion machines do everything; add flour, eggs, and water and the machine does the rest. It mixes, kneads, and shapes at the touch of a button. For the occasional pasta maker, the most practical machine is the hand cranked Italian model that attaches to a table-top. The dough is kneaded and stretched then cut into desired shapes. Hands and a rolling pin will produce surprisingly good results if a machine is not available. Cranked or rolled pasta is more tender than machine-worked dough. As is often the case, we pay the price for convenience.

As a rule of thumb, cream-based sauces are good with flat or hollow pastas like *fettucine, tagliatelle, spaghetti, or macaroni. The sauce clings to and coats the large surfaces of these cooked noodles. Thick tomato-based sauces are best with shaped pastas like shells, fusili, or farfalle. These will hold the more textured sauce rather than simply coating the pasta as with a cream sauce. Don't be afraid to cross these boundaries. Many sauces work with both kinds.*

We've included a final section on pasta dishes from Asia. Tastes and textures from kitchens throughout the world have made an impact on the modern American diet. Japan, China, and Thailand have introduced us to noodle dishes that fit perfectly into the way we eat today. Light, flavorful, and surprisingly satisfying, these dishes are healthful, easy to digest, and simple to prepare. American grocery stores used to have just a few shelves of Asian foodstuffs offered exclusively by one or two nationally known brand names. Today there is a larger selection of these foods, found fresh, canned, bottled, and frozen, so they don't seem as exotic as they might have even ten years ago. Noodle dishes are an easy way to enjoy these flavors.

FRESH PASTA

2 cups flour	2 eggs, well beaten
½ teaspoon salt	2 tablespoons warm water

1. Sift flour and salt onto a pastry board, make a well in the center, and add eggs and water. Work the flour into the egg mixture, adding more water if necessary to make a stiff but malleable dough. Or, place flour and salt in the bowl of a food processor fitted with the metal blade. Pulse briefly to mix. Combine eggs and water in a small mixing bowl. Pour through feed tube with the blades in motion. Process until dough forms into a solid mass.

2. Knead on a floured work surface until smooth and pliable. Divide dough in half and let it rest for 30 minutes, covered with damp cotton tea towel.

3. Use a rolling pin or a pasta machine to roll out as thin as possible. Cut into desired shapes. Spread pasta on the board and let dry thoroughly before using. Use immediately if pasta is to be filled.

To Cook Fresh or Homemade Pasta

Drop dried noodles in boiling salted water using about 6 quarts per pound of pasta. Boil until just tender, about 5 to 7 minutes. Drain well. If pasta is to be used in baked dishes, slightly undercook and rinse with cold water to prevent sticking. Drain again.

FILLED PASTAS

There are all sorts of excellent ready-to-cook filled pastas on the market today. Meat-and-cheese-filled tortelloni, seafood-stuffed ravioli, or pop-in-the-oven filled cannelloni are great convenience foods. They can be held in the freezer and boiled or baked in a matter of minutes to provide the base for a nutritious, tasty meal. Many specialty food markets sell very good fresh ravioli, tortellini, and cannelloni with exotic fillings like pumpkin, crabmeat, or wild mushrooms. Buy or prepare a tomato sauce or simply toss the cooked filled pastas with butter, olive oil, fresh herbs, or cheese and serve as a main course. Make a large green salad, provide good bread, and a light, cool dessert for a perfect last-minute dinner.

PASTA SAUCES

An interesting sauce can make a sensational pasta dish. As versatile as bread, pasta needs only a flavorful accompaniment to provide satisfying results. Try mixing any cooked pasta with one of the following selections or use your imagination. Remember that creamy sauces are usually better with flat or hollow pastas and tomato-based and other textured sauces go best with shaped pastas. One pound serves 4 people. Suggested amounts of sauce to use per pound follow each recommendation.

Basic Tomato Sauce, page 405 (2 cups)
Mornay Sauce, page 400 (1 cup)
Creole Sauce, page 402 (1 cup)
Cucumber Cream Sauce, page 408 (1 cup)
Tapenade, page 45 (1 cup)
Mushroom Sauce, page 401 (2 cups)
Anchovy Sauce, page 402 (1 cup)
Parsley-Butter Sauce, page 407 (1 cup)

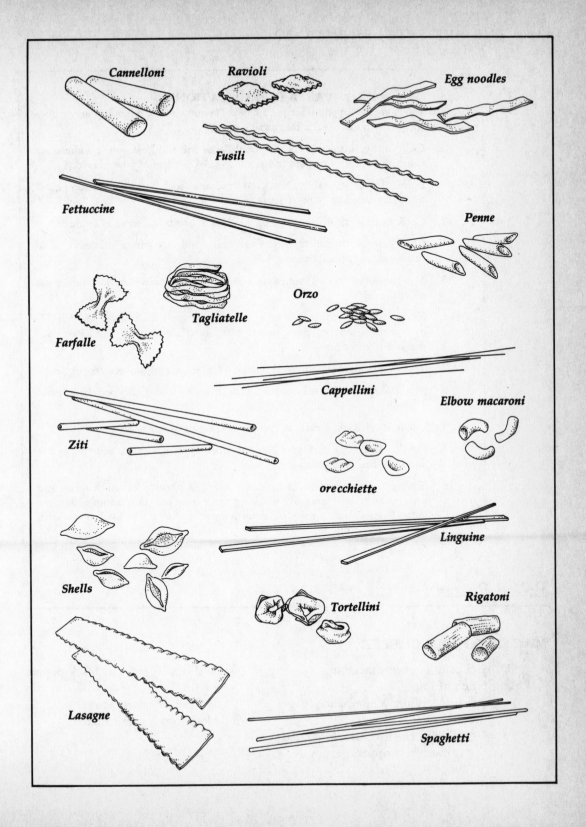

PASTA IMPROVISATIONS

Use pasta to augment any ingredients on hand. Try some of the following suggestions for making a last-minute meal a memorable one.

1. Cube or dice any leftover meat, poultry, or fish and bind with a white sauce (page 399). Season to taste and serve on cooked pasta of your choice.

2. Puree leftover vegetables, heat, and thin with stock or cream. Season generously to make a tasty pasta sauce.

3. Cook pasta shells in a hearty beef or chicken broth and serve as a side dish.

4. Chop drained, canned anchovies and capers and mix with a little olive oil to make a delicious pasta sauce.

5. Mix chunks of drained canned tuna and halved black olives with cooked pasta and olive oil.

6. Finely chop a generous amount of parsley, add some fresh herbs, and sprinkle over drained, cooked pasta tossed with butter or olive oil. Add Parmesan cheese and serve hot.

7. Toss cooked pasta with toasted sesame seeds, sesame oil, and red pepper flakes.

8. Mix cooked, dried beans and pasta then toss with freshly chopped shallots and olive oil.

9. Use leftover cooked pasta in stuffings for meats or vegetables.

10. Toss cooked pasta with very ripe tomatoes—peeled, seeded, and chopped—and fresh basil and olive oil.

11. Flavored butters that might have been made in advance for another dish and kept in the freezer can make a savory sauce for pasta. For example, leftover butter flavored with a red wine reduction and shallots can be used to toss with cooked, drained pasta.

Baked Pastas

MACARONI AND CHEESE

2 cups uncooked macaroni
pinch of salt
2 cups Medium White Sauce (page 399)
1 cup sharp cheddar cheese, grated
½ cup freshly chopped parsley (optional)

salt and freshly ground black pepper to taste
1 cup fresh breadcrumbs
3 tablespoons butter, melted

1.   Preheat oven to 350° F. Butter a baking dish just large enough to hold the cooked pasta.

2.   In a large pot of boiling water, add macaroni and a pinch of salt. Bring back to a boil and cook until tender, about 7 to 10 minutes. Drain.

3.   In a large mixing bowl, combine the cooked pasta, the white sauce, ¾ cup of the cheese, the parsley (if desired), and salt and pepper to taste. Pour into baking dish just large enough to hold the noodles in a thick layer. Sprinkle over the remaining ¼ cup cheese and the breadcrumbs. Drizzle melted butter over the top. Bake in the oven until browned and the sauce is bubbling, about 30 minutes.

MACARONI BAKED IN TOMATO SAUCE WITH HERBS

2 cups uncooked macaroni
pinch of salt
4 tablespoons olive oil
1 medium onion, diced
2 cloves garlic, peeled and finely
   chopped
2 28-ounce cans whole tomatoes,
   drained, seeded, and chopped

½ cup loosely packed shredded
   fresh basil or 1 teaspoon dried
2 tablespoons finely chopped
   parsley
¼ cup grated Parmesan cheese
¼ cup dry breadcrumbs

1.   Preheat over to 350° F.

2.   In a large pot of boiling water, add macaroni and a pinch of salt. Bring back to a boil and cook until tender, about 7 to 10 minutes. Drain.

3.   Heat 2 tablespoons of the oil in a small, nonreactive saucepan. Add the onion and garlic. Cook over low heat until soft, about 5 minutes. Stir in the tomatoes and cook until the vegetables are soft and the tomatoes have begun to give off liquid, about 10 minutes.

4.   In a large bowl, mix the tomato sauce, macaroni, and herbs. Stir to blend. Pour into a buttered baking dish and cover with the Parmesan cheese and breadcrumbs. Drizzle the remaining 2 tablespoons of olive oil over the top and bake until browned and sauce is bubbling, about 30 minutes.

MACARONI AND OYSTERS

2 cups uncooked macaroni
1 pint oysters, shucked and drained
2 cups Medium White Sauce (see
  page 399)

salt and freshly ground black pepper
  to taste
1 cup fresh breadcrumbs
3 tablespoons butter, melted

1. Preheat oven to 400° F. Butter a baking dish just large enough to hold the cooked pasta.

2. In a large pot of boiling water, add the macaroni and a pinch of salt. Bring back to a boil and cook until done, about 7 minutes. Drain well. Pour into a large mixing bowl.

3. Add the oysters and the white sauce. Stir well. Season with salt and pepper to taste. Pour into baking dish.

4. Cover the top with the breadcrumbs. Drizzle the melted butter over the top. Bake until browned, about 20 minutes.

NOODLE KUGEL

1 pound broad noodles
1 cup fat (chicken, goose, or butter)

4 eggs, beaten
salt and freshly ground black pepper
  to taste

1. Preheat oven to 400° F. Butter a baking dish just large enough to hold the cooked noodles.

2. In a large pot of salted boiling water, cook the noodles until done. Drain.

3. In a large bowl, combine the cooked noodles with the fat and the eggs. Season to taste. Transfer to the baking dish. Bake until top is well browned, 15 to 25 minutes.

Boiled Pastas

SPAGHETTI WITH MEAT SAUCE

2 tablespoons butter or olive oil
4 medium onions (1½ pounds),
  thinly sliced
½ cup warm water
1 red pepper (about ½ pound),
  diced
1 pound ground beef or pork or an
  equal mixture of both
2 small cloves garlic, minced

2 28-ounce cans tomatoes, drained,
  seeded, and chopped
2 tablespoons tomato paste
¼ teaspoon red pepper flakes
  (optional)
salt and freshly ground black pepper
  to taste
1 pound spaghetti
grated Parmesan cheese

1. In a large saucepan, heat the butter or oil over moderately high heat. Add the onions and cook until soft, about 5 minutes. Add the water and the red pepper. Increase heat and cook until water has evaporated. Add the meat and the garlic. Cook over high heat until meat has browned. Add the tomatoes, the tomato paste, and the red pepper flakes, if desired. Reduce heat to moderate and cook, uncovered, until sauce is rich and thickened, about 1 ½ hours, stirring occasionally. Season with salt and pepper.

2. In a large amount of boiling, salted water cook the spaghetti until tender, about 7 to 10 minutes. Drain well. Toss a small amount of the sauce and the pasta in a large bowl. Top with more sauce and Parmesan cheese.

Variation: Substitute 1 pound ground turkey for the beef.

SPAGHETTI AND MEAT BALLS

1 recipe Meat Balls (Koenigsberger
  Klops) (page 288)
2 cups beef stock (page 59)
Spaghetti Meat Sauce (see recipe
  above)

1 pound spaghetti
grated Parmesan cheese

1. Prepare Meat Balls and cook until done in boiling stock to cover. Remove from cooking liquid and add balls to the meat sauce and cook for 30 minutes.

2. In a large amount of boiling salted water cook the spaghetti until tender, about 7 to 10 minutes. Drain well. Serve the sauce over the cooked pasta and surround with meat balls. Sprinkle with grated cheese.

SPAGHETTI WITH SWEETBREADS AND MUSHROOMS

2 pounds Boiled Sweetbreads (page 329)
1 pound spaghetti
salt and freshly ground black pepper to taste

½ cup butter
1 pound mushrooms, cleaned and trimmed
2 tablespoons flour
1 cup milk or cream

1.   Prepare the sweetbreads. Set aside.
2.   In a large pot of boiling, salted water, cook the spaghetti until tender, about 7 to 10 minutes. Drain and season with salt and pepper to taste. Mix well. Pack into a well-buttered mold and keep hot.
3.   In a medium sauté pan, melt the butter. Add the mushrooms and cook over moderately high heat. Add the flour and when slightly browned, add the milk or cream. Stir over low heat until smooth.
4.   Turn spaghetti out of mold and surround with sweetbreads. Top with the mushroom sauce.

PASTA PRIMAVERA

2 medium carrots (about ½ pound), trimmed, peeled and cut into ¼-inch dice
¼ pound green beans, trimmed and cut into ½-inch pieces
1 cup yellow squash (about ½ pound), diced
½ cup fresh peas (or thawed frozen)
¼ cup olive oil
1 clove garlic, crushed, peeled, and finely minced

1 medium onion (about ½ pound), thinly sliced
1 small red pepper (preferably less than ½ pound), stemmed, cored, and cut into ¼-inch dice
1 pound shaped pasta (wheels, fusilli, rotelle, or bowties)
salt and freshly ground black pepper to taste
¼ cup (tightly packed) shredded fresh basil or 1 tablespoon dried basil
grated Parmesan cheese (optional)

1.   Plunge the carrots into a large pot of boiling, salted water and cook until soft, about 5 to 7 minutes. Remove to a large mixing bowl with a slotted spoon. Repeat this procedure with the green beans, the squash, and the peas, bringing the water back to a full boil each time. Set the cooked vegetables aside. Alternatively, follow manufacturer's instructions for cooking vegetables in the microwave oven.
2.   In a large sauté pan, heat the oil over moderate heat. Add the garlic, the onions, and the red peppers. Cook over moderately low heat until very soft,

about 15 minutes. Drain any water that has accumulated from the cooked vegetables and add to the sauté pan.

3. In a large amount of boiling, salted water cook the pasta until tender,
about 7 to 10 minutes. Heat the vegetables in the sauté pan over moderately
high heat, stirring frequently. Season with salt and black pepper to taste. In a
large mixing bowl, toss the pasta, the basil, and the vegetables to mix well.
Serve immediately with Parmesan cheese if desired.

PASTA WITH CHICKEN AND ROASTED PEPPERS   *Serves 8.*

1 whole chicken, 4 to 6 pounds,
    trimmed of excess fat
4 cups rich chicken stock (page 59)
2 medium onions, peeled and cut in
    half
2 carrots, peeled and cut into 2-inch
    pieces
1 stalk celery, chopped
2 large red peppers

2 large yellow peppers
4 tablespoons butter
4 tablespoons flour
salt and freshly ground black pepper
    to taste
2 pounds fettucine
chopped fresh parsley for garnish
    (optional)

1. Place chicken in large pot. Add chicken stock, onions, carrots, and celery.
Season with a large pinch of salt. Bring to a boil over high heat, reduce to a
simmer, and cook gently until done, about 45 minutes. Leave to cool in its own
liquid.

2. Roast and peel peppers (page 385). Remove seeds and membrane. Cut
into long, thin strips.

3. Remove chicken from pot when cool enough to handle. Pull away all
meat from bones, discarding skin, gristle, and fat. Cut into 1- to 2-inch cubes.
You should have about 4 cups of cleaned, boned chicken. Cover and set aside.

4. Strain the chicken broth, discarding all vegetables, and measure. You
should have about 4 cups liquid. If you have more than this amount, pour into
a large saucepan and reduce over high heat until you have 4 cups. If you have
less than this amount, add water to measure 4 cups.

5. Melt butter in a large saucepan. Stir in flour and cook over low heat until
lightly golden, about 3 minutes. Pour in chicken broth all at once, whisking
constantly. Bring to a simmer stirring frequently. Let cook gently until thickened
and creamy, about 10 minutes. Remove from heat and add chicken and peppers,
season to taste with salt and pepper. (Recipe can be prepared in advance up to
this point. Cool to room temperature, cover, and refrigerate for up to 2 days.)

6. Bring sauce to a simmer when ready to assemble dish. In a large pot of
boiling salted water, cook fettucine until tender, about 7 to 10 minutes. Drain
pasta well and divide between warmed plates. Top with sauce and serve at once.
Garnish with chopped parsley if desired.

PASTA WITH BROCCOLI, ANCHOVIES, AND GARLIC

1 pound pasta (ziti, rigatoni, fusilli,
   or shells)
¼ cup olive oil
4 cloves garlic, peeled and thinly
   sliced

2 tablespoons anchovy paste
4 cups cooked broccoli florets
   (removed from large stalks)
freshly ground black pepper to taste

1. Bring a large amount of salted water to a boil. Cook the pasta until tender, about 7 to 10 minutes. Drain well.

2. In a large sauté pan, heat the olive oil over moderate heat. Add the garlic and cook until softened, 3 to 5 minutes. Stir in the anchovy paste and mix well. Combine with the cooked broccoli, stirring gently to coat.

3. In a large mixing bowl, toss together the broccoli mixture with the cooked pasta. Season with a generous amount of black pepper. Serve at once.

PASTA WITH LAMB AND EGGPLANT

1 medium eggplant (about 1
   pound), peeled, and cut into 1-
   inch cubes
2 tablespoons olive oil
1 small onion (about 4 ounces),
   thinly sliced
2 cloves garlic, peeled and finely
   minced
1 pound ground lamb

2 teaspoons cumin
salt and freshly ground black pepper
   to taste
1 pound hollow or shaped pasta
   (ziti, penne, or shells)
2 tablespoons chopped fresh
   oregano or 1 tablespoon dried

1. Place the eggplant in a large saucepan and cover with cold water. Bring to a boil, reduce heat, and cook until soft, about 10 minutes. Drain.

2. In a sauté pan, heat the olive oil over medium-high heat. Add the onion and the garlic. Cook until soft, about 3 minutes. Stir often to prevent scorching. Stir in the ground lamb and the cumin. Cook just until all traces of pink are gone, about 7 to 10 minutes. Season with salt and pepper to taste.

3. In a large amount of lightly salted boiling water, cook pasta until tender, about 7 to 10 minutes. Drain well.

4. In a large mixing bowl, toss together the eggplant, the lamb mixture, the pasta, and the oregano. Serve at once.

PASTA WITH WHITE BEANS, TOMATOES, AND HERBS

2 tablespoons butter
2 tablespoons finely chopped
  shallots
2 cloves garlic, finely chopped
3 to 4 medium fresh tomatoes (1½
  pounds), peeled, seeded, and
  chopped, or 1 28-ounce can,
  drained and chopped

1 cup cooked white beans (navy or
  Great Northern) (page 179)
salt and freshly ground black pepper
  to taste
1 pound shaped or hollow pasta
  (fusilli, rigatoni, ziti, or shells)
½ cup fresh parsley, finely chopped

1. In a medium saucepan, melt the butter over medium-high heat. Add the shallots and garlic. Cook until soft but not brown. Add the tomatoes and cook until they begin to give off liquid and are warmed through, about 10 minutes. Stir in the cooked beans. Season to taste with salt and pepper.

2. In a large amount of boiling salted water, cook the pasta until tender, about 7 to 10 minutes. Drain and empty into a large mixing bowl. Toss with the tomato and bean mixture, the fresh parsley, and more salt and pepper to taste. Serve at once.

PASTA WITH KALE, BACON AND BLACK-EYED PEAS

½ pound slab bacon
1 small onion, thinly sliced
2 pounds cooked kale, fresh or
  frozen, chopped
freshly ground black pepper to taste

1 cup cooked black-eyed peas (page
  179)
1 pound shaped pasta (shells, ziti,
  penne, or wheels)
2 tablespoons red wine vinegar

1. Remove rind from the bacon, if necessary. Cut into chunks about ¼ inch thick and 1 inch long. Cook in a large sauté pan over moderately high heat until well browned. Remove with a slotted spoon, set aside.

2. Drain off all but 2 tablespoons bacon fat. Add the onions to the sauté pan. Over moderately high heat, cook until soft but not browned. Add the chopped kale and stir to blend. Season with freshly ground black pepper. Add the peas and warm through.

3. In a large pot of boiling salted water, cook the pasta until tender, about 7 to 10 minutes. Drain well.

4. Just before serving, add the vinegar to the kale and peas. In a large bowl, combine the bacon, the kale and peas, and the pasta. Toss well and serve at once.

PASTA WITH SUN-DRIED TOMATOES, OLIVES, AND GOAT CHEESE

½ cup sun-dried tomatoes
½ pound fresh goat cheese, chilled
½ cup pitted oil-cured black olives
1 pound shaped or hollow pasta

¼ cup olive oil
2 tablespoons chopped fresh
 rosemary or 1 tablespoon dried
freshly ground black pepper to taste

1. Cut the tomatoes into strips and place in a large mixing bowl. Crumble the cheese over the tomatoes and let come to room temperature. Chop the olives and add to the bowl.

2. In a large amount of boiling salted water, cook the pasta until tender, about 7 to 10 minutes. Drain well.

3. Toss together the tomatoes, goat cheese, olives, and pasta with the olive oil and the rosemary. Season with black pepper to taste. Serve at once.

PASTA WITH TURKEY, CELERY, AND SAGE

1 cup heavy cream
2 tablespoons chopped fresh sage,
 or 1 tablespoon dried
2 tablespoons butter
3 ribs celery, thinly sliced
1 medium onion, thinly sliced

1 pound fettucine or spaghetti
2 cups cooked turkey, cut into
 small cubes
salt and freshly ground black pepper
 to taste
several leaves of fresh sage for
 garnish (optional)

1. In a heavy saucepan, heat the cream with the sage. Remove from heat, cover and let infuse for 15 minutes.

2. In a large skillet, melt the butter. Add the celery and the onion. Cook over low heat until the onions are transparent and the celery is soft, about 15 minutes.

3. Strain the cream into the skillet with the celery and onions. Bring to a boil and reduce over high heat until slightly thickened, 3 to 5 minutes.

4. In a large amount of boiling, salted water, cook the pasta until tender, about 7 to 10 minutes. Drain well.

5. In a large bowl, combine the sauce, pasta, and cooked turkey. Toss well, season to taste, and serve hot. Garnish with fresh sage leaves if desired.

Filled Pastas

LASAGNE   *Serves 4 to 6.*

2 tablespoons olive oil
1 pound ground beef
1 clove garlic, finely minced
1 large can (28 ounces) tomatoes, drained and coarsely chopped
salt and freshly ground black pepper to taste

1 tablespoon chopped fresh oregano or 1 teaspoon dried
½ pound lasagne noodles
1 pound ricotta or dry cottage cheese
½ cup grated Parmesan cheese
½ pound mozzarella cheese, sliced

1.   In a large skillet or sauté pan, heat the olive oil. Add the beef and garlic. Cook over moderately high heat until meat is browned. Tip the pan and drain off as much fat as is possible. Add the tomatoes and season with salt, pepper, and oregano. Simmer until thickened, about 30 minutes. Preheat the oven to 350° F.

2.   In a large pot of boiling, salted water, cook the noodles until tender, about 7 to 10 minutes. Drain well. Set aside.

3.   Line a large, greased baking dish with ½ cup of the beef mixture. Cover with a single layer of the cooked lasagne noodles. Spread ½ of the ricotta cheese on the noodles, sprinkle with ½ of the Parmesan cheese, and place over this ⅓ of the mozzarella. Repeat ending with the remaining beef mixture and mozzarella.

4.   Bake until bubbling and slightly browned on top, about 45 minutes. Let stand for 15 minutes after removing from the oven. Cut into squares.

LASAGNE WITH SAUSAGE AND PEPPERS

½ pound curly edge lasagne noodles
3 tablespoons olive oil
5 Italian sausages (about 1 pound)
1 medium red pepper, cored and seeded
1 medium yellow pepper, cored and seeded
1 medium green pepper, cored and seeded

1 large onion, thinly sliced
2 cloves garlic, finely minced
1 pound ricotta cheese
1 egg
1 teaspoon dried oregano
1½ cups plus 2 tablespoons strained Basic Tomato Sauce (page 405)
8 thin slices (about ¼ pound) fresh mozzarella cheese

1.   Preheat oven to 375° F. In a large pot of boiling, salted water, cook the noodles until tender, about 7 to 10 minutes. Drain and set aside.

(continued)

2. In a medium skillet, heat 2 tablespoons of the oil. Cut the sausages into ½-inch slices and sauté over moderate heat until lightly browned, about 1½ minutes on each side. Remove with a slotted spoon and drain on paper towels. Reserve the pan drippings with any rendered fat.

3. Slice the peppers lengthwise into ¼-inch strips. Add the peppers, onion, and garlic to the skillet and cook over moderate heat until softened, about 20 minutes. Stir often.

4. In a small mixing bowl, beat together the ricotta cheese, the egg, and the oregano.

5. Grease a small baking dish (8 inch by 11 inch) with the remaining tablespoon of olive oil. Add 2 tablespoons of the tomato sauce to moisten the bottom of the dish. Top with a layer of the cooked noodles. Place half of the sausage slices over the bottom of the dish, make a layer of the cooked vegetables and the ricotta cheese mixture. Add another layer of noodles and repeat the fillings. Top with another layer of noodles and pour the remaining tomato sauce over all. Top with the mozzarella cheese slices and bake until set and lightly browned on top, 30 to 35 minutes.

SEAFOOD LASAGNE

½ pound curly lasagne noodles
2 cups fish stock (page 60) or bottled clam juice
1 pound medium shrimp, peeled, deveined, and coarsely chopped (reserve shells)
2 tablespoons butter
3 tablespoons flour
1 teaspoon chopped fresh tarragon or ½ teaspoon dried

1 pound flounder fillets, cut in half
1 pound skinned catfish fillets, cut into 1-inch chunks
freshly ground black pepper to taste
2 cloves garlic, peeled and finely minced
¼ cup finely chopped parsley
1 to 2 teaspoons finely grated lemon zest
¼ cup dry breadcrumbs

1. Preheat oven to 375° F. In a large pot of boiling, salted water, cook the noodles until tender, about 7 to 10 minutes. Drain and reserve.

2. In a small saucepan, combine fish stock or clam broth and reserved shrimp shells. Bring to a boil over moderate heat. Cover and keep warm.

3. In a heavy saucepan, melt the butter. Add flour and cook over moderate heat for 2 minutes. Strain stock or broth into flour and butter. Discard shells. Beat vigorously over high heat and stir until mixture comes to a boil. Boil for 1 minute. Add the tarragon.

4. Combine half of the sauce with the shrimp. Reserve.

5. Spread 2 tablespoons of the sauce over the bottom of a small baking dish (8 inch by 11 inch). Layer with noodles, flounder fillets, and catfish chunks.

Season with pepper. Spread over half of the shrimp mixture. Repeat. Pour the remaining sauce on top.

6. Combine garlic, parsley, lemon zest, and breadcrumbs. Sprinkle evenly over the top. Bake in the preheated oven for 30 minutes.

MEAT RAVIOLI

2 recipes of Fresh Pasta (page 149)
1½ cups chopped cooked beef
½ cup chopped cooked spinach
¾ cup grated Parmesan or Romano cheese

¾ cup dry breadcrumbs
½ pound pork sausage
2 eggs
salt and freshly ground black pepper to taste

1. Make Fresh Pasta. Let rest for 30 minutes, divide in half, and roll into sheets as thin as possible. While preparing the filling, let dry on a cloth sprinkled with cornmeal.

2. Combine the cooked beef with the spinach, cheese, breadcrumbs, sausage, eggs, and salt and pepper to taste.

3. Put filling by teaspoonfuls on one sheet of dough, 2 inches apart. Cover with second sheet, pressing well between the mounds to seal the edges. Cut into squares with a moistened pastry cutter. Drop ravioli into boiling salted water and cook 20 minutes or until dough is cooked through. Cut into edge of ravioli to test. Remove with skimmer to serving dish. Toss with butter, olive oil, or tomato sauce and serve at once.

Variation:

Cheese Ravioli:

Mix 1 pound ricotta cheese, 3 eggs, ½ cup grated Parmesan or Romano cheese, and salt and pepper to taste. Make and fill ravioli following basic recipe replacing cheese mixture for meat. Cook as directed and serve with a sauce of melted butter and additional grated cheese or tomato sauce.

KREPLACH OR PIEROGI

2 recipes Fresh Pasta (page 149)
1 pound cooked meat, chopped
2 teaspoons grated onion
1 egg

salt and freshly ground black pepper
  to taste
2 tablespoons hot fat or melted
  butter
browned cracker crumbs, for
  garnish

1. Make Fresh Pasta. Roll out in very thin sheets and spread on cloth sprinkled with cornmeal to dry.

2. Combine the meat, onion, egg, salt, and pepper.

3. Cut the dough into 2-inch squares, place a teaspoon of meat mixture on every square, and then fold each to make a triangular shape, pressing edges together well. Drop into boiling soup or salted water. Cook for 15 minutes. Drain, place on hot platter, and pour hot fat or butter over them. Garnish with browned cracker crumbs.

CHEESE KREPLACH OR PIEROGI

2 recipes Fresh Pasta (page 149)
1 pound ricotta or cottage cheese
1 egg
1 tablespoon heavy cream, sour
  cream, or butter

salt and freshly ground black pepper
  to taste
2 tablespoons hot fat or melted
  butter

1. Make Fresh Pasta. Roll out in thin sheets and spread out on cloth sprinkled with cornmeal to dry.

2. In a small bowl, mix together the cheese, egg, and cream or butter. Season with salt and pepper.

3. Cut the dough into 2-inch squares. Place a teaspoon of cheese mixture on each square, and fold into a triangular shape. Press edges together well to seal. Drop into boiling salted water or soup and cook for 15 minutes. Drain and drizzle with the fat or melted butter.

Variation: If sweet kreplach are desired, omit salt and pepper. Use cottage cheese and flavor with sugar, lemon rind, or cinnamon.

Asian Noodle Dishes

SOBA NOODLES WITH RED PEPPERS AND SNOW PEAS

8 ounces soba noodles (buckwheat noodles)
2 tablespoons vegetable oil
8 ounce (½ pound) snow peas
1 small red pepper, seeded and cut into thin strips
2 teaspoons finely chopped fresh ginger
1 tablespoon sesame oil
1 tablespoon toasted sesame seeds
¼ cup thinly sliced scallions

1. In a large pot of boiling water, cook the soba noodles until tender, about 5 minutes. Drain well.

2. In a large skillet or wok, heat the vegetable oil. Add the snow peas and red pepper. Cook for about 2 minutes, stirring constantly.

3. Combine noodles, cooked vegetables, and ginger in a large mixing bowl and toss well. Coat noodles with sesame oil and garnish with sesame seeds and scallions.

PAD THAI

¼ cup distilled white vinegar
3 tablespoons fish sauce
2 tablespoons sugar
¼ cup dried shrimp
9 ounces dried rice sticks (rice noodles)
2 tablespoons peanut oil
2 red serrano chili peppers, seeded and very finely minced
4 cloves garlic, smashed, peeled, and minced
1 pound lean pork (loin, tenderloin, butt, or shoulder), cut into thin slices ⅜ inch by 2 inches
½ pound small shrimp, cooked, shelled, and deveined
2 eggs, lightly beaten
2 cups fresh bean sprouts
1 tablespoon fresh lime juice
¼ cup roasted, peanuts, coarsely chopped
¼ cup thinly sliced basil
¼ cup thinly sliced scallions

1. In a small bowl, combine the vinegar, fish sauce, sugar, and dried shrimp. Mix well to blend. Set aside.

2. In a large bowl, soak the noodles in enough hot water to cover until softened, about 20 minutes. Drain. In a large pot of boiling water, cook the noodles until tender, about 2 minutes. Drain and rinse well. Spread them out to drain on paper towels.

(continued)

3. In a large skillet or a wok, heat the peanut oil. Add the peppers and garlic and cook until the peppers are slightly wilted, about 30 seconds. Add the pork and cook until browned. Stir in the dried and the cooked shrimp. Make a well in the center of the mixture and pour in the eggs. When they are almost set, scramble them evenly. Add half the noodles, thoroughly incorporating them into the mixture. Stir in the remaining noodles and half the bean sprouts. Cook until sprouts are nearly wilted. Add the lime juice.

4. Heap the meat and noodles onto a platter. Cover one half with the peanuts and the other half with the remaining uncooked bean sprouts. Garnish with basil and scallions.

CHINESE EGG NOODLES WITH SPICY PEANUT SAUCE

2 cups peanut oil
1 cup raw, peanuts
½ cup strong freshly made tea, preferably Chinese
6 cloves garlic, smashed, peeled, and minced
1 tablespoon minced fresh ginger
2 red serrano chili peppers, seeded and finely chopped
¼ teaspoon salt
2 teaspoons sugar

1 tablespoon tamari
¼ cup fresh lemon juice
2 tablespoons sesame oil
1 tablespoon chili oil
2 whole, boneless, skinless chicken breasts
8 ounces (½ pound) Chinese egg noodles
1 pound cucumber, peeled, seeded, and thinly sliced
¼ cup cilantro, coarsely chopped

1. In a large skillet or wok, heat the oil until nearly smoking. Add the peanuts, stir gently for a few seconds, then remove from heat. Allow the peanuts to sit for 10 minutes. With a slotted spoon, transfer the peanuts to the work bowl of a food processor. Reserve the oil.

2. Grind the peanuts to a coarse paste. Add a dash of the tea, the garlic, ginger, and chilies. Pulse to blend. Pour in the remaining tea and the salt, sugar, tamari, and lemon juice. Process until smooth.

3. Scrape the peanut sauce into a mixing bowl and stir in the sesame and chili oils. Mix thoroughly.

4. In a wok or large skillet, add 2 tablespoons of the reserved peanut oil. Quickly fry the chicken breast in the hot oil just until it begins to brown. Remove from pan. Drain on paper towels, then shred.

5. In a large pot of boiling water, cook the egg noodles just until tender, about 5 minutes. Drain well.

6. In a large mixing bowl, toss together the noodles and peanut sauce. Add the chicken and mix well. Place on serving dishes, garnish with sliced cucumber and cilantro. Serve hot or cold.

GRAINS AND LEGUMES

Nutritionists have recently been urging us to include more whole grains and legumes in our diet. High in fiber and complex carbohydrates, low in fat, full of earthy flavor that satisfies and fortifies, such foods can be a welcome menu addition rather than a dietary obligation.

There are a wide variety of grains on the market now that provide the essentials for lots of appealing dishes, and many are available in the local supermarket. In addition, health-food stores usually carry an array of barley, buckwheat, bulgur, corn, millet, oats, rye, and wheat. The textures range from the whole kernel to ground or polished seeds and berries. Bought in bulk, they can be kept on hand almost indefinitely to provide all sorts of low-cost, healthy, and flavorful foods for meals or snacks.

That old favorite rice now comes in many forms. Brown rice, sticky rice, and short-grain Arborio rice are almost as common as plain white rice. As interest in ethnic food has grown, so has the appreciation for some previously unknown dishes. Versatile and easy to prepare, rice is increasingly known as an economical and natural convenience food.

Dried beans, peas, and lentils have been around since man started cultivating land long ago. Today, these legumes (also known as "pulses") are making a comeback as an alternative source of protein. When mixed with other foods, like rice or pasta, the lowly dried vegetable becomes either the focus of or a companion to an extremely satisfying and tasty meal.

Grains

Grains come to us in many forms. Husks are almost always removed and the remaining kernels or bran are processed into a variety of common products. The following list of the most common grains and how to prepare them provides an endless array of edible possibilities. Once thought of as only for the die-hard health-food enthusiast, grains are replacing potatoes as savory side dishes.

Barley: Comes in whole kernels or ground into fine, medium, and coarse grades. Soak overnight for best results. *Whole barley* is chewy. *Pearl barley* simply refers to the process used for removing the hard, outer husk. Boil either in plenty of salted water until soft, 45 minutes to 1 hour. Then drain. Cook *ground* *barley* in the same manner but shorten cooking time by approximately 15 minutes. Wonderful in soups.

Buckwheat: Toasted, either whole in kernels (groats) or cracked and ground into coarse and fine textures. Finely ground buckwheat is known as buckwheat *grits*. *Kasha* is a popular dish made from cracked or whole roasted seeds. For "grits," simmer 1 part finely ground buckwheat in 2½ parts water for 12 to 15 minutes. (See recipe, page 169, for Buckwheat Kasha.)

Bulgur: Wheat berries are steamed, dried, and cracked to produce this whole wheat grain. Cook 1 part bulgur in 2 parts water until liquid is absorbed, about 30 minutes. Use in soup, for stuffings, or in salads.

Cornmeal and Hominy: Ground dried white or yellow corn is used to make these traditionally Southern staples. The tough kernel of corn is removed by machine or by soaking in a lye solution to yield the whole berries known as *hominy*. *Grits* are hominy ground very fine. Blue cornmeal from the American Southwest is increasingly popular because of its visual novelty.

Millet: A small, roundish hard cereal grain cultivated from the earliest times. Cook in twice its volume of milk or water for 30 to 45 minutes.

Quinoa: An ancient grain from South America. It is a hard, whole grain that is very high in protein and particularly easy to digest. This versatile grain can be used in soups, salads, or as a side dish. Follow package instructions. The rule of thumb is 2 parts water to 1 part quinoa.

Oats: *Raw oats (groats)* come in unpolished kernels that can be cooked in twice the volume of water for about an hour. *Rolled oats* are steamed groats that have been rolled or steel cut to remove the husk. The thickness determines whether they are quick cooking or not. These flakes cook quickly either way. Follow package directions for best results. *Oatmeal* is husked groats ground into coarse, medium, and fine textures used primarily for making porridge. Simmer uncovered in twice the volume of water until thick, about 12 minutes, unless package directions state otherwise.

Rye: This grain's kernels come cracked and polished. The grain is mostly used finely ground for flour but coarsely cracked rye groats can be delicious. Cook 1 part rye in 2 parts water until soft, about 15 minutes. Ground rye can also be made into porridge. Cook according to package directions or 1 part rye in 4 times the volume of water for about half an hour.

Semolina: Semolina comes from grinding a hard, durum wheat into a fine texture. Semolina is used for making couscous, pasta, polenta, and as a porridge. Simmer 1 part semolina in 4 parts water for making porridge. Because it comes from such a hard grain, the cooking time is relatively long, about 30 minutes.

Wheat: Abundant and versatile, wheat has been a mainstay of the human diet for centuries. The *wheat berry* is the whole kernel, which can be boiled in water for about an hour. *Cracked wheat* comes in coarse, medium, and fine grinds. Simmer coarse or medium grinds in 2 parts water until softened, about 45 minutes. Finely ground wheat can be made into porridge. Simmer uncovered in 4 parts water until thick and creamy, about 30 minutes.

CRACKED WHEAT PILAF

1 medium onion, finely chopped	½ teaspoon salt
2 carrots, peeled and chopped	freshly ground black pepper to taste
2 ribs celery, chopped	several sprigs fresh thyme (or 1
2 tablespoons olive oil	teaspoon dried thyme)
1 cup cracked wheat	1 fresh bay leaf, crumpled (or 2
2 cups beef stock (page 59)	dried bay leaves)

1. In a medium covered pan, combine the onions, carrots, celery, and the olive oil. Cook over moderately high heat until vegetables are soft. Stir often to prevent scorching.

2. Add the cracked wheat and stir to blend. Continue cooking over moderately high heat for about 2 minutes. Pour in stock, add salt, pepper, and herbs. Bring to a boil, reduce heat, and cover. Simmer until wheat is tender, about 35 minutes.

3. When done, remove from heat and discard sprigs of thyme and bay leaf. Fluff with a fork. Replace cover and let stand for 5 more minutes before serving.

BUCKWHEAT GROATS (KASHA)

1 medium onion, diced	2½ cups fine-grind buckwheat
2 tablespoons butter or fat	groats
1 teaspoon salt	2 cups boiling water
a little paprika	(approximately)
	1 egg

1. Preheat oven to 450° F. In a small sauté pan, fry the onion in the fat until translucent. Set aside.

(*continued*)

2. In a small mixing bowl, mix together the salt, paprika, and buckwheat. Place in a greased baking dish. Slowly stir in as much boiling water as it will absorb. Add the onion, fat, and egg. Cover and bake in the preheated oven for about 20 minutes.

CORNMEAL MUSH

2 teaspoons salt	1 cup cornmeal
4 cups boiling water	

Add salt to boiling water in the upper part of a double boiler. Add the meal slowly in a thin stream, stirring constantly. Cover and steam over boiling water from 1 to 3 hours. Alternatively, mix the meal with 1 cup of cold water and add to 3 cups of boiling, salted water. Proceed as for above. Cornmeal mush served with cottage cheese and sour cream is a delicious Romanian supper dish.

POLENTA

Follow instructions above for Cornmeal Mush. Add a pinch of red pepper and 1 cup grated Parmesan cheese while hot. Pour into a loaf pan and chill until firm. Unmold and cut into slices. Either brown in olive oil or bake in a hot oven (450° F) until crisp and browned on edges. Serve plain with additional cheese or with Basic Tomato Sauce (page 405).

GRITS

1 cup fine hominy	4 cups boiling water
1 teaspoon salt	

Stir hominy slowly, in a thin stream, into salted boiling water. Reduce heat, cover, and simmer, stirring occasionally, until tender and thick, about 1 hour.

COUSCOUS

Traditionally part of an elaborate North African dish with stewed meats and vegetables, a simplified version makes a delectable side dish. Instant brands come with their own instructions. Try adding scallions, toasted pine nuts or walnuts, currants, or halved raisins for added flair.

1 cup couscous (available in health-food stores)
1 cup boiling water

salt and freshly ground black pepper to taste

1. Rinse the couscous in cold water and strain through a stainless-steel sieve. Repeat until water runs clear. Leave the couscous in the sieve and let sit for 15 to 20 minutes. Rake and comb the grains to break up lumps as the grains swell.

2. Place the couscous over a pan with the boiling water. Steam the grains until softened, 10 to 15 minutes. Empty into a serving bowl and season with salt and pepper to taste.

Note: The cooked grains can be molded into small, lightly buttered ramekins and tightly packed. Simply reheat in water bath just before serving. Unmold as individual servings.

RICE

Many kinds of rice are described below. Processed rice comes with separate directions that should be carefully followed.

 Several methods of cooking ordinary rice are given in this chapter. Whatever method is used, the grains of rice should be just cooked through but not soft and mushy. To test rice, press a grain between the fingers or bite into it. The grains should be separate and distinct and there should be no hard center. Let rice stand over hot water for a few minutes, uncovered, to dry. To keep rice hot, or to reheat it, put it in a colander over hot water, uncovered, or set it in a pan of hot water in a moderate oven. If reheating in a microwave oven, cover and cook on high power about 1 minute per cup of rice. Frozen rice may be cooked 2 minutes on high power. One cup raw rice makes about 3 cups cooked.

All forms of cooked rice can be refrigerated for 6 to 7 days and frozen for 6 months. Keep stored in airtight, covered containers or sealable plastic bags to prevent drying out.

Some rice terms are defined below:

Long-Grain Rice: Rice that is long and slender, as much as 4 to 5 times long as it is wide.

Medium-Grain Rice: Rice that is plump in shape but not round. These grains are more moist and tender than long-grain rice.

Short-Grain Rice: Rice that is almost round. This tends to be a sticky rice with grains that cling together when cooked.

Brown Rice: Whole or broken kernels of rice from which only the hull has been removed. Brown rice may be eaten as is or mixed with regular-milled white rice. Cooked brown rice has a slightly chewy texture and a nutty flavor. The light brown color is caused by the presence of the seven bran layers that are rich in minerals and vitamins.

Parboiled Rice: This term refers to rice soaked in warm water under pressure, steamed, and dried before milling. This process gelatinizes the starch in the grain, forces vitamins into the center, and insures a separateness of grain. It retains more nutrients than regular-milled white rice but it takes a few more minutes to cook.

Precooked Rice: Rice that is milled, completely cooked, and then dehydrated. Preparation takes only a few minutes. Also called *quick-cooking* and *instant* rice. To prepare, follow the package instructions exactly.

Basmati Rice: Indian rice with a slender and long grain. It is delicate with a distinctively flowerlike fragrance and subtle flavor.

Arborio Rice: A short-grain rice from Italy, most commonly used for making Risotto (see recipe below). It is a starchy rice that gives off a creamy liquid when cooked over low heat for a long time.

Wild Rice: Not genuinely a rice but grain from a grass native to North America. It has a long, brown grain that can be quite chewy. It is often mixed with white or brown rice for a more balanced texture.

Rice easily absorbs flavors. Try using beef or chicken stock for the cooking liquid. A small amount of fresh herbs, grated lime or lemon rind, or a pinch of saffron can give a subtle dimension to plain rice.

BOILED RICE

1 cup rice   2 teaspoons salt
4 cups boiling water

1. Wash rice in cold running water until liquid runs clear.
2. Sprinkle rice slowly into rapidly boiling, salted water so as not to check the boiling. Stir with a fork. Boil rapidly, uncovered, until grains seem soft when pressed between fingers, about 20 minutes.
3. Drain in coarse strainer, pouring the boiling water through rice. Put strainer over hot water, uncovered, and rest 5 to 10 minutes so grains will be whole, dry, and fluffy.

QUICK BOILED RICE

1 cup rice   1 teaspoon salt
2 cups cold water

Wash and rinse rice in cold running water. Place ingredients in pan with tight-fitting cover. Bring to a vigorous boil. Reduce heat to low and cook for 15 minutes. Turn off heat. Leave rice covered for 5 minutes before removing lid.

STEAMED RICE

1 cup rice   1 teaspoon salt
3 cups boiling water

Wash rice in cold water and drain. Put boiling, salted water in top of a double boiler. Set over direct heat and gradually add rice. Boil 5 minutes. meanwhile, heat water in the bottom of the double boiler. Place rice over hot water and steam, covered, 40 minutes or until water is absorbed and grains are tender. Uncover to dry. Suitable for molds or rings.

BROWN RICE

1 cup brown rice   2 teaspoons salt
4 cups boiling water

Follow recipe for steamed or boiled rice but increase cooking time to 40 to 60 minutes.

WILD RICE

 Wash in fresh water many times until free from grit. Boil or steam like brown rice, until just tender, 40 to 60 minutes. Lift with fork but do not stir; grains break easily.

RICE IN THE MICROWAVE

1 cup rice	1 teaspoon salt
1¼ cups water	

Combine all ingredients in a microproof baking dish. Cover and cook on high for 5 minutes or until boiling. Reduce setting to 50 percent power and cook 15 minutes for white rice and 20 minutes for parboiled rice. For brown rice, increase water to 2 cups and reduce power setting to 30 percent. Cook 45 to 55 minutes. Fluff with a fork.

GREEN RICE RING

1 cup rice	1 cup heavy cream, whipped
4 eggs, separated	4 to 5 tablespoons Parmesan cheese
1 cup parsley, minced	1 teaspoon salt
1 green pepper, finely chopped	paprika
1 small onion, finely chopped	

Preheat oven to 375° F. Boil rice (page 173). Beat yolks until lemon colored and mix with cooked rice. Add parsley, green pepper, onion, and cream. Beat egg whites to a froth and fold into rice mixture. Add cheese, salt, and paprika. Pack into a buttered ring mold. Set filled mold into a pan of hot water. Bake until set, about 45 minutes.

BASIC FRIED RICE

¼ cup vegetable oil	salt and freshly ground black pepper
1½ cups cooked rice	to taste
⅔ cup slivered scallions	cooked chicken or pork, cut into
1 tablespoon soy sauce	fine strips
	fried bean sprouts

1. In a large skillet or wok, place the oil. Add rice, scallions, soy sauce, salt, and pepper. Cook over low heat, stirring lightly, until rice becomes lightly colored.

2. Add chicken or pork, bean sprouts, or any combination of meat and vegetables. Heat through and serve at once.

SHRIMP FRIED RICE

4 cups cold, cooked rice
2 eggs, well beaten
½ pound cooked baby shrimp
3 tablespoons peanut or other oil

1 small onion, thinly sliced
1 clove garlic, minced
2 tablespoons soy sauce
4 tablespoons sherry
freshly ground black pepper to taste

1. Add a little water to cooked rice to loosen grains. In a mixing bowl, combine the beaten eggs and the shrimp.

2. In a large skillet or wok, heat the oil. Add the onion and cook until onions are slightly softened. Add garlic and continue cooking until it just begins to color.

3. Pour in the shrimp and eggs. Cook over moderate heat, stirring constantly. Add rice and cook 2 minutes, stirring constantly.

4. Add soy sauce, sherry, and pepper to taste. Stir and toss to heat through. Serve at once.

RISOTTO

While somewhat labor intensive, risotto is an amazingly versatile dish. Cooked in a hearty stock, it can be used to provide a side dish with a subtle flavor of beef, chicken, or fish. The addition of chopped, cooked meat, vegetable, or seafood can turn risotto into a memorable main dish. Fat, round Arborio rice is the preferred grain for preparing this celebrated Italian specialty. Serve risotto as soon as possible after preparing. If left to cool, the cooked rice can turn gummy and unpleasantly sticky.

3 tablespoons butter
1 small onion, chopped
1½ cups rice (preferably Arborio)

3 cups concentrated beef, chicken, or fish stock (page 59 or 60)
½ cup grated Parmesan cheese
salt and freshly ground black pepper to taste

1. In a heavy casserole, melt the butter. Add the onion and cook gently until softened. Pour in the rice and stir until rice is transparent.

2. Add ½ cup of the stock and stir over moderately high heat until liquid is absorbed. Add ½ cup more stock and stir again until absorbed. Continue this process until all liquid is used. (The process should take about 20 minutes.)

3. Add the cheese and stir to blend. Add salt and pepper to taste. Place in a warmed bowl. Serve at once with additional Parmesan cheese if desired.

RICE PILAF

Rice takes on a subtle distinctiveness when cooked with a liquid that imparts flavor. Rice pilaf is the perfect accompaniment for a varied list of chicken, fish, and meat dishes. Use the stock that best suits your needs in the following recipe.

2 tablespoons butter or olive oil
1 medium onion, finely chopped
1 cup rice, washed

2 cups richly flavored fish, chicken, or beef stock (page 60 or 59)
salt to taste

1. In a covered saucepan, melt the butter. Add the onion and cook over moderately low heat until softened. Add the rice and cook, stirring constantly, until rice is shiny and translucent.

2. Bring stock to a boil. Pour into rice with onions. Bring back to a boil. Add salt. Reduce heat and simmer, covered, for 20 minutes. Remove cover, stir gently with a fork, replace cover, and let sit for 5 minutes. Serve right away.

---

10 WAYS TO DRESS UP PLAIN RICE
All amounts are based on 3 cups cooked rice (1 cup raw)

1. Add 1 cup smoked or cured ham cut into small cubes to hot rice or mix with 2 tablespoons chopped fresh parsley and 2 tablespoons finely chopped scallions.

2. Toss hot cooked rice with ¼ cup snipped fresh herbs (thyme, chervil, basil, chives, rosemary, or coriander), 2 tablespoons freshly grated Parmesan cheese, and ½ cup toasted pine nuts.

3. Add a small pinch of saffron threads and 1 cup finely chopped red pepper to rice as it cooks.

4. Cook rice with 1 small onion finely chopped in 2 tablespoons olive oil or butter before adding liquid. Remove pits from 1 cup oil-cured olives and chop coarsely with 2 tablespoons capers. Add to cooked rice and let stand, covered, for 5 minutes to heat through.

5. Cook ½ cup finely chopped green pepper and ¼ cup chopped onion in 2 tablespoons butter or olive oil until soft. Add 1 pound fresh tomatoes, peeled, seeded, and chopped. Cook until tomatoes start to give off liquid. Drain well and add to hot cooked rice. Let stand for 5 minutes, covered, before serving.

6. Cut 1 small zucchini or 1 small yellow squash into small dice. Blanch in boiling salted water for 1 to 2 minutes. Drain, refresh under cold, running water. Add to hot cooked rice. Cover and let heat through for 5 minutes.

7. Slice 1 pound cleaned and trimmed mushrooms and cook in 2 tablespoons butter or olive oil with a clove of minced garlic for 5 minutes over moderately high heat. Drain and add to hot cooked rice.

8. Cook ½ pound chicken livers in butter or olive oil for 7 to 10 minutes then cool. Puree in the bowl of a food processor. Mix with rice and ¼ teaspoon red pepper flakes. Warm through. Season with additional salt if desired.

9. Remove tough stems from 1 pound of fresh spinach. Blanch in a large amount of boiling, salted water for 2 minutes. Drain, refresh under cold, running water, then squeeze out excess moisture. Chop coarsely and add to hot cooked rice. Stir in 1 teaspoon grated lemon rind and freshly ground black pepper. Heat through and serve at once.

10. To cooked rice add ¼ cup currants, ½ cup slivered, toasted almonds, and the peel of an orange julienned into very thin strips.

CEREALS

There has been an explosion in the variety of breakfast cereals in today's marketplace. The overwhelming choices call for a certain amount of discrimination on the part of the modern consumer. High-fiber, cholesterol-reducing claims abound as the competition between food companies increases. Although over-processed, highly sugared products are selling as fast as ever, healthy alternatives are increasingly within reach. Don't be misled by fancy packaging. Read labels carefully to avoid unwanted chemicals and additives.

Making breakfast cereal at home is surprisingly easy and quite economical. Most of the makings can be found in supermarkets and health-food stores. Make large quantities and freeze some to enjoy for weeks. Keep all cereals tightly covered in a dry, cool spot. Serve with lowfat milk or yogurt and fresh fruit for a particularly light, satisfying morning meal or snack.

Cooked cereals are convenient winter foods. Packaged wheat, corn, and oat cereals come with exact directions that often include microwave instructions. Dried fruit added during the cooking of the cereal can be a delightful enhancement. Serve with cream or milk, with or without sugar or syrup, or with butter and brown sugar.

GRANOLA   *Makes about 10 cups.*

The following recipe is just a guide. Try using your favorite combinations of cereals, grains, and nuts. The quality of dried fruit is better today than ever before. Dried cherries, dried cranberries, and even dried blueberries make colorful and tasty supplements. Substitute the honey called for below with maple syrup or molasses and vary the nuts to include pecans, hazelnuts, or pine nuts. Create your own custom cereal that will be pure and more healthful than any commercially available product.

It helps if you have a large bowl and a large roasting pan when making this granola. The mixing and stirring can be messy if your equipment is too small. Simply halve the recipe if this is the case.

3 cups old-fashioned oats
1 cup raw sunflower seeds
½ cup lightly toasted sesame seeds
1 cup wheat bran
½ cup oat bran
½ cup wheat germ
½ cup coarsely chopped walnuts

1 cup raw peanuts
½ cup coarsely chopped almonds
1 cup shredded or flaked
    unsweetened coconut (optional)
¼ cup safflower oil
1 cup honey
2 cups mixed dried fruit (apricots,
    prunes, raisins, golden raisins,
    currants, dates, or figs), cut or
    sliced into small pieces

1.   Preheat oven to 300° F. In a very large mixing bowl, combine the oats, sunflower seeds, sesame seeds, wheat bran, oat bran, wheat germ, nuts, and coconut (if desired). Mix well. Pour over the oil and honey. Stir to blend evenly.

2.   Empty into a large baking or roasting pan with high sides. Bake until grains and nuts are lightly colored and thoroughly cooked, about 45 minutes. Stir every 5 to 10 minutes to insure even cooking. Let cool completely. Stir and break up any clumps that form as the granola cools. Add mixed dried fruit and blend. Store in airtight container.

Legumes

Dried beans, peas, and lentils are low in fat, high in fiber, protein, phosphorus, iron, and vitamin B. When mixed with certain other foods, notably rice, these foods become "perfect foods" containing all the essential amino acids. Known collectively as "legumes" from their botanical grouping Leguminosae, these foods are becoming a staple of the trend toward healthier eating. Not only are they an inexpensive source of protein but some nutritionists claim that increased consumption of dried legumes can actually reduce cholesterol levels. Aside from all the wholesome reasons to enjoy these foods, they have a wonderful flavor that can be enhanced with little effort. Used in soups, salads, purees, or served as a main course, these legumes can be one of the most varied and appealing items found in anyone's menu repertoire.

One word of caution: Although dried beans, peas, and lentils are relatively easy to prepare, they can be a little tricky. The first step to achieve best results is to choose the right ingredient. We have no way of knowing the age and shelf life of the vegetables in question, and the American consumer can rarely identify the locale of origin. The best advice for choosing from the dried legumes available is to know your grocer. These foods do have a long shelf life but not as long as some marketplaces would have us believe. A store with a large turnover of inventory is a good bet for fresher selections. Look for vibrant-colored legumes of plump, glossy healthiness rather than choosing the dull-hued ones with a powdery pallor. Let the grocer know if you don't find the quality you're looking for. Ask for and expect the best.

TIPS FOR COOKING DRIED LEGUMES

1. Purchase a quality product (see above).
2. Wash thoroughly. Sort through carefully and remove any chipped or broken pieces and any small rocks. Leave in cold water and collect any legumes that float to the top.
3. Soaking: Some peas and beans come presoaked and need little attention before cooking. These come in packages that give clear instructions. Lentils don't need any soaking. Otherwise, you can't go wrong by soaking most legumes in plenty of soft, cold water for an extended amount of time. Change water and rinse beans often to reduce flatulence.

   Overnight is standard for soaking but here is a time-saving shortcut. Cover vegetables with cold water and bring to a boil. Reduce heat and simmer for about 3 minutes. Cover and let stand for 1 hour. Drain and rinse with cold water before proceeding.

4. Cooking times vary. Younger beans and all peas and lentils cook more quickly than older ones. Follow recipes for guidelines but always taste for texture before terminating cooking. Undercooked legumes are unpleasant tasting and indigestible. Look for a soft but not mushy feeling without a trace of grittiness. The skin should break easily while tightly holding the legume together.

5. Never boil legumes, simmer instead to prevent disintegration of the bean, pea, or lentil. Add boiling water as needed to replenish cooking liquid. Stir gently to prevent skins from breaking.

6. Add salt at the end of cooking. Salt added at the start of cooking can cause the skin to split and the inside to toughen and never become tender.

7. While not healthy by some modern standards, a bit of fat will give a pleasant character to most cooked legumes. A piece of salt pork or bacon is tasty but even a tablespoon of vegetable oil (especially olive oil) will produce a smoother, less farinaceous end result.

8. Do not keep dried beans, peas, or lentils on the shelf for more than a year. Use them as pie pastry weights and purchase new ones. They become tough and hard when old. Not even a long soaking and cooking can bring them to life.

9. As a rule of thumb, 1 cup dried beans, peas, or lentils will yield about 2 cups of coaked, cooked legumes.

10. The microwave can be useful for soaking and cooking dried legumes. Consult manufacturer's instructions for your particular make or model. Generally, for *soaking* the following procedure is best: 1 cup of dried beans or peas can be tightly covered in a casserole containing 2 cups cold water. Set microwave setting at high and let cook for 5 minutes. Stir, then cook at medium for 3 minutes. Let stand, covered, for 1 hour. For *cooking,* try this formula: add 1 cup presoaked dried peas or beans to a large casserole containing 1½ cups cold water. Cover and cook on high setting for 10 to 15 minutes. Remove and stir. Add salt. Cover again and cook on medium until tender, about 45 minutes. Stop and stir once about halfway through cooking. Let stand, covered, for about 10 minutes after cooking. Drain off any excess liquid.

SOME POPULAR LEGUMES

Adzuki   beans are said to be one of the most digestible of dried beans. A small, dark red bean native to Japan, the adzuki is cooked like the lentil. It has a distinctive sweetness not found in most dried beans. A fairly recent arrival in the West, it is slightly more expensive and difficult to find.

Black beans (also known as *turtle* beans) are a staple of South and Central American cooking. Ink black, sometimes with a purple hue, these beans are mixed with chilies, cumin, ham, garlic, and fresh herbs like cilantro to produce some of the finest legume dishes. A popular soup is the most famous of these (page 66). Thick and hearty, the soup is traditionally served with chopped onion and sliced eggs.

Black-Eyed Peas are a specialty of the South. With an oval shape containing a black spot in the middle of the curved side, this pea is moist and full of character when cooked slowly with pungent seasonings to complement its earthy flavor.

Cannellini is an Italian bean found in specialty-food stores throughout the country. Plump and meaty, this is the bean used in Tuscan soups or in Italian bean soups and salads.

Chick Peas (also known as *garbanzo* beans) are large peas with a fleshy hue and a rough-textured outer skin that resembles a hazelnut. These beans usually need a long soaking and a particularly long cooking. When cooked, they lend themselves to all sorts of purees, dips, soups, and salads. In the Middle East and in India, this is a very important crop.

Cranberry beans are smooth, round beans with dark red marks. Cooked as for pinto or kidney beans, these have a woody flavor and a rather gritty texture.

Fava beans (also known as *broad* beans) are brown when dried and have a rippled surface. Strong and distinctive, these beans are widely used in Middle Eastern cooking. They require a long soaking.

Flageolets are recent French imports to the American dried bean market. These are pale green or white beans known for their delicacy, fine texture, and low starch content. The fresher ones need little soaking. Older *flageolets* have less flavor and are easy to spot: the skins become crinkly as old age causes them to lose moisture.

Great Northern beans are probably our most popular dried legume. Milky white and smooth textured, they are often cooked with onion, garlic, and/or herbs of distinctive flavor to bring out their rather bland taste.

Kidney beans are an earthy reddish brown color and take their name from the organ they resemble. Popular in Mexico and other Central American countries where they are valued for their nutritional benefits and low cost, these are one of America's most popular dried legumes. The recent interest in Cajun cooking has enhanced their image as well. Kidney beans are praised in Louisiana where rice, the natural accompaniment to these rather farinaceous beans, is a staple. These beans, like the black bean mentioned above, take well to the fiery seasonings so prevalent in Cajun cuisine.

Lentils are botanically different from peas and beans but are served in much the same way. Red, brown, and green varieties usually need little or no soaking. They cook quickly and lend themselves to a minimum of flavoring due to their assertive taste and satisfying allure. Soft and quite juicy, lentils make wonderful soups and purees.

Lima beans are actually dried *butter* beans. The smaller ones can be delicious but tend to become soft when overcooked even slightly. Avoid larger dried limas as they tend to be mushy and mealy when reconstituted. Cooked dried lima beans make a wonderful puree or soup.

Mung beans are one of the most varied of beans. They come whole, split, or skinless. They are available in green, gold, and sometimes black varieties. They can be sticky when cooked. They are often cultivated for their sprouts. These beans generally need no soaking.

Navy beans (also known as *Yankee* beans) are similar to Great Nothern beans but smaller and rounder, more like a pea. These are the beans used for making traditional American Baked Beans. Like the Great Northern, these almost tasteless legumes lend themselves to flavorings of sugar and spice.

Pinto beans are speckled and come in various shades of red and brown. Similar in taste and texture to the kidney bean, the pinto bean is earthy flavored and sometimes quite tough.

Soissons are another French import of distinctive flavor. Small, white, and smooth textured, they are often used in making the great French bean dish, Cassoulet.

Soybeans, one of man's oldest known foods, has been a staple in China and Japan for centuries. Used to produce oil, flour, and other products for sustenance, the dried soybean can be treated as for any dried legume. There are thousands of varieties but only two that are mass cultivated for commercial and fresh consumption. Yellow, green, and black soybeans are used primarily in soups and salads. They are very high in protein and one of the most digestible of all dried vegetables.

Split Peas are the skinned and split dried form of our field or garden peas. They come mostly in bright green or yellow forms. These peas need soaking and long, slow cooking before being made into soup or purees to serve as a side dish with almost any hearty entrée.

BAKED BEANS   *Serves 4 to 6.*

4 cups navy beans
1½ pounds brisket of beef or ½
   pound fat salt pork
½ tablespoon mustard

1 tablespoon salt
3 tablespoons sugar
2 tablespoons molasses
1 cup boiling water

1. Wash beans, cover with cold water, and soak overnight. Drain and rinse. Place beans in a large casserole and cover with cold water. Heat slowly and simmer until tender, 1½ to 2 hours.

2. Drain beans and put in pot with the brisket of beef. If pork is used, scald it, cut through rind in ½ inch strips, and bury it in the beans leaving rind exposed. Mix mustard, salt, sugar, molasses, and water. Pour over beans. Add enough boiling water to cover. Bake, covered, in a slow oven (300° F) for 6 to 8 hours. Uncover during the last hour so that pork will brown and be crisp.

REFRIED BEANS

1½ cups dry kidney beans
1 cup chopped onions
2 medium tomatoes, peeled, seeded,
   and chopped
1 small clove garlic, minced

1 teaspoon chili powder
dash of cayenne pepper
1 teaspoon salt
2 tablespoons vegetable oil

1. Soak the beans overnight. Drain. Cook beans in 5 cups of water with half of the onions, half of the tomatoes, the garlic, chili powder, and cayenne until beans are tender. Then add salt. Drain.

2. Heat oil in a large skillet. Sauté remaining onions until clear. Add remaining tomatoes and cook 2 to 3 minutes. Gradually mash the beans into the skillet. Mash only a small quantity at a time and mix well before adding more beans. Fry until heated through.

BEANS AND BARLEY

1½ cups navy beans	2 cups vegetable broth or chicken
1 quart boiling water	stock (page 61 or 59)
½ cup barley	salt and freshly ground black pepper
2 teaspoons salt	

1.   Soak navy beans in cold water overnight. Drain and rinse. Add boiling water and cook gently, until nearly tender but not broken, 1½ to 2 hours.

2.   Add barley and salt. Cook slowly until barley is almost tender. Add stock and continue cooking until water evaporates. Season to taste and bake in medium oven (350° F) until dry but not browned, about ½ hour.

BAKED LIMA BEANS

1 pound dried lima beans	2 tablespoons flour
salt	salt pork, or back or neck of a fat
paprika	chicken
2 tablespoons fat or buter	

1.   Wash beans thoroughly. Soak in lukewarm water to cover for 2 hours. Bring quickly to a boil, reduce heat, and simmer until tender, about 1 hour. Add salt and paprika to taste.

2.   Drain the liquid from the beans and reserve.

3.   Heat fat or butter in a skillet. Add the flour and stir until brown. Add 1 cup of the cooking liquid to flour mixture and cook, stirring, until smooth and thick. Add the beans.

4.   Turn into a casserole. Bury salt pork or chicken in beans and bake for 1 hour at 350° F. Add more bean liquid as necessary.

PEA PUREE

2 cups dried peas	2 thick slices smoked bacon
½ teaspoon sugar (optional)	1 large onion, chopped
pinch of white pepper	

1.   Wash the peas. Soak for several hours in cold water. Drain and rinse. Place in a large saucepan and cover with cold water. Bring to a simmer, stirring frequently. Cook until peas are soft. Rub through a strainer or puree in a food processor fitted with the metal blade. Season to taste with sugar and pepper.

2.   Cut bacon into small cubes. Fry until lightly browned. Add the onion

and continue cooking until golden brown. Pour the bacon and onion over puree just before serving.

Note: The above recipe can be prepared with lentils or navy beans as well.

LENTILS WITH TOMATO SAUCE

1½ cups lentils
1 tablespoon salt
3 to 4 tomatoes, peeled, seeded, and chopped
2 carrots, peeled and chopped

1 clove garlic, minced
1 bay leaf
1 large onion, chopped
2 tablespoons shortening

1. Rinse the lentils and drain. Add salt, tomatoes, carrots and garlic, and bay leaf to lentils. Add cold water to cover.
2. Bring to a simmer, reduce heat, and cook until tender.
3. Sauté the onions in the shortening. Add the lentils with only enough of the liquid so that the mixture is fairly dry. Heat thoroughly.

CHICK PEA LOAF

2 cups celery, diced
2 cups cauliflower, diced
1 green pepper, diced
2 cups cooked chick peas
4 tablespoons flour

1 cup water
½ teaspoon soy sauce
½ teaspoon thyme
½ teaspoon marjoram

1. Preheat oven to 350° F.
2. Steam vegetables until just tender. Mash chick peas and vegetables. Mix in flour and water. Stir until smooth. Season with soy sauce, thyme, and marjoram.
3. Place in greased loaf pan. Bake for 45 minutes.

CURRIED RED LENTILS

2 cups (1 pound) red lentils
2 tablespoons oil
1 small onion, chopped
2 teaspoons curry powder

6 cups water, chicken stock (page 59) or mixture of the two
freshly ground black pepper

(continued)

1. Rinse lentils and drain.
2. In a large saucepan or soup kettle, heat the oil. Add the onions and cook over moderately high heat until slightly softened, about 3 minutes. Add the curry powder and cook for a minute or two to take off the raw edge. Then add the lentils and toss to coat.
3. Pour in the water or stock and bring to just below the boiling point. Reduce heat and simmer slowly until lentils are tender, about 30 minutes. Season to taste with pepper.

SPICY BEANS

2 cups Great Northern or navy beans
1 medium onion, quartered
2 tablespoons grated fresh ginger (or 1 teaspoon ground ginger)
¼ teaspoon ground cloves
¼ teaspoon ground cumin
1 dried red pepper pod, crushed but in one piece
1 teaspoon grated lemon rind

1. Wash and pick over beans. Soak in cold water overnight, changing the water often. Drain.
2. Place the soaked beans in a large soup kettle or casserole. Add the onion and enough cold water to cover (about 4 cups). Bring to just below the boiling point, reduce heat, and simmer uncovered until beans are tender, about 2 hours.
3. Thirty minutes before the beans are done, add the ginger, cloves, cumin, red pepper pod, and lemon rind. Stir well to blend. Cook for the remaining 30 minutes. Remove from heat, cover, and let infuse for an additional 10 to 15 minutes. Remove the red pepper pod.

WHITE BEANS WITH TOMATO AND HERBS

2 cups Great Northern or navy beans
1 onion, quartered
3 to 4 medium tomatoes, peeled, seeded, and chopped
several sprigs fresh thyme (or 1 teaspoon dried)
1 fresh bay leaf (or 2 dried)
1 clove garlic, minced
about 4 cups chicken stock (page 59) or water and chicken stock mixed
2 tablespoons mixed fresh herbs, chopped (parsley, thyme, marjoram, oregano, or sage) or 1 tablespoon dried
1 teaspoon salt
freshly ground black pepper to taste

1. Wash and pick over beans. Soak in cold water overnight, changing the water frequently. Drain.

2. Cover with cold water in a medium pot, add the onion and bring to just below the boiling point. Reduce heat to a simmer and cook beans gently until tender, about 2 hours. Drain and rinse.

3. In a soup pot or large casserole, combine the cooked beans with the tomatoes, thyme sprigs, bay leaf, and garlic. Pour in enough stock or stock and water to cover. Bring to just below the boiling point. Reduce heat and cook, covered, for an additional 30 minutes so that beans absorb the flavor of the herbs and seasonings. Remove the sprigs of thyme and the bay leaves. Remove from heat, cover, and let beans stand for an additional 10 to 15 minutes. Just before serving, stir in the chopped herbs. Season to taste with salt and pepper.

TEXAS PINTO BEANS

1 pound pinto beans	1 tablespoon chili powder (or to
½ pound slab bacon, rind removed	taste)
2 onions, chopped	6 cups water
3 to 4 tomatoes, peeled, seeded, and	1 teaspoon salt
chopped	

1. Wash and pick over beans. Cover with cold water. Let soak overnight. Drain and rinse.

2. Cut the bacon into pieces about ¼ inch wide and 1 inch long. Place in a large casserole and cook over moderately high heat until browned and fat is rendered. Remove the bacon and set aside.

3. Add the onions to the casserole. Cook over moderately low heat until softened. Add the tomatoes and continue cooking for another minute or two. Add the chili powder and mix to blend. Add the beans.

4. Pour on the water and bring almost to a boil. Add the bacon pieces and salt. Reduce heat to low and simmer uncovered until beans are softened and liquid is slightly thickened, about 2 hours.

FISH AND SEAFOOD

Fish

Fish consumption is increasing nationwide. As the predilection for red meat declines, the American public is learning that fish is a desirable protein alternative to pork or beef. The health benefits are without question. High in protein, full of vitamins and minerals, and relatively low in fat, fish is a timely food. In fact, eating fish could save your life. Recent studies show that certain fish contain omega-3, a polyunsaturated fatty acid that reduces the chance of a clot in coronary arteries and could prevent hardening of the arteries in general.

Over-fishing and industrial pollution are taking their toll on our fragile sea world. More and more, our market fish are coming from deeper waters that are free of the wastes found in local areas. As a result, we have a larger variety of species to choose from than ever before. Pollution has increased the popularity of aquaculture as well. More fish than ever is being farmed to keep up with the demand, providing the modern consumer with a even wider array of fresh untainted fish.

Selecting Fish

Modern methods of flash freezing on large vessels in deep waters has become popular. Much of the fish found in supermarkets these days has probably been frozen. While this is a convenient and harmless procedure, no one can deny that there is a certain loss of taste and texture suffered in the process. Look for fresh fish when possible. If frozen fish is used, be sure to defrost carefully. Follow package instructions where applicable. If thawing home-frozen fish, let stand in the refrigerator overnight, dry, and cook at once. Be careful when defrosting fish in the microwave. It dries out the juices too quickly. Use it to initially thaw the ice surrounding the fish if desired. After that, let the thawing process be done conventionally—slowly in the refrigerator.

Whatever the species, there are some guidelines that will be helpful when confronted with choices at the marketplace. Remember that fish is least expensive and most appealing when it is freshly caught, in season. Look for bright, clear eyes and red gills. There should be a clean, ocean smell. Avoid fish with a strong odor. As a general rule, count on ¾ pound per person when buying whole fish with the bone and head intact. For dressed or pan-dressed fish, count on ½ pound per person. Buy ⅓-pound fillets or steaks per person.

PREPARING FRESH WHOLE FISH

Most fish is purchased ready to use, cleaned and scaled, skinned, boned, or filleted. The fish man will be glad to prepare your choice of fresh fish for the cooking method you plan to use. When the family fisherman or woman brings home a catch of fresh fish, or decides to give the monger a day off, follow these simple procedures:

Scaling and Cleaning

Lay fish on heavy paper. Use fish scaler, ordinary grater, or knife. Hold the fish by the tail. Scrape from tail end to head, slanting knife toward you to prevent scales from flying. Remove gills, cut through the skin of the abdomen, and take out the entrails. Wash thoroughly in cold water.

Skinning

Lay the fish flat and with a small sharp knife cut through the skin close to the fins down both sides of the back. Pull out the fins, and, if desired, cut off head. Loosen flesh close to skin on one side and strip off toward tail. Turn and skin the other side.

Scale fish if skin is to be reserved and used. Bend head backward and, beginning at the base of the head, separate flesh from skin with small sharp knife, working toward the tail. It can then be stuffed to restore its original shape, for Stuffed Fish (page 198).

Boning

Scale and clean the fish. Beginning just below the head, cut along the spine as close to the backbone as possible down to the tail. Push the flesh on that side away from the backbone with the back of the knife. Separate the backbone in the same manner from the remaining half of the fish. Pick out small bones remaining in the fish.

Alternatively, after gutting and washing the fish, cut close to fins on both sides of fish, pull out fins. On both sides of backbone make an incision from head to tail. Separate flesh from backbone with the back of a knife. Remove backbone and bones attached to it. Pick out remaining bones carefully.

Cooking Different Types of Fish

Cooking methods for fish can be used according to their fat content. While there are shady areas when it comes to classification, we can make generalizations that will help assure that fish is cooked to perfection.

Oily fish are usually dark-fleshed species like mackerel, bluefish, or mullet. Moderately oily fish are harder to define. Some examples include carp, catfish, and hake. Leaner fish are usually white fleshed and include kinds like sole, flounder, tilefish, or whiting. Each of these categories is best treated by different methods of cooking.

BROILING

Larger and oilier fish are best broiled or grilled. (See the Outdoor Cooking chapter, page 341, for information on grilling fish.) Lean fish are good broiled but need added fat. Here is a list of fish ideal for broiling.

Black Bass	Salmon
Bluefish	Sea Bass
Bloater	Shad
Cod	Shad Roe
Halibut	Sturgeon
Pike	Swordfish
Pompano	Trout
Porgy	Whitefish

Broiling Method

Preheat broiler. Sprinkle fish cut to be broiled with salt and pepper, spread with a little butter. Lightly dredge with flour if desired (skin side only). Place on well-greased broiler rack, flesh side up, about 4 inches from the heat. Broil until flesh is firm and delicately browned, basting occasionally. Whole fish and fish steaks should be turned and browned on both sides. Serve on hot platter. Spread with additional butter if desired and garnish with parsley and lemon. For an added twist, try serving your favorite broiled fish with one of the compound butters listed on page 363.

LEMON HERB BROILED MACKEREL

4 tablespoons butter
1 tablespoon lemon juice
1 teaspoon lemon zest
1 tablespoon finely chopped fresh
 herbs (parsley, chives, chervil,
 and/or thyme)

4 mackerel fillets with skin on,
 about 6 ounces each
melted butter for brushing
salt and freshly ground black pepper
 to taste

1. Either chop finely by hand or use a food processor fitted with the metal blade to blend together the butter, lemon juice, zest, and herbs. Place on a large piece of plastic wrap and form into a 2-inch-diameter cylinder. Twist tightly on both ends to close. Chill for at least several hours.

2. Just before serving time, preheat broiler. Brush mackerel fillets with melted butter and season with salt and pepper. Place on a well-greased broiling pan and broil about 4 inches from the heat until opaque and firm to the touch, about 5 minutes. Serve immediately with slices of the seasoned butter on the side.

BROILED HALIBUT STEAK

Marinate each 1-inch, 6-ounce halibut steak in 1 tablespoon salad oil and 2 tablespoons lemon juice for ½ hour. Just before serving time, preheat broiler. Wipe fish dry and broil until flesh is white and firm, turning carefully when first side begins to brown. Before serving, spread with butter if desired.

DILL BUTTER SALMON STEAKS

8 tablespoons butter
2 teaspoons dill seed
2 tablespoons lemon juice

4 teaspoons fresh chives and/or
 parsley
pinch of freshly ground black
 pepper
4 salmon steaks, about 6 ounces
 each

1. In the bowl of a food processor fitted with the metal blade, combine the butter, dill seed, lemon juice, and herbs. Process until well blended, scraping down the sides of the bowl as necessary. Season to taste with pepper. Place on a large piece of plastic wrap and form into a 2-inch-diameter cylinder. Twist tightly on both ends to close. Chill for at least several hours.

(continued)

2.   Just before serving time, preheat broiler. Broil salmon steaks about 4 inches from the source of heat, basting with dabs of the chilled butter mixture, about 2 minutes on each side. Serve with thick slices of the remaining butter on the side.

BROILED SHAD

Clean and split a 3-pound shad. Spread all over with a little olive oil and sprinkle with a little salt and pepper. Let stand 1 hour. Put on well-greased pan in broiler, flesh side up. Brown well, then turn, broil slowly until flesh flakes easily. If desired, spread with additional butter and salt and pepper; reheat and serve.

BROILED SHAD ROE

Cook shad roe 15 minutes in enough simmering salted water to cover, with ½ teaspoon vinegar. Drain, cover with fresh cold water, and let stand 5 minutes. Remove from water. Drain and dry well.Brush with melted butter mixed with a few drops of lemon juice. Place in greased pan under broiler, broil slowly for about 15 minutes, then turn. Baste with additional butter. Serve with lemon quarters.

BROILED SWORDFISH STEAKS WITH SOY AND GINGER

¼ cup dark soy sauce	1 tablespoon sesame oil
1 tablespoon finely chopped fresh ginger	4 swordfish steaks, ½ inch thick, about 6 ounces each

1.   Combine soy sauce, ginger, and oil in a flat dish large enough to hold the fish in an even layer. Add the fish steaks and cover. Marinate for 1 hour at room temperature or 2 to 3 hours in the refrigerator, turning occasionally.

2.   Just before serving time, preheat broiler. Broil about 4 inches from the heat source until firm and opaque, about 2½ minutes on each side, basting several times with the marinade. Serve at once garnished with fresh dill, parsley, or watercress.

BOILING AND POACHING

This is the best way to cook leaner fish that sometimes need added moisture as their fat levels are low. Some fish suitable for boiling or poaching are:

Cod	Red Snapper
Carp	Sole
Halibut	Sea Bass
Haddock	Tilefish
Monkfish	Trout
Pickerel	Weakfish
Pike	Whitefish
Pompano	

Use a shallow pan, wide enough to hold fish without overlapping. Barely cover the fish with a flavored liquid like Court Bouillon (see recipe below) or water seasoned with salt, herbs or spices, milk, or a mixture of either with wine. Be careful not to overcook fish when using this method. These are usually more delicate species with fragile flesh that can be tough and chewy when cooked longer than is necessary. Learning by touch is the best way to determine when fish is done. The flesh should be tender, flaky, and soft. Use the Canadian Fish-Cooking Method as a guide (see box on page 221).

COURT BOUILLON   *Makes about 1½ quarts. Keeps about 1 week.*

2 onions, sliced	2 bay leaves, crumpled
2 carrots, peeled and coarsely chopped	2 quarts water
	2 cups dry white wine
2 leeks, white part only (optional)	½ teaspoon salt
2 stalks celery, coarsely chopped	10 whole peppercorns
several sprigs of fresh parsley	
several sprigs of fresh thyme or 1 teaspoon dried	

Combine the ingredients in a large, nonreactive pot. Bring to a boil over moderately high heat. Reduce heat and let simmer for 30 to 45 minutes. Let cool to room temperature. Strain through a colander and reserve in the refrigerator, covered, until ready to use.

BASIC BOILED OR POACHED FISH

3 pounds lean fish (see list above), whole cleaned or cut into large pieces or steaks

salt and freshly ground black pepper to taste

1½ quarts Court Bouillon (see recipe above)

Season fish with salt and pepper to taste. Bring the Court Bouillon to a simmer in a pot large enough to hold the fish flat. Add the fish, a few pieces at a time, and simmer just until the flesh is opaque and easily flakes. Carefully remove the fish to a platter with a slotted spoon and serve with a butter or tomato-based sauce of choice. (See Sauce chapter for suggestions.)

Note: Boned fish fillets or whole fish, unboned, may be cooked in this manner. To remove a whole fish from the pan without breaking, wrap the fish in cheese-cloth before cooking.

BASIC BOILED FISH

This is a recipe from the old edition that is simple and probably more suited to the days before refrigeration when transportation was less reliable. Older fish benefit from soaking in salt to remove the odors and "freshen up" the flesh. If your fish is fresh, eliminate this step.

3 pounds cleaned whole fish, cut in slices and sprinkled with salt

1 quart water

2 tablespoons vinegar

¼ teaspoon whole pepper

1 tablespoon finely chopped onion

1 tablespoon finely chopped celery

1 tablespoon finely chopped carrot

Let fish stand in salt several hours. Boil water, vinegar, pepper, and vegetables until the water is well flavored. Add the fish, a few slices at a time, and let simmer until the flesh is firm and begins to leave the bones. Remove slices and bones with a slotted spoon, discarding the bones. Arrange fish on platter. Strain and reserve the fish stock, if desired.

BOILED SALMON TROUT

3½ pounds salmon trout

¼ of a cabbage, thinly sliced

1 carrot, peeled and finely chopped

1 onion, finely chopped

14 ounces (½ can) canned whole tomatoes, drained

5 bay leaves

¼ teaspoon peppercorns

1 celery root, trimmed, peeled, and cut into small pieces

2 potatoes, peeled and cut into small pieces

1 quart boiling water

2 or 3 egg yolks

½ cup cream

chopped fresh parsley

1. Salt the fish and let stand several hours.

2. Meanwhile, cook the vegetables, canned tomatoes, bay leaves, and peppercorns in the boiling water and boil until the water is well flavored, about 1 hour. Add the fish and slowly boil until the flesh separates from the bones.

3. Place fish on platter. Strain the fish liquid and return to saucepan. Beat yolks well, add cream. Pour the egg mixture, gradually, into the hot fish liquid over low heat, stirring constantly until thickened. Then pour over the fish. Set in the oven with oven door open to keep hot if not serving immediately and serve garnished with parsley.

Note: The sauce will curdle if left too long on stove or if stove is too hot.

POACHED SEA BASS WITH RED PEPPER SAUCE

2 tablespoons olive oil

1 medium onion, peeled and thinly sliced

2 cloves garlic, peeled, mashed, and coarsely chopped

2 large red peppers, about ½ pound each, seeded and thinly sliced

whole black sea bass, about 3 pounds

salt and freshly ground black pepper to taste

3 to 4 cups fish stock (page 60) or bottled clam juice

1. In a sauté pan large enough to hold the fish flat, heat the olive oil. Add the onion, garlic, and peppers. Cook over moderately high heat until vegetables are limp and slightly softened.

2. Season fish with salt and pepper. Wrap in a single layer of cheesecloth to facilitate handling. Place on top of the vegetables and pour on enough fish stock or clam juice to half cover. Cook over moderate heat for five minutes, carefully lift and turn to continue cooking for five more minutes on the other side. When done, lift the cooked fish to a warm platter and set aside while preparing the sauce.

3. Pour the contents of the sauté pan into a fine-meshed strainer. Discard the cooking liquid. Place the cooked vegetables in the bowl of a food processor fitted with the metal blade or in a blender. Process until smooth. Season to taste with salt and pepper. Remove fish from cloth and fillet. Spoon some of the sauce on the fish and serve the rest on the side.

FISH À LA TARTARE

3½ pounds fish, pike or trout	1 tablespoon powdered sugar
4 hard-cooked yolks of eggs	1 tablespoon vinegar
1 teaspoon mustard	1 teaspoon chopped parsley
1 tablespoon salad oil	1 cup strained fish liquid
1 tablespoon capers	salt and pepper to taste
¼ cup Boiled Mayonnaise Dressing (page 131)	4 hard-cooked whites of eggs, chopped
1 tablespoon catsup	1 tablespoon pickles, finely chopped

Boil (see above) and bone the fish, leaving it whole or cut in portions for serving. Rub the yolks smooth with the mustard and oil, add the rest of the ingredients, the chopped ingredients last. Season to taste.

COLD POACHED TROUT WITH HORSERADISH SAUCE

Cold fish can make a pleasant luncheon or first-course dish. Trout farming is a booming business and good, fresh fish is easy to find. Try the following recipe with any other mild-flavored, sweet-fleshed fish.

2 to 3 pounds whole trout	1 cup heavy cream
salt and freshly ground black pepper to taste	2 tablespoons prepared horseradish
1½ quarts Court Bouillon (page 193)	

1. Season the fish with salt and pepper. Wrap each in a single layer of cheesecloth with extending ends to facilitate handling. Place in a sauté pan large enough to hold the fish in a flat layer and pour in enough bouillon to half cover. Bring to a simmer and cook until done, about 10 minutes, turning once. Gently lift out the fish and transfer to a platter. Remove the cheesecloth. Cool to room temperature, cover, and chill in the refrigerator for at least 2 hours, or overnight.

2. Just before serving, whip the cream just until soft peaks are formed. Fold in the horseradish. Season with pepper. Serve the cold fish in fillets or whole, with the sauce on the side.

Note: Do not overbeat the cream. Most prepared horseradish is packed in vinegar that can turn cream. Use very fresh cream and beat it only until soft peaks are formed.

GEFILLTE FISH

 This is an heirloom recipe that must be included in any version of The Settlement Cookbook. *What would Passover be without this most classic of dishes? We find pike the best choice, but any fresh-water fish with firm, white flesh is traditional.*

3 pounds white-fleshed fresh-water fish
2 medium onions, peeled
1 slice of bread or ¼ cup matzo meal or crackers
salt and pepper to taste

1 egg
1 cup cold water
¼ celery root or 1 stalk celery, finely chopped

1. Clean fish, remove skin whole and bone. Grind 1 onion with flesh of fish. Add bread soaked in cold water and squeezed dry or add cracker crumbs or matzo meal. Add salt and pepper to taste, egg, and cold water. Mix thoroughly until smooth.

2. Wash fish skin and fill with the mixture.

3. Boil fish bones, remaining onion and celery for 20 minutes in water to cover. Sprinkle fish with salt and pepper and add to kettle. Simmer 1 hour or longer until well done. Add water as necessary to prevent burning.

4. Remove fish carefully to a platter. Reduce broth until it is very thick. Strain and pour it over fish. Serve hot or cold.

BAKING

Fatty fish do well by baking. The fat content makes up for the lack of liquid used in poaching or boiling. A hot oven is essential, 400° to 500° F is optimum. Whole fish should be scaled and cleaned, but skin and bones should not be removed. Sprinkle fish with salt and pepper, fill with stuffing if desired, and sew or skewer opening together. Bake in greased pan in a hot oven just until flesh separates easily from bone, allowing 10 minutes for each inch thickness of fish (see Canadian Fish-Cooking Method, page 221). Basting with melted butter or good-quality olive oil will prevent drying out. Fish best for baking are:

Black Bass	Mackerel	Sea Bass
Bluefish	Mullet	Shad
Carp	Perch	Sturgeon
Cod	Pickerel	Trout
Flounder	Pike	Swordfish
Haddock	Red Snapper	Weakfish
Hake	Salmon	Whitefish
Halibut		

BASIC STUFFING FOR BAKED FISH

1½ cups breadcrumbs
¼ teaspoon salt
¼ cup butter, melted
1 teaspoon chopped onion
1 teaspoon chopped parsley

1 whole egg, lightly beaten
1 teaspoon capers (optional)
1 teaspoon chopped pickles
  (optional)
freshly ground black pepper to taste

 Combine all ingredients and mix well. For moist stuffing use soft breadcrumbs.

Variations:

Stuffing with Shrimp: Chop ½ pound cooked, peeled, and deveined shrimp. To basic stuffing add the chopped shrimp, 2 extra teaspoons parsley, and 1 clove peeled, minced garlic. Mix as for above.

Stuffing with Mushrooms and Scallions: Add ¼ pound cleaned, finely chopped mushrooms sprinkled with the juice of ½ lemon to the mixture above. Substitute ½ cup finely chopped scallions (white part only) for the onions.

Stuffing with Raisins and Almonds: Soak ¼ cup raisins in boiling water for 10 minutes. Drain well. Add along with ½ cup toasted, slivered almonds to the stuffing above, omitting the capers and pickles.

BAKED HALIBUT STEAK

 This recipe was in the original edition of the Settlement Cookbook. It called for cooking the fish in "bread pans." We tried it in the microwave oven as well with excellent results—what goes around, comes around.

1.   Preheat oven to 400° F. Marinate 2 to 3 pounds halibut steaks in juice of 2 lemons for 2 hours.

 2.   Place strips of salt pork, 2 bays leaves, ½ teaspoon peppercorns and allspice, and 2 or 3 cloves in a baking dish. Lay the fish steaks over these. Sprinkle with salt, pepper, and 2 tablespoons melted butter. Bake about 20 minutes in the preheated oven. Serve with Basic Tomato Sauce (page 405).

BAKED TROUT

 Another original recipe that seems old-fashioned but full of the warmth and goodness of days gone by.

3 pounds trout	1 tablespoon flour
1 can tomatoes (or several fresh tomatoes in season), peeled, seeded, and chopped	1 tablespoon butter
1 onion, finely chopped	1 egg yolk
1 piece celery root, chopped	½ cup heavy cream
	½ teaspoon Worcestershire sauce (optional)

Salt fish and let stand several hours. Preheat oven to 400° F. Place fish in baking pan large enough to hold fish in one layer with tomatoes, onion, celery root, flour, and butter. Bake for ½ hour. Strain the sauce, drain vegetables, and just before sending it to the table, thicken with the egg yolk, cream, and Worcestershire sauce if desired.

Note: Omit the salting of the fish if you wish.

TUNA BAKED WITH TOMATO AND CELERY

2 pounds fresh tuna, cut into 1-inch chunks	2 large tomatoes, peeled, seeded, and chopped
salt and freshly ground black pepper to taste	several sprigs of fresh thyme or ½ teaspoon dried
2 tablespoons butter	2 medium celery roots, trimmed, peeled, and cut into 1-inch pieces
2 tablespoons vegetable oil	lemon juice
2 medium leeks, white part only, cleaned, trimmed, and thinly sliced	

1. Preheat oven to 450° F. Season tuna with salt and pepper.
2. In a large sauté pan, heat the butter and oil. Add the tuna and brown over moderately high heat. Carefully turn the pieces constantly to insure that they do not stick and that they are uniformly browned. Remove to drain on paper towels.
3. Pour off all but 2 tablespoons of the cooking fat. Add the leeks and cook over moderate heat until softened, stirring often to prevent them from browning. Add the tomatoes, increase heat, and continue cooking until the liquid from the tomatoes has been rendered and subsequently boiled off. Season with thyme, salt, and pepper.

(continued)

4. Place the celery root in a small saucepan and cover with water, a pinch of salt, and several drops of lemon juice to prevent discoloration. Bring to a boil, reduce heat, and cook until soft. Drain and sprinkle with additional lemon if not to be used right away.

5. In a covered baking dish, combine the leeks, tomatoes, celery root, and tuna. Season with more salt and pepper to taste. Stir carefully to blend. Cover and bake in the preheated oven for about 15 minutes or until bubbling hot.

Notes: Substitute 2 onions for the leeks if desired. If celery root is not available, use 2 stalks of celery, peeled and trimmed into 1-inch pieces. Use canned tomatoes if fresh ones are out of season. Serve with a bright green vegetable like broccoli, zucchini, or green beans.

BAKED BLUEFISH "EN PAPILLOTE"

3 pounds bluefish fillets, cut into 4 pieces
½ pound mushrooms, thinly sliced
2 tablespoons lemon juice

½ teaspoon fresh rosemary or ¼ teaspoon dried
salt and freshly ground black pepper to taste

1. Preheat oven to 450° F. Place individual servings of fish on large squares of parchment paper. Cover with equal portions of the mushrooms. Sprinkle with lemon juice. Evenly distribute rosemary over the top. Season with salt and pepper to taste.

2. Fold the parchment paper over the fish and crimp or fold over the edges well to seal. Bake for 15 minutes.

3. Open with the tip of a knife and pull back the paper. Transfer contents to warm plates and serve fish in the paper.

BAKED RED SNAPPER WITH FENNEL

whole red snapper about 3 pounds
2 small bulbs fennel with branches
1 lemon, very thinly sliced
several sprigs fresh thyme or 1 teaspoon dried

2 cloves garlic, peeled and crushed
salt and freshly ground black pepper to taste
olive oil for brushing

1. Preheat oven to 450° F. Place the snapper in a lightly oiled baking dish large enough to hold the fish flat. Trim the fennel, reserving the wispy branches, and slice the bulb paper thin. Surround the fish with the lemon slices and sliced fennel and insert the branches in the cavity of the snapper. Place the sprigs of thyme around the fish or sprinkle over dried thyme. Add the crushed garlic and season with salt and pepper.

 2. Brush the fish with olive oil and bake until done, about 15 minutes. Brush with additional oil during cooking to prevent drying out. (Use the Canadian Fish-Cooking Method found on page 221 for accuracy of doneness.) Serve hot garnished with the cooked fennel.

FRYING

It is best only to deep-fry fish that have a low fat content, although almost any fish can be pan fried. In these days of health-conscious dieting, a properly treated, succulent piece of fried fish with a crusty outside and a moist inside can be a treat worth the extra calories. Some specific fish well suited for frying are:

Black Bass	Pike
Brook Trout	Pollock
Bullhead	Pompano
Butterfish	Porgy
Carp	Red Snapper
Catfish	Salmon steaks
Cod	Sole
Flounder	Swordfish
Haddock	Trout
Halibut	Whitefish
Perch	Whiting
Pickerel	

BASIC PAN-FRYING

Clean whole or filleted fish. Sprinkle with salt and pepper, dredge in flour, breadcrumbs, or cornmeal. Cook in heavy skillet with ¼ inch of hot but not smoking fat. Shake the pan often to prevent sticking. Cook until well browned on both sides.

BASIC DEEP-FRYING

Clean whole or filleted fish, wipe dry as possible. Salt and pepper, dip in flour, crumbs, or cornmeal. If a thicker crust is desired, dip in beaten egg and again in crumbs. Fry fillets golden brown in deep hot fat, 375° F, for 2 to 3 minutes.

When a cube of white bread browns in 30 seconds, the fat is ready for frying small fish or fillets. Larger fish should be fried at 350°, when bread cubes will brown in 35 seconds, and they will take a little longer. Use good-quality, polyunsaturated fats like safflower and sunflower oils or corn oil for a healthy alternative to lard or hydrogenated shortenings. Serve fried fish sprinkled with lemon juice.

FRIED CATFISH

Long an American favorite, catfish is enjoying a boom in popularity due in part to the phenomenal growth in the fish-farming industry.

2 pounds catfish, whole or fillets
2 cups whole milk
coarse, yellow cornmeal, about 1
   cup
salt and freshly ground black pepper
   to taste

corn oil for frying
chopped parsley
lemon wedges

   1. Soak fish in milk for 15 minutes. Drain well.

   2. Just before cooking, dredge in a shallow bowl full of cornmeal mixed with salt and pepper. Shake off excess and fry in hot (375° F) oil until golden brown. Do not overcrowd the pan or pieces will not brown properly. Let oil come back to 375° before starting again if working in two batches.

   3. Drain on paper towels and serve at once, garnished with parsley and lemon wedges.

<u>**Note:**</u> While deep-frying is particularly good for catfish, any firm-fleshed hearty fish will do nicely when prepared in this manner.

PAN-FRIED TROUT

4 medium (about 8 ounces) trout,
   cleaned, fins removed
salt and freshly ground pepper to
   taste
cornmeal, flour, or dry
   breadcrumbs, about 1 cup

4 tablespoons butter
2 tablespoons vegetable oil

   1. Pat dry the fish and season well with salt and pepper. Dredge in one of the above coatings and shake off excess.

2.   Heat butter and oil in a large, heavy sauté pan or skillet. When very hot, add fish and cook until golden brown and firm to the touch. Serve at once with wedges of lemon, chopped herbs, or one of the fish sauces listed on pages 362.

PAN-FRIED SHAD ROE WITH BACON

roe of 1 shad
½ teaspoon salt
6 ounces thickly sliced bacon

¼ cup red wine vinegar
2 tablespoons drained, chopped
  capers
chopped parsley for garnish

1.   Rinse the roe under cold running water. Bring 2 cups of water to a boil with the salt. Add the roe and reduce the heat. Simmer until roe turns brown and firm, about 5 minutes. Drain well.

2.   In a heavy skillet, cook the bacon until crisp. Remove to drain. Turn the roe in the same pan just to heat through, about 2 minutes. Drain and pour out any excess fat. Place roe on heated platter.

3.   Carefully pour the vinegar into the hot pan. Stir over high heat to pick up any bits from cooking the bacon and roe. Add the capers and pour this sauce over the roe. Serve at once with the crisp bacon and garnish with chopped parsley.

FRIED SMELTS

Clean smelts, leave on heads and tails, if desired. Sprinkle with salt and pepper, roll in flour, dip in beaten egg then in bread or cracker crumbs, and fry in deep hot fat (375° F) 5 to 8 minutes, until brown. Drain well and season with additional salt and pepper if desired.

FISH CAKES

1 pound scrod fillets, cut into 1-
  inch pieces
4 tablespoons butter
1 small onion, peeled and chopped
1 celery rib, peeled and finely
  chopped
1 tablespoon finely chopped parsley

1 teaspoon grated lemon rind
½ cup fresh breadcrumbs
1 teaspoon salt
freshly ground black pepper to taste
cornmeal for dusting
2 tablespoons vegetable oil for
  frying

(continued)

1. Place fish in the workbowl of a food processor fitted with the metal blade. Process until the fish is completely ground and almost fluffy. Scrape down sides as is necessary.

2. In a small sauté pan, melt 2 tablespoons of the butter. Add the onions and the celery. Cook over moderately high heat until soft but not brown.

3. In a large mixing bowl, use a rubber spatula to combine the cooked onion with the processed fish. Carefully fold in the parsley, lemon rind, breadcrumbs, salt, and pepper. Be careful not to overmix.

4. Divide the mixture into 4 equal balls. Gently shape each one into a patty, handling as little as possible. Lightly dust in cornmeal.

5. Heat the remaining butter with the oil in a large sauté pan or skillet. Cook the cakes until golden brown and quite firm to the touch, about 5 minutes on each side. Drain on paper towels.

Notes: Substitute 1 cup cold mashed potatoes for the breadcrumbs if desired. Serve with fresh Basic Tomato Sauce (page 405), your favorite bottled salsa sauce, or dipping sauce.

Variations:

Santa Fe Fishcakes: Add 1 tablespoon chopped, red mild chili pepper. Replace the parsley with fresh cilantro and the lemon rind with lime rind.

Curry Fishcakes: Sauté the onions and celery with 1 to 2 teaspoons curry powder and proceed as for above. Serve with a tasty chutney.

Fishcakes aux Fines Herbes: Add 1 teaspoon chopped, fresh thyme, 1 teaspoon chopped chives, and 1 teaspoon chopped rosemary to the basic recipe. Serve with Mustard Sauce (page 409) but slightly reduce the amount of mustard used so as to not overpower the fishcakes.

SALTED, PICKLED, AND SMOKED FISH

Before the days of refrigeration, preserving fish was done by salting, pickling, or smoking. The original Settlement book gave the following instructions for such treatments.

PICKLED FISH

1 pint vinegar	18 allspice
1 pint water	5 bay leaves, broken up
salt to taste	5 sliced onions
20 peppercorns	4 slices lemon

Boil vinegar and water ½ hour with salt, peppercorns, allspice, bay leaves, and 4 slices of onion. Add lemon slices, cook 5 minutes, then remove them. Simmer the fish in this liquid until you can pull out a fin. Cook only a few small fish or slices of fish at one time. Pack fish as cooked into a stone crock with one or more raw sliced onions between layers. Pour over the hot liquid with seasonings. Cover and keep in a cool place. In a few days the liquid will form a jelly around the fish. This liquid is enough for ½ gallon of fish. Will keep several weeks.

In these days of sodium nitrate and chemical stabilizers, this sort of procedure seems almost quaint. The smokehouse was turned into a bomb shelter in the '50s, and nowadays who buys 20 pounds of fish at a time? Is there a need to keep fish in a crock for several weeks? Times have changed.

Nowhere is this more evident than with the herring. The early Settlement immigrants brought with them from Europe a great tradition of pickled herring. How luscious the recipes sound. Salt herring was soaked in cold water to remove the strong taste, then drained and rinsed to serve with boiled potatoes. In the early editions of the book, there were two recipes for pickling herring in cream and three recipes for Rollmops or herring rolls. Today, fresh herring are hard to come by. The closest we come to enjoying these relics of the past is when we're lucky enough to find some of the better brands of bottled herring in the grocery store. In case fresh herring is available in the local fish market, or should you receive a windfall of 20 pounds of fish and you feel nostalgic for some of these foods you might have enjoyed long ago, by all means follow the methods described above. Otherwise, ready-to-eat pickled herrings may be purchased at the dairy counter of many of today's supermarkets.

In addition to herring, salt cod preparations and Finnan Haddie are characteristic fish dishes that have long been in The Settlement Cookbook. Be sure to read the packer's directions to determine whether the fish called for below has been treated in any way. Revise the soaking and cooking times accordingly. Keep in mind, too, that there are some excellent new varieties of pickled and smoked fish with low sodium content.

CODFISH BALLS

6 ounces salt codfish
2½ cups potatoes, peeled and cut
   into pieces
½ tablespoon butter

¼ teaspoon freshly ground black
   pepper
1 egg, beaten well
oil or fat for frying

1.   Wash the fish in cold water. Soak until softened, and desalted—about 24 hours—changing the water often. Drain. Remove the bones and shred. Cook the fish and the potatoes together in boiling water until the potatoes are tender. Drain and dry out by stirring over heat.

2.   In the bowl of a food processor fitted with the metal blade, puree the mixture until light and fluffy. Add butter, pepper, and the egg. Process just to blend. Alternatively, chop fish very fine. Work into a paste using mortar and pestle. Stir in remaining ingredients.

3.   Shape the mixture on a spoon and drop into deep, hot fat (about 375° F). Fry until brown and drain on paper towels. If they break apart, add a little more egg.

CREOLE CODFISH

1 cup salt codfish
4 medium boiled potatoes, peeled,
   sliced, and cooled
1 medium red pepper, coarsely
   chopped
salt and freshly ground black pepper
   to taste

1 tablespoon fresh thyme or 1
   teaspoon dried
1 cup Basic Tomato Sauce (page
   405)
buttered bread or cracker crumbs

1.   Wash the fish in cold water. Soak until softened and desalted—about 24 hours—changing the water often. Drain. Remove the bones and shred.

2.   Preheat oven to 350° F. Into a buttered baking dish, place a layer of the cold boiled potato slices, a layer of the shredded fish, some of the red pepper, and season with salt, pepper, and thyme. Repeat until all of the ingredients are used.

3.   Pour the Tomato Sauce over and cover with bread or cracker crumbs. Bake until hot, bubbling, and browned on top.

FINNAN HADDIE

Soak smoked haddock in cold water for several hours. Drain well and cover with hot water. Bake at 350° F until tender, about 30 minutes. Drain, spread with 2 tablespoons butter.

FINNAN HADDIE IN CREAM

 Cover smoked haddock with cold water, bring slowly to the boiling point, keep hot for 25 minutes. Drain well and flake. To each cup of fish, add 1 tablespoon butter, 2 or 3 hard-cooked eggs, thinly sliced, ½ cup heavy cream, and some chopped parsley. Heat gently.

BROILED FINNAN HADDIE

 Soak smoked haddock overnight and drain. Brush with butter and broil 15 to 20 minutes, depending on the thickness of the fish. Serve with melted butter and chopped parsley.

Seafood

Despite overfishing and pollution, we have as much seafood as ever to provide our marketplaces with an abundance of clean, safe products that lend themsleves to creative culinary endeavors. Interestingly enough, recent studies show that most of the seafood consumed in America is done outside of the home. What are we afraid of? What follows are some recipes that will hopefully inspire us all to head back to the kitchen in pursuit of a venture to make the best use of the glistening seafood so prominently displayed in our local stores. Some of these are timeless, original Settlement recipes that have been enjoyed by many people since the book was first published at the turn of the century. Others are new ideas that combine contemporary ingredients with modern techniques.

OYSTERS AND CLAMS

Shucking Oysters and Clams

Hold an oyster or clam firmly against a towel on the table, large side down. Insert a blunt-tipped, sturdy oyster knife between the shells and twist to force open. Sever the muscles that attach the meat to the top and bottom shells. Pick out any bits of shell. Be careful to reserve the interior liquid or "liquor." Serve raw oyster in the deep side of the shell with a cocktail or vinegar sauce or lemon wedges and freshly ground black pepper.

Steaming Open Oysters or Clams

When oysters or clams are to be served cooked, they may first be steamed open. Put a small amount of water in the bottom of a large kettle, add the oysters, and cover. Steam rapidly for just a few minutes, just until the shells open. Strain the liquid before using it.

When oysters are served in cooked dishes, it is important to avoid overcooking. Oysters are cooked when they swell or plump slightly and the edges begin to curl. Overcooked oysters are tough and rubbery.

Usually plan to serve 3 to 6 oysters or clams per person as an appetizer, and 6 to 12 pieces as a main course.

BROILED OYSTERS

1 pint selected oysters
¼ cup melted butter

⅔ cup seasoned bread or cracker crumbs

1. Shuck oysters and dry between towels. Lift with fork by the tough muscles and dip in butter, then in crumbs.

2. Place in a buttered baking dish and cook under a preheated broiler until juices flow, turning once while broiling. Serve with lemon wedges.

PAN-BROILED OYSTERS

2 tablespoons butter
1 pint oysters, shucked, juices
　reserved and strained
1 cup hot cream

pinch of cayenne pepper
1 teaspoon salt
⅛ teaspoon white pepper

1. In a large frying pan, melt the butter over high heat. Add the oysters, cover, and shake until oysters are plump.

2. Add the cream and reserved juices from the oysters. Season with cayenne, salt, and pepper. Serve hot.

FRIED OYSTERS

24 large oysters
½ cup breadcrumbs or cornmeal
1 teaspoon salt

⅛ teaspoon freshly ground black pepper
1 egg, beaten

1. Shuck and drain select oysters. Season breadcrumbs or cornmeal with salt and pepper, and roll oysters in mixture. Let stand 15 minutes.

2. Dip in beaten egg, roll in crumbs again, and let stand again for 15 minutes in a cool place.

3. Fry one minute or until golden brown in deep, hot fat (375° F). Drain on paper towels, serve on hot platter garnished with parsley, pickle, or lemon.

SCALLOPED OYSTERS

½ cup dry breadcrumbs
1 cup cracker crumbs
½ cup melted butter
1 pint shucked oysters

2 tablespoons reserved oyster liquor
salt and freshly ground black pepper
  to taste
2 tablespoons milk or cream

Preheat oven to 400° F. Mix bread and cracker crumbs and stir in the butter. Put a third in the bottom of a buttered, shallow baking dish. Cover with half of the oysters and season with salt and pepper. Add half of the oyster liquor and half of the cream. Repeat, cover top with remaining crumbs. Bake 30 minutes in the hot oven.

OYSTERS ROCKEFELLER

2 dozen large oysters
½ cup butter
1 tablespoon each parsley and
  scallions
juice of one lemon
salt and freshly ground black pepper
  to taste

pinch of cayenne pepper
¼ cup cooked spinach, water
  squeezed out and finely chopped
several slices of thinly sliced bacon
  cut into 1-inch squares
rock salt

1. Preheat oven to 400° F. Scrub the oysters thoroughly. Shuck and leave oysters on bottom of shells and arrange them on a large baking sheet.

2. In a small bowl, mix together the butter, parsley, scallions, lemon juice, salt, pepper, and cayenne. Put some of this mixture on each oyster and top with a little of the cooked spinach. Place a piece of bacon on each oyster.

3. Place the oysters in the oven and heat until oysters swell. Set shells in heavy pie plate filled with rock salt to preserve heat and serve at once.

STEAMED OYSTERS OR CLAMS

 Scrub shells of 2 dozen oysters or clams to remove all sand. Lay them in a large covered kettle, add ½ cup boiling water for 2 dozen medium-size shells. Cover and steam until shells partially open (5 to 10 minutes). Serve with melted butter.

CLAMS À LA ST. LOUIS

1 onion, finely chopped
2 tablespoons butter
1 tablespoon flour
30 clams, shucked, cleaned, and
    chopped, all juices reserved
½ teaspoon salt

½ teaspoon cayenne pepper
½ teaspoon dry mustard
4 egg yolks
2 tablespoons cold water
chopped parsley for garnish

1. Preheat oven to 350° F. In a sauté pan, cook the onions in the butter over moderately high heat. Stir in the flour and blend. Add the clams and their juices. Season with salt, cayenne, and mustard. Cook for 10 minutes over moderately low heat.

2. Beat the egg yolks with the water until lemon colored. Remove the clam mixture from the heat and add the egg yolks. Pile mixture back into shells. Heat in the oven for 5 to 10 minutes. Garnish with parsley.

SCALLOPS

Scallops come shucked in two forms: 1. bay scallops, which are small, cylindrical pellets about ½ inch long and 2. sea scallops, which are larger, sweeter morsels about 1 inch in circumference. Either are delicious when simply sautéed and served as a first course, or served over rice or pasta for a main course. Marinated, broiled scallops are mighty tasty as well. Allow 6 to 8 ounces shucked scallops per person.

SAUTÉED SCALLOPS   *Serves 2.*

Pat dry 1 pound scallops. Season with salt and pepper. Drop into a large sauté pan with a small amount of olive oil or butter. Toss or stir constantly over moderately high heat until the scallops lose their translucency and are firm to the touch, 3 to 5 minutes. Season again to taste and serve at once.

Variations:

With Tomato, Garlic, and Herbs: Follow directions above. After scallops have cooked for about 1½ minutes, add 1 peeled, seeded, and chopped medium tomato, 1 finely minced clove of garlic, and 2 tablespoons mixed herbs (parsley, thyme, rosemary, chervil, chives, or oregano). Continue cooking over moderately high heat until done. Serve at once.

With Cream and Saffron: In a large sauté pan, combine the scallops with ½ cup heavy cream. Add a small pinch of saffron. Toss or stir over moderately high heat until cream has slightly thickened and saffron has blended, 3 to 5 minutes. Season to taste with salt and pepper. Serve at once. Garnish with freshly chopped parsley.

BROILED SCALLOPS   *Serves 2.*

Pat dry 1 pound of scallops. In a nonreactive bowl just large enough to hold the scallops, combine ¼ teaspoon salt, ⅛ teaspoon paprika, ⅛ teaspoon white pepper, 1½ tablespoons white wine vinegar, 1½ tablespoons lemon juice, and 6 tablespoons olive oil. Marinate the scallops in this mixture, refrigerated, for 1 hour. Roll in seasoned breadcrumbs, brush with melted butter, broil until golden brown. Serve with melted butter and lemon juice.

LOBSTER

Boiling Lobster

Put whole live lobsters, head first, one at a time, in a large kettle of boiling, salted water to cover. (Use about 2 tablespoons salt to 1 quart water.) Bring back to a simmer and cook 5 minutes for the first pound and 3 minutes for each additional pound. Drain and cool quickly by plunging into ice water.

Opening Boiled Lobster

Take off the claws. Separate large claws at joints, crack with a mallet or nutcracker, or cut shell and remove the meat. Separate the tail from the body. Draw out the tail meat and split it open slightly through the center. Take out the intestinal vein. Hold the body shell firmly, draw out the body, and remove the stomach and green liver. Pick out the meat from body bones. The stomach and intestinal vein are not edible.

Preparing and Cleaning Lobster

Cut off the thin legs and insert knife into the abdomen of cooked lobster. Cut through undershell toward the head of the lobster. Then cut toward the tail. Separate the halves. Remove the sand sac from the head and the intestinal tract in the middle. To split lobster in half, cross large claws and hold with left hand. With the right hand draw a sharp pointed knife quickly through the body lengthwise from head to tail. Crack claws slightly with the handle of a large knife or a mallet.

Broiling or Grilling Lobster

Heat oven to 400° F. Split the lobster with a large knife and glaze with olive oil. Broil about 4 inches from the heat source, meat side toward the fire, about 10 minutes, depending on size. Season with salt, cayenne, and brush with melted butter. Serve with lemon and melted butter.

Baking Lobster

Split and clean a 2-pound live lobster. Brush with melted butter. Heat oven to 450° F. Place lobster in a baking pan, flesh side up. Bake for 5 minutes. Then brush with melted butter. Reduce heat to 350° and bake for 10 or 15 more minutes. Gently probe the flesh of the lobster at the thickest part of the tail. The flesh should be white and firm, the carcass bright red. Do not overcook. Serve with melted butter.

LOBSTER À LA THACKERAY

Walnut catsup seems to be the key ingredient for the following recipe. If this is not available, try substituting your favorite store-bought or homemade relish. This recipe has been in every Settlement edition.

2 boiled lobsters	3 dashes cayenne pepper
½ cup butter	1 tablespoon walnut catsup
¼ teaspoon salt	1 teaspoon paprika

1. Remove the meat from the lobsters, set aside, and discard the shells. Remove the liver or tomalley.
2. In a small, nonreactive saucepan, place the liver. Add the butter, salt, cayenne, catsup, and paprika. Cook over moderately high heat for 5 minutes.
3. Add the lobster meat and heat through. Serve with rice or pasta.

LOBSTER THERMIDOR

3 or 4 boiled lobsters	1 tablespoon tomato concentrate
2 tablespoons butter	2 cups Medium White Sauce (page
½ small onion, finely chopped	399)
¼ cup dry white wine	grated Parmesan cheese
½ pound mushrooms, finely chopped	

1. Preheat oven to 450° F. Split the lobsters in half and pick out the meat. Leave the main body shell intact. Dice the meat into large bite-size pieces.
2. In a large sauté pan or skillet, heat the butter. Add the onions, lobster pieces, and wine. Cook for 5 minutes, stirring constantly. Add the mushrooms and the tomato concentrate. Continue cooking for 5 more minutes.
3. Fill the shells with the mixture. Pour over Medium White Sauce and sprinkle with the cheese. Bake in the hot oven until thoroughly heated and bubbly, or brown topping quickly under the broiler.

LOBSTER NEWBURG   *Serves 2.*

This is an adaptation of the original Settlement recipe. We've substituted olive oil for butter and eliminated the egg yolk enrichment to lighten it up. The reduction process is rather long and requires complete concentration. This is a rather expensive, special dish that is meant for special occasions. Rice is the traditional accompaniment.

2 boiled lobsters, about 1 pound
   each
2 tablespoons olive oil
2 small onions, thinly sliced
1 cup fish stock (page 60), bottled
   clam juice, or water

1 cup heavy cream
salt and freshly ground pepper to
   taste
1 tablespoon sherry (optional)
parsley for garnish (optional)

1.   Remove the flesh from the tail and the claws of the lobster, reserving any juices. Set aside. Cut the carcass into small pieces.

2.   In a large sauté pan, heat the olive oil. Add the onion and cook over moderately high heat until translucent. Do not brown. Add the carcass of the lobster and any reserved juices. Pour in the fish stock, clam juice, or water. Partially cover and cook over high heat for 10 minutes, stirring often.

3.   Strain into a heavy saucepan. (There should be about 1½ cups liquid at this point. If not, add additional fish stock to equal this amount. Pour off excess if there is more than this amount.) Discard the carcass and cooked onions. Reduce the liquid over high heat until about 3 tablespoons of liquid remain in the pan. The consistency should be syrupy and quite concentrated. Immediately pour in the cream. Stir over high heat until reduced by half. Season with salt, pepper, and sherry if desired.

4.   Slice the reserved lobster tail into even slices. Arrange attractively on individual plates with the claw meat. Nap the lobster lightly with the sauce and garnish with parsley, if desired. Serve immediately.

CRAB

Boiling Hard-Shell Crabs

Bring water to a boil in a large pot. Add salt (2 teaspoons per quart of water). Drop in the crabs and bring back to a boil. Cook over high heat until they change color and come back to the surface, about 5 minutes. Drain and wash carefully. Remove the claws, pull off the hard shell, and remove the spongy part. Crack claws with nutcracker and remove meat. Serve the remaining soft shell with the claws.

FRIED SOFT-SHELL CRABS

Prepare the crabs by first removing their sand bags. Raise the apron and cut it from the crab. Remove the spongy substance surrounding the apron. Wash and wipe crab dry. Season with salt and pepper. Dip in crumbs, beaten egg, and again in crumbs. Fry in deep, hot fat about 3 to 5 minutes. Serve immediately, with Tartar Sauce (page 408).

DEVILED CRABS

2 tablespoons butter
2 ribs celery, peeled and finely chopped
1 small onion, finely chopped
1 green pepper, trimmed, seeded, and finely chopped
1 teaspoon dry mustard
½ teaspoon salt
½ teaspoon cayenne

½ teaspoon red pepper flakes (optional)
2 tablespoons chopped parsley
1 hard-boiled egg, chopped
1 cup fresh breadcrumbs, plus more for browning
1 pound fresh lump crabmeat
2 tablespoons milk
melted butter for drizzling

1. Preheat oven to 425° F. In a sauté pan, melt the butter. Add the celery, onion, and green pepper. Cook over moderately high heat until softened but not browned. Transfer to a mixing bowl. Add mustard, salt, cayenne, red pepper flakes if desired, parsley, and chopped egg. Gently fold in the breadcrumbs and crab. Moisten with the milk.

2. Pack the mixture into emptied crab shells or small ramekins. Top with breadcrumbs and drizzle over melted butter. Bake in the hot oven until golden brown. Serve at once.

CRAB CAKES

4 tablespoons butter
1 small onion, finely chopped
2 ribs celery, peeled and finely chopped
1 small, sweet red pepper, finely chopped
1 cup dry white wine
1 pound fresh lump crabmeat
1 cup fresh breadcrumbs

1 tablespoon parsley
1 teaspoon grated lemon zest
1 tablespoon lemon juice
½ teaspoon salt
¼ teaspoon freshly ground black pepper
cornmeal for dusting
2 tablespoons vegetable oil

(continued)

1. In a small sauté pan, melt 2 tablespoons of the butter. Add the onion, celery, and pepper. Cook over moderately high heat until softened but not browned. Pour in the wine and increase heat to high. Boil until liquid is reduced by half. Transfer the contents of the pan to a mixing bowl.

2. Add the crabmeat, breadcrumbs, parsley, lemon zest and juice, salt, and pepper. Gently blend. Using wet hands, form small balls of the mixture. Pat down to make cakes 2 to 3 inches in diameter. Rewet hands as is necessary while shaping the mixture.

3. Place the cornmeal in a shallow bowl. Roll each cake in the meal, shaking off any excess. Melt the remaining 2 tablespoons of butter with the vegetable oil over high heat. When very hot, add the cakes and quickly sauté until golden brown. Serve at once with Basic Tomato Sauce (page 405) or your favorite bottled salsa sauce.

SHRIMP

Shrimp come in different sizes, categorized according to the number per pound. Jumbos come 10 to 15 per pound, large 16 to 20 per pound, mediums come 21 to 25 per pound, and small shrimp about 31 to 35 per pound. Medium is always a good choice. The amount to buy per serving depends on how they are to be prepared. Remember that 2 pounds of unpeeled, headless shrimp will yield about 1 pound cleaned and trimmed. Look for firm, fresh-smelling shrimp. Avoid those that have a sharp, ammonia-like smell. Always clean and devein shrimp. The black line that runs along the back of the shrimp should be removed with the tip of a sharp-bladed knife. This can be done either before or after cooking.

Boiling Shrimp

Bring a large amount of water, 1 tablespoon salt, and 1 tablespoon caraway seeds or pickling spices to a boil (at least 1½ quarts for each pound). Add the shrimp. Bring back to the boil. Cook at a full boil for 1 minute. Shrimp will be bright pink. Turn off heat and let stand for another two minutes. Drain immediately. When cool enough to handle, peel and devein. Reheat in preferred sauce, serve with melted butter, or chill and serve cold with seafood Cocktail Sauce (page 36).

Frying Shrimp

Wash, rinse, and pat dry shrimp. Peel and remove the black vein that runs along the back. Chill thoroughly. Dip shrimp into beaten and seasoned egg, roll in flour or cracker meal, and fry a few at a time in deep, hot fat (350° F) for 2 to 3 minutes, until golden. Serve hot with lemon wedges or a spicy, tomato-based sauce like the Cocktail Sauce found on page 36.

Serving Cold Shrimp

Boil 4 to 5 pounds of shrimp as for above. Chill thoroughly. Peel and carefully devein. Spread an assortment of cleaned, crisp lettuce leaves on a large serving platter. Pile the shrimp in the middle. Surround with sliced or quartered tomatoes, hard-boiled eggs, olives, lemon wedges, celery sticks, and fresh parsley. Serve a bowl of Green and/or Red Mayonnaise (page 130) on the side.

THREE QUICK SHRIMP SAUTÉES

SHRIMP WITH TOMATOES AND HERBS

2 tablespoons olive oil
2 small onions, thinly sliced
1 green pepper, seeded and cut into thin slices
2 pounds shrimp, peeled and deveined
2 large tomatoes, peeled, seeded, and chopped

½ teaspoon red pepper flakes (optional)
salt and freshly ground black pepper to taste
¼ cup chopped fresh herbs (parsley, thyme, chervil, cilantro, or chives)

1. In a sauté pan, heat the olive oil and add the onions and the peppers. Cook until softened without browning the onions.

2. Add the shrimp, tomatoes, and seasonings. Cook over high heat until shrimp are firm and pink and juices have reduced and thickened, about 7 minutes. Turn or toss often to assure even cooking. Add herbs just before serving. Serve at once with rice or pasta.

SAUTÉED SHRIMP WITH ORANGE

2 tablespoons olive oil
2 small onions, thinly sliced
2 pounds shrimp, peeled and
   deveined
juice of 1 orange, about ½ cup
1 tablespoon grated orange zest

⅛ teaspoon cumin
salt and freshly ground black pepper
2 tablespoons butter (optional)
1 medium orange, peeled and cut
   into sections

1. In a sauté pan, heat the olive oil and add the onions. Cook until softened. Add the shrimp and cook quickly over moderately high heat until firm and bright pink, about 7 minutes. Stir or toss constantly to assure even cooking and to prevent the onions from browning. Remove the shrimp and keep warm.

2. Add the orange juice and the zest to the sauté pan. Boil over high heat to reduce by half. Add the cumin. Season with salt and pepper to taste. Whisk in butter to enrich if desired.

3. Add the orange sections to the sauce. Leave on heat long enough to just warm through. Spoon the sauce over the shrimp on a serving platter. Serve at once with boiled white rice.

SHRIMP CURRY

2 tablespoons butter
2 pounds shrimp, peeled and
   deveined
1 small onion, peeled and thinly
   sliced

1½ teaspoons curry powder
1 cup heavy cream

1. In a nonreactive skillet, melt 1 tablespoon of the butter. Add the shrimp and stir constantly. Cook the shrimp just until it turns pink, about 3 minutes. Remove the shrimp from the skillet and place on a serving platter. Cover with foil to keep warm.

2. Melt remaining tablespoon butter, add onions and curry powder and cook until the onions are soft. Add cream and reduce over high heat until thick. Add shrimp and cook for 2 minutes more until shrimp is heated through. Serve immediately with rice or Asian noodles.

Mussels, Frog Legs, and Crawfish

MUSSELS

To clean mussels scrub them well with a vegetable brush and chip off any barnacles with a sharp knife or with your finger. If that doesn't work, try pulling at it gently with a pair of pliers. Don't worry if you can't remove all the beard, just pull off what you can and leave the rest. Never remove the beard until just before cooking or the mussels will spoil and die.

MUSSELS IN WHITE WINE

3 quarts fresh mussels	6 peppercorns
1 cup white wine	1 bay leaf
3 shallots or 1 onion, very finely chopped	3 sprigs thyme
1 bunch parsley	2 tablespoons coarsely chopped parsley

1. Clean the mussels. In a large, nonreactive pan combine the wine, shallots, parsley bunch, peppercorns, bay leaf, and thyme sprigs. Bring to a boil and simmer for 2 minutes. Add mussels, cover, and cook over a high fire, stirring occasionally, for 5 to 7 minutes, or until the mussels open. (Discard any that do not open.)

2. Remove the mussels to soup bowls. Strain the cooking liquid and taste for seasoning. Spoon cooking liquid over mussels, sprinkle with chopped parsley, and serve hot.

FROG LEGS

FROG LEGS À LA NEWBURG

Boil 4 pairs frog legs in salted water and drain. Heat 2 tablespoons butter, add ½ cup chicken stock (page 59), ½ cup madeira, salt, and cayenne pepper to taste. Boil 3 minutes, stirring constantly, and pour over frog legs.

FRIED FROG LEGS

Scald the frog legs in boiling water for just a moment, then drain and dry. Dust with salt and pepper, dip in beaten egg, then in rolled cracker crumbs. Let stand 10 minutes. Fry quickly in hot fat (375° F) for about 10 minutes or until juices run clear.

CRAWFISH

Crawfish, also known as mud bugs and crayfish, have enjoyed a renewed popularity recently. The two kinds native to the United States are almost identical. Louisiana crawfish are smaller and slimmer than the West Coast variety. They are prepared in the same way.

To clean live crawfish rinse them under cold running water. Grab the middle flap at the end of the tail fan between your thumb and forefinger. Sharply twist it clockwise and pull. It will draw the entrails out of the crawfish, leaving it clean and ready to cook.

BOILED CRAWFISH

Put live crawfish in 2 quarts boiling water with 1 tablespoon each salt and caraway seeds. Boil until bright red, about 5 minutes. Drain and serve hot or cold.

MICROWAVE FISH COOKERY

Because fish's delicate flavor benefits from simple preparations and quick cooking it is an ideal food for the microwave. Unlike conventional cooking methods, microwaves cook the inside and outside of the fish at the same time resulting in tender, flavorful, and evenly cooked fish. Where some methods—like oven baking—often dry out the flesh, microwaves keep it moist. Browning, so often a problem when using the microwave, isn't an issue for fish cooking.

Fish can be cooked without fat or heavy sauces in the microwave, making a meal that is already low in calories and high in nutrition an even healthier choice. Simply put your fillet, steak, or cleaned whole fish on a dish or serving platter, season it lightly, cover tightly with microwave-proof plastic, and follow instructions designed for your particular microwave. You can add a small amount of vegetables if you wish—less than half a cup will not affect the cooking time—but for the most effective microwave cooking keep your preparations simple. As the fish cooks, it lets off water and creates its own cooking liquid, which can be used as a mild fish stock for sauces.

Many of the recipes in this chapter can be easily adapted for the microwave. Baked Red Snapper with Fennel, Baked Trout, Baked Bluefish, and Lemon Herb Mackerel were some of our favorites. Because microwave ovens vary in power and size, we aren't able to give specific instructions for each recipe. We urge you to become familiar with your particular machine and its well-suited capacity for creating perfectly cooked, healthy fish dishes.

SMOKED SALMON

Smoked salmon has long been a deluxe European product. Colorful, versatile, and deliciously salty/sweet, Americans are finding that this subtly smoky delicacy can be an elegant offering for special occasions.

There are several choices for serving smoked salmon. With drinks before dinner, it can be sliced thin and served simply with small pieces of brown bread or crisp toasts accompanied by a crock of butter. The slices can be rolled with cream cheese mixed with chives or dill. Arranged decoratively and served with lemon wedges or with a mild horseradish sauce, smoked salmon makes an enticing first course.

However you choose to serve smoked salmon, the kind you buy is important. Imported salmon is always a good choice. The best is Scotch salmon, which has a captivating pink/orange sheen that promises a unique flavor. Danish smoked salmon is slightly darker and can be very good but lacks the flavor of the Scotch. Norwegian salmon is a good compromise between the two. It has a pink/copper color with more flavor than the Danish but less finesse than the Scotch. All three are expensive but worth the extravagance for particular celebrations or holidays.

Increasingly common is Canadian smoked salmon. Sold either vacuum packed or frozen, this product is more readily available than the Scotch, Danish, or Norwegian varieties that are available in fine specialty stores. It is relatively inexpensive, usually comes presliced, and has a more-than-acceptable flavor. It can be mixed with equal parts of butter and seasoned with dill or lemon to make a delicious, spreadable mousse. This is the best smoked salmon to use in salads, sandwiches, scrambled eggs, or omelettes.

THE CANADIAN FISH-COOKING METHOD

Cooking fish seems to intimidate even accomplished cooks. While not quite as daunting as it seems, finding that moment of succulent perfection is an art. Overcooked fish is dry and rubbery. Undercooked fish is unpleasantly chewy and may even be dangerous. Here are some helpful criteria.

"The Canadian Cooking Method" is an outgrowth of experimentation and testing done by the Department of Fisheries of Canada. Excellent results are obtained if fish is measured at its thickest point then cooked for 8 to 10 minutes per inch or fraction thereof. It works with all kinds of fish: fillets, whole fish, and fish steaks. It applies to every method of cooking: broiling or grilling, baking, frying, sautéing, and poaching.

Simply lay the fish (or cut of fish) flat and measure at the widest point with a ruler. For example, if a whole fish measures 1½ inches, cook for 12 to 15 minutes. If a fillet measures only ½ inch thick, cook it for 4 to 5 minutes. This principle works with frozen fish as well. Cook unthawed frozen fish for 15 to 20 minutes per inch and results will be practically guaranteed.

Only experience will teach how to master the art of perfectly cooked fish. The Canadian Method should serve only as a guideline. Learn what fish looks and feels like when it is cooked exactly to your liking. Don't be put off if results are disappointing at first. Keep trying, using this handy method as a beginning standard.

POULTRY AND GAME

Consumption of poultry has increased dramatically in the last few years. Part of this increase can be attributed to the demise of fatty red meats and pork in the modern American diet. Low in fat, easy to prepare, and versatile, poultry is the main source of protein in many households today.

Most poultry is now sold eviscerated, completely pre-cleaned, ready for cooking or freezing. You may buy poultry whole for roasting, cooking on the rotisserie, boiling, or braising; split for broiling or barbecuing; cut up into serving-size pieces for frying or sautéing.

PREPARING A WHOLE BIRD

How Much to Buy

A small broiler, split, serves 2; larger broilers may be quartered to provide 4 servings. Fryers serve 3 to 4. So does the average duckling. If buying goose, allow 1 pound per serving. Plan on ¾ to 1 pound of turkey, dressed weight, per serving.

Trussing

Tuck end of neck skin under at the back and secure with poultry pin or skewer. Turn wings back under and secure tips against body. Tie drumsticks together, crossing thread under tail of bird and securing legs close to the body. Or, if flap of skin is slit at front of bird above tail, cross legs and tuck them under this band of skin to secure.

Disjointing

Buying a whole bird is the most economical way to purchase poultry. Supermarkets often run specials on whole birds, and the little time spent cutting them into various parts can mean big savings in the food budget.

Cutting and boning poultry is easy once a few simple techniques have been

CUTTING UP A WHOLE CHICKEN

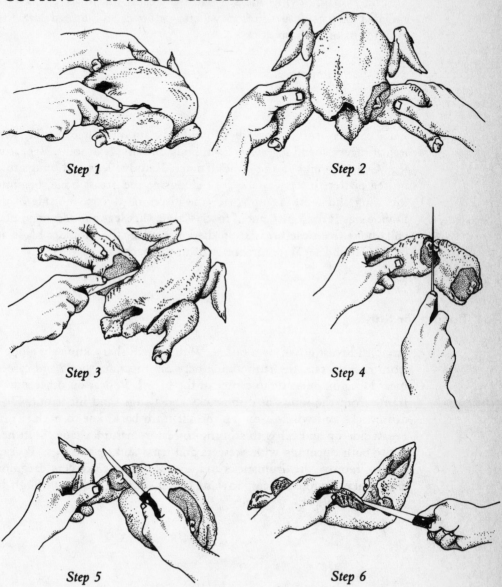

Step 1

Step 2

Step 3

Step 4

Step 5

Step 6

mastered. For best results, the National Broiler Council offers three tips: 1. be confident, 2. work quickly, and 3. use a sharp knife.

Whole birds can be halved, quartered, cut into parts, or even cut into smaller pieces. Bone the breast or thighs or cut into strips or nuggets. Cut the meatier portion from the wing and store in the freezer until enough have been accumulated for party drumettes. Save leftover bones and unused parts (neck, back, etc.) to make soup or stock.

Carving

Place chicken, turkey, or other fowl breast up on heated platter, with neck to left of carver. Bend leg away from body and divide at joint. Repeat with other leg. Cut off wings in the same manner. Remove legs and wings to a separate heated platter. Insert carving fork alongside the breast bone, beginning above the wing and working up. Place the pieces neatly on one side of the platter. Divide legs at the joints, and if fowl is large, slice legs and second joints. Separate collarbone from the breast, slip the knife under the shoulder blade and turn it over. Cut and separate the breast from the back.

Boning for Stuffing

Lay bird breast down on a board. With a small sharp knife slit along backbone from neck to tail. Insert the knife between meat and bone and carefully work meat loose on one side to center of the breast. Repeat on other side. Sever the frame from the joints at drumsticks and wings, and lift it out. Do not bone drumsticks and wings. Sew up the slit from backbone to neck. Turn the bird breast side up and fill with stuffing to restore natural shape. Stuff neck cavity. Close both openings with skewers and truss and tie the legs. To carve boned poultry remove the drumsticks and wings. Remove skewers. Beginning at one end, make diagonal slices, toward center, cutting down through breast and stuffing.

QUARTERING A CHICKEN

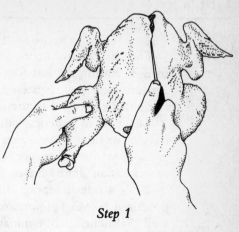

Step 1

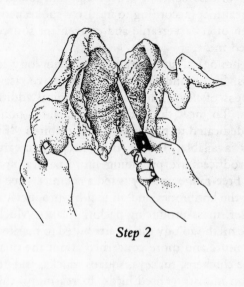

Step 2

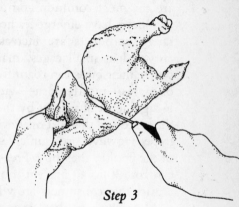

Step 3

BONING HALF A CHICKEN BREAST

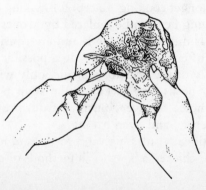

Step 1

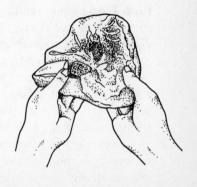

Step 2

Chicken

The chicken industry has enjoyed a remarkable period of growth and expansion during the last four decades. A record high of 60.3 pounds per capita consumption was registered in 1987, up from 41 pounds in 1977. This can be attributed to several factors.

Advances in genetics, nutrition, disease control, processing, and marketing have made poultry a cheaper and healthier (according to industry spokespeople) product for the consumer. Chicken offers a versatile and convenient source of protein as an alternative to fatty red meat.

While strides in more efficient biological and engineering technology have produced record amounts of birds, health and quality concerns have risen as well. Salmonella contamination, loss of flavor, and use of chemical additives are the most common complaints. To meet the demand for quality, poultry producers have emerged who are dedicated to providing superior birds. "Free-range" products are increasingly available. Rather than keeping creatures crowded in small cages, many producers are providing more natural spaces where their birds can roam freely. Free-range poultry is fed a chemical-free diet of grains—mostly corn—without the antibiotics and animal by-products used in significant quantities by the larger, mass-producing packing plants. Much of the success of this sort of alternative methodology can be attributed to marketing hype. However, consumers seem more and more concerned about the quality of the poultry they buy. Free-range chickens, turkeys, squabs, ducks, and geese can cost 30 to 40 percent more than industry-raised birds. Increasingly, this is a price that consumers are willing to pay for assured quality and flavor.

Most chickens that come to market now are *broiler-fryers,* only nine weeks old. They weigh from 3 to 4 pounds and are usually tender and juicy. The *roaster,* marketed at 12 weeks, weighs between 3½ and 5 pounds. It costs more per pound and takes longer to cook. The *stewing hen,* fowl, or bro-hen, is an egg layer that has finished producing. They are marketed at 1½ years, weigh from 4 to 6 pounds, and require even longer cooking. Except for making chicken soups, many cooks feel that the stewing hen can be replaced by broiler-fryers. *Capons,* altered roosters, can weigh as much as 7 pounds and are considered a luxury roast. Broiler-fryer parts are often sold separately. It is possible to buy only breasts, for a party meal, or only drumsticks for a picnic, only wings for a fricassee or for grilling, or thrifty necks and backs for the soup pot. The broiler-fryer is the best all-around choice for every purpose from broiling or frying to roasting, cooking in a casserole, and oven baking.

Chicken has excellent value nutritionally; it is high in protein and lower in calories than most meats. In addition, chicken adapts to all methods of cooking and seasoning.

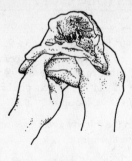

Step 3

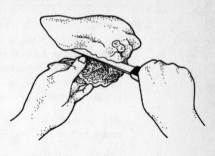

Step 4

CHICKEN THIGH

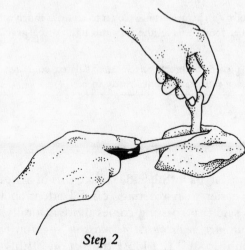

Step 2

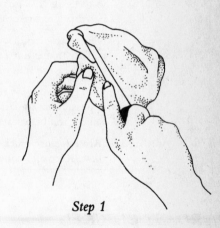

Step 1

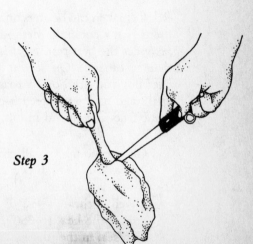

Step 3

PRACTICAL GUIDELINES FOR SAFETY

---

1. Always cook poultry well done, not medium or rare. Salmonella is heat sensitive and is easily destroyed at temperatures of 140° F or more. The U.S. Department of Agriculture recommends cooking until the meat reaches a temperature of 180° F to ensure the destruction of any Salmonella that may be present. Boneless parts may be cooked to an internal temperature of 160° F. When poultry is cooked properly, all juices from the meat should run clear, not pink.

2. Always thaw chicken in the refrigerator, or in the microwave, never on the kitchen counter. Bacteria multiply rapidly at room temperature.

3. Always wash hands, countertops, and utensils in hot, soapy water between each step of food preparation. Bacteria present on raw meat and poultry can get into other food if exposed to the same utensils. For example, be sure the platter that carries the cooked meat to the table is not the same platter that carried raw meat to the grill. Do not cut up raw poultry and then use the same knife or cutting board to prepare other foods unless the utensils are washed thoroughly.

4. Never leave poultry out at room temperature for more than 2 hours. Cooked poultry that is not eaten immediately should be kept either hot (between 140° to 165° F) or brought to room temperature and then refrigerated at 40° F or less.

5. Always thoroughly reheat leftovers before eating. Cover to retain as much moisture as possible and guarantee that food heats all the way through. Bring gravies to a rolling boil before serving.

6. Always store chicken for picnics or luncheons in an insulated container or ice chest. Keep all cooked poultry refrigerated until ready to eat.

ROAST CHICKEN

Roast chicken can be an economical, flavorful, and creative part of a meal. While there is no cooking method easier than roasting, careful attention to detail provides the best results. It is said that roasting comes more naturally to some than to others. *"On devient cuisinier, mais on est né rôtisseur"*—"you become a chef but you are born a roasting cook" is a loose translation of this proverb attributed to the nineteenth-century French gastronome, Brillat-Savarin. Keep some facts and tips in mind:

1. Choose young, small chickens for roasting. The following recipes call for 3½- to 5-pound chickens that serve 4 to 6 people.
2. Know your oven. Use a thermometer to verify the temperature. Start with a well preheated 450° F oven. As soon as you put the bird in the oven, reduce the heat to 350° F. The initial high heat will sear the chicken and help seal in the juices.

CARVING A ROAST CHICKEN, A CAPON, OR A TURKEY

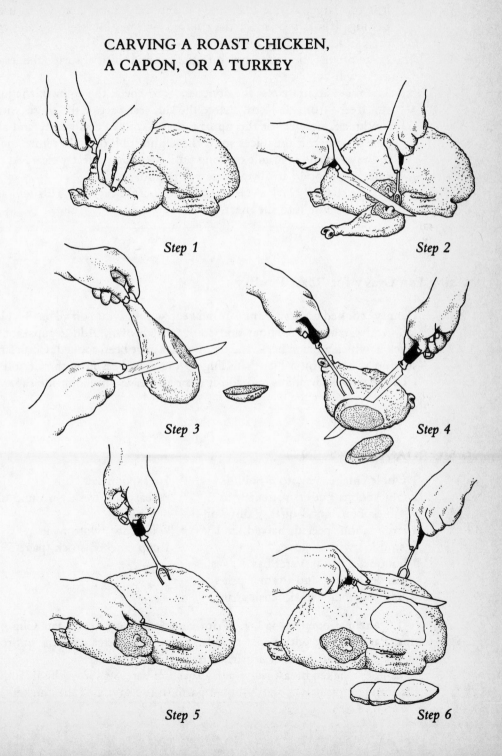

Step 1

Step 2

Step 3

Step 4

Step 5

Step 6

3. Use a roasting pan that is just large enough to hold the chicken snugly. If it is too large, all the juices will evaporate leaving nothing to use for the basting. If it is too small, the chicken will not cook evenly and collecting the pan juices will be difficult.

4. Baste often. The more moisture the cooking bird absorbs, the less dry the meat will be.

5. The most accurate test for doneness is to check the color of the juices that run freely from the bird. Pierce the thickest part of the thigh with a long toothpick, skewer, or the tip of a sharp knife. Press gently and allow the juices to flow. If the juices show the slightest bit of pink, return the chicken to the oven and continue cooking until they run perfectly clear. As a general rule, cook for 18 to 20 minutes per pound.

6. Let the roasted chicken rest 10 minutes before carving. This will allow the juices to settle into the meat.

Making Pan Gravy for Roast Poultry

Remove cooked poultry from pan and keep warm. Drain off all but 4 tablespoons fat. Add 4 tablespoons flour and cook until brown. Add 2 cups hot chicken stock in which giblets, neck, and tip of wings have been cooked. Cook 5 minutes, stirring in the brown bits that cling to the pan. Season with salt and pepper. Chop the cooked giblets and add if desired. Serve hot alongside carved meat.

BASIC ROAST CHICKEN

1 whole chicken, 3½ to 5 pounds	1 teaspoon salt
2 tablespoons butter, softened, or 2 tablespoons good–quality olive oil	½ teaspoon freshly ground black pepper
1 large onion, peeled, halved, and studded with 2 cloves	½ cup dry white wine
1 bouquet garni (several bay leaves, parsley stems, and thyme sprigs tied together with kitchen string)	1 cup chicken stock (page 59)

1. Preheat oven to 450° F. Trim chicken of any excess fat. Clip off wing tips. Pat bird dry with paper towels. Smear the butter over the entire surface of the chicken. (Or use a brush to coat with olive oil.)

2. Set chicken breast side up in a roasting pan. Season with salt and pepper. Place the onion halves and bouquet garni in the cavity of the chicken.

3. Place in the oven and immediately lower the temperature to 350° F. Cook until a fork can be easily inserted into the thickest part of the thigh and the juices run clear showing no trace of pink, 1 to 1½ hours. Baste often with the accumulating pan drippings.

4. When chicken is done, remove from oven, place on a platter, and cover to keep warm. Skim off the fat in the roasting pan and set the pan over high heat. Carefully pour in the wine and stir with a wire whisk to remove any cooked bits stuck to the bottom of the pan. Add the chicken stock and cook until reduced by half. Strain into a serving bowl and skim off any fat that rises to the top.

5. After the chicken has rested for at least 10 minutes, carve as shown on page 229. Serve hot with pan juices on the side.

ROAST CHICKEN WITH PARSLEY, PARMESAN, AND PINE NUTS

1 whole chicken, 3½ to 5 pounds
1 cup (loosely packed) parsley
   leaves, stems removed
¼ cup pine nuts, toasted
1 clove garlic, finely chopped
¼ cup grated Parmesan cheese

1 teaspoon red pepper flakes
¼ cup butter, cut into small pieces
2 tablespoons olive oil
salt and freshly ground black pepper
   to taste

1. Preheat oven to 450° F. Trim chicken of any excess fat. Clip off wing tips. Pat bird dry with paper towels.

2. In the workbowl of a food processor fitted with a metal blade, combine the parsley, pine nuts, garlic, and cheese. Process until the parsley is chopped, about 10 seconds. Add the red pepper flakes and butter and process until the mixture forms a paste.

3. Use your fingers to loosen the skin from the breast and tops of the legs of the chicken. Be careful not to break the skin. Gently force the butter under the skin and cover as much of the surface of the meat as is possible. Continue until all of the mixture is under the skin. Brush the olive oil over the top of the skin and season with salt and pepper.

4. Set the chicken breast side up in a lightly oiled roasting pan. Place in the oven and immediately lower the temperature to 350° F. Cook until a fork can be easily inserted into the thickest part of the thigh and the juices run clear showing no trace of pink, 1 to 1½ hours. Baste often with the accumulating pan juices.

5. When chicken is done, remove from oven, place on a platter, and cover to keep warm. After the chicken has rested for at least 10 minutes, carve as shown on page 229. Serve hot.

CURRY ROAST CHICKEN

1 whole chicken, 3½ to 5 pounds	½ teaspoon dry mustard
3 tablespoons plain yogurt	1 tablespoon lemon juice
2 to 3 teaspoons good-quality curry powder	salt and freshly ground black pepper to taste

1. Trim chicken of any excess fat. Clip off wing tips. Pat bird dry with paper towels.

2. Combine yogurt, curry powder, mustard, and lemon juice to make a paste. Completely cover chicken with this paste. Salt and pepper the bird. Let marinate, refrigerated, for 2 to 4 hours.

3. Preheat oven to 450° F. Set the chicken breast side up in a lightly oiled roasting pan. Cover with foil. Place in oven and immediately lower the temperature to 350° F. Cook until a fork can be easily inserted into the thickest part of the thigh and the juices run clear showing no trace of pink, 1 to 1½ hours. Baste often with the accumulating pan juices. Remove foil during the final 10 to 15 minutes of cooking.

4. When chicken is done, remove from oven, place on a platter, and cover to keep warm. After the chicken has rested for at least 10 minutes, carve as shown on page 229. Serve hot.

ASIAN ROAST CHICKEN

¼ cup soy sauce	1-by-2-inch piece fresh ginger, peeled and grated, or 1 teaspoon ground ginger
2 tablespoons dark sesame oil	
2 tablespoons rice vinegar	
2 cloves garlic, peeled and finely chopped	1 whole chicken, 3½ to 5 pounds
	¼ to 1½ cups water

1. In a small mixing bowl, combine soy sauce, sesame oil, vinegar, garlic, and ginger. Let stand at room temperature for several hours to blend flavors. Strain, if using fresh ginger, push down on solids to extract as much juice as possible.

2. Trim chicken of any excess fat. Clip off wing tips. Pat bird dry with paper towels. Brush evenly with prepared marinade. Refrigerate for 2 to 4 hours, brushing often with the marinade. Preheat oven to 450° F.

3. Set the chicken breast side up in a lightly oiled roasting pan. Place in oven and immediately lower the temperature to 350° F. Check every 10 to 15 minutes to be sure there is enough liquid in the bottom of the pan. If the juices cook away, add ¼ cup water. Repeat as necessary, adding only ¼ cup of water at a time. Baste often with the accumulating pan juices. Cook until a fork can be easily inserted into the thickest part of the thigh and the juices run clear showing no trace of pink, 1 to 1½ hours.

4. When chicken is done, remove from oven, place on a platter and cover to keep warm. After the chicken has rested for at least 10 minutes, carve as shown on page 229. Serve hot.

FRENCH ROAST CHICKEN

1 whole chicken, 3½ to 5 pounds	1 teaspoon salt
½ cup butter, softened	½ teaspoon freshly ground black
½ cup chopped fresh parsley	pepper
2 cloves garlic, chopped	2 tablespoons olive oil
1 teaspoon grated lemon rind	3 whole cloves garlic, peeled

1. Preheat oven to 450° F. Trim chicken of any excess fat. Clip off wing tips. Pat bird dry with paper towels.

2. Combine butter, parsley, chopped garlic, lemon rind, salt, and pepper. Blend well to make a thick paste. Use your fingers to loosen the skin from the breast and tops of the legs of the chicken. Be careful not to break the skin. Gently force the butter under the skin and cover as much of the surface of the meat as possible. Continue until all of the mixture is under the skin. Brush the olive oil over the top of the skin and season with salt and pepper. Set the chicken breast side up in a lightly oiled roasting pan.

3. Place in the oven and immediately lower the temperature to 350° F. Add whole cloves of garlic to the pan. Cook until a fork can be easily inserted into the thickest part of the thigh and the juices run clear showing no trace of pink, 1 to 1½ hours. Baste often with the accumulating pan juices.

4. When chicken is done, remove from oven, place on a platter, and cover to keep warm. After the chicken has rested for at least 10 minutes, carve as shown on page 229. Serve hot.

BROILED CHICKEN

Split a small broiler-fryer (1½ pounds) in half. Sprinkle with salt and pepper, rub with softened butter. Place rack as far away as possible from the heating unit of the preheated broiler. Broil until well browned and cooked through, 30 to 45 minutes. Watch carefully, turn often, and brush with butter or olive oil and drippings.

The compound butters found on page 363 are especially well suited for broiling chicken. Split small chickens in half and season with salt and pepper. Lift the skin carefully without tearing and use fingers to force the flavored butter over the flesh. Broil as for above.

For a lighter taste, try brushing the broilers with a savory mix of soy sauce, rice wine vinegar, and ground ginger just before cooking. Brush with the mixture several times when turning and broiling.

BROILED CHICKEN WITH ORANGE, HONEY, AND CRACKED PEPPER MARINADE

1 tablespoon cracked peppercorns
1 shallot, finely chopped
2 teaspoons finely grated orange
 zest
1 tablespoon honey

2 tablespoons fresh orange juice
2 tablespoons white wine vinegar
½ cup olive oil
1 orange, thinly sliced

1. In a mixing bowl, combine the peppercorns, shallot, orange zest, honey, juice, and vinegar. Mix well. Stirring constantly with a wire whisk, slowly add the olive oil.

2. Place chicken in a shallow dish. Tuck a few of the orange slices under the skin. Scatter the remaining ones on top. Pour marinade over the chicken halves and tightly cover with plastic wrap. Refrigerate for 4 to 12 hours, turning frequently. Broil as directed above.

Variation:

Herb Marinade: Combine 2 tablespoons finely chopped fresh herbs (thyme, rosemary, sage, chives, or parsley) with ¼ cup lemon juice, 1 clove crushed garlic and mix well. Stirring constantly with a wire whisk, slowly add ½ cup olive oil. Place chicken in a shallow dish. Place a thinly sliced small onion over chicken. Pour marinade over the chicken halves and tightly cover with plastic wrap. Refrigerate for 4 to 12 hours, turning frequently. Broil as directed above.

POACHED CHICKEN

Choose a stewing chicken that weighs 5 to 7 pounds. Trim off excess fat and cut into pieces or leave whole. Place in a large pot with quartered onions, peeled carrots cut into 1-inch pieces, celery cut into 1-inch pieces, crumpled bay leaves, salt, and whole peppercorns. Cover with cold water and bring almost to the boiling point over moderately high heat. Reduce heat and regulate so that the chicken barely simmers. Do not allow to boil. Cook until a fork can be inserted in the chicken with ease, about 1 hour. Skim often to remove scum that will come to the top. Let cool in broth. Strain broth and discard vegetables. When at room temperature, chill for several hours or overnight. Remove congealed fat from top. Serve the broth as a first course with a slice of bread (sprinkled with Parmesan cheese, if desired) on top. Remove the chicken from the bones and cut flesh into large chunks. Reheat in a small amount of the broth and serve with fresh, seasonal vegetables as a main course. The meat can be sliced cold for salads and sandwiches, too. The broth can be used as a base for any number of soups. (See the Soup Chapter, page 58.)

For Chicken and Dumplings, first follow procedures above. Make a Fricassee Sauce (page 401) using the cooking broth from the poached chicken. Combine chicken with the sauce. Season with salt and pepper. Top with Baking Powder Biscuits (page 475). Bake in hot oven until well browned.

OVEN-BROWNED POACHED CHICKEN

Prepare Poached Chicken, above. Sprinkle outside of cooked bird with salt, paprika, and ginger to taste and dredge well with flour. Heat 3 tablespoons chicken fat or butter in a roasting pan. Roll chicken in the melted fat. Bake in hot oven 10 or 20 minutes, basting often, until browned. If browned before ready to serve, reduce heat and cover closely, to keep meat juicy. Remove bird to a serving platter. Add 1 cup of water or chicken stock (page 59) to the pan and cook a few minutes, stirring in the brown bits that cling to the pan.

BRAISED CHICKEN

Braising is one of the most versatile and delicious ways to prepare poultry. In general, braising describes combining meat and vegetables with liquid and cooking them in a slow oven or simmering over very low heat. Stews and fricassees are types of braises. While the preparation of these dishes often differs in detail, the basic technique remains the same.

Low-priced legs, thighs, and wings, as well as whole chickens, are good for braising. Begin by browning the pieces in fat or oil. Remove the chicken from the pan and add chopped vegetables—usually carrots, onions, and celery. Cook until the vegetables are soft and beginning to color. Add the cooking liquid and scrape the bottom of the pan to incorporate the rich pan deposits. Return the meat to the pan and cover with a tight-fitting lid. Cook very gently until the meat is tender. A braise should never be allowed to boil. Too high a heat will toughen the chicken.

When done, strain the cooking liquid and cool it. When all the fat has come to the surface carefully skim it off. Once the braising liquid is clean, boil it over a very high heat to concentrate the flavors and give it a rich, sumptuous body. To make a classic fricassee, enrich the cooking liquid with egg yolks, cream, or flour.

OVEN-BRAISED CHICKEN

2 small broiling chickens, each cut
   into 4 pieces
¾ cup butter
¾ cup dry white wine

salt and freshly ground black pepper
   to taste
1 teaspoon chopped fresh tarragon
   (½ teaspoon dried)
1 cup chicken stock (page 59)

1. Preheat oven to 325° F. Trim chickens of excess fat and place skin side up in a large, shallow metal baking dish or roasting pan.

2. Melt butter, add wine and seasonings. Pour a bit over the chickens.

3. Bake in preheated oven until tender, about 1 hour. Baste frequently.

4. Remove chicken to a serving platter and keep warm. Pour off fat from the pan and on top of the stove, pour in the chicken stock. Use a wire whisk to pick up any bits left in the bottom of the pan. Bring to a boil over high heat to reduce slightly. Spoon a bit of concentrated juice over the chicken and serve any that remains on the side.

Variations:

Braised with Tomatoes and Garlic: Add 1 cup peeled, seeded, and coarsely chopped tomatoes and 1 clove finely minced garlic to the pan when the chicken goes into the oven. Proceed as for above. Add a teaspoon of tomato paste to the deglazed sauce if desired.

Braised with Lemon and Fennel: Add 2 lemons cut in half and 2 bulbs sliced fennel to the chicken in the baking pan above. Remove the fennel and lemon with the chicken when done. Discard the lemon. Use ¾ cup chicken stock and 1 tablespoon Pernod to deglaze the pan. Drain as much fat as is possible from the cooked fennel and puree in a food processor. Season to taste with salt and pepper and serve with the chicken and sauce.

Braised Barbecue Chicken: Prepare chicken as for above. Omit butter, wine, and chicken stock. Substitute Easy Barbecue Sauce on page 346. Use half of the sauce and cook as for above, basting frequently. Serve with remaining sauce.

Many braised dishes, stews, casseroles, and similar long-cooked preparations that generate their own sauce are perfect "do-ahead" dishes. Easily done in stages that can be carried out days in advance, these sauced preparations can be done in earthenware or glass baking dishes, refrigerated or frozen, and reheated in the oven or microwave. They make welcome additions to "bring-a-covered-dish" affairs as well as thoughtful comforting offerings to friends and neighbors. Use your imagination to mix in rice, potatoes, or cooked noodles to provide a one-dish meal. Fresh bread crumbs or olive oil drizzled on top will provide a crunchy, brown topping when reheated.

CHICKEN BRAISED IN RED WINE (COQ AU VIN)

½ pound slab bacon, cut into ½-inch pieces

3 carrots, peeled and coarsely chopped

2 ribs celery, coarsely chopped

2 small onions, peeled and coarsely chopped

2 3- to 5-pound chickens, cut into serving pieces

salt and freshly ground black pepper to taste

3 tablespoons flour

3 cups hearty red wine

2 bay leaves, crumpled

2 cloves garlic, crushed

several sprigs fresh thyme, or 1 teaspoon dried

20 to 25 pearl onions, peeled

2 tablespoons butter

pinch of salt

1 teaspoon sugar

1 tablespoon vegetable oil

½ pound mushrooms, halved or quartered

2 tablespoons chopped parsley

1. Cook bacon over moderately high heat until brown. Remove bacon from pan, drain on paper towels, and reserve. Add carrots, celery, and onions to the pan. Cook over low heat until soft, 10 to 15 minutes. Remove the vegetables and reserve.

2. Season the chicken pieces with salt and pepper. Place them in the pan and cook over moderately high heat until browned, turning frequently. Return the cooked vegetables to the pan. Sprinkle with flour and continue to cook, stirring, until the flour is lightly colored.

3. Pour in the wine and bring to a boil. Scrape the bottom of the pan with a wooden spoon to loosen all the cooked-on bits. Add bay leaves, garlic, and thyme. Reduce to a low simmer. Cover and cook gently until chicken is very tender, 45 minutes to an hour. Skim top of fat that rises to the surface.

4. When done, remove the chicken to a platter and keep warm. Strain the cooking liquid, pressing down hard on the cooked vegetables to extract flavor. Discard the vegetables.

5. Skim off all surface fat from the cooking liquid. In a saucepan, boil until slightly reduced and thickened. Season to taste with salt and pepper. (Note: Can be done in advance to this point. Let chicken and sauce come to room temperature. Refrigerate until ready to finish the dish.)

6. In a small sauté pan, combine the pearl onions with 1 tablespoon of the butter, a pinch of salt, and the sugar. Pour on enough cold water to barely cover. Cook over high heat, uncovered. Shake and stir the pan often. The water will boil away, allowing the onions to cook. When all liquid has evaporated, the sugar will start to caramelize the onions. Shake and stir constantly at this point. Allow onions to brown nicely but do not burn. Remove to drain on paper towels. Melt the remaining butter with the vegetable oil. Add the mushrooms and cook over high heat until well browned. Season to taste with salt and pepper and drain on paper towels.

7. Just before serving, combine the chicken, the cooked bacon bits, the browned onions, and the mushrooms with the sauce in a covered casserole. Bring to a simmer and season to taste with salt and pepper. Sprinkle the chopped parsley over for garnish. Serve very hot with noodles, rice, or potatoes.

CHICKEN FRICASSEE

1 stewing chicken, 5 to 7 pounds, cut into pieces
salt and freshly ground black pepper to taste
½ teaspoon ground ginger
1 small onion, peeled and coarsely chopped

2 ribs celery, trimmed and coarsely chopped
1 carrot, peeled and coarsely chopped
1 slice lemon
3 tablespoons chicken fat (page 243)
4 tablespoons flour

1. Begin this dish 24 hours before serving. Season chicken well with salt, pepper, and ginger.

2. In a large kettle or stew pot, cover the chicken with boiling water. Add the onion, celery, carrot, and lemon slice. Simmer until tender, about 1 hour.

3. Let chicken cool in the broth. Remove chicken and strain broth. Allow them to come to room temperature then refrigerate overnight. Remove the fat that has hardened on the surface of the broth.

4. In a skillet or frying pan large enough to hold all the chicken, melt the fat. Add the flour and stir well. Gradually add 2 cups of the chicken broth, stirring constantly to prevent lumps. Add chicken, cut into large pieces and reheat.

BRAISED CURRIED CHICKEN LEGS

8 chicken legs, about 2 pounds
salt and freshly ground black pepper to taste
2 tablespoons butter
2 tablespoons vegetable oil

1 medium onion, thinly sliced (about 1 cup)
4 tablespoons flour
1 to 2 tablespoons mild curry
2 cups chicken stock (page 59)

1. Preheat oven to 350° F. Season the chicken legs with salt and pepper to taste. In a large, covered, oven-proof casserole, combine the butter and oil. Melt over high heat. Add the chicken and cook over high heat until well browned, about 5 minutes, turning often. Remove and set aside.

2. Pour off all but 2 tablespoons of the cooking fat. Add onion, flour, and curry powder. Reduce heat to medium and stir until curry is slightly cooked and onions are barely softened, about 5 minutes. (Do not be alarmed if mixture seems dry at this point.) Add chicken stock all at once and whisk vigorously. (Lumps will appear but will be strained out at the end.) Bring mixture to a slow simmer, add chicken legs, cover and place in the center of the preheated oven. Cook until tender, about 35 minutes. Stir occasionally to insure even cooking.

3. When chicken is done, remove to a serving platter. Strain sauce over and serve immediately.

Panfried Chicken

Panfrying is a particularly good way to preserve the natural tenderness of young chicken. The chicken pieces are first seared in a hot pan to seal in the juices then finished over reduced heat. When done, the cooked chicken is removed. Fat is poured off and a delicious sauce made by deglazing with a flavorful liquid. The sauce can be enriched with butter, cream, or by reduction. A suitable garnish, usually a vegetable, can be added to cook with the chicken.

Boneless breast halves, fillets, and cutlets make quick meals when pan fried in a small amount of fat over medium-high heat, 3 to 5 minutes per side.

BASIC SAUTÉED CHICKEN BREASTS

4 halved, boneless, skinless chicken breasts	2 tablespoons oil
salt and freshly ground black pepper to taste	¼ cup wine, brandy, or any fortified wine
2 tablespoons butter	½ cup chicken stock (page 59)
	½ cup heavy cream

1. Trim breasts of any excess fat or gristle. Season well with salt and pepper.
2. In a sauté pan large enough to hold the breasts flat, melt the butter and oil. When sizzling hot, add the chicken. Cook over moderately high heat until well browned and cooked throughout, 3 to 5 minutes per side. Remove to a serving platter and cover to keep warm.
3. Pour off the fat. Place the pan back on the heat. Carefully pour in the wine. Stir vigorously with a wire whisk to loosen any cooked bits stuck to the bottom of the pan. Add the chicken stock. Reduce over high heat until only about 2 tablespoons of liquid remain. Add the cream and cook until reduced by half.
4. Pour off any accumulated juices from the chicken platter. Spoon the sauce over and serve hot.

(continued)

Variations:

With Balsamic Vinegar: Prepare chicken breasts as above through Step 2. Pour off the fat. Place the pan back on the heat. Omit the wine. Instead, carefully pour in ½ cup Balsamic vinegar (or any flavored vinegar). Add 2 minced shallots and cook over moderately high heat until vinegar is reduced by half and shallots are soft. Spoon over cooked chicken as for above.

With Tomato, Garlic, and Basil: Prepare chicken breasts as above through Step 2. Pour off the fat. Place the pan back on the heat. Omit the wine. Carefully pour in the chicken stock. Stir vigorously with a wire whisk to loosen any cooked bits stuck to the bottom of the pan. Add 1 cup peeled, seeded, coarsely chopped tomatoes and 2 cloves finely chopped garlic. Cook over high heat until sauce is thick and garlic is cooked through, about 3 minutes. Remove from heat and add 1 cup loosely packed, shredded basil. Stir to blend. Spoon over chicken as for above.

With Mushrooms and Cream: Prepare chicken breasts as above through Step 2. Pour off the fat. Place the pan back on the heat. Add 1 cup thinly sliced mushrooms and cook until they begin to brown, 1 to 1 ½ minutes. Carefully pour in ½ cup white wine and cook over high heat until only 2 tablespoons of liquid remain. Stir frequently. Add ½ cup heavy cream and cook until reduced by half. Spoon over chicken as for above.

With Mustard: Prepare chicken breasts as above through Step 2. Pour off the fat. Place the pan back on the heat. Carefully pour in ½ cup chicken stock. Stir vigorously with a wire whisk to loosen any cooked bits stuck to the bottom of the pan. Cook over high heat until only 2 tablespoons of liquid remain. Add ½ cup heavy cream and cook until reduced by half. Remove from heat and stir in 2 tablespoons Dijon mustard. Spoon over chicken as for above.

CHICKEN SAUTÉ WITH 40 CLOVES OF GARLIC

1 broiler-fryer, 3 to 5 pounds, cut into 8 pieces	2 tablespoons butter
	2 tablespoons oil
salt and freshly ground black pepper to taste	40 cloves of garlic, unpeeled
	½ cup chicken stock (page 59)

1. Season chicken to taste with salt and pepper. In a large sauté pan with a cover, melt the butter with the oil over moderately high heat. When very hot, add the seasoned chicken and brown well.

2. Reduce heat to a simmer and add the garlic. Cover tightly and let cook until chicken is tender, 30 to 45 minutes.

3. Remove the chicken to a serving platter and keep warm. Pour off fat from pan. Empty the garlic into a sieve and drain off as much fat as possible.

4. Return the sauté pan to the stove. Pour in the chicken stock, bring to a boil, and reduce by half. Use a spatula or spoon to work the cooked garlic through the sieve. Add to the reduced pan juices.

5. Drain off excess liquid from the serving platter. Pour over the pan juices with garlic and serve at once.

CHICKEN WITH PEPPERS, OLIVES, AND TOMATOES

1 broiler/fryer, 3 to 5 pounds, cut into 8 pieces
salt and freshly ground black pepper to taste
2 tablespoons olive oil
3 sweet peppers (assorted colors), cored, deveined, and cut into strips
1 medium onion, thinly sliced
4 cloves garlic, coarsely chopped

1 pound ripe tomatoes, peeled, seeded, and chopped, or 1 small can whole tomatoes, drained
¼ teaspoon dried red pepper flakes (optional)
4 ounces black olives, pitted and coarsely chopped
2 tablespoons finely chopped fresh parsley

1. Season chicken to taste with salt and pepper. In a large sauté pan with a cover, heat the oil over moderately high heat. When very hot, add the seasoned chicken and brown well. When the chicken is browned on all sides, remove from pan and drain on paper towels.

2. Add the peppers, onions, and garlic to the pan. Cook just until soft. Be careful not to let the onions or garlic brown. Remove the cooked vegetables from the pan and reserve.

3. Add the tomatoes and cook for several minutes over high heat. Stir to incorporate the cooked bits of meat on the bottom of the pan. Add the chicken pieces and peppers, onions, garlic, and red pepper flakes, if desired. Reduce heat to a simmer. Cover tightly and let cook until chicken is tender, about 30 minutes.

4. Remove chicken to a serving platter and pour the cooked vegetables on top. Sprinkle with olives and parsley. Serve immediately.

RENDERED CHICKEN FAT

Wash fat. Cut into small pieces and place in a small saucepan or skillet with ½ inch of water. Cook over very low heat until most of the fat is melted. Add ½ onion, diced, and continue cooking until fat pieces are crisp. Strain fat into jars, cover, and store. To make crisp cracklings, cook a little longer, until brown. Drain on paper towels and season with salt and pepper. Cracklings may be added to chopped liver and pâtés for an interesting texture and flavor.

Note: Duck, goose, or turkey fat may be rendered in the same way. Can be frozen in small containers and defrosted as needed.

CHICKEN PAPRIKA

2 broiler-fryer chickens, cut up
1 teaspoon salt
¼ cup flour
1 tablespoon paprika

¼ cup butter
1½ cups hot water or milk
2 to 3 tablespoons sour cream

1. Season chicken with salt. Combine flour and paprika. Roll chicken pieces in flour.
2. In a frying pan, melt the butter. When sizzling, add chicken pieces and cook over medium heat until brown, turning often. Add hot water or milk. Cover and simmer until tender, about 30 minutes. Just before serving, stir in sour cream. Do not heat after this or sauce will curdle.

DEEP-FRIED CHICKEN

All parts of the chicken can be deep-fried. Crisp on the outside and tenderly moist on the inside, great fried chicken calls for more careful time and attention than any other technique. Keep the following points in mind:

The oil used must be one that can withstand high temperatures. Most vegetable oils on the market are satisfactory but peanut, safflower, cottonseed, and corn oils are best as they are less likely to break down or smoke when subjected to intense heat. Chicken should be fried at 350° F for best results.

Be sure to carefully monitor the process. Most chicken pieces will cook within 15 to 20 minutes. Regulate the heat to insure that the chicken is not browning too fast. The outside should not be too brown before the inside is cooked. Too little heat will render the chicken soggy and heavily greasy. A thermometer for the oil is helpful for beginners.

Do not overcrowd the pan. If the pan is too full, the excess moisture will produce steam and prevent crispiness. Season well with salt and pepper before frying. Drain thoroughly when cooked and serve as soon as possible for maximum effect.

FRIED CHICKEN

The original Settlement recipe called for frying in butter. While imparting good flavor, butter is more likely to break down and burn at the desired temperature (350° F).

½ cup flour
salt and freshly ground black pepper
　to taste
½ teaspoon ground ginger

1 broiler-fryer chicken (1½ to 2
　pounds), cut into parts
½ cup cooking oil or butter

1. In a paper or plastic bag, combine flour with salt, pepper, and ginger. Add chicken pieces, a few at a time, and shake to coat thoroughly.

2. In a large skillet or frying pan, heat oil to 350° F. Add chicken, skin side down, cook about 10 minutes, turning to brown all sides. Reduce heat to medium low, cover, and cook until a fork can be easily inserted, about 20 minutes.

OVEN-FRIED CHICKEN

1 broiler-fryer chicken (1½ to 2 pounds), cut into serving pieces
salt and freshly ground black pepper to taste

¼ cup butter, softened, or poultry fat
½ cup finely ground breadcrumbs

1. Preheat oven to 400° F. Season chicken pieces with salt and pepper. Rub with softened butter and coat with breadcrumbs.

2. Place chicken in an even layer in a shallow roasting pan. Bake until crispy and cooked through, about 30 minutes.

BUFFALO CHICKEN WINGS

The following recipe is an American specialty that was created in a Buffalo, N.Y. tavern to serve with drinks at the bar. It is now a popular appetizer or first course that makes good use of one of the most tender, flavorful, and economical parts of the chicken. The cool crispness of the celery and the creaminess of the dressing help cut the spiciness of the hot pepper flavorings.

Cut tips off 25 to 30 chicken wings, discard, and cut remaining 2 sections in half at the joint. One part should look like a miniature drumstick and the other one wider with 2 small bones. Prepare as for fried chicken, but add ½ teaspoon cayenne pepper to the flour before dredging. Fry as is directed, shortening the cooking time to 10 to 15 minutes. Drain well and pour over the following sauce: Melt ½ cup butter and add ¼ cup vinegar and 1 teaspoon hot pepper sauce (or more if desired). Stir to blend and pour over hot chicken wings.

Arrange wings on a large serving platter. Serve with a doubled recipe of Roquefort Dressing (page 132) in a bowl for dipping. Peel 5 to 6 stalks of celery and cut into 3-inch-long, ¼-inch-thick pieces and chill. Serve to dip with wings. Provide a bottle of hot sauce for those who desire to shake on extra heat.

CHICKEN LIVERS

SAUTÉED CHICKEN LIVERS

1 pound chicken livers, cut in half
½ teaspoon salt
⅛ teaspoon paprika
flour

3 tablespoons butter
1 onion, finely chopped
½ cup chicken stock (page 59)

1. Season livers well with salt and paprika. Dredge in flour.
2. In a frying pan, melt butter over medium heat. When sizzling, add onion and cook until soft and beginning to brown. Add livers and cook until evenly browned. Pour in chicken stock, heat to the boiling point. Serve on toast if desired.

CHICKEN LIVER TIMBALES

1 tablespoon butter
12 chicken livers
½ small onion, finely chopped
salt and freshly ground black pepper
  to taste

pinch of cayenne pepper
1 teaspoon chopped parsley
5 eggs, separated
2 tablespoons breadcrumbs

1. Preheat oven to 350° F. In a frying pan, melt the butter over medium heat. When sizzling, add the livers and chopped onion. Cook over low heat until the livers are evenly browned and the onion is soft, about 5 minutes. Remove from heat.

2. Press liver and onions through a sieve or puree in a food processor fitted with a metal blade. Season paste with salt, pepper, and cayenne. Stir in parsley, egg yolks, and 1 tablespoon breadcrumbs and mix well.
3. Beat egg whites until stiff. Gently fold into the liver mixture.
4. Fill greased timbale molds with the mixture. Sprinkle remaining breadcrumbs on top.
5. Bake molds on a pan half filled with hot water for ½ hour. Unmold and serve hot with Mushroom Sauce (page 401).

CHICKEN LIVERS WITH MUSHROOMS

4 slices bacon, cut into small dice
½ pound chicken livers, cut in half
½ pound mushrooms, sliced
salt and freshly ground black pepper
    to taste

2 teaspoons flour
½ cup light cream

   1. In a frying pan, cook the bacon until crisp. Remove from pan and drain on paper towels. Sauté livers and mushrooms in remaining fat just until the livers begin to brown and the mushrooms start to soften, about 4 minutes. Season with salt and pepper.

   2. Combine flour and cream. Pour over livers and cook until smooth. Add bacon and serve hot on toast.

CHICKEN POT PIE

1 small chicken, 3 to 5 pounds,
   trimmed of excess fat
1 medium onion, peeled and quartered
2 stalks celery, sliced
4 to 5 carrots, peeled
1 cup fresh or frozen green peas

½ pound mushrooms
3 tablespoons butter
salt and freshly ground black pepper to
   taste
2 tablespoons flour

   1. Place the chicken in a large pot. Add the onion, celery, and 2 of the carrots coarsely chopped. Pour in enough cold water to barely cover. Bring to a boil over moderately high heat. Reduce heat to a simmer and cook gently until very tender, about 45 minutes. Remove from heat and let the chicken cool to room temperature in the broth.

   2. Preheat oven to 450° F. Transfer the chicken to a work surface. Strain the cooking liquid, discarding the vegetables. You should have about 2 cups liquid. If you have more than this amount, boil over high heat and reduce to this measure. If you have less than this amount, add enough water to measure 2 cups. Remove the chicken from the bones and cut or shred into large chunks. Set aside.

   3. Cut the remaining carrots into ¼ inch cubes. Blanch in boiling water for 2 minutes. Refresh under cold running water. Set aside. If using fresh green peas blanch them in boiling water for 2 minutes. Refresh under cold running water. Set aside.

   4. Cut the mushrooms into halves or quarters. Melt 1 tablespoon of the butter in a sauté pan. Add the mushrooms and brown over moderately high heat. Season with salt and pepper. Set aside.

   5. In a saucepan, melt the remaining butter and add the flour. Stir until well blended and lightly colored. Pour in the 2 cups of cooking liquid and stir vigorously with a wire whisk. Bring to a boil and cook over moderately high heat until thickened.

(continued)

Season to taste with salt and pepper. Add the chicken, the carrots, peas, and mushrooms. Blend and season to taste again.

6. Pour into a 6-cup oven-proof baking dish or soufflé mold. Top with Baking Powder Biscuits (page 475). Make slashes and crimp edges. Bake in preheated oven until crust is golden brown. Serve immediately.

Leftovers

CHICKEN HASH

2 tablespoons butter
½ cup celery, thinly sliced
½ cup onion, finely chopped
2 tablespoons flour
2 cups chicken stock (page 59)

4 cups cooked chicken (or turkey), minced
salt and freshly ground black pepper to taste
2 tablespoons chopped parsley

1. Melt the butter in a small saucepan. Add the celery and onion. Cook over low heat until vegetables are soft and translucent, stirring often.

2. Sprinkle with the flour. Stir to blend and cook gently over low heat until slightly cooked but not browned, about 3 minutes. Pour in the chicken stock. Increase heat to medium-high. Stir and cook until thickened to a creamy consistency. Add chicken and season to taste with salt and pepper. Remove from heat and add the parsley.

3. Serve hot in pastry shells, on toast, or with Rice Pilaf (page 176).

CHICKEN CROQUETTES

3½ cups cooked chicken, very finely ground
2 cups Thick White Sauce (page 400)
2 teaspoons lemon juice
1 tablespoon chopped parsley
salt and freshly ground black pepper to taste

pinch of cayenne pepper
very finely chopped onion, to taste
dry bread or cracker crumbs for coating
1 egg, lightly beaten

1. Combine chicken and sauce. Add lemon juice, parsley, salt, peppers, and onions. Spread mixture on a platter to cool.

2. When cool enough to handle, shape into cylinders about 2 to 3 inches long. Roll in bread or cracker crumbs and let stand 5 minutes.

3. Dip croquettes in egg and again in crumbs. Fry in deep hot fat (375° F) until golden brown and crusty, about 3 minutes. Drain on paper towels.

POULTRY STUFFINGS

Small birds require about 1 cup stuffing per pound of weight; larger birds slightly less. Extra stuffing may be baked in a greased casserole alongside the bird for about 1 hour. Stuffing expands during cooking so fill birds lightly. Fill the body and neck cavity with the same or different stuffings. Ingredients for stuffings may be prepared ahead and chilled until needed, but the bird must not be filled until just before roasting. Stuffing should be removed from the bird immediately after roasting and always kept separately to prevent the growth of harmful bacteria.

Most stuffings are based on bread but rice or potatoes may also be used. Bread for stuffing should be several days old. When the bread is soaked in milk or water before blending, the stuffing will be moist and compact. If the bread is simply tossed with fat, seasonings, and other ingredients, the stuffing will be crumbly.

BREAD STUFFING

4 cups dry bread cubes
salt and freshly ground black pepper
  to taste
⅛ teaspoon ground ginger
¼ teaspoon poultry seasoning

1 tablespoon chopped fresh herbs
  (thyme, parsley, or sage),
  optional
2 tablespoons butter or fat, melted
1 egg, slightly beaten
1 small onion, finely chopped

Soak bread in cold water and squeeze dry. Season with salt, pepper, ginger, poultry seasoning, and herbs. Pour in melted butter and mix thoroughly. Stir in the egg and onion. Or, heat the butter in a large skillet. Add the soaked and dried bread and stir until the butter is absorbed. Add the seasonings and herbs. Stir in the egg and onion. Cool before filling bird.

Note: The liver, heart, and gizzard of the bird can be cooked until tender, finely chopped and added to this dressing. Or add ¼ pound browned pork or liver sausage.

Variations:

Orange Stuffing: Add 2 tablespoons orange juice and grated rind of 1 orange to the above recipe. Orange juice and rind may also be added to the pan gravy.

Potato Stuffing: Add 2 cups hot, mashed white potatoes or sweet potatoes to the above recipe. Use for turkey or goose. This stuffing is also suitable for lamb or veal breast.

CORN BREAD STUFFING

8 cups corn bread crumbs
½ teaspoon dried thyme
¼ teaspoon dried oregano
salt and freshly ground black pepper
   to taste

¾ cup butter or fat
1 onion, chopped
½ cup chopped celery
3 tablespoons chopped parsley

1.   Combine crumbs with thyme and oregano. Add salt and pepper to taste.

2.   In a skillet, melt butter or fat. Add onion and cook until translucent. Stir in crumbs and toss well. Add celery and parsley. Cool thoroughly before stuffing bird.

Variation:

Corn Bread Oyster Stuffing: Add 1 dozen large oysters, coarsely chopped, and a little bit of oyster liquid to the above recipe.

ALMOND STUFFING FOR TURKEY

4 cups dry breadcrumbs
¾ cup milk
1 cup butter, melted
3 eggs, well beaten
2 cups diced celery

½ onion, grated
1 cup chopped almonds
salt and freshly ground black pepper
   to taste
¼ teaspoon ginger

Soak breadcrumbs in milk and squeeze dry. Stir in the butter and eggs. Add the celery, onions, and almonds. Season with salt and pepper. Add the ginger.

CHESTNUT STUFFING FOR TURKEY

4 cups large chestnuts
¼ cup butter, melted
salt and freshly ground black pepper
   to taste

1 egg, beaten
2 cups breadcrumbs, or hot mashed
   sweet potatoes
turkey liver, finely chopped

1.   Blanch and shell chestnuts. Cook until tender in boiling salted water, about 15 minutes. Drain and rice.

2.   Add butter to riced chestnuts. Season with salt and pepper. Stir in egg. Add breadcrumbs or potatoes and liver. Cool before stuffing bird.

LIVER STUFFING FOR SQUABS   *Makes enough for 6 squabs.*

2 tablespoons butter
2 eggs
6 squab livers, lightly sautéed and finely chopped

salt and freshly ground black pepper to taste
about ⅓ cup fresh breadcrumbs

With an electric or hand mixer, cream butter. Add eggs and beat well. Using a rubber spatula, fold in the livers. Season well with salt and pepper. Add enough breadcrumbs to form a soft dressing that will drop from the spoon.

BREAD STUFFING FOR GOOSE OR DUCK

4 cups dry bread cubes
2 tablespoons butter or fat
1 small onion, finely chopped
¼ cup celery root, peeled and diced
goose or duck liver, gizzard, and heart, lightly sautéed and finely chopped

½ cup strained tomatoes
salt and freshly ground black pepper to taste
⅛ teaspoon ginger
⅛ teaspoon nutmeg
1 egg, well beaten

1. Soak bread in cold water and squeeze dry.
2. In a large skillet, melt the butter or fat. Add the onion and celery root. Cook until soft and the onion is translucent. Add bread cubes and cook until the cubes begin to brown. Stir often.
3. Add the organ meats and tomatoes. Season well with salt and pepper. Add the ginger and nutmeg. Stir in egg and toss well. Cool stuffing before filling bird.

PRUNE AND APPLE STUFFING FOR DUCK OR GOOSE

¼ pound pitted prunes
5 sour apples, peeled, cored, and quartered
1 cup breadcrumbs

½ teaspoon poultry seasoning
salt and freshly ground black pepper to taste

1. Follow directions for Stewed Prunes, page 413. Cut prunes into quarters.
2. Cook apples in a very small amount of water until half done. Add prunes, breadcrumbs, and poultry seasoning. Season well with salt and pepper. Mix well. Cool before stuffing bird.

STUFFING FOR GAME

1 slice wheat bread, soaked in milk
2 hard rolls, crumbled
1 onion, finely chopped
3 or 4 slices of lightly cooked
   bacon, crumbled
1 tablespoon butter, melted
3 eggs, beaten

1 teaspoon finely chopped orange
   rind
1 teaspoon finely chopped lemon
   rind
3 apples, peeled, cored, and cut into
   cubes
salt and freshly ground black pepper
   to taste

Combine soaked bread and crumbled rolls with the onion and bacon. Stir in butter and eggs. Add the orange and lemon rind and apple cubes. Season well with salt and pepper. Stuff bird just before cooking.

CHICKEN AND THE MICROWAVE

Like fish, chicken cooks well in the microwave because the meat retains its natural nutrients and flavor. Frozen chicken is speedily defrosted in the microwave and leftovers may be quickly reheated.

Helpful Hints
(Microwave information courtesy of the National Broiler Council.)

* Microwave ovens vary, so always follow manufacturer's instructions. In general allow 6 minutes per pound for cooking chicken.
* Chicken parts microwave best on high, whole birds on medium.
* Place meatier parts toward outside of the dish, bony parts to the center.
* Rearrange and/or turn parts halfway through microwaving to promote even cooking.
* Cook whole bird breast side down for first half of cooking time, then breast side up until done.
* Cover chicken with wax paper or plastic wrap.
* For best results, add salt after instead of before cooking.
* Check for doneness after the bird has rested for 10 minutes. (The bird continues to cook in its own heat outside of the microwave.) When microwaving chicken, it is best to undercook and test for doneness. If a fork cannot be inserted with ease, return to oven briefly for additional cooking time.

Roasting Whole Birds
Whole chickens can be microwaved plain or brushed with melted butter or with a variety of sauces or glazes.

For best results dry chicken with paper towel and place breast side down on roasting rack or inverted saucer in a microwave dish. If desired, brush on butter or sauce; cover loosely with waxed paper and microwave on medium 15 minutes more. Rotate dish several times during cooking.

Sprinkle chicken with salt or seasoning, if desired, cover tightly, and let stand 5 minutes before checking for doneness. Return to oven for additional cooking if fork cannot be easily inserted and juices do not run clear.

Reheating Cooked Chicken

To reheat, place cooked chicken in casserole or serving dish. Cover with paper towel or waxed paper. Microwave on high 1½ to 2 minutes per serving or until heated through.

If microwave temperature probe is used, insert in chicken and then microwave on high until the probe registers 150° to 160° F.

Defrosting

Defrosting is quick and easy in the microwave but times vary according to the form in which the chicken is frozen—whole, cut up, or select parts. In general, follow these steps:

- Remove chicken from freezer wrapper.
- Place on roasting rack in shallow microwave dish.
- Cover with waxed paper or freezer paper.
- Microwave on defrost or medium-low 2 minutes; let stand 2 minutes. Repeat.
- Turn chicken as it thaws, taking care that it does not begin to cook.
- Giblets defrost quicker than other parts; remove when pliable.
- Bonier parts such as wings thaw before meatier parts. A whole chicken requires more time than parts.
- Defrosted chicken feels soft, moist, and cold, not hard and stiff.

Turkey

TURKEY TIPS

Turkey is not just a roasted bird served only on Thanksgiving Day anymore. Producers have found that there is a market for the tender, lean flesh of this easy-to-raise poultry. By careful marketing, the turkey industry has made available all sorts of parts that can be bought separately at fairly reasonable prices. Ground turkey, huge turkey legs with meat hearty enough to treat like beef, and plump breasts for white meat enthusiasts are readily available. The following information will be helpful for choosing and preparing new ideas when "talking turkey" in today's modern kitchen, no matter what time of year.

Selection

- Choose fresh or frozen turkey that is tightly wrapped in packaging free of tears.
- Check label to identify "expiration," "sell by," and "best if used by" dates.

Handling and Defrosting

- Take fresh or frozen turkey home immediately after purchasing and keep frozen or refrigerated until ready to use.
- Thaw whole bird or turkey parts in the refrigerator, *never on kitchen countertops*.
- Only refreeze turkey if ice crystals are still present in meat; otherwise cook immediately.
- To thaw a whole turkey, place wrapped turkey on a tray in refrigerator. Allow 5 hours per pound to completely thaw.

Preparation

- All equipment and materials used for thawing, storage, preparation, and serving of poultry must be clean.
- Wash hands thoroughly with hot, soapy water before and after handling raw poultry.
- Wash dishcloth or sponge after cleaning up raw poultry juices.
- Clean cutting surfaces, knives, pans, cutting equipment, and thermometers after and between preparation steps of raw poultry and other foods.
- Use hard plastic or acrylic cutting boards instead of wooden surfaces to prepare poultry.
- Use a clean plate for serving cooked poultry.

Cooking

- Cook turkey immediately after thawing.
- Do not partially cook turkey. Finish the cooking once it is started.
- Stuff turkey just before cooking, or cook stuffing separately.

Storage

- Store turkey in coldest part of refrigerator or freezer.
- Uncooked turkey, like any other perishable meat, should never be held at room temperature for more than two hours.
- To store turkey in the freezer, rewrap prepackaged turkey in freezer paper or heavy foil. Label and date. Keep frozen turkey at 0° F.
- Fresh turkey parts will keep in the freezer for up to 6 months, whole turkey for 12 months. Turkey deli products keep 1 to 2 months frozen. Leftover cooked turkey can be frozen up to 4 months.
- Keep turkey in the refrigerator at 40° F or below. Allow space around food for circulation of cool air.
- Fresh turkey in its original wrapping will keep 3 to 4 days. Leftover cooked turkey will keep 1 to 2 days.
- Always refrigerate cooked turkey in covered containers.
- Keep hot turkey dishes hot (140° F or above) and cold foods cold (40° F or below).
- Remove stuffing from turkey right after cooking and place in separate container before storing uneaten turkey in the refrigerator.
- Reheat leftovers thoroughly to at least 165° F. Boil leftover gravy for one minute before serving.

All information courtesy of the National Turkey Federation.

TURKEY PARTS AND HOW LONG TO COOK THEM

Exact cooking times will vary depending on weight and thickness of turkey parts used, and intensity of heat. Here is a general guideline.

Cutlets: Sauté a ¼–inch-thick cutlet 2 to 3 minutes on each side over medium-high heat.

Breast Steaks: Broil a ¾-inch steak 6 inches from source of heat, or braise 5 to 7 minutes on each side.

Tenderloins: Bake at 400° F for 18 to 30 minutes; broil or grill 6 inches from source of heat, 8 to 12 minutes per side.

Drumsticks, Wings, Wing Drumettes, and Thighs: Bake at 325° F for 1 to 1¾ hours; braise covered for 1 to 1½ hours over low heat, or in a 350° F oven. Barbecue on covered grill or in foil wrap 1 to 1¾ hours.

Breast and Breast Portions: Roast at 325° F for 15 to 20 minutes per pound. Barbecue 4 to 6 inches from heat source on covered grill or in foil wrap 11 to 18 minutes per pound.

Boneless Turkey Roasts: Roast at 325° F 35 to 45 minutes per pound.

Stir Fries: 5 minutes over medium-high heat.

Kebabs: Grill or broil 1-inch cubes 6 inches from source of heat, 4 to 5 minutes per side.

Stew, Goulash, or Ragout: Brown 1½-inch cubes over medium-high heat before adding to remaining ingredients. Heat 10 to 12 minutes.

All information courtesy of the National Turkey Federation.

ROAST TURKEY

Preheat oven to 325° F. Season bird with salt, pepper, and ground ginger. Stuff if desired and truss like a chicken (page 222). Place turkey on a rack in a shallow roasting pan, breast side up. Brush skin with ½ cup melted butter or fat. To keep turkey moist, cover top with a double thickness of cheesecloth or aluminum foil and baste often during roasting. Roast according to timetable (page 258). Turkey is done when thickest part of drumstick feels soft when pressed between fingers or when thermometer inserted in thickest part of drumstick registers 180° F. (Be careful that the thermometer does not touch the bone.) Remove strings and skewers and serve turkey garnished as desired.

TURKEY ROASTED IN FOIL

A whole turkey of any size may be cooked at a high oven temperature wrapped in aluminum foil. This method is particularly suitable for cooking larger birds, weighing 16 to 24 pounds. Preheat oven to 450° F and prepare turkey as for Roast Turkey, above. Place turkey in center of a foil strip long enough to meet on top of bird, plus 12 inches. If the standard 18-inch foil is not wide enough, splice two sheets of foil with a double fold pressed flat. Bring ends of foil together over breast of turkey and make double fold to fasten above the bird. Bend sides of foil up high enough to prevent drippings from escaping into pan, but do not seal. Package should not be airtight. Place turkey—breast up—in shallow pan, but not on a rack. Cook to within 30 to 40 minutes of total cooking time given in chart below. Carefully open foil. Continue cooking until bird tests done and is browned.

COOKING TIMES FOR ROASTING STUFFED TURKEY WRAPPED IN FOIL AT 450° F

(Turkey is done when meat thermometer inserted in drumstick registers 180° F.)

Size of Bird	Cooking Time
6 to 8 pounds	2¼ to 3¼ hours
8 to 12 pounds	3 to 4 hours
12 to 16 pounds	3½ to 4½ hours
16 to 20 pounds	4 to 5 hours

ROAST HALF-TURKEY

Rub cavity of uncooked half-turkey with salt or seasoning. Place cut side down on rack in shallow pan. Brush top with melted butter and cover with cheesecloth or aluminum foil, as for whole turkey, and baste often with additional butter and/or pan drippings. Roast according to timetable (page 258). If stuffing is desired, remove turkey to a platter when half done. Place a double thickness of well-greased aluminum foil on rack. Shape a mound of dressing on the foil the shape of the cavity, put the turkey half over it, and finish roasting.

BROILED TURKEY

4- to 6-pound turkey, split in half
½ lemon
butter, melted

salt and freshly ground black pepper
to taste

1. Cut off wing tips or fold them back against the cut side of the bird. Rub with lemon, melted butter, and season well with salt and pepper.

2. Lay turkey on broiling pan, skin side down. Broil as far as possible from the source of heat, 8 to 10 inches. The surface should begin to brown after about 20 minutes. Cook until well browned, about 40 minutes. Turn skin side to the heat and continue to broil until skin is browned and crisp and the turkey cooked through, about 40 minutes longer. Baste occasionally with pan drippings and more butter to keep surface moist. When done the drumstick should be soft to the pressure of a finger and the leg should move easily in the joint. If necessary, turn again and finish cooking. Divide into quarters for serving.

BRAISED TURKEY LEGS

4 turkey legs, about 3 pounds
salt and freshly ground black pepper
to taste
¼ pound slab bacon, cut into small
dice

1 large onion, chopped
2 carrots, peeled and chopped
2 celery ribs, thinly sliced
1 clove garlic, crushed
½ cup rich chicken stock (page 59)

1. Preheat oven to 325° F. Trim legs of any excess fat. Season with salt and pepper. In a sauté pan, cook the bacon over moderately high heat. When browned and fat is rendered, remove cooked bacon and set aside.

2. Brown the legs in the hot bacon fat. Remove to a heavy, oven-proof casserole with a lid. Pour off all but 2 tablespoons of the fat. Add the onions, carrots, celery, and cooked bacon. Cook over moderately high heat until vegetables are softened, stirring often to prevent scorching. Add to the turkey in the casserole along with the clove of garlic.

3. Pour the chicken stock into the pan in which the turkey and vegetables have browned. Stir to pick up any bits left in the bottom of the pan. Bring to a boil then pour over the chicken and vegetables in the casserole. Cover tightly.

4. Cook in the preheated oven until turkey is very tender, about 1½ hours. Remove the legs and set aside. Strain the cooking liquid through a sieve, pressing down to extract as much flavor as possible. Discard the solids. Let the strained liquid come to room temperature. Skim off fat that accumulates on top. (If time permits, after liquid has come to room temperature, refrigerate several hours or overnight. Fat will be congealed and easy to remove.)

Recipe can be done ahead to this point. Chill braising liquid and legs tightly covered in the refrigerator. Let come to room temperature before proceeding.

5. Bring cooking liquid to a boil over high heat in a heavy saucepan. Reduce by half over high heat. Season to taste with salt and pepper.

6. Return legs to an oven-proof casserole. Spoon over a small amount of the sauce, cover, and reheat gently in 350° F oven for 15 to 20 minutes. Arrange on a serving platter, spoon over a spoonful or two of sauce, and pour the rest of the sauce in a sauce boat to pass separately. Serve hot with rice.

TURKEY AND MUSHROOM MEAT LOAF

1 pound mushrooms, cleaned and
   cut in halves or quarters
juice of 1 lemon
1 onion, finely chopped
1 medium red pepper, finely diced
2 celery ribs, thinly sliced

1 pound ground turkey
¾ cup fresh breadcrumbs
2 tablespoons freshly chopped
   parsley
1 egg
salt and freshly ground black pepper
   to taste

1. In the bowl of a food processor fitted with the metal blade, combine the mushrooms with the lemon juice and the onion. (This might have to be done in 2 batches if the food processor is small. Simply add half the lemon juice and half the onion with each batch.) Process with quick pulses several times, scrape down sides, and repeat until mushrooms are finely chopped and onion is incorporated.

2. In a heavy-bottomed, nonreactive saucepan, combine the mushroom mixture with the red pepper and celery. Cook over moderately high heat until mushrooms start to exude moisture. (Mushrooms will give off much liquid. This evaporates quickly and will result in a smooth paste that will help bind the meat loaf.) Stir constantly until mixture is very thick and all liquid has cooked off, about 10 minutes. Empty into a bowl and allow to cool to room temperature before proceeding.

This recipe can be done in advance to this point. After coming to room temperature, cover tightly and refrigerate until ready to use.

3. In a bowl, combine the cooked mushroom mixture, turkey, breadcrumbs, parsley, and egg. Work quickly, stirring and/or mixing just enough to blend. Do not overwork or meat loaf will be tough. Season with salt and pepper. (To avoid eating raw turkey, cook a spoonful or two in vegetable oil before adjusting the seasoning.)

4. Preheat oven to 350° F. Lightly oil a 1-quart loaf pan with olive oil. Gently pack in the turkey and mushroom mixture. Cover loosely with an oiled piece of aluminum foil. Bake until there are no traces of pink and juices run clear, 45 minutes to 1 hour. Let rest in pan for 10 minutes. There will be an excess amount of liquid given off by the vegetables as the loaf cooks. Use a spatula or a small plate to hold the meatloaf in place as you tilt the pan to pour off excess liquid. Carefully unmold onto a serving platter. Pour off excess liquid again and spoon over a small amount of warmed Basic Tomato Sauce (page 405). Serve the remaining sauce on the side. Garnish with additional chopped parsley if desired.

TURKEY ROASTING TIMES
Open Roasting Pan Method at 325° F

Internal Temperatures
To Be Reached:
Thigh 180—185° F
Breast—170° F
Stuffing—160° to 165° F

Type of Turkey	*Ready to Cook Weight* *(pounds)*	*Roasting Time* *(hours)*
Whole Turkey	6 to 8	2¼ to 3¼
(Unstuffed)	8 to 12	3 to 4
	12 to 16	3½ to 4½
	16 to 20	4 to 5
	20 to 24	4½ to 5½
Whole Turkey (Stuffed)	6 to 8	3 to 3½
	8 to 12	3½ to 4½
	12 to 16	4 to 5
	16 to 20	4½ to 5½
	20 to 24	5 to 6½
Frozen Prestuffed Turkey	7 to 9	5 to 5½
	9 to 11	5½ to 6
	11 to 14	6 to 6½
	14 to 16	6½ to 7
Turkey Breast and Parts	2 to 4	1½ to 2
	3 to 5	1½ to 2½
	5 to 7	2 to 2½

Standing Time Before Slicing:
Whole Turkey   15 minutes
Turkey Breast   10 minutes

Duck

ROAST DUCKLING

1 5-pound duckling
salt and freshly ground black pepper
   to taste

ground ginger
1 cup hot duck stock (page 260) or
   water

   1. Preheat oven to 450° F. Wipe duckling with paper towels inside and out. Season well with salt, pepper, and ginger. If desired, wings and legs may be tied together under the back, but trussing is not necessary, especially if wing tips are cut off.

   2. Place bird on a rack and roast in the preheated oven. After 15 minutes, reduce heat to 350° F and continue to roast until tender, about 20 minutes per pound. Pour off fat as it accumulates and reserve for other uses. Baste duckling often with hot stock or water and drippings.

   3. Remove duckling to a platter and cover loosely with foil to keep warm. Pour off the fat and make pan gravy from the drippings. Add minced neck meat and giblets to the gravy if desired.

Note: Allow at least 1 pound of duck per person, as there is a rather large ratio of fat and bone to meat.

Variations: Trim off the neck and wing tips of the duckling and fill the body cavity with the following stuffings: Prune and Apple Stuffing (page 249); Bread Stuffing for Goose or Duck (page 249); or Corn Bread Stuffing (page 248) with an addition of ½ pound cooked sausage. Season and roast as for above.

DUCKLING À L'ORANGE

1 5-pound duckling
salt and freshly ground black pepper
   to taste
ground ginger
1 unpeeled orange, sliced thin
1 small onion, sliced

¼ cup honey
slivered zest and juice of 2 oranges
1 tablespoon flour
dash of red wine (optional)
orange slices for garnish

   1. Preheat oven to 450° F. Wipe duckling with paper towels inside and out. Season well with salt, pepper, and ginger. Stuff cavity with orange and onion slices.

   2. Roast on a rack in the preheated oven, about 20 minutes. Reduce heat to 350° F and continue to roast until tender, about 20 minutes per pound. Pour off fat as it accumulates and reserve for other uses. Combine honey and orange juice. Pour over duckling and baste often.

3. In a small saucepan, cover orange zest with water and boil 10 minutes. Drain and reserve zest. Spoon 2 tablespoons fat from the roasting pan over the zest, add flour, and cook a few minutes, stirring often.

4. Remove duckling to a platter and cover loosely with foil to keep warm. Pour off fat. Measure drippings and add enough water to make 1½ cups fat-free liquid. Set roasting pan on top of the stove, add drippings, and cook over high heat, stirring to incorporate any cooked bits stuck to the bottom of the pan. Strain the liquid into the saucepan with the orange zest and cook, stirring until the sauce is smooth and slightly thickened. Add a little red wine, if desired.

5. Arrange the duckling on a warm serving platter. Garnish with orange slices. Spoon a little of the sauce over the bird and serve the remainder separately.

DUCK STOCK

A simple duck stock can be made from the neck, wing tips, and giblets of the bird. Simply cover with cold water, season with salt and pepper to taste, and bring to a boil. Skim off any scum that rises to the surface. Add a celery stalk and half an onion and reduce to a simmer. Cook until vegetables are tender, about 2 hours. Strain. Remember that duck stock is very fatty. Carefully skim off the fat before using.

Goose

ROAST GOOSE

1 12- to 14-pound goose	2 teaspoons caraway seeds
salt and freshly ground black pepper to taste	Prune and Apple Stuffing (page 249)

1. Preheat oven to 350° F. Wipe goose inside and out with paper towels. Season well with salt, pepper, and caraway seeds. Stuff cavity of the bird with Prune and Apple Stuffing and truss.

2. Place trussed bird on a rack in a shallow pan. Roast in a moderate oven until goose is tender, about 3½ hours. The skin should be very crisp and brown. Drain off fat as it accumulates during cooking. Baste bird occasionally with pan drippings mixed with hot water.

3. Remove goose to a platter and cover loosely with foil to keep warm. Remove stuffing immediately. Pour off the fat and make Pan Gravy (page 230) from the drippings. Serve hot with stuffing and gravy.

GAENSEKLEIN (FRICASSEED GOOSE)

back, wings, neck, gizzard, and
   heart of goose
salt and freshly ground black pepper
   to taste
ground ginger
garlic clove, peeled (optional)

½ onion, thinly sliced
piece of celery root
2 tablespoons butter
2 tablespoons flour
1 teaspoon chopped parsley

   1. Season meat well with salt, pepper, and ginger. If desired, rub with garlic. Cover and let stand overnight in the refrigerator.

   2. In a large pot, cover meat with boiling water. Simmer for 2 hours. Add onion and celery root and continue to simmer until the meat is tender. Strain the broth and skim off the fat that rises to the surface. Remove any bones from the meat and set the meat aside. Discard the other solids.

   3. In a saucepan, melt the butter and add the flour. Stir for a few minutes over low heat until well combined. Slowly pour in 1 cup of the hot goose stock. Cook, stirring constantly, until smooth and slightly thickened. Taste and correct seasoning if necessary. Add the goose pieces and gently reheat.

   4. Transfer to a serving platter. Garnish with parsley and serve hot with Spatzen (page 79).

GOOSE CRACKLINGS (GRIEBEN)

Cut the fat skin of a goose into 1- to 1½-inch squares. Season well with coarse salt and refrigerate overnight. Rinse and drain. In a deep pot, combine with the rest of the goose fat and cover with cold water. Cook over moderately high heat until all the water has evaporated. If chewy cracklings are desired, remove them with a slotted spoon as soon as the fat is clear and season with salt. For crispy cracklings, cook until well browned, season well, and place in a warm oven for a few minutes.

Cornish Hens and Squabs

Cornish hens are small birds with an average weight of 1½ pounds. Their flavor is a cross between chicken and game birds. Technically wild fowl, squabs are the same size as Cornish hens and have a similar flavor. Both are usually served whole, 1 to a serving. In addition to the following preparations, try hens in any of the recipes for chicken earlier in this chapter.

ROASTED CORNISH GAME HENS

4 Cornish hens, about 1 pound each	butter, melted
1 lemon, cut in half	2 cups chicken stock (page 59)
salt and freshly ground black pepper to taste	

1. Preheat oven to 450° F. Rub hens thoroughly with lemon and season well with salt and pepper. Brush with melted butter.
2. Set hens on a rack in an open roasting pan. Roast in preheated oven until tender, 30 to 40 minutes. Baste frequently with pan drippings and stock. When done, the legs should move easily in their sockets and the flesh should feel soft.
3. Use the drippings to make Pan Gravy (page 230). Serve hens hot with gravy on the side.

STUFFED ROASTED CORNISH GAME HENS

4 Cornish hens, about 1 pound each	¾ cup raw rice
salt and freshly ground black pepper to taste	2 cups chicken stock (page 59)
1 tablespoon butter	1 teaspoon fresh thyme, or ½ teaspoon dried
1 small onion, finely chopped	

1. Season hens well with salt and pepper.
2. In a frying pan, melt the butter. Add the onion and cook until soft. Add rice and stir over medium heat until colored. Add stock and salt to taste, stir, and bring to a boil. Reduce to a low simmer, and cover. Cook until liquid is absorbed and rice is tender. Remove from heat and fluff with a fork. Add thyme and salt and pepper to taste. Cool to room temperature. Stuff hens with cooled rice.
3. Roast hens in a preheated 350° F oven until tender and legs move easily in their sockets, 30 to 45 minutes. Baste occasionally with pan drippings and butter.
4. When hens are done, remove stuffing immediately. Use the drippings to make Pan Gravy (page 230). Serve hens hot with gravy on the side.

ROASTED SQUABS

Prepare Liver Stuffing for Squabs, page 249. Preheat oven to 450° F. Loosen breast skin from wishbone almost down to bottom of breastbone to form a pocket. Fill pocket and neck with stuffing. Tie at the top. Or stuff the body cavity as for other poultry. Fasten legs together at the back. Place squabs closely together in a roasting pan and spread with softened, butter. Roast for 5 minutes. Reduce heat to 375° F and roast until tender, about 30 minutes. When hens are done, remove stuffing immediately. Use the drippings to make Pan Gravy (page 230). Serve hens hot with gravy on the side.

BROILED SQUABS

Cut along the backbone of squabs with a small, sharp knife and split in half. Season well with salt and pepper. Brush with melted butter. Flatten breastbone and place bird on broiler, skin side to the heat. When skin is crisp and beginning to brown, turn and broil 4 to 6 inches from flame 10 to 12 minutes longer, until done.

SQUABS EN CASSEROLE

6 squabs, trimmed
salt, freshly ground black pepper,
   and paprika to taste
3 tablespoons butter
2 tablespoons sherry
several sprigs parsley

1 small carrot, peeled and chopped
1 onion, thinly sliced
1 bay leaf, crumbled
2 cups chicken stock (page 59)
1 tablespoon flour
12 mushrooms, sautéed

1. Preheat oven to 350° F. Season birds with salt, pepper, and paprika. In a large frying pan, melt 2 tablespoons of the butter. Gently brown the birds on all sides, in two batches if necessary. Remove the browned birds to a heavy, oven-proof casserole with a tight-fitting lid. Pour out the fat from the pan and add the sherry. Cook over high heat, stirring vigorously to incorporate all the cooked-on bits. Pour the sherry over the birds in the casserole.
2. Add the parsley, carrot, onion, bay leaf, and stock. Cover and cook in oven until tender, about 1 hour.
3. When done, transfer the birds to a serving platter and cover loosely with foil to keep warm. Strain the cooking liquid and discard the solids. Skim off fat.
4. In a small saucepan, melt the remaining tablespoon butter. Add the flour and cook until lightly colored. Pour in the cooking liquid and cook over moderately high heat until smooth.
5. Drain platter of any liquid given off by the birds. Spoon a small amount of the sauce over the birds. Serve the rest in a sauce boat on the side along with the sautéed mushrooms.

Game Birds

While once available to friends and families of hunters, game birds are being farmed to meet increasing demands for lean, flavorful poultry. Many of the following Settlement recipes give instructions for preparing freshly killed game. Though most farmed game comes dressed and ready to cook, the information on preparation is useful for friends and families of sportsmen who still bring home their coveted catch.

TO PLUCK WILD DUCK

Dissolve ¾ pound paraffin in 7 quarts of boiling water. Dip duck in and out of boiling mixture 4 or 5 times. Cool until paraffin has coated the feathers, about 3 to 5 minutes. Pluck. Feathers of game birds may also be loosened by plunging the birds into boiling water for about 10 seconds. Clean and draw as usual.

ROAST WILD DUCK

1 wild duck
salt and freshly ground black pepper
   to taste
1 tablespoon vinegar

1 small onion, peeled and cut in half
flour
2 tablespoons butter

1. Clean duck thoroughly and draw. Season inside and out with salt and pepper, and sprinkle with vinegar. Place onion inside cavity of the bird. Refrigerate overnight.
2. Preheat oven to 400° F. Remove onion. If duck is old and tough, cook slowly in boiling water until tender before roasting. Season again with salt and pepper.
3. Dredge with flour. Place duck in a shallow roasting pan with butter. Roast until browned, basting often. Serve hot with wild rice and currant jelly.

GUINEA HENS

Treat guinea hens just like chicken. They are best done simply roasted. Try one of the stuffings found on pages 247–250.

ROAST PARTRIDGE

Pluck, draw, and wash the birds. Secure a slice of bacon on the breast of each bird. Place in a shallow roasting pan and roast in a hot oven, 450° F, for 15 minutes. Remove bacon and season birds well with salt and pepper to taste. Reduce oven to 350° F, and continue cooking birds until tender. Serve with Pan Gravy (page 230), or, pour 1 cup heavy cream over birds and sprinkle with toasted breadcrumbs.

BRAISED PHEASANT

2 pheasants	1 tablespoon flour
salt and freshly ground black pepper	½ cup white wine
2 tablespoons butter	1 cup sour cream
2 cups water or cream	

1. Pluck feathers; clean and singe. Wash birds. Cut off wings and legs. Split back. Leave breasts whole. Season lightly with salt and pepper.
2. In a large sauté pan, melt the butter. Add the pheasant pieces and cook until well browned on all sides. Add water or cream and cover. Cook on the stove over a low flame or in a 325° F oven until tender. Baste and turn pieces often. Add more water or butter as necessary.
3. When done, remove to a serving platter and cover loosely with foil to keep warm. Pour off fat from the pan. Add the flour and the wine and on top of the stove, bring to a boil stirring constantly with a wire whisk. Let reduce slightly. Remove from heat, add sour cream and pour over birds.

ROAST PHEASANT

Prepare birds as above, leaving wings and legs. Stuff body cavity and inside of neck with Bread Stuffing (page 247) if desired. Roast as for Roast Chicken (page 228), until tender.

QUAIL

Cut along the backbone of birds with a small, sharp knife and split in half. Season well with salt and pepper. Brush with melted butter. Flatten breastbone and place bird on broiler, skin side to the heat. When skin is crisp and beginning to brown, turn and continue cooking, until done. Allow 10 to 20 minutes for young, tender birds. For older, tougher birds, prepare as for Squabs en Casserole (page 263).

POTTED QUAIL

Season birds well with salt and pepper. Sauté in butter, turning often to brown all sides. Cover with hot water or chicken stock (page 59). Cover and cook over a low flame or in a moderately slow oven, 325° F, until tender. Baste and turn pieces often. Add more liquid as necessary. Deglaze pan with white wine and reduce slightly. Serve quail on toast points, garnished with currant jelly.

Rabbit

Rabbits can be prepared like chicken—stewed, fricasseed, or roasted. Lean and flavorful, rabbit is being enjoyed now more than ever.

BELGIAN HARE FRICASSEE

1 rabbit, cleaned and cut into serving pieces
salt and freshly ground black pepper to taste

flour, for dredging
¼ pound salt pork, sliced

1. Season rabbit pieces well with salt and pepper. Dredge in flour.
2. In a large sauté pan, fry the salt pork. When the pieces of pork begin to dry out, remove them from the pan with a slotted spoon. Brown the rabbit pieces very quickly in the hot pork fat. Cover and cook over very low heat until tender, about 30 minutes.
3. Remove rabbit pieces to a serving platter and cover loosely with foil to keep warm. Pour off fat from the pan. Add a small amount of water and stir to incorporate the brown bits that cling to the pan. Pour sauce over the rabbit. Serve hot with gooseberry jelly, or any other tart preserves, or with Horseradish Sauce (page 400).

HASENPFEFFER

1 rabbit, cleaned and cut into
   serving pieces
white wine vinegar
1 small onion, peeled and sliced
salt and freshly ground black pepper
   to taste

1 teaspoon cloves
2 bay leaves, crumpled
2 tablespoons butter
1 cup thick sour cream

1.   In a large jar or crock, place the rabbit pieces. Cover with equal parts water and vinegar. Add onion slices, salt and pepper, cloves, and bay leaves. Cover and refrigerate for 2 days.

2.   Remove meat from marinade and pat dry. Strain the marinade and reserve. In a large sauté pan, melt the butter. When sizzling hot, add the meat. Quickly brown on all sides, turning often. Gradually add enough of the marinade to cover. Simmer over a low flame until meat is tender, about ½ hour.

3.   Remove the cooked rabbit pieces to a serving platter and cover loosely with foil to keep warm. Just before serving, boil the cooking liquid to thicken and add thick sour cream. Pour a small amount of the sauce over the rabbit and serve the rest on the side.

RABBIT WITH PRUNES

Marinade
1 cup hearty red wine
several sprigs parsley
2 bay leaves
1 large onion, quartered
1 carrot, peeled and coarsely
   chopped
10 whole peppercorns
1 tablespoon olive oil

Rabbit
1 rabbit, cut into 6 pieces
½ pound pitted prunes
2 tablespoons oil
2 tablespoons butter
2 tablespoons flour
1 cup red wine
1 cup chicken stock (page 59)
1 clove garlic
salt and freshly ground black pepper
   to taste
chopped parsley for garnish

1.   In a nonreactive bowl, combine the ingredients for the marinade. Add the rabbit and cover. Refrigerate for 10 to 12 hours (or overnight) turning several times.

2.   Meanwhile, place prunes in a bowl and cover with tepid water. Let soak for at least 6 hours. (If pressed for time, cover with boiling water and let sit for 1 to 2 hours.)

(continued)

3. Drain the rabbit and dry with paper towels. Combine oil and butter in a heavy, covered casserole. Over moderately high heat, brown the rabbit and set aside. Add the onion and carrot from the marinade and cook until soft. Sprinkle over the flour and stir until lightly browned. Add the rest of the marinade, the cup of red wine, the stock, and the garlic. Bring to a boil. Add the rabbit pieces.

4. Drain the prunes and add to the casserole. Bring to a boil, reduce heat, and simmer until tender, about 45 minutes.

5. When done, remove rabbit and prunes to a serving platter. Strain the sauce into a heavy, nonreactive saucepan. Bring to a boil and let reduce by half. Correct the seasoning and spoon over the rabbit. Garnish with chopped parsley.

Venison

Farm-raised venison is a growing business. Today's consumer is finding a healthy, lean meat of superior quality in many marketplaces and in restaurants throughout the country. High in protein and usually produced without added hormones, steroids, or antibiotics, the increased demand is being met by some industrious farmers who started breeding for large-scale production almost 2 decades ago. Saddles, chops, loins, and steaks are found in supermarkets and specialty food stores either fresh or frozen. Lacking the gaminess of wild deer, farm-raised venison is mild in flavor and quite adaptable to most beef and veal recipes.

Venison roast should always be served rare, although it may be served more well done when stewed or braised. Prepare Venison Roast like Crown Roast of Lamb (page 321), allowing for a shorter cooking time. Prepare Venison Cutlets like veal cutlets (page 297), or simply fried in a skillet. Serve with Currant Jelly Sauce (page 406) or Port Wine Sauce (page 403). Cook Saddle of Venison like Hasenpfeffer (page 267), or Sauerbraten (page 290). Venison steaks may be broiled like beef steak (page 278).

VENISON STEW

3 pounds cubed venison
salt and freshly ground black pepper
  to taste
2 tablespoons oil
2 tablespoons butter
2 onions, peeled and chopped
2 carrots, peeled and sliced
2 celery stalks, sliced

2 cloves garlic, crushed
2 tablespoons flour
1 cup tomatoes, peeled, seeded, and
  chopped
2 cups beef stock (page 59)
several sprigs of fresh thyme (or 1
  teaspoon dried)
2 bay leaves, crumbled
2 tablespoons chopped parsley for
  garnish, if desired

1. Preheat oven to 325° F. Season meat with salt and pepper. In a large, oven-proof casserole, melt the oil and butter. Brown venison over moderately high heat. Remove and pour off all but 2 tablespoons fat.

2. Add the onions, carrots, celery, and garlic to the casserole. Cook over moderately high heat until onions are translucent. Replace meat and sprinkle all with the flour. Allow to cook until flour is slightly browned, stirring constantly. Add the tomatoes. Pour in stock and bring to a boil. Season with salt, pepper, thyme, and bay leaves. Cover tightly and place in the preheated oven. Cook until meat is very tender, about 2 hours. The meat should be very soft and shred easily when held between two fingers.

3. Remove meat to a serving dish and keep warm. Strain cooking liquid and discard vegetables. Reduce slightly if sauce seems too thin. Thin out with water or additional stock if sauce seems too thick. Taste for seasoning and pour over meat in dish. Garnish with chopped parsley if desired. Serve with rice, potatoes, or buttered noodles.

MEAT

When buying meat it is important to select the right cut for the desired cooking method. (See charts throughout this chapter.) Keep in mind that when properly prepared, the least expensive cuts of meat are as high in nutritional value and as good to eat as the most expensive cuts.

Remove the market wrappings from fresh meat, wrap it in moisture-proof paper or plastic wrap, and store in the coldest part of the refrigerator. Frozen meat should be wrapped in freezer paper and stored in the freezer compartment at 0° F or lower until ready to defrost. Smoked meats should be stored in the refrigerator, as should canned hams, unless otherwise stated on the label. Leftover cooked meat should be cooled to room temperature, then closely covered before refrigerating.

Meat may be cooked with dry heat: roasted or baked in the oven or on the grill or rotisserie, broiled or pan-broiled in a hot skillet without fat. It may be cooked in moist heat—like pot roast or stews—when the meat is braised in a covered kettle with a little liquid, either in the oven or on top of the range; or it may be simmered submerged in water or stock. Thin cuts of tender meat may be flash-cooked in a small amount of fat, a process called panfrying or sautéeing. To deep-fry, cook the meat quickly in fat deep enough to cover it completely.

To cook frozen meat roasts without defrosting, increase the cooking time by one third to one half. The extra time needed to cook frozen steaks, chops, and hamburgers depends upon the thickness and size of the meat. Don't forget that the microwave oven is useful for defrosting even large cuts of meat in a short amount of time.

We are passing along the recommendations for cooking meat supplied by the National Meat Board. The charts that follow give specific times for cooking meat that comes straight from the refrigerator, because among the generation of instant cooks, few people have time to bring the evening's roast beef to room temperature before cooking. Bacteria grow easily in that murky area of tepidness when the meat is neither chilled nor cooked. The oven is usually not preheated, either. Cooking slowly and evenly is a foolproof way to roast.

By no means is the more accomplished cook tied to these suggestions. If you are used to beginning a roast in a hot oven, then turning down heat to finish at a moderate temperature, please do so. Simply compensate in the time charts that follow by reducing the cooking time per pound by 2 to 3 minutes.

MEAT AND THE MICROWAVE

Repeated tests have shown the key to success when microwaving meat is using a medium-low or 30 percent power (approximately 200 watts). The rapid heat penetration of microwave cooking on high does not allow adequate time for the development of tenderness and flavor in many beef cuts. However, at a lower power setting, the heat penetration is slowed, and more tender, flavorful meat is the result. While cooking at a lower power setting will increase cooking time, the improvement in overall eating quality is worth the extra minutes. It should be noted that even when roasts are cooked at medium-low power, there is a substantial time savings over conventional cooking.

General Tips for Microwaving Meat
(adapted courtesy of National Meat Board)

- Remember small pieces of meat cook faster than large pieces; thin portions cook faster than thick portions; and small quantities cook faster than large quantities.
- Shape ground meat into uniform-sized ½-inch-thick patties. Form a ¾-inch hole in the center of each for even cooking.
- Arrange uniform meat shapes like beef patties or meatballs in a circle. Leave the center of the platter empty.
- Leftover meat retains its flavor with reheating. Overlap or shingle slices of precooked meat for even reheating.
- Stir meat dishes with high liquid content occasionally to redistribute the heat from the outside to the inside.
- Shield irregularly shaped edges of roasts that may overcook with small pieces of foil.
- Collect meat drippings with microwave-safe utensils. Use a trivet or rack for roasts; a colander over a bowl or container for ground meat.
- When planning meals, remember that vegetables can be cooked in the microwave oven during standing time.

TO TEST FOR DONENESS

Many professionals determine when a steak, chop, or cutlet is properly cooked by touch. With practice, you can learn to gauge the amount of cooking needed without consulting timetables or cutting into the meat. The soft part of your hand between the thumb and the index finger approximates the feel of raw meat. Meat contracts as it cooks just as your muscles do when you make a fist. The soft, flabby texture of an open hand feels like raw meat. Closed feels rare, tightened is medium, and clenched is well done.

HAND TEST FOR DONENESS

Beef

Today's beef is lower in fat and calories than ever before. New breeding and feeding techniques combined with closer trimming of fat at the retail level are results of consumer demands for a healthier product.

Beef is graded by the U.S. Department of Agriculture. Of U.S.D.A.-stamped beef, *Prime* is sold to restaurants, hotels and specialty food stores. *Choice* and *Select* (formerly graded as *Good*) are those generally most available in retail meat markets. Select has the least fat, and therefore is somewhat less juicy and tender. It is usually the least expensive of these three grades.

An attempt by the meat industry to provide the kind of product the modern consumer demands has resulted in some innovative concepts. Brand-name beef—sold as *lean* or *lite*—spans the rankings from *choice* down to the lowest two U.S.D.A. grades, *cutter* and *canner*. Not only do these varieties contain less fat, they generally cost more. In addition they proclaim to come from animals that haven't been raised on hormones, antibiotics, or the other chemicals that have been used to increase productivity for the better part of this century.

Since fat is what gives beef flavor and juiciness, we have lost something valuable in our efforts to be healthier. A fair amount of *marbling* (the distribution of fat throughout the flesh of the meat) was considered a sign of a desirable piece of beef before the days of cholesterol concern. However, those of us attempting to reduce our intake of saturated fat must learn how to cook the increasingly available leaner products with equally excellent results.

There is a tendency for lean beef to be tough and dry when overcooked. Better to roast, broil, or pan-fry lean cuts only to the rare or medium stage. Well-done lean meat is best when braised or stewed. The liquid will add needed moisture and break down the tough fibers during a longer, slower cooking process. Lean beef can also be tenderized by marinating in an acidic base like wine, lemon, or vinegar. Consult the following listings for cuts suitable to various cooking methods.

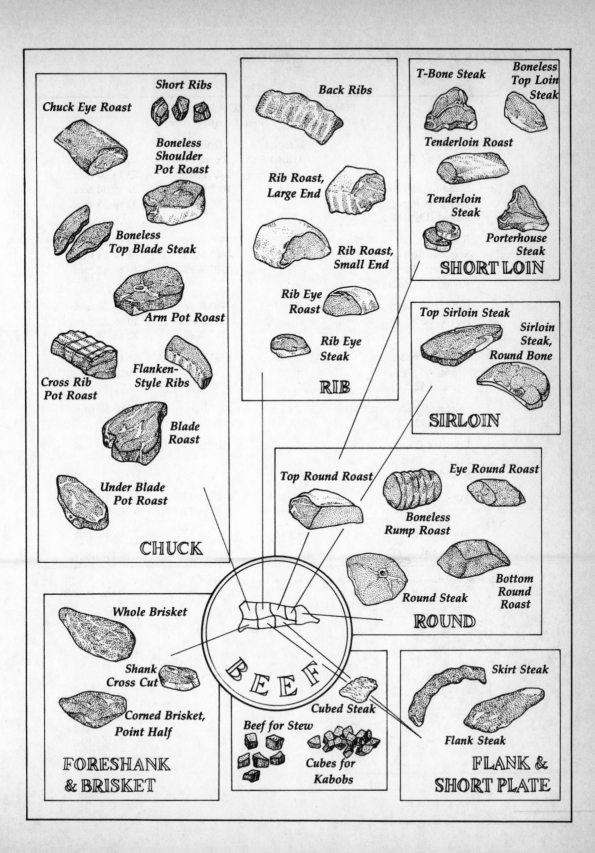

Short Ribs

Chuck Eye Roast

Boneless Shoulder Pot Roast

Boneless Top Blade Steak

Arm Pot Roast

Cross Rib Pot Roast

Flanken-Style Ribs

Blade Roast

Under Blade Pot Roast

CHUCK

Back Ribs

Rib Roast, Large End

Rib Roast, Small End

Rib Eye Roast

Rib Eye Steak

RIB

T-Bone Steak

Boneless Top Loin Steak

Tenderloin Roast

Tenderloin Steak

Porterhouse Steak

SHORT LOIN

Top Sirloin Steak

Sirloin Steak, Round Bone

SIRLOIN

Top Round Roast

Eye Round Roast

Boneless Rump Roast

Round Steak

Bottom Round Roast

ROUND

Whole Brisket

Shank Cross Cut

Corned Brisket, Point Half

FORESHANK & BRISKET

Cubed Steak

Beef for Stew

Cubes for Kabobs

Skirt Steak

Flank Steak

FLANK & SHORT PLATE

BEEF

TIMETABLE FOR ROASTING
(300° F to 325° F Oven Temperature)

Cut	Weight (Lbs.)	Internal Temp. (F)	Time* per pound
Rib	4 to 6	140° Rare	23 to 25 min.
Standing Rib Roast		160° Med.	27 to 30 min.
Newport Roast		170° Well	32 to 35 min.
Rolled Rib Roast			
Rib	6 to 8	140° Rare	26 to 32 min.
Standing Rib Roast		160° Med.	34 to 38 min.
Newport Roast		170° Well	40 to 42 min.
Rolled Rib Roast			
Rib Eye Roast	4 to 6	140° Rare	18 to 20 min.
(roast at 350° F)		160° Med.	20 to 22 min.
		170° Well	22 to 24 min.
Fillet or Tenderloin, whole	4 to 6	140° Rare	45 to 60 min. (total)
(roast at 425° F)			
Fillet or Tenderloin, half	2 to 3	140° Rare	45 to 50 min. (total)
(roast at 425° F)			
Boneless Rump	4 to 6	150° to 170°	25 to 30 min.
Standing Rump			
Rolled Rump			
Tip	3½ to 4	140° to 170°	35 to 40 min.
	6 to 8	140° to 170°	30 to 35 min.
Top Round	4 to 6	140° to 170°	25 to 30 min.
Ground Beef Loaf	1½ to 2½	160° to 170°	1 to 1½ hours

Based on meat taken directly from the refrigerator and an oven that is not preheated.

ROASTING

The choice of cut used for roasting is most important. Tender cuts from the rib, short loin, and sirloin are best for this dry-heat method. Other cuts from the chuck, round, flank, or brisket can be prepared by moist *or* dry-heat cooking.

A foolproof method is to roast beef at an even temperature for the duration of cooking time. Roast according to chart above, starting in a cold oven. Whatever method is employed, place the beef fat side up and season well with pepper. Sprinkle with salt during the last half hour of cooking. (Salt will draw out juices as the beef cooks so add it only toward the end of roasting when moisture is already sealed in.) When done let meat rest, covered loosely with foil, for 10 to 15 minutes before carving.

Alternatively, start the cooking in a very hot oven (500° F) and sear the roast for 5 to 10 minutes, turning several times to brown. Turn down the heat to 300° F to 325° F and continue cooking according to the "Beef Roasting Chart" above. Adjust the cooking time per pound by a few minutes to compensate for the initial searing technique. The searing and browning of a beef roast adds color and a somewhat crackling texture to the roast. This must be done quickly and efficiently and with extra attention.

Yorkshire Pudding is a traditional accompaniment for roast beef (see recipe below). Some other serving suggestions are: Baked Potatoes (page 386), Braised Green Peas (page 383), Lemon Carrots (page 371), Creamed Spinach (page 391), Cauliflower Au Gratin (page 372), or Sautéed Summer Squash (page 392).

CARVING A ROLLED RIB ROAST

Step 1

Step 2

CARVING A CROWN ROAST

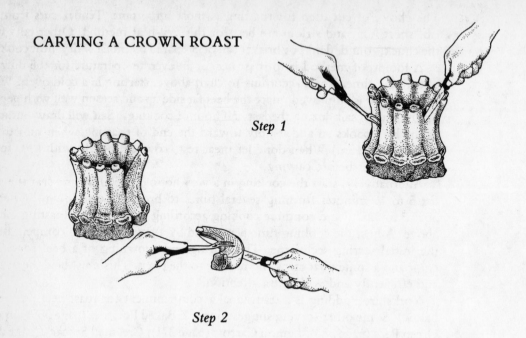

Step 1

Step 2

CARVING A STANDING RIB ROAST

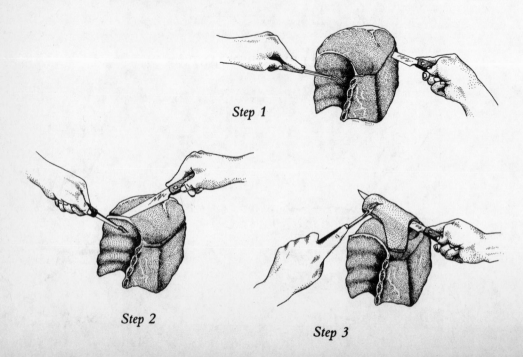

Step 1

Step 2

Step 3

YORKSHIRE PUDDING

1½ cups flour
¼ teaspoon baking powder
½ teaspoon salt

1½ cups milk
2 eggs
⅓ cup beef drippings

1. Mix dry ingredients. Gradually add the milk and then the eggs. Beat well. Place hot beef drippings in an oblong pan and pour in the batter ½ inch deep.

2. Twenty to 30 minutes before the Roast Beef is done, remove it from the pan and place directly on the oven rack. Place the pan containing the pudding batter underneath the roast and allow the juices to drip on the pudding while baking. Bake in a moderate oven, 350° F, 20 to 30 minutes, gradually decreasing the heat.

3. Cut pudding into squares and serve with Roast Beef.

Saucing Roast Beef

An excellent sauce for roast beef can be made by simply deglazing the roasting pan. Pour off the fat, add stock, wine, or water to the hot pan. Place on top of the stove and over low heat; use a whisk to blend and pick up any of the savory bits left from the roasted beef. Increase heat and let boil until slightly thickened. Enrich with softened, butter if desired. Season to taste with salt and pepper.

Pan gravy can be made in a similar way. Pour off all but two tablespoons of fat, add 2 tablespoons flour and gradually add 1 cup or more of boiling stock or water. Cook over moderate heat on top of the stove until thickened, about 5 minutes. Season with salt and pepper. Strain to remove lumps if necessary.

MICROWAVING BEEF ROASTS
(adapted courtesy of National Meat Board)

1. Place 2- to 3-pound beef roast, fat side down (if fat layer is present), on rack in microwave-safe dish. Place a 2-pound beef rib or top loin roast cut side down so roast is stable and will not tip over. Do not add liquid. Season as desired.

2. Place waxed paper over top of roast; microwave at medium-low or 30 percent power (approximately 200 watts). Estimate the cooking time for the type of roast. (See chart below.) Specific times vary with weight, shape, and composition of roast as well as differences in microwave ovens.

3. At midpoint of cooking time, rotate dish ¼ turn and invert roast. Shield edges that appear to be overcooking with small pieces of foil.

4. To determine doneness during cooking, use a microwave thermometer or probe. When roast is 5 to 10 degrees below doneness desired, remove from oven, tent with foil, and allow to stand 10 minutes before carving. To determine doneness after roast has been removed from microwave oven use a quick-recovery or regular meat thermometer. (See chart on page 274 for temperature ranges.)

5. Cook roasts from beef round only to rare or medium rare. Carve into thin slices. More tender roasts from the rib and loin can be cooked to rare, medium, or well done.

Type of Beef Roast	Raw Weight	Power Level	Mid-Size and Full-Size (minutes per pound)
Beef Rib Eye	2 to 3 lbs.	Medium-Low	16 to 20
Beef Top Loin	2 to 3 lbs.	Medium-Low	16 to 18
Beef Eye Round	2 to 3 lbs.	Medium-Low	14 to 16
Beef Top Round	2 to 3 lbs.	Medium-Low	19 to 22
Beef Tip (Cap Off)	3 lbs.	Medium-Low	20 to 22
Beef Rump	2 to 3 lbs.	Medium-Low	20 to 22

BROILING, PAN BROILING, AND PANFRYING

TIMETABLE FOR BROILING, PAN BROILING, AND PANFRYING
(times based on meat taken directly from refrigerator)
Note: For well-done meats, add 5 to 10 minutes to time suggested for medium.

Cut	Weight	Inches from Heat	Time Rare	Med.
Chuck Steak				
¾ inch	1¼ to 1¾ lbs.	2 to 3	14	20
1 inch	1½ to 2½ lbs.	3 to 4	20	25
1½ inch	2 to 4 lbs.	4 to 5	30	35
Rib Steak				
¾ inch	11 to 14 ozs.	2 to 3	8	12
1 inch	1 to 1½ lbs.	3 to 4	15	20
1½ inch	1½ to 2 lbs.	4 to 5	25	30
Rib Eye Steak				
¾ inch	7 to 8 ozs.	2 to 3	8	12
1 inch	9 to 10 ozs.	3 to 4	15	20
1½ inch	12 to 14 ozs.	4 to 5	25	30

Cut	Weight	Inches from Heat	Time Rare	Time Med.
Top Loin Steak				
¾ inch	11 to 14 ozs.	2 to 3	8	12
1 inch	1 to 1½ lbs.	3 to 4	15	20
1½ inch	1½ to 2 lbs.	4 to 5	25	30
Sirloin Steak				
¾ inch	1¼ to 1¾ lbs.	2 to 3	10	15
1 inch	1½ to 3 lbs.	3 to 4	20	25
1½ inch	2¼ to 4 lbs.	4 to 5	30	35
Porterhouse Steak				
¾ inch	12 to 16 ozs.	2 to 3	10	15
1 inch	1½ to 2 lbs.	3 to 4	20	25
1½ inch	2 to 3 lbs.	4 to 5	30	35
Tenderloin (Filet Mignon)	4 to 8 ozs.	2 to 4	10 to 15	15 to 20
Ground Beef Patties				
½ inch × 4 inch	4 ozs.	3 to 4	8	12
1 inch × 4 inch	5⅓ ozs.	3 to 4	12	18
Top Round Steak				
1 inch	1¼ to 1¾ lbs.	3 to 4	20	30
1½ inch	1½ to 2 lbs.	4 to 5	30	35
Flank Steak	1 to 1½ lbs.	2 to 3	12	14

Tender, quick-cooking cuts of beef are best for broiling, panbroiling, and panfrying. Because they require minimum treatment, the results will be directly related to the quality of meat.

Flame broiling requires a heat source of substantial intensity. Lightly brush meat with oil, season with salt and pepper, and set broiling pan 2 to 5 inches from heat source. Cook according to the chart. Pour off accumulating fat to avoid the risk of fire.

For panbroiling or panfrying, choose a heavy pan that will evenly distribute heat. The pan or skillet should be large enough to allow plenty of room for the piece of beef being cooked. Do not overcrowd; too much meat will produce excess moisture resulting in steam that will prevent proper browning. Cook in batches if necessary, pouring off fat before beginning again.

For pan broiling, place meat directly in a sizzling hot skillet. Cook slowly, turning occasionally. Pour off excess fat as it accumulates to broil rather than to fry.

For panfrying, brown meat in butter melted with oil. Cook over moderate heat, turning occasionally until done.

For a quick sauce, deglaze pan or skillet used for pan-broiled or panfried beef with stock, wine, or flavored vinegar. Reduce over high heat until thick and syrupy. Enrich with butter if desired and nap meat with a small amount of this concentrated reduction.

Top broiled beef with one of the compound butters found on page 363. Some side dish serving suggestions include: Baked Potatoes (page 386), Sautéed Mushrooms (page 379), Onions Au Gratin (page 381), or Rice Pilaf (page 176).

CARVING A STEAK

Step 1

Step 2

Step 3

STEAK WITH PEPPERCORNS

4 small steaks (about 6 ounces each, 1½ inches thick)
1 tablespoon each green, red, and black peppercorns
2 tablespoons butter

2 tablespoons oil
¼ cup brandy
1 cup heavy cream
salt and additional freshly ground black pepper to taste

1. Trim excess fat from steaks. Crush the peppercorns lightly with the back of a large, heavy knife. Use the heel of the palm to gently press the crushed peppers into each steak.

2. In a sauté pan large enough to hold the steaks in one flat layer, melt the butter with the oil. When sizzling hot, add the steaks. Brown over moderately high heat. Lower heat and cook until done, using the chart on page 278 as a guide. (Do in 2 batches if necessary.)

3. Remove the steaks to a platter and keep warm. Pour off excess fat from the sauté pan. Return to the heat and carefully pour in the brandy. Use a wire whisk, stirring vigorously, to pick up the bits left behind from the cooking of the steaks. Bring to a boil and reduce by half over high heat. Pour in the cream and reduce by half again. Season with salt and freshly ground black pepper, if desired.

4. Top each steak with a spoonful of the sauce.

STEAK WITH REDUCTION OF RED WINE AND SHALLOTS

4 tablespoons butter
2 tablespoons oil
4 small beef fillets (4 to 6 ounces
   each, 1½ inches thick)
salt and freshly ground black pepper
   to taste

1 cup red wine
2 shallots, finely chopped
fresh chopped parsley or small
   leaves of watercress for garnish

1. In a skillet or frying pan large enough to hold the steaks flat, melt 2 tablespoons of the butter and the oil. Cut the remaining 2 tablespoons of butter into small pieces and keep chilled. Season the steaks with salt and pepper to taste. When fat is sizzling hot, add the meat. Cook over medium-high heat until done, about 2 minutes on each side for rare. Remove to a serving platter and keep warm.

2. Drain off the fat from the pan. Carefully pour in the wine. With a wire whisk, stir to pick up any bits in the bottom of the pan. Bring to a boil and add the shallots. Reduce over high heat until all but 1 tablespoon of the liquid remains, stirring frequently. Working on and off the heat, add the chilled pieces of butter little by little. Whisk constantly until sauce is smooth and emulsified. Season with salt and pepper.

3. Spoon a tablespoon or two of the sauce over each fillet. Garnish with sprigs of parsley or watercress if desired. Serve at once.

HAMBURG STEAK

 This forerunner to the modern hamburger has been in The Settlement Cookbook *since the earliest editions and still has a place in the modern kitchen. Try deglazing the pan after cooking with some wine or stock to make a sauce.*

1 pound round steak
1 teaspoon chopped onions
salt and freshly ground black pepper

fresh celery tops or parsley and thin
   slices of lemon for garnish

(continued)

1. Salt and prepare meat as desired. Cut off fat, bone, and stringy pieces, and very finely chop. Combine meat with onions, season to taste. Shape meat into round cakes a little less than ½ inch thick.

2. Heat pan or skillet to very hot and grease lightly. Add meat and count to 60, turn and cook on the other side until brown.

3. Serve hot and garnish with celery tops or parsley and two or three slices of lemon. Pour the fat and drippings from the pan over the meat.

BRAISING AND STEWING

TIMETABLE FOR BRAISING

Cut	Weight or Size	Approx. Total Cooking Time
Blade Pot Roast	3 to 5 lbs.	2 to 2½ hours
Arm Pot Roast	3 to 5 lbs.	2½ to 3½ hours
Boneless Chuck Roast	3 to 5 lbs.	2½ to 3½ hours
Short Ribs	2 × 2 × 4-inch pieces	1½ to 2½ hours
Flank Steak	1½ to 2 lbs.	1½ to 2½ hours
Round Steak	¾ inch to 1 inch thick	1 to 1½ hours
Swiss Steak	1½ inches to 2½ inches thick	2 to 3 hours

TIMETABLE FOR STEWING

Cut	Approx. Weight	Approx. Total Cooking Time
Fresh or Corned Brisket	4 to 6 lbs.	3½ to 4½ hours
Shank Cross Cuts	¾ to 1¼ lbs.	2½ to 3 hours
Beef for Stew	3 to 4 lbs.	2 to 3 hours

Less expensive cuts of beef contain connective tissue that breaks down during a long, slow cooking process. Large cuts of beef are especially tasty cooked in a variety of liquids that renders them moist and succulent with a velvety, gelatinous sauce.

Braising means browning in hot fat and cooking in a minimum amount of liquid. The pan or casserole should be just large enough to hold the meat flat in one layer and must be fitted with a lid that covers it tightly. It holds in the steam needed to soften and make the beef more tender. Allow the meat to cook slowly for a long time. Stock, wine, or water can be combined with aromatic vegetables—onions, carrots, or celery—to add flavor. Herbs and spices like bay leaves, thyme, parsley stems, and peppercorns are pleasant additions too. Beef that is particularly tough, full of sinews and gristle might benefit from marinating. (See "Marinades" in the Outdoor Cooking chapter for suggestions.)

Pot Roasting is a similar technique but browning is optional. The meat is cooked immersed in liquid, which can later be thickened with flour, cornstarch, or by reducing to provide a hearty sauce at the end of cooking. While almost any cut of beef can be pot roasted, it is a technique good for large cuts of tough meat whose texture is made extraordinary by a long, slow simmer. A *stew* consists of smaller pieces of meat cooked in the same manner.

BEEF COOKED IN BEER AND ONIONS

2 pounds chuck or round, cut into 6 to 8 slices
salt and freshly ground black pepper to taste
2 tablespoons butter
2 tablespoons oil
5 to 6 medium onions, peeled and thinly sliced

1½ tablespoons flour
2 cups dark beer
2 to 3 sprigs fresh thyme (or 1 teaspoon dried)
1 bay leaf, crumpled

1. Season the beef with salt and pepper. In an oven-proof covered casserole, melt the butter and oil. Brown the meat in the fat over high heat and remove. Add the onions, lower heat, and cook slowly until soft, stirring frequently. Add the flour and stir to blend. Keep stirring over moderately high heat until flour begins to brown.

2. Pour in the beer. Stir until thickened and simmering. Return the browned beef to the pan, add thyme and bay leaf. Cover and cook over low heat until beef is very tender, about 2½ hours. Check often to make sure that there is enough liquid to cover the meat. Add more beer or water as needed.

3. Correct the seasoning with salt and pepper. Serve very hot with rice or buttered noodles.

BRAISED AND GRILLED OXTAILS

2½ to 3 pounds oxtail, cut into 2-
   inch pieces
2 tablespoons oil
1 onion, peeled and coarsely
   chopped
4 cloves garlic, peeled and coarsely
   chopped
2 carrots, peeled and coarsely
   chopped
2 ribs celery, diced

2 bay leaves
sprig of thyme
1 cup dry white wine
1 cup beef stock (page 59)
salt and freshly ground black pepper
   to taste
mustard for spreading
fresh, soft breadcrumbs for coating
melted butter for drizzling

1. In a large pot, cover the oxtail pieces with cold water and bring to a boil. Simmer for 10 minutes and drain.

2. In a heavy casserole or Dutch oven, heat the oil. Add onions and garlic and cook over low heat until soft, but not brown, about 10 minutes. Add the carrots, celery, and herbs. Set the blanched oxtail pieces on top of the vegetables, pour in the wine and stock. Bring to a boil, then lower to a simmer. Cover and braise over very low heat until the meat is tender and beginning to come away from the bones, about 3 hours.

3. Let the oxtail pieces cool in the braising liquid. Remove them to a platter. Strain and degrease the braising liquid and discard the vegetables. In a saucepan, reduce the braising liquid to a thick syrup.

4. Season the oxtails with salt and pepper. Brush each piece generously with mustard and cover with breadcrumbs. Arrange on a broiling pan and drizzle melted butter over breaded meat. Set the pan 6 inches from the heat and brown. Turn pieces often until they are crisp on all sides.

5. Drizzle reduced pan juices over the oxtail pieces and serve.

BEEF STEW

3½ pounds boneless beef, cut into
   small pieces
salt and freshly ground black pepper
   to taste
¼ cup flour
oil for frying
½ onion, thinly sliced
2 small white turnips, cut into small
   pieces

2 small carrots, peeled and cut into
   small pieces
2 medium potatoes, peeled and cut
   into small pieces
½ cup strained tomatoes, if desired
2 tablespoons butter mixed with 2
   tablespoons flour

1. Season meat well with salt and pepper. Dredge with flour.

2. In a heavy casserole or Dutch oven, brown seasoned meat in hot fat with the onion. Add enough water to barely cover.

3. Simmer until almost tender, about 2 to 3 hours. Check periodically. If too much liquid seems to be evaporating, pour in enough to keep the meat almost covered with liquid. Add the vegetables during last half hour of stewing. Cook until done.

4. Strain cooking liquid into a small saucepan and add any beef drippings stuck to bottom of casserole. Return meat and vegetables to casserole. Blend small amounts of butter and flour mixture into the liquid and whisk over moderate heat until slightly thickened. Season with salt and pepper. Pour sauce over the vegetables and meat and bring to a simmer. Correct seasonings and serve.

BRISKET WITH SAUERKRAUT

2 tablespoons butter
2 tablespoons oil
3 pounds brisket of beef
1 onion, thinly sliced
salt to taste

2 pounds sauerkraut
1 raw potato, peeled and grated, or
  2 tablespoons flour
1 apple, peeled, cored, and sliced
1 tablespoon caraway seeds

1. In a heavy casserole or Dutch oven with a cover, melt butter with oil. When sizzling hot, add meat and brown on all sides. Remove meat and pour off excess fat.

2. Return the meat to the pan and add enough cold water to cover. Bring to a boil over high heat and skim off any foam. Add onion, and salt to taste. Simmer until tender, about 2 hours.

3. Remove meat to a serving platter and keep warm. In a saucepan, combine ¼ of the cooking liquid with sauerkraut, grated potato or flour, and sliced apple. Sprinkle with caraway seeds and simmer 10 to 15 minutes.

4. Slice brisket and serve hot with sauerkraut. (The remaining cooking liquid makes a delicious broth to serve first as soup.)

BRISKET OF BEEF WITH BEANS

1 pound navy or dried lima beans
2 pounds brisket of beef
salt and freshly ground black pepper
   to taste
¼ cup brown sugar

¼ cup molasses
½ teaspoon dry mustard
2 tablespoons butter
2 tablespoons flour

1. Soak beans overnight in cold water, changing water several times.

2. Season meat with salt and pepper. Drain beans, cover with fresh water, and heat slowly. Add meat and simmer until meat and beans are tender, about 2½ hours. Add sugar, molasses, and mustard.

3. Measure out 1 cup of the cooking liquid. In a saucepan, heat the butter, add the flour, and gradually stir in the liquid. Stir constantly and cook until smooth and thickened. Pour this sauce over meat and beans and cook until the beans are brown. Remove brisket, allow to settle for a few minutes, then slice and serve alongside beans in sauce.

BEEF EN CASSEROLE

2½ pounds chuck or round
salt and freshly ground black pepper
   to taste
1 tablespoon flour
2 tablespoons oil or beef drippings

1 small carrot, peeled and diced
1 small onion, peeled and sliced
1 cup strained tomatoes
1 bay leaf

1. Preheat oven to 325° F. Season meat well with salt and pepper and dust with flour. In a heavy casserole or Dutch oven, heat oil or fat and brown meat on all sides.

2. When meat is browned, add remaining ingredients, cover, and simmer in the oven until tender, about 2½ hours. Remove bay leaf and serve hot with mashed or baked potatoes.

PAUPIETTES (MOCK BIRDS)

These thin slices of meat spread with seasonings are rolled up and tied to resemble little birds. The term "mock bird" has been in The Settlement Cookbook *since its first edition. This probably comes from a famous Flanders dish called "oiseau sans tête" (bird without a head) in French.*

1 pound round steak, or veal steak,
    ¼ inch thick, cut into 4 pieces
salt and freshly ground black pepper
    to taste
¼ teaspoon prepared mustard
1 tablespoon chopped cooked bacon
1 teaspoon finely chopped onion
1 tablespoon chopped pickle

1 large pinch paprika
2 tablespoons fat drippings
flour for dredging
2 cups boiling water
1 bay leaf
1 cup sour cream (optional)

1. Flatten meat and sprinkle with salt and pepper. Combine mustard, bacon, onion, pickle, and paprika and spread evenly over the meat slices. Roll each slice and tie with a string or fasten with a toothpick.

2. In a heavy casserole or Dutch oven, heat the fat drippings. Lightly dust each roll with flour and brown on all sides. Add boiling water and bay leaf, cover tightly, and simmer until tender, 2½ to 3 hours. Remove from heat and add sour cream if desired. Remove strings or toothpicks before serving.

Note: Veal does not require as long a cooking time as beef.

Many braised dishes, stews, casseroles, and similar long-cooked preparations that generate their own sauce are perfect "do-ahead" dishes. Easily done in stages that can be carried out days in advance, these sauced preparations can be done in earthenware or glass baking dishes, refrigerated or frozen, and reheated in the oven or microwave. They make welcome additions to "bring-a-covered-dish" affairs as well as thoughtful comforting offerings to friends and neighbors. Use your imagination to mix in rice, potatoes, or cooked noodles to provide a one-dish meal. Fresh bread crumbs or olive oil drizzled on top will provide a crunchy, brown topping when reheated.

BRAISED SHORT RIBS OF BEEF

2 tablespoons butter
2 tablespoons oil
3 pounds short ribs of beef
1 cup chopped celery

½ cup sherry vinegar
1 tablespoon caraway seeds
salt and freshly ground black pepper
    to taste

1. Preheat oven to 325° F. In a heavy covered casserole, melt the butter with oil. When sizzling hot, quickly brown the ribs on all sides.

2. Remove the meat and pour off all but 1 tablespoon of the fat. Add the celery and cook over moderate heat until soft and translucent, about 5 minutes.

(continued)

Stir often to prevent scorching. Carefully pour in the vinegar and bring to a boil over moderately high heat. Return the ribs to the pan. Add the caraway seeds and salt and pepper to taste, cover, and place in the oven.

3. Cook until very tender and meat is pulling away from the bones, about 1 hour. Watch carefully. The meat should exude enough liquid to prevent scorching. If the pan seems too dry, add small amounts of water as needed. Serve the ribs with rice or potatoes with the pan juices alongside.

CLASSIC MEAT LOAF

1 pound beef	onion and celery salt
½ pound veal	½ cup canned tomatoes
small piece suet	¼ pound bread (4 to 5 sandwich
1 egg	slices), soaked in water and
¼ cup chopped walnuts (optional)	squeezed dry
1 teaspoon salt	several strips of thinly sliced bacon

1. Preheat oven to 350° F. In a food processor fitted with a metal blade, grind meat and suet. (Or have the meat ground at the market.)

2. Beat egg well, add meat, walnuts if using, seasonings, tomatoes, and squeezed-dry bread. Mix thoroughly, form into loaf, lay strips of bacon on top.

3. Place in roasting pan in which 1 tablespoon fat has been melted. Bake in oven for 1 hour.

Notes: The suet may be omitted from this recipe, but if it is available, it can add a wonderful flavor. If desired, cook in a loaf pan to retain shape.

KOENIGSBERGER KLOPS (MEAT BALLS)

Meat Balls	*Sauce*
1 pound beef, ground	3 cups water
1 pound pork, ground	1 onion, finely chopped
1 onion, grated	4 bay leaves
⅓ cup breadcrumbs	1 tablespoon sugar
salt and freshly ground black pepper	1 teaspoon salt
to taste	½ teaspoon each allspice and
nutmeg	peppercorns
5 egg whites, beaten	¼ cup tarragon vinegar
	1 tablespoon flour
	5 egg yolks, beaten
	1 lemon, sliced
	capers

1. To prepare the meat balls, mix all ingredients, adding beaten egg whites last. Form into 1-inch balls. Set aside.

2. Boil first 6 sauce ingredients for about 30 minutes. Strain, return liquid to boiling point, add meat balls and simmer 15 minutes.

3. Remove balls to a hot platter and keep them hot. Add vinegar to liquid.

4. Dissolve flour in small amount of water, and to this, add beaten yolks. Add gradually to liquid, stirring constantly until smooth and thick. Do not boil. Pour sauce over meat balls and garnish with lemon slices and capers.

GROUND BEEF IN CABBAGE LEAVES

8 large leaves of cabbage
1 pound lean raw beef, ground
salt and freshly ground black pepper
   to taste
1 small onion, grated
½ cup cooked rice

2 cups tomatoes, peeled, seeded,
   and chopped
1 onion, chopped
2 tablespoons vinegar
2 tablespoons sugar

1. Pour boiling water over the cabbage leaves to make them soften. Set aside.

2. Season the meat with salt and pepper, add grated onion and rice. Roll a portion of the meat mixture in each leaf. Fasten with toothpicks.

3. Place them fold side down in the bottom of a covered kettle. Add the rest of the ingredients, a little water, and simmer until cabbage is tender, 45 minutes to 1 hour.

POT ROAST

2 tablespoons butter
2 tablespoons oil
3 to 4 pounds chuck, shoulder, top
   or bottom round, brisket, blade,
   or rump
salt and freshly ground black pepper
   to taste
1 carrot, peeled and chopped
1 rib celery, diced
1 medium onion, peeled and stuck
   with 4 cloves
1 leek, trimmed, washed, and sliced
   (optional)

1 cup peeled canned tomatoes,
   drained
4 to 6 cloves of garlic, peeled and
   crushed
2 cups red wine, beef stock (page
   59), or water
1 fresh bay leaf (or 2 dried and
   crumpled)
several sprigs fresh thyme (or 1
   teaspoon dried)
2 tablespoons butter mixed with 2
   tablespoons flour

(continued)

1. In a heavy skillet or casserole with a tight-fitting lid, melt the butter and the oil. Season the beef with salt and pepper. When the fat is sizzling hot, brown the meat on all sides.

2. Add the vegetables, garlic, cooking liquid, and herbs. Cover and cook over low heat 2½ to 3 hours. Turn the meat several times while cooking and add additional liquid if necessary to keep barely covered.

3. When the meat is done, skim off excess fat that rises to the surface, remove the bay leaf, place the pot roast on a platter, and cover to keep warm. Strain the cooking liquid into a small saucepan. (You should have about 2½ cups of liquid. If not, add enough water or stock to measure this amount. If you have more than 2½ cups, reduce over high heat to reach this amount.) Discard the vegetables and herbs.

Note: The pot roast can be done a day or two ahead to this point. Let the roast and the sauce come to room temperature. Tightly wrap the cooked beef in plastic wrap or foil. Reserve the sauce separately in the refrigerator. This is a good way to insure that most of the fat is removed. After refrigerating, the fat will congeal on the surface. It is easy to skim this off in its hardened form. Proceed as for below.

4. Bring the cooking liquid to a boil on top of the stove. Whisk in the mixed butter and flour. Blend and heat until thickened. Season to taste with salt and pepper.

5. Return the meat to the casserole. Pour over the sauce. Cook for 10 to 15 more minutes. Remove the roast to a cutting board. Carefully slice (meat will shred easily) and overlap on a serving platter. Pour over some of the sauce. Serve the rest in a sauce boat on the side.

SAUERBRATEN

2 carrots, peeled and finely chopped

2 ribs celery, finely chopped

1 leek, trimmed, washed, and finely chopped (optional)

6 peppercorns

6 juniper berries

2 whole cloves

2 cups red wine

½ cup wine vinegar

2-pound rump roast

salt and freshly ground black pepper

1 tablespoon butter

1 tablespoon oil

2 tablespoons softened butter mixed with 2 tablespoons flour

3 tablespoons raisins

1. In a nonreactive saucepan, combine the vegetables and spices with the red wine and vinegar. Boil for 5 minutes, remove from heat, cover and allow to come to room temperature.

2. Pat the beef dry and place in a bowl small enough to hold the meat totally immersed. Pour over the marinade. Refrigerate for 3 to 5 days, turning the meat occasionally.

3. Preheat oven to 325° F. Remove the beef from the marinade. Dry with paper towels and season with salt and pepper. Heat the butter and oil in a large sauté pan and brown the meat on all sides. Place the browned meat in a heavy, covered oven-proof casserole. Pour over the marinade, cover, and cook in the oven until tender, about 1½ hours.

4. When the meat is done, remove the roast from the casserole and set aside. (Leave the oven on.) Strain the cooking liquid into a small saucepan, pressing down hard on the vegetables to extract as much flavor as possible. (You should have about 2 cups of liquid. If not, add enough water or beef stock to measure this amount. If you have more than 2 cups, boil over high heat to reduce to this amount.) Skim off fat.

Note: The Sauerbraten can be done a day or two ahead to this point. Let the meat and the sauce come to room temperature. Tightly wrap the cooked beef in plastic wrap or foil. Reserve the sauce separately in the refrigerator. This is a good way to insure that most of the fat is removed. After refrigerating, the fat will congeal on the surface. It is easy to skim this off in its hardened form. Proceed as for below.

5. Bring the strained sauce to a boil. Whisk in the mixture of butter and flour. Blend until thickened. Season with salt and pepper to taste. (If lumps appear, strain again after thickening.) Return both the meat and the sauce to the casserole and add the raisins. Return to the oven and cook for 15 to 20 more minutes, covered.

6. Remove the roast and slice carefully (meat will shred easily). Arrange on a serving platter and pour over some of the sauce. Serve the rest in a sauce boat on the side.

Veal

Veal is the meat of the calf. When it comes from a young animal up to 14 weeks of age, it is very tender. Much of the veal on the market today comes from older animals and may require long, moist cooking to insure tenderness. Naturally lean, its flavor and texture are improved by cooking with added fat or liquid.

Veal was always served well done in the past. Today, we've discovered that increasing the degree of doneness actually reduces the tenderness and juiciness, especially when cooked by dry-heat methods. Nowadays veal should be roasted to an internal temperature of 160° F to 170° F which is 10° lower than the charts found in the original editions of *The Settlement Cookbook*.

ROASTING

	TIMETABLE FOR ROASTING *(300° F to 325° F Oven Temperature)*		
Cut	Approx. Weight (Lbs.)	Internal Temp.	Approx. Total Cooking Time (Min. per Lb.)
Loin	3 to 4	160° F (Med.) 170° F (Well)	34 to 36 38 to 40
Loin, Boneless	2 to 3	160° F (Med.) 170° F (Well)	18 to 20 22 to 24
Rib	4 to 5	160° F (Med.) 170° F (Well)	25 to 27 29 to 31
Crown (12 to 14 ribs)	7½ to 9½	160° F (Med.) 170° F (Well)	19 to 21 21 to 23
Rib Eye	2 to 3	160° F (Med.) 170° F (Well)	26 to 28 30 to 33
Rump, Boneless	2 to 3	160° F (Med.) 170° F (Well)	33 to35 37 to 40
Shoulder, Boneless	2 to 3	160° F (Med.) 170° F (Well)	31 to34 34 to 37

Veal is delicate and needs to be handled with care. A quick browning in hot fat before roasting gives an appealing look to the finished roast, although such treatment is optional. A veal roast can successfully be browned in the oven, straight from the refrigerator. Whereas beef is hardy enough to stand a rigorous tossing about and high heat when browning, the tender flesh of veal requires a more gentle approach. Turn carefully with tongs over a moderate heat.

Veal roasts are lean and therefore need some fat added during the dry-heat roasting. Larding with fat using an instrument made specifically for this purpose is best, but perhaps not practical for most modern households. Alternatively, layer strips of bacon over the roasting veal or simply brush with vegetable oil before roasting. Baste frequently with accumulated pan juices. Let veal stand at room temperature for 10 to 15 minutes before carving.

RIB

Rib Roast

Rib Chop

Boneless Rib Chop

Boneless Rib Roast

Crown Roast

Butterfly Chop

Loin Chop

Kidney Chop

Boneless Loin Roast

Loin Roast

LOIN

Boneless Sirloin Roast

Sirloin Steak

Sirloin Roast

Top Sirloin Steak

SIRLOIN

Round Steak

Leg Cutlet

Boneless Rump Roast

LEG/ROUND

Cubed Steak

Stew Meat

Cubes for Kabobs

SHOULDER

Boneless Shoulder Arm Roast

Arm Roast

Boneless Shoulder Eye Roast

Blade Roast

Arm Steak

Blade Steak

VEAL

Breast

Cross-Cut Shank

Shank

Riblet

Boneless Breast Roast

FORESHANK & BREAST

HERB ROASTED VEAL ROAST

1 tablespoon fresh thyme, coarsely
 chopped
5 small leaves fresh sage, torn in
 half
1 tablespoon fresh rosemary,
 coarsely chopped
2 fresh bay leaves, torn in half

1 small piece chilled salt pork
 (about 2 ounces), rind removed
3-pound veal rump roast or
 boneless veal shoulder roast
freshly ground black pepper
½ cup dry white wine

1.　Preheat oven to 325° F. In the bowl of a food processor, combine the herbs with the salt pork. Process to blend. Scrape down sides and process again. Repeat this procedure until a thick, spreadable paste is formed.

2.　Season the roast with black pepper. Spread the herb mixture evenly all over the roast.

3.　Lay roast in a pan just large enough to hold it snugly. Place in the oven uncovered and cook until meat reaches 160° F on a thermometer inserted in the thickest part of the roast, about 1½ hours.

4.　Remove the roast from the pan and keep warm, covered loosely with foil.

5.　Pour off any excess fat from the roasting pan. Place pan over burner on top of the stove. Add wine and adjust heat to medium-high. Use a wire whisk to pick up any roasting bits from the pan. Increase heat and let boil vigorously until pan juices and wine have reduced by half.

6.　Slice veal thinly and arrange on a serving platter. Spoon over the deglazed pan juices and serve immediately.

Note:　Dried herbs can be substituted but the flavor will not be the same. Reduce amounts called for by half if using dried herbs.

STUFFED ROAST VEAL BREAST

Select a small veal breast and have the butcher slice a pocket on the underside. Stuff with Bread Stuffing (page 247) or Potato Stuffing (page 247) and sew up pocket with a trussing needle. Season breast with salt, freshly ground black pepper, and ground ginger. Dredge with flour.

In a very large skillet or fry pan, heat 2 tablespoons fat (a combination of vegetable oil and butter is best). Gently brown the breast on all sides and remove from pan.

Place breast, fat side up, on a rack in a shallow roasting pan. Insert meat thermometer so bulb is centered in thickest part not touching fat. Roast, un-covered, in a slow oven (300 ° F to 325° F), about 1 hour and 30 minutes or until thermometer registers 155° F.

Transfer roast to a warm platter and let stand 15 minutes before carving. Temperature should rise to 160° F, during standing.

Note: Lamb breast may be prepared the same way.

BROILING, PAN BROILING, AND PANFRYING

TIMETABLE FOR BROILING

Cut	Approx. Weight	Inches from Heat	Approx. Total Cooking Time in Minutes	
			Med. (160° F)	Well (170° F)
Loin/Rib Chops				
1 inch	8 ozs.	4	14	17
1½ inches	11 ozs.	5	21	25
Arm/Blade Steak				
¾ inch	16 ozs.	4	14	16
Ground Veal Patties				
½ inch	4 ozs.	4	8	12

TIMETABLE FOR PAN BROILING
(Cook over Medium-Low to Medium Heat)

Cut	Approx. Weight	Approx. Total Cooking Time in Minutes	
		Med. (160° F)	Well (170° F)
Loin/Rib Chops ¾ inch to 1 inch	7 to 8 ozs.	10	14
Blade/Arm Steak ¾ inch	16 ozs.	13	15
Ground Veal Patties ½ inch (medium to medium-high heat)	4 ozs.	6	9

(continued)

TIMETABLE FOR PANFRYING
(Cook over Medium-High Heat)

Cut	Approx. Thickness	Approx. Total Cooking Time (Min. per Lb.)
Cutlets	⅛ inch	3 to 4
	¼ inch	5 to 6
Ground Veal Patties	½ inch	5 to 7
Veal Steaks (Loin)	1 to 2 inches	5 to 6

Follow guidelines for panfrying and broiling beef (page 278) but be especially careful to choose the right cut of veal. Only the most tender cuts should be used for quick-cooking techniques. For example, cutlets from the leg do well when seasoned then quickly cooked in hot fat or butter. Pounding these kinds of cutlets between 2 sheets of waxed paper aids tenderization by breaking down connective tissue. Chops can be panfried if particularly thin and of exceptional quality. (Otherwise, follow instructions for braising). Do not overcook veal when panfrying; most cuts require a simple browning and a quick but moderate finishing. Marinating in a seasoned liquid containing a food acid such as lemon juice, vinegar, or wine for 6 to 24 hours helps to tenderize quick-cooking cuts of veal.

MEDALLIONS OF VEAL IN SORREL SAUCE

3 cups (loosely packed) whole sorrel leaves, large stems removed
4 boneless veal steaks (from the loin), about 2 inches thick
salt and freshly ground black pepper to taste

2 tablespoons butter
2 tablespoons oil
1 cup heavy cream
several drops of lemon juice, if needed

1. Bring a large amount of salted water to a boil in a large, nonreactive pot. Plunge in the sorrel and blanch for 1 minute. Drain well. When cool enough to handle, squeeze out as much liquid as possible using your hands. Coarsely chop and set aside.

2. Season veal steaks with salt and pepper. In a large sauté pan, melt the butter and oil over moderately high heat. When sizzling, add the steaks and cook until done, about 5 minutes on each side. Turn frequently. Remove to a serving platter and keep warm.

3. Pour off fat from the sauté pan. Add cream. Stir vigorously with a wire whisk and bring to a boil. Reduce by half over high heat. Turn down heat and stir in the chopped sorrel. Do not allow cream to boil again. Season to taste with salt and pepper. Off the heat, add several drops of lemon juice just before serving. (This depends on the acidity of the sorrel being used.)

4. Pour off any liquid that has accumulated on the meat platter. Spoon over the sauce and serve at once.

Variation: If sorrel is not available, a good substitution is watercress. Use the same amount but remove as many of the hard, tough stems as possible from the watercress as they are very bitter. Proceed as for above.

VEAL CUTLETS

Use slices of veal from the ribs or the leg cut ¼ inch thick. Have the butcher flatten to a uniform thickness or place between pieces of waxed paper and make smooth with the back of a large knife. Season well with salt and freshly ground black pepper. Dredge cutlets in breadcrumbs and let sit for 15 minutes. Dip in lightly beaten egg, and then in breadcrumbs again. Fry slowly until well browned in hot oil and butter, about 3 minutes on each side. Drain well and serve while still very hot.

Variations: Spread the cutlets lightly with Dijon mustard before the initial breading for a more pungent flavor. Alternatively, cook cutlets in a mixture of butter and oil without breading. Do not overcook. The cutlets should be firm and moist but not tough and dried out.

Notes: Deglazing the pan with the addition of an acidic flavoring such as wine, vinegar, or lemon juice makes a quick and tasty sauce. Cutlets take well to marinating, too. Simply drizzle with good olive oil and a small amount of lemon juice or white wine an hour or so before cooking. Refrigerate and turn every 10 or 15 minutes. Be sure to dry them well before browning.

WIENER SCHNITZEL

Cook breaded veal cutlets as for above. When done, sprinkle with lemon juice. Garnish each serving with lemon slices, capers, anchovy fillets, and a fried or poached egg, if desired.

PARPRIKA SCHNITZEL

4 boneless veal cutlets, cut from the
   leg (about ¼ pound each)
flour, salt, and freshly ground black
   pepper, for dredging
2 tablespoons butter

2 tablespoons oil
1 tablespoon paprika
3 medium onions, sliced
½ cup sour cream

1. Pound cutlets to a ¼-inch thickness (see Veal Cutlets, above). Dip in flour mixed with salt and pepper.

2. Heat butter and oil in a large sauté pan. Stir in paprika. Add the sliced onions and cook until soft and translucent.

3. Add cutlets and cook until brown on both sides. Stir in sour cream, cover, and cook until meat is tender, about 10 minutes.

QUICK VEAL CUTLET SAUTÉS

4 boneless veal cutlets, cut from the
   leg (about ¼ pound each)
salt and freshly ground black pepper
   to taste
2 tablespoons butter
2 tablespoons oil
1 cup chicken stock (page 59)

½ cup marsala (or port or any other
   fortified wine)
½ teaspoon cornstarch dissolved in
   1 teaspoon water
freshly chopped parsley for garnish
   (optional)

1. Place veal between 2 pieces of waxed paper. Use the handle of a large knife to pound the meat flat. Season to taste with salt and pepper.

2. In a large sauté pan or nonstick skillet, melt butter and oil. Over moderately high heat, quickly brown the veal on both sides (about 1½ minutes on each side). Remove to a platter and keep warm.

3. Pour off the fat from the browning of the veal. Place the pan back on the heat and pour in the chicken stock and the wine. Stir to remove any browned bits and reduce over high heat until slightly thickened, about 2 minutes.

4. Turn down heat to a slow simmer. Pour in the cornstarch mixture and stir to dissolve. Turn off heat and continue stirring until sauce is creamy.

5. Drain off any accumulated moisture from the meat platter. Spoon the sauce over the cutlets, garnish with freshly chopped parsley if desired, and serve at once.

<u>**Variations:**</u>

Balsamic Vinegar: After browning the veal above, pour off all but 1 tablespoon of the cooking fat. Add one finely chopped shallot (one heaping tablespoon) and cook over moderate heat until translucent. Replace the wine with ½ cup balsamic vinegar. Proceed with the basic recipe.

Ginger and Cream: After browning the veal as for above, omit the chicken stock. Instead, pour off fat and deglaze the pan with ¼ cup dry white wine. Boil over high heat to reduce by half. Pour in 1 cup heavy cream and 2 to 3 tablespoons chopped, fresh ginger. Omit the cornstarch mixture. Turn up heat and let boil vigorously until reduced by half. Sauce should be thick and creamy. Off heat, gently stir in 1 teaspoon cider vinegar. Season well with salt and pepper. Proceed with the basic recipe.

Curry Sauce: After browning the veal as for above, pour off all but 2 tablespoons cooking fat. Add 1 tablespoon finely chopped onion and 1 tablespoon mild curry powder. Cook over moderately low heat until onions are translucent and slightly softened, about 2 minutes. Pour in the cup of chicken stock, add one tablespoon tomato paste and increase the heat. Omit the cornstarch mixture. Boil vigorously, stirring with a whisk until reduced by half. Proceed with the basic recipe.

 Red Pepper Sauce: After browning the veal as for above, pour off all but 2 tablespoons cooking fat. Add 2 tablespoons finely chopped onion and cook over moderately low heat until onions are translucent and slightly softened, about 2 minutes. Add 1½ cups diced red pepper and cook for an additional 2 minutes. Pour in 1 cup of chicken stock. Omit the cornstarch mixture. Boil vigorously, stirring with a whisk until reduced by half. Season with ¼ teaspoon cumin and a pinch of cayenne pepper. Pour mixture into a blender or food processor and puree until smooth. Pass sauce through a fine sieve back into the pan. Correct seasoning and proceed with the basic recipe.

BRAISING AND STEWING

TIMETABLE FOR BRAISING

Cut	Weight or Thickness	Approx. Total Cooking Time
Boneless Breast, Stuffed	2 to 2½ lbs.	1¼ to 1½ hours
	4 to 4½ lbs.	2 to 2½ hours
Boneless Breast, Rolled and Tied	2 to 3 lbs.	1½ to 2½ hours
Riblets	2 to 3 lbs.	50 to 70 minutes

(continued)

TIMETABLE FOR BRAISING

Cut	Weight or Thickness	Approx. Total Cooking Time
Arm/Blade Steak	¾ inch to 1 inch thick	45 to 60 minutes
Round Steak	¼ inch thick	30 minutes
Boneless Shoulder Roast	3½ to 4 lbs.	2 to 2½ hours
Loin/Rib Chops	½ inch thick	8 to 10 minutes
	¾ inch to 1 inch thick	20 to 25 minutes

TIMETABLE FOR STEWING

Cut	Approx. Size	Approx. Total Cooking Time
Boneless Breast	1-inch cubes or pieces	1¼ to 1½ hours
Cross Cut Shanks	1½ inches thick	1 to 1¼ hours
Veal for Stew	1- to 1½-inch cubes or pieces	45 to 60 minutes

Braising is the choice technique for less tender and generally more economical cuts of veal. (For guidelines on braising, see page 282). The veal is first slowly browned in hot oil for flavor and color, then leisurely cooked with a small amount of liquid such as water, stock, wine, or fruit/vegetable juice until tender. Remember that a slower and more gentle browning is advised for veal than for beef. Stewing is particularly good for veal. Less tender but richly flavored cuts are usually cut into small pieces and simmered for a relatively long time. This differs from braising in that the meat is covered with liquid, or a combination of liquids, and gently simmered over low heat until tender. The resulting broth can be reduced or thickened and served as a sauce.

BRAISED VEAL CHOPS

4 veal chops (from the loin or rib,
　¾ to 1 inch thick)
salt and freshly ground black pepper
flour for dredging
2 tablespoons butter

2 tablespoons oil
1 medium onion, thinly sliced
1 cup chicken stock (page 59) or
　water

1. Preheat oven to 325° F. Season chops with salt and pepper. Dredge lightly in flour.

2. In a large skillet, heat the butter and oil. Gently brown the chops over moderately high heat, about 2 minutes on each side. Remove to drain on paper towels.

3. Pour off all but 2 tablespoons of fat. Add the onion and cook over moderate heat until wilted and transparent, about 5 minutes.

4. Place chops in a heat-proof covered baking dish. Cover with the cooked onions.

5. Place the pan the onions were cooked in back on the stove. Gradually add the chicken stock and stir vigorously with a wire whisk to remove any browned bits. Allow liquid to come to a boil. Pour over the chops and onions. Season with additional salt and pepper. Cover tightly and cook in oven until chops are very tender, 45 minutes to 1 hour. Check regularly and add small amount liquid if necessary.

OSSO BUCCO (BRAISED VEAL SHANKS)

2 pounds meaty veal shanks, about 2 inches thick
salt and freshly ground black pepper to taste
2 tablespoons butter
2 tablespoons oil
½ cup dry white wine
2 small onions, finely chopped
3 medium carrots, finely chopped

2 stalks celery, thinly sliced
several sprigs of fresh thyme (or 1 teaspoon dried)
1 clove garlic, thinly sliced
1 cup whole tomatoes in puree, chopped
1 cup chicken or beef stock (page 59)

1. Trim any gristle from veal and season with salt and pepper. Melt butter and oil in a large sauté pan. When sizzling hot, add meat and brown well on both sides. Remove to an oven-proof casserole with a tight-fitting cover.

2. Pour off excess fat from the sauté pan. Add the wine and stir with a whisk over moderately high heat. Reduce by half. Add the onions, the carrots, and the celery. Cook until vegetables are slightly softened, stirring to prevent scorching.

3. Preheat oven to 325° F. Cover meat with cooked vegetables along with any accumulated pan juices from the sauté pan. Add the thyme, garlic, and the tomatoes. Pour on enough stock to reach halfway up the meat.

4. Cover the casserole in the oven and cook until veal shreds easily when pierced with a fork, about 2 hours.

5. Remove the cooked veal to a platter. Strain the contents of the casserole over the meat, pressing hard on the vegetables to extract as much flavor as possible. Serve with buttered noodles, boiled potatoes, or rice.

Note: If the sauce seems too thin, strain the contents into a heavy saucepan and cook vigorously until reduced. The sauce should be just thick enough to coat the back of a spoon.

VEAL FRICASSEE

Veal

2 pounds lean cubes of veal
1 yellow onion, quartered
2 carrots, peeled, halved, and cut into 2-inch pieces
1 stalk celery, peeled and cut into 2-inch pieces
1 quart chicken stock (page 59)
salt to taste
3 tablespoons butter
3 tablespoons flour

Onions

20 to 25 pearl onions, peeled
1 tablespoon butter, at room temperature
1 teaspoon sugar

Mushrooms

½ pound mushrooms, trimmed, cleaned, and quartered
1 tablespoon butter
1 tablespoon oil
salt and freshly ground black pepper to taste

1. In a large pot, place the veal, onion, carrots, and celery. Pour in the stock and season lightly with salt. (Be careful if using canned stock; it can be very salty.)

2. Bring to a simmer over moderately high heat. Reduce heat and cook slowly, uncovered, until meat is very tender, 1 to 1½ hours.

3. Drain meat and vegetables. Reserve the meat and cooking liquid; discard the aromatic vegetables. There should be about 3 cups of the liquid. If there is more than this amount, return to the stove and reduce over high heat until it measures 3 cups. If there is less than this amount, add enough water or stock to reach this measure.

4. Melt the butter in a large saucepan. Add the flour and blend. Cook over low heat for a minute or two to remove the raw flour taste. Pour in the reserved 3 cups liquid. Increase heat and stir until thickened. Add the cubes of veal. Remove from heat and set aside.

5. To prepare the onions: Place the onions in a small sauté pan. Pour in enough cold water to half cover. Add the butter and the sugar. Cook over high heat until all of the water has evaporated, stirring and shaking the pan often. When the water has boiled out, the onions should be soft and cooked through. The sugar will caramelize the onions. They must be watched carefully at this point. Toss and stir as they turn a rich, amber color. Drain on paper towels. Set aside until ready to assemble the dish.

6. To prepare the mushrooms: Pat dry the mushrooms. In a sauté pan, melt the butter and the oil. Increase heat to moderately high. Add the mushrooms and toss to coat in the mixture of butter and oil. Season well with salt and pepper. Keep the heat high and stir or toss constantly until the mushrooms just begin to give off water. They should be well browned and glistening. Remove from heat and drain on paper towels. Set aside until ready to assemble the dish.

Just before serving, bring the veal and sauce to a simmer. Add the caramelized pearl onions and the browned mushrooms. Warm through over moderate heat. Season again with salt and pepper to taste. Serve with noodles or rice.

Notes: The pearl onions and mushrooms can be done 24 hours in advance. Proceed as is indicated above. Let cool completely and cover with plastic wrap. Keep in a cool spot but do not refrigerate.

Pork, Ham, and Bacon

Today's pork is leaner and lower in fat and calories than ever before. New breeding and feeding practices as well as closer trimming of retail cuts makes pork an attractive choice for the modern cook. Pork cuts that come from the "loin" or "leg" (such as pork loin, tenderloin, center cut loin chops, and selected leg roasts) are leaner than the average pork cut and have less fat.

PORK AND THE MICROWAVE
(See also General Tips for Microwaving Meat, page 271)
(courtesy of National Meat Board)

1. Cook pork in a closed container such as a loosely sealed cooking bag or a covered microwave-safe container. The closed container produces a moist atmosphere, which reduces heat loss and provides more even cooking.

2. Cook at medium-low or medium power setting to ensure even cooking. The improvement in overall eating quality is worth the extra minutes. In a microwave oven with full power output of 650 watts, medium-low is 30 percent of power or 200 watts. Medium is 50 percent power or 325 watts.

3. Rotate cooking dish and rearrange pork halfway through cooking. Turn roasts, ribs, or chops and stir cubes for more even cooking.

4. Select compact, evenly-shaped boneless and bone-in pork roasts for microwave cooking. Roasts should weigh 3 to 3½ pounds and be about 4 inches in diameter. Suggested bone-in roasts include pork loin center roasts (rib or loin) and pork shoulder blade Boston roasts.

5. Ask your meat retailer to cut country-style ribs into 1-inch-thick portions and spareribs or back ribs into 3- to 4-rib portions. Ribs may weigh up to 3 to 3½ pounds.

6. Select pork chops weighing 5 to 7 ounces each and cut ¾ to 1 inch thick. Boneless top loin, center cut rib or center cut loin chops are all good choices.

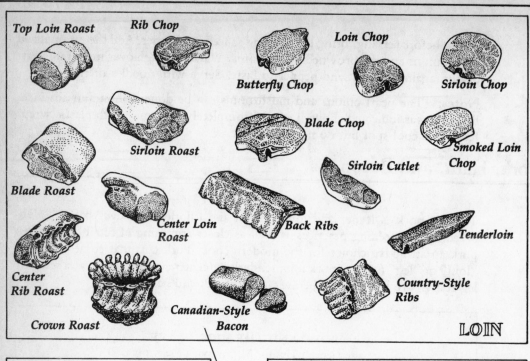

Top Loin Roast

Rib Chop

Loin Chop

Butterfly Chop

Sirloin Chop

Sirloin Roast

Blade Chop

Smoked Loin Chop

Blade Roast

Sirloin Cutlet

Center Loin Roast

Back Ribs

Tenderloin

Center Rib Roast

Country-Style Ribs

Crown Roast

Canadian-Style Bacon

LOIN

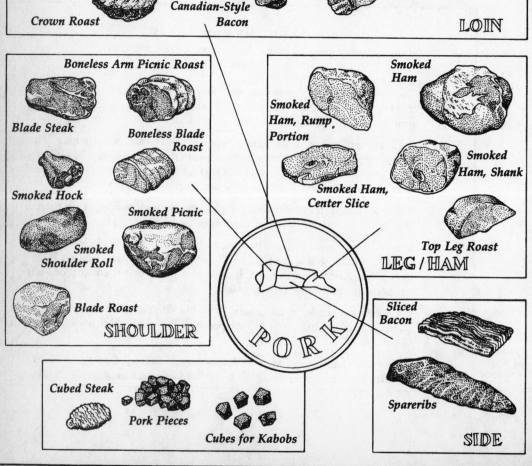

Boneless Arm Picnic Roast

Blade Steak

Boneless Blade Roast

Smoked Hock

Smoked Picnic

Smoked Shoulder Roll

Blade Roast

SHOULDER

Smoked Ham

Smoked Ham, Rump Portion

Smoked Ham, Shank

Smoked Ham, Center Slice

Top Leg Roast

LEG / HAM

PORK

Sliced Bacon

Spareribs

SIDE

Cubed Steak

Pork Pieces

Cubes for Kabobs

ROASTING

	TIMETABLE FOR ROASTING		
	(325° F Oven Temperature)		
Cut	Approx. Weight or Size	Internal Temp.	Approx. Total Cooking Time (Min. per Lb.)
Loin Center (bone-in)	3 to 5 lbs.	160° F 170° F	20 to 25 26 to 31
Blade/Loin/Sirloin (boneless tied)	2½ to 3½ lbs.	170° F	33 to 38
Boneless Rib End	2 to 4 lbs.	160° F 170° F	26 to 31 28 to 33
Top (double)	3 to 4 lbs.	160° F 170° F	29 to 34 33 to 38
Top	2 to 4 lbs.	160° F 170° F	23 to 33 30 to 40
Crown	6 to 10 lbs.	170° F	20 to 25
Leg			
Whole (bone-in)	12 lbs.	170° F	23 to 25
Top (inside)	3½ lbs.	170° F	38 to 42
Bottom (outside)	3 ½ lbs.	170° F	40 to 45
Blade Boston (boneless)	3 to 4 lbs.	170° F	40 to 45
Tenderloin	½ to 1 lb.	160° F 170° F	27 to 29 30 to 32
Backribs		tender	1½ to 1¾ hours (total cooking time)
Country-Style Ribs	1-inch slices	tender	1½ to 1¾ hours (total cooking time)
Spareribs		tender	1½ to 1¾ hours (total cooking time)
Ground Pork Loaf	1 to 1½ lbs.	170° F	55 to 65
Meatballs	1 inch	170° F	25 to 30
	2 inches	170° F	30 to 35

Recommendations for roasting pork used to call for an internal temperature of 185° F, which often meant a dry, tough piece of meat. Nutritionists agree that a temperature of 160° F is perfectly safe for the modern consumer. A well-done roast registers about 170° F on the meat thermometer. The result of not overcooking is a moist, succulent piece of pork, especially when roasted.

Loin, tenderloin, shoulder, or leg (fresh ham) are good choices for roasting. Pork should be roasted at a low temperature for most of the time that it cooks. A quick browning in hot fat will give an appealing look to the finished meat. After that, the pork should cook at an even pace until the internal temperature measures at least 160° F on a meat thermometer when placed at the thickest part of the roast, away from the bone. To check the doneness of the pork roast without a thermometer, pierce with a long needle, skewer, or the tip of a thin-bladed knife. The juices should run clear, without a trace of pink.

CARVING A PORK LOIN

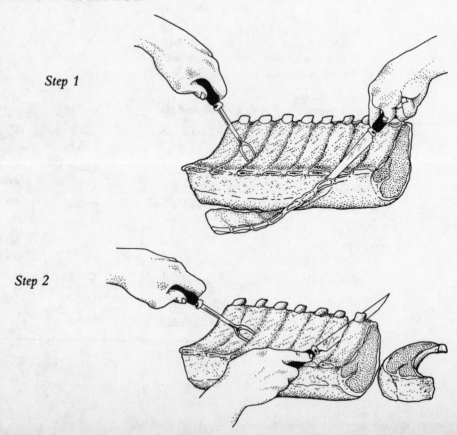

Step 1

Step 2

SHERRY-GLAZED PORK

2-pound pork loin
salt and freshly ground black pepper
2 tablespoons butter
2 tablespoons oil

½ cup sherry
¼ cup firmly packed brown sugar
1 teaspoon freshly ground cloves
   (or 2 teaspoons bottled ground
   cloves)

1. Preheat oven to 325° F. Season the pork with salt and pepper. In a large sauté pan, melt the butter and oil. Brown the pork in the sauté pan over high heat. Remove to a covered oven-proof casserole.

2. In a saucepan, combine the sherry, sugar, and cloves. Bring to a boil and cook until syrupy, about 3 minutes.

3. Spoon glaze over roast. Place in oven and roast until internal temperature reaches 160° F to 170° F (see chart above). Baste frequently with the glaze and accumulated pan juices. Let sit, covered loosely with foil, 10 to 15 minutes before slicing.

Note: If you have a spice grinder, simply grind several whole cloves to a fine powder. Store-bought ground cloves are less pungent.

Variation:

Molasses Bourbon Glaze: Follow the recipe above. Substitute ½ cup bourbon for the sherry and ½ cup dark molasses for the brown sugar. Add 1 teaspoon fresh thyme and ½ teaspoon ground ginger in place of the ground cloves.

ROAST PORK TENDERLOINS WITH MUSTARD SAUCE

2 pork tenderloins, about ¾ pound
   each
salt and freshly ground black pepper
   to taste
2 tablespoons vegetable oil

½ cup dry white wine
½ cup heavy cream
¼ cup Dijon mustard
chopped fresh parsley for garnish
   (optional)

1. Preheat oven to 325° F. Pat tenderloins dry and season with salt and pepper. Place 1 tablespoon of the oil in a baking dish. Brush the tenderloin with the remaining tablespoon of oil. In an oven-proof pan, brown on top of the stove. Place in oven and cook until the roast reaches an internal temperature of 160° F to 170° F, about 30 minutes. (Meat should be firm to the touch and juices should be clear, not pink, when pierced at the thickest part of the roast.)

2. Meanwhile, in a medium-size, nonreactive saucepan, pour in the wine. Over high heat, boil until reduced by half, about 3 minutes. Pour in the cream and continue boiling over high heat until it thickly coats the back of a spoon, about 5 minutes.

3. Remove sauce from heat, stir in the mustard and season to taste with salt and pepper.

4. Slice tenderloin into 1-inch-thick slices on the diagonal. Place on a serving platter and spoon over sauce. Garnish with chopped parsley if desired.

Variation:

With Dried Fruit: Prepare the pork tenderloin as for above but to the roasting pan add ¼ cup golden raisins, 4 to 6 pitted prunes cut in half, and 4 to 6 dried apricots cut into slivers. Omit the mustard sauce. Remove the cooked roast to a platter and keep warm. Pour 1 cup dry white wine into the roasting pan with the dried fruit. Cook over high heat on top of the stove until reduced by half, carefully stirring to pick up any bits left in the bottom of the pan from roasting. Cut the pork as indicated above. Serve on a platter surrounded with the dried fruit. Garnish with chopped parsley if desired.

BAKING HAM

TIMETABLE FOR BAKING HAM
(325° F Oven Temperature)

Cut	Approx. Weight in Lbs.	Internal Temp.	Approx. Total Cooking Time (Min. per Lb.)
Whole Ham (with bone)	10 to 15	170° F	23 to 25
Shank Half (or Butt portion, bone-in)	3 to 5	170° F	38 to 42
Picnic	4 to 10	170° F	35 to 40

Baking pork usually refers to ham. For tenderized commercial hams, follow directions on the wrapper. For regular hams, refer to the chart for cooking times.

CLASSIC BAKED HAM

 Place a whole fresh ham thick side up on a rack in an open pan. Bake at 325° F according to Timetable for Baking Ham (above). About 45 minutes before ham is done, remove from oven. Take off all rind except a collar around the shank bone. Score the fat to form diamonds. Moisten 1 cup brown sugar with fat drippings and 2 tablespoons flour, if desired, and rub over ham. Stud with whole cloves. Return to oven. Add 1 cup cider or robust red wine and baste ham often, increasing the heat to 400° F for the last 20 minutes to brown the ham. Let rest for 15 to 20 minutes before carving.

CARVING A HAM SHANK

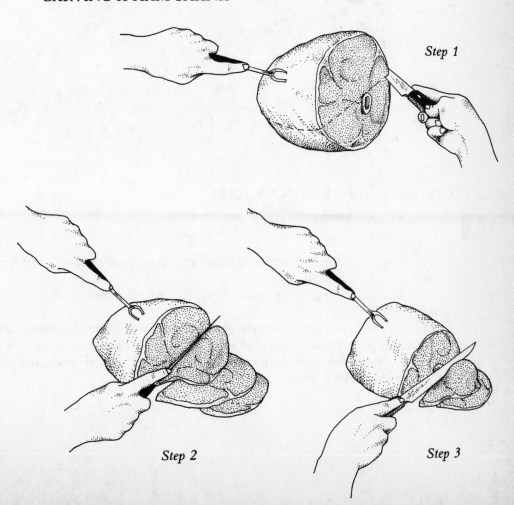

Step 1

Step 2

Step 3

CARVING BUTT END OF HALF HAM

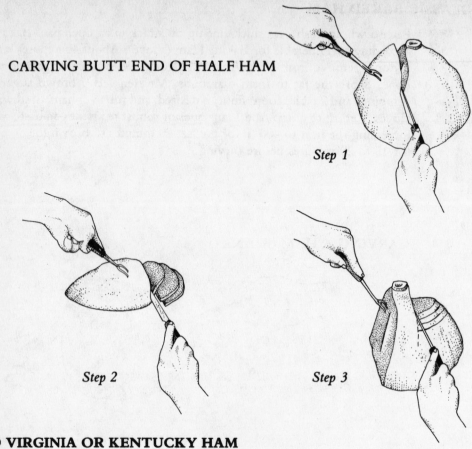

Step 1

Step 2

Step 3

BAKED VIRGINIA OR KENTUCKY HAM

1 country-style smoked ham, 10 to 12 pounds	brown sugar whole cloves

1. Soak ham for 12 hours in cold water, changing the water 2 or 3 times. Drain and scrub thoroughly.

2. Place in boiling water and simmer, covered, 25 minutes per pound. Let cool slightly.

3. Lift from kettle and remove rind. Score fat in a diagonal pattern. Spread thoroughly with brown sugar and stud with cloves. Place in roasting pan and bake uncovered for 20 or 30 minutes at 375° F, basting with cider, red wine, or concentrated fruit juice.

BAKED COUNTRY HAM IN CRUST

 Soak and scrub a country-style ham as directed above. Make a thick paste of rye flour and water. Spread all over ham. Set on a rack in pan. Bake in hot oven (400° F) to brown paste, then lower temperature and bake about 4 hours at 300° F. Make a hole in paste and pour in a cup of hot cider and the pan drippings. Repeat twice if needed. Bake 1 hour longer, slit crust, and remove it. Remove rind. Brush the fat with beaten yolk of egg, sprinkle with brown sugar and rye bread crumbs, and brown. Save crust and use to keep leftover ham moist.

HAM SLICE BAKED WITH APPLES

1 ham slice, ½ inch thick, about 1¼ pounds
3 Granny Smith apples, peeled, cored, seeded, and cut into quarters
¼ cup calvados or applejack (optional)
1 cup cider

1. Preheat oven to 350° F. Pat ham slice dry. Evenly brown the ham in a large skillet over high heat. (It should give off enough fat to properly brown the slice. If not, add a tablespoon or two of all-purpose vegetable oil.) Remove to a baking dish and keep warm.

2. Add the apples to the skillet and brown quickly on all sides. Remove to the baking dish with the ham.

3. Pour all excess fat from the skillet. Add calvados or applejack if desired and stir to pick up any bits left from the browning of the ham and apples. Add cider and bring to a boil. Reduce by half. Empty baking dish of any accumulated juices. Pour sauce over ham and apples.

4. Bake until ham is tender and sauce is thick and syrupy, about 30 minutes. Baste frequently with the pan juices. If the apples become too soft, remove and replace just to heat through at the end of the baking.

5. Arrange the ham on a large platter. Surround with the apples. Spoon over a bit of the sauce and serve the rest on the side.

Note: If cooking liquid is still not thickened enough at the end of baking, drain into a heavy saucepan and reduce over high heat until it reaches desired consistency.

BAKED SAUSAGE

1½ pounds sausage meat
1 cup flour
3 teaspoons baking powder

½ teaspoon salt
3 tablespoons shortening
½ cup milk

1. Preheat oven to 450° F. Put the meat into a shallow baking pan. In a bowl, toss together the flour, baking powder, and salt. Cut in shortening until mixture looks like cornmeal. Add milk and stir to make a soft dough. Knead 5 or 6 times and pat or roll into a sheet the size of the pan.

2. Lay the dough on the sausage, mark in squares for serving and bake until biscuit topping is well browned and sausage is cooked through, 10 to 15 minutes. Pour off excess fat.

BROILING, PAN BROILING, AND PANFRYING

TIMETABLE FOR BROILING, PAN BROILING, AND PANFRYING
(4 Inches from Heat)

Cut	Approx. Thickness/ Weight	Internal Temp.	Approx. Total Cooking Time in Minutes
Loin/Rib Chop (bone-in)	¾ inch	160° F	8 to 11
		170° F	11 to 14
	1½ inches	160° F	19 to 22
		170° F	23 to 25
Boneless Loin Chop	1 inch	160° F	11 to 13
		170° F	13 to 15
	1½ inches	160° F	16 to 18
		170° F	18 to 20
Butterflied Chop	1 inch	160° F	11 to 13
		170° F	13 to 15
	1½ inches	160° F	16 to 18
		170° F	18 to 20
Blade Chop (bone-in)	¾ inch	170° F	13 to 15
	1½ inches	170° F	26 to 29
Shoulder Chop (bone-in)	¾ inch	170° F	13 to 18
	1½ inches	170° F	18 to 20
Pork Cube Kebabs Loin/Leg	1 inch	160° F	9 to 11
		170° F	11 to 13
Tenderloin	1 inch	160° F	12 to 14
		170° F	16 to 18
Tenderloin	½ to 1 lb.	160° F	16 to 21
		170° F	20 to 25

TIMETABLE FOR BROILING, PAN BROILING, AND PANFRYING
(4 Inches from Heat)

Cut	Approx. Thickness/ Weight	Internal Temp.	Approx. Total Cooking Time in Minutes
Ground Pork Patties	½ inch	170° F	7 to 9
Country-Style Ribs (5 inches from heat)	1 inch slices	tender	45 to 60
Spareribs (5 inches from heat)		tender	45 to 60
Backribs (5 inches from heat)		tender	45 to 60
Butterflied Single Loin Roast (boneless)	3 lbs.	160° F	22 to 24
		170° F	26 to 28

Small, lean cuts of pork and fatty cuts like bacon are best for broiling, pan broiling, and panfrying. Because pork needs a rather slow and gentle cooking, only the thinnest and leanest of chops are candidates for broiling or quick frying. Thicker chops can be browned first but then must be cooked slowly for a long period of time (see "Braising" below).

Bacon

Place bacon slices in a cold skillet, cook slowly over medium heat until crisp. Turn frequently with tongs or a fork. Press slices during cooking to prevent buckling and curling. Drain on paper towels.

Or place thin slices of bacon close together on rack over dripping pan. Broil until crisp, about 3 minutes per side.

 Bacon can be cooked successfully in the microwave oven. Follow manufacturer's instructions for your particular oven. Place bacon between sheets of paper towel to absorb fat. Cook on a microwavable plate or on a microwavable roasting rack.

Canadian Bacon

Canadian bacon is smoked boneless pork loin with only a small amount of fat. It should be sliced thin and broiled or panfried. Canadian bacon may be used in recipes like other cooked bacon.

Sausages

FRIED LIVER SAUSAGES .

 Fry fresh liver sausage in 2 tablespoons fat until browned. Serve with sauerkraut and boiled potatoes, or with fried onions.

FRIED PORK SAUSAGE

 Prick sausage with a fork. Place in skillet with a little boiling water, cook until water is evaporated and fry until brown and cooked through.

BRAISING AND STEWING

	TIMETABLE FOR BRAISING	
Cut	**Approx. Weight or Thickness**	**Approx. Total Cooking Time**
Loin/Rib Chop (bone-in)	¾ inch	30 minutes
Boneless Loin Chop	1½ inches	45 minutes
Spareribs/Backribs		1½ hours
Country-Style Ribs		1½ to 2 hours
Tenderloin Whole	½ to 1 lb.	40 to 45 minutes
Slices	½ inch	25 minutes
Shoulder Steaks	¾ inch	40 to 50 minutes
Cubes	1 inch to 1¼ inches	45 to 60 minutes
Leg Steaks (inside)	⅛ to ¼ inch	5 to 7 minutes
Blade Boston (boneless)	2½ to 3½ lbs.	2 to 2½ hours
Blade Boston (bone-in)	3 to 4 lbs.	2¼ to 2¾ hours
Sirloin (boneless)	2½ to 3 lbs.	1¾ to 2¼ hours

SAUSAGE AND PEPPERS

Prepare Fried Pork Sausage as described above (page 314). Roast red, yellow, or green peppers as described on page 385. Cut into thin strips. Remove cooked sausage to a serving platter and keep warm. Drain fat from pan and toss pepper strips with chopped garlic to taste until pepper strips are heated through and garlic is softened, about 2 minutes. Strew peppers over sausage and serve at once.

TIMETABLE FOR STEWING

Cut	Approx. Thickness	Approx. Total Cooking Time
Spareribs		2 to 2½ hours
Country-Style Ribs		2 to 2½ hours
Cubes	1 to 1¼-inch cubes or pieces	45 to 60 minutes

Braising pork is one of the best ways to treat this naturally moist meat from the pig. As for beef, veal, or lamb, a braise works best with a minimum amount of liquid. Long cooking times will break down the tough fibers characteristic of meat meant to be braised or stewed. Different liquids may be used to add flavor and character to the meat (see the "Braised Pork Chops" below).

BRAISED PORK CHOPS

4 pork chops, 1 to 2 inches thick
salt and freshly ground black pepper
   to taste
2 tablespoons butter
2 tablespoons oil

1 small onion, thinly sliced
1½ cups chicken or beef stock (page 59)
chopped fresh parsley (optional)

1.   Preheat oven to 325° F. Trim chops and pat dry. Season to taste with salt and pepper. In a large sauté pan, melt the butter with the oil. Over moderately high heat, brown quickly on both sides. Remove chops to a covered, oven-proof casserole.
2.   Pour off all but 1 tablespoon of fat from sauté pan. Add the onion and cook over moderately high heat until soft and translucent. Pour in the stock and bring to a boil.
3.   Pour the contents of the sauté pan over the pork chops. Cover tightly. Place in the oven and cook until tender. (Refer to charts above for cooking time.)
4.   Remove chops to a serving platter and keep warm. Strain liquid into a

saucepan. Skim off fat from the surface. Reduce until thickened over high heat. Spoon sauce over chops and serve at once. Garnish with chopped parsley if desired.

Variations:

Beer and Onions: In the basic recipe above, increase the onions to 2. Replace the liquid called for with 1½ cups dark beer. Add 1 teaspoon fresh rosemary and proceed with the basic recipe, except simply strain the cooking liquid over the chops and do not reduce further. Garnish with fresh sprigs of rosemary, if desired.

Red Cabbage: Follow the basic recipe with these additions. After browning the onions, add 1 small head of shredded red cabbage (about 5 cups, loosely packed) to the sauté pan. Pour in ½ cup red wine vinegar and cook over moderately high heat until cabbage is wilted. Add 1 tablespoon caraway seeds. Spread over the chops and cook as for above. Check every 15 minutes or so to make sure there is enough liquid given off by the cabbage to keep the chops moist. Add ¼ cup water or stock at a time, if necessary. When done, omit the last step and simply remove chops to a serving platter. Season cabbage to taste with salt and pepper. Serve very hot alongside the chops.

Lemon and Thyme: Marinate pork chops for ½ hour in a mixture of ½ cup olive oil, ¼ cup lemon juice, and 1 tablespoon fresh thyme (or 1 teaspoon dried). Reserve marinade and prepare pork chops according to the first step of the basic recipe. After browning, replace the stock with ¼ cup of the marinade, ¾ cup of chicken stock, and ½ cup lemon juice. Add several sprigs of fresh thyme (or 1 teaspoon dried) and 1 small clove of finely chopped garlic. Cover and cook as for above. Remove chops to a platter and strain cooking liquid into a saucepan. Dilute 1 scant teaspoon of cornstarch in 1 teaspoon of cold water. Stir into sauce slowly over low heat. Warm just until sauce is thickened. Remove from heat and spoon over chops. Garnish with sprigs of fresh thyme if desired.

Cider and Green Apples: Prepare the chops as for the basic recipe with the following substitutions. Add three Granny Smith apples—peeled, cored, and cut into small cubes—to the onions. Cook until golden. Pour ¼ cup calvados or applejack into the pan and bring to a boil. Stir to pick up any bits from the browning of the chops, onions, and apples. Pour this mixture over the pork chops in the casserole. In place of the chicken stock, add enough cider to half cover, about 1 cup. Braise as for above. When done, remove chops to a serving platter and keep warm. Work the contents of the casserole through a fine-meshed sieve, blender or food processor. Add 2 tablespoons heavy cream to lightly bind the sauce. Spoon over chops and serve at once.

PORK STEWS AND BRAISES

Pork lends itself to long, slow cooking. The tough fibers break down and moisture is absorbed to produce a luscious, flavorful stew or braise. Today's pork is leaner than in days gone by. Adding an extra piece of bacon, salt pork, or ham hock can replace some of the reduced fat content of leaner cuts. Choose pork shoulders, legs, loins, or ribs for best results.

FRENCH COUNTRY PORK STEW WITH CABBAGE

1 pound dried white beans (Great Northern or Navy)
4 to 5 pound piece of pork shoulder or butt (fresh ham or shank)
½ pound piece slab bacon, rind removed
1 large cabbage, cored and shredded into large pieces
2 carrots, peeled and diced
1 onion, peeled and quartered
2 stalks celery, coarsely chopped
2 turnips, peeled and quartered
4 to 5 medium potatoes (about 1½ pounds), peeled and diced
½ pound green beans, trimmed and cut into 1-inch pieces
salt and freshly ground black pepper to taste
2 tablespoons olive oil
2 tablespoons chopped fresh parsley, if desired

1. Soak the beans overnight in cold water. Drain, rinse, and place in a large casserole or soup kettle.

2. Add the pork, bacon, cabbage, carrots, onion, and celery. Add enough cold water to cover. Bring to a boil, reduce heat and simmer until beans are tender and pork is cooked through, about 2 hours.

3. Place the turnips and potatoes in a large pot. Cover with cold water, season with salt and bring to a boil. Reduce heat and cook until done, about 20 minutes. Drain and keep warm.

4. Plunge green beans into a large pot of boiling, salted water. Cook rapidly until firm but not limp, 5 to 7 minutes. Drain and refresh under cold, running water. Set aside.

 5. Remove cooked pork and keep warm. Discard the bacon piece. Puree vegetables in a food processor fitted with the metal blade. Pour into a saucepan and warm over moderately low heat. Season to taste with salt and pepper.

6. Cut meat into thick slices. Arrange on a large serving platter. Add water if necessary to thin out vegetable puree to a saucelike consistency and spoon ovr pork. In a large sauté pan or skillet, quickly sauté the potatoes, turnips, and green beans in the olive oil to heat through. Season with salt and pepper to taste. Use vegetables to surround the pork and puree. Sprinkle with chopped parsley if desired. Serve at once.

BRAISED PORK RIBS

2 to 3 pounds pork ribs, cut into serving pieces
2 tablespoons olive oil
2 onions, thinly sliced
1 carrot, peeled and coarsely chopped
1 celery stalk, chopped

1 clove garlic, finely chopped
½ cup chicken stock (page 59)
several sprigs fresh thyme (or 1 tablespoon dried)
salt and pepper to taste

1. Preheat oven to 325° F.
2. In a large casserole or dutch oven, brown the ribs in the olive oil over moderately high heat. Remove and drain. Add the onions, carrot, and celery. Stir and quickly cook until vegetables are softened and slightly browned. Add the garlic. Place ribs back into pot and pour in the chicken stock.
3. Add the thyme and salt and pepper to taste. Cover and cook in preheated oven until ribs are tender, about 1 hour. Garnish with a sprinkle of fresh thyme if desired.

Lamb and Mutton

Lamb is the meat of the sheep under 1 year of age. It is firm-textured but tender, pink to dark red in color, with a considerable amount of firm white fat. Most lamb is marketed when it is about 6 to 8 months old. While lamb was once available primarily in the spring, it can now be enjoyed year-round. You may still find some lamb labeled "spring lamb," which indicates that it was produced between March and October when the quality is especially good. Mutton comes from sheep over 1 year of age. Its texture is softer and its flavor is distinctly stronger than that of lamb. Mutton is less popular in this country and thus less widely available than lamb. Where it is sold in any substantial quantity, as in England, it is actually cheaper than lamb.

LAMB AND THE MICROWAVE

Lamb can be cooked quickly and conveniently in the microwave oven. Ground lamb is especially suited to microwave cooking and can be made into patties, balls, loaves, and casseroles. Strips and cubes of tender lamb from the shoulder can be deliciously cooked by microwaves.

Lamb roasts can also be successfully cooked in the microwave oven. Appropriate for microwave cookery are boneless leg and loin roasts and bone-in center leg roasts. For the most tender, juicy, and flavorful results, use low power (about 30 percent) and follow the microwave meat roasting recommendations found on page 271.

RIB

Rib Roast

Rib Chop

Frenched Rib Chop

Crown Roast

SHOULDER

Arm Chop

Boneless Shoulder Roast

Square-Cut Shoulder, Whole

Blade Chop

Presliced Shoulder

Neck Slice

LEG

Center Leg Roast

Whole Leg

Short Cut Leg

Shank-Portion Roast

Center Slice

Boneless Sirloin Roast

French-Style Roast

Boneless Leg Roast

Hind Shank

American-Style Roast

Sirloin Chop

LAMB

FORESHANK & BREAST

Boneless Rolled Breast

Shank

Riblets

Spareribs

Cubes for Kabobs

Stew Meat

LOIN

Double Loin Chop

Loin Chop

Loin Roast

ROASTING

TIMETABLE FOR ROASTING			
(325° F Oven Temperature—NOT PREHEATED)			
Cut	**Approx. Weight in Lbs.**	**Internal Temp.**	**Approx. Total Cooking Time (Min. per Lb.)**
Leg	7 to 9	140° F (Rare)	15 to 20
		160° F (Med.)	20 to 25
		170° F (Well)	25 to 30
Leg	5 to 7	140° F (Rare)	20 to 25
		160° F (Med).	25 to 30
		170° F (Well)	30 to 35
Leg, Boneless	4 to 7	140° F (Rare)	25 to 30
		160° F (Med.)	30 to 35
		170° F (Well)	35 to 40
Leg, Shank, Half	3 to 4	140° F (Rare)	30 to 35
		160° F (Med.)	40 to 45
		170° F (Well)	45 to 50
Leg, Sirloin, Half	3 to 4	140° F (Rare)	25 to 30
		160° F (Med.)	35 to 40
		170° F (Well)	45 to 50
Shoulder, Boneless	3½ to 5	140° F (Rare)	30 to 35
		160° F (Med.)	35 to 40
		170° F (Well)	40 to 45
Square-Cut Shoulder (or Cushion Shoulder)	3 to 5	140° F (Rare)	30 to 35
		160° F (Med.)	35 to 40
		170° F (Well)	40 to 45
Crown Roast	4 to 6	160° F	25 to 30

Lamb roasts best cooked at moderate temperatures, between 300° F and 325° F. Trim off excess fat and remove fell, if desired. (This thin paper-like covering on the outer fat helps retain shape and juiciness during cooking. However, it makes carving difficult if left on.) Season with salt and pepper before placing in a roasting pan large enough to snugly hold the meat. Roast gently until cooked to desired doneness. Let meat rest, covered loosely with foil, for 15 to 20 minutes before carving.

If desired, use the tip of a sharp knife to make incisions all over the lamb just before roasting. Peel and slice several cloves of garlic and cut into thin slivers.

Gently force garlic into the flesh with finger. For other flavoring, try rubbing surface of roast with Dijon mustard mixed with a small amount of oil or a mild curry pomade made of softened butter and curry powder. Lamb is excellent when marinated. (See Outdoor Cooking chapter for some ideas.) Oven roasted potatoes, rice pilaf, or any seasonal vegetable like fresh spinach, green beans, grilled eggplants, zucchini and yellow squash, or broiled tomatoes are favorites with roast lamb. Mint jelly is a traditional accompaniment.

CROWN ROAST OF LAMB

 Sprinkle roast with salt and pepper. Place ribs down in an open roasting pan so that the ends of the rib bones from a rack. Cook according to table above. Place on hot platter rib ends up. Deglaze pan with white wine to make a sauce to pass alongside if desired. The classic presentation is to garnish rib ends with paper frills. Fill center of crown with mashed potatoes, potato balls, or any fresh, green vegetable like peas or green beans.

CARVING A LEG OF LAMB

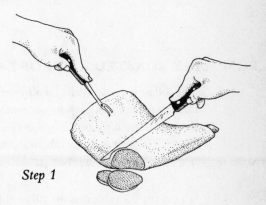

Step 1

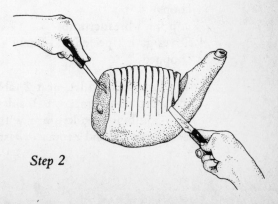

Step 2

ROAST LEG OF LAMB

5- to 7-pound leg of lamb
2 cloves garlic, sliced into thin
  slivers
olive oil
salt and freshly ground black pepper
  to taste

fresh crumbled thyme or rosemary
  (optional)
½ cup dry white wine

1. Trim lamb of excess fat. Remove fell if desired. With the tip of a sharp knife, make small incisions in the flesh. Gently force the slivers of garlic into the slits.

2. Brush the roast with olive oil. Season with salt and pepper. Rub the surface with the herbs, if desired. Place in a roasting pan just large enough to hold the meat snugly.

3. Roast in the oven at 325° F according to the chart above. Do not cover.

4. Remove the roast and keep warm. Pour off any excess fat. Place the pan on top of the stove and carefully add the wine. Use a whisk to stir and pick up any bits from the bottom of the pan. Let reduce by half over high heat.

5. Slice the roast and serve the deglazed pan juices on the side.

ROSEMARY ROASTED RACK OF LAMB

The following recipe calls for a hotter temperature than the table above suggests. Because it is a traditional recipe from the south of France where lamb is cooked faster and quicker, the results are different. The inside will be very rare and the outside crisp. Roasting in a very hot oven requires careful attention. Cook according to the times suggested above if a more moderate approach is desired.

¼ cup plus 2 tablespoons olive oil
young rack of lamb (rib end of the
  saddle or double loin with 8
  chops)
½ cup fresh breadcrumbs
4 cloves garlic, peeled and finely
  chopped

1 tablespoon fresh rosemary, finely
  chopped
salt and freshly ground black pepper
  to taste
1 tablespoon Dijon mustard

1. In a large skillet, heat 2 tablespoons of the olive oil over high heat and quickly brown the rack on all sides.

2. Combine breadcrumbs with garlic, rosemary, and remaining olive oil. Season with salt and pepper to taste.

3. Spread the mustard evenly over the fat side of the rack. Gently pat on the breadcrumbs to form an even crust.

4. Bake at 450° F until a meat thermometer registers 140° F for rare, or 160° F for medium, about 20 to 25 minutes.

BROILING, PAN BROILING, AND PANFRYING

TIMETABLE FOR BROILING, PAN BROILING, PANFRYING

Cut	Approx. Thickness	Approx. Weight in Ounces	Inches from Heat (For Broiling)	Approx. Total Cooking Time in Minutes
Shoulder Chops	¾ inch to 1 inch	5 to 9	3 to 4	7 to 11
Rib Chops	1 inch	3 to 5	3 to 4	7 to 11
	1½ inches	4½ to 7½	4 to 5	15 to 19
Loin Chops	1 inch	3 to 5	3 to 4	7 to 11
	1½ inches	4½ to 7½	4 to 5	15 to 19
Sirloin Chops	¾ inch to 1 inch	6 to 10	3 to 4	12 to 15
Leg Steaks	¾ to 1 inch	11 to 18	3 to 4	14 to 18
Cubes for Kebabs	1 inch to 1½ inches		4 to 5	8 to 12
Ground Lamb Patties	½ inch × 4 inches	4	3	5 to 8

Select chops of uniform thickness for broiling. Remove skin and extra fat. If desired they may be boned, rolled, and wrapped in strips of bacon. Follow directions for broiling beef (page 278).

Use rib, loin, or shoulder chops cut about 2 inches thick for pan broiling or panfrying. To pan broil, have skillet sizzling hot. Put in chops and cook 1 minute, turn and sear the other side. Reduce and cook chops slowly until done. Pour off extra fat so that chops will broil, not fry.

For panfrying, melt 2 tablespoons butter and 2 tablespoons oil in a skillet large enough to hold chops or steaks flat in one layer. Cook over moderate heat, turning occasionally until done. See chart above for approximate times.

BROILED LAMB CHOPS

 Season chops with salt and freshly ground black pepper. Trim excess fat and use it to grease broiling pan. Broil until cooked to desired doneness. (See chart above for approximate cooking times).

STUFFED LAMB CHOPS

boned lamb chops, rib or loin, cut 2 inches thick, 2 per person (2 to 4 ounces each)
chicken livers, liver sausage, or large fresh mushrooms to taste

salt and freshly ground black pepper to taste

1. Make a small incision in each chop and insert a mushroom in each. Or, place a chicken liver or thick slice of sausage near the long end, drawing end of chop into round flat piece with string.
2. Place chops in a greased broiling pan under a hot flame and brown on both sides. Broil until cooked to desired doneness (see chart above.)
3. Remove string, sprinkle with salt and pepper. Dot with butter, remove to a hot platter and serve.

PANFRIED LOIN CHOPS WITH TOMATO AND GARLIC

4 loin chops, ½ to 1 inch thick
salt and freshly ground black pepper to taste
2 tablespoons olive oil
1 to 2 cloves garlic, finely minced

1 cup tomatoes, peeled, seeded, and chopped
1 tablespoon fresh thyme, or 1 teaspoon dried

1. Season chops with salt and pepper to taste.
2. In a large skillet or sauté pan, heat oil. Add chops and over moderate heat cook until done 6 to 8 minutes per side.
3. When done remove from pan, set aside, and cover loosely with foil to keep warm. Pour off all but 1 tablespoon of the fat. Add garlic and cook over low heat until soft but not brown. Add tomatoes and thyme. Increase heat and cook until moisture has evaporated and sauce is quite thick, about 5 minutes. Correct seasoning. Spoon sauce over chops.

PAN-BROILED RIB CHOPS WITH TARRAGON SAUCE

8 trimmed rib chops, ½ to 1 inch
    thick
1 cup white wine
1 tablespoon fresh tarragon, finely
    chopped, or 1 teaspoon dried

4 tablespoons butter, cut into small
    pieces and chilled
salt and freshly ground black pepper
    to taste

1. Rub a heavy skillet or sauté pan with a bit of the fat from the lamb.
Cook the chops over moderately low heat until done, 6 to 8 minutes per side.
Turn frequently.

2. Remove the chops and cover loosely with foil to keep warm. Carefully
pour in the wine. With a wire whisk, stir to pick up any bits in the bottom of
the pan. Bring to a boil and add the tarragon. Reduce over high heat until all
but 2 tablespoons of the liquid remain, stirring constantly. Working on and off
the heat, add the chilled pieces of butter piece by piece. Whisk constantly until
sauce is smooth and emulsified. Do not boil. Season with salt and pepper.

3. Nap each chop with a small amount of the sauce and serve hot.

BRAISING AND STEWING

TIMETABLE FOR BRAISING

Cut	Weight or Thickness	Approx. Total Cooking Time
Neck Slices	¾ inch	1 hour
Shoulder Chops	¾ inch to 1 inch	45 to 60 minutes
Breast, Stuffed	2 to 3 lbs.	1½ to 2 hours
Breast, Rolled	1½ to 2 lbs.	1½ to 2 hours
Riblets	¾ to 1 lb. each	1½ to 2 hours
Shanks	¾ to 1 lb. each	1½ to 2 hours
Lamb for Stew	1½-inch pieces	1½ to 2 hours

Braising lamb cuts is similar to braising beef. See "Braising" in the beef
section, page 282. Dredging is optional with lamb. Shanks of lamb are highly
underrated. The succulent meat of this cut turns into a savory, gelatinous treat

when cooked slowly for a long time. Serve almost any braised lamb with potatoes, rice, or buttered noodles. A fresh green vegetable like leaf spinach, brussels sprouts, or green beans adds a refreshing crunchy texture to the long-cooked meat.

BRAISED LAMB SHANKS WITH WHITE BEANS

4 lamb shanks, about ¾ pound each
salt and freshly ground black pepper to taste
2 tablespoons butter
2 tablespoons oil
1 medium onion, thinly sliced

½ cup dry white wine
1 cup peeled, seeded, and crushed tomatoes
several sprigs fresh rosemary
½ pound white beans, presoaked overnight

1. Season the lamb shanks with salt and pepper to taste. In a heavy skillet, melt the butter with the oil. When sizzling hot, quickly brown the lamb on all sides. Remove the browned shanks to a heavy casserole with a lid.
2. Add the onions to the skillet and cook over moderately high heat until soft and translucent but not browned. Carefully pour in the wine. Add the tomatoes and rosemary. Bring to a boil. Add the beans and stir to blend.
3. Pour beans over the lamb shanks. Cover and bake until beans are tender and meat is beginning to fall away from the bone, 1½ to 2 hours. Watch carefully and add water, ¼ cup at a time, as needed. Beans should be kept moist but not submerged in liquid.
4. Remove shanks to a large serving platter. Season beans to taste with salt and pepper. Surround the shanks with the beans and serve hot.

LAMB STEAK WITH CURRIED SQUASH

4 small lamb steaks, ½ inch thick (4 to 6 ounces)
salt and freshly ground black pepper to taste
2 tablespoons butter
2 tablespoons oil
2 small onions, thinly sliced

1 to 2 tablespoons curry powder
½ cup water, chicken stock (page 59), or dry white wine
2 pounds acorn squash, peeled, seeded, and cut into 2-inch chunks
chopped fresh parsley for garnish

 1. Season the lamb steaks with salt and pepper to taste. In a large heavy skillet, melt the butter with the oil. When sizzling hot, quickly brown the lamb on all sides. Remove to a heavy casserole with a lid.

2. Pour off all but 1 tablespoon fat from the skillet. Add the onions and curry powder. Cook over moderate heat until onions are slightly softened and well coated with curry powder. Carefully pour in the water, stock, or wine. Add the squash and toss or stir to blend.

3. Pour the squash and onion mixture over the lamb steaks. Cover and cook until meat is tender, about 1 hour. Watch carefully and add water if necessary to prevent scorching, ¼ cup at a time.

4. Remove meat and keep warm. Scrape cooked squash and onions into the workbowl of a food processor fitted with a metal blade. Process until mixture is smooth, scraping down sides as necessary.

5. Wipe casserole dry. Arrange steaks overlapping. Season squash purée to taste and pour over steaks. Cover and gently reheat. Garnish with chopped parsley and serve with rice.

	TIMETABLE FOR STEWING	
Cut	**Average Size**	**Approx. Total Cooking Time**
Lamb or Mutton for Stew	1-inch to 1½-inch pieces	1½ to 2 hours

Review the comments about stewing in beef and veal sections (page 282 and 299). Remember that mutton has a texture that is softer and marbled with creamy-colored fat with flavor that is distinctly stronger than that of lamb. It is often used in stews that are highly spiced (like curry) to mask the somewhat gamey taste.

LAMB STEW

2 pounds lamb from shoulder, neck, or breast cut into 1½-inch cubes
salt and freshly ground black pepper to taste
2 tablespoons butter
2 tablespoons oil
2 tablespoons flour
4 tomatoes, peeled, seeded, and chopped (or 1 cup canned)
1 clove garlic, crushed
2 bay leaves, crumbled

15 to 20 pearl onions, peeled
4 to 5 carrots, peeled and cut into 1-inch pieces
3 to 4 small white turnips, peeled and quartered
10 small new potatoes, cut in half
1 cup fresh green beans, cut into 1-inch pieces
1 cup green peas
chopped fresh parsley for garnish (optional)

(continued)

1. Trim meat and season with salt and pepper. In a covered casserole or Dutch oven, melt the butter and oil. Over moderately high heat, brown the lamb in the hot fat. Pour off fat and sprinkle the meat with the flour. Stir until flour starts to brown. Add enough water to barely cover, about 2 cups. Stir in the tomatoes, garlic, and bay leaves. Bring to a slow simmer and cook gently for 1 hour.

2. With a slotted spoon, remove the pieces of cooked meat. Strain the sauce. Wipe out the casserole and return the meat and strained sauce. Add the pearl onions, carrots, turnips, and potatoes. Bring back to a simmer and cook slowly for another hour. About ½ hour before stew is done, add the green beans and peas.

3. Season with salt and pepper to taste. Serve hot garnished with chopped parsley, if desired.

CURRIED MUTTON STEW

2 pounds mutton cut into large cubes	2 small onions, thinly sliced
salt and freshly ground black pepper to taste	1 to 2 tablespoons curry powder
2 tablespoons butter	2 cups water or chicken stock (page 59)
2 tablespoons oil	1 tablespoon tomato paste
2 tablespoons flour	1 clove garlic, crushed

1. Preheat oven to 350° F. Season the mutton with salt and pepper. In a large, oven-proof casserole or Dutch oven, melt the butter and oil. When sizzling hot, add the mutton and brown on all sides. Pour off all but 2 tablespoons of fat. Add the flour and onions and curry powder. Stir to blend. Cook over moderate heat until onions are softened and flour begins to brown.

2. Pour in the water or stock. Stir to blend. Add the tomato paste and garlic. Cover tightly and place in the oven. Cook for 1 hour.

3. Remove the meat, strain the sauce, and skim off fat that rises to the surface. Wipe out the casserole and return the meat to it along with the strained sauce. Season to taste with salt and pepper. Serve with rice or potatoes.

Variety Meats

Sweetbreads, brains, tongue, kidneys, heart, and tripe are known collectively as variety meats or offal. They may be expensive like sweetbreads or very inexpensive like heart or tripe. Although known for their high nutritional value—especially liver—organ meats are rich in cholesterol. Variety meats are very perishable and should be carefully refrigerated and used soon after purchase.

Variety meats have lost some importance in the modern kitchen. The recipes from the original Settlement editions are classic, perhaps even old-fashioned when compared to today's lighter, healthier mode of cooking. When properly prepared, however, these meats can be surprisingly flavorful. While perhaps not ideal as a part of every cook's repertoire, an occasional meal centered around one of these delicacies can be a welcome and sometimes nostalgic change of pace.

SWEETBREADS

Sweetbreads are the thymus glands of calf, steer, or lamb. Both kinds, the round heart sweetbreads and the longish throat sweetbreads, come in pairs. Everything except the thin covering membrane and the tubes and veins is edible. Sweetbreads should be chilled in cold water to degorge them of any impurities. Soak again in cold water after a brief parboiling to firm up the soft flesh. The cooked sweetbreads are then heated with a sauce or browned in the oven, under the broiler, or in melted butter. A pound of sweetbreads serves 4.

BOILED SWEETBREADS

1 pound sweetbreads
½ teaspoon salt

1 tablespoon vinegar or lemon juice
2 cups boiling water

1. Soak the sweetbreads in enough cold water to cover for 20 minutes. Drain.
2. Add salt and vinegar or lemon juice to boiling water. Add the sweetbreads and boil for 20 minutes.
3. When sweetbreads are cooked, immediately drain and plunge them into cold water. Remove and discard the tubes and membranes.
4. Slice sweetbreads. Heat in simmering Medium White Sauce, page 399, or Creole Sauce, page 402. Serve hot on toast, with pasta, or with chicken, mushrooms or peas in pastry shells. Or, wrap the boiled sweetbreads in bacon and broil or panbroil slowly until bacon is crisp.

BAKED SWEETBREADS

1 pound Boiled Sweetbreads (page 329), cleaned and left whole

2 tablespoons butter, melted
about 1 cup fresh breadcrumbs

1. Preheat oven to 350° F. Dip Boiled Sweetbreads in butter and cover with crumbs.

2. Bake until crisp and well browned, 30 to 40 minutes, basting occasionally with butter. Cut in slices and serve with fresh, seasonal vegetables and rice or pasta.

FRIED SWEETBREADS

¼ cup fine breadcrumbs
½ teaspoon salt
⅛ teaspoon freshly ground black pepper
⅛ teaspoon ground ginger

1 pound Boiled Sweetbreads (page 329), cleaned and sliced
1 egg, beaten

1. Season breadcrumbs with salt, pepper, and ginger. Roll sweetbread slices in seasoned crumbs, dip in egg, and in crumbs again.

2. Fry in deep hot fat or sauté until brown on all sides. Drain on paper towels and serve immediately.

BRAISED SWEETBREADS

3 tablespoons butter
1 onion, chopped
2 pounds Boiled Sweetbreads (page 329), cleaned and left whole
1 cup sweetbread cooking liquid

salt and freshly ground black pepper to taste
½ teaspoon mustard
1 tablespoon flour
2 tablespoons sherry

1. Preheat oven to 350° F. In a heavy casserole or Dutch oven, melt the butter. Add the onions and gently cook over high heat until they begin to brown, about 3 minutes. Remove onions from the pan and reserve. Add the sweetbreads and brown on all sides. Pour in the reserved cooking liquid, season with salt and pepper, and add mustard.

2. Bake, basting occasionally, adding more liquid as it cooks down until sweetbreads are cooked through, about 30 minutes.

3. When sweetbreads are done, remove to a serving platter and cover loosely with foil to keep warm. Skim off fat from cooking juices in pan. Thicken with 1 tablespoon flour dissolved in a little water. Flavor with sherry and season with salt and pepper. Drain off any accumulated juices from the meat platter. Pour sauce over sweetbreads and serve at once.

SWEETBREADS WITH MUSHROOMS

2 tablespoons butter
2 tablespoons flour
½ cup milk or cream
½ cup chicken broth (page 59)
2 tablespoons blanched almonds, chopped
½ pound mushrooms, trimmed, sliced, and quickly sautéed

2 cups diced cooked and cleaned sweetbreads
salt and freshly ground black pepper to taste
¼ teaspoon ground ginger
1 teaspoon chopped parsley
1 cup buttered breadcrumbs

1.   Preheat oven to 375° F. Melt the butter. Add the flour and gradually stir in milk or cream and the broth. Stir constantly and cook until smooth.

2.   Remove from heat and add almonds, mushrooms, and sweetbreads. Season with salt, pepper, ginger, and parsley. Spread in a buttered baking dish or casserole, or divide among individual buttered ramekins. Sprinkle top with crumbs.

3.   Bake until browned on top, about 30 minutes.

LIVER

Liver is recognized as a valuable source of iron, Vitamin A, and many B vitamins. All kinds of liver have the same nutritional quality, from the expensive delicately flavored veal and the calf's liver to lamb, beef, and inexpensive pork liver. Liver should be cooked very quickly in a little fat to the medium-rare stage for most tender results. Beef and pork liver are less tender and may need to be braised. Allow 1 pound of liver for 4 servings. Before cooking, remove the skin and any veins that can be cut out without spoiling the appearance of the slice.

SAUTÉED LIVER

1 pound calf's liver or baby beef liver	2 tablespoons flour
	2 tablespoons butter
salt and freshly ground black pepper to taste	

1.   Wipe liver dry and slice thin. Season with salt and pepper to taste and dredge with flour.

2.   In a skillet, melt the butter. When sizzling hot, add the liver and fry the slices until brown, a few minutes on each side. Reduce heat and cook a few minutes longer until medium-rare. Serve hot with fried onions or crisp bacon.

Variation: Follow the above recipe. When the liver is done, remove to a platter and keep warm. Pour off the fat from the skillet and return to the stove. Carefully add ½ cup balsamic vinegar. Bring to a boil, using a whisk to stir and pick up any bits that remain in the bottom of the pan. Reduce by half over high heat. Nap each slice of liver with a small amount of the reduction.

BAKED CALF'S LIVER

whole calf's liver, washed, trimmed, and skinned	2 tablespoons flour
	2 tablespoons butter
salt and freshly ground black pepper to taste	2 onions, thinly sliced

1.   Preheat oven to 400° F. Season liver with salt and pepper to taste and dredge with flour.

2.   In an oven-proof skillet, melt the butter. Add the liver and sliced onions. Spoon some of the melted butter on top of the liver.

3.   Cover and bake in the oven for 15 minutes. Uncover, reduce heat to 325° F and bake until tender and well browned, 45 minutes to an hour.

Many braised dishes, stews, casseroles, and similar long-cooked preparations that generate their own sauce are perfect "do-ahead" dishes. Easily done in stages that can be carried out days in advance, these sauced preparations can be done in earthenware or glass baking dishes, refrigerated or frozen, and reheated in the oven or microwave. They make welcome additions to "bring-a-covered-dish" affairs as well as thoughtful comforting offerings to friends and neighbors. Use your imagination to mix in rice, potatoes, or cooked noodles to provide a one-dish meal. Fresh bread crumbs or olive oil drizzled on top will provide a crunchy, brown topping when reheated.

BRAISED CALF'S LIVER

Although the following slow cooking method may seem more old-fashioned than today's quickly cooked calf's liver, we find this braised liver nostalgically enticing.

⅛ pound sliced bacon
2½ pounds whole calf's liver, skinned
salt and freshly ground black pepper to taste
pinch of mace
2 tablespoons goose fat or butter
1 small carrot, peeled and sliced
1 small onion, peeled and sliced

1 rib celery, sliced
1 bay leaf
6 black peppercorns
3 whole cloves
2 cups beef stock (page 59) or water
lemon juice to taste
chopped parsley

1. Preheat oven to 325° F. Wrap the bacon slices around the liver and season well with salt, pepper, and sprinkle with mace.

2. In a casserole with a tight-fitting lid, heat the goose fat or butter and quickly brown the liver on both sides. Add the vegetables, bay leaf, peppercorns, and cloves. Add the stock or water, cover, and bake 2 hours. Uncover the casserole during the last 20 minutes.

3. When ready to serve, strain the cooking liquid and season with lemon juice and finely chopped parsley.

Note: If desired, liquid can be thickened with 2 tablespoons flour made smooth with a little cold water and cooked for 5 minutes.

BRAISED PORK LIVER

1 pound pork liver, cut into ½-inch slices
¾ teaspoon salt
⅛ teaspoon freshly ground black pepper
2 tablespoons flour
4 tablespoons butter

2 carrots, peeled and diced
2 potatoes, peeled and sliced
1 onion, diced
1 cup boiling water
1 cup tomato juice

1. Season liver with salt and pepper and dredge with flour.

2. In an oven-proof casserole with a cover, melt the butter. Add the liver and quickly brown on all sides. Add the carrots, potatoes, onions, and liquids. Cover and simmer over low heat until tender, about 1½ hours.

BRAINS

All brains may be cooked in the same manner. Calf's brains are more expensive than beef or pork brains and have a more delicate flavor and texture. Two calf's brains weigh about 1 pound, enough for 4 servings.

CALF'S BRAINS

1 pound calf's brains
½ teaspoon salt

1 tablespoon vinegar or lemon juice
2 cups boiling water

1.   Soak the brains in enough cold water to cover for 20 minutes. Drain.
2.   Add salt and vinegar or lemon juice to boiling water. Add the brains, reduce heat, and cook gently for 20 minutes.
3.   When brains are cooked, immediately drain and plunge the brains into cold water. Remove and discard the tubes and membranes.
4.   Cut into cubes or slices. Use like sweetbreads, or add to scrambled eggs or use in a soufflé.

CALF'S BRAINS IN VINAIGRETTE SAUCE

1 pound calf's brains
½ teaspoon salt
1 tablespoon vinegar or lemon juice
5 whole peppercorns

2 cups boiling water
Vinaigrette Sauce (page 129)
2 tablespoons finely chopped
    parsley

1.   Soak the brains in enough cold water to cover for 20 minutes. Drain.
2.   Add salt, vinegar or lemon juice, and peppercorns to boiling water. Add the brains and reduce heat and cook gently for 20 minutes.
3.   When brains are cooked, remove brains from cooking liquid and immediately plunge into cold water. Remove and discard the tubes and membranes.
4.   Cut into ¼-inch slices. Pat dry between sheets of paper toweling. Chill thoroughly. Decoratively arrange on a serving platter. Combine the Vinaigrette Sauce and the parsley. Spoon over some of the sauce and serve the rest on the side.

TONGUE

Beef or ox tongue is widely available in several forms: fresh, pickled, or smoked. Calf's tongues and lamb tongues are sold fresh; the calf's tongue is considered the choicer of the two. Allow 1 pound of tongue for 4 servings.

BOILED SMOKED BEEF TONGUE

1 smoked beef tongue, washed
6 bay leaves
1 teaspoon whole peppercorns

1 teaspoon whole cloves
1 onion, peeled and sliced

1. If the tongue is very salty soak in cold water overnight. In a large pot of fresh cold water, combine the tongue with the bay leaves, peppercorns, cloves, and onion. Simmer slowly until tender, when the bone moves easily and the skin curls back at the root, 3 to 5 hours.

2. Slit and pull off the outer skin, cut off root and let tongue cool in the stock. Tongue may be sliced and served cold or served hot with puréed chestnuts or mashed potatoes.

CALF'S TONGUE

3 fresh calf's tongues
3 bay leaves
1 onion, peeled and sliced
1 teaspoon whole peppercorns

1 tablespoon salt
1 tablespoon flour
2 tablespoons prepared horseradish

1. In a large pot, combine tongues, bay leaves, onion, peppercorns, and salt and cover with cold water. Simmer until tongues are tender (20 minutes per pound).

2. Remove tongues from the kettle. Slit and pull off the skin. Cut tongues lengthwise.

3. Strain cooking liquid into a saucepan. Add flour blended with a little cold water and the horseradish. Cook until smooth and thick.

4. Pour sauce over tongue and serve hot.

BRAISED CALF'S TONGUE

2 calf's tongues
1 tablespoon vinegar or lemon juice
2 tablespoons oil
2 onions, peeled and sliced
2 carrots, peeled and sliced

1 cup beef stock (page 59)
salt and freshly ground black pepper
  to taste
2 tablespoons flour
½ cup milk or sour cream

1. In a large pot of boiling salted water, add the tongues and vinegar or lemon juice and parboil for 20 minutes. Drain and skin the tongues.

2. In a covered casserole, heat the oil and lightly brown the tongues with the onions and carrots. Stir often to prevent burning. Add beef stock and salt and pepper to taste. Cover and simmer gently over moderate heat until tongue is very tender, about 1 hour. Add more stock if necessary.

3. When tongue is cooked, remove to a platter and cover loosely with foil to keep warm.

4. Strain the cooking liquid, pressing down hard on the vegetables to extract as much flavor as possible. Wipe out the casserole and return to the stove. Blend the flour with the milk or sour cream and add to the casserole along with the strained cooking liquid. Stir until thick and smooth. Correct seasoning. Pour over tongues and serve hot.

BEEF'S TONGUE À LA JARDINIERE

beef's tongue, about 1 pound
1 small carrot, peeled and sliced
1 small turnip, peeled and sliced
1 rib celery, sliced
1 potato, peeled and sliced

½ pound fresh peas
¼ pound string beans, cleaned and
  trimmed
¼ pound pearl onions, peeled
¼ pound cherry tomatoes, stemmed
1 tablespoon flour

1. In a large pot, boil tongue for 1 hour. Remove tongue and reserve the cooking liquid. Skin the tongue.

2. In a large roasting pan, spread the vegetables across the bottom and place the skinned tongue on top. Moisten with some of the reserved cooking liquid, cover, and cook slowly at 300° F until tender, about 2 hours.

3. Remove the tongue and vegetables to a hot platter and cover to keep warm. Thicken the pan juices with the flour, as in Pan Gravy, page 403. Slice the tongue and serve hot with the cooked vegetables and gravy.

OTHER VARIETY MEATS

KIDNEYS

6 lamb or 4 veal kidneys
salt and freshly ground black pepper
  to taste

2 tablespoons butter
1 tablespoon chopped onion

1. Plunge the kidneys in boiling water. Drain and remove skins. Soak in cold salted water for 30 minutes. Drain. Remove and discard the tubes and membranes. Slice kidneys. Season with salt and pepper to taste.

2. In a large skillet, melt the butter. Add the onion and cook over moderate heat until just beginning to soften, about 2 minutes. Add kidneys and cook for 5 minutes. Be careful not to overcook or kidneys will become tough.

3. Serve hot with Mushroom Sauce, page 401.

CALF'S HEART

1 cup dry breadcrumbs
salt and freshly ground black pepper
  to taste
½ teaspoon chopped parsley
1 tablespoon finely chopped onion

1 tablespoon butter, melted
1 calf's heart
flour, for dredging
2 tablespoons oil

1. Soak the crumbs in cold water and squeeze dry. Season with salt and pepper to taste. Add parsley and onion. Stir in butter.

2. Wash the heart. Remove veins and blood clots and stuff with prepared breadcrumbs. Season heart with salt and pepper to taste. Dredge with flour.

3. In a large skillet, heat the oil. When hot, quickly add the heart and brown on all sides.

4. Remove heart to a deep casserole with a lid. Pour in boiling water to half cover the heart. Cover and bake at 300° F until tender, about 2 hours.

STUFFED DERMA (KISHKE)

1½ cups flour, or flour mixed with
  matzo meal
¾ cup rendered chicken fat, plus
  more for brushing
1 medium onion, finely chopped
salt and freshly ground black pepper
  to taste

¼ teaspoon paprika
3-foot piece of beef casing, washed
  and scraped, 1 end sewn closed
2 onions, thinly sliced
1 cup boiling water

(continued)

1. Preheat oven to 350° F. Blend flour, fat, and chopped onion. Season well with salt, pepper, and paprika. Stuff casing lightly to allow for expansion and sew closed.

2. In the bottom of a large baking dish, layer the sliced onions. Lay the derma on top of the onions and brush with additional chicken fat. Add boiling water.

3. Cover and bake. Baste often and cook until tender, about 2 hours.

HONEYCOMB TRIPE

1 pound fresh tripe, washed and cut into 1-inch squares	¼ teaspoon sugar
	¼ teaspoon Dijon mustard
¼ teaspoon salt	1 tablespoon flour

1. In a large saucepan, combine the tripe with the salt, sugar, and mustard. Pour in 2 cups water and bring to a boil. Skim carefully. Simmer until tender, about 2 hours. Watch closely to prevent sticking and skim again if necessary.

2. Stir in flour mixed with a little water. Simmer ½ hour longer. Correct seasoning. Serve hot with boiled potatoes and a pinch of chopped parsley.

Leftovers

Leftover meats have endless uses, limited only by the imagination of the cook. It is often a real economy of time, as well as of money, to buy and cook more meat than is needed for a single meal and to base another meal, more quickly prepared, on the "planned over" meal.

To Store Leftover Cooked Meats

Remove cooked meat from bones as soon as possible, trim and discard fat and other inedible portions. Wrap meat in moisture-proof paper to prevent drying. Use within 2 days or freeze, in meal-size portions, for up to 6 weeks.

Sliced Leftover Meats

Avoid recooking meats that should be served rare. Let leftover rare roast beef and steak slices come to room temperature. Just before serving cover with very hot gravy and serve at once on warmed plates, or on toast as a hot sandwich. Or serve slices of cold meat with salads or hot vegetables. Reheat lamb, veal, pork, or pot-roasted beef in hot gravy, barbecue sauce, or other sauces.

Bits and Pieces of Leftover Meat

Leftover meat too small to slice may be cut into uniform pieces and added to a mixed salad. Use in sauces, as stuffing for vegetables, filling for meat pies, or serve with pasta or rice. The meat may be ground to make rissoles, croquettes, or a meat soufflé. Leftover lamb makes an excellent curry. Reheat veal in sour cream sauce with mushrooms to make Veal Stroganoff. Use leftover pork for an Asian style stir-fry.

Leftover Stew

Supplement leftover stew with freshly cooked beans or vegetables, or shred the meat, extend the sauce, and serve as a sauce for pasta or rice.

BAKED ROAST BEEF HASH

2 cups chopped roast beef or steak
2 cups chopped boiled potatoes
2 tablespoons tomato puree
½ cup milk, cream, or gravy
salt and freshly ground black pepper to taste

1. Preheat oven to 375° F. In a mixing bowl, combine meat and potatoes. Add tomato puree and moisten with milk, cream, or gravy. Season well with salt and pepper. Pack in a greased casserole.
2. Bake until heated throughout and top is browned, about 30 minutes.

CORNED BEEF HASH

2 cups chopped corned beef
3 cups chopped boiled potatoes
1 onion, minced
½ cup beef stock (page 59)
salt and freshly ground black pepper to taste
2 tablespoons oil

(continued)

1.   In a mixing bowl, combine meat and potatoes. Add onion and moisten with beef stock. Season well with salt and pepper.

2.   In a heavy skillet, heat the oil. Add hash, cook slowly until browned crisp on the bottom. Fold like an omelet and serve.

RED FLANNEL HASH

2 cups chopped corned beef
6 boiled potatoes, chopped
1 onion, minced
6 cooked beets, chopped

½ cup beef stock (page 59)
salt and freshly ground black pepper
   to taste

1.   Preheat oven to 375° F. In a mixing bowl, combine meat, potatoes, onions, and beets. Moisten with stock. Season well with salt and pepper. Pack in a greased casserole.

2.   Bake until heated throughout and top is browned, about 30 minutes.

SHEPHERD'S PIE

2 cups cold cooked meat
⅔ cup gravy
salt and freshly ground black pepper
   to taste

2 small onions, coarsely chopped
2 tablespoons fresh parsley, finely
   chopped
mashed potatoes

1.   Preheat oven to 350° F. In the workbowl of a food processor fitted with a metal blade, coarsely grind the meat. Stir in the gravy. Season with salt and pepper. Add onions and parsley.

2.   Place in a buttered baking dish and spread mashed potatoes over the meat. Bake until potatoes are golden brown, about 15 minutes. Or, cover with Potato Crust (recipe follows).

POTATO CRUST

2 cups flour
½ teaspoon salt
2 teaspoons baking powder

½ cup vegetable shortening
1 cup cold mashed potato
milk or water

1.   Sift together flour, salt, and baking powder. Cut in the shortening until the dough resembles coarse meal. Add the potatoes and enough milk or water to form a soft dough.

2.   On a floured board, roll out the dough to an even thickness. Cover pie and slash crust with a knife to create steam vents. Bake until potatoes are golden brown, about 15 minutes.

Outdoor Cooking

In this day of freezer-to-microwave-oven cooking, nothing appeals to our primitive instincts more than the charcoal grill. Whether using an elaborate gas-electric variety that resembles a mini-oven or a simple hibachi that suits the smallest of spaces, outdoor cooking is easy, fun, and practical. The array of barbecue cookers on the market is vast. The following recipes were tested on a medium-sized kettle grill with a cover and a nonadjustable rack, although the techniques carry over to other grills. Follow manufacturer's instructions if you own a more sophisticated model.

There are also a variety of charcoals around these days. Briquets are by far the most common. They are usually made from pounded charcoal with certain additives—coal, oil, sawdust, lime, and even sodium nitrate—that might affect flavor. For the purist, there are increasingly available brands of 100 percent charcoal made from the finest of hardwoods. While briquets are somewhat easier to ignite and burn longer, the true hardwood kinds impart no chemical aftertaste. The same choices are available when it comes to starters. The convenience of lighter fluid is offset by the artificial taste it leaves behind. Twigs and newspaper work fine if you have some patience. By far the less fussy, messy method is an electric starter. Left for 8 to 10 minutes beneath a pile of charcoal, it is a fast, efficient, and easy way to start a fire. Another handy implement is a metal cylinder starter. Newspaper is put in the bottom part, charcoal on top, and all is ignited with a single match.

Determining when to place foods on the grill to cook depends on many factors. Be sure to read through each recipe to decide on the degree of heat intensity required. Allow plenty of time to begin the fire well in advance if foods are to be cooked slowly. The temperature can be regulated somewhat using the top and bottom vents and by covering. Opening vents underneath the bed of coals will increase the heat. Covering the grill will hold heat in enough to create the same effect of a conventional oven. Once the fire has started, spread the coals out to fit an area about 1 inch wider than the food that is being cooked on the grill.

Hardwoods in the fire are increasingly popular additions to outdoor cooking. Mesquite, hickory, and grapevines that have been soaked in water can be thrown over the coals a few minutes before grilling to impart subtle flavors to the food.

Cooking on a grill is a breeze if a few guidelines are followed. First, the grill should be oiled before using. Rubbing with a piece of fat, applying a no-stick cooking spray, or brushing with a small amount of vegetable oil will keep most foods from adhering to the surface. It is also important to know that most nonadjusting grills are situated about 5 inches from the source of heat. If you have an adjustable unit, be aware of the distance from the fire and make modifications where necessary according *to the recipe being used. Remember, fat will often splatter onto the coals causing un-wanted flare-ups of flames that will char the food being cooked. Watch carefully for this irritation and calm the flames with water. Dousing is another way of controlling the heat. Don't be afraid to carefully sprinkle or spray a mist of water over if the heat is too intense. Finally, covering the grill will produce a smokiness that is sometimes desirable, especially for cuts of meat that require a longer cooking time.*

Maintaining and cleaning the grill is necessary to insure good results from your outdoor cooking adventures. Remove the ashes that accumulate in the bottom of the cooker from time to time. Keep the grill itself clean. Scrub with a stiff wire brush after each use. Use oven cleaner for particularly stubborn, burned-on foods. The vents should be kept movable and easily opened. Hose down and wipe out the cooker at regular intervals. Keep covered and stored in a well-protected spot.

Marinades and Barbecue Sauces

Marinades can provide an added dimension to outdoor cooking. They serve to tenderize and flavor meats as well as to help keep them moist. Some of the marinades that follow can be used with either poultry, steaks, chops, or roasts except where noted. Timing is important. Be sure to allow enough time for marinating foods that require tenderizing or extra flavor enhancing. Less expensive, tougher cuts of meat like a chuck roast or brisket benefit from a day or two in a marinade while vegetables and fish can break down or start to decompose if left in an acidic marinade for too long.

There are basically three kinds of marinades: (1) cooked, (2) uncooked, and (3) rubs. Although they can often be used interchangeably, there are some differences to keep in mind.

Cooked marinades are rich and hearty but result in a more subtle reward. For example, aromatic vegetables like onion, celery, and carrot are cooked for a long time with wine. The resulting concoction is full of a gentle blend of flavors. They are often used for large, strong cuts of beef, venison, or game.

Uncooked marinades are robust in content and serve to flavor lighter meats like pork and veal, and chicken as well as some fish. These are quick, easy combinations of wine, vinegar, or citrus juice with spices and herbs.

Rubs work well with steaks, chops, and cutlets that will cook for a shorter amount of time. Because the spicy mixture is worked into the flesh, most rubs are quite intense and are meant to produce sharp flavor in a short amount of time.

Barbecue sauces are sacred in some American regions. The cultural attachments are downright sentimental for those of us whose memory is full of summer days of sweet, smoky meats and greasy napkins. Although the variety of sauces is endless we've limited our selection to two basic types. One is tomato-based and the other is a clear vinegar blend. We refuse to take a stand on such a personal choice.

The following recipes are meant to give inspiration, not to serve as pat rules. A couple of generalizations are permitted, however. Sugar-based sauces will caramelize and leave a bitter aftertaste if taken too far. Wine-, vinegar-, or citrus-based sauces will tenderize tough cuts of meat while imparting flavor. Use your imagination and what is at hand to provide interesting concoctions for your outdoor cooking endeavors. The same marinade may be used as a basting sauce as well. Some marinades may also be served as a sauce with the meat, chicken, or fish they have flavored.

RED WINE MARINADE   *Makes about 5 cups.*

This recipe is good for hearty beef and tangy game. The wine will help tenderize tough cuts of meat. Be sure to use a wine that is full of body and character.

½ cup olive oil
1 medium onion, peeled and
    chopped
2 medium carrots, peeled and
    chopped
3 ribs of celery, chopped
3 cups red wine
2 cups water
3 bay leaves

2 tablespoons fresh thyme, chopped
    (or 1 tablespoon dried)
2 tablespoons fresh basil, chopped
    (or 1 tablespoon dried)
½ cup (tightly packed) parsley,
    chopped
4 cloves garlic, coarsely chopped
10 to 12 whole black peppercorns

1. In a large nonreactive saucepan, heat the olive oil. Add the onion, carrots, and celery. Cook over low heat until the vegetables are soft, about 15 minutes. Stir often and do not allow onions to brown.

2. Pour in the wine and water. Season with the bay leaves, the herbs, the garlic, and the peppercorns. Bring to a simmer over moderately high heat, reduce heat, and simmer, uncovered, for 1 hour. Strain and let come to room temperature before using.

3. Combine with the meat for 12 to 24 hours in a shallow dish and keep covered in the refrigerator. Turn the meat several times while marinating.

BEER AND GINGER MARINADE *Makes about 2 cups.*

This is a good marinade for flank steak. The bitterness of the beer marries well with the sharpness of ginger. The orange peel adds a third dimension.

1½ cups flat beer
½ cup olive oil
2 tablespoons finely chopped fresh
  ginger

2 cloves garlic, coarsely chopped
1-by-3-inch piece of orange peel

1. In a nonreactive bowl, combine the beer, oil, ginger, garlic, and orange peel.

2. Use a receptacle large enough to snugly hold the meat (beef, lamb, or game) but not too large or flavor will not penetrate. Cover tightly and be sure to leave the meat in the marinade long enough to pick up the flavors of the liquid, at least 6 hours and up to 48. Turn frequently so that the marinade is evenly distributed. Strain and use as a basting sauce if desired.

BUTTERMILK, GARLIC, AND ROSEMARY MARINADE *Makes about 2 cups.*

The acidity of the buttermilk adds flavor and tenderizes just about any meat. Butterflied leg of lamb works especially well. Try inserting the garlic into tiny holes in the meat rather than just mixing it with the buttermilk. Another suggestion is to soak rabbit in this mixture and substitute fresh sage for the rosemary.

2 cloves garlic, peeled and thinly
  sliced
several sprigs fresh rosemary or 2
  teaspoons dried

freshly ground black pepper to taste
2 cups buttermilk

1. Combine the ingredients in a large nonreactive bowl. Season meat with salt and pepper and toss in the mixture to coat. Place meat and marinade in a plastic bag with a zipper-like enclosure and seal tightly. Marinate in the refrigerator for 1 to 2 days, turning often.

2. Remove meat and let come to room temperature before grilling. Discard marinade.

CURRY MARINADE   *Makes about ¼ cup.*

This is a paste for adding a pungent flavor to hearty red meats. It makes only a limited quantity, enough for a small roast or for 1 or 2 pounds of cubed meat.

1 tablespoon Dijon mustard
1 to 2 tablespoons curry powder
1 teaspoon cumin

2 tablespoons lemon juice
1 tablespoon olive oil

In a medium mixing bowl, combine all ingredients. Stir until smooth.

Note: Try tossing the marinade with 1-inch chunks of lamb (cut from the leg or shoulder) to use on skewers alternating with eggplant and peppers.

CITRUS MARINADE   *Makes 1⅓ cups.*

This is a light and simple marinade that imparts a great deal of flavor. Try marinating veal, skinless, boneless chicken breasts, or white-fleshed fish like sole or flounder.

½ cup fresh lime juice
½ cup freshly squeezed orange juice
⅓ cup olive oil

¼ teaspoon salt
⅛ teaspoon black pepper

1.   Combine the ingredients and pour over chicken, veal, or fish in a non-reactive shallow dish.
2.   Leave to marinate in the refrigerator for 4 to 12 hours, covered. Turn often. Wipe meat dry before grilling.

SPICY CHILI RUB

1 small jalapeño pepper
1 tablespoon tomato paste
2 teaspoons chili powder

1 tablespoon olive oil
1 teaspoon fresh lemon juice

1.   Spear the jalapeño pepper with a fork. Hold over a flame on top of the stove. Roast the pepper until it is charred, turning until evenly blackened. Let cool slightly, peel and seed. Chop very finely on a large work surface. Use the back of a knife to smear the chopped pepper into a paste.
2.   Add the tomato paste, chili powder, olive oil, and lemon juice. Stir until smooth. Use a brush—not your hands—to apply to pork chops, small steaks, or chicken breasts an hour or two before grilling.

EASY BARBECUE SAUCE   *Makes about 2 cups.*

2 cups catsup
1 cup distilled white vinegar
2 tablespoons brown sugar
1 small lemon, seeded and coarsely
 chopped
4 cloves garlic, peeled and finely
 chopped
1 medium onion, peeled and finely
 chopped

2 tablespoons Worcestershire sauce
1 teaspoon cumin
1 tablespoon chili powder
Tabasco sauce, to taste
salt and freshly ground black pepper
 to taste

Combine all of the ingredients in a large, nonreactive saucepan. Bring to a boil over high heat, reduce to a simmer. Cook over medium-low heat until rich and dark, 20 to 30 minutes. Stir occasionally. Strain and cool to room temperature. Use to baste large cuts of meat while cooking over a charcoal grill.

TWIN LAKES BARBECUE SAUCE

1 cup white wine vinegar
⅓ cup olive oil
¼ cup (tightly packed) chopped
 fresh herbs or 2 tablespoons dried
 herbs

1 small clove of garlic, finely
 chopped
salt and freshly ground black pepper
 to taste

In a pint jar with a tight-fitting lid, pour the vinegar and the oil. Add the herbs, garlic, and salt and pepper to taste. Cover and shake vigorously until well blended. Let sit at room temperature for at least 1 hour before using. Good for pork, chicken, or veal. Use as a basting sauce for fish steaks.

Hotdogs and Hamburgers

Hotdogs and hamburgers done on a grill are long-standing American favorites. To prepare them is no mystery. Using good-quality franks, the right meat and seasonings for the burgers, and a proper charcoal fire will guarantee success for any outdoor cooking enthusiast.

HOTDOGS

Hotdogs come in many sizes and shapes. They can be made from beef, pork, veal, chicken, turkey, or even tofu. Low in fat and surprisingly flavorful, hot dogs made from veal, chicken, turkey, and tofu can be used just like pork or beef franks. Use well-spiced condiments to zip up the mild nature of these modern hotdogs. Hotdogs are almost always fully cooked and require only warming up. Try serving grilled franks on different kinds of rolls and breads for variety. Broil on an oiled grill over red-hot coals. Franks will swell and ooze slightly when heated through. Alternatively, broil in a hinged grill or spear the hotdogs on long forks or sticks for self-service over an open fire. Chopped onion, sauerkraut, pickles, and spicy relishes are good classic accompaniments for hotdogs, and don't forget the mustard and catsup!

TEXAS RED HOTS (CHILI DOGS) *Serves 4 to 6.*

1 pound lean ground beef
¼ cup oil
1 large can (28 ounces) canned
   tomatoes, drained
1 clove garlic

1 to 2 teaspoons chili powder
salt and freshly ground black pepper
   to taste
12 good-quality hot dogs
1 cup chopped onion for garnish

1. In a large sauté pan or skillet, brown the meat in the oil. Stir in the tomatoes, garlic, and chili powder. Cover and simmer until rich and thickened, about 20 minutes, stirring often. Season with salt and pepper to taste. Add additional chili powder if desired.

2. Grill the hot dogs over hot coals. Place in rolls or buns and spoon over the chili sauce. Top with chopped onions.

STUFFED FRANKS

Cut long slit in frankfurter to make a pocket. Insert strip of cheddar cheese. Wrap with bacon, secure with toothpicks. Broil until bacon is brown and crisp. Brush with mustard and serve on a toasted bun.

HAMBURGERS

Hamburgers should be lightly shaped into patties of uniform thickness. Try using a mixture of ground turkey for a healthy but drier alternative. Broil 3 inches from the coals, about 4 to 5 minutes each side for medium-rare. Serve with garnishes to taste: catsup, chili sauce, mustard, pickles, sliced raw onion or tomato, or a barbecue sauce. Serve on toasted buns, English muffins, French, Italian, or rye bread by simply molding the patty to the necessary shape.

GRILLED CHEESEBURGER

Grill hamburgers on one side, turn and top with a slice of cheddar cheese, a slice of Swiss cheese, or crumbled blue cheese. When bottom is browned and meat is cooked to desired doneness, cheese will be melted.

GRILLED PIZZABURGERS

Grill hamburgers as usual on one side, turn, top with a slice of mozzarella cheese, a spoonful of spaghetti sauce, and a pinch of oregano. Serve on toasted English muffins.

GRILLED BURGUNDY BURGERS

Sauce
¼ cup butter, melted
2 tablespoons red wine
1 clove garlic, finely minced
salt, freshly ground black pepper,
  and cayenne pepper to taste

Burgers
1 pound ground beef
½ cup fresh breadcrumbs
¼ cup hearty red wine
1 teaspoon salt
¼ teaspoon freshly ground black
  pepper
½ small onion, finely chopped

1. In a small nonreactive bowl, combine sauce ingredients. Set aside.
2. In a large mixing bowl, break up meat with a fork. Add the breadcrumbs, the wine, salt, pepper, and onion. Mix quickly and shape into 4 patties. Brush lightly with sauce.
3. Grill as for the burgers above, basting with more sauce. Serve on slices of French bread with some of the basting sauce spooned over.

Beef, Pork, and Lamb

BEEF

GRILLED BEEF STEAKS

Choose tender steaks 1 to 3 inches thick, well marbled. Fillets, strip steaks, sirloin, and T-bone are excellent grilling steaks. Less tender cuts such as top round or rump roast must be marinated before broiling and usually benefit from slower cooking. Slash fat edge of steak to prevent curling. Rub grill with a piece of fat or spray cold grill with nostick cooking spray before grilling. Make sure grill has had enough time to heat so that the steak sears slightly before cooking. Grill 1-inch steak 2 to 3 inches from heat, 5 to 6 minutes each side for medium-rare, 2-inch steak takes 10 to 12 minutes each side. Or, sear steaks on both sides, raise grill and cook to desired degree of doneness. To test, make small cut with sharp kinfe in thickest part near the bone or learn to gauge doneness using the hand test found on page 271.

GRILLED FLANK STEAK

A marinade is almost essential to tenderize and flavor this particular piece of beef. The beer and ginger recipe on page 344 is a good choice. Grill on hot coals, 6 to 8 inches from the source of heat until rosy pink in the center, about 7 minutes per side. Slice very thinly on the diagonal.

BARBECUED POT ROAST

2 cups Red Wine Marinade (page 343), cooled to room temperature
1 bottom or top round roast (about 2 pounds), 2½ inches high
2 bay leaves, crumpled

10 to 12 whole black peppercorns
1 medium onion studded with 2 or 3 whole cloves
salt and freshly ground black pepper to taste

1. In a nonreactive, shallow bowl wide enough to hold the roast flat, pour the marinade over the meat. Add the bay leaves, the peppercorns, and the studded onion. Cover tightly and let stand in the refrigerator for at least 6 hours and up to 2 days, turning frequently and re-covering each time. Alternatively, place the marinade and the meat with seasonings in a plastic bag that closes with a zipper-like seal that will prevent any seepage. Simply turn the bag from time to time to insure that the meat is evenly marinated.

2.   An hour before you're ready to cook the roast, remove the meat from the refrigerator and prepare a fire in your charcoal grill. When charcoals are covered with gray ash and fire is moderately low, place the roast on the hot grill. Season lightly with salt and pepper. Strain the marinade into a saucepan and bring to a boil, reduce heat, and keep hot. Cook roast covered with the vents open until well browned on the outside and rosy pink on the inside, about 15 minutes each side, basting from time to time with the marinade if desired. Flames that result from fat dripping on the hot coals tend to burn the outside of meat, keeping the inside uncooked. Check often and douse with water as needed to prevent unwanted flames. Let roast stand for 10 minutes. Slice thinly across the grain and serve with the marinade sauce on the side.

PORK

PORK CHOPS

Choose either meatier, more tender loin chops or less moist, less expensive shoulder chops about 1 inch thick. Trim off excess fat. Season with salt and pepper or rub with a spicy marinade (pages 342–346). Cook on a low charcoal fire that has been started about 1 hour in advance. Cook 6 to 8 inches from the fire if you have an adjustable rack. Douse the fire if it is too hot. The chops should cook slowly and evenly until well done but not dry. (See cooking chart for pork, page 305, for guidelines. But remember that the degree of heat is not as easily regulated or measured as is the case in a kitchen oven. Use a meat thermometer to insure that chops are done if in doubt.) The chops may be marinated with a cooked or uncooked marinade and basted during the cooking with the same liquid.

Note: When pork is on the barbecue, the plentiful fat drippings tend to catch fire. Keep the sprinkler handy to douse the flames.

GRILLED PORK TENDERLOINS

This boneless, succulent piece from the inside of the loin is the perfect choice for outdoor grilling. The trick is to cook it very slowly over the grayest of charcoal embers. Be sure to have the meat at room temperature, not straight from the refrigerator, before beginning. Marinate the tenderloin, if desired, and serve with a piquant sauce like Mustard Sauce (page 409).

2 whole pork tenderloins, about
   1½ pounds each
2 cloves garlic, peeled and slivered

salt and freshly ground black pepper
   to taste

1. Spray the grill with no-stick cooking spray or rub with pieces of fat. Prepare a fire in the charcoal grill about an hour and a half before cooking the tenderloin. The coals should be gray, not red hot. Douse lightly with water and wait a few minutes before proceeding if the coals are too hot.

2. Make ½-inch incisions all over the surface of the pork. Insert the slivers of garlic into the tenderloin pushing gently with the fingers until well studded all over. Season with salt and pepper. Cook uncovered over low heat turning frequently, until lightly browned on the outside and inside shows no further signs of pink, about 45 minutes according to the heat of the charcoal grill. A meat thermometer should read 160° F when positioned at its thickest point. Let rest 10 minutes before slicing.

SPARERIBS

Marinate meaty spareribs or baby back ribs with any desired marinade for at least 2 hours and up to 24. Cook over gray embers of charcoal about 6 inches from the source of heat until done, about 1 hour. Turn frequently and baste with the marinade only during the last 20 minutes to prevent the sauce from caramelizing. Parboil ribs for 20 minutes or so to reduce the outdoor cooking time; or they may be oven roasted ahead of time and finished on the grill, with frequent basting. Three whole racks of ribs is approximately enough for 4 people.

LAMB

GRILLED LAMB CHOPS

Choose loin, rib or shoulder chops, 1½ to 2 inches thick. Or have butcher cut lamb steaks from the leg, about 2 inches thick. Marinate if desired, season and grill on an oiled rack about 5 inches from the coals, 5 to 7 minutes per side for medium-rare. Be careful not to overcook.

GRILLED LEG OF LAMB

Carefully bone a leg of lamb, making an effort to keep the meat intact. Or have the butcher "butterfly" the leg for grilling. Place meat in a shallow dish and pour over a marinade of choice or use a seasoned rub. Keep in refrigerator for 1 to 2 days, turning often. Start a charcoal fire about 1 hour before ready to cook. Remove the lamb from the marinade and wipe dry. Grill uncovered over the hot coals until desired degree of doneness is obtained, about 20 minutes per side for medium-rare. Internal temperature of meat should read about 165° F. Let sit for 10 minutes before slicing.

Poultry and Game

CHICKEN

If you're lucky enough to have a grill equipped with an electrically turned spit or rotisserie, the best way to use it is with chicken. Truss bird carefully and balance on the spit. Brush with butter and season with salt and pepper. Or use a barbecue sauce basting frequently only at the end of the cooking to prevent the sauce from caramelizing. Cook until there are no traces of pink in the juices that run when pierced at the thigh, about 1 hour depending on the size of the chicken and the degree of heat.

The next best way to cook chicken outside is to split broilers or small fryers in half and grill over moderately low heat. Rub with butter and season with salt and pepper. Place bone side down on grill, then turn to brown skin side. Baste frequently with melted butter. A butter that has been seasoned with herbs, lemon, or any other assortment of flavors (page 363) can be tucked under the skin just above the flesh of the chicken. Grill the halves until golden brown and cooked through, about 30 minutes depending on the size of the bird and the degree of heat. Be sure to check often to prevent flare-ups of flames that will occur from the dripping of butter onto the hot coals. Douse with water as necessary to prevent the outside of the chicken from charring.

Chicken breasts can be an excellent food for outdoor cooking. However, a few guidelines are important to follow. Boneless, skinless breasts are great for marinades. Their delicate flesh picks up flavor and becomes tender when kept for even a few hours in a savory mixture of herbs and spices. The grill must be very hot and well oiled or the breasts will stick. Brush the breasts with olive oil just before placing on the grids. Grill for about 2 minutes on each side over moderately-high heat. The internal temperature should read 160° F. Remove immediately and keep covered until ready to serve. The breasts will dry out if cooked for too long.

Chicken legs, thighs, and wings can be grilled, too, but benefit from a slightly slower, less-intense cooking.

TURKEY

Small turkeys (6 to 8 pounds) can be cooked on a spit. Follow directions for spit-roast chicken above. A meat thermometer inserted into thickest part of breast should read 185° F and the meat of the drumstick should feel soft when pressed.

A whole breast can be grilled as well. It should be cut in half, marinated if desired, and cooked uncovered slowly over very gray coals until done all the way through. Do not overcook. Time will vary according to size and heat of the grill. Test for doneness by inserting a sharp knife into the center of the breast. The flesh should show no traces of pink. A meat thermometer should read 175° F when checked at its thickest point.

Turkey cutlets should be treated as for the chicken breasts above. Turkey drumsticks, thighs, and wings benefit from a longer, slower cooking on a moderately low fire.

Ground turkey makes good mock hamburgers. The meat is drier than beef but can be made less so by a quick, even cooking with a brushing of melted butter or olive oil (see hamburger recipes for cooking times).

GRILLED CORNISH HENS

Whole or split Cornish hens should be cooked like broiler-fryers (see above).

RABBIT

Because rabbit is usually a very tough animal, it benefits from marinating for a long time in an acidic sauce. The meat is full of protein and low in fat, so brushing frequently with the marinade will help prevent drying out. Cook, covered, over low heat—very gray coals—until browned but still moist. Cooking too long will dry out the tender flesh. A younger, smaller rabbit will do better on a grill than an older, tougher one. Make an effort to find one that has not been frozen. Freezing seems to make the somewhat tough fibrous structure of the animal even more so. A covered grill will enhance the smoky flavor.

Fish and Shellfish

Fish takes naturally to outdoor cooking. The smoky, charcoal flavor marries well with the delicate flesh of most fish.

Coals for cooking fish should be white ash, not red hot. If you have an adjustable grill, it should be set at least 6 inches from the source of heat. Make sure that it is well oiled to prevent sticking. A hinged wire grill is best for larger pieces and truly a necessity for whole fish. Fragile fillets do better when cooked in envelopes of foil with seasonings and a bit of oil or butter. Hardwood chips can impart a delicious flavor but can be overpowering if too many are used. A small handful of mesquite is more than adequate for several pieces of grilled fish.

Marinades are useful when cooking fish outdoors. They are more beneficial for adding and enhancing taste than for tenderizing. A half hour at room temperature or two hours in the refrigerator is long enough to leave fish or shellfish to marinate. Any longer and the acidic nature of most marinades can break down the soft fibers, causing fish or shellfish to decompose.

The best way to test for doneness is to measure the fish fillet, steak, or whole fish at its thickest point. Cook over medium-low heat for 10 minutes per inch or fraction thereof. (See page 221 for further information.) This prevents probing through the skin and flesh to check for flakiness or opaque color and thereby destroying the presentation of a perfectly grilled fish.

Oily fish like bluefish, mackerel, and salmon do especially well on the grill. Leaner, flatfish species like flounder, sole, or snapper do best when filleted and cooked in foil (see recipe below). Round fish like bass and trout are often done whole with their skins intact. Steaks from large fish like tuna, salmon, and swordfish are excellent for grilling. Whatever the species or cut, all fish will benefit from a brushing of olive oil or butter to prevent drying out.

Shellfish are outstanding choices for open-air cooking. Shrimp and lobster in their shells can be cooked directly on the grill. Bivalves like oysters, mussels, and clams can be heated until they open and then cooked through. Specific instructions follow.

GRILLED FISH STEAKS

Choose steaks of salmon, halibut, haddock, tuna, or cod. Brush on both sides with oil or melted butter and lemon juice. Season to taste with salt and pepper. Let stand ½ hour at room temperature. Arrange directly on an oiled grill or an oiled hinged grill with a long handle. Grill 10 to 12 minutes in all, turning several times, basting frequently to keep fish moist. Do not overcook. Serve with lemon wedges.

GRILLED WHOLE FISH

Clean fish, season inside and out with salt and pepper. Stuff with onions, lemon slices, or fresh herbs if desired. Brush with butter or oil. Wrap in foil and grill 5 to 6 inches from the coals. Alternatively, use an oval-shaped, oiled hinged grill made for this purpose and cook on a grill set over white ash coals until golden brown on the outside and tenderly moist on the inside, 10 minutes per inch of fish when measured at its thickest point. (See page 221.)

GRILLED FISH FILLETS

Be sure to leave skins on. Arrange as above and cook 6 inches from the grill over moderately low heat until browned. Fish fillets done in this manner cook quickly. Care should be taken to not overcook. If very fragile, cook in foil as described below.

FISH FILLETS IN FOIL

Lay fish fillets on a square of foil. Season with salt, pepper, and fresh herbs of choice, add lemon juice or white wine and seal tightly. Cook close to the fire until firm and all traces of translucence are gone, about 5 to 7 minutes if fillets measure ½ inch thick, longer if thicker. Let flavors develop for 1 minute then open and carefully remove. Serve hot.

GRILLED SHRIMP

Split shrimp down the back and remove the vein without peeling. Marinate in lemon juice, vinegar, or white wine with seasonings for ½ hour at room temperature or 2 hours in the refrigerator. Drain and arrange on grill or in a hinged broiler and cook, 3 inches from the source of heat, until bright pink and slightly firm to the touch, about 5 minutes. Serve with melted butter or a chilled, tomato-based sauce of choice.

GRILLED WHOLE LOBSTER

Insert a sharp knife between the body and tail shell of a live lobster. Cut down to sever the spinal cord and kill the lobster. Lay on grill close to coals and grill 15 to 20 minutes, turning often. Split lengthwise, remove the stomach from behind the head and the black intestinal vein that runs from the stomach to the tip of the tail, the green liver, the pink coral, and the roe. Serve with melted butter and lemon.

GRILLED SPLIT LOBSTER

Sever spinal cord as above and split lobsters lengthwise. Remove intestines and stomach. Brush with melted butter, season with salt and pepper. Broil, shell side down, 4 inches from coals, until meat is cooked through, about 12 minutes. Serve with melted butter and lemon.

GRILLED OYSTERS

Place unopened oysters on the grill. Cook until shells open, 6 to 8 minutes. Serve with melted butter or any flavored butter sauce.

BUTTER-GRILLED OYSTERS

Open oysters. Discard the flat side of the shell. Loosen from the deep shell. Replace in deep shell with butter or desired sauce. Grill, shell side down, for 8 to 10 minutes.

CLAMS ON THE GRILL

Hard-shell clams may be roasted on the grill like oysters. The thin-shelled clams called "steamers" are always cooked in the following manner: Wash clam shells thoroughly, and put into kettle with ½ cup water. Cover tightly and steam 5 minutes or longer, until clam shells open. Serve with melted butter for dipping, and cups of the clam broth for sipping.

SCALLOPS

Marinate sea scallops in a lemon- or wine-based marinade for ½ hour at room temperature. Season with salt and pepper and arrange on a metal skewer. Brush with marinade and broil over moderately high heat until lightly browned and cooked through, about 7 minutes. Turn frequently and baste often.

Vegetables

POTATOES

Wrap medium-size white baking potatoes or sweet potatoes in heavy-duty aluminum foil. Bake in hot coals, turning occasionally. Bake about 45 minutes, depending on size of potatoes.

For covered grill, wrap potatoes as above. Place directly on grill, cover, leaving vents open, and bake for about 45 minutes.

GRILLED SCALLOPED POTATOES

For each serving, peel a medium-size potato, slice very thin, lay slices in overlapping layers on square of aluminum foil. Dot with 1 tablespoon butter, salt and pepper. Add 2 tablespoons milk. Seal package carefully with double fold. Cook on grill, close to coals, about 15 minutes. Open package to test for tenderness, reseal for longer cooking if necessary.

GRILLED NEW POTATOES

Boil small red-skinned new potatoes in salted water until tender. Drain well and skewer. Brush with oil and grill over moderately low coals until well dried out and hot, about 3 minutes. Season to taste with salt and pepper.

HUSK-ROASTED CORN

Pull husks back carefully leaving them attached at the base of the ear of corn. Remove silk. Twist husks tightly around ears. Soak in salted water for 30 minutes. Roast on grill for 10 to 15 minutes, turning to roast evenly.

FOIL-ROASTED CORN

Remove husks and silk. Brush corn generously with melted butter. Wrap in aluminum foil. Cook directly on coals for 10 to 15 minutes. Turn once or twice during cooking. Season butter with fresh herbs or slivered garlic if desired.

GRILLED TOMATOES

Use ripe tomatoes in season. Cut firm ones in half crosswise. Brush cut side with melted butter. Season with salt and pepper. Arrange on an oiled, hinged rack. Broil over hot coals until heated through and softened, about 10 minutes.

GRILLED PARSLIED TOMATOES

Make a mixture of chopped parsley, finely minced garlic, and dry breadcrumbs. Prepare tomatoes as for above and arrange cut side up on a grill. Sprinkle with the parsley mixture and cover grill. Cook until tomatoes are hot and tops have started to brown, about 10 minutes. Serve at once.

GRILLED EGGPLANT

Cut medium-size eggplants into thick slices. Brush with olive oil and season with salt and pepper. Grill over hots coals until brown on both sides.

GRILLED PEPPERS

Brush red, yellow or green peppers with olive oil and grill over hot coals until very hot and blistered. Remove to a plastic bag with a zipper-like, tight-closing seal. Let rest for 1 hour. Skin will be loosened and easy to peel. Carefully cut in half, remove core and skin, reserving juices. Slice peppers into strips and cover with olive oil if not to be used right away.

GRILLED MUSHROOMS

Choose large mushrooms and clean them well. Brush with melted butter and season with salt and pepper. Sprinkle with fresh herbs, if desired. Place on an oiled, hinged grill and cook close to the coals until browned and cooked through.

GRILLED ONIONS

Cut thick slices from large, sweet onions. Brush with butter and season with salt, pepper, and herbs of choice. Arrange on an oiled hinged grill and broil over hot coals until browned and slightly caramelized. Turn often, brushing with more melted butter if desired.

GRILLED MIXED VEGETABLES

Place a mixture of quick-cooking vegetables that will be done at the same time on a large square of foil. Julienned, small green beans, snow peas, tiny dice of carrots, potatoes or turnips, zucchini or squash are a few possibilities. Choose vegetables of contrasting color and texture. Dot with softened butter, salt and pepper to taste, and fresh herbs. Seal edges tightly and place on grill over hot coals. Cook, turning occasionally, until vegetables are softened, about 15 minutes over a moderately hot fire. Open carefully and serve at once.

Skewer Cooking

Any foods suitable for grilling or broiling may be cut into uniform pieces and cooked on skewers over an outdoor grill. Choose foods that take the same amount of time to cook. Partly cooked foods may be combined with raw foods that cook quickly. Select foods with an eye for harmony and interesting contrast of flavors, colors, and textures. Many skewered foods can be marinated before cooking and basted with oil or butter during cooking for maximum effect. Here are some general suggestions:

Meats: beef, lamb, or veal cut into uniform cubes; ham, slab bacon, or sausages cut into small morsels; chunks of chicken or turkey; chicken livers.

Seafood: fish fillets, scallops, shrimp, clams, oysters, lobster tails.

Vegetables: mushrooms; tomato wedges or cherry tomatoes; parboiled small onions or potatoes; red, yellow, or green peppers; eggplant; zucchini, or summer squash.

SHISH KEBABS

1 cup wine vinegar
½ teaspoon ground cinnamon
½ teaspoon ground cloves
1 medium onion, chopped

1 garlic clove, minced
1 cup olive oil
2 pounds leg of lamb, cut into 1 ½-inch cubes
cherry tomatoes or tomato wedges

1.   In a medium nonreactive saucepan, heat the vinegar with the spices. Remove from heat and let cool. Add the onion, the garlic, and the oil. Pour into a bowl.

(continued)

2. Add lamb cubes to the bowl, turn to coat, and let stand for 2 hours at room temperature. Turn occasionally to season evenly.

3. Thread lamb cubes on skewers alternately with tomatoes. Brush with marinade and broil over hot coals several inches from heat until meat is crusty on the outside but medium-rare inside.

Variations:

1. Use the Curry Marinade on page 345. Use cherry tomatoes and proceed as for above.

2. Substitute cubes of lean beef for the lamb. Use quartered, large mushrooms for the vegetables and proceed as for above.

3. Cut pieces of smoked sausage into 1-inch pieces. Alternately use 1-inch squares of red and yellow peppers (roasted and peeled if desired) with the sausage. Marinate and grill as for above.

SHASHLIK

1 cup oil
3 to 4 garlic cloves, grated
1 onion, grated
2 pounds leg of lamb, cut in 1½-inch cubes

salt
freshly ground black pepper

1. In a large mixing bowl, mix the oil, garlic, and onion. Turn lamb cubes in mixture to coat. Cover and let stand overnight in refrigerator.

2. About 2 hours before cooking, remove bowl from refrigerator. Continue to marinate meat, turning occasionally.

3. Thread on skewers, broil close to coals until lamb is crusty on outside but still pink inside. Season with salt and pepper to taste.

CHICKEN KEBABS

2 whole boneless, skinless chicken breasts (¾ to 1 pound), cut into 1-inch chunks
2 tablespoons Worcestershire sauce
1 tablespoon grated gingerroot
1-by-2-inch piece of lemon peel

1 large clove garlic, thinly sliced
1-by-2-inch piece of lemon peel
1 small zucchini, sliced into ½-inch-thick slices, parboiled
1 medium onion, cut into quarters
salt and freshly ground black pepper to taste

1. In a medium mixing bowl, toss the chicken chunks with the Worcestershire sauce, ginger, lemon peel and sliced garlic. Cover and keep for 2 to 4 hours in the refrigerator, turning often to distribute the marinade.

2. Drain the chicken pieces and reserve any liquid from the marinade. On skewers, alternate the chicken with the parboiled zucchini and pieces of the onion quarters that have been separated into 2 or 3 layers. Season to taste with salt and pepper.

3. Broil the kebabs over moderately hot coals, turning often and brushing frequently with the marinade if it has rendered any liquid. (If there is not a sufficient amount, brush with a small amount of additional Worcestershire sauce.) They are done when the chicken is slightly browned and vegetables are softened and tender, about 10 minutes.

FISH KEBABS

We strongly recommend roasting and peeling the peppers (page 385) for the following recipe for delightful results.

1½ pounds firm-flesh fish fillets
   (swordfish, tuna, or salmon), cut
   into 1- to 1½-inch cubes
2 tablespoons lemon juice
2 tablespoons olive oil
1 tablespoon grated onion
¼ teaspoon red pepper flakes
salt and freshly ground black pepper
   to taste

1 medium red pepper (about ½
   pound), cut into 1-inch squares
   (roasted and peeled if desired)
1 medium yellow pepper (about ½
   pound), cut into 1-inch squares
   (roasted and peeled if desired)

1. In a medium, nonreactive bowl, combine fish chunks with the lemon juice, olive oil, grated onion, pepper flakes, salt and pepper. Cover and marinate for ½ hour at room temperature or for 2 hours in the refrigerator.

2. Remove fish from the marinade and wipe dry. Reserve any liquid from the marinade. Arrange on skewers alternating peppers and fish. Broil over hot coals, brushing with any liquid from the marinade. Fish should be flaky and devoid of all translucent appearance when done. The peppers should be softened and slightly wrinkled, about 10 minutes.

SHRIMP AND SNOW PEAS ON SKEWERS

1 pound medium shrimp, split
down the back through the shell
and vein removed
Citrus Marinade (see page 345)

½ pound snow peas, trimmed and
blanched for 1 minute in boiling,
salted water, refreshed under cold
running water and drained

1. In a medium, nonreactive bowl, marinate shrimp for ½ hour at room temperature or 2 hours in the refrigerator. Drain well, reserving the liquid from the marinade.

2. Arrange the shrimp on skewers, alternating with the snow peas. Broil over moderately hot coals, turning often and brushing frequently with the marinade until shrimp are bright pink and tender to the touch, about 5 minutes.

---

5 QUICK SAUCES TO ACCOMPANY GRILLED STEAKS, CHOPS, CHICKEN, OR FISH

BALSAMIC SAUCE

In a heavy, nonreactive saucepan, reduce 1 cup balsamic vinegar with 1 very finely chopped shallot over very high heat. When only 2 tablespoons of liquid remain, carefully whisk in 4 tablespoons cold butter that has been cut into small pieces. Add 1 piece at a time, working the pan on and off the heat, whisking constantly, until the sauce is thick and emulsified. Season to taste with salt and pepper. Serve with beef, pork, or lamb.

LEMON-CHICKEN SAUCE

Reduce 1 cup chicken stock (page 59) as for above with 1 heaping teaspoon grated lemon rind. Add 4 tablespoons butter in the same manner as above and serve with grilled chicken breasts or charcoal-cooked, halved broilers.

APPLE SAUCE FOR GRILLING

Reduce 1 cup good-quality apple cider as for above. When only 2 tablespoons of liquid remain, add ½ cup heavy cream and reduce until thick and rich. Spoon a small amount over grilled pork chops and garnish with sautéed apple slices.

HERB AND EGG SAUCE

In a medium mixing bowl, combine 2 very finely chopped hard-boiled eggs with ¼ cup (tightly packed) chopped fresh herbs and 2 tablespoons mayonnaise. Season to taste with salt and pepper and serve at room temperature with grilled fish.

MINT GRILLING SAUCE

In a heavy, nonreactive saucepan, combine ½ cup finely chopped fresh mint with 1 cup cider vinegar. Add 1 tablespoon sugar and bring to a boil over high heat. Remove from heat and let cool. Serve with grilled lamb.

COMPOUND BUTTERS FOR STEAKS, CHOPS, CHICKEN, AND FISH

Butter is a natural accompaniment for grilled meat, poultry, and fish. Try using one of the following compound butters to add a special touch to your outdoor grilling adventure. The butters are easy to do in a food processor but certainly possible to execute with a hand-held mixer or even a large bowl and a whisk. In any case, make sure that you start out with butter that is at room temperature. Work quickly so that the butter stays soft but does not melt. The following recommendations are for ½ cup butter (1 stick). A little goes a long way, a tablespoon per serving is enough for one. Use any left over with vegetables, potatoes, rice, or pasta.

CITRUS/HERB BUTTER

Combine butter with 1 teaspoon grated lemon or lime peel with 1 heaping tablespoon chopped fresh herbs (parsley, basil, tarragon, thyme, or savory), salt and pepper to taste. Place on a small piece of plastic wrap, form into a round bar about 2 inches in diameter and several inches long. Tightly twist the ends closed and refrigerate until ready to use.

MUSTARD BUTTER

Add 2 tablespoons Dijon mustard, ¼ teaspoon ground cumin, salt, and pepper to butter. Prepare the seal in plastic as for above.

HORSERADISH BUTTER

Add 1 tablespoon drained, prepared horseradish to the softened butter. Proceed as for above.

JALAPEÑO AND CILANTRO BUTTER

Carefully peel and seed a small jalapeño pepper. Chop very finely. Combine with butter and ¼ cup finely chopped fresh cilantro. Proceed as for above.

ITALIAN BUTTER

Mix ¼ cup Parmesan cheese with 2 tablespoons chopped fresh parsley and 1 clove finely minced garlic. Proceed as for above.

VEGETABLES

Whenever possible, choose fresh, locally grown vegetables. Modern transportation and farming techniques bring more variety of produce to the marketplace than ever before. Although almost any vegetable is available all year round, buying seasonal produce is still an economical and flavorful way to shop. Many urban areas now have farmer's markets, and farm stands often appear in both rural and suburban communities. These are excellent sources for premium vegetables.

Buy in small quantities that you can use within a day or two. Even vegetables from your own garden lose freshness rapidly and should be picked just before cooking, if possible.

STORING VEGETABLES

To store, lettuce should be trimmed, washed, and dried in a salad spinner. Pat dry with paper towels then refrigerate in airtight containers or plastic bags.

Cabbage, root vegetables, unshelled peas and beans need no refrigeration. Store in a dark, dry area in a basket or bin that allows air to circulate around them. (Freshly shelled peas and beans can be refrigerated or left in a very cool spot.)

Tomatoes should not be refrigerated and will ripen if left in a sunny spot like a window sill. Sweet and hot peppers stay fresh in the vegetable crisper in the refrigerator. They should be consumed fairly soon after picking unless they are to be roasted. (Even shriveled-skin peppers can be charred and the skin removed.)

Squash are hearty vegetables that will keep almost anywhere. Discard if soft spots begin to appear.

Mushrooms can be refrigerated but will do fine in a dark, cool corner of the kitchen. Do not wash until just before using.

Gently wash fresh herbs and wrap the stems in wet paper towels. Store in plastic bags in the refrigerator.

PREPARING VEGETABLES

(General Rules from the earliest edition of *The Settlement Cookbook*)

Wash vegetables thoroughly, pare and scrape if skins must be removed. Keep in cold water until they are to be cooked to keep them crisp and to prevent their being discolored. Cook in boiling water. The water must be kept at the boiling point. Use 1 teaspoon salt with 1 quart of water. Put the salt into the water when the vegetables are partially cooked. The water in which vegetables are cooked is called vegetable stock.

Fresh, green vegetables require less water than others.

Cabbage, cauliflower, onions, and turnips should be cooked uncovered in a large amount of water.

All vegetables must be drained as soon as possible. Season with salt and pepper and serve hot with butter or sauce.

The color may be kept in green vegetables by pouring cold water through them after draining.

Cold vegetables may be used for salads, or may be placed in a baking dish with one half again the quantity of a favorite sauce. Cover with buttered crumbs and brown in a hot oven.

COOKING VEGETABLES

Vegetables, more than any other food, require proper cooking and seasoning to bring out their maximum appeal. To preserve vitamins and minerals, pare them as thinly as possible. Vegetables look and taste best when they are cooked until just tender. Test doneness by inserting a knife tip into the vegetable's thickest part; there should still be some resistance.

Use an adequate amount of water when boiling. Pressure cooking and steaming are particularly good methods of cooking vegetables. The microwave oven can be a time and energy saver (see page 395). Whatever the method used, it is important to avoid overcooking, which destroys flavor, color, and texture. Remember that seasonings and sauces should bring out, not disguise, the flavor of vegetables.

Artichokes

French artichokes have a large scaly head, like the cone of a pine tree. The edible portion consists of the thickened portion at the base of the scales and the receptacles are the "bottoms." The parts of the flower in the center of the bud are called the choke and must be removed.

When the artichoke is very young and tender the edible parts may be eaten raw as a salad. When it becomes hard, as it does very quickly, it must be cooked.

When boiled it may be eaten as a salad or with a sauce. The scales are pulled with the fingers from the cooked head, the base of each leaf dipped in the sauce, and then eaten.

The "bottom," which is the most delicate part, may be cut up and served as a salad or stewed and served with a sauce.

STEWED ARTICHOKES

4 large or 8 small artichokes	2 tablespoons vinegar
3 tablespoons salt	4 quarts water

1.   With a sharp knife or kitchen shears, trim about an inch from the top of the artichoke. Add salt and vinegar to water. Cook artichokes 20 to 30 minutes, or until leaves pull out easily.

2.   Drain and cut each artichoke in half lengthwise, or serve whole, removing the white fuzzy fiber or "choke."

3.   Serve cold as a first course with Vinaigrette Sauce (page 129) or serve hot with melted butter and lemon.

ROASTED ARTICHOKES

Cut six fine, green artichokes into quarters and remove the chokes. Trim the leaves neatly and parboil them five minutes in salted water. Drain. Lay them in a casserole, season with salt, pepper, and ¼ cup butter. Cover and cook in a moderate oven 25 minutes. Serve with any desired sauce.

Jerusalem Artichokes

Jerusalem artichokes look like small potatoes, but are not so mealy. Wash and scrape, soak 2 hours in cold water with a little vinegar. Drain. Cover with boiling salted water and boil until tender. Drain immediately or they will harden again. Or, boil with the skins on and when tender, peel. Serve with Medium White Sauce (page 399). Use instead of potatoes in your favorite potato salad, or puree in the food processor.

Asparagus

Select asparagus with tightly closed buds. Wash thoroughly. Snap off lower tough ends of stalks and peel tough skin from stems. Tie in bunches with string. Bring enough salted water to cover stalks to a rapid boil in lower half of double boiler. Stand the bunches, leaving tips out of water. Cook for 5 minutes and then cover with the inverted upper half of double boiler until stalks are tender, about 10 minutes. Serve at room temperature with Vinaigrette Sauce (page 129) or warm as a side dish with roasts or grilled meats.

White asparagus stalks must be pure white at tips. If pink they are apt to be bitter. Snap off tough ends. Cut waxy thick skin on lower end and peel rest of stalk very thin. Parboil, drain, add fresh, salted boiling water, and cook rapidly until tender. Best served tepid with Vinaigrette Sauce (page 129) and chopped hard-boiled eggs as a first course.

Fresh Beans

Green beans and wax beans may be used interchangeably. Most varieties now sold do not have strings, so the name "string bean" is out of date. If there are strings (some are still grown in home gardens), snap the ends and pull down the pod to remove. Imported haricots verts are small and need shorter cooking time. Larger green and wax beans can be trimmed on the ends before cooking if desired.

DRESSED GREEN BEANS

The original recipe for cooking green, wax, or string beans called for a cooking time of one to three hours. Today's tastes are for a crisper, fresher bean with more flavor and nutritive value. The following method of cooking reflects this trend. Bright green and lively, the beans need just a quick tossing in butter with plenty of salt and pepper for a perfect side dish with roasts, chops, chicken, or fish. They are delicious cold in salads as well.

Wash beans, remove strings as necessary, trim ends, and cut into 1-inch lengths or thin, slanting slices. Or leave the beans whole. Place beans in rapidly boiling salted water to cover. Cook until just tender, 10 to 15 minutes. Drain and refresh under cold running water. Just before serving, toss with hot butter or olive oil and season with salt and pepper.

Beets

Wash beets, but do not cut them, as that destroys the sweetness and color. Cook in boiling water until tender. Young beets will cook in 1 hour or less, older ones in 1 to 2 hours. When cooked, put them in a pan of cold water and rub off the skin. Young beets are cut in quarters and served hot with butter, salt, pepper, and hot vinegar. Old beets are often sliced and pickled in vinegar.

Beet tops, if young and fresh, may be prepared like spinach.

COLD PICKLED BEETS

1 quart cold boiled beets, peeled (about 2 pounds)
1 teaspoon salt
⅛ teaspoon freshly ground black pepper

1 pint vinegar
caraway seeds or onion slices (optional)

Slice the beets, place in a large jar, and cover with the seasoning and vinegar. Add a little caraway seed or raw onion slices if desired. Pickled beets keep for 2 weeks in the refrigerator.

Broccoli

DRESSED BROCCOLI

Wash well. Cut off tough ends of stalks. Trim into small florets of uniform size. (Save stalks for making stock or soup.) Cook uncovered in rapidly boiling water or steam until tender, about 5 minutes. Drain and refresh under cold running water. Just before serving, toss in hot butter or olive oil until heated through and season with salt and pepper.

Brussels Sprouts

Choose firm, compact heads of uniform size. Discard any wilted leaves. Cut the stalks close to the heads. Cut a shallow cross in the bottoms and soak in cold salted water for 10 minutes. Drain well and cook in rapidly boiling water or steam until easily pierced with a fork, 10 to 20 minutes depending on size. Drain. Just before serving, toss in hot butter or olive oil until heated through and season with salt and pepper.

BRUSSELS SPROUTS AND CHESTNUTS

1 pound Italian chestnuts
1 quart cooked brussels sprouts
  (about 1 pound)

⅓ cup butter
salt and freshly ground black pepper
  to taste

1. Preheat oven to 350° F. Put chestnuts in saucepan of cold water and boil until the shells and skins are easily removed.

2. Butter a large baking dish, put in a layer of sprouts, then one of chestnuts. Dot with butter, sprinkle sparingly with pepper and add a little salt if necessary. Continue in this way until all ingredients are used.

3. Add enough boiling water to just moisten and bake for 30 minutes.

Cabbage

Green cabbage, savoy or curly cabbage, and Chinese or stalk cabbage are all cooked the same way. Remove and discard the core of the round heads and the root end of the stalk cabbage. Cut into wedges and boil or steam until tender. Or cut into large or small shreds and sauté in hot butter or oil until wilted and just tender. Red cabbage takes slightly longer to cook than the green and white varieties, and a little lemon juice or vinegar should be added to preserve its color.

CHOPPED CABBAGE

2 tablespoons butter or olive oil
1 onion, finely chopped
1 quart cabbage, chopped (about 1
  pound)

boiling water
1 teaspoon salt
⅛ teaspoon freshly ground black
  pepper
2 tablespoons flour

1. Heat fat in a large casserole or skillet. Add the onions and lightly brown. Add the cabbage, cover and let steam for 10 minutes.

2. Pour over enough boiling water to barely cover, add salt and pepper, and cook until tender. Sprinkle with flour, boil a little longer, and serve hot. Savoy or curly cabbage may be prepared in the same way.

CABBAGE AND APPLES

1 quart shredded red or white
  cabbage (about 1 pound)
2 tablespoons butter, olive oil, or
  chicken fat
2 sour apples, peeled and sliced

2 teaspoons caraway seeds
2 teaspoons salt
½ teaspoon paprika
1 small onion, thinly sliced

Soak cabbage 10 minutes in salted water. Drain well. Heat the fat in a large skillet. Add the cabbage and apples, caraway seeds, salt, paprika, and onion. Cover and cook slowly about 1 hour.

SWEET AND SOUR CABBAGE

1 cabbage (red or white)
salt and freshly ground black pepper
2 sour apples, sliced
2 tablespoons butter or fat

boiling water
2 tablespoons flour
4 tablespoons brown sugar
2 tablespoons vinegar

Finely shred the cabbage, add salt and pepper to taste and the apples. Heat fat or butter in a large skillet. Add the cabbage and apples. Add boiling water to cover and cook until tender. Sprinkle with flour, add sugar and vinegar. Simmer 10 minutes.

CABBAGE AND SAUSAGES

6 sausages
4 cups cabbage, finely shredded

½ teaspoon freshly ground black
  pepper
salt to taste

Fry the sausages crisp and brown. Remove sausages and pour off all but 3 tablespoons of the fat. Put cabbage in pan, cover and cook until tender. Add seasonings. Arrange on a hot dish and garnish with the sausages. Serve with mashed potatoes.

DRESSED SAUERKRAUT

Sauerkraut, which is made by salting cabbage and allowing it to ferment, may be eaten raw or cooked before eating. Canned sauerkraut is cooked during the canning process and is prepared in a shorter time than the raw variety, which is purchased in bulk or in plastic bags.

2 tablespoons shortening or fat
1 onion, diced
1 quart sauerkraut (about 1 pound)
1 raw potato, grated

1 teaspoon caraway seeds
boiling water or chicken stock (page 59)
brown sugar or grated apple (optional)

Heat the fat in a large skillet. Cook onion until translucent, add sauerkraut. Cook 5 minutes, add potato and caraway seeds. Cover with boiling stock or water. Brown sugar and a grated apple may be added if desired. Cover well and cook slowly ½ hour on top of range or in moderate (350° F) oven.

Carrots

Carrots come in various shapes and sizes. Most are the long, slender root-like cultivated ones available year-round. Small, knobby round ones are sometimes found in early spring and are good for glazing. Baby carrots are newly popular and are served peeled and boiled with a small amount of the stem attached for color.

Carrots need not be peeled if thoroughly scrubbed before using. However, the appearance is often a brighter, vibrant orange if peeled and served in soups, stews, or sliced and boiled.

LEMON CARROTS

Old carrots may be used for this dish. Pare and cut carrots into dice, and simmer in salted water until tender but not pulpy. Drain, return to the heat, and for every pint of carrots add a teaspoon of minced parsley, a pinch of sugar, ½ teaspoon paprika, one tablespoon of butter, and the juice of ½ lemon. Heat through, shaking the dish now and then so that each piece of the vegetable will be coated with the dressing.

FLEMISH CARROTS

1 pound carrots
1 quart boiling water
1 teaspoon salt
2 tablespoons butter or fat
1 small onion, finely chopped

pinch of sugar (optional)
¼ teaspoon salt
⅛ teaspoon white pepper
1½ cups chicken stock (page 59)
1 teaspoon chopped parsley

(continued)

Scrape, slice, and cook the carrots in the boiling, salted water until tender. Drain. Heat butter or fat in a skillet, add onion and brown lightly. Add the carrots and seasonings. Shake well over the heat for 10 minutes, add the stock, cover and simmer for ½ hour. Add the parsley and serve hot.

CARROTS AND PEAS

½ pound carrots
1 pint green peas, cooked (about ½ pound)
2 tablespoons flour
salt and freshly ground black pepper to taste

pinch of sugar (optional)
2 tablespoons butter or fat
½ cup chicken stock (page 59)

Wash, scrape, and cut carrots into ½-inch cubes. Cook until tender, drain, and reserve ½ cup carrot water. Mix carrots well with cooked peas. Sprinkle with flour, salt and pepper, and sugar if desired. Add butter or fat, stock, and carrot water. Boil a little longer and serve.

Cauliflower

Select cauliflower with unblemished white head and fresh green leaves. Or use the more delicately flavored blue variety. Cut off the greens, trim the stalk level with the flower, and soak, head down, in cold salted water for 30 minutes. Drain before cooking. Cauliflower may be steamed, boiled, or parboiled and then baked or fried.

CAULIFLOWER POLONAISE

Boil or steam a cauliflower to desired doneness. Meanwhile, brown 2 tablespoons fine soft breadcrumbs in ¼ cup butter. Drain the cauliflower and sprinkle with the crumbs just before serving.

CAULIFLOWER AU GRATIN

Preheat oven to 350° F. Cover separated florets from 1 boiled cauliflower with 1 cup Medium White Sauce (page 399) in buttered baking dish, top with buttered crumbs and grated cheddar cheese. Bake until crumbs are brown.

Celery

Celery is a strong-flavored vegetable. Use it sparingly when employed as an aromatic vegetable in salads, soups, or stews. Cooked celery can be a delicious side dish to be served with hearty red meats like beef or lamb.

Celery root is full of intense earthiness. It can be pureed with potatoes or served cold as suggested below. This root vegetable tends to darken quickly when exposed to air and certain metals. Use a stainless-steel knife to cut and rub with cut lemon during preparation to prevent discoloration.

CREAMED CELERY

1 bunch celery

1 cup Medium White Sauce (page 399)

Wash, scrape, and cut the celery stalks into pieces 1½ inches long. Cook, covered, in a small amount of rapidly boiling salted water until tender. Drain and serve with Medium White Sauce.

BRAISED CELERY

Wash, scrape, and cut outer stalks of celery into 3-inch pieces. Dry thoroughly. Sauté in 2 tablespoons butter in a heavy skillet until lightly browned. Add ½ cup chicken or beef stock (page 59) and simmer until liquid is almost absorbed.

Celeriac or Celery Root

The root and not the stalks of this vegetable are eaten. Scrub, peel, slice, and cook in boiling water until tender, about 30 minutes. Drain and serve with Thick White Sauce (page 400) or chill, cut into slices, and serve as salad with Vinaigrette Sauce (page 129).

Chestnuts

To shell and blanch chestnuts, make ½-inch slit on flat side of chestnuts with a sharp knife. Cover chestnuts with boiling water and let stand for 30 minutes. Carefully remove shell and skin.

BRAISED CHESTNUTS

Remove shells from chestnuts as described above. Then boil very slowly in water until about half done, drain off any remaining water, and add one cup of chicken stock (page 59) and one cup of brown sugar. Let this simmer until it is soft, then add 2 tablespoons butter. Reduce liquid and serve piled in the center of a serving dish surrounded with meat.

CHESTNUT PUREE

1 pound chestnuts, shelled
hot milk
2 tablespoons butter

salt and freshly ground black pepper to taste

Cover chestnuts with boiling salted water and cook until tender. Drain and mash or put through a ricer. Add enough hot milk to make a smooth puree. Then add the butter and salt and pepper to taste. Beat until light and smooth.

Corn

Fresh corn on the cob should have light-green, moist husks and a brown silky tassel. The ears should be full of kernels and the kernels so juicy that when you cut into one with a fingernail, it bursts with milky juice. Do not husk corn until just before cooking, since it loses freshness rapidly. Golden and white varieties are equally delicious, but the white is more delicate in texture.

BOILED CORN ON—OR OFF—THE COB

Remove husks and silk threads, drop ears in a large amount of rapidly boiling water with a little sugar (if desired), and boil 2 to 5 minutes. Remove from water and serve with butter, salt, and pepper.

Cut the cooked corn from the cobs and serve heated with butter, salt, and pepper.

CREAM-STYLE CORN

Scrape corn from cobs, cook slowly 2 to 5 minutes in its own juice with a little butter, salt, and pepper. Add some milk if necessary.

BAKED CORN

Soak corn still in the husks in cold water for 10 minutes. Bake in 400° F oven for 10 to 15 minutes. Remove husks.

ESCALLOPED CORN

6 ears of fresh-cooked corn	1 teaspoon sugar (optional)
1 teaspoon salt	½ cup corn cooking liquid
⅛ teaspoon freshly ground black pepper	1 tablespoon butter
	1 cup breadcrumbs
2 tablespoons flour	

1. Preheat oven to 350° F. Cut boiled corn from the cob. Mix kernels with the salt, pepper, flour, sugar if desired, and corn liquid.

2. Melt the butter, mix with the breadcrumbs, and cover bottom of a baking dish with ½ of the crumbs. Add the corn mixture and cover with the rest of the crumbs. Bake about 20 minutes and serve hot.

PUFFY CORN FRITTERS

2 eggs, separated	3 tablespoons milk
2 cups fresh corn pulp (from about 6 ears)	2 tablespoons flour
	vegetable oil for deep-frying
½ teaspoon salt	

1. Beat the egg yolks and combine with the corn. In a separate bowl, beat the egg whites until stiff. Set aside.

2. Add the salt, milk, and flour to the corn mixture. Last of all, fold in beaten egg whites.

3. Drop by teaspoonfuls in deep, hot fat and fry until brown. Or drop on a hot, greased griddle or frying pan.

SUCCOTASH

1 cup cooked corn kernels	salt and freshly ground black pepper to taste
1 cup cooked lima beans	1 tablespoon butter
2 ripe tomatoes, peeled, seeded, and coarsely chopped	

Combine corn, beans, and tomatoes in a heavy, nonreactive saucepan. Boil over high heat until tomatoes give off liquid that boils away and thickens. Season to taste with salt and pepper. Add butter, blend, and serve very hot.

Cucumbers

Cucumbers are usually served raw with salad dressing or pickled in brine. They can be cooked to serve as a side dish, as well. Most are coated with wax and should therefore be peeled. The seeds are bitter and difficult to digest. Cut cucumber in half lengthwise and use a small spoon to scrape out seeds.

CUCUMBERS WITH MINT

2 medium cucumbers, peeled and
    seeded
2 tablespoons butter
½ cup chicken stock (page 59)

salt and freshly ground black pepper
    to taste
2 tablespoons freshly chopped mint

Cut cucumbers into uniform, 1-inch pieces. Sauté in butter until slightly softened. Add stock and increase heat to high. Toss and stir until almost all of the liquid has evaporated and cucumbers are translucent. Season with salt and pepper. Sprinkle over mint just before serving.

Eggplant

Eggplant should be dark purple and firm fleshed when purchased. Large ones tend to be bitter and thick skinned. To draw out some of the bitterness, cut large eggplants in half and score with the tip of a sharp-bladed knife. Sprinkle with a large amount of salt and let sit undisturbed for 30 minutes. Rinse off salt and liquid and pat dry with paper towels. Baby eggplants have the same color but are at least half the size. Because their flavor is sweet, they do not need to have the bitterness extracted with salt as suggested for the larger variety. Small white eggplant are sometimes seen on the market and are known for their sweet flesh and subtle flavor.

STUFFED EGGPLANT

2 medium eggplants (or four baby
    eggplants)
1 cup olive oil
2 medium onions, finely chopped
2 cloves garlic, minced
3 medium tomatoes, peeled, seeded,
    and chopped

2 tablespoons chopped parsley
salt and freshly ground black pepper
    to taste
¼ cup fresh breadcrumbs
¼ cup grated Parmesan cheese

1.   Preheat oven to 425° F. Trim ends of eggplant but leave unpeeled. Cut in half lengthwise and score with the tip of a sharp-bladed knife. Sprinkle with salt and let sit for 30 minutes to draw out bitter juices. Rinse and pat dry with paper towels.

2.   Lightly oil a baking dish large enough to hold the eggplant in one flat layer. Place the eggplant cut side up and pour over ½ cup of the olive oil. Bake in the preheated oven until flesh is soft, about 20 minutes. Remove from the oven and use a large spoon to scoop out the flesh, leaving the shell intact. Chop the flesh and set aside. Reserve the shells. Leave the oven on.

3.   Heat ¼ cup of the olive oil in a large sauté pan. Add the onion and cook until translucent. Add the garlic and cook until softened, about 1 more minute. Add the tomatoes and cook over high heat until liquid has evaporated, about 15 minutes. Stir often. Add the parsley and chopped flesh of the eggplant. Season to taste with salt and pepper.

4.   Season the eggplant shells with salt and pepper and spoon in the filling. Sprinkle over the breadcrumbs and cheese. Dribble over the remaining ¼ cup olive oil and set in the preheated oven. Cook until top is browned and filling is heated through, about 15 minutes.

FRIED EGGPLANT

1 cup olive oil
2 medium eggplants, cut into ½-
  inch slices
1 cup flour for dredging

2 eggs, lightly beaten with 1
  teaspoon of milk or water
salt and freshly ground black pepper
  to taste

In a medium sauté pan over moderately high heat, heat the olive oil. Working quickly, dredge the eggplant in flour then dip in the beaten egg. Fry until golden brown and cooked through, about 5 minutes on each side. Drain on paper towels and season with salt and pepper while hot.

Greens

To prepare greens such as collard, kale, mustard, or turnip, if greens are young and tender, wash well in several changes of cold water. Transfer to a large, nonreactive pot and set over high heat. Quickly cook and stir constantly until greens are wilted. Cover, reduce heat, and let cook slowly until tender but not overcooked, about 5 minutes. Season to taste with salt and pepper.

If greens are older or meat is to be served with them, simmer the meat in just enough water to cover. When meat is tender, add greens and simmer until just tender. The length of time will depend upon the age of the greens. Test at the end of 30 minutes.

DANDELION GREENS

Select dandelions early in the spring before they begin to blossom. Wash thoroughly and remove roots. Cook in boiling salted water for a minute, covered. Stir, uncover and cook rapidly until tender. Drain, season with butter, salt, pepper, and vinegar. (Or serve raw like a salad green.)

CURLY ENDIVE, KALE, OR ESCAROLE

Prepare any of these greens as for cooking Spinach (page 391). Cook in rapidly boiling salted water until just tender, 15 to 20 minutes. Drain, chop, and season. Add butter, cream, or cream sauce. Or substitute any of these greens for the cabbage in the recipe for Chopped Cabbage (page 369).

BOILED KOHLRABI

1 quart kohlrabi (about 2 pounds)	2 tablespoons flour
2 tablespoons butter or fat	salt and freshly ground black pepper to taste

1. Wash, peel, and cut the kohlrabi root in slices and cook in rapidly boiling salted water for 5 minutes. Then cover and boil until tender.
2. Cook the greens or tops in boiling, salted water only until tender. Drain and chop very fine, reserving 1 cup cooking liquid.
3. Heat the butter or fat, add the flour, then the chopped greens and 1 cup cooking liquid. Add the kohlrabi slices, season, and reheat.

Note: Kohlrabi may also be served raw, thinly sliced and salted.

Mushrooms

Fresh, cultivated mushrooms are naturally white. They discolor easily when exposed to air. Use lemon juice to keep them from turning brown while working with them. Small mushrooms are served whole or stemmed. Larger mushrooms,

---

WILD MUSHROOMS

Wild or exotic mushrooms are showing up in markets all over the country. Cultivated mushrooms provide us with an ample supply of the classic kind year-round. Seasonal field mushrooms have a subtle flavor that most of us would prefer. There is some danger in foraging for wild mushrooms. Some species are poisonous; edible varieties must be correctly identified.

Many field mushrooms are supplied by growers today. Some enthusiasts seek them in the damp, spring forests where they naturally spring up. However they are procured, these delicacies are one of nature's most flavorful offerings. A few of the ones commonly available are listed here. Look for more wild mushrooms to arrive on the market as demand for these gifts of nature increases.

Morels are dome shaped and dark brown with a sponge-like texture. Rich and full flavored, they are often cooked with cream and served in a sauce. These are readily available in dried form, too.

Oyster mushrooms have large, flat heads and are bark-brown with a white, fleshy texture that is almost meaty. These can be employed in the same way as the cultivated or button variety as they are mild in flavor.

Chanterelles are early summer mushrooms with a siphon-shaped head and thick swollen ribs hanging over a thick stem. They are as versatile as most other mushrooms but can be tough if cooked too long.

Ceps or *Boletus edulis* are a European delicacy with a dark brown head and a solid, thick stem. Highly prized among gourmets, this usually imported variety is a fall delight for those lucky enough to find a place that sells them.

Shiitakes have a large earth-colored level top with a pleasant, nutty flavor. They are often used in Oriental cooking.

---

except when they are to be stuffed or broiled for garnish, should be sliced. Wild mushrooms can offer an interesting change of pace to mushroom appetizers, stuffings, fillings, and salads. (See the box that follows for specific information.)

The following heirloom recipes are traditional ways of serving mushrooms. Used in rice or pasta dishes, mixed with other vegetables, added to stews and sauces, the lowly mushroom is a versatile fungus. Their earthy flavor can add interesting dimensions to ordinary fare.

SAUTÉED MUSHROOMS

1 pound mushrooms
2 tablespoons butter
¼ teaspoon salt
⅛ teaspoon freshly ground black
   pepper

juice of ½ lemon
1 teaspoon parsley, chopped
toast

1. Wash the mushrooms, remove and discard stems, peel caps, and thinly slice. Place in a skillet with butter, salt, and pepper.

2. Cook over moderately high heat until mushrooms give off liquid, tossing and stirring frequently. Increase heat and cook until all liquid has boiled away and mushrooms are browned and done, again stirring and tossing frequently. Add the lemon juice and parsley. Serve on hot slices of toast.

BROILED MUSHROOMS

12 large mushrooms
2 tablespoons butter
¼ teaspoon salt

⅛ teaspoon freshly ground black
   pepper
toast rounds

1. Wash mushrooms, remove stems, and place caps in a buttered broiling pan. Broil 5 minutes, round side up, during first half of broiling.

2. Turn mushrooms over and put a small piece of butter in the hollow of each cap. Sprinkle with salt and pepper and serve as soon as butter is melted. Keep mushrooms hollow side up to hold in the juices and serve on rounds of buttered toast.

BAKED MUSHROOMS

12 large mushrooms
2 tablespoons butter
salt and freshly ground black pepper
   to taste

⅔ cup light cream
toast

Preheat oven to 425° F. Wash the mushrooms, remove and discard stems (or reserve them for other uses). Place in a buttered baking dish, hollow side up. Sprinkle with salt and pepper, dot with butter, and add the cream. Bake 10 minutes. Arrange mushrooms on toast and pour over the pan juices and cream from baking dish.

Okra

Okra came to us from Africa. Long popular in the South, it is increasingly found throughout the country. Okra has a fuzzy green skin with a wet, sticky center filled with round, white seeds. It is often served sliced, breaded, and fried. Pickled okra is a surprisingly interesting condiment.

BOILED OKRA

1 pound okra	2 tablespoons butter
salt and freshly ground black pepper	

Wash okra, cut off stem ends. Cut into ½-inch pieces. Cook uncovered in boiling, salted water to cover until tender, 7 to 10 minutes. Drain, season with salt and pepper, add butter, and serve over rice.

Onions

The onions that are commonly available in the market are dried, with the exceptions of the scallions, or green onions. Very small onions, both white and yellow, are used for pickling or cooked and glazed for garnishing stews and other vegetables. White onions about the size of large walnuts are used for boiling. Yellow onions are the least expensive and most widely used. The Vidalia onion is a mild, sweet yellow-skinned variety from Georgia that is best served raw in salads. The large, red Spanish or Bemuda onions, which are milder and more delicate in flavor, are used mostly in salads, too.

BAKED ONIONS

Preheat oven to 350° F. Select even-sized medium onions. Wipe but do not peel. Cut each in half crosswise and place in baking dish, cut side down. Add 2 tablespoons melted butter, salt, and pepper. Pour in a little water to prevent scorching. Bake until tender, about 30 minutes.

BOILED ONIONS

Cut a cross at root end of medium-size onions. Pour boiling water over them and let stand 2 minutes. Drain and peel. Boil in a covered, nonreactive saucepan in one inch of rapidly boiling salted water only until tender. Drain, add butter, and season to taste with salt and pepper. Or cover with Medium White Sauce (page 399).

ONIONS AU GRATIN

Preheat oven to 350° F. Peel and boil onions as above until nearly done. Drain and place in a baking dish. Make 1 cup Medium White Sauce (page 399) and pour over the onions. Add a layer of buttered cracker crumbs and ½ cup grated Swiss or cheddar cheese. Bake until top is golden brown and sauce is bubbling, about 20 minutes.

GLAZED PEARL ONIONS

Place 1 pint of pearl onions in a heat-proof container. Pour over boiling water to cover. Let sit for 5 minutes. Drain and when cool enough to handle, pinch root ends to remove skins. Trim off root end and make a small cross with the tip of a sharp knife. In a skillet large enough to hold the onions in one flat layer, place the onions and add water to barely cover. Add 1 tablespoon of butter, ½ teaspoon salt, and 1 teaspoon sugar. Bring to a rapid boil. As the water boils off, the onions will cook. The butter and sugar will remain leaving a caramelizing glaze that will coat the onions. Once the water has boiled away, watch carefully and toss or stir as onions caramelize. Remove to drain on paper towels.

Note: This is a wonderful garnish for stews. The pan can be deglazed with wine or stock and added to the stew for additional flavor.

Parsnips

This cream-colored root vegetable is best during the fall months. Parsnips are prepared much like carrots or turnips. Choose small, young ones if possible. Avoid the large, thick parsnips as they can be woody and too strongly flavored.

BOILED, FRIED, AND MASHED PARSNIPS

 Wash young parsnips, scrape, cut in pieces and cook, covered in boiling, salted water until tender. Drain and serve with hot butter, Drawn Butter (page 407), or Medium White Sauce (see page 399). Or wash and cook whole in boiling, salted water until tender, about 45 minutes. Drain and plunge in cold water and slip off skins. Cut in slices lengthwise and fry in butter. Or mash and season with butter, salt, and pepper. Or shape into flat, round balls, roll in flour or dip in molasses, and fry until crisp and nicely browned in butter or other fat.

PARSNIP PUREE

2 to 3 pounds young parsnips, trimmed, scraped, and cut into 1-inch pieces
½ teaspoon salt

2 tablespoons butter, at room temperature
pinch of freshly grated nutmeg

1. Place parsnips in a large, nonreactive saucepan and cover with cold water. Bring to a boil, add the salt, and cook until tender, about 30 minutes. Drain well.
2. Work the cooked parsnips through a fine sieve or puree in a food processor. Return to saucepan and set over moderately low heat. Stir in the butter and season lightly with nutmeg. Serve at once with broiled or grilled meats.

Peas

Small round green peas are the delight of many devoted gourmets. Some peas can be consumed while still in the pod, like snow peas and sugar snap peas. Peas straight from the pod should be shelled and cooked as soon as possible. Try braising with thinly shredded lettuce or add a handful of finely chopped fresh mint just before serving.

BRAISED GREEN PEAS

 3 pounds green peas in pod
1 teaspoon salt
2 tablespoons butter or fat

dash of freshly ground black pepper
small pinch of sugar (optional)

Remove peas from pods and let stand ½ hour in cold water. Skim off undeveloped peas from top of water and then drain. Cook until soft in a small quantity of boiling water, add salt when nearly tender. (Cooking time varies greatly. Older, larger peas can take up to 45 minutes while tender young ones can be done in 10-20 minutes.) Let the water boil away and without draining, add butter or fat. Season with pepper and add a pinch of sugar if desired.

SNOW PEAS SAUTÉ

2 tablespoons olive oil
1 pound snow peas, ends and
  strings removed

½ red pepper, sliced into thin
  julienne strips
salt and white pepper to taste

In a large sauté pan or wok, pour in the olive oil. Add the peas and the red pepper and cook over very high heat until softened but still crisp, about 2 minutes. Stir constantly. Season to taste with salt and pepper. Serve at once with broiled or grilled meat, chicken, or fish.

Peppers

Red, yellow, purple, and green sweet or bell peppers are found in markets throughout the country. Domestic varieties are increasingly plentiful during the summer and imported peppers are seen more and more throughout the year. Flavorful, colorful, and versatile, this vegetable evokes a modern light touch so sought after in home kitchens and restaurants these days.

Many cooks prefer to roast peppers for adding to stuffings, sauces, or to serve cold in salads. (See box on roasting peppers.) Cooked peppers can add a festive touch as a side dish as in the sauté that follows.

COLORFUL PEPPER SAUTÉ

2 pounds (3 to 4 medium) mixed
  sweet peppers (red, yellow, or
  green)
½ cup olive oil
1 medium onion, thinly sliced

1 clove garlic, finely minced
¼ teaspoon cumin
salt and freshly ground black pepper
  to taste

Cut peppers in half. Remove seeds and membranes. Slice lengthwise into very thin julienne strips. Pour the oil into a large sauté pan or skillet. Add the prepared peppers, the onion, and the garlic. Cook over moderately high heat until wilted, about 10 minutes. Stir constantly. Do not allow onions or garlic to burn. Season with cumin, salt and pepper. Reduce heat and simmer gently until peppers and onions are very soft, about 20 minutes. Stir occasionally. Season again with salt and pepper before serving.

ROASTING PEPPERS

(See Outdoor Cooking chapter for instructions on how to roast peppers on a charcoal grill.)   Line an oven broiler pan with aluminum foil. Brush lightly with oil. Place red, green, or yellow peppers flat on top and position pan about 5 inches from the source of heat. Broil under direct heat until peppers are charred all over. Turn often to insure even charring. When completely blackened, remove to paper or plastic bags and close tightly. Allow skins to loosen in the steam sealed in the bag, 30 to 45 minutes. Remove and peel off skin. Peeling can be done under cold running water if desired. (Some cooks prefer to hold the peppers over a bowl to capture any juices that are extruded during the peeling process.) When peel is removed, cut peppers in half to remove all seeds and membrane. Keep covered in olive oil if not to be used immediately.

PEPPERS STUFFED WITH MEAT

6 green peppers
2 cups cooked chicken, beef, ham, veal, or lamb (or a combination), chopped
2 cups boiled rice
1 cup strained tomatoes

1 tablespoon grated onion
2½ tablespoons butter
2 tablespoons fresh breadcrumbs
¾ cup chicken or beef stock (page 59)

1.   Preheat oven to 350° F. Cut off stem ends and remove seeds and veins from peppers. Boil 2 minutes and drain.

2.   Mix together meat, rice, tomatoes, and onion. Fill peppers with this mixture.

3.   Add butter to crumbs and spread over peppers. Place in a baking dish and pour in the stock. Bake until peppers are tender, about 25 minutes.

PEPPERS STUFFED WITH CORN

6 green peppers
2 cups cooked corn
1 teaspoon salt

⅛ teaspoon pepper
½ cup grated Swiss or cheddar
   cheese
2 tablespoons butter

1. Preheat oven to 350° F. Cut off stem ends and remove seeds and veins from peppers. Boil 2 minutes and drain.

2. Mix corn with salt, pepper, cheese, and butter. Fill peppers with this mixture.

3. Bake in a pan with a little water added until peppers are tender, about 25 minutes.

Potatoes

All-purpose potatoes are available year-round but are freshest in the fall when fully ripe. They keep best in a cool, dark, dry space. When sprouts appear, they should be removed; receiving their nourishment from the starch, they deteriorate the potato.

Choose the long russet potatoes for baking and french frying; these are mealier and fluffier than other varieties. For boiling, whole, new potatoes, either red or white, are an excellent choice when in season. These potatoes are also particularly good for salads, since they are moist, firm, and hold their shape well.

BOILED POTATOES IN JACKETS

Scrub 6 potatoes well and let stand in cold water with a little salt ½ hour. Place in a large pot, pour boiling water over them to cover (about 1 quart), add 1 tablespoon salt. Boil until fork will easily pierce them. Drain, shake gently over the fire to dry.

BOILED NEW POTATOES

Scrape new potatoes and let stand in cold water ½ hour. Boil until tender in salted, boiling water (add 1 tablespoon salt for every 1 quart water). Drain. Add 2 tablespoons melted butter, 1 tablespoon chopped parsley, or, if desired, 1 teaspoon caraway seeds or chopped chives. Shake well over heat and serve hot. May also be served with Medium White Sauce (page 399).

MASHED POTATOES

6 hot, boiled potatoes	1 teaspoon salt
2 tablespoons butter	freshly ground black pepper to taste
⅓ cup hot milk	

Rub the hot potatoes through a ricer or mash well. Add the butter, milk, salt, and pepper to taste. Beat well until light and creamy.

Variation:

Mashed Potatoes with Onions or Garlic: Prepare potatoes as for above. Cook 1 finely chopped onion or 1 finely minced clove garlic in a little butter or olive oil until golden. Pour over or stir into mashed potatoes.

BAKED POTATOES

In choosing potatoes for baking, select those of uniform size and shape. Scrub well and dry. Rub with any desired fat. Place in a preheated hot oven (400° F) and bake until tender when pressed with a finger, about 1 hour. Cut a 2-inch cross at the center broadside top. Press toward the center with both hands and the skin will burst open, allowing steam to escape. Serve buttered. Or top with grated cheese, sour cream, or cottage cheese, and sprinkle with chopped chives, parsley, or other fresh herbs.

POTATOES ON THE HALF SHELL

6 baked potatoes	¼ cup hot milk
2 tablespoons butter	1 cup grated cheese (cheddar or
1 teaspoon salt	Swiss)

Cut baked potatoes in half lengthwise and scoop out the inside. Mash and mix with the butter, salt, and milk. Return to the shells and sprinkle with the cheese. Place in moderate oven (350° F) and bake until hot and lightly browned, 5 to 10 minutes.

BOSTON BROWNED POTATOES

 Peel and quarter 6 medium-size potatoes. Place in a shallow baking dish with 4 tablespoons melted butter. Coat potatoes, season well with salt, paprika, and pepper. Bake in hot oven (400° F) 30 to 45 minutes. Or add to roasting pan 1 hour before meat is done and toss to coat with drippings.

SARATOGA POTATOES

 Pare and slice potatoes paper thin. Soak in cold, salted water and drain dry between paper towels. Fry only a handful at a time in deep, hot fat until a delicate brown and crisp. Drain on paper towels and sprinkle with salt.

FRENCH-FRIED POTATOES

 Using long thin potatoes, peel if desired, wash, and cut lengthwise into lengths of uniform size. Soak in cold, salted water. Drain and dry. Fry in deep, hot fat (375° F) until tender and golden brown. Sprinkle with salt and serve hot.

POTATO CROQUETTES

2 cups riced boiled potatoes	1 egg yolk
⅛ teaspoon white pepper	1 teaspoon chopped parsley
¼ teaspoon celery salt	onion juice
2 tablespoons butter	breadcrumbs
½ teaspoon salt	1 egg, beaten
	oil for deep-frying

1.   Combine the potatoes, pepper, celery salt, butter, and salt. Add the egg yolk and mix well. Rub through a sieve and add the parsley and a few drops of onion juice. Chill the mixture to make it easier to work with.

2.   Shape into smooth balls, then into cylinders. Dip each in breadcrumbs, then in the beaten egg. Dip in crumbs again. Fry in deep, hot fat (375° F). Drain on paper towels.

POTATO PUFFS

2 cups riced boiled potatoes
1 cup sour cream
about 1 cup flour

½ teaspoon salt
oil for deep-frying

Blend potatoes with sour cream, add enough flour to make a dough. Add salt and knead for a minute or two. Roll out very thin on a floured board. Cut into rounds with a biscuit cutter and fry until brown in deep, hot fat (375° F). Drain on paper towels.

LYONNAISE POTATOES

Slice cold leftover boiled new potatoes about ¼ inch thick. Season with salt and pepper. Fry a small onion in beef fat or butter until light brown. Add the potatoes and brown on one side. Turn and brown on the other. Sprinkle with chopped fresh parsley.

HASHED BROWN POTATOES

Preheat oven to 475° F. Chop cold, boiled potatoes (new ones are best) into bits the size of a peanut. Season with salt and pepper, and for each quart of chopped potatoes, allow 3 tablespoons butter. Heat the butter and toss the potatoes in it till they begin to show a little brown. Add ½ cup cream and place in oven to brown. Serve in the baking dish.

POTATO CAKES

Shape cold, mashed potatoes into rounds ½ inch thick. Put them in a hot, greased frying pan. Fry until well browned on one side. Turn and brown on the other and serve hot.

BAKED MASHED POTATOES

2 tablespoons butter, melted
2 cups mashed potatoes, cold
2 eggs, well beaten

1 cup milk or cream
salt and freshly ground black pepper
  to taste

(continued)

Preheat oven to 425° F. Stir the butter well with the potatoes, add the eggs and then the milk or cream. Season with salt and pepper. Beat all together well. Place in a greased pudding dish and bake until brown.

SCALLOPED POTATOES

4 cups sliced raw potatoes
1 teaspoon salt
¼ teaspoon freshly ground black
  pepper

1 tablespoon chopped parsley
1 cup Medium White Sauce (page
  399)
1 cup buttered cracker crumbs

Preheat oven to 350° F. Season potatoes with salt, pepper, and add parsley. Butter a baking dish, put in the potatoes and pour on the Medium White Sauce. Cover with crumbs and bake until browned, about 1 hour.

Sweet Potatoes

Sweet potatoes are yellow and dry. Yams are orange, moist, and sweet. The two can be used in recipes interchangeably. Look for unblemished vegetables and wash carefully. The skin of a sweet potato is more fragile than that of a regular potato.

BAKED SWEET POTATOES

Gently wash and rinse potatoes. Rub with butter or oil. Bake on a rack in a hot oven (400° F) until tender when pierced with a fork, about 45 minutes.

BOILED SWEET POTATOES

Select potatoes of uniform size. Wash, pare, and cook in boiling, salted water to cover until tender, about 20 minutes.

GLAZED SWEET POTATOES

6 medium-size sweet potatoes
½ cup brown sugar

¼ cup water
3 tablespoons butter

1. Preheat oven to 350° F. Wash and pare potatoes. Cook 10 minutes in boiling, salted water. Drain, cut in halves lengthwise, and put in a buttered pan.

2. Make a syrup by boiling the sugar and water for 3 minutes. Stir in the butter. Brush potatoes with a third of the syrup and bake until glazed, about 15 minutes, basting twice with remaining syrup.

SCALLOPED SWEET POTATOES WITH GREEN APPLES

2 to 3 medium boiled sweet
potatoes
3 to 4 small green apples, peeled,
cored, and cut into ¼-inch slices
½ cup brown sugar

2 tablespoons butter
salt to taste

Preheat oven to 350° F. Slice potatoes ¼ inch thick. Put half the potatoes in a buttered baking dish, cover with half the fruit, sugar, and butter. Season with salt. Repeat using all the ingredients. Bake until apples are cooked and mixture is bubbling.

SWEET POTATO CROQUETTES

2 cups mashed sweet potatoes
¼ teaspoon freshly ground black
pepper
2 tablespoons butter, melted
½ teaspoon salt
1 egg yolk

1 teaspoon chopped parsley
dried breadcrumbs
1 egg, beaten
oil for deep-frying

1. Mix together the potatoes, pepper, butter, and salt. Beat until light. Add the egg yolk and mix well. Rub through a sieve or puree in a food processor. Add the parsley. Chill the mixture to make it easier to work with.

2. Shape into smooth balls, then into cylinders. Dip in breadcrumbs, then in beaten egg, then in crumbs again.

3. Fry in deep, hot fat (375° F). Drain on paper towels.

Spinach

Choose young, tender leaves of spinach. Two pounds serves 3 to 4 people. Cut off and discard the roots and any withered leaves. Remove large, tough stems. Wash the leaves in a large basin of lukewarm water and shake the leaves to dislodge the sand. Let it settle to the bottom. Lift out the greens and discard the water and sand. Repeat until the water is clear.

Cook spinach in a nonreactive pan. There should be enough liquid from washing to provide necessary moisture. Stir quickly over high heat until leaves are wilted. Drain well.

CHOPPED SPINACH

2 pounds spinach, washed
2 tablespoons butter or fat
1 teaspoon grated onion
2 tablespoons breadcrumbs
½ teaspoon salt
¼ teaspoon freshly ground black
  pepper

dash of nutmeg
1 cup chicken stock (page 59)
lemon wedges
sliced hard-cooked eggs (optional)

1. Put washed spinach into a large, nonreactive pot without water. Let cook slowly until some of the juice is drawn out, then increase heat and boil until leaves are tender.

2. Drain and chop very fine. Heat butter in skillet, add onion, crumbs, and seasonings and brown lightly. Add stock gradually, stirring constantly. Add spinach and heat. Serve garnished with lemon wedge and sliced hard-cooked egg if desired.

CREAMED SPINACH

Cook and drain spinach as directed above. Add ½ cup heavy cream and gently heat. Do not boil. Season with additional salt and pepper.

Squash

The many varieties of squash fall into two categories. The first is the watery, tender varieties that cook quickly, such as the yellow crookneck, the green zucchini that resembles cucumber, and the white scalloped cymling or pattypan. The other type is the hard shelled, dark-green acorn and Hubbard, the tan butternut, and pumpkin, which must be peeled and freed from seeds and stringy pith before cooking.

Tender varieties of squash are best cooked in rapidly boiling water, quickly steamed, or sautéed in oil or butter. Hard-shelled squash and pumpkin are better cooked until their tough fibers are broken down by either boiling, steaming, or baking for a relatively long amount of time.

BAKED ACORN SQUASH

Preheat oven to 350° F. Cut small acorn squash in two lengthwise. Remove seeds and strings. Parboil, then place in pan with just enough water to cover bottom. Into each half place 1 teaspoon butter and 1 tablespoon brown sugar. Bake until soft, about 45 minutes. If desired, remove baked pulp from shell, mash, season with butter, salt, and pepper. Refill shells and serve.

SAUTÉED SUMMER SQUASH

2 tablespoons butter or olive oil
1 pound summer squash, washed
  and thickly cut

salt and freshly ground black pepper
  to taste

Use small, young and fresh squash only. Heat butter or oil in a large skillet. Add squash and season with salt and pepper. Stir and shake the pan over moderately high heat until squash is softened and slightly translucent, 7 to 10 minutes. Adjust seasoning and serve at once.

Tomatoes

Hot-house tomatoes are available year-round. They may look like a perfect specimen from the outside, but inside the pulp is often woody with a watery flavor to boot. Italian plum tomatoes (Roma) tend to have more flavor out of season. Otherwise, canned tomatoes are often an acceptable substitution for sauces, soups, casseroles, and stuffings.

In the summer, look for varieties locally home-grown. Growing seasons vary from climate to climate. Jersey beefsteak, Early Girl, Big Boy, Supersteak, Delicious, and small cherry tomatoes are but a few of the many varieties that abound. To the enthusiast, there is nothing like growing your own. For non-gardeners, the effort put into searching out the perfect tomato at the height of ripe perfection is worth the time and trouble.

Take as many ripe, smooth tomatoes as you desire. Wash and wipe and serve with or without the skin. To remove skin, cut out core on one end. On the other end, make a cross with the tip or a thin-bladed knife. Plunge into boiling water for about 30 seconds. Drain and slip off skin under running, cold water. To remove seeds, cut the tomatoes in half. Squeeze gently in the palm of one hand and shake off the exuding seeds.

BASIC STEWED TOMATOES

Skin tomatoes following the directions above. Cut in pieces, put in a nonreactive stew pot, and cook slowly until softened, about 20 minutes. Stir occasionally. Season with butter, salt, and pepper.

STUFFED TOMATOES

6 good-quality firm tomatoes
2 tablespoons butter
1 cup rye or white breadcrumbs
1 small onion, grated

1 tablespoon chopped parsley
salt and freshly ground black pepper
2 egg yolks

1. Preheat oven to 350° F. Wash and dry tomatoes. Cut off tops. Remove pulp with a small spoon, and rub through a fine sieve.
2. Put butter in pan, add breadcrumbs, cook a few minutes. Add the onion, parsley, salt, and pepper, and the tomato pulp. Stir in the egg yolks and toss to combine. Fill the tomatoes with the mixture. Top with additional breadcrumbs or cracker crumbs, dot with butter, and place in a buttered baking dish. Bake for about 30 minutes.

STUFFED TOMATOES WITH CHICKEN LIVERS

8 firm tomatoes
salt and freshly ground black pepper
    to taste
1 tablespoon butter
1 medium onion, chopped

6 fresh mushrooms, sliced
½ pound chicken livers, chopped
½ cup breadcrumbs
chopped parsley

1. Wash and dry tomatoes. Cut through top without detaching to serve as a cover. Scoop out pulp. Season inside with a little salt and pepper.

2. Melt butter, add onion, and fry until lightly browned, about 3 minutes. Add the mushrooms and the chicken livers. Season to taste with salt and pepper. Cook for 3 minutes, stirring occasionally. Add pulp, breadcrumbs, and parsley. Cook 2 minutes longer. Cool. Preheat oven to 350° F.

3. Stuff tomato shells with mixture and top with tomato "lids." Cover and bake in a buttered baking dish for 20 minutes.

Variation: Sausage meat or chicken may be used in place of livers.

Turnips

Turnips are best in fall and winter. The rutabagas (a large yellow variety), the large white, and the small flat purple top are all used interchangeably. Wash, peel, and cut into uniform pieces. Cook 3 cups turnip cubes in boiling, salted water until soft, about 15 minutes. Drain, mash, season with fat or butter, salt, a little sugar if desired, and pepper. Or mix with an equal quantity of hot, mashed potatoes.

VEGETABLES AND THE MICROWAVE

The microwave may seem like an odd choice for making the most of fine-flavored, fresh produce. The still somewhat synthetic concept of a quick-cooking box without visible heat seems antithetical to the natural offerings we get from the earth.

However, water allows microwave energy to penetrate efficiently through a vegetable's soluble structure. This results in a bright-colored, lively vegetable that retains many of its essential vitamins and minerals. And without heating the kitchen!

The broad category of vegetables and the many kinds of microwave ovens on the market make it difficult to generalize cooking times and techniques. While we encourage the use of this appliance for preparing vegetables, we suggest that the reader find ways to proceed that are best for his or her particular oven. Powers vary greatly and cooking times for one oven are not suitable for another. We direct the reader to the manufacturer's instructions as well as to two books that are devoted to this kind of cooking. (See the Bibliography.)

VEGETABLE STEWS

We think of stews as only applicable to meat. A savory assortment of vegetables with contrasting colors, tastes, and textures can provide the same satisifaction as a meat stew.

Ratatouille is a regional French dish that combines many elements of sun-drenched summer bounty. Eggplants, tomatoes, onions, peppers, zucchini, and the essential garlic are the components for this vegetable stew that can be served hot or cold. The Winter Vegetable Stew is made up of carrots, turnips, celery root, leeks, and potatoes. The Mixed Vegetable Spring Stew makes use of peas, asparagus, new potatoes, baby carrots, and spring onions all bound in a light cream sauce.

Don't be restricted by a set format for making a vegetable stew. Substitutions are encouraged! Choose the best of what is in season, what looks good in the marketplace, and what goes best with the rest of the meal. Parsnips, salsify, beets, dried beans, brussels sprouts, fennel, and cabbage are good winter vegetables to consider. Spinach, snow peas, and baby artichokes are available in the spring. Summer vegetables are plentiful. Red, yellow, and green peppers are at their best then. Green beans, okra, and sweet corn can all go into a stew. One word of caution: Be careful not to overcook the stew. Vegetables should be tender and digestible but not limp and without character. Using pieces of uniform size will help insure even cooking. Begin with the vegetables that take the longest to cook. Be imaginative with the seasonings. Serve vegetable stews as a first course or as a side dish with meat, fish or chicken.

RATATOUILLE

This recipe makes enough for 10 to 12 people. Making a large amount is as easy as making a small amount provided that the utensils you use are of the same scale. It lasts for days and can be eaten hot or cold.

olive oil

2 onions, peeled and sliced

6 cloves garlic, finely chopped

2 yellow peppers, roasted, peeled, and cut lengthwise into thin strips (page 385)

2 red peppers, roasted, peeled, and cut lengthwise into thin strips (page 385)

5 tomatoes, peeled, seeded, and coarsely chopped

3 eggplants, peeled and cut into ½-inch cubes

salt and freshly ground black pepper to taste

3 yellow squash, halved and sliced ¼ inch thick

3 zucchini, halved and sliced ¼ inch thick

½ cup finely chopped fresh herbs (thyme, parsley, rosemary, oregano, or marjoram), tightly packed

1. In a large, heavy pan heat enough olive oil to thinly cover the bottom. Add the onions and cook over moderately high heat until translucent but not browned, about 10 minutes. Stir often. Add the garlic and the peppers, continue cooking until garlic is slightly softened, about 2 more minutes. Add the tomatoes and reduce heat. Let simmer until tomatoes have given off moisture. Increase heat and cook until mixture is slightly reduced, stirring often.

2. In a separate pan or skillet, heat more olive oil. Add the eggplants and season with salt and pepper. Cook until oil is absorbed and eggplant is soft, about 10 minutes. (Do not overcrowd the pan; do in two or three batches if necessary.) Set aside.

3. In a large pot of boiling, salted water, cook the yellow squash and zucchini until tender, about 3 minutes.

4. Combine the eggplant and the cooked squash with the tomatoes and peppers. Heat through to blend flavors. Add the herbs, season to taste with additional salt and pepper.

WINTER VEGETABLE STEW

2 tablespoons butter
2 medium onions, peeled and
    quartered
2 leeks, white part only, trimmed
    and cleaned
2 medium potatoes, peeled and cut
    into ½-inch cubes
3 carrots, peeled and cut into 1-inch
    slices
2 small turnips, peeled and cut into
    ½-inch cubes

1 celery root, peeled and cut into
    ¼-inch slices
½ cup chicken stock (page 59) or
    water
2 tablespoons lemon juice
salt and freshly ground black pepper
    to taste
1 tablespoon chopped parsley

1. In a heavy pan, melt the butter. Add the onions, leeks, potatoes, carrots, turnips, and celery root. Stir and toss over high heat until vegetables are coated with butter. Add the chicken stock or water and lemon juice. Season with salt and pepper. Reduce heat, cover and let cook slowly until all vegetables are tender, 30 to 45 minutes.

2. Uncover and turn heat up as high as possible. Cook, stirring constantly, until moisture is reduced and juices are syrupy. Taste for seasoning. Add chopped parsley just before serving.

MIXED VEGETABLE SPRING STEW

2 tablespoons butter
½ pound new potatoes, scrubbed
    and cut in half
10 to 12 baby carrots, scrubbed
1 pound spring onions, white parts
    only, trimmed, blanched, and cut
    in half
2 cups shredded lettuce

2 cups shelled fresh green peas
1 pound fresh asparagus, trimmed,
    stem peeled, and cut into quarters
½ cup heavy cream
salt and freshly ground black pepper
    to taste
1 tablespoon chopped parsley

1. In a heavy pan with a lid, melt the butter over moderately high heat. Add the potatoes, carrots, onions, and lettuce. Shake the pan to coat the vegetables and cover. Reduce heat to a simmer and let the vegetables cook very slowly until tender. Shake the pan often and watch to see that they are cooking in their own juices. Add a tablespoonful or two of water if liquid has evaporated to prevent scorching.

2. Cook the peas in a large pot of boiling salted water. Drain and refresh under cold running water.

3. Cook the asparagus until tender and drain well.

4. Combine the peas and asparagus with the other vegetables. Add the cream and gently stir to blend. Increase heat and let cream reduce slightly. Season with salt and pepper. Add the parsley.

SAUCES

Gone are the days of thick sauces to cover food of lesser quality or to add bulk to a meal or a particular dish. With the advent of lighter cooking and healthier eating, sauces have been streamlined to accent and pick up subtle flavors rather than to mask and hide. For example a light butter sauce is used just to nap a piece of grilled fish, chicken, or beef to add a sheen of intensity. Essences of flavor can be achieved with a quick deglazing of a pan. A trend toward simplicity is the order of the day.

We're also including many of the traditional sauces found in the original Settlement editions. While flour-based sauces are used less today as are those bound with egg yolks and heavy cream, they are part of a certain tradition that is time honored and true. The basic white and brown sauces here are frequently referred to as part of recipes in this book.

Many of the sauces given in this chapter are multipurpose. They can be used with everything from eggs and spaghetti to vegetables, fish, and meat. Some of them are made with the liquid from the dish they are to accompany—pan gravy and fricassee sauce are examples of this. Other sauces require milk, stock, wine, or fruit juices as bases.

White Sauces

THIN WHITE SAUCE   *Makes 1 cup.*

2 tablespoons butter
1½ tablespoons flour
1 cup hot milk

¼ teaspoon salt
⅛ teaspoon white pepper

Melt the butter in a saucepan. Remove from heat and mix the butter with flour. Return to low heat and cook until it bubbles, then add ⅔ of the hot milk at once and the rest gradually. Increase heat and boil, stirring constantly, until the mixture thickens. Season with salt and pepper and serve hot.

MEDIUM WHITE SAUCE   *Makes 1 cup.*

2 tablespoons butter
2 tablespoons flour
1 cup hot milk

½ teaspoon salt
⅛ teaspoon white pepper

(continued)

Melt the butter in a saucepan. Remove from heat and mix the butter with flour. Return to low heat and cook until it bubbles, then add ⅔ of the hot milk at once and the rest gradually. Increase heaat and boil, stirring constantly until the mixture thickens. Season with salt and pepper and serve hot.

THICK WHITE SAUCE   *Makes about 1 cup.*

2½ tablespoons butter
⅓ cup flour
1 cup hot milk or beef, chicken, or
   vegetable stock (page 59 or 61)

¼ teaspoon salt
⅛ teaspoon white pepper

Melt butter in hot frying pan, add flour and stir well. When it bubbles add ⅔ of the hot liquid at once and the rest gradually, stirring constantly until smooth. Season with salt and pepper.

CHEESE SAUCE

Add ½ cup of grated cheddar cheese to 1 cup hot Medium or Thick White Sauce (above).

MORNAY SAUCE

Add ¼ cup each of grated Parmesan and Swiss cheese to 1 cup of hot Medium White Sauce (above). Stir until melted.

HORSERADISH SAUCE

Add 3 to 4 tablespoons prepared horseradish to every 1 cup of Medium White Sauce (above). Season with salt and white pepper. Blend well.

MUSTARD SAUCE

Add 1 to 2 tablespoons Dijon mustard to 1 cup Medium White Sauce (above) just before serving. A teaspoon of vinegar can be added for extra tangy flavor if desired.

MUSHROOM SAUCE

Trim and clean ½ pound mushrooms. Remove stems and slice for sauce. Caps may be sautéed separately in a little butter and used to garnish the dish. Or use mushrooms whole, sliced or quartered. Sauté in a little butter. Make Medium White Sauce (above) using mushroom liquid instead of part of the milk. Add mushrooms and parsley and serve.

RAVIGOTE SAUCE   *Makes about 1 cup.*

2 green onions
2 tablespoons butter
2 tablespoons tarragon vinegar
1 cup Thin White Sauce (above)

1 tablespoon lemon juice
½ tablespoon chopped parsley
½ tablespoon chopped chives
salt and freshly ground black pepper
    to taste

Slice onions, add butter and vinegar. In a small saucepan cook until vinegar is reduced to half. Add remaining ingredients. Serve hot with poultry and fish.

FRICASSEE SAUCE   *Makes 2 to 2½ cups.*

¼ cup chicken fat
¼ cup flour
1½ to 2 cups hot chicken stock
    (page 59)

½ cup half-and-half
1 teaspoon salt
¼ teaspoon white pepper

Heat fat in double boiler, add flour when it bubbles. Add stock at once, stir until thick, then add the half-and-half and stir until smooth. Season to taste. Serve with chicken.

Brown Sauces

BROWN SAUCE   *Makes about 1 cup.*

2 tablespoons butter or fat
1 small onion, chopped (optional)
2 tablespoons flour

1 cup hot water, or beef, chicken,
    fish, or vegetable stock (page 59,
    60, or 61)
½ teaspoon salt
⅛ teaspoon pepper

Brown the butter or fat and if desired add the onion. When brown, add the flour, let brown. Add ⅔ cup of the hot liquid at once and gradually add the rest of the liquid along with the seasonings. Let cook 5 minutes stirring often and serve with hot meat, vegetables, dumplings, etc.

ANCHOVY SAUCE

Add 1 tablespoon of anchovy paste to the Brown Sauce recipe above. Season with lemon juice to taste.

CAPER SAUCE

Add ¼ cup of capers, drained, to 1 cup Brown Sauce (above). Serve hot with tongue, calf's brains, sweetbreads, mutton, or fish.

CREOLE SAUCE   *Makes about 2 cups.*

1½ cups Brown Sauce (above)
2 tablespoons butter
2 tablespoons onion, chopped
2 tablespoons chopped green pepper
3 tablespoons chopped tomato
¼ cup mushrooms

½ teaspoon salt
¼ teaspoon paprika
1 teaspoon catsup
½ cup blanched sliced almonds
   (optional)

Heat Brown Sauce. In a separate pan, melt butter, add onion, and fry lightly. Add the peppers, tomatoes, and mushrooms. Cook for a few minutes. Add vegetables to Brown Sauce along with seasonings and catsup. Simmer 20 minutes. If desired, add blanched almonds. Serve hot.

PIQUANT SAUCE   *Makes about 1 cup.*

1 cup Brown Sauce (above)
½ small onion, finely chopped
2 tablespoons lemon juice, vinegar,
   sherry, or claret

1 tablespoon each capers and
   pickles, chopped

Heat Brown Sauce, add remaining ingredients. Serve hot with beef or fish.

PORT WINE SAUCE   *Makes about 1¼ cups.*

 Prepare 1 cup Brown Sauce (above). Add ¼ cup currant jelly and 2 tablespoons port wine. Cook until jelly is dissolved and serve hot with venison.

RAISIN SAUCE   *Makes about 1½ cups.*

 1 Cup Brown Sauce (above) made   sherry or Madeira to taste
    with fruit juice
½ cup seeded raisins

Heat Brown Sauce. Add raisins, simmer 10 minutes. Add wine to taste. Serve with ham or tongue.

Pan Juices

A pan gravy may be made for any roasted meat or poultry, or for any sautéed or panfried meat. Pour off the pan juices and skim off excess fat. Return 2 tablespoons fat to the roasting pan or skillet or use butter. Add 2 tablespoons flour and cook, stirring, until golden. Add the pan juices plus stock or water to make 1 cup liquid and cook, stirring in the brown bits that cling to the pan, until blended. Simmer 5 minutes, stirring often, and strain into a sauceboat. Season to taste with salt and pepper.

To deglaze, pour off the pan juices as for above. Remove all fat and return the roasting pan or skillet to top of stove. Carefully pour in ¼ cup white wine, flavored vinegar, a fortified wine like brandy or cognac, cider, cream, or any flavorful liquid that will complement the meat being roasted or panfried. Reduce slightly over high heat. Add the pan juices plus stock or water to make 1 cup liquid and cook, stirring in the brown bits that cling to the pan. Simmer 5 minutes, stirring often, and strain into a sauceboat. Season to taste with salt and pepper. This is essentially the same procedure for pan gravy but without the flour. This procedure is known as meat served "au jus." While thin and not bound, the resulting juice will be concentrated enough to spoon over carved meat.

Hollandaise Sauces

Somewhat reluctantly, we are including this heirloom recipe for Hollandaise Sauce and a quick version. Remember that undercooked eggs are a risk in these days of increasing Salmonella contamination (see page 86). In the following recipes, the yolks will not be cooked sufficiently to kill this germ if it is present in the eggs you use. However, the sauce is such a part of traditional cooking that we cannot simply discard it. The recipe here has been in *The Settlement Cookbook* since the first edition, before the era of mass food production and concern about undercooked eggs.

HOLLANDAISE SAUCE   *Makes about 1½ cups.*

2 tablespoons white wine vinegar
¼ teaspoon white pepper
¼ cup water
1 cup butter

4 egg yolks
juice of ½ lemon
salt to taste

1.   Boil vinegar, pepper, and water until liquid is reduced by half.

2.   Divide butter into 3 parts. Place 1 part into top of a double boiler with egg yolks and lemon juice. Stir constantly over boiling water until butter is melted.

3.   Add second part of butter, stir until melted, and as sauce thickens, the third part. Add the vinegar-water reduction and cook for 1 minute. Season with salt. Serve with vegetables and fish.

QUICK HOLLANDAISE SAUCE   *Makes about 1¼ cups.*

½ cup butter, at room temperature
2 or 3 egg yolks
1 tablespoon lemon juice

¼ teaspoon salt
a few grains cayenne pepper
½ cup boiling water

1.   With a wooden spoon, cream the butter. Add the yolks, one at a time. Beat well and add the lemon juice, salt, and cayenne pepper. About 5 minutes before serving add the boiling water and stir rapidly.

2.   Cook the mixture over hot water in the top of a double boiler, stirring constantly, until it thickens.

Tomato Sauces

BASIC TOMATO SAUCE   *Makes about 1¾ cups.*

½ can tomatoes or 1¾ cups fresh
   stewed tomatoes
2 slices onion
8 peppercorns
1 bay leaf
2 cloves

2 tablespoons butter or other fat
2 tablespoons flour
1 tablespoon sugar (optional)
½ teaspoon salt

  1. Cook tomatoes 15 minutes with the onion and spices. Strain.

  2. Heat the butter in a frying pan, add flour and ⅔ cup of the hot, strained tomatoes, then the rest. Cook until thick. Season to taste with sugar, if desired, and salt. May be thickened with grated gingerbread.

ITALIAN-STYLE TOMATO SAUCE   *Makes about 2 cups.*

1 onion, finely chopped
1 clove garlic, finely chopped
1 tablespoon oil

1 quart fresh tomatoes, sieved
salt and freshly ground black pepper
   to taste

Fry onion and garlic in oil until light brown. Add tomatoes and let cook until slightly thickened, about 30 minutes. Season with salt and pepper.

BASIC BARBECUE SAUCE   *Makes about 2 cups.*

1 cup diced onion or 1 clove garlic,
   finely chopped
2 tablespoons fat
1 cup chopped tomato
1 cup green pepper, diced
1 cup diced celery
2 tablespoons brown sugar

½ tablespoon dry mustard
2 cups hot chicken or beef stock
   (page 59)
salt and freshly ground black pepper
   to taste
1 cup catsup

Fry the onion or garlic lightly in fat. Add the remaining ingredients and cook slowly for 1 hour, uncovered. Liquid should be reduced by half and sauce should be well blended. Dip any meat in sauce before roasting or broiling or baste with sauce during roasting.

SPANISH CHILI SAUCE   *Makes about ½ cup.*

10 fresh hot peppers, seed and pith
    removed
1 teaspoon salt

1 onion, chopped
1 clove garlic, minced
½ teaspoon marjoram

Cook peppers until soft in boiling water to cover. Mash or press through colander. Add remaining ingredients. If a hotter sauce is desired, leave seeds in the peppers.

Sweet and Sour Sauces

GINGERSNAP SAUCE   *Makes about 1½ cups.*

4 to 6 large gingersnaps, crumbled
½ cup brown sugar, firmly packed
¼ cup vinegar
½ teaspoon onion juice

1 cup hot water, or beef or chicken
    stock (page 59)
1 lemon, sliced
¼ cup raisins

Mix all ingredients together and cook until smooth. Pour hot over cooked fish, meat, or tongue. Or chill and serve with leftover meat or chicken.

SWEET AND SOUR SAUCE   *Makes about 1 cup.*

2 tablespoons butter
2 tablespoons flour
½ teaspoon salt
¼ teaspoon pepper

1 cup hot vegetable broth (page 61)
2 tablespoons vinegar
2 tablespoons sugar

Brown butter well and add the flour. Continue browning slightly over moderately high heat. Add the seasonings and ⅔ cup of stock. Stir, then add the rest with the vinegar and sugar. Cook until smooth. Serve hot with cooked string beans, carrots, soup meat, or roasts.

CURRANT JELLY SAUCE   *Makes about 1 cup.*

½ lemon, diced
1 tablespoon chopped citron
1 teaspoon butter
½ cup sherry

½ cup (4 ounces) currant jelly
salt and freshly ground black pepper
    to taste

Heat all ingredients together, strain, and stir smooth. Serve hot with game.

MINT SAUCE   *Makes about ½ cup.*

1 tablespoon confectioners' sugar or
  ½ cup strained honey

½ cup cider vinegar
¼ cup chopped mint leaves

Dissolve sugar or honey in vinegar. Pour over mint and let stand 30 minutes over low heat, covered. If vinegar is strong, dilute with warm water to taste. Serve hot over hot lamb. Or boil sugar and vinegar, add the mint leaves, and let boil up once. Cover and set aside to steep.

Butter Sauces

PARSLEY-BUTTER SAUCE

1 tablespoon butter
1 teaspoon minced parsley
1 teaspoon lemon juice

salt and freshly ground black pepper
  to taste

Cream butter. Add parsley, lemon juice, salt, and pepper. Spread over hot broiled fish or steak.

ANCHOVY SAUCE

Follow recipe for Parsley Butter Sauce above, using anchovy paste instead of parsley.

DRAWN BUTTER SAUCE   *Makes 2½ cups.*

8 tablespoons butter
4 tablespoons flour
2 cups boiling water, milk, or fish
  stock (page 60)

½ teaspoon salt
⅛ teaspoon white pepper

Melt 4 tablespoons of the butter in a heavy saucepan. Add flour and blend well. Add the liquid, stirring constantly. Add the remaining butter and season with salt and pepper. Boil 5 minutes and serve immediately.

Mayonnaise and Cream Sauces

TARTAR SAUCE   *Makes about 1 cup.*

1 cup bottled mayonnaise
1 tablespoon chopped capers
1 tablespoon vinegar
1 tablespoon chopped olives

1 tablespoon chopped pickles
minced onions or chives to taste
(optional)

Combine mayonnaise with the rest of the ingredients. Serve cold with hot fish or cold meat. Add minced chives or onions if desired.

CUCUMBER CREAM SAUCE   *Makes about 1 cup.*

1 fresh cucumber
½ cup heavy cream
¼ teaspoon salt

pinch of freshly ground black
pepper
3 tablespoons vinegar or lemon
juice

Pare, seed, and coarsely chop cucumber. Whip cream until stiff. Add the salt and pepper and gradually the vinegar or lemon juice. When ready to serve, fold in the cucumber.

WHIPPED HORSERADISH CREAM SAUCE   *Makes about 1½ cups.*

1 cup heavy cream
salt and white pepper
¾ cup grated horseradish root,
drained

1 tablespoon sugar
1 tablespoon vinegar or lemon juice

Whip cream stiff, gradually beat in rest of the ingredients. Season to taste.

SAUCES BY REDUCTION

A wonderful sauce with a delicate, light touch can be made by reducing wine, stock, cider, or cream. Boiling over high heat will evaporate moisture resulting in a smooth sauce thick enough to coat the back of a spoon. The time required to reach the consistency desired will vary according to the amount and density of the liquid used. Reducing can be a tricky technique. It requires total attention to stop the process at just the right time. Not enough time will leave the sauce thin and without character. Too much time will bring about a thick and cloying sauce.

While some of the following suggestions call for cream and butter, keep in mind that just a tablespoon or so per serving is all that is required for an intense burst of flavor. All of these reductions work best in a nonreactive, heavy saucepan when stirred with a wire whisk.

RED WINE AND SHALLOTS

Chill 2 tablespoons butter cut into small cubes. Reduce 1 cup red wine with one finely chopped shallot over high heat. When only 2 tablespoons of the wine remain, add the butter in small amounts. Work the saucepan on and off the heat, whisking constantly. The butter should emulsify as it is incorporated. (The degree of heat is important. If the saucepan becomes too hot, the butter will break down. If not hot enough, the butter will not blend easily into the reduction.) When thickened, season to taste with salt and pepper. Serve immediately over grilled or panfried meats.

APPLE CIDER SAUCE

Reduce 1 cup apple cider over high heat. When reduced to 2 tablespoons, add ½ cup chicken stock (page 59) and reduce again by half. Add ¼ cup heavy cream, reduce slightly, and season with salt and pepper to taste. Serve with roast pork along with caramelized apples.

MUSTARD SAUCE

Reduce ½ cup white wine until only 2 tablespoons remain. Pour in ½ cup cream and reduce again by half. Remove from heat and stir in ¼ cup Dijon mustard. Season to taste with salt and pepper. Serve at once with grilled or roasted beef, veal, or pork.

BALSAMIC VINEGAR

Chill 2 tablespoons butter cut into small cubes. Reduce ½ cup balsamic vinegar to 2 tablespoons. Add ½ cup chicken stock (page 59) and reduce again by half. Add the chilled butter bit by bit. Work the saucepan on and off the heat, whisking constantly. The butter should emulsify as it is incorporated. (The degree of heat is important. If the saucepan becomes too hot, the butter will break down. If not hot enough, the butter will not blend easily into the reduction.) When thickened, season to taste with salt and pepper. This sauce is perfect with sautéed calf's liver or sautéed chicken breasts.

TOMATO FISH SAUCE

Reduce 1 cup fish stock (page 60) with 2 tablespoons finely chopped onion. When only 2 tablespoons liquid remain, add 1 peeled, seeded, and chopped tomato. Boil over high heat until moisture is evaporated. Work in 2 tablespoons chilled butter as is described above. Season well with salt and pepper. Add 1 tablespoon chopped fresh tarragon before serving. This sauce is good with grilled fish steaks like tuna or swordfish.

FRUIT

Modern *means of distribution, refrigeration, new farming techniques, and health considerations have changed the way we eat fruit.*

Although many fruits are available year-round, nothing can take the place of seasonal, locally grown produce. Grocery store chains bring in grapefruit during the summer, strawberries in the winter, asparagus in the fall, and apples in the late spring. The resulting displays are visually appealing often at the expense of flavor. Buy in season! Farmer's markets are good places to find the best of what your area has to offer.

Pesticides and chemical additives have also made much fruit available year-round. It is always a good idea to thoroughly wash and rinse produce before using to avoid any harmful effects of such chemicals.

Nutritionists encourage consumption of fruit to provide all sorts of needed vitamins and minerals. Eating a variety of citrus fruit, apples, bananas, melons, and dried fruits is a flavorful way to keep a healthy constitution.

The following chapter is divided into fresh fruits and cooked fruits. An attempt has been made to honor the serving suggestions as well as specific recipes from the earliest editions of the book. Simple but honest and time honored, the recipes are as applicable for today's kitchen as they were almost a hundred years ago.

Fresh Fruit

Fresh fruit makes a light, satisfying dessert. Choose seasonal, ripe fruit bursting with flavor. Arrange in a large bowl and use as a decorative centerpiece at dinner. Guests can help themselves to the fruit at the close of the meal.

STRAWBERRIES AU NATUREL

Pick over berries, but do not remove stems. Place carefully in colander in a pan of cold water, so the water will cover the berries. Lift the colander up and down, change the water and thus wash the berries. Drain thoroughly.

Place berries in small plate, on rose geranium leaves, if desired, and at the side put one large leaf heaped with a tablespoon of powdered sugar. Or omit the leaves, have small mound of powdered sugar in center of plate, and surround with the berries. Or stem and wash the berries, place in sauce dish, and serve sprinkled with sugar or with sugar and cream.

ORANGES

For a simple presentation, cut an orange in half crosswise and place on an attractive dish. With a small sharp knife cut around each section so guests can easily scoop out the juice and pulp with a spoon. Sweeten if necessary.

West Indian Method

Peel the oranges, taking off as much membrane as possible. With a very sharp knife cut out the orange sections in wedges all around as you would an apple— leaving the seeds, tough, stringy central part, and most of the inner skin together. This is a much less tedious process than removing skin by sections. Arrange the sections on a small plate in the form of a daisy. Put a mound of white sugar in center.

Oranges with Coconut

Pare the oranges, slice crosswise as thin as possible, and place in small saucers. Cover the fruit thickly with fine shredded coconut, then add powdered sugar. For every six dishes of the fruit squeeze the juice of one orange over the dishes of fruit. Let stand half an hour before serving.

GRAPEFRUIT

Cut in half with a sharp knife, remove seeds, loosen pulp and thick, pithy white center, and sprinkle with sugar. Wipe knife after each cutting so that the bitter taste may be avoided. Or pour in white wine or sherry, sprinkle with powdered sugar, and let stand several hours in refrigerator to ripen. Serve cold in the shell. Decorate with mint leaves, if desired.

FRESH PINEAPPLE

Cut pineapple in thick slices, crosswise, peel off the rind, and then slice in small slices or chop, discarding the hard core in the center. Place in fruit dish, sprinkle well with sugar, add the juice of a lemon, and let stand a few hours to ripen. Serve cold.

MELONS

Cut melons in half, in sections, or slices, remove seeds and fibers. Serve ice cold with salt or sugar at the beginning of a meal, or fill with ice cream and serve as a dessert. Or cut flesh into cubes or balls and serve in the melon shells or in sherbet glasses.

WATERMELON

Cut a chilled watermelon in slices and remove the shell. Or cut out the red portion with tablespoon or divide into cubes an inch square and remove seeds. Pour over a little wine or have ready a mixture of ½ tablespoon ground cinnamon to ½ cup powdered sugar and sprinkle this over the melon. Refill the melon shell and let stand a few moments. A hollowed-out watermelon shell makes an attractive bowl for fruit salad.

Cooked Fruit

BAKED APPLES

Wipe and core sour apples such as Granny Smith. Place them in an earthen dish and fill the center of each apple with sugar and cinnamon, if desired. Measure 1 tablespoon of water for each apple and pour it around the apples. Bake in a hot oven (400° F) until soft, but not mushy, 20 to 30 minutes. Serve with milk or cream.

STEAMED APPLES

1

Wipe, core, and pare sour apples (Granny Smith, Greenings, or Winesap). Put on a plate in a steamer and cook until the apples are tender. The juice may be strained and made into syrup using ¼ cup sugar to ½ cup juice. Boil for 5 minutes, add 1 teaspoon lemon juice and strain over the apples.

2

Select 8 red apples (Red Delicious, Rome Beauty, or McIntosh), cook in boiling water halfway up the fruit until soft, turning often. Remove skins carefully so that the red color may remain.

To the water add 1 cup sugar, grated rind of a lemon, and juice of 1 orange. Simmer until reduced to 1 cup. Cool and pour over apples.

APPLESAUCE

10 to 12 apples (about 2½ pounds)	1 tablespoon lemon juice
½ cup sugar	nutmeg or cinnamon (optional)

Wash, quarter, and core cooking apples. Add water to barely cover. Cook until nearly soft, add sugar, lemon juice, and nutmeg or cinnamon, if desired. Cook a few minutes longer, press through a strainer, and cool.

RHUBARB SAUCE

Skin and cut stalks of rhubarb in ½-inch pieces. Scald with boiling water. Let stand ten minutes and drain. In a nonreactive heavy-bottomed pan cook until soft, adding water as necessary to keep them from burning, then sweeten. Flavor with the grated rind of an orange.

STEWED PRUNES

½ pound prunes	¼ cup sugar
½ lemon, sliced	

Wash the prunes and soak them in cold water overnight. In a heavy-bottomed, nonreactive pan cook slowly with lemon until tender. Add sugar and cook 5 minutes longer.

Dried apricots or any other dried fruit may be prepared the same way and mixed with the prunes.

CRANBERRY SAUCE

The following recipe is a Settlement original. The amount of sugar can be halved if desired. The result will yield a tart, lively sauce with less calories. Try adding a pinch of grated lemon, lime, or orange rind for variation.

2 cups water   1 quart cranberries
2 cups sugar

Boil water and sugar to a syrup about 10 minutes. Add the cranberries, washed and picked over. Cover and cook until the cranberries are clear. Serve cold with meat or poultry.

JELLIED CRANBERRY SAUCE

4 cups cranberries   2 cups sugar
2 cups water

Wash the cranberries. Cook in the water until they are soft and the skins pop open. Strain, add the sugar and stir until the sugar is dissolved. Boil 5 to 8 minutes or until a drop jells on a cold plate. Skim. Pour into individual wet molds or ring mold and cool.

FRESH CRANBERRY RELISH

1 pound cranberries   2 cups sugar
1 large orange, seeded but not
    peeled

In the bowl of a food processor fitted with the metal blade, grind the cranberries and orange. Add sugar and mix thoroughly. Let stand several days before using. Keeps well in the refrigerator or freezer. Serve with poultry or meat.

CRANBERRY COMPOTE

1 quart cranberries   1 cup sugar
2 cups strawberry preserves

Cover cranberries with water, bring to a boil and cook, uncovered, for about 5 minutes. Then add strawberry preserves and sugar and cook about 5 minutes longer. Serve cold.

FRESH PEACH OR PEAR COMPOTE

1½ cups sugar	4 small pieces stick cinnamon
1½ cups water	2 dozen peaches or 1 dozen pears

Boil sugar and water to a syrup. Add the cinnamon and fruit, peeled and sliced. Simmer until tender. Serve cold with meat.

GINGERED FIGS

1 pound dried figs	sugar
juice and grated rind of ½ lemon	1 tablespoon lemon juice
1 large piece gingerroot	

Wash figs and remove stems. Cover with cold water and add lemon juice and rind and gingerroot. Simmer until the figs are puffed and soft. Remove figs. Strain and measure juice and add one-half as much sugar. Boil until thick and add 1 tablespoon lemon juice. Pour juice over figs. Serve cold with whipped cream, if desired.

BAKED BANANAS

Pull down a section of the skin of each banana, loosen the fruit from the skin and remove all coarse threads that adhere to the fruit. Return the banana to the skin in its original position. Lay the prepared fruit in a nonreactive pan and bake in a hot oven until the skins are blackened and the pulp is softened. Remove pulp from the skin without injury to shape. Bend in a half circle in a serving dish. Sprinkle with powdered sugar and finely chopped, blanched pistachio nuts and serve as a dessert.

BAKED APRICOTS AND RAISINS

½ pound dried apricots	½ cup sugar
1 cup seedless raisins	juice of 1 lemon
2 cups water	1 orange, peeled and sliced

Wash apricots and raisins. Add water and place in baking dish. Cover and bake 2½ hours at 325° F. Add sugar, lemon juice, and orange slices. Stir until sugar is dissolved. Chill.

BROILED GRAPEFRUIT

Cut grapefruit in half. Cut out center core and loosen sections from membrane. Cover each half with 2 tablespoons brown sugar and ½ tablespoon butter or sprinkle with granulated sugar and cinnamon to taste. Broil 15 minutes, 3½ inches from heat. Serve hot.

Fruit Desserts

Fruit desserts can be festive and fanciful. In addition to the heirloom recipes found in this chapter, here are some others designed for modern entertaining. All of these can be done in advance. This leaves extra time for garnishing and last-minute embellishing.

ORANGES IN CARAMEL

8 large oranges
2 cups sugar
3 cups water
2 tablespoons orange liqueur (Grand Marnier or Cointreau)

½ cup orange juice
fresh mint leaves or candied violets for garnish (optional)

1. Using a vegetable peeler, carefully remove just the orange part of the peels from the oranges. (Avoid the white pith as it is bitter.) Julienne into very thin strips. Blanch in boiling water for 2 to 3 minutes. Drain and refresh under cold, running water.

2. Combine ½ cup of the sugar and 2 cups of the water in a heavy, non-reactive saucepan. Bring to a boil with one tablespoon of the orange liqueur. Add the blanched rind and let cook over moderately high heat until rinds are softened and sugar is syrupy, about 10 minutes.

3. Remove any remaining peel and all white pith from the oranges. Cut crosswise into ½-inch slices. Arrange attractively in a glass bowl and chill.

4. Combine the remaining 1½ cup sugar and cup of water in a heavy, nonreactive saucepan. Boil over high heat until dark amber. Pour half onto an oiled baking sheet. Return the remaining caramel to the heat and carefully pour on the orange juice. Bring back to a boil, stir to dissolve, and add the orange rind with the syrup and the remaining tablespoon of orange liqueur. Cool completely.

5. When the caramel has hardened on the baking sheet, break up into large pieces and place in the bowl of a food processor. Grind into coarse pieces.

6. Serve the oranges in glass bowls with the cooled rinds and syrup spooned over evenly. Sprinkle with the caramel and serve at once. Garnish with mint leaves or candied violets if desired.

PEARS IN RED WINE

½ cup sugar
4 cups hearty red wine
2-inch-long piece of lemon rind
1 cinnamon stick
2 whole cloves

4 to 6 firm pears, peeled and cored
  with stem intact
mint leaves, cinnamon, or toasted
  almonds for garnish

1. In a nonreactive saucepan large enough to hold the pears upright, combine the sugar, wine, lemon rind, and spices. Bring to a boil. When sugar has dissolved, let syrup cook down over high heat for 5 to 7 minutes.

2. Immerse the pears in the syrup. Weigh down with a heat-proof plate so that all fruit is submerged. Reduce heat to a steady simmer and let pears cook until softened, 30 to 45 minutes. Let them cool completely in the liquid.

3. Remove pears to a serving dish. Strain the liquid and return to a nonreactive saucepan. Reduce over high heat until the consistency of a thick syrup, about 10 minutes. Cool, then chill for at least several hours in the refrigerator.

4. Just before serving, spoon the syrup over the cooked fruit. Garnish with mint leaves, a dusting of ground cinnamon, or finely chopped toasted almonds. Serve with whipped cream on the side.

CLAFOUTIS

This is a rustic but very versatile, simple French dessert. The traditional recipe calls for cherries. Almost any fruit could be substituted. Try it with dried apricots, peaches, prunes soaked in brandy or cognac, fresh berries or plums. The Clafoutis is attractive when done in a fairly deep porcelain quiche mold with scalloped edges.

1 pound sour cherries (or the
  equivalent amount of fruits
  suggested above)
3 tablespoons flour
⅛ teaspoon salt

¼ cup sugar
4 eggs
2 cups milk
2 egg yolks

(continued)

1. Preheat oven to 375° F. Arrange the fruit in the bottom of a shallow, 2-quart baking dish.

2. In a mixing bowl, combine the flour, salt, and sugar. Add the eggs, one at a time, alternating with the milk. Beat in the extra yolks.

3. When smooth and well blended, strain the egg mixture over the fruit. Bake in the preheated oven until set and golden brown, about 45 minutes. Let cool before serving.

TROPICAL FRUITS

Fruit shipped from far corners of the world is providing modern markets with abundant choices. Ethnic groups living closely together are introducing all sorts of new foods to their neighbors. Many products once considered hard to find are as abundant today as apples, oranges, or bananas.

Here are some guidelines for selecting and serving some of the increasingly available tropical and exotic fruits:

Carambola: (Also called *starfruit*.) Blond-yellow and long with protruding ribs, the carambola is unpeeled, cut and eaten fresh with seeds discarded. The fruit is shaped like a star with flesh that is juicy but sharp. This native of the West Indies and Brazil is sweet when very ripe. The same fruit can be eaten with a vinaigrette sauce as for a salad like an avocado.

Cherimoya: Used in native South and Central America for drinks and sherbets, this light green, rough-textured exotic fruit can be eaten raw if very ripe. Discard the seeds before eating or cooking.

Feijoa: (Also called *pineapple guava*.) Mostly exported from New Zealand, this second name is appropriate for its characteristically tart-but-sweet taste. Its about 3 inches long with dark green skin and white flesh.

Kiwi: Also grown abundantly in New Zealand, the kiwi is one of the modern kitchen's most well-known exotic fruits. Green with bursts of black seeds, the kiwi is used to adorn desserts, salads, and some savory meats like pork, veal, or game. High in vitamin C and juicy, the kiwi has a hairy outer skin and should be soft to the touch when mature.

Kumquat: Originally from Asia, the kumquat is cultivated in many parts of the world today. It is orange, oval, and fragrant with an acidic, tart center. The kumquat makes wonderful jellies and jams.

Loquats: Also native to Asia, the Loquat is a yellow/orange fruit about the size of an apricot. Found mostly in the spring, the flesh is acidic and bracing. It is also used for making jams and jellies.

Mango: This is an oblong tropical fruit with skin color that varies from green to purplish red as it ripens. Its tough fibrous flesh clings to a large, flat kernel. Ripe mangos can be served sliced and chilled, in a salad or as a contrasting ingredient in a savory dish like duck or pork. Mangos make wonderful sherberts and can be used for pastries, soufflés, and puddings.

Papaya: With a bright orange flesh and a greenish yellow skin, the papaya is one of the most flavorful of tropical fruits. The center is filled with a cluster of black seeds that should be discarded before consuming. Serve chilled as for a melon as a first course or sliced in salads with contrasting elements of sweet and savory. Or sprinkle papaya with sugar for dessert.

Passion Fruit: About the size of an egg, the passion fruit is wrinkled and dark brownish-red on the outside when mature. The pulp is sharp and intensely flavored and is firmly attached to the small, edible seeds. The juice is often extracted and used for pastries, jams and jellies, drinks, and sherbets.

Pomegranate: The skin of this round fruit is burnished red and smooth. The inside reveals crimson red flesh surrounding small seeds. Usually the fruit is eaten unadorned as any fresh fruit. The juice is also extracted, sweetened and known as grenadine. Pomegranate is attractive when a few loosened seeds are sprinkled over a composed salad.

Prickly Pears: This is actually the edible fruit of a cactus plant. Roundish with an orange-red hue, the fruit has prickles that necessitate careful handling. Eaten raw after cautiously peeling, the prickly pear can also be cooked and used in preserves and pastry making.

Tamarind: An ancient fruit found in the cuisines of many tropical countries, the tamarind is brown and long with a sweet-and-sour-tasting flesh. Used for making chutneys and other preserves, it is found in curries, salads, sherberts, drinks, and vegetable concoctions throughout the world.

GRIDDLE CAKES, WAFFLES, DOUGHNUTS, FRITTERS, AND COFFEE CAKES

The basic ingredients in the batter that make a quick bread when baked become a griddle cake or pancake when cooked on a hot flat iron, or a waffle when cooked between two textured irons. And similar batters become a doughnut or a fritter when fried in deep fat. In sweetened form, yeast bread dough is used to make coffee cakes or Kuchen (their German name). The results are an array of breakfast treats good enough to eat all day long.

Griddle Cakes and Pancakes

Any of these hot cakes may be served as main courses at luncheon or supper, and pancakes and waffles make delicious desserts, as well.

Griddle cake batters are thick enough to hold their shape, so that they can be poured from a pitcher or the tip of a spoon to make perfect round cakes. Pancake batters tend to be thinner, and often take the shape of the skillet. You can make several at a time and keep them warm in a low oven. While practical when cooking for a crowd, they are never as good as when fresh off the iron or griddle.

To Make Griddle Cakes

Heat a griddle or skillet and test temperature by sprinkling with a few drops of water. If the water disappears at once, the griddle is too hot. If it flattens out and boils, the griddle is not hot enough. If the drops bounce, the griddle is just right. Brush the griddle lightly with fat, using a pastry brush. Pour batter in uniform amounts from a pitcher, or from the tip of a large spoon. When cakes are full of bubbles turn with a spatula or pancake turner and brown the other side. Turn only once.

Griddle cakes are usually served with butter and syrup or sauce. Maple sugar, honey, fruit preserves, as well as whipped cream, sweetened sour cream, or yogurt make excellent accompaniments. For recipe ideas, see section Syrups and Sauces for Griddle Cakes and Waffles on page 431.

Griddle cakes can be savory, too. Rice and corn cake recipes that follow here can be served with a savory sauce for a different twist. Traditional crêpes can be filled with any of the suggestions mentioned on page 424. Griddle cakes are versatile menu items that can turn an ordinary meal into something special.

PLAIN GRIDDLE CAKES

1 cup flour	1 egg, lightly beaten
2 teaspoons baking powder	1 cup milk
¼ teaspoon salt	1 teaspoon butter, melted

1. Sift the dry ingredients together. Add egg and milk and stir gradually to make a smooth batter. Add the butter.
2. Bake on a hot griddle according to directions above.

BUTTERMILK GRIDDLE CAKES

In the following recipe sour cream may be substituted for the buttermilk and the butter omitted.

2½ cups flour	2 tablespoons butter, melted, or
½ teaspoon salt	vegetable oil
1½ teaspoons baking soda	1 egg, lightly beaten
2 cups buttermilk	

1. Sift dry ingredients together. Combine the buttermilk, melted butter, and egg. Add to the dry ingredients and stir to make a smooth batter.
2. Bake on a hot griddle according to the directions on page 420 and serve at once.

SOUR CREAM GRIDDLE CAKES

1 teaspoon baking soda	½ cup flour
1 cup sour cream	2 tablespoons cottage cheese
2 eggs, lightly beaten	

1. Combine the baking soda and sour cream. Add the eggs and stir in the flour and cottage cheese.
2. Bake on a hot griddle according to the directions on page 420.

RICE GRIDDLE CAKES

2 cups flour	2 cups hot cooked rice
3 teaspoons baking powder	2 eggs, separated
1 teaspoon salt	2 cups milk

1. Sift the dry ingredients together and mix with the rice. Lightly beat the egg yolks, add the milk, and combine with the rice mixture.

2. Beat the egg whites until they hold stiff peaks and gently fold into the rice batter.

3. Bake on a hot griddle according to the directions on page 420 and serve at once.

CORNMEAL GRIDDLE CAKES

1 cup flour	1½ teaspoons salt
1 cup cornmeal	1 or 2 eggs, well beaten
1 tablespoon baking powder	2 cups milk

1. Sift the dry ingredients together. Combine the egg and the milk and mix with the dry ingredients to make a smooth batter.

2. Bake on a hot griddle according to the directions on page 420 and serve at once.

YEAST GRIDDLE CAKES

1 package active dry yeast	1 teaspoon salt
2 cups lukewarm milk (110° F) and	1 teaspoon baking soda
1 cup lukewarm water mixed	3 tablespoons syrup
1 cup white flour	2 eggs
1 cup barley flour	2 tablespoons butter, melted, or
1 cup cornmeal	vegetable shortening

1. Dissolve yeast in ¼ cup of the warm milk-water mixture and allow to stand 3 to 5 minutes until tiny bubbles appear on the surface.

2. Add the remaining warm liquid, flours, cornmeal, and salt and stir to make a thin batter. Cover and let rise overnight.

3. The next morning, stir in the soda, syrup, eggs, and butter. Cover and let rise for 15 minutes.

4. Bake on a hot griddle according to the directions on page 420 and serve at once.

BUCKWHEAT CAKES

½ package active dry yeast
4 cups lukewarm water (110° F)
1 teaspoon sugar
½ cup flour

3¼ cups buckwheat flour
1 teaspoon salt
2 tablespoons molasses

1.   Dissolve yeast in ¼ cup of the warm water with the sugar and allow to stand 3 to 5 minutes until tiny bubbles appear on the surface.

2.   Add the remaining water, flours, and salt and stir to make a thin batter. Cover and let rise overnight. Stir in molasses.

3.   Bake on a hot griddle according to the directions on page 420 and serve at once.

BAKED PANCAKE

2 eggs, lightly beaten
¾ cup flour
½ teaspoon salt

1 cup milk
2 teaspoons butter or shortening

1.   Preheat oven to 425° F. Combine the eggs, flour, salt, and milk. Blend well.

2.   Heat skillet in oven and add the butter. When butter is melted, pour in the batter. Bake for 15 minutes. Reduce heat to 325° F and bake until brown. Serve on hot platter with confectioners' sugar and lemon slices or lemon juice.

CRÊPES

Crêpes are among the most versatile of foods. Serve them as a main dish for lunch or supper rolled around savory fillings (a good way to use leftovers) and heated in a sauce. Use the sweet crêpes recipe from the Crêpes Suzette (see below) spread with jam and sprinkled with sugar as dessert after a light meal of soup or salad. Crêpes freeze well, filled or unfilled.

3 eggs
1½ cups milk
1 cup flour

½ teaspoon salt
2 tablespoons butter, melted

1.   Combine eggs and milk. Add flour, salt, and, finally, the melted butter. Beat until smooth. Cover and place in the refrigerator for 1 to 2 hours.

2.   Heat a 6-inch greased skillet or special crêpe pan. Add 1 tablespoon of

batter and tip the skillet from side to side until the batter covers the bottom of the skillet. Lift one edge then gently loosen. Quickly turn over with fingers or tongs. Brown the crêpes on both sides. Keep crêpes warm in a very low oven while cooking off all the batter. Place desired filling in the center of each crêpe and roll. Spoon sauce over filled crêpes and serve at once.

SUGGESTED CRÊPE FILLINGS
Deviled Crabs, page 215
Creamed Spinach, page 391
Ratatouille, page 396
Chicken Hash, page 246

SUGGESTED CRÊPE SAUCES
A dash of wine added to the sauce adds flavor. Parmesan cheese sprinkled over the top also enhances the flavor.

Thin White Sauce, page 399
Cheese Sauce, page 400
Mornay Sauce, page 400
Mushroom Sauce, page 401

CRÊPES SUZETTE

1 cup flour	2 eggs, separated
⅓ cup confectioners' sugar	1 cup milk
¼ teaspoon salt	grated rind of one lemon

1. Sift dry ingredients. Beat egg yolks, add milk, dry ingredients, and the lemon rind. Beat the egg whites until stiff but not dry and gently fold into the batter.

2. Heat a 6-inch greased skillet. Add 1 tablespoon of batter and tip the skillet from side to side until the batter covers the bottom of the skillet. Brown the crêpes on both sides and roll. Keep crêpes warm in a very low oven while cooking off all the batter. Serve with the Sauce, below.

SUZETTE SAUCE FLAMBÉ

½ cup butter	2 tablespoons grenadine
3 tablespoons confectioners' sugar	1 tablespoon each cognac, rum, and
juice of 1 orange	Cointreau

1. In a chafing dish, melt the butter, add the sugar and allow to cook for a few minutes. Add the orange juice and grenadine and stir constantly.

2. Add the rolled crêpes, turning each in the sauce until well covered. Pour in the liqueurs. Off heat, carefuly light with a match and turn the crêpes in the flaming sauce until the flame burns out.

GERMAN PANCAKE

3 eggs, very lightly beaten	½ cup milk
½ teaspoon salt	2 tablespoons butter
½ cup flour	confectioners' sugar and lemon juice

1. Preheat oven to 450° F. Combine eggs with salt and flour and gradually add the milk, beating all the time.

2. Spread the bottom and sides of a 10-inch skillet thickly with the butter and pour in the batter. Bake 20 minutes; reduce the heat to 350° F and continue baking until crisp and brown. Place on a hot platter and sprinkle with confectioners' sugar and lemon juice.

BOHEMIAN PANCAKES

½ package active dry yeast	grated rind of ½ lemon
¼ cup lukewarm water (110° F)	2 eggs, well beaten
1¼ cups flour	¾ cup lukewarm milk
1 tablespoon sugar	Prune Filling (page 449)
½ teaspoon salt	

1. Dissolve yeast in the warm water and allow to stand 3 to 5 minutes until tiny bubbles appear on the surface.

2. Combine the flour, sugar, salt, and lemon rind, add the eggs and milk and beat well. Stir in the dissolved yeast. Cover and let rise in a warm place until very light.

3. Lift the dough by spoonfuls from the top of the mixture so as not to deflate the remainder. Spread on a moderately hot griddle with the back of a spoon, reduce heat and bake slowly so they will rise again; turn and bake on the other side.

4. Spread pancakes with a thick layer of Prune Filling, cover generously with crumbled gingersnaps, and spread with sweetened whipped cream. Or, cover with sour cream and riced, dry cottage cheese. Serve cold.

POTATO PANCAKES

Use your food processor for grating potatoes.

1

2 cups raw grated potatoes	1 tablespoon flour, breadcrumbs, or
2 eggs, well beaten	matzo meal
⅛ teaspoon baking powder	freshly ground black pepper to taste
1½ teaspoons salt	

   1. Combine potatoes and eggs and stir in the remaining ingredients.

   2. Drop by spoonfuls onto a hot greased skillet into small cakes. Brown on both sides. Serve hot with applesauce, or alongside braised meats.

2

4 large potatoes, washed and peeled	½ teaspoon salt
½ cup sour cream or hot milk	2 eggs, separated

   1. Soak the peeled potatoes in cold water for several hours. Grate the potatoes, place in a colander set over a bowl, and let drain. When the starch has settled in the bottom of the bowl, drain off the water and reserve the starch.

   2. In a mixing bowl, combine potatoes, starch, sour cream or hot milk, and salt. Beat the yolks well and add to the potato mixture. Beat the whites until stiff and gently fold in.

   3. Drop by spoonfuls onto a hot greased skillet into small cakes. Brown on both sides. Serve hot with applesauce, or alongside braised meats.

Variation:

Baked Potato Pancakes: Mix as above. Heat a generous amount of fat in a skillet, add the potato batter, and bake in a hot oven (400° F) for 15 minutes. Turn and bake 15 minutes on the other side. Serve hot with applesauce, or alongside braised meats.

COMBINATION PANCAKES

1 teaspoon baking soda	1 tablespoon butter
2½ cups buttermilk	1 tablespoon sugar
1 cup white flour	2 eggs, well beaten
1 cup barley (or rye) flour	½ teaspoon salt
1 cup cornmeal	

1. Dissolve the soda in buttermilk. Set aside. Sift the flours and cornmeal together.

2. Cream the butter and the sugar, and add the eggs, salt, and buttermilk mixture. Gradually stir in the flours to make a smooth batter.

3. Bake on a hot griddle according to directions on page 420 and serve at once.

BLINTZES

4 eggs, well beaten	1 cup flour
1 cup milk	1 teaspoon salt

1. Combine eggs and milk. Gradually stir in the flour and the salt to make a smooth batter.

2. Heat a heavy 6-inch skillet and grease lightly. Pour only enough batter to make a very thin pancake, tipping the pan from side to side until the batter covers the bottom of the pan. Bake on one side only until it blisters. Toss on a board, fried side up. Repeat until all the batter is used, setting each aside.

3. Place a rounded tablespoon of the desired filling (see below) in the center of each pancake. Fold over both sides and roll into envelope shape. Just before serving, fry on both sides or bake until golden brown. Serve hot with sugar and cinnamon or with sour cream.

CHEESE FILLING FOR BLINTZES

1½ pounds dry cottage cheese	1 tablespoon butter, at room
salt to taste	temperature
2 egg yolks, beaten	1 tablespoon sugar

Press cheese through a colander or sieve. Add salt and combine with remaining ingredients.

POTATO FILLING FOR BLINTZES

1 small onion, finely chopped	1 egg
1 tablespoon butter	salt and freshly ground black pepper
2½ cups mashed potatoes	to taste

Fry the onion in the butter until soft but not brown. Combine the mashed potatoes, egg, salt, and pepper and add the fried onion.

MATZO PANCAKES

boiling water	¼ teaspoon freshly ground black
3 matzos, broken	pepper
2 eggs, well beaten	goose fat, or butter
1 teaspoon salt	

1. Pour boiling water over matzos to cover. Let stand for 15 minutes. Squeeze the matzos dry and add the egg, salt, and pepper.

2. Melt the goose fat on a hot griddle and drop batter by spoonfuls into small cakes. Brown on both sides and serve hot with Sugar Syrup (page 431) or jelly.

MATZO MEAL PANCAKES

Leftover pancakes may be cut into noodles and served in soup.

½ cup matzo meal	2 eggs, separated
1 teaspoon salt	1 cup milk or water
1 tablespoon sugar	

1. Combine dry ingredients. Beat the egg yolks with the milk and mix with the dry ingredients. Let stand for a half hour to swell. Beat egg whites until stiff but not dry and gently fold into the batter.

2. Bake on a hot, greased griddle and serve hot with sugar or Sugar Syrup (page 431).

Waffles

Waffles are part of a northern European heritage that found an avid following here in the New World. Belgium is the home of the crisp almost cookie-like waffles that are spread with jam or cream just as they come off the griddle. Our waffles have a cake-like texture. A good one should be crisp outside but moist in the center. To insure this consistency, have an iron well preheated before adding batter.

Care and Use of Waffle Irons

Preheat until warm—not more than 5 minutes. Brush a thin coating of melted butter over the entire inner surface. Pour in enough batter to make a thick waffle. Remove when brown, and discard the first waffle. Wipe off surplus grease with a piece of dry cheesecloth.

Do not grease an electric iron once it is tempered. An electric iron must be thoroughly heated before pouring in the batter. To prevent sticking, swab dampened cloth before each baking. Place 1 tablespoon or more of the batter near the center in each section of the iron, sufficient to touch the top of the grid. Close quickly so waffles brown on top. Bake until waffle stops steaming. Follow manufacturer's instructions for other types of irons.

Waffle Batters

Waffles will stick to the waffle iron when there is not sufficient fat in the batter. Buttermilk makes a more tender waffle than regular milk. If buttermilk or cream is used, use ½ teaspoon baking soda for each cup of liquid.

Waffles are done when steam stops escaping from the iron and there is no resistance when opening.

SERVING WAFFLES

Waffles are usually served hot topped with syrup, honey, or sweet preserves. While pure maple syrup is the best, try substituting cane syrup or corn syrup for a more economical choice.

Most waffles are sweet, though they can also be made savory. Simply omit the sugar in the recipe and serve warm with creamed chicken, beef, or fish.

BASIC WAFFLE RECIPE

2 cups flour
2 teaspoons baking powder
2 tablespoons sugar
½ teaspoon salt

2 eggs, separated
2 cups milk
4 to 6 tablespoons butter, melted

1. Sift flour, baking powder, sugar, and salt twice. Beat egg yolks, add milk, and mix with dry ingredients just enough to blend them. Add the butter. Beat egg whites until stiff but not dry and gently fold into the batter.
2. Bake in a preheated waffle iron.

MAPLE PECAN WAFFLES

2½ cups flour
2 teaspoons baking powder
½ teaspoon salt
2 eggs, separated
2 cups buttermilk

2 tablespoons maple syrup
4 to 6 tablespoons butter, melted
1 cup toasted pecans, coarsely
   chopped

1. Sift flour, baking powder, and salt twice. Beat egg yolks, add buttermilk and maple syrup, and mix with dry ingredients just enough to blend them. Add the butter. Beat egg whites until stiff but not dry and gently fold into the batter with the pecans.
2. Bake in a preheated waffle iron.

CHOCOLATE WAFFLES

¼ cup butter or shortening
⅔ cup sugar
2 ounces unsweetened chocolate,
   melted
3 eggs, separated

1½ cups flour
1 tablespoon baking powder
¼ teaspoon salt
1¼ cups milk
½ teaspoon vanilla

1. Cream butter and sugar until light. Add chocolate and egg yolks and beat well. Sift the flour, baking powder, and salt together and add to the batter alternately with the milk mixed with the vanilla. Beat egg whites until stiff but not dry and gently fold into the batter.
2. Bake in preheated waffle iron. Serve hot with butter and powdered sugar.

GINGERBREAD WAFFLES

3 eggs
¼ cup sugar
½ cup molasses
1 cup buttermilk
1½ cups flour
1 teaspoon ground ginger
½ teaspoon ground cinnamon, if
   desired

½ teaspoon ground cloves, if
   desired
½ teaspoon salt
1 teaspoon baking soda
1 teaspoon baking powder
⅓ cup butter, melted

1. Beat eggs until light. Add sugar, molasses, and buttermilk. Sift dry

ingredients together and add to the batter. Stir until smooth and add the melted butter.

2. Bake in a preheated waffle iron. Serve hot with butter and powdered sugar.

CHEESE WAFFLES

2 cups flour	1 cup grated cheddar cheese
2 teaspoons baking powder	2 eggs, separated
1 teaspoon salt	1½ cups milk
2 tablespoons sugar	¼ cup butter, melted

1. Sift dry ingredients together and add the cheese. Beat the egg yolks and stir in along with the milk and butter. Beat egg whites until stiff but not dry and gently fold into the batter.

2. Bake in a preheated waffle iron.

CORNMEAL WAFFLES

2 cups cake flour	3 tablespoons sugar
2 cups yellow cornmeal	4 eggs, separated
2 tablespoons baking powder	2 cups milk
2 teaspoons salt	½ cup butter, melted

1. Sift dry ingredients together. Beat the egg yolks and stir in along with the milk and butter. Beat egg whites until stiff but not dry and gently fold into the batter.

2. Bake in a preheated waffle iron.

Syrups and Sauces for Griddle Cakes and Waffles

SUGAR SYRUP

2 cups sugar (white, brown, or maple)	⅔ cup boiling water

Combine sugar and boiling water and stir just until sugar dissolves. Boil gently until clear and cool before serving.

HONEY SAUCE

½ cup honey
¼ cup butter, softened

½ teaspoon ground cinnamon
(optional)

Blend honey and butter together until smooth. Add cinnamon if desired.

BROWN SUGAR SAUCE

1 cup brown sugar, firmly packed
1 cup white sugar

1 cup water

Combine sugars and water in a small saucepan and boil until clear.

ORANGE HARD SAUCE

⅓ cup butter, at room temperature
1 cup confectioners' sugar

2 teaspoons orange juice
¼ cup finely chopped candied
orange peel

Cream butter and sugar together. Add orange juice and stir in candied orange peel.

CURRANT JELLY SAUCE

1 cup currant jelly
½ cup boiling water

2 teaspoons finely minced fresh
orange peel

Combine jelly and water and mix until smooth. Stir in orange peel.

Doughnuts

To fry doughnuts, the fat must be hot enough to brown a cube of bread in one minute, about 360° to 375° F, the hotter temperature for yeast raised doughs. Place the doughnuts in a bath of hot fat, deep enough to rise them off the bottom of the pan. They should float quickly to the top. Brown the doughnuts on one side, turn and brown the other. If the fat is too cool, the doughnuts will absorb the fat. If it is too hot, the doughnuts will brown before they have sufficiently raised. When the doughnuts are done, drain on paper towels or unglazed brown paper.

PLAIN DOUGHNUTS   *Makes 18 doughnuts.*

2 cups flour
½ cup sugar
1 teaspoon salt
1 tablespoon baking powder
¼ teaspoon cinnamon

⅛ teaspoon grated nutmeg
2 tablespoons butter, melted
½ cup milk
1 egg, well beaten
oil for deep-frying

1. Sift dry ingredients. Combine the butter, milk, and egg and add to the dry ingredients.

2. Knead lightly on a well-floured board. Roll out to ¼ inch thick and cut out dough with a doughnut cutter or shape by hand. Roll scraps into small balls.

3. Fry in deep, hot fat as directed above.

SOUR CREAM DOUGHNUTS   *Makes 36 doughnuts.*

3 eggs
1 cup sugar
1 cup sour cream
1 teaspoon baking soda
4 cups flour

⅛ teaspoon grated nutmeg
1 teaspoon salt
oil for deep-frying
powdered sugar

1. Beat eggs until light, add sugar and beat until creamy. Combine sour cream and baking soda and stir into the egg mixture. Gently fold in the flour, nutmeg, and salt.

2. Knead lightly on a well-floured board. Roll out to ¼ inch thick and cut out dough with a doughnut cutter or shape by hand. Roll scraps into small balls.

3. Fry in deep, hot fat as directed on page 432. When partially cooled, dust with powdered sugar.

BUTTERMILK DOUGHNUTS   *Makes 36 doughnuts.*

2 eggs
1¼ cups sugar
2 tablespoons shortening
½ teaspoon salt
1 teaspoon grated nutmeg
1 teaspoon baking soda

2 teaspoons baking powder
4 cups flour
1 cup buttermilk
oil for deep-frying
powdered sugar

(continued)

1. Beat eggs until light, add sugar and shortening and beat until creamy. Sift dry ingredients together and add to the egg and butter mixture alternately with the buttermilk. (Note: To make a lighter dough use ½ cup less flour and place in the refrigerator overnight.)

2. Knead lightly on a well-floured board. Roll out to ¼ inch thick and cut out dough with a doughnut cutter or shape by hand. Roll scraps into small balls.

3. Fry in deep, hot fat as directed on page 432. When partially cooled, dust with powdered sugar.

DOUGHNUT DROPS

2 eggs	1½ cups flour
¼ cup sugar	4 teaspoons baking powder
1 teaspoon salt	oil for deep-frying
2 tablespoons butter, melted, or shortening	1 ounce unsweetened chocolate, melted (optional)
⅓ cup milk	powdered sugar

1. Beat eggs until light, add sugar, salt, butter or shortening, and milk. Mix flour and baking powder together and gently stir into the batter until evenly combined. Stir in chocolate, if desired.

2. Drop by tablespoonfuls into deep, hot fat as directed on page 432. Dip spoon into the hot fat before taking up each spoonful to keep the batter from sticking. When partially cooled, sprinkle with powdered sugar.

RAISED DOUGHNUTS

Prepare any Kuchen Dough, Number 1, 2, or 3 (page 438) and let rise until doubled. Roll out to a thin sheet and cut into rings with a doughnut cutter. Cover and let rise again until nearly doubled in bulk. Fry in deep, hot fat as directed on page 432. Drain on paper towels. When cool enough to handle, roll in powdered sugar.

BERLINER PFANN KUCHEN (FILLED DOUGHNUTS)

 Prepare any Kuchen Dough, Number 1, 2, or 3 (page 438) and let rise until doubled. Roll out to a sheet 1 inch thick and cut into rounds. Place a teaspoon of preserves or a stewed prune in the center of half of them. Brush the edges with beaten egg white and cover with the other half. Press edges neatly together. Or, cut dough into large rounds. Place a teaspoon of preserves, a stewed prune, or 1 teaspoon of chopped dried fruit in the center of each. Shape and roll so that the filling is completely covered. Place on a well-floured board, cover and let rise again until very light. Fry in deep, hot fat as directed on page 432. Drain on paper towels. When partially cooled, sprinkle with powdered sugar.

CRULLERS

 Prepare Plain Kuchen Dough (page 438). After first rising, roll out ½ inch thick. Cut into strips 8 inches long, ¾ inch wide. Place on a well-floured board, cover and let rise until doubled. Twist ends, turning hands in opposite directions, and pinch the ends together. Fry in deep, hot fat as directed on page 432. Drain on paper towels. When partially cooled, sprinkle with powdered sugar.

SPRITZ KRAPFEN (FRENCH CRULLERS)

2 cups water
1 tablespoon butter
2 cups flour
¼ cup sugar
juice and finely grated rind of 1
   lemon

4 eggs
oil for deep-frying
powdered sugar

1. In a saucepan, combine water and butter. Bring to a boil and add the flour all at once. Stir vigorously until the dough comes away from the sides of the pan. Remove from heat, add the sugar, lemon juice, and finely grated rind. Add the eggs one at a time, beating constantly between each addition.

2. Drop by spoonfuls, or drop from a large pastry bag into deep, hot fat and fry as directed on page 432. When partially cooled, dust with powdered sugar.

KRINGLES

1 teaspoon butter
¼ teaspoon salt
1 tablespoon sugar
1 egg, beaten
1 tablespoon cream

1 teaspoon lemon juice
1 cup flour, approximately
oil for deep-frying
powdered sugar

(continued)

1.   Mix butter, salt, and sugar with the egg. Add the cream, lemon juice, and enough flour to make a stiff dough.

2.   Knead lightly on a floured board. Roll out very thin and cut into pieces 3 inches long and 2 inches wide. Make four 1-inch slits at equal intervals on each piece. Gather up the dough by running a fork in and out of the slits.

3.   Lower into deep, hot fat and fry until light brown. When partially cooled, sprinkle with powdered sugar.

HESTERLISTE

3 eggs, well beaten	2 teaspoons baking powder
5 tablespoons butter	8 cups flour
1 cup sugar	oil for deep-frying
2 cups milk	powdered sugar

1.   Mix eggs with butter and sugar. Add the milk, baking powder, and flour.

2.   Knead lightly on a floured board. Roll out very thin and cut into pieces 3 inches long and 2 inches wide. Make four 1-inch slits at equal intervals on each piece. Gather up the dough by running a fork in and out of the slits.

3.   Lower into deep, hot fat and fry until light brown. Sprinkle with powdered sugar.

ROSETTES (SWEDISH WAFERS)

1 egg	¼ teaspoon salt
1 teaspoon powdered sugar	oil for deep-frying
2 cups milk	powdered sugar
2¼ cups flour	

1.   Beat egg very lightly, add sugar, milk, and flour mixed with salt, alternately, beating all together until smooth.

2.   Put fancy iron wafer mold in a small saucepan of deep, hot fat; when well heated, remove from the fat and dip into the batter. Be careful not to allow the batter to run over the top of the mold. Dip the iron again into the hot fat and fry until crisp and brown. Remove from fat and let wafer slip off and drain on paper towels. Wipe iron occasionally to remove excess fat. Sprinkle with powdered sugar, or fill with jam or fresh fruit and top with whipped cream. Serve hot or cold.

Fritters

Like pancakes and waffles, fruit fritters may be served as main courses at lunch or supper, or as desserts. Fritters may be sautéed in butter, but they are better fried in deep fat. Some fritters involve coating pieces of fruit in batter and others call for folding bits of fruit directly into the mix.

To fry fritters, heat fat in a heavy pan to a temperature of 350° to 360° F. Test temperature with a deep-fat thermometer, or by browning a cube of soft white bread in the fat; it should be golden brown within 35 seconds. Dip prepared fruit in the batter, using a fork or slotted skimmer; drain off excess batter. Fry fritters until golden brown; those made with uncooked fruit should take about 5 minutes, with cooked fruit about 4 minutes. Drain on paper towels. Serve hot and sprinkle with confectioners' sugar if desired.

BASIC FRITTER BATTER

1⅓ cups flour
2 teaspoons baking powder
¼ teaspoon salt

⅔ cup milk
1 egg, well beaten

Sift dry ingredients together. Gradually add the milk and egg. Use to coat fruit according to the directions above.

APPLE FRITTERS

2 large tart apples, peeled, cored, and cut into ⅓-inch slices
sugar and cinnamon to taste

1 recipe Basic Fritter Batter (see above)
oil for deep-frying

Sprinkle apple slices with cinnamon and sugar. Dip in fritter batter and fry in deep, hot fat according to the directions on page 437.

Variations:
Fresh peaches, apricots, oranges, pineapples, bananas, or pears may be cut in slices or in large pieces, dipped in fritter batter, and fried using this technique.

CHERRY FRITTERS

1 cup flour	⅓ cup milk
½ teaspoon salt	¾ cup sour cherries, stemmed and
1 teaspoon baking powder	pitted
1 egg, lightly beaten	oil for deep-frying
1 tablespoon butter, melted	2 tablespoons sugar for dusting

1. Sift dry ingredients together. Add egg and butter. Combine with milk and add to dry ingredients. Fold in cherries.

2. Drop by teaspoonfuls into deep, hot fat. Fry until brown, about 4 to 5 minutes. Drain and dust with sugar.

QUEEN FRITTERS

¼ cup butter	2 eggs
½ cup milk	oil for deep-frying
½ cup flour	fruit preserves
pinch of salt	powdered sugar

1. Combine butter and milk and bring to a boil, add flour and salt and stir until the mixture comes away from the sides of the pan. Remove from heat and add eggs, one at a time, beating constantly.

2. Drop by teaspoonfuls into deep, hot fat and fry until puffed and brown. Drain. Fill a pastry bag with the fruit preserves. With the tip of the pastry bag, poke a small hole in the bottom of the fritter and fill with the preserves. When partially cooled dust with powdered sugar.

Kuchen (or Coffee Cakes)

A sweetened yeast bread served with coffee or tea is a pleasant, informal way of entertaining or treating the family on weekends. Recipes for coffee cakes have originated in many parts of the world, especially in Scandinavian and German-speaking countries. The German word for coffee cake, *kuchen*, is used in this section of our book because many of the recipes are of German origin, contributed by the original Settlement cooks.

The methods for making these yeast-dough coffee cakes resemble those for making bread, so the general rules for making bread, page 452, may be helpful.

Chilled kuchen doughs are easier to handle. If time permits, reduce the flour by ¼ to ½ cup. Put the dough in a greased bowl, large enough to allow for rising, grease the dough, cover with a damp towel and let sit in a warm place until doubled in bulk, then punch down. Cover tightly again with plastic wrap and chill for 24 hours. When ready to use, form into desired shapes and top with one of the fillings found on pages 448–449. Let rise slowly until doubled in bulk and bake.

PLAIN KUCHEN DOUGH

1 package active dry yeast
2 cups scalded milk, cooled to
   110°F
½ cup butter, at room temperature
¾ cup sugar

1 teaspoon salt
pinch of grated nutmeg
1 egg, or 2 yolks
finely grated rind of 1 lemon
6 cups flour

1.   Dissolve yeast in ¼ cup of the warm milk and allow to stand 3 to 5 minutes until tiny bubbles appear on the surface.

2.   Combine the butter, sugar, salt, nutmeg, egg or yolks, and lemon rind with the remaining milk. Stir in the dissolved yeast and enough flour to make a soft dough.

3.   Toss onto a floured board and knead until smooth and elastic (or in a mixer fitted with the dough hook attachment).

4.   Put dough in a greased bowl, cover with a damp towel, and let rise until doubled in bulk.

5.   Punch dough down. Shape, rise, and bake according to the boxed recipes (page 440).

SWEET KUCHEN DOUGH

1 package active dry yeast
2 cups lukewarm (110° F) milk
8 cups flour
1 cup butter, at room temperature

1 cup sugar
4 eggs
1 teaspoon salt
finely grated rind of 1 lemon

1.   Dissolve yeast in the warm milk, add 1 cup of the flour, cover and let sit until doubled in bulk.

2.   Cream the butter, add the sugar and the eggs, one at a time, stirring well after each addition. Add the salt and lemon rind. Stir in the remaining flour

alternately with the yeast mixture and mix well. (If dough is too soft to knead, add more flour as needed.)

3. Toss onto a floured board and knead until smooth and elastic (or in a mixer fitted with the dough hook attachment).

4. Put dough in a greased bowl, cover with a damp towel, and let rise until doubled in bulk.

5. Punch dough down. Shape, rise, and bake according to the boxed recipes (below).

RICH KUCHEN DOUGH

1 package active dry yeast	3 eggs
1¼ cups lukewarm (110° F) milk	1 teaspoon salt
1 cup butter, at room temperature	finely grated rind of 1 lemon
½ cup sugar	4 to 5½ cups flour

1. Dissolve yeast in the warm milk and allow to stand 3 to 5 minutes until tiny bubbles appear on the surface.

2. Cream the butter, add the sugar and the eggs, one at a time, stirring well after each addition. Add the salt and lemon rind. Stir in the flour alternately with the yeast mixture and mix well. (If dough is too soft to knead, add more flour as needed.)

3. Toss onto a floured board and knead until smooth and elastic (or in a mixer fitted with the dough hook attachment).

4. Put dough in a greased bowl, cover with a damp towel, and let rise until doubled in bulk.

5. Punch dough down. Shape, let rise, and bake according to the boxed recipes below.

SHAPING AND BAKING KUCHEN DOUGH

PLAIN COFFEE KUCHEN

Make any desired Kuchen Dough (above). When risen and light, spread dough ½ inch thick in a shallow buttered pan. Cover and let rise again until double in bulk. Before baking, melt 2 tablespoons butter and spread over dough. Sprinkle with sugar, cinnamon, and chopped nuts or with Streusel Crumb Topping, page 450. Preheat oven to 350° F. Bake 15 to 20 minutes until coffee cake sounds hollow when tapped.

CURRANT BUNS

Prepare Kuchen Dough, above, kneading in 1 cup currants. When risen and light, shape into smooth balls. Place close together in lightly greased tin. Brush tops with butter. Cover well. Let rise until fully 2½ times original size. Preheat oven to 400° F. Bake about 20 minutes, until golden brown. Glaze top before removing from oven with ½ cup milk sweetened with 1 tablespoon of sugar. Bake 2 additional minutes.

HOT CROSS BUNS

Prepare like Currant Buns. When half risen in pans, cut two slits in the shape of an X across tops of buns. Let rise until 2½ times original bulk, then bake like Currant Buns. While still warm, fill cross with Confectioners' Sugar Icing, page 597.

KIPFEL (TURNOVERS OR POCKETBOOKS)

Prepare any Kuchen Dough (above) or make Short Pastry (page 521) or Cookie Dough for Oven Pies (page 522). Roll out ¼ inch thick (if using Kuchen Dough wait until after first rising). Cut dough into 3-inch squares. Place 1 tablespoon jam or any desired pie or kuchen filling, pages 448–449, in center of each square. Bring the four corners of each square over the filling and pinch together on top and at corners so that the juice won't escape. Or lightly wet two edges of the squares, fold over to form a three-cornered little pie. Pinch the edges well together. Lay in greased pan and if Kuchen Dough is used, let stand in warm place to rise. Preheat oven to 400° F. Bake about 20 minutes until well done and browned.

KUCHEN TARTS

Roll a piece of any raised Kuchen Dough (above) 1 inch thick on a floured work surface. Cut with biscuit cutter and place close together in a buttered pan. Let rise until very light. Dip fingers in flour and make a cavity in center of each biscuit. Drop in a bit of jelly or preserves. Preheat oven to 400° F. Bake 15 to 20 minutes until lightly browned.

PURIM CAKES (HAMAN POCKETS)

After first rising, roll out any Kuchen Dough (above) to ¼-inch thickness. Cut into 4-inch squares. Brush with oil, spread Poppy Seed Filling (page 449) or Cheese Filling (page 427) on each square. Fold in half diagonally over filling and pinch together to make a three-cornered cake. Brush top with warm honey, let rise until doubled in bulk. Preheat oven to 400° F. Bake about 20 minutes, until golden brown.

BOHEMIAN KOLATCHEN

Make any Kuchen Dough (above). Add a little cinnamon and mace and 1 teaspoon anise seed, well pounded. Let rise until very light, roll out ½ inch thick. Cut in 3-inch rounds, lay on a well buttered pan, pressing down the center of each so as to raise a ridge around the edge. Place 1 tablespoon Prune Filling (page 449) or jam in the center of each cake. Let rise until double in bulk, then brush with stiffly beaten egg white and sprinkle with sugar. Preheat oven to 400° F. Bake for 20 minutes until lightly browned.

BUTTER HORNS

Make any Kuchen Dough (above) and cut into 10 pieces. Roll each piece to a 9-inch round about ¼ inch thick. Brush well with softened butter, then with Pecan Filling (page 609), or with almond paste, softened with sugar and cream. Cut each round in half, each half into equal triangles. Roll from wide end to opposite point. Roll into crescent shape. Place in greased or buttered tin, point side down, let rise again until light, about 2 hours. Preheat oven to 400° F. for 15 to 20 minutes until lightly browned. While warm ice with Confectioners' Sugar Icing (page 597) flavored with almond.

SCHNECKEN (PLAIN CINNAMON ROLLS)

Make any Kuchen Dough (above). When light, roll ¼ inch thick, into an oblong sheet about 9 inches wide. Brush well with melted butter. Sprinkle with sugar, cinnamon, and ½ cup of seedless raisins. Roll up like a jelly roll. Cut into 1-inch slices. Brush sides with melted butter. Place close together, cut side down, in shallow, buttered pan. Brush tops with butter, sprinkle with sugar and cinnamon. Let rise until light. Preheat oven to 400° F. Bake for about 25 minutes until golden brown.

CARAMEL SKILLET ROLLS

Prepare plain Cinnamon Rolls as above. Place 3 tablespoons melted butter in a heavy skillet. Cover with a thick layer of brown sugar, sprinkle with broken pecan meats or sliced almonds. Place rolls, sides brushed with butter, close together, flat side down in pan. Let rise until doubled in size. Preheat oven to 400° F. Bake about ½ hour until browned. Invert pan, remove rolls at once. Serve caramel side up.

YEAST KRANTZ (COFFEE CAKE RING)

Prepare Rich Kuchen Dough (above) and knead in ¼ cup raisins. Let rise in a warm place until doubled in bulk. Divide into 3 or 4 parts. Roll each part into a long strand. Braid the strands. Form in a circle, or twist the braid to resemble the figure 8. Place in greased or buttered baking pan. Let rise again in a warm place until doubled. Preheat oven to 375° F. Bake ½ hour or until well browned. Brush with beaten egg and sugar. Sprinkle with a few chopped almonds. Return to the oven to brown nuts slightly.

PECAN ROLLS

any Kuchen Dough (pages 438–440)
½ cup butter, melted
2 tablespoons sugar
1 teaspoon cinnamon
½ cup raisins

1 cup pecans, coarsely chopped
additional melted butter for
   preparing muffin pans
½ cup honey, warmed
¾ cup brown sugar
whole pecan halves, for garnish

1. After first rising, roll dough into oblong sheet, ¼ inch thick. Spread with melted butter. Sprinkle with sugar, cinnamon, and raisins. Add chopped nuts.

2. Roll up like a jelly roll, pinching outer edge when finished. Cut into 12 slices.

3. Prepare muffin pans by placing 1 teaspoon melted butter and 1 teaspoon warmed honey in bottom of each cup. Cover with 1 tablespoon brown sugar. Press 5 pecan halves, rounded side down, on sugar. Place cut rolls, flat side down, on this. Cover loosely with damp towel and let rise until more than doubled in size.

4. Preheat oven to 400° F. Bake about 15 minutes, then reduce to 325° F for 10 minutes more until well browned. Let cool 1 minute, then remove from pan. Replace any pecans if necessary and let cool, bottom side up.

SHORT-CUT COFFEE CAKE

½ package active dry yeast
¼ cup lukewarm (110° F) water
2 cups sifted flour
¼ cup sugar
3 teaspoons baking powder

¾ teaspoon salt
¼ cup butter, chilled
½ cup milk
1 egg, beaten

1. Dissolve yeast in the warm water and allow to stand 3 to 5 minutes until tiny bubbles appear on the surface.

2. Sift the dry ingredients twice. Cut in the butter until it is as fine as cornmeal.

3. Add the milk and the egg to the dissolved yeast and combine with the flour mixture. Beat well.

4. Let stand in a buttered and floured shallow 8-inch square pan ½ hour.

5. Preheat oven to 350° F. Cover dough with Streusel Crumb Topping (page 450) and bake 30 to 40 minutes.

FILLED WALNUT KIPFEL

5 eggs, separated
½ cup sugar
1 teaspoon vanilla
½ cup cream or milk

1 package active dry yeast
1½ cups butter
4 cups flour
1 recipe Walnut Filling (page 499)

1. Beat the egg whites until stiff. Set aside. Beat together the egg yolks, the sugar, vanilla, and half of the cream or milk.

2. Heat the remaining ¼ cup cream or milk to 110° F and sprinkle the yeast over it. Let sit for 5 minutes to dissolve.

(continued)

3. Cut the butter into the flour with fingertips, two knives, or a food processor.

4. Combine the three mixtures, adding more flour if needed to form a solid dough.

5. Roll the dough quite thin. Cut into small squares. Place a small portion of filling in the middle of each square. Roll, beginning at one corner and form into crescent shapes. Place in pan and frost with the beaten egg whites. Let rise 2 or more hours. Preheat oven to 400° F. Bake for 20 minutes then reduce the heat to 325° F and continue baking 10 more minutes.

KOLATCHEN (SOUR CREAM BUNS)

1 package active dry yeast
¼ cup warm (110° F) water
½ cup butter
5 egg yolks
2 tablespoons sugar
grated rind of 1 lemon

1 cup thick sour cream
3 cups flour
2 egg whites
¼ pound raisins or candied cherries
sugar for sprinkling

1. Sprinkle yeast over warm water. Let sit for 5 minutes or until dissolved.

2. Cream the butter. Add the egg yolks, sugar, lemon rind, sour cream, and the dissolved yeast. When well blended, add the flour and stir just to blend.

3. Drop the mixture from a teaspoon on well-greased pans. Let rise in a warm place until doubled in bulk.

4. Preheat oven to 375° F. Beat the egg whites until stiff. Place a raisin or cherry on the top of each cake and spread with beaten egg whites. Sprinkle with sugar and bake 15 to 20 minutes.

BUNDT KUCHEN

1 package active dry yeast
1 cup lukewarm (110° F) milk
3 cups flour
½ cup butter
1 cup sugar

4 eggs
⅛ teaspoon salt
grated rind of 1 lemon
⅛ teaspoon grated nutmeg
blanched whole almonds

1. Dissolve yeast in the warm milk, add 1 cup of the flour, cover and let sit until doubled in bulk.

2. Cream the butter, add the sugar and the eggs, one at a time, stirring well after each addition. Add the salt, lemon rind, and nutmeg. Add the yeast mixture and stir in the remaining 2 cups flour. Mix well.

3.   Grease a bundt pan with soft butter. Decorate the bottom with blanched almonds. Place the dough in the pan, cover and let rise until almost doubled in size. Preheat oven to 350° F. Bake until done, 45 minutes to 1 hour.

ICEBOX BUNDT KUCHEN WITH ALMOND FILLING

1 package active dry yeast
1 cup lukewarm (110° F) milk
4 cups flour
1 cup butter
½ cup sugar
⅛ teaspoon salt
grated rind of 1 lemon
3 egg yolks

Almond Paste
3 egg whites
¾ cup sugar
1 cup grated (or finely chopped)
   almonds
¾ teaspoon cinnamon

1.   Dissolve yeast in the warm milk, add 1 cup of the flour, cover and let sit until doubled in bulk.

2.   Cream the butter, add the sugar, salt, and lemon rind. Add the egg yolks, one at a time, stirring well after each addition. Beat until very light. Add the yeast mixture alternately with the remaining 3 cups flour. Mix well.

3.   Place dough in a well-greased bowl, cover tightly and store in the refrigerator overnight.

4.   For the filling, beat the egg whites until stiff but not dry. Add the sugar and gently fold in the almonds and cinnamon.

5.   Remove dough from the refrigerator and roll out to ½-inch thickness. Spread with Almond Paste (see below). Roll dough up like a jelly roll, working quickly to keep the dough cool. Place in a greased bundt pan, cover and let rise in a cool place 3 to 4 hours. Preheat oven to 350° F. Bake 1 hour.

SAVARIN

Savarin is a lovely sponge cake drenched in syrup. The cake can be prepared several days in advance, refrigerated, and soaked a few hours before serving.

2 packages active dry yeast
1 cup lukewarm (110° F) milk
4 cups flour
1 cup butter
1 cup sugar
5 eggs
1 teaspoon salt
grated rind of 1 lemon
¼ cup seedless raisins (optional)
1 cup toasted almonds, coarsely
   chopped

Syrup
1 cup sugar
½ cup water
¼ cup rum

1. Dissolve yeast in the milk and allow to stand 3 to 5 minutes until tiny bubbles appear on the surface. Add 1 cup of the flour, cover and let rise until doubled in bulk.

2. Cream the butter and sugar. Add 3 eggs and the yolks of the 2 remaining eggs, one at a time, stirring well after each addition. Add the salt and lemon rind. Stir in the remaining 3 cups flour, the yeast mixture, and the raisins, if desired. Mix well. Beat the egg whites until stiff but not dry, and fold into the dough. Beat until smooth and light.

3. Butter two 10-inch bundt pans, sprinkle each with ½ cup of the almonds. Add the dough, cover loosely with a damp towel, and let rise until nearly to the top of the forms. Preheat oven to 375° F. Bake for 15 minutes, reduce heat to 350° F and bake until done, about 15 minutes more.

4. To make the syrup, boil the sugar with the water for 5 minutes, then add the rum. When the Savarins are done remove them from their pans. Pour syrup into the hot, empty forms, return the cake to the forms and let stand until all the syrup is absorbed. Remove from the forms and baste with any remaining syrup.

Note: If cakes have been done in advance, warm in a 350° F oven for 10 to 15 minutes. Set over cake racks and pour on the syrup.

STOLLEN

 A Christmas specialty, Stollen always makes a good coffee cake no matter what season.

2 packages active dry yeast
2 cups lukewarm (110° F) milk
8½ cups flour
1 pound butter, softened
1 cup sugar
4 whole eggs
1 teaspoon salt
grated rind of 1 lemon

½ teaspoon nutmeg
½ cup candied orange peel, finely chopped
½ cup candied citron, finely chopped
¾ pound raisins
½ pound chopped almonds (optional)
¼ cup rum
melted butter for brushing

1. Dissolve yeast in the milk and allow to stand 3 to 5 minutes until tiny bubbles appear on the surface. Add 1 cup of the flour, cover and let rise until doubled in bulk.

2. Cream the butter and sugar. Add eggs one at a time, stirring well after each addition. Add the salt and lemon rind and combine with the yeast mixture. Stir in 7 cups flour and the nutmeg.

3. Toss onto a floured board and knead until smooth and elastic (or in a mixer fitted with the dough hook attachment). Sprinkle the remaining ½ cup flour over the candied fruit, raisins, and chopped nuts, if using, and add to the dough with the rum.

4. Put dough in a greased bowl, cover with a damp towel, and let rise until doubled in bulk, about 2 hours.

5. Toss dough onto a floured board and divide into 3 or more parts. Roll out slightly and spread the top of the dough with melted butter. Press down the center, and fold over in half. Set on greased and floured baking sheets. Brush melted butter over the tops. Cover loosely with a damp towel and let rise until doubled. Preheat oven to 350° F. Bake about 45 minutes. When cool, cover with Confectioners' Sugar Icing (page 597).

SPICE YEAST CAKE

3 cups flour	½ teaspoon nutmeg
1 package active dry yeast	¼ teaspoon ginger
1 cup brown sugar, firmly packed	1¼ cups milk
1 cup granulated sugar	¼ cup water
1 teaspoon baking soda	1 cup butter
½ teaspoon salt	3 eggs
1 teaspoon cinnamon	

1. In a large mixing bowl, combine all the dry ingredients, including the yeast. Combine the milk, water, and butter and heat to about 120° F. Add the liquid and eggs to the dry ingredients and mix well.

2. Grease the bottom of a 9-by-13-inch cake pan. Pour in the batter, cover with a damp towel, and let rise for 30 minutes. It will not rise much. Preheat oven to 350° F. Bake for 45 to 50 minutes. Remove from pan and cool completely on a rack. Frost with Brown Butter Brandy Frosting (page 600).

Coffee Cake Fillings and Toppings

The following recipes are to be used as fillings and toppings for the preceding doughs. Store-bought almond paste mixtures, prune and apricot fillings, as well as good-quality preserves and jams are all fine, but homemade fillings almost always have much better flavor without the additives, extra sugar, and even salt that are usually contained in such products. Nowadays, frozen bread dough is available in many grocery stores. The following fillings and toppings will turn this convenient item into a special breakfast, brunch, or tea in a hurry.

Note: Use the food processor for chopping nuts and blending toppings.

ALMOND FILLING

3 tablespoons butter	grated rind of ½ lemon
½ cup sugar	1 egg, slightly beaten
½ cup almonds, blanched and finely chopped	

Cream butter and sugar. Add the almonds, lemon rind, and only enough egg to make a stiff paste.

WALNUT FILLING

2 cups finely chopped walnuts ¼ cup syrup or honey
¼ cup sugar

Mix the nuts with the sugar. Add enough syrup or honey to make a paste.

GINGERGBREAD FILLING

5½ cups flour 1 tablespoon baking soda
2 cups molasses 1 cup warm water
2 tablespoons butter or goose fat

Place the flour in a bowl. Add the molasses, butter or goose fat, and soda dissolved in the warm water. Mix well and beat thoroughly about 20 minutes. Preheat oven to 400° F. Pour into buttered bread pans and bake about 1 hour. Will keep for months, covered, in a dry place.

POPPY SEED FILLING

1 cup black poppy seeds 1 tablespoon chopped citron
1 cup milk ½ cup raisins
2 tablespoons butter ¼ cup sugar
5 tablespoons honey or syrup 1 tart apple, grated, or ¼ cup
½ cup chopped almonds   currant or raspberry jelly or jam
grated rind of ½ lemon

Crush poppy seeds with the back of a large knife. Boil with milk and all other ingredients except the apple until thick. If not sweet enough, add more sugar. When cool, add grated apple or the jelly or jam.

PRUNE FILLING

1 pound pitted prunes, boiled 1 tablespoon lemon juice
½ cup sugar

Rub boiled prunes through a colander or sieve. Mix well with any accumulated juices, sugar, and lemon juice. Use to fill turnovers (Kipfel) or coffee cakes or as a filling for two-crust or open-faced pies.

STREUSEL CRUMB TOPPING

½ cup flour
2 to 4 tablespoons butter
5 or 6 tablespoons sugar

½ teaspoon cinnamon
almonds, chopped or pounded

Mix flour, butter, sugar, and cinnamon by rubbing well with the fingertips until small crumbs are formed. Add a few almonds. Sprinkle over any unbaked coffee cake that has been brushed with melted butter.

APRICOT GLAZE

¼ cup sugar
¼ pound dried apricots (preferably unsulphured)

1 cup water

Add sugar to apricots and water. Cook gently until tender and thick. Strain through a fine sieve. Bottle while hot. When ready to use, dilute with water. Use to glaze coffee cakes or to glaze open fruit pies or tarts.

BREADS, QUICK BREADS, BISCUITS, AND MUFFINS

For the beginning cook, the great variety of breads and bread names sometimes causes confusion. In general, yeast breads include all the standard and more exotic types of loaves made with white, whole wheat, rye, and other flours. The basic doughs can be shaped and seasoned to produce a variety of rolls and loaves. The key element is the yeast, which causes the dough to "rise." Quick breads are those using baking powder or soda as a leavening agent instead of yeast. Sweetened quick breads are often known as tea breads and they are generally in loaf rather than ring form. Quick breads also include biscuits, muffins, popovers, corn bread, and spoon bread.

INGREDIENTS

The most basic bread doughs are made from flour, water and salt. Some recipes call for sugar, shortening, and other liquids in place of or in addition to the water.

Flour: Flour is classified as "hard" or "soft" according to the variety of the botanical plant used and the amount of protein contained in each particular strain. The amount of gluten that can be developed as the proteins are worked in a dough is determined by the flour. A high degree of gluten is desired for bread making and a softer, less glutenous variety is desired for making pastries. All-purpose flour is a blend of hard and soft flours uniformly sold throughout the country. This ubiquitous blend comes either "bleached" or "unbleached." Chemicals are added to bleached flour to make it whiter and to increase shelf life. Chemical-free, unbleached flour is increasingly available. Most flour today is sold presifted. Enriched flour is wheat flour that contains added vitamins and minerals.

Some flours specifically called for in this section on bread making are:

Bread Flour: White flour made from hard wheat. The gluten develops easily resulting in an airy but firm-textured bread. Because softer flour has more flavor, some bakers prefer to mix bread flour with a softer one in order to obtain a loaf that has an appealing look with minimum effect on taste.

Whole Wheat and Graham Flour: These two flours are technically the same. When milling white flour, only the endosperm of the wheat is used. In flour ground from the whole kernel, the germ, endosperm, and bran are incorporated.

Rye Flour: Rye is a different grain from wheat that contains only a small amount of gluten. It is usually a good idea to mix rye flour with some wheat flour to make a less dense bread. It can be bought in light, medium, and dark grinds, usually in health-food stores, but increasingly in supermarkets.

Pumpernickel: Also from the rye grain, this flour is ground whole with the bran and germ left in as with whole wheat flour. Most recipes call for mixing it with other, lighter flours for better results.

Salt and Sugar: Sugar, in limited amounts, can quicken the action of the yeast; salt will retard the action.

Shortening: Use butter, margarine, emulsified vegetable shortenings, meat fat, or vegetable oil.

Liquid: Use water, milk, whey, potato or rice water, alone or mixed with water. Liquid should be 110° F before adding yeast.

Potato Water: Helps keep bread moist and hastens the rising. To make 1 cup potato water: wash and peel 1 or 2 potatoes, cover with boiling water, and when thoroughly cooked, drain off and save potato water. Finely mash potato and add to potato water.

Yeast: There are two types used in home baking: compressed fresh or cake yeast, and active dry granulated yeast. Both are living substances and must be activated in warm liquid. One package dry yeast may be used in place of 1 cake of yeast in ¼ cup water that feels warm to the touch (110° F.), usually somewhat warmer than the liquid for cake yeast. Then follow any recipe using yeast. Cake yeast is perishable and must be kept in the refrigerator. Dry yeast will keep for several months on the pantry shelf; check the package for expiration date. One package active dry yeast contains about 1 tablespoon.

MAKING BREAD

To Mix

By Hand: There are several methods of mixing bread dough by hand. For the *straight dough method,* all the flour is added to make a stiff dough. For the *sponge dough method,* a sponge is made first with liquids, yeast, and part of the flour and allowed to rise. The rest of the flour is added later to make a stiff dough.

With an Electric Mixer: Most multipurpose mixers sold today have an attachment called a dough hook that is perfect for kneading. To make bread in a mixer, blend yeast with other dry ingredients using one half of the flour. Heat liquid ingredients and shortening until warm (110° F). Add liquid to dry ingredients, then add egg and blend mixture at low speed until moistened. Add the rest of the flour in small amounts along with other ingredients such as fruits or nuts. Knead dough with the hook attachment as for any other recipe.

In the Food Processor: Unless you have a large-capacity processor, do not attempt to use this machine for making yeast breads. While the processor is useful for small batches, these recipes are for old-fashioned breads that call for larger amounts of flour than most household processors can accommodate. Neither do we suggest tampering with the following recipes to make smaller amounts of dough. The proportions are precise quantities for breads made years ago. To change the amounts would mean changing the integrity of the finished loaf. However, use the processor for the side tasks, like chopping nuts or fruits.

To Proof Yeast

Mix yeast with warm water and allow to stand 3 to 5 minutes to be certain that the yeast is active. A small pinch of sugar will give the live yeast something to feed on and will quicken the action. The small bubbles that appear on the surface are proof that the yeast is active and ready to use. Water temperature for active dry yeast is 110° to 115° F, for compressed yeast 85° F.

To Knead

Toss dough on a floured board. Fold edges of the dough toward the center and press down and away with the palm of your hand, turning dough around and around as you knead until it no longer sticks to your hands or the board. Dough is ready when it is smooth and elastic, full of blisters, and springs back when lightly pressed with the fingers.

To Raise

Place dough in a lightly greased bowl and then flip it over so that all of it is covered with grease. Cover bowl with plastic wrap or a damp towel and let the dough rise at room temperature in a spot free from drafts. When the dough has doubled in size punch it down or shape as directed in recipe or as desired and set it aside to rise again. When your dough has doubled in bulk, gently poke your fingers into it; if the dent remains, the dough is ready.

To Shape

For loaves gently roll out dough like a jelly roll, pinch ends to seal. Place seam side down in a lightly oiled 5-by-9-inch bread or loaf pan (some standard loaf pans measure 4½ inches by 8½ inches). Do not fill pans more than half full. Cover lightly and allow dough to rise almost to top of pan.

Alternatively, free-form shapes can be interesting and creative. Instead of placing in a loaf pan, try working dough into cylinders and then into long and thin "baguettes." Or divide dough into three even coils and braid into an intricate patterned loaf. Scissors and razor blades can be used to form ridges and gashes that will cook into textured edges of golden crust.

To Bake

Most breads bake in a moderately hot oven, 350° to 400° F. To test whether a loaf is done, rap the bottom of it with your knuckle. If it sounds hollow your loaf is done. If not, return it to the oven for another 10 minutes.

When the loaves are done, take them from the oven, and if you have baked your loaves in pans remove them from the pans, and place them on racks to cool. For a soft crust, lightly cover the loaves with a damp towel during cooling.

For the enthusiast, tiles are available in many specialty-food stores that help home ovens recreate the ideal conditions of a professional bread oven. Modify your oven by lining the shelves with these unglazed quarry tiles. Like bricks, they give off radiant heat for even cooking, so conducive to bread baking. Once preheated, you can bake your loaves directly on the tiles.

For even better results, set a wide pan on the oven bottom and fill it with water. The steam this creates will delay formation of the crust during cooking and produce a lighter, fuller loaf. Also try using a plant sprayer to spray the loaves with fresh water as they go into the oven.

Bread

FRENCH BREAD   *Makes 3 loaves.*

Straight Dough Method

1 package active dry yeast
2 cups warm (110° F) water, potato water (page 452), or scalded milk
6 to 6½ cups flour

1 tablespoon salt
1 egg white mixed with 1 teaspoon water, for glazing

1. Dissolve yeast in ¼ cup of the warm liquid and allow to stand 3 to 5 minutes until tiny bubbles appear on the surface.

2. Combine flour and salt. Add half the flour and the remaining liquid to the dissolved yeast and beat well. Gradually add remaining flour.

3. Toss onto a floured board and knead until smooth and elastic (or in a mixer fitted with the dough hook attachment).

4. Put dough in a greased bowl, cover and let rise until doubled in bulk.

5. Punch dough down and divide into 3 equal parts. Shape each piece into a long, narrow loaf. Place loaves on greased cookie sheets, far apart to allow for rising. Using a razor or sharp knife, slash ⅛ inch deep along top of the loaves, lengthwise. Cover with a towel and allow to rise until doubled in bulk.

6. Preheat oven to 400° F. Brush the loaves with the egg white mixed with water and bake 15 minutes, then lower the temperature to 350° F and continue baking until crisp and well browned, about 30 more minutes.

Sponge Method

1 package active dry yeast
1 cup scalded water or potato water (page 452), cooled to warm temperature (110° F)
1 cup scalded milk, cooled to warm temperature (110° F)

6 cups flour
1 tablespoon salt
1 egg white mixed with 1 teaspoon water, for glazing

1. Dissolve yeast in warm water or potato water and allow to stand 3 to 5 minutes until tiny bubbles appear on the surface. Beat in 2 cups of the flour to make a smooth batter, cover and let rise at room temperature until doubled in bulk.

2. Add the warm milk to the sponge and gradually stir in the remaining 4 cups flour and the salt.

3. Toss onto a floured board and knead until smooth and elastic (or in a mixer fitted with the dough hook attachment).

4. Put dough in a greased bowl, cover and let rise until doubled in bulk.

5. Punch dough down and divide into 3 equal parts. Shape each piece into

a long, narrow loaf. Place loaves on greased cookie sheets, far apart to allow for rising. Using a razor or sharp knife, slash ⅛ inch deep along top of the loaves, lengthwise. Cover with a towel and allow to rise until doubled in bulk.

6. Preheat oven to 400° F. Brush the loaves with the egg white mixed with water and bake for 15 minutes, then lower the temperature to 350° F and continue baking until crisp and browned, about 30 minutes.

BASIC WHITE BREAD   *Makes 2 loaves.*

Straight Dough Method

1 package active dry yeast
2 cups warm (110° F) water, potato
    water (page 452), or scalded milk
2 tablespoons shortening
2 tablespoons sugar

1 tablespoon salt
6 to 6½ cups flour
1 egg white mixed with 1 teaspoon
    water, for glazing

1. Sprinkle yeast over 1 cup of the warm liquid and allow to stand 3 to 5 minutes until dissolved and tiny bubbles appear on the surface.

2. Pour the rest of the liquid over the shortening, sugar, and salt. Add half the flour to the dissolved yeast and beat well. Gradually add remaining flour and liquid.

3. Toss onto a floured board and knead until smooth and elastic (or in a mixer fitted with the dough hook attachment).

4. Put dough in a greased bowl, cover and let rise until doubled in bulk.

5. Preheat oven to 350° F. Punch down and shape dough into 2 loaves. Place in prepared pans according to the directions on page 454. Bake for about 45 minutes, or until golden and hollow sounding when tapped. Glaze with egg white mixture while warm.

Sponge Method

1 package active dry yeast
1 cup scalded water or potato
    water, cooled to warm
    temperature (110° F)
1 tablespoon plus 1 teaspoon sugar

6 cups flour
1 cup scalded milk, cooled to warm
    temperature (110° F)
2 tablespoons shortening
1 tablespoon salt

1. Dissolve yeast in warm water with 1 teaspoon sugar and allow to stand 3 to 5 minutes until tiny bubbles appear on the surface. Beat in 2 cups of the flour to make a smooth batter, cover and let rise at room temperature until doubled in bulk.

2. Pour the warm milk over the shortening, salt, and remaining 1 tablespoon sugar. Add to the sponge and gradually stir in the remaining 4 cups flour.

3. Toss onto a floured board and knead until smooth and elastic (or in a mixer fitted with the dough hook attachment).

4. Put dough in a greased bowl, cover and let rise until doubled in bulk.

5. Preheat oven to 350° F. Punch down and shape dough into 2 loaves and place in prepared pans according to the directions on page 454. Bake for about 45 minutes, or until golden and hollow sounding when tapped.

CHALLA (SABBATH TWISTS)   *Makes 2 loaves.*

1 package active dry yeast	2 tablespoons vegetable oil
¼ cup warm (110° F) water	2 eggs, beaten
2 cups hot water	8 cups flour
1 tablespoon salt	1 egg yolk, beaten
1 tablespoon sugar	poppy seeds

1. Dissolve yeast in warm water and allow to stand 3 to 5 minutes until tiny bubbles appear on the surface.

2. In a mixing bowl, pour hot water over the salt, sugar, and vegetable oil. When cooled to lukewarm (110° F), add dissolved yeast, eggs, and gradually beat in the flour.

3. Toss onto a floured board and knead until smooth and elastic (or in a mixer fitted with the dough hook attachment).

4. Put dough in a greased bowl, cover and let rise until doubled in bulk.

5. Punch dough down and divide in half. Cut each half into 4 equal parts and roll each piece 1½ inches thick. Twist 3 lengths into a braid; fasten ends well and place in a floured loaf pan. Repeat with 3 more lengths. Cut each remaining quarter into 3 parts, roll each part ½ inch thick and braid. Lay each braid on top of the loaves in the pans, cover and let rise until doubled in bulk.

6. Preheat oven to 400° F. Brush loaves with beaten egg yolk and sprinkle with poppy seeds. Bake for 15 minutes, reduce heat to 350° F and continue baking until done, about 45 minutes. For a hard crust, cool unwrapped.

BARCHES (RAISIN BREAD)   *Makes 1 oversized loaf or 2 smaller ones.*

1 package active dry yeast	¼ cup raisins
2 cups warm (110° F) milk or water	8 cups flour
⅓ cup butter or fat	½ teaspoon powdered anise
½ cup sugar	1 egg yolk, beaten
1 teaspoon salt	poppy seeds (optional)
1 egg, beaten	

1. Dissolve yeast in ¼ cup of the warm milk or water and allow to stand 3 to 5 minutes until tiny bubbles appear on the surface.

(continued)

2. In a mixing bowl, pour the remaining warm milk or water over butter, sugar, and salt. Add dissolved yeast and the egg. Mix in the raisins, flour, and anise.

3. Toss onto a floured board and knead until smooth and elastic.

4. Put dough in a greased bowl, cover and let rise until doubled in bulk.

5. To form into a large loaf, punch down and divide dough into 4 parts, roll into long strands and with 3 of the strands make a braid. Place in an oversized greased and floured loaf pan. Fold the remaining strand double, twist like a rope and lay lengthwise down the center of the loaf. Cover and let rise until doubled in bulk. To make 2 smaller loaves, begin instead by dividing the dough into eight pieces.

6. Preheat oven to 375° F. Brush with beaten egg yolk and sprinkle with poppy seeds, if desired. Bake 1 hour, until well browned.

MILWAUKEE RYE BREAD   *Makes 3 to 4 loaves.*

1½ cups cold water	1 package active dry yeast
¾ cup cornmeal	¼ cup lukewarm (110° F) water
1½ cups boiling water	2 cups mashed potatoes
1½ tablespoons salt	6 cups rye flour
1 tablespoon sugar	2 cups whole wheat flour
2 tablespoons fat	1 tablespoon caraway seeds

1. Stir the cold water and cornmeal until smooth. Add the boiling water and cook, stirring constantly, for about 2 minutes.

2. Add salt, sugar, and fat and let stand until lukewarm. Dissolve yeast in the ¼ cup lukewarm water. Set aside. To the cornmeal mixture, add potatoes, the dissolved yeast, and then the rye and wheat flours and caraway seeds.

3. Mix and knead to a smooth, stiff dough, using whole wheat flour or cornmeal on the board. Place in a lightly oiled bowl.

4. Cover, set aside in warm place until doubled in bulk. Punch down and shape into 3 or 4 loaves and place in greased pans according to the directions on page 454. Let rise to top of pans.

5. Preheat oven to 375° F. Bake for about 1 hour, until done.

PUMPERNICKEL BREAD   *Makes 3 or 4 loaves.*

1½ cups cold water	1 package active dry yeast
¾ cup cornmeal	¼ cup lukewarm (110° F) water
1½ cups boiling water	2 cups mashed potatoes
1½ tablespoons salt	6 cups medium rye flour
1 tablespoon sugar	2 cups white flour
2 tablespoons fat	1 tablespoon caraway seeds

1. Stir the cold water and cornmeal until smooth. Add the boiling water and cook, stirring constantly for about 2 minutes.

2. Add salt, sugar, and fat and let stand until lukewarm. Dissolve yeast in the ¼ cup lukewarm water. Set aside. To the cornmeal mixture, add potatoes and the dissolved yeast, and then the rye and white flours and caraway seeds.

3. Mix and knead to a smooth, stiff dough, using white flour or cornmeal on the board. Place in a lightly oiled bowl.

4. Cover, set aside in warm place until doubled in bulk. Punch down and shape into 3 or 4 loaves, place in greased pans. Let rise to top of pans.

5. Preheat oven to 375° F. Bake about 1 hour until done.

SOUR DOUGH FOR RYE BREAD

Place 1 cup of rye bread dough (see recipe for Milwaukee Rye Bread, page 458) in a stone crock. Cover and set aside a few days to ferment. Before baking a fresh batch of bread, stir this sour dough down and add ½ cup of it to the lukewarm water in place of fresh yeast. Starter will last for years if kept covered in a cool dry spot and periodically replenished.

NORWEGIAN RYE BREAD   *Makes 2 loaves.*

1 package active dry yeast
¼ cup warm (110° F) water
1 cup graham (whole wheat) flour
¼ cup brown sugar, firmly packed

3 cups rye flour
1 tablespoon salt
hot water

1. Dissolve yeast in the ¼ cup warm water and allow to stand 3 to 5 minutes until tiny bubbles appear on the surface.

2. Combine dry ingredients. Pour in as much hot water as the flour will take up to make a stiff batter. Cover and let stand until lukewarm.

3. Add the dissolved yeast and just enough flour to knead.

4. Put onto a floured board and knead until smooth and elastic (or in a mixer fitted with the dough hook attachment).

5. Put dough in a greased bowl, cover and let rise until doubled in bulk.

6. Punch dough down and shape into 2 loaves according to directions on page 454. Cover and let rise again until doubled in bulk.

7. Preheat oven to 375° F. Bake until done, about 1½ hours.

OATMEAL BREAD   *Makes 3 loaves.*

1 package active dry yeast
¼ cup lukewarm (110° F) water
1½ cups rolled oats
2 teaspoons salt

¼ cup sugar
2 cups boiling water
4½ to 5 cups white flour

1.   Dissolve yeast in the ¼ cup lukewarm water and allow to stand 3 to 5 minutes until tiny bubbles appear on the surface.

2.   In a mixing bowl, combine oats, salt, and sugar. Add boiling water and let stand until lukewarm.

3.   Add the dissolved yeast to the oatmeal mixture and gradually stir in the flour.

4.   Put onto a floured board and knead until smooth and elastic (or in a mixer fitted with the dough hook attachment).

5.   Put dough in a greased bowl, cover and let rise until doubled in bulk.

6.   Punch dough down and shape into 3 loaves according to the directions on page 454. Cover and let rise again until doubled in bulk.

7.   Preheat oven to 350° F. Bake until done, about 45 to 60 minutes.

COMBINATION BREAD   *Makes 4 loaves.*

1 cup rolled oats
1 cup cornmeal
1 tablespoon salt
2 tablespoons sugar
1 tablespoon fat
2 cups boiling water

2 packages active dry yeast
½ cup lukewarm (110° F) water
1 cup rye flour
1 cup whole wheat flour
1¾ cups white flour

1.   In a mixing bowl, combine oats, cornmeal, salt, sugar, and fat. Add boiling water and let stand 1 hour.

2.   Dissolve yeast in the ½ cup warm water and allow to stand 3 to 5 minutes until tiny bubbles appear on the surface.

3.   Add the dissolved yeast to the oat mixture and gradually stir in the flours.

4.   Put onto a floured board and knead until smooth and elastic (or in a mixer fitted with the dough hook attachment).

5.   Put dough in a greased bowl, cover and let rise until doubled in bulk.

6.   Punch dough down and shape into 4 loaves according to the directions on page 454. Cover and let rise again until doubled in bulk.

7.   Preheat oven to 350° F. Bake until done, about 45 minutes.

Rolls

SEMMEL (CRISP ROLLS)   *Makes about 24 rolls.*

1 package active dry yeast
2 cups warm (110° F) water, potato
  water (page 452), or scalded milk
6 to 6½ cups flour

1 tablespoon salt
1 egg white mixed with 1 teaspoon
  water, for glazing

   1. Dissolve yeast in ¼ cup of the warm liquid and allow to stand 3 to 5 minutes until tiny bubbles appear on the surface.

   2. Combine flour and salt. Add half the flour and the remaining liquid to the dissolved yeast and beat well. Gradually add remaining flour.

   3. Toss onto a floured board and knead until smooth and elastic (or in a mixer fitted with the dough hook attachment).

   4. Put dough in a greased bowl, cover and let rise until doubled in bulk.

   5. Punch dough down and cut into small, equal pieces. Knead each piece into a patty 1 inch high and 3 inches in diameter. Set the rolls 2 inches apart on a lightly oiled baking sheet. Cover and let rise slightly, about 20 minutes. Dip the handle of a table knife in flour and press down through the center of each roll lengthwise, rolling the knife back and forth to make a deep crease down the middle of each piece. Cover and let rise again until double in bulk.

   6. Preheat oven to 400° F. Brush the rolls with the egg white mixed with water and bake for 15 minutes, then reduce heat to 350° F and continue baking until crisp and well browned.

BAGELS   *Makes about 24 bagels.*

¼ tablespoon butter, softened
1½ tablespoons sugar
½ teaspoon salt
1 cup scalded milk

1 egg, separated
1 package active dry yeast
3¾ cups flour

   1. In a mixing bowl, combine butter, sugar, and salt. Add milk and cool to lukewarm.

   2. Beat the egg white until soft peaks form. Add the egg white, yeast, and gradually stir in the flour.

   3. Toss onto a floured board and knead until smooth and elastic (or in a mixer fitted with the dough hook attachment).

   4. Put dough in a greased bowl, cover and let rise until doubled in bulk.

5. Punch dough down and cut into small, equal pieces. Roll each piece the width of a finger and twice the length, tapering at the ends. Shape into rings or pretzels, pinching the ends together well. Let stand on a floured board, only until they begin to rise.

6. Fill a large, shallow pan half full of water; when very hot, but not boiling, carefully drop in bagels, one at a time. The bagels should sink and then rise again after a few seconds. Simmer for 1 minute, turning over once. Using a skimmer lift out the bagels and let drain briefly on a paper towel, then place on a thin, greased baking sheet.

7. Preheat oven to 400° F. Brush the tops of the bagels with the beaten egg yolk and sprinkle with onion bits, coarse salt, sesame, caraway, or poppy seeds, if desired. Bake until crisp and golden brown, first on one side then the other, about 25 to 30 minutes altogether.

RYE YEAST ROLLS   *Makes about 24 rolls.*

1½ packages active dry yeast
2 cups warm (110° F) potato water
   (page 452)
4 cups rye flour
2 cups white flour
1 cup cooked, riced potatoes,
   solidly packed

1 egg white beaten with 1 teaspoon
   cold water, for glaze
1 teaspoon caraway seeds
1 tablespoon coarse salt

1. Dissolve yeast in ¼ cup of the potato water and allow to stand 3 to 5 minutes until tiny bubbles appear on the surface.

2. Add the flours and riced potatoes and mix well.

3. Toss onto a floured board and knead until smooth and elastic.

4. Put dough in a greased bowl, cover and let rise until doubled in bulk.

5. Cut and shape into small loaves, 1½ inches wide by 3 inches long. Place far apart on a floured pan, cover and let rise until doubled in bulk.

6. Preheat oven to 400° F. Brush the tops lightly with egg white glaze and sprinkle with a little caraway seeds and a little salt. Bake until brown and crisp, about 25 minutes.

RYE SALT STICK VARIATION

Follow recipe above. After first rising, punch down dough, cut into even pieces and roll shapes the size of a lead pencil. Bake as for above.

ZWIEBACK   *Makes about 12 toasts.*

1 package active dry yeast	3 eggs
½ cup milk, scalded and cooled to lukewarm (110° F)	½ teaspoon salt
¼ cup sugar	½ teaspoon powdered anise
¼ cup butter, melted	flour

   1.   Dissolve yeast in the milk and allow to stand 3 to 5 minutes until tiny bubbles appear on the surface.

   2.   Add the sugar, butter, eggs, salt, anise, and enough flour to handle. Mix well.

   3.   Toss onto a floured board and knead until smooth and elastic.

   4.   Put dough in a greased bowl, cover and let rise until doubled in bulk.

   5.   Divide dough into small equal pieces and shape into 3-inch oblong rolls. Place close together on a buttered baking sheet in rows 2 inches apart. Cover and let rise again until doubled in bulk.

   6.   Preheat oven to 400° F. Bake for 20 minutes. Cool on a rack, and when room temperature cut into ½-inch slices and return to oven until evenly browned on each side.

SHAPING AND BAKING ROLLS

Take any roll recipe made with yeast and, when dough is light, cut in small pieces and shape as follows. For crusty rolls, place far apart on a greased baking sheet. For soft rolls, place closer together. Preheat oven to 450° F. Bake for 15 to 20 minutes or follow the specific instructions below. Remove from oven and brush tops with melted butter.

TEA ROLLS   *Makes about 12 rolls.*

1 package active dry yeast	1½ teaspoons salt
1 cup scalded milk, cooled to lukewarm (110° F)	⅓ cup butter, softened
1½ cups flour	¼ cup sugar
	2 eggs

   1.   Dissolve yeast in the milk and allow to stand 3 to 5 minutes until tiny bubbles appear on the surface.

   2.   Gradually add the flour to the dissolved yeast. Beat thoroughly, cover and allow to stand until light.

   3.   Add salt, butter, sugar, and eggs and stir until well combined.

   4.   Toss onto a floured board and knead until smooth and elastic (or in a mixer fitted with the dough hook attachment).

5. Put dough in a greased bowl, cover and let rise until doubled in bulk.

6. Punch dough down and cut into small, equal pieces. Shape each piece into balls or small finger rolls; place close together on a greased baking sheet, cover and let stand until risen and light.

7. Preheat oven to 400° F. Bake until lightly browned, about 15 minutes.

Notes: For crustier rolls, set far apart on the baking sheet. If desired, brush the tops of the rolls while still hot with ¼ cup confectioners' sugar mixed with 2 tablespoons rum.

POPPY SEED HORNS   *Makes about 24 crescents.*

1 package active dry yeast
2 cups warm (110° F) water, potato
    water (page 452), or scalded milk
2 tablespoons shortening
2 tablespoons sugar
1 tablespoon salt

6 to 6½ cups flour
½ cup butter, melted
1 egg yolk mixed with 1 teaspoon
    cold water, for glazing
poppy seeds

1. Sprinkle yeast over 1 cup of the warm liquid. Let stand 3 to 5 minutes until dissolved and bubbles are beginning to show on the surface.

2. Pour the rest of the liquid over the shortening, sugar, and salt. Add half the flour and the dissolved yeast and beat well. Gradually add remaining flour.

3. Toss onto a floured board and knead until smooth and elastic (or in a mixer fitted with the dough hook attachment).

4. Put dough in a greased bowl, cover and let rise until doubled in bulk.

5. Roll into a round sheet ¼-inch thick. Spread with melted butter, then cut from center to outer edge in wedges like a pie. Beginning at the wide end roll up to the point. Draw ends around into crescents. Place far apart in greased pans, brush tops with egg yolk glaze and sprinkle tops of horns with poppy seeds. Cover loosely with a towel and set aside to rise until doubled in bulk.

6. Preheat oven to 400° F. Bake until brown and crusty, about 20 minutes.

EVER-READY ROLLS

1 package active dry yeast
1¾ cups lukewarm (110° F) milk
2 tablespoons plus 1 teaspoon sugar
1 medium potato, boiled and riced
    while hot

2 tablespoons butter
1 teaspoon salt
4 cups flour

1. Dissolve yeast in ¾ cup of the milk with 1 teaspoon of the sugar and allow to stand 3 to 5 minutes until tiny bubbles appear on the surface.

2. Mix the hot riced potato with the butter, salt, and remaining sugar. Alternately mix in the flour and the remaining 1 cup milk. Stir in the yeast and let rise until very light, doubled in bulk.

3. Toss onto a floured board and knead until smooth and elastic (or in a mixer fitted with the dough hook attachment).

4. Put dough in a greased bowl, cover, and let rise until very light.

5. Shape as desired (see below) and bake 450° F for 12 to 15 minutes.

PARKER HOUSE ROLLS

1 *Makes about 40 to 50 rolls.*

Pat or roll dough ⅓ inch thick and cut into rounds 2½ inches across. Brush well with melted butter. Fold over double so that the edges meet, or dip handle of a knife in flour and make a crease through the middle. Press edges together at the middle to keep the shape. Place in rows close together in greased pans, let stand until slightly raised, then bake in a preheated 450° F. oven 12 to 15 minutes.

2 *Makes about 20 to 25 rolls.*

Roll ¼ inch thin and cut with a 2-inch biscuit cutter. For each roll, stack 2 biscuits, one on top of the other, in a greased pan, and let stand until slightly raised. Brush the tops of each stack lightly with water and sprinkle with sugar. Bake in a preheated 375° F oven until done, about 20 minutes.

PLAIN ROLLS   *Makes about 40 to 50 rolls.*

Roll out 1 inch thick and cut with a biscuit cutter, or cut off small pieces, fold sides under until top of roll is round and smooth. Bake as directed above.

FINGER ROLLS   *Makes about 20 to 25 rolls.*

Roll dough size and shape of finger. Place close together on well-greased pans and brush in between with melted butter. Bake as directed above.

CRESCENT ROLLS   *Makes about 40 to 50 rolls.*

Roll dough ¼ inch thick in round sheets the size of a plate. Spread with melted butter, cut dough in wedges like a pie. Beginning at the wide end roll up to the point. Draw ends around into crescents. Bake as directed above.

LEAFLET ROLLS   *Makes about 24 rolls.*

Pinch off amount of dough desired; roll into an oblong sheet ¼ inch thick and spread well with melted butter. Cut into 8 strips, each strip as wide as the bottom of each muffin cup. Lay one strip on top of the other and cut through the layers to form squares. Alternate the corners of each stack of squares and place one stack of 8 in each muffin cup, with the layers pointing upward. Place in greased muffin tins about 1½ inches deep and 1¾ inches across the bottom. Cover and let rise until light. Bake in a preheated oven at 425° F for 10 to 20 minutes, until well done.

CLOVER LEAF ROLLS   *Makes about 24 rolls.*

Roll dough into 1-inch balls and place 3 in each cup of a greased muffin tin. Brush with melted butter before baking as directed above.

ROSE ROLLS   *Makes about 12 rolls.*

Roll dough into 1-inch balls and place 5 to 7 in each cup of a greased muffin tin. Brush with melted butter before baking as directed above.

BRAIDED ROLLS   *Makes about 12 rolls.*

Roll 3 or 4 pieces of dough each the width of a finger and twice as long. Lay side by side, pinch top ends together and twist into a loose braid. Press bottom ends together. Bake on a baking sheet as directed above.

TWISTS   *Makes about 12 twists.*

Roll the dough into cylinders ½ inch thick and 7 inches long with palm of hand. Hold one end in each hand and twist the ends in opposite directions. Bring the two ends together thus forming a shape like a rope. Bake on greased pans ½ inch apart according to directions above.

Toasts

Toast is made from any sliced bread. Tight-textured, close-grained bread makes the best toast. It should be crisp, freshly made, and uniformly golden brown.

Bread that has been cut into triangles, fingers, or other fancy shapes and toasted can be used for garnishes.

To Toast Bread

In Automatic Toaster: Follow manufacturer's instructions.

Under Broiler: Preheat broiler for 5 minutes. Place bread in pan on rack 2 to 3 inches from source of heat. Brown on one side, turn and continue on other side. Watch carefully, turning the pan often to insure even coloring.

MILK TOAST

2 cups milk
2 teaspoons butter

½ teaspoon salt
4 slices bread (preferably homemade)

1. Heat milk, butter, and salt. Bring just to a boil and remove from heat.
2. Toast bread. Place toast in hot bowl, accompanied by a pitcher of the hot milk. Pour milk over toast and serve immediately.

Variation:
Butter the dry toast, sprinkle with sugar and cinnamon, add ½ teaspoon salt to 1 cup of hot milk, and pour it over the toast. Serve hot.

MELBA TOAST

Cut bread as thin as possible. Preheat oven to 325° F. Arrange in pan, place in oven, and let dry out until crisp. Turn often to insure uniform coloring.

TOASTED BREAD LOAF

Remove crust from top and sides of a small loaf of white bread. With a very sharp knife, cut thin slices down to but not through bottom crust, which is left intact. Spread melted butter between slices, and over top, sides, and ends. Preheat oven to 250° F. Place in pan and toast in oven until golden brown, about 45 minutes. Serve whole.

FRENCH TOAST

2 eggs	⅔ cup milk
½ teaspoon salt	6 slices stale bread

Beat the eggs, salt, and milk slightly. Dip the bread in the mixture. Have a griddle hot and well buttered. Brown the bread on either side. Serve with cinnamon and sugar, powdered sugar, honey, or syrup.

MATZOS À LA FRENCH TOAST

6 eggs	4 matzos (unleavened bread)
½ tablespoon salt	sugar and cinnamon
2 tablespoons fat or olive oil	rind of 1 lemon, grated

Beat eggs until very light, add salt. Heat the fat or olive oil in a skillet. Break the matzos into large, equal pieces. Dip each piece in the egg mixture and fry a light brown on both sides. Serve hot, sprinkled with sugar, cinnamon, and a little grated lemon rind.

CINNAMON TOAST

Quickly toast ¼-inch slices of bread on both sides. Spread with butter, sprinkle with a mixture of ½ cup granulated sugar mixed with 1 teaspoon cinnamon. Broil until sugar melts and forms a crust. Serve hot.

Variations:

Maple Toast: Scrape soft maple sugar and use in place of the sugar and cinnamon.

Butterscotch Toast: Use brown sugar, free from lumps, in place of the granulated sugar.

ORANGE TOAST

6 slices bread	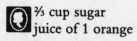 ⅔ cup sugar
butter	juice of 1 orange
grated rind of 1 orange	

1. Toast bread quickly so it will not harden. Butter well.
2. Mix grated orange rind and sugar. Moisten with the juice.
3. Spread mixture on the buttered toast and place under preheated broiler for a few minutes until the coating begins to sizzle. Serve hot.

Quick Breads

Quick breads are so called because they use baking powder rather than yeast as a leavening agent and therefore require no rising time. Virtually all baking powders today are double acting. That means gases are released first on contact with moisture, and then a second time during baking. Baking powder contains alkaline and other chemicals that can leave a bitter aftertaste in baked goods. To make your own, combine 2 teaspoons cream of tartar with 1 teaspoon baking soda; add 1 teaspoon cornstarch if it is to be held on the shelf for an extended period of time.

Some of the breads that follow are served hot, with a meal; others are sliced to be served either warm or cold with butter, cream cheese, or preserves at tea. Many are delicious when served for breakfast, too.

BUTTERMILK BREAD

4 cups flour
¼ teaspoon salt
1 teaspoon sugar
1 teaspoon baking soda

2 teaspoons cream of tartar
1 egg, beaten
1½ cups buttermilk

Preheat oven to 350° F. Sift the dry ingredients, add the egg and buttermilk. Mix well but do not overwork the batter. Place dough in well-buttered loaf pan and bake for about 35 minutes.

BRAN BREAD

4 cups white flour
2 teaspoons salt
4 teaspoons baking soda
4 cups bran flour

1 cup molasses
4 cups milk
chopped nuts and raisins (optional)

Preheat oven to 350° F. Sift together the white flour, salt, and baking soda. Add the bran flour and mix well. Stir in the molasses and milk. Fold in chopped nuts and raisins, if desired. Pour batter into 3 greased loaf pans. Bake for about 1 hour.

CORN BREAD OR CORN STICKS

2 cups yellow cornmeal	2 cups buttermilk
1 teaspoon salt	2 eggs, lightly beaten
1 tablespoon baking powder	2 tablespoons butter, melted

Preheat oven to 425° F. Mix the cornmeal, salt, and baking powder together until blended. Add the buttermilk, eggs, and butter. Stir quickly to combine ingredients. Pour into a square 8-inch greased pan and bake until a toothpick comes clean when pierced in the middle, 30 to 40 minutes. Alternatively, pour batter into hot, greased corn stick molds and bake until golden brown, 15 to 20 minutes.

Variations:

Jalapeño and Cheese: To the above recipe, add 3 small jalapeño peppers that have been halved, seeded, and finely chopped. Stir in 1 cup grated cheddar cheese.

Corn Kernels and Red Pepper: To the above recipe, add 1 medium roasted red pepper (see page 385) cut into small cubes and 1 cup whole kernels of corn.

SOUTHERN SPOON CORN BREAD

1 cup cornmeal	2 eggs, well beaten
2 cups boiling water	1 teaspoon salt
1 tablespoon vegetable shortening, melted	2 cups milk
	2½ teaspoons baking powder

1.   Preheat oven to 350° F. Scald cornmeal with water, stir thoroughly and then cool. Add melted shortening, eggs, salt, and milk. Stir in the baking powder. The batter should be quite thin.

2.   Pour into a greased baking dish and bake from 30 to 40 minutes. Leave in dish and serve with a spoon.

BOSTON BROWN BREAD

1 cup rye flour
1 cup cornmeal
1 cup graham (whole wheat) flour
1 teaspoon salt

2 cups sour milk with ¾ tablespoon baking soda or 1¾ cups sweet milk with 5 teaspoons baking powder
¾ cup molasses

1. Mix and sift rye flour, cornmeal, graham flour, and salt. Add milk and molasses. Stir until well mixed.
2. Fill greased loaf pans or 1-pound food cans ⅔ full. Cover with foil and steam. Large molds should take 2½ hours and small ones, about 1 hour.

To Steam: Place molds on rack inside a large kettle or canning bath that has a tight-fitting lid. Add warm water to half the height of mold. Cover kettle, let water gradually come to boiling point. Boil gently, adding more boiling water when necessary.

BROWN NUT BREAD

1½ cups graham flour (whole wheat flour)
¾ cup white flour
1½ teaspoons baking soda

1½ cups buttermilk
⅓ cup New Orleans (dark) molasses
½ teaspoon salt
¼ cup broken walnuts

Preheat oven to 325° F. Mix flours and baking soda. Add the buttermilk to the molasses then stir in salt. Blend well to make a smooth batter. Fold in nuts. Pour batter into greased loaf pan and bake about 1 hour.

DATE BREAD

1 cup boiling water
1 cup dates, pitted and finely chopped
½ cup white sugar or firmly packed brown sugar
1½ cups flour

1 teaspoon baking powder
1 teaspoon baking soda
1 teaspoon salt
1 egg, beaten
½ cup pecans, coarsely chopped

1. Pour water over dates. Let stand until cool and dates are plumped.
2. Preheat oven to 350° F. Sift together sugar, flour, baking powder, soda, and salt. Combine with the dates and their soaking liquid and mix in the beaten egg.
3. Fold in nuts. Place in buttered loaf pan and bake until toothpick comes clean when pierced in the center, 45 minutes to 1 hour.

PRUNE, DATE, OR RAISIN BREAD

1 cup whole prunes, dates, or
   raisins
2½ cups graham (whole wheat)
   flour
¼ cup sugar
1 teaspoon salt

4 teaspoons baking powder
1 cup milk
1 tablespoon shortening, melted

1. Soak prunes or raisins in cold water for several hours. Drain, remove prune pits, and chop. Chop dates if used.

2. Mix dry ingredients, add milk, and beat well. Add the prunes, dates, or raisins, and melted shortening.

3. Put in greased loaf pan, let stand 25 minutes in warm place. Preheat oven to 350° F and bake for about one hour.

APRICOT NUT BREAD

½ cup dried apricots
1 egg, lightly beaten
1 cup sugar
2 tablespoons butter, melted
2 cups flour
2 teaspoons baking powder

¼ teaspoon baking soda
¾ teaspoon salt
½ cup orange juice
¼ cup water
1 cup chopped Brazil nuts

1. Preheat oven to 350° F. Wash and coarsely chop apricots. Beat egg until light, stir in sugar and mix well. Stir in butter.

2. Sift flour with baking powder, soda, and salt. Add alternately with the orange juice and water to the sugar mixture. Add Brazil nuts and apricots. Mix well.

3. Pour into a buttered loaf pan. Bake until toothpick comes clean when pierced in the center, about 1 hour.

ORANGE AND NUT BREAD

2 cups white flour
2 cups whole wheat flour
4 teaspoons baking powder
2 teaspoons salt
½ cup sugar

½ cup candied orange peel
½ cup finely chopped pecans
2 cups milk
1 egg, well beaten

1. Preheat oven to 350° F. Mix together flours, baking powder, salt, and sugar. Add orange peel and nuts.

2. Add milk to eggs and combine with the dry ingredients. Stir until smooth, then beat well.

3. Pour into two shallow buttered loaf pans (about 8 inches by 4 inches). Bake about 45 minutes.

BANANA BREAD

2 cups sifted flour	½ cup sugar
2 teaspoons baking powder	2 eggs
½ teaspoon baking soda	2 medium-size ripe bananas,
½ teaspoon salt	mashed with a fork
¼ cup butter	½ cup buttermilk

1. Preheat oven to 350° F. Sift flour, baking powder, soda, and salt three times.

2. Cream butter and sugar, add eggs one at a time.

3. Add bananas to the buttermilk and mix alternately with the flour mixture and the butter mixture.

4. When well blended, pour into a greased loaf pan. Bake about 45 minutes.

PUMPKIN BREAD

3 cups sifted all-purpose flour	1 cup vegetable oil
½ teaspoon baking powder	3 eggs
1 teaspoon baking soda	1 16-ounce can pumpkin (or 2 cups
1 teaspoon ground nutmeg	fresh pumpkin, boiled and
1 teaspoon ground cloves	pureed)
1 teaspoon ground cinnamon	1 cup coarsely chopped dark
½ teaspoon salt	seedless raisins
3 cups sugar	½ cup chopped walnuts

1. Preheat oven to 350° F. Butter a 10-inch fluted, tube baking pan with butter or vegetable shortening and dust lightly with flour.

2. In a medium-size bowl sift together flour, baking powder, baking soda, nutmeg, cloves, cinnamon, and salt.

3. In a large mixing bowl, place sugar, oil, and eggs. Stir until well blended. Stir pumpkin into egg mixture.

(continued)

4. Gradually add sifted dry ingredients to egg mixture, stirring well after each addition. Fold in raisins and nuts.

5. Pour batter into prepared pan and bake until a toothpick inserted into center comes out clean when pierced in the center, about 1 hour and 15 minutes. Cool on a wire rack for 10 minutes before removing from pan. Then cool completely on a rack.

6 oz = 1 cup zucchini = 1 zucchini

ZUCCHINI BREAD

3 cups flour *1½*   2 cups sugar *1¾ c*
1 teaspoon salt *½*   1 cup oil *½*
1 teaspoon baking soda *½*   2 cups grated raw zucchini *1*
¼ teaspoon baking powder *1¼*   2 teaspoons vanilla *1½*
2 teaspoons cinnamon *½*   1 cup chopped walnuts *½*
3 eggs *2*   *375°*

1. Preheat oven to 350° F. Combine flour, salt, baking soda, baking powder, and cinnamon. *SMALLER BOWL*

2. Beat eggs until light. Stir in sugar, oil, zucchini, and vanilla. Add dry ingredients and then the nuts. Pour into 2 small buttered loaf pans. Bake for about ~~1 hour.~~

LARGER BOWL

50" cover w/ damp towel while cooling

Baking Powder Biscuits

It is important to remember that when making biscuits all measurements must be level. That is to say, that flour should be scooped up with a measuring cup, filled and the top leveled off with the back of a knife. Most flour is presifted these days. Check the package and if not marked as such, sift the flour with the other dry ingredients. Sifting is used to insure proper blending in many of the following recipes. Work butter or other fat into flour with a fork, with two knives, a pastry blender, or a food processor.

Preheat oven well before baking. Most biscuit doughs do best when cooked in a hot oven (450° F) immediately after mixing. Be sure that the baking sheet is greased before beginning. When baked, turn them out onto racks and let them cool for 20 to 30 minutes.

BISCUIT BATTERS AND DOUGHS

When a flour mixture is moistened stiff enough to knead, it is called a *dough*. If thin enough to be beaten, it is called a *batter*.

Pour Batter: 1 measure of liquid to 1 measure of flour as in griddle cakes (page 420). Batter may be stirred and beaten with a spoon.

Drop Batter: 1 measure of liquid to 2 measures of flour as in muffins or cake.

Soft Dough: 1 cup of liquid to 3 cups of flour makes a soft dough that can be kneaded. Mix thoroughly with a knife.

Stiff Dough: 1 cup liquid to 4 cups of flour makes a stiff dough that can then be rolled thin.

BAKING POWDER BISCUITS *Makes about 24 1½-inch biscuits.*

2 cups flour
4 teaspoons baking powder
1 teaspoon salt

2½ tablespoons shortening
¾ cup milk or water

1. Preheat oven to 450° F. Sift together the dry ingredients. Work the shortening into flour mixture with a fork or tips of fingers. Make a well in the center. Into this pour the milk all at once. Stir well for 20 seconds until all the flour is moistened. Alternatively, place the dry ingredients in the bowl of a food processor fitted with the metal blade. Cut in the shortening with several quick pulses. Do not overwork. Pour the milk in with the blade in motion. Process just until the mixture forms a solid dough.
2. Quickly toss on a floured board. Knead gently for 20 seconds, pat or roll until ½ inch thick. Cut into rounds, place in pan, and bake until golden brown, 10 to 15 minutes. Turn out onto racks and cool.

Note: For best results use as little flour as possible on the board when shaping the dough.

DROP BISCUITS

Follow recipe for Baking Powder Biscuits, above, increasing the milk to 1 cup for a softer dough. Drop by spoonfuls on greased pan or in muffin pan, and bake until golden brown, 10 to 15 minutes.

Sandwich Biscuits Preheat oven to 475° F. Roll Baking Powder Biscuit dough, above, ¼ inch thick and cut with a small biscuit cutter. Spread half the rounds with creamed butter and top with any chopped meat. Cover with remaining rounds. Press together and brush tops and sides with milk. Bake 10 to 12 minutes.

New England Tea Biscuits Preheat oven to 400° F. Follow the recipe for Baking Powder Biscuits, above, doubling the amount of shortening. Press a sugar cube dipped in orange juice or orange marmalade on top of each biscuit. Bake 10 to 15 minutes.

SOUR CREAM OR SODA BISCUITS   *Makes about 24 1½-inch biscuits.*

2 cups flour
½ teaspoon soda
1 tablespoon baking powder

½ teaspoon salt
2 tablespoons butter
¾ cup sour cream

1.   Preheat oven to 400° F. Sift together dry ingredients. Work in the butter with a fork, add sour cream quickly to make a soft dough.
2.   Pat, roll out, and cut into biscuits or drop by spoonfuls on greased pan or in muffin pan. Bake for 15 to 20 minutes.

BISCUIT DOUGH FOR SHORTCAKE   *Makes about 6 4-inch biscuits or 2 8-inch biscuits.*

2 cups flour
4 teaspoons baking powder
½ teaspoon salt

2 tablespoons sugar
½ cup shortening
¾ cup milk

1.   Preheat oven to 450° F. Mix together flour, baking powder, salt, and sugar. Work in shortening with a fork, pastry blender, or in a food processor. Add milk all at once and quickly blend.
2.   Toss on floured board. Pat, roll out, and cut with large (4 inch) biscuit cutter or roll to fit two 8-inch round cake pans and bake until golden brown, 12 to 15 minutes. Split biscuits and fill with crushed, sweetened fruit or berries and top with whipped or plain heavy cream.

BRAN BISCUITS   *Makes about 24 1½-inch biscuits.*

1 cup white flour	1 cup bran flour
1 tablespoon baking powder	2 tablespoons shortening
½ teaspoon salt	¾ cup milk

    1. Preheat oven to 450° F. Mix and sift the white flour, baking powder, and salt. Add the bran flour, work in the shortening with knife, fork, pastry blender, or food processor. Add milk, mixing quickly until you have a soft dough.

    2. Toss lightly on a floured board until smooth and roll out to ½-inch thickness. Cut with a biscuit cutter. Place in a buttered pan and bake 12 to 15 minutes.

POTATO BISCUITS   *Makes about 12 1½-inch biscuits.*

1 cup flour	2 tablespoons shortening
1 tablespoon baking powder	1 cup mashed potatoes
1 teaspoon salt	½ cup water or milk

    1. Preheat oven to 400° F. Sift together dry ingredients. Work in the shortening with knife, fork, or pastry blender. Add potato and mix thoroughly. Add liquid, mixing quickly until you have a soft dough.

    2. Roll out lightly to ½-inch thickness. Cut with a biscuit cutter. Place on a buttered pan and bake 12 to 15 minutes.

SWEET POTATO BISCUITS   *Makes about 12 1½-inch biscuits.*

1¼ cups flour	¾ cup mashed sweet potato
4 teaspoons baking powder	⅔ cup milk
1 tablespoon sugar	4 tablespoons butter, melted
½ teaspoon salt	

    1. Preheat oven to 450° F. Sift together dry ingredients. Combine the sweet potato, milk, and melted butter and mix well with dry ingredients to make a soft dough.

    2. Drop batter into greased muffin pans. Or knead lightly on a floured board, until smooth, roll out to ½-inch thickness, and cut with a biscuit cutter. Place on a buttered pan. Bake 12 to 15 minutes.

CHEESE BISCUITS   *Makes about 24 1½-inch biscuits.*

2 cups flour	2 tablespoons butter
4 teaspoons baking powder	¾ to 1 cup milk
1 teaspoon salt	¾ cup grated cheddar cheese

1. Preheat oven to 450° F. Sift dry ingredients together. Work in the butter with knife, fork, pastry blender, or food processor. Add milk, mixing quickly, and stir in the cheese.

2. Toss lightly on a floured board until smooth and roll out to ½-inch thickness. Cut with a biscuit cutter. Place on a buttered pan and bake 12 to 15 minutes. Or, roll out dough, dot with butter, and sprinkle with additional grated cheese. Roll up as for a jelly roll, cut into 1-inch slices, and bake cut side down.

RYE BISCUITS   *Makes about 12 biscuits.*

4 cups rye flour	1 tablespoon shortening, melted
1 teaspoon salt	1 egg white mixed with 1
2 tablespoons baking powder	tablespoon cold water
1½ cups milk or water	1 tablespoon caraway seeds

1. Sift together dry ingredients. Combine the milk or water and melted shortening and mix well with dry ingredients to make a soft dough.

2. Knead lightly on a floured board until smooth and shape into rolls 1¼ inches thick by 2½ inches long. Place on a buttered pan 2 inches apart, brush tops with egg white glaze and sprinkle with caraway seeds. Cover lightly with a towel and let stand in a warm place for 30 minutes. Meanwhile, preheat oven to 450° F. Bake for 12 to 15 minutes.

Muffins and Popovers

Here are the two ways to mix the following muffin batters:

Dry Method: Mix dry ingredients. Slightly beat the eggs and add milk and melted shortening. Combine wet and dry ingredients as quickly as possible only until the dry ingredients are moistened.

Cake Method: Mix dry ingredients. Cream butter and sugar, add eggs and beat well. Alternately stir in the flour and the milk, always starting and finishing with the flour.

The crumb of the dry-method muffin will be crispier and "short." The cake method will yield a coarser, larger-crumb muffin.

Let muffins cool slightly (about 5 minutes) then turn out onto racks to cool.

BASIC MUFFINS   *Makes about 24 2-inch muffins.*

2 cups flour
½ teaspoon salt
4 teaspoons baking powder
2 tablespoons sugar

1 cup milk
1 egg
3 tablespoons butter, melted

1. Preheat oven to 450° F. Sift together dry ingredients. Mix milk, egg, and butter. Combine wet and dry ingredients quickly, only until flour is moistened.
2. Pour into greased muffin tins. Bake 15 to 20 minutes.

Variations:

Cornmeal, rye, or whole wheat muffins can be made the same way, by mixing ¼ to ½ the quantity of cornmeal, rye, or whole wheat flour with the white flour.

BRAN MUFFINS   *Makes about 24 2-inch muffins.*

2 tablespoons butter or shortening
¼ cup sugar or dark molasses
1 egg, slightly beaten
1 cup bran

¾ cup milk
1 cup flour
2½ teaspoons baking powder
¼ teaspoon salt

1. Cream butter or shortening with sugar or molasses. Add the egg, bran, and milk. Let stand until most of the moisture is absorbed.
2. Preheat oven to 400° F. Stir in flour, baking powder, and salt. Bake in buttered muffin tins until a toothpick comes out clean when inserted in the center, 20 to 30 minutes. Leave in pan for 5 minutes, remove and cool on wire rack.

SOUR CREAM MUFFINS   *Makes about 24 2-inch muffins.*

1¾ cups flour
2 teaspoons baking powder
2 tablespoons sugar
½ teaspoon salt

1 egg, well beaten
1 cup sour cream
½ teaspoon baking soda mixed with
    1 tablespoon water

(continued)

1. Preheat oven to 450° F. Sift together dry ingredients. Combine egg, sour cream, and baking soda mixed with water. Combine wet and dry ingredients quickly, only until flour is moistened.

2. Pour into greased muffin tins. Bake 15 to 20 minutes.

SALLY LUNN (HOT BREAD)   *Makes about 24 2-inch muffins.*

¼ cup butter	4 teaspoons baking powder
⅓ cup sugar	1 teaspoon salt
2 eggs, separated	¾ cup milk
2 cups bread flour	

1. Preheat oven to 400° F. Cream the butter and sugar. Beat until light and fluffy. Drop the unbeaten egg yolks into the mixture and beat until thick and lemon colored. Sift together dry ingredients and add to the butter mixture, alternately with the milk, starting and finishing with the flour. Stiffly beat the egg whites and fold in.

2. Pour into greased muffin tins. Bake about 25 minutes.

HONEY AND NUT BRAN MUFFINS   *Makes about 24 2-inch muffins.*

1 cup flour	1 tablespoon butter, melted
½ teaspoon baking soda	1½ cups milk
½ teaspoon salt	½ cup honey
2 cups bran	¾ cup finely chopped walnuts

1. Preheat oven to 425° F. Combine dry ingredients. Mix together butter, milk, and honey. Stir wet and dry ingredients quickly, only until flour is moistened. Fold in nuts.

2. Pour into greased muffin tins. Bake 25 to 30 minutes.

WHOLE WHEAT MUFFINS   *Makes about 12 to 15 2-inch muffins.*

½ cup white flour	3½ teaspoons baking powder
1 cup whole wheat flour	1 egg, well beaten
¼ teaspoon salt	¾ cup milk

1. Preheat oven to 425° F. Sift together the flours and discard any bran left in the sifter. Sift again with the salt and baking powder. Mix egg and milk

together. Combine wet and dry ingredients quickly, only until flour is moistened.

2. Pour into greased muffin tins. Bake 25 to 30 minutes.

BLUEBERRY MUFFINS   *Makes about 24 2-inch muffins.*

2 cups flour
1 cup blueberries, washed and
    drained
¼ cup butter
¼ cup sugar

1 egg, well beaten
½ teaspoon salt
4 teaspoons baking powder
1 cup milk

375°/1doz *½*

1. Mix ¼ cup of the flour with the blueberries and let stand for 1 hour.
2. Preheat oven to 425° F. Cream the butter and sugar. Beat until light and fluffy. Add the egg. Sift together remaining flour, salt, and baking powder and add to the butter mixture, alternately with the milk, starting and finishing with the flour. Fold in the floured berries last.
3. Pour into greased muffin tins. Bake about 20 to 25 minutes.

check them with toothpick

Variations:

Cranberry-Orange Muffins: Substitute 1 cup of cranberries for blueberries in the above recipe. Add 1 tablespoon finely grated orange zest and 1 tablespoon orange juice to the butter and sugar and proceed as above.

Banana-Pecan Muffins: Add 2 large ripe bananas and 1 tablespoon lemon juice to the butter and sugar in the above recipe. Fold in ½ cup toasted and coarsely chopped pecans and omit blueberries.

POTATO FLOUR MUFFINS   *Makes about 12 to 15 2-inch muffins.*

4 eggs, separated
¼ teaspoon salt
1 tablespoon sugar

½ cup white potato flour
1 teaspoon baking powder
2 tablespoons ice water

1. Preheat oven to 400° F. Beat egg whites until stiff; beat egg yolks lightly. Add salt and sugar to the beaten yolks and fold in the whites. Sift flour and baking powder twice and beat thoroughly into the eggs. Add the ice water.
2. Pour into greased muffin tins. Bake about 15 to 20 minutes. These are best served warm.

APPLE MUFFINS   *Makes 12 3- to 4-inch muffins or 24 2-inch muffins.*

2 cups flour	1 cup finely chopped apples
¾ teaspoon salt	1 egg, well beaten
4 tablespoons sugar	½ cup milk
2 teaspoons baking powder	12 apple slices
2 tablespoons butter	½ teaspoon cinnamon

1.   Preheat oven to 400° F. Combine flour, salt, 2 tablespoons of the sugar, and the baking powder. Cut in the butter with a fork, add chopped apples and mix. Combine the egg and milk and mix the wet and dry ingredients quickly, only until flour is moistened.

2.   Drop by spoonfuls into 12 greased muffin tins. Place 1 slice of apple on each muffin. Mix remaining sugar with the cinnamon and sprinkle over the tops of the muffins. Bake about 20 minutes.

SCOTCH SCONES   *Makes about 12 to 15 scones.*

1 teaspoon cream of tartar	½ teaspoon salt
2 cups flour	¼ cup lard or butter
½ teaspoon baking soda	½ cup buttermilk

1.   Sift together dry ingredients. Cut in lard or butter. Make a well in the center of the flour and pour in the buttermilk to form a soft dough. Mix thoroughly.

2.   Roll out to ½ inch thick, cut into squares, and bake on a hot griddle, browning both sides. Serve hot or cold.

CORN PONES OR DODGERS   *Makes about 12 to 24 cakes.*

2 cups cornmeal	2 teaspoons fat
1 teaspoon salt	1¾ cups boiling water

1.   Combine cornmeal, salt, and fat. Add the boiling water. Beat well. Preheat oven to 400° F.

2.   When cool, form into thin cakes and bake until crisp, about 30 minutes. Serve with butter or gravy.

POPOVERS   *Makes 9 to 10 popovers.*

1 cup flour	1 cup milk
¼ teaspoon salt	1 tablespoon butter, melted
2 eggs	

1.   Preheat oven to 450° F. Sift flour and salt into a bowl. Beat eggs, add milk, butter, and add flour and salt. Beat only enough to make a smooth batter.

2.   Fill hot, greased popover pans or muffin pans one third full of the mixture. Bake for 30 minutes, then lower heat to 350° F and continue baking for 15 minutes or until firm, brown, and raised or popped.

Note: Keep oven door closed during the first 30 minutes of baking.

CHEESE POPOVERS   *Makes 9 to 10 popovers.*

1 egg	1 cup flour
¼ teaspoon salt	¼ pound cheddar cheese, grated
1 cup milk	

1.   Preheat oven to 450° F. Beat the egg slightly with the salt and milk. Stir gradually into flour to make a smooth batter. Beat until full of air bubbles.

2.   Have popover or muffin pans hot and well greased. Into each, drop a rounded teaspoon of this batter. Spread with a teaspoon of cheese and cover with another teaspoon of batter.

3.   Bake for 20 minutes, reduce heat to 350° and bake 20 minutes until brown, crisp, and popped over.

IRISH POTATO CAKES   *Makes about 24 squares.*

2 cups flour	1 teaspoon caraway seeds
4 teaspoons baking powder	2 cups mashed potatoes
1 teaspoon salt	½ cup milk
1 tablespoon butter	

1.   Mix together the flour, baking powder, and salt. Cut in the butter. Add the caraway seeds, the mashed potatoes, and the milk.

2.   Roll out to about ¼-inch thickness and cut into squares.

3.   Brown slowly in a small amount of fat in a heavy skillet over moderate heat. Split and serve with butter.

COOKIES

A *full cookie jar is a sign of a hospitable household—and great-tasting homemade cookies may range from the plainest sugar cookie to the most elaborate filled bar.*

Certain basic rules and techniques apply to all cookie baking. First, follow recipes accurately. Unless otherwise directed, always grease cookie sheets lightly. It is more efficient to work with two or more large shallow pans, so that some of the cookies can be in the oven while others are being arranged on the extra baking sheets. Remove the baked cookies to a rack to cool.

Wipe the baking sheet with a paper towel, grease again, and begin to shape the next batch.

The baking times given for these cookies are offered as guidelines. Remember that it is important not to overbake cookies. Soft cookies are done when they are firm and spring back from the pressure of a finger. Crisp cookies are done when they are very lightly and evenly browned. Learn to know your oven by using. Use an oven thermometer to insure accuracy.

Cookies keep very well if they are properly packed: soft cookies should be stored in an airtight container, and crisp cookies in a jar that permits air to enter. Between each layer of cookies, use waxed paper to keep tops from sticking to bottoms. If the crisp cookies become soft, they may be recrisped in the oven. A piece of apple or potato packed with soft cookies helps to keep them moist and chewy.

The food processor can be useful when making cookies. Learn how to work in short, quick pulses when blending ingredients. Cookies can become tough as gluten develops as a result of overworking the dough. The processor is especially handy for grinding nuts when you want them finely chopped. Adding a spoonful of sugar to the nuts will help prevent them from becoming too oily.

While we don't encourage baking in the microwave, it is a convenient way to melt butter, chocolate, or to make simple syrups and certain glazes. Follow manufacturer's instructions for specifics concerning your particular machine.

Virtually all of these recipes for cookies are heirloom. Rather than add new recipes, we've re-worked them to make the best possible use of modern equipment.

Rolled Cookies

Cookie dough that is to be rolled out should be well chilled for easier handling. This varies according to the amount of dough. Two hours is a good rule of thumb. When in doubt, err on the side of overchilling rather than not chilling enough. A soft dough is hard to work with and will result in a tough cookie. When the dough is too soft from being warm, it is necessary to add more flour to make a stiffer dough, and this results in a tough cookie, too. Begin by dusting a rolling pin with flour and roll the chilled dough out on a lightly floured board, half or one third at a time. Do not overwork the dough. Work quickly to insure as little handling as possible. Remember the thinner you roll the dough the crisper the cookie. Soft cookies are always the thickest. Use a floured knife to cut the dough into squares, diamonds, or bars, or cut fancy shapes with a floured cookie cutter. Try to cut the cookies as closely together as you can to get the most cookies from your dough. The trimmings may be rerolled, but they are not as delicate. Design your own cookie shapes from patterns cut from cardboard. Lay the cardboard pattern on the dough and cut around it with a sharp, floured knife.

ALMOND STICKS   *Makes 12 to 15 sticks.*

1 cup butter	2 cups almonds, finely chopped
1 cup sugar	1 teaspoon finely grated lemon rind
2 eggs plus 1 yolk	2 cups flour

1. Cream the butter until light. Add ¾ cup of the sugar, the 2 eggs, all but ¼ cup of the almonds, the lemon rind, and flour and mix until all the ingredients are thoroughly combined. Gather the dough together in one lump, cover in plastic wrap, and chill for 2 hours.

2. Preheat oven to 350° F. On a lightly floured board, roll out ½ of the dough at a time to a sheet ⅛ inch thick. Cut into strips ¾ inch wide and 4 inches long. Lightly beat the egg yolk and brush it on the tops of the cookies. Sprinkle with the remaining ¼ cup each sugar and almonds.

3. Place about 1 inch apart on greased cookie sheets and bake for 10 to 12 minutes.

MUERBE (BASIC BUTTER COOKIES)   *Makes about 80 small cookies.*

1 pound butter	2 tablespoons lemon juice or brandy
1¼ cups sugar	6 cups flour
2 eggs, separated	1 teaspoon baking powder
½ teaspoon finely grated lemon rind	1 cup almonds, finely chopped

1. Cream butter, add 1 cup of the sugar and beat until light. Lightly beat the egg yolks and add along with the lemon rind, lemon juice or brandy, and the flour mixed with the baking powder. Mix until all the ingredients are well combined. Gather the dough together in one lump, cover in plastic wrap, and chill for 2 hours.

2. Preheat oven to 350° F. On a lightly floured board, roll out ½ of the dough at a time to a sheet ⅛ inch thick. Cut into desired shapes. Lightly beat the egg whites and brush on the tops of the cookies. Sprinkle with the remaining ¼ cup sugar and the almonds.

3. Bake on greased cookie sheets for 10 to 15 minutes.

<u>Variation:</u>

Filled Crescents:

½ recipe Muerbe (see above)
1 pound seedless raisins, chopped
1-inch slice citron, chopped
½ teaspoon finely grated lemon rind
¼ teaspoon mace

½ pound unblanched almonds, coarsely chopped
½ cup butter, melted
Ginger Snaps, crushed (page 491)
brandy, to taste

Prepare the Muerbe dough. Roll out as in Step 2, above, and cut the cookies into 2-inch rounds. Mix together the remaining ingredients and place 1 teaspoon filling in the center of each cookie and fold in half to form crescents. Pinch edges together tightly to seal. Brush lightly with slightly beaten egg yolk instead of egg whites. Omit the sugar and almonds for sprinkling. Bake as above.

MERINGUE-TOPPED BUTTER COOKIES   *Makes about 60 small cookies.*

2 cups flour
1 teaspoon baking powder
1 cup butter
4 eggs, separated
1 cup sugar

½ pound blanched almonds, finely chopped
1 teaspoon finely grated lemon rind
1 tablespoon fresh lemon juice
confectioners' sugar, for dusting

1. Sift together flour and baking powder and set aside. Cream the butter and egg yolks and mix in the flour. Gather the dough together in one lump, cover with plastic wrap, and chill for 2 hours.

2. Preheat oven to 350° F. On a lightly floured board, roll out ½ of the dough at a time to a sheet ⅛ inch thick and cut into rounds.

3. Beat the egg whites until frothy. Gradually add the sugar and continue beating until the whites hold soft peaks. Fold in the almonds, grated lemon rind and juice, and carefully cover the cookies with this meringue.

4. Bake on greased cookie sheets 15 minutes. Cool on racks and dust lightly with confectioners' sugar.

CARDAMOM COOKIES   *Makes about 100 small cookies.*

1 cup butter	4 cups flour
1 cup sugar	1 teaspoon cardamom seeds,
2 eggs	crushed
	1 teaspoon finely grated lemon rind

1. Cream butter and sugar until light. Mix in the other ingredients and beat until well combined. Gather the dough together in one lump, cover with plastic wrap, and chill for 2 hours.

2. Preheat oven to 400° F. On a lightly floured board, roll out ½ of the dough at a time to a sheet ⅛ inch thick and cut into rounds.

3. Bake on greased cookie sheets for 10 to 12 minutes.

BASIC CHOCOLATE COOKIES   *Makes about 40 small cookies.*

2½ cups flour	¼ teaspoon salt
2 teaspoons baking powder	2 ounces unsweetened chocolate,
½ cup butter	melted
1½ cups sugar	¼ cup milk
1 egg, well beaten	

1. Sift together flour and baking powder and reserve. Cream butter and sugar until light. Add egg, salt, and chocolate and beat well. Alternately mix the sifted ingredients and the milk into the butter mixture. Beat until thoroughly combined. Gather the dough together in one lump, cover with plastic wrap, and chill for 2 hours.

2. Preheat oven to 350° F. On a lightly floured board, roll out ½ of the dough at a time to a sheet ⅛ inch thick and cut into shapes with a small cookie cutter.

3. Bake on greased cookie sheets for 10 minutes.

CHOCOLATE ALMOND COOKIES   *Makes about 80 small cookies.*

½ pound sweet chocolate	¼ teaspoon cloves
¼ pound unblanched almonds	3 tablespoons milk
1¼ cups sugar	4 cups flour
1 cup butter	1 teaspoon baking powder
2 eggs plus 1 egg white	sugar for sprinkling (optional)
½ teaspoon cinnamon	

1. In the workbowl of a food processor, coarsely grind the chocolate and the almonds with ¼ cup of the sugar and reserve.

(continued)

2. Cream the butter with the remaining 1 cup sugar. Add the whole eggs one at a time. Blend in the spices, milk, flour, and baking powder. Add the chocolate and almonds. Mix well. Gather the dough together in one lump, cover with plastic wrap and chill for 2 hours.

3. Preheat oven to 350° F. On a lightly floured board, roll out ½ of the dough at a time to a sheet ⅛ inch thick and cut into shapes with a small cookie cutter. Lightly beat the egg white and brush on top of the cookies. Sprinkle lightly with additional sugar if desired.

4. Bake on greased cookie sheets for 10 minutes.

CHOCOLATE LEMON COOKIES   *Makes about 40 small cookies.*

1 cup butter
2 cups flour
3 eggs
½ pound sweet chocolate, coarsely chopped

1 cup sugar
1 teaspoon finely grated lemon rind
½ teaspoon vanilla
1 cup almond halves

1. Cream the butter, add the flour and blend well. Beat in 2 of the eggs, chocolate, sugar, lemon rind, and vanilla and mix until thoroughly combined. Gather the dough together in one lump, cover with plastic wrap, and chill for 2 hours.

2. Preheat oven to 350° F. On a lightly floured board, working quickly with just a small amount of dough at a time, roll out to a sheet ⅛ inch thick and cut into shapes with a small cookie cutter. Beat the remaining egg; brush the cookies lightly with the egg, and place 1 almond half on top of each.

3. Bake on greased cookie sheets for 10 minutes.

CHOCOLATE STICKS   *Makes 15 to 20 sticks.*

3 cups flour
1 teaspoon baking powder
1 cup blanched almonds, coarsely chopped
2 ounces citron, coarsely chopped
4 eggs

2 cups brown sugar, firmly packed
½ teaspoon cinnamon
¼ teaspoon allspice
¼ teaspoon ground cloves
¼ pound sweet chocolate, coarsely chopped

1. Sift together flour and baking powder and mix in the almonds and citron. Reserve. Beat the eggs and sugar until light. Add the spices and chocolate. Combine the two mixtures. Chill until firm, about 2 hours.

2. Preheat oven to 350° F. On a lightly floured board, roll out ½ of the dough at a time to a sheet ⅛ inch thick and cut into strips 3½ inches long.

3. Bake on greased cookie sheets for 10 minutes.

MANDELCHEN   *Makes about 24 small cookies.*

2 cups whole raw almonds   butter
½ cup sugar   confectioners' sugar

  1.   Blanch almonds and let dry overnight. Grind fine, add sugar and enough butter to knead into a very stiff paste.
  2.   Preheat oven to 350° F. Working very quickly roll the dough thin and cut into small rounds.
  3.   Bake on greased cookie sheets for about 10 minutes. Dust with confectioners' sugar while warm.

Note: Watch carefully during baking as these cookies burn easily.

CHRISTMAS SPICE COOKIES   *Makes about 50 small cookies.*

2 cups brown sugar, firmly packed   ⅛ teaspoon nutmeg
½ cup honey or syrup   2 ounces citron, very finely ground
¼ cup butter   1 egg
2½ cups flour   2 teaspoons lemon juice
1 tablespoon baking powder   ½ teaspoon finely grated lemon rind
1 teaspoon cinnamon   2 tablespoons milk
½ teaspoon cloves

  1.   In a small saucepan, combine sugar and honey or syrup and cook over low heat until the sugar is dissolved. Remove from heat, add butter and set aside to cool. Sift together flour, baking powder, cinnamon, cloves, and nutmeg.
  2.   In a large mixing bowl, mix the dry ingredients with the cooled sugar and butter, add the citron, egg, lemon juice and rind, and the milk. Mix well. Gather the dough together in one lump, cover with plastic wrap, and chill for 2 hours.
  3.   Preheat oven to 350° F. On a lightly floured board, roll out ½ of the dough at a time to a sheet ⅛ inch thick and cut into desired shapes.
  4.   Bake on greased cookie sheets for 10 minutes.

CINNAMON STARS   *Makes about 24 stars.*

6 egg whites   1 teaspoon cinnamon
2 cups confectioners' sugar   1 pound almonds, coarsely chopped
finely grated rind of 1 lemon

  1.   Beat egg whites until stiff. Fold in the sugar and finely grated lemon rind. Set aside ¼ of this mixture and to the remainder add the cinnamon and almonds and mix well.

(continued)

2. Preheat oven to 350° F. Lightly dust a pastry board with confectioners' sugar to prevent sticking and roll out the dough to a thin sheet. Cut into star shapes and on top of each cookie place a small portion of the reserved egg mixture.

3. Bake on greased cookie sheets until crusty, about 20 minutes.

FIG COOKIES   *Makes about 40 small cookies.*

1 teaspoon baking soda
2 tablespoons sour cream
½ cup butter
1 cup brown sugar, firmly packed

2 eggs, beaten
½ teaspoon cinnamon
1 cup dried figs, chopped
2 cups flour

1. Sprinkle the baking soda over the sour cream and stir to dissolve. Cream butter and sugar, add eggs, sour cream and soda, cinnamon, figs, and flour. Mix well. Gather the dough together in one lump, cover with plastic wrap, and chill for 2 hours.

2. Preheat oven to 350° F. On a lightly floured board, roll out ½ of the dough at a time and cut into desired shapes.

3. Bake on greased cookie sheets for 10 minutes.

SUGAR COOKIES

One of the most versatile of all cookies, this simple recipe and its variations can be used to form all sorts of shapes and sizes. (Remember to allow extra cooking time for larger, thicker cuts of dough.) Fresh eggs and good butter make an exceptional cookie.

BASIC SUGAR COOKIES   *Makes about 40 small cookies.*

2 cups flour
2 teaspoons baking powder
½ cup butter
1 cup sugar

1 egg, beaten
¼ cup milk
¼ teaspoon vanilla, nutmeg, or any
    other flavoring

1. Sift the flour. Mix the baking powder with 1 cup of the flour and reserve. Cream the butter and sugar. Add the egg, milk, vanilla or other flavoring, and the 1 cup flour with the baking powder. Mix well. Stir in the remaining 1 cup flour. Gather the dough together in one lump, cover with plastic wrap, and chill for 2 hours.

2. Preheat oven to 375° F. On a lightly floured board, roll out ½ of the dough at a time to a sheet ¼ inch thick and cut into desired shapes. Sprinkle with cinnamon, sugar, or chopped nuts, if desired.

3. Bake on greased cookie sheets for 8 to 10 minutes.

Variations:

Fruit-Filled Cookies:

1 recipe Basic Sugar Cookies	1 cup cold water
1 cup raisins	1 tablespoon flour
1 cup dates, finely chopped	½ cup chopped nuts
1 cup sugar	

Prepare the cookie dough, above. Preheat oven to 350° F. Roll out as in Step 2, but cut cookies into rounds and omit any topping. Combine remaining ingredients and boil over medium heat until thick, stirring constantly. Cool. Place a teaspoonful of the fruit filling on half the rounds and cover with the remaining halves, pinching edges together tightly. Bake on greased cookie sheets for 8 to 10 minutes.

Jelly-Filled Cookies:
Prepare dough for Basic Sugar Cookies, above. Preheat oven to 350° F. Roll out, as in Step 2, but cut half the dough into rounds and the remainder with a doughnut cutter of the same outer diameter. Omit any topping. Place the doughnut-shaped cookie over the round and fill the center with your favorite jelly or preserves. Bake on greased cookie sheets for 10 to 12 minutes.

Date Pinwheels:
Prepare dough for Basic Sugar Cookies, above. Preheat oven to 375° F. Roll into 1 large, thin sheet, brush generously with melted butter. Sprinkle with chopped dates, walnuts, cinnamon, and sugar. Roll like a jelly roll and cut into 1-inch slices. Bake slices flat on greased cookie sheets for 20 minutes. Makes about 40 pinwheels.

GINGER SNAPS   *Makes 20 to 30 small cookies.*

¼ cup butter	¼ tablespoon ginger
¼ cup sugar	¼ teaspoon baking soda
1 egg	1½ cups flour
¼ cup molasses	

1. Cream the butter and sugar, add egg and molasses. Mix in the ginger, soda, and flour. Gather the dough together in one lump, cover with plastic wrap, and chill for 2 hours.

(continued)

2. Preheat oven to 350° F. On a lightly floured board, roll out ½ of the dough at a time to a sheet ¼ inch thick and cut into desired shapes.

3. Bake on greased cookie sheets for 15 to 20 minutes.

GINGER WAFERS   *Makes about 40 small cookies.*

2½ cups flour	½ teaspoon ginger
¼ teaspoon baking soda	½ cup butter
⅛ teaspoon salt	½ cup dark molasses
½ teaspoon cinnamon	½ cup sugar
¼ teaspoon cloves	1 egg

1. Sift together the flour, baking soda, and spices. In a large saucepan, combine butter and molasses and heat over a low flame until the butter melts. Stir in the sugar and remove from heat. Cool to lukewarm. Stir in the egg and the dry ingredients. Mix well. Gather the dough together in one lump, cover with plastic wrap, and chill for 2 hours.

2. Preheat oven to 350° F. On a lightly floured board, roll out ½ of the dough at a time to a sheet ⅛ inch thick and cut into rounds.

3. Bake on greased cookie sheets for 15 to 20 minutes.

HERMITS   *Makes about 60 small cookies.*

1 cup butter	3 cups flour
1½ cups sugar	1 teaspoon cloves
1 cup chopped raisins	1 teaspoon nutmeg
3 eggs	1 teaspoon baking soda

1. Cream butter and sugar until light. Add raisins and eggs, beat well. Sift the dry ingredients and add to the mixture. Gather the dough together in one lump, cover with plastic wrap, and chill for 2 hours.

2. Preheat oven to 325° F. On a lightly floured board, roll out ½ of the dough at a time to a sheet ⅛ inch thick and cut into rounds.

3. Bake on greased cookie sheets for 15 minutes.

MOLASSES HERMITS   *Makes about 60 small cookies.*

2½ cups flour
2 teaspoons baking powder
¼ teaspoon salt
1 teaspoon cinnamon
¼ teaspoon cloves
1 teaspoon nutmeg

½ cup butter or shortening
1 cup sugar
2 eggs, beaten
½ cup molasses
1 cup raisins, chopped
2 tablespoons milk

1. Sift together the flour, baking powder, and spices. Cream butter or shortening and sugar, add eggs and molasses. Mix in the dry ingredients, raisins, and milk. Gather the dough together in one lump, cover with plastic wrap, and chill for 2 hours.

2. Preheat oven to 350° F. On a lightly floured board, roll out ½ of the dough at a time to a thin sheet and cut into desired shapes.

3. Bake on greased cookie sheets for 10 minutes.

LEBKUCHEN   *Makes 20 to 30 cookies.*

4 eggs
2 cups light brown sugar, firmly packed
2 cups flour
1 teaspoon ground cinnamon

¼ pound finely chopped almonds or pecans
2 ounces finely chopped citron
1 recipe Confectioners' Sugar Glaze (page 597)

1. Preheat oven to 375° F. Beat the eggs and sugar until light and fluffy. Combine flour and cinnamon with the finely chopped nuts and citron. Mix well with the eggs and sugar.

2. Spread dough ½ inch thick in greased 10-by-15-inch pan. Bake for 25 minutes. Cool in the pans. Frost with Confectioners' Sugar Glaze and cut into strips.

HONEY LEBKUCHEN   *Makes 40 to 50 cookies.*

6 cups flour
2 teaspoons baking soda
1 teaspoon cinnamon
½ teaspoon ground cloves
⅛ to ¼ pound chopped citron
4 eggs, slightly beaten
2 cups sugar

¾ cup honey
¾ pound almonds, coarsely chopped
3 tablespoons rum, wine, or lemon juice
1 recipe Confectioners' Sugar Glaze (page 597)

(continued)

1. Sift together the flour, baking soda, and spices. Stir in the citron. Combine the eggs, sugar, honey, and almonds. Stir in the rum, wine, or lemon juice and mix well with the flour and spices.

2. On a floured board, roll the dough ¼ inch thick and cut into 2-by-3-inch squares. Set on greased cookie sheets and let stand in a cool place overnight.

3. Preheat oven to 325° F. Bake for 25 minutes. Cool on a rack and frost with Confectioners' Sugar Glaze.

Note: The original recipe called for "powdered carbonate of potassium" as a leavening agent. This is no longer readily available in pharmacies. We've had good results substituting baking soda.

MATZO COOKIES   *Makes 15 to 20 small cookies.*

½ cup shortening
1 cup sugar
2 eggs

½ cup potato flour
½ cup matzo meal
½ cup ground almonds

1. Preheat oven to 375° F. Cream shortening and sugar until light. Beat in the eggs. Add the remaining ingredients and mix well. Chill for 2 hours.

2. On a board sprinkled with potato flour and sugar, roll out the dough to a sheet ⅛ inch thick. Cut into desired shapes.

3. Bake for 10 to 12 minutes.

ORANGE COOKIES   *Makes about 40 small cookies.*

2 cups flour
2 teaspoons baking powder
¼ cup butter
1 cup sugar

4 egg yolks, lightly beaten
2 tablespoons orange juice
½ teaspoon grated orange zest

1. Preheat oven to 375° F. Sift the flour and baking powder together. Cream butter and sugar, add the yolks, orange juice, and zest. Mix in the dry ingredients. Chill for 2 hours.

2. On a well-floured board, roll out dough and cut into desired shapes.

3. Bake for 8 to 10 minutes.

SOUR CREAM COOKIES   *Makes about 60 small cookies.*

1 cup sugar
3 cups flour
1 teaspoon salt
1 teaspoon baking soda

1 teaspoon nutmeg
1 cup butter
2 eggs, well beaten
1 cup thick sour cream

1.   Sift the dry ingredients together. Blend in the butter. Gradually add the eggs and sour cream. Gather the dough together in one lump, cover with plastic wrap, and chill for 2 hours.

2.   Preheat oven to 425° F. On a well-floured board, roll out dough and cut into desired shapes.

3.   Bake on greased cookie sheets for 6 to 8 minutes.

BUTTERMILK COOKIES   *Makes about 60 small cookies.*

The original Settlement recipe calls for sour milk. We have substituted buttermilk.

¼ cup butter
2 cups sugar plus more for
    sprinkling
2 eggs

4 cups flour
1 teaspoon baking soda
1 cup buttermilk

1.   Cream the butter and sugar, add the eggs, mix well. Add in the flour. Dissolve the baking soda in the buttermilk and stir into the dough. Gather the dough together in one lump, cover with plastic wrap, and chill for 2 hours.

2.   Preheat oven to 375° F. On a well-floured board, roll out dough to a sheet ⅛ inch thick. Sprinkle the dough with sugar and press the sugar lightly into the dough with a rolling pin. Cut into desired shapes.

3.   Bake on greased cookie sheets for 6 to 8 minutes.

SPRINGERLE   *Makes 30 to 45 squares.*

2 eggs
1 cup sugar, sifted

2 cups flour, sifted
1 to 2 tablespoons anise seeds

1.   Beat eggs and sugar until very light. Gradually add flour stirring until the dough is thick. Chill for 2 hours.

2.   On a well-floured board, roll out dough to a sheet ⅛ inch thick. Press a floured Springerle board down very hard on the dough to emboss the designs.

3.   Cut out the squares and let dry for 10 hours on a floured board at room temperature.

4.   Preheat oven to 325° F. Sprinkle with the anise seeds and bake on greased cookie sheets until pale and golden.

ROLLED WAFERS   *Makes about 20 wafers.*

¼ cup butter
½ cup confectioners' sugar
¼ cup milk

1 cup flour
½ teaspoon vanilla
almonds, finely chopped

1. Preheat oven to 325° F. Cream the butter and sugar. Very slowly add the milk, then stir in the flour and vanilla.

2. Spread dough thin on a greased cookie sheet. Sprinkle with almonds. Mark in 3-inch squares.

3. Bake for 15 minutes. Cut squares with a sharp knife. While still hot, roll the wafers over the handle of a wooden spoon, or shape into cornucopias. Fill with whipped cream if desired.

Molded Cookies

These cookies need not be rolled and cut out; they are quickly shaped by rolling bits of dough between the palms to make balls, or against a floured board with the palm of the hand to make fingers or sticks. Or they may be forced through a cookie press fitted with tubes to make decorative shapes.

CRISS-CROSS BROWN SUGAR COOKIES   *Makes about 60 small cookies.*

2 cups flour
1½ teaspoons baking powder
½ cup brown sugar, firmly packed
2 cups butter

1 egg
1 egg white, lightly beaten
¼ cup chopped nuts

1. Preheat oven to 400° F. Sift together the flour and baking powder. Cream sugar and butter and add the egg. Add the sifted dry ingredients and mix to a smooth dough.

2. Roll into small balls and place on greased cookie sheets 1 inch apart. Flatten criss-cross style with a fork dipped in flour. Brush with beaten egg white and sprinkle with chopped nuts. Bake for 10 to 12 minutes.

CRISS-CROSS PEANUT BUTTER COOKIES   *Makes about 80 small cookies.*

3 cups flour
½ teaspoon salt
1½ teaspoons baking powder
1 cup butter or shortening
1 cup white sugar
1 cup brown sugar, firmly packed

2 eggs, well beaten
1 teaspoon vanilla
1 cup peanut butter
1 egg white, lightly beaten
chopped nuts (optional)

1.   Preheat oven to 400° F. Sift together the flour, salt, and baking powder and set aside. Cream butter or shortening and sugars, add the eggs and vanilla. Add the dry ingredients and the peanut butter. Mix well and knead.

2.   Roll into ¾-inch balls and place on greased cookie sheets, 1 inch apart. Flatten criss-cross style with a fork dipped in flour. Brush with egg white and sprinkle with chopped nuts if desired. Bake for 10 to 12 minutes.

BUTTER BALLS   *Makes about 30 small cookies.*

½ cup butter
¼ cup sugar
1 egg, separated
½ teaspoon vanilla
½ teaspoon finely grated lemon rind

½ teaspoon finely grated orange
   rind
1 tablespoon lemon juice
1 cup flour
½ cup filberts, finely ground
12 candied cherries, coarsely
   chopped

1.   Cream butter and sugar well. Add the egg yolk, vanilla, citrus rinds, and lemon juice. Stir in the flour and beat until very light. Tightly cover the bowl and chill overnight.

2.   Preheat oven to 350° F. Roll into small balls and dip into the slightly beaten egg white. Roll in the ground nuts. Place on greased cookie sheets, 1 inch apart. Press a bit of cherry on top of each. Bake for 20 to 30 minutes.

GINGER COOKIES   *Makes about 60 small cookies.*

2 cups sifted flour
2 teaspoons baking powder
1 teaspoon ground cinnamon
1 teaspoon ground ginger
1 teaspoon ground cloves

¼ cup butter
1¼ cups sugar
1 egg
¼ cup dark molasses

(continued)

1. Preheat oven to 350° F. Sift together the flour, baking powder, and spices. Cream butter and 1 cup of the sugar, add the egg, molasses, and the dry ingredients. Mix well.

2. Form into small balls and roll in the remaining sugar. Place 2 inches apart on a greased cookie sheet. Bake for 10 to 12 minutes.

TEIGLACH   *Makes about 80 cookies.*

4 cups flour
1 teaspoon baking powder
1 teaspoon salt
3 tablespoons vegetable oil
5 eggs

1½ cups honey
½ cup sugar
½ pound filberts, finely chopped
ground ginger

1. Preheat oven to 375° F. Combine flour, baking powder, salt, oil, and eggs and knead until smooth.

2. Divide dough into 8 parts, roll each into a ¼-inch-thick rope, and cut into ½-inch pieces. Boil honey and sugar, pour into baking pan, add pieces of dough and place in oven. When dough is well puffed and beginning to brown, add chopped nuts and bake until brown, about 45 to 50 minutes, stirring occasionally.

3. Remove from the oven. Turn out onto a wet board; cool slightly. Dip hands in hot water and pat cookies flat. Sprinkle with a little ginger and refrigerate.

MOLDED SUGAR COOKIES   *Makes about 60 small cookies.*

1½ cups flour
½ teaspoon baking powder
¼ teaspoon cream of tartar
pinch of salt
½ cup butter or shortening

1 cup sugar
1 egg
1 teaspoon vanilla
cinnamon and sugar

1. Preheat oven to 400° F. Sift together flour, baking powder, cream of tartar, and salt. Cream the butter and gradually add the sugar. Add the egg and beat well. Gradually mix in the sifted ingredients and the vanilla.

2. Roll the dough into small balls and place 1 inch apart on a greased cookie sheet. Gently flatten the top of each cookie with the bottom of a glass. Sprinkle with cinnamon and sugar. Bake for 10 to 12 minutes.

PFEFFERNUESSE *Makes about 60 small cookies.*

2 cups corn syrup
2 cups dark molasses
1 cup butter or shortening
1 teaspoon finely grated lemon rind
1 tablespoon lemon juice
1 cup brown sugar, firmly packed
10 cups flour

1 teaspoon baking soda
2 teaspoons ground cinnamon
¼ pound citron, finely chopped
⅓ pound almonds, finely chopped
1 egg white, lightly beaten
confectioners' sugar

1. Preheat oven to 350° F. In a saucepan, warm the syrup and molasses. Add the butter, lemon rind and juice, and the brown sugar. Sift together the flour, baking soda, and cinnamon and gradually stir in to the other ingredients. Fold in the citron and almonds.

2. Roll dough into small balls and place far apart on a greased cookie sheet. Brush with egg white.

3. Bake until lightly browned, about 15 minutes. Remove from oven, roll in confectioners' sugar, and cool on racks.

CHOCOLATE PRETZELS *Makes about 60 pretzels.*

1 cup butter
⅔ cup sugar
1 egg
2 ounces unsweetened chocolate, melted

1½ cups flour
⅛ teaspoon cinnamon
1 teaspoon vanilla
½ cup almonds, finely chopped

1. Preheat oven to 375° F. Cream butter and sugar; add the egg and the remaining ingredients, except the almonds. Chill thoroughly.

2. Roll small pieces of dough into pencil-thick ropes. Shape into pretzels.

3. Place on greased cookie sheets and sprinkle with finely chopped almonds. Bake for 10 to 15 minutes.

MARZIPAN COOKIES *Makes about 45 cookies.*

1¼ pounds whole raw almonds
(sweet almonds, if available)

5 cups confectioners' sugar
2 egg whites

1. Blanch almonds and let dry overnight. Preheat oven to 325° F. Grind the almonds very fine, sift sugar over the ground almonds, and add egg whites.

(continued)

2. On a board lightly dusted with confectioners' sugar, knead dough to a stiff paste. Add more egg whites if necessary. Shape into a roll and, working with pieces the size of a walnut, roll each piece into a rope ½ inch thick. Form into rings, crescents, hearts, bow knots, and pretzels.

3. Bake on greased cookie sheets until slightly browned, about 15 minutes.

PECAN FINGERS   *Makes about 60 small cookies.*

1 cup butter
¾ cup confectioners' sugar
2 cups pecans, coarsely chopped
1 teaspoon vanilla

2 cups flour
1 tablespoon ice water
⅛ teaspoon salt

1. Preheat oven to 325° F. Cream butter and sugar; add the nuts, vanilla, flour, water, and salt. Mix well.

2. On a board lightly dusted with flour, shape the dough into a roll. Working with pieces the size of a walnut, roll into finger lengths.

3. Bake on greased cookie sheets for 20 to 30 minutes. Roll in confectioners' sugar while still warm.

SPRITZ COOKIES   *Makes 45 to 60 cookies.*

1 cup butter
1 cup sugar
1 whole egg or 2 yolks

1 teaspoon vanilla
2½ cups flour

Preheat oven to 375° F. Cream butter and sugar; add the egg or yolks, vanilla, and flour. Mix well. Shape with a cookie press directly onto ungreased cookie sheets. Bake for 15 minutes.

ALMOND BREAD SLICES   *Makes 45 to 60 cookies.*

2 eggs, well beaten
½ cup sugar
1 teaspoon lemon juice
½ teaspoon finely grated lemon rind
½ teaspoon vanilla
1⅔ cups flour

¼ cup blanched almonds, split lengthwise
¼ cup butter, at room temperature, or vegetable oil
2 teaspoons baking powder

1. Preheat oven to 325° F. Beat eggs and sugar until light. Add lemon juice and rind, vanilla, and 1 cup of the flour. Mix in the almonds, butter or oil, and the remaining flour mixed with the baking powder.

2. Turn the dough out onto a lightly floured board and knead until smooth. Roll into 2 long loaves about 2 inches thick.

3. Bake on greased cookie sheets for 20 to 30 minutes. Remove from the oven and while still warm cut into ½-inch slices.

Variation:

Cocoa Almond Bread Slices: Prepare as above through Step 1. Divide the dough into four parts and add 2 teaspoons cocoa to 1 part of the dough. Knead until smooth and blended and shape into a roll ½ inch thick. Combine the remaining 3 pieces of dough, knead and divide into 2 parts. Roll into 2 sheets ½ inch thick. Cut the cocoa dough into 2 pieces and wrap the plain dough around it. Bake and slice as directed above.

Refrigerator Cookies

Refrigerator or icebox cookies are among the quickest to make; the dough is molded into oblongs or uniform rolls, and thoroughly chilled. The roll is then sliced. Be sure to use a gentle sawing motion that does not distort the shape. Refrigerator cookie dough keeps well, and the cookies may be sliced and baked in small quantities, as needed.

RUM SLICES   *Makes 45 to 60 cookies.*

4 egg whites
2 cups confectioners' sugar
½ pound pecans, ground
½ pound walnuts, ground

1 teaspoon vanilla or rum
1 recipe Confectioners' Sugar Glaze (page 597)

1. Beat the egg whites until stiff; beat in the sugar and nuts. Add the vanilla or rum.

2. Shape into rolls ¾ inch across. Cover with plastic wrap and chill for 45 minutes.

3. Preheat oven to 350° F. Cut into ½-inch slices and place on greased cookie sheets. Bake for about 15 minutes. Remove from oven and while still warm ice with Confectioners' Sugar Glaze flavored with rum.

ALMOND CRESCENTS   *Makes about 60 crescents.*

1¼ cups flour
1 cup blanched almonds, or blanched Brazil nus, finely chopped
¼ cup confectioners' sugar

½ cup butter, creamed
1 egg yolk, lightly beaten, as needed
Vanilla Sugar, see below

1. Combine the flour with the nuts and sugar. Add the butter and, on a lightly floured board, knead until smooth and well blended. If the dough is too crumbly, add a little egg yolk.

2. Shape into rolls 2 inches thick. Cover with plastic wrap and chill for 45 minutes.

3. Preheat oven to 325° F. Cut crosswise into ½-inch slices, roll up and shape into crescents. Bake on greased cookie sheets for about 20 minutes. The cookies should remain almost white. Remove from the oven and dip in Vanilla Sugar while still hot.

VANILLA SUGAR

Break one vanilla bean in small pieces or finely grind in a nut grinder or food processor. In a paper bag or a jar, combine ground vanilla bean with 1 cup confectioners' sugar or granulated sugar and shake well. Let stand for at least 24 hours. Keep tightly covered in a cool, dry place. Lasts indefinitely.

OATMEAL CRISPS   *Makes 45 to 60 cookies.*

1½ cups flour, sifted before measuring
1 teaspoon baking soda
1 teaspoon salt
1 cup butter
1 cup granulated sugar

1 cup brown sugar, packed
2 eggs, well beaten
1 teaspoon vanilla
3 cups uncooked quick-rolled oats
½ cup chopped nut meats

1. Sift together flour, soda, and salt. Beat butter, gradually add the sugars and cream until very light. Add eggs, vanilla, oats, and nuts, mixing well after each addition. Stir in the dry ingredients.

2. Form the dough into 4 rolls, about 2½ inches thick. Wrap in waxed paper and chill for 45 minutes.

3. Preheat oven to 400° F. Slice thin and bake on greased cookie sheets for about 10 minutes.

PEANUT OR ALMOND ICEBOX COOKIES *Makes 60 to 80 cookies.*

1 pound butter
1 cup sugar
1 cup brown sugar, firmly packed
3 eggs, well beaten
½ pound peanuts or almonds,
    chopped

5 cups flour
1 tablespoon cinnamon
2 teaspoons baking soda

1. Cream butter and sugars well. Add eggs, chopped nuts, and dry ingredients.
2. Form the dough into rolls, about 2½ inches thick. Wrap in waxed paper and chill for 45 minutes.
3. Preheat oven to 350° F. Slice thin and bake on greased cookie sheets for about 10 minutes or until crisp.

PIN WHEEL COOKIES *Makes about 60 cookies.*

½ cup butter
½ cup sugar
1 egg yolk
1½ cups flour
1½ teaspoons baking powder

3 tablespoons milk
½ teaspoon vanilla
1 ounce unsweetened chocolate,
    melted

1. Cream butter and sugar; add egg and beat well. Sift flour and baking powder and add to mixture with milk and vanilla. Divide dough in half and add chocolate to one part.
2. Wrap in waxed paper and chill for 45 minutes. Pat each piece into a thin, oblong sheet on waxed paper. Place the chocolate dough over the plain dough and roll tightly. Wrap in waxed paper and chill until firm.
3. Preheat oven to 375° F. Slice thin and bake on greased cookie sheets for about 10 minutes.

Drop Cookies

The dough for drop cookies is soft and cannot be rolled or molded. Scoop up a teaspoonful of the dough and scrape it from the spoon onto a greased baking sheet with another teaspoon or with a rubber spatula. Use a pastry bag with a wide tip if desired. Allow at least 2 inches between cookies, since they spread during baking.

ANISE COOKIES   *Makes about 60 cookies.*

The original recipe calls for hand stirring the eggs and sugar for 45 minutes. This will certainly make for a perfect cookie. For most of us, the use of an electric mixer for 20 minutes is a fine alternative.

3 eggs, at room temperature
1 cup sugar
1½ to 2 cups cake flour

½ teaspoon baking powder
1 tablespoon anise seed

1.   With an electric mixer, beat eggs and sugar for 20 minutes at low speed, add the other ingredients and beat for 3 minutes longer.

2.   Drop from a teaspoon onto well-greased and floured cookie sheets, 2 inches apart. Let stand overnight or about 10 hours at room temperature to dry. Preheat oven to 350° F. Bake 10 to 15 minutes.

DELICATE CHOCOLATE COOKIES   *Makes about 60 small cookies.*

2 cups cake flour
1 teaspoon baking powder
¾ cup butter
1 cup confectioners' sugar
2 ounces unsweetened chocolate, melted
1 egg, beaten
¼ cup milk
1 teaspoon vanilla

Frosting
¾ cup confectioners' sugar
1 teaspoon butter, melted
1 teaspoon vanilla
half-and-half

1.   Preheat oven to 350° F. Sift together flour and baking powder. Cream butter and sugar; add chocolate and egg. Add sifted ingredients, milk, and vanilla.

2.   Drop by spoonfuls onto well-greased cookie sheets, 2 inches apart. Bake 8 to 10 minutes.

3.   Meanwhile, prepare frosting by combining sugar, butter, and vanilla. Slowly add enough half-and-half to make mixture thin enough to spread. Frost cookies when cooled.

COCONUT DROPS   *Makes 45 to 60 cookies.*

1½ cups flour
3 teaspoons baking powder
4 eggs

2 cups confectioners' sugar
¼ pound shredded coconut

1. Preheat oven to 350° F. Sift the flour and baking powder together. Beat eggs until light, add sugar, and beat well. Add sifted ingredients and stir in the coconut.

2. Drop from a teaspoon onto well-greased cookie sheets, 3 inches apart. Bake 10 to 15 minutes.

LACE COOKIES *Makes about 45 to 60 cookies.*

¼ cup butter
2 cups brown sugar, firmly packed
2 eggs, well beaten
1 teaspoon vanilla

1 teaspoon baking powder
½ cup flour
½ pound pecans, coarsely chopped

1. Cream butter and sugar. Add eggs, beat well; add vanilla. Add baking powder to flour and mix with nuts. Combine the two mixtures.

2. Preheat oven to 400° F. Drop by ½ teaspoonfuls onto well-greased and floured cookie sheets 3 inches apart.

3. Bake about 8 minutes. Let cool slightly on the pan before removing.

MOLASSES LACE COOKIES *Makes 45 to 60 cookies.*

½ cup molasses
½ cup sugar
½ cup butter

1 cup flour
¼ teaspoon baking powder
½ teaspoon baking soda

1. Preheat oven to 325° F. Boil molasses, sugar, and butter for 1 minute. Remove from heat. Add remaining ingredients and place in a double boiler over hot but not boiling water so the batter doesn't solidify.

2. Drop by ½ teaspoonfuls onto well-greased and floured cookie sheets, 3 inches apart.

3. Bake about 15 minutes. Let cool slightly on the pan before removing.

OATMEAL LACE COOKIES *Makes 45 to 60 cookies.*

½ cup butter, melted
2½ cups rolled oats
1 cup brown sugar, firmly packed

2 teaspoons baking powder
1 egg, beaten

1. Preheat oven to 350° F. Melt butter and combine with dry ingredients. Add egg and mix well.

2. Drop by teaspoonfuls onto well-greased cookie sheets. Bake about 8 to 10 minutes. Let cool slightly on the pan before removing.

CLASSIC OATMEAL COOKIES   *Makes about 60 cookies.*

1 cup butter
1 cup sugar
2 eggs, beaten
2 cups flour
1 teaspoon baking powder
½ teaspoon baking soda

¼ teaspoon salt
1 teaspoon cinnamon
2 cups uncooked quick-rolled oats
1 cup raisins or dates, chopped
1 cup walnuts, chopped
¼ cup milk

1. Preheat oven to 350° F. Cream butter and sugar, add eggs. Sift together the flour, baking powder, soda, salt, and cinnamon, combine with the oats and sprinkle over the raisins and nuts. Add to the butter mixture along with the milk.

2. Drop from a teaspoon onto well-greased cookie sheets, 1 inch apart. Bake 10 to 15 minutes.

SPICE COOKIES   *Makes about 60 cookies.*

5 eggs, beaten
2 cups brown sugar, firmly packed
2 teaspoons cinnamon
1 teaspoon ground cloves

1 teaspoon vanilla
1 teaspoon ginger
1 teaspoon baking soda
3 cups flour

1. Preheat oven to 375° F. Combine all the ingredients in order.

2. Roll into small balls or drop by teaspoonfuls onto well-greased cookie sheets. Bake 10 to 15 minutes.

RAISIN COOKIES   *Makes about 60 cookies.*

⅔ cup butter
1½ cups granulated or firmly
   packed brown sugar
2 eggs
1 cup raisins, chopped
1 teaspoon cloves

½ teaspoon mace
¼ teaspoon salt
1 teaspoon baking soda
3 tablespoons buttermilk
2½ cups flour

1. Preheat oven to 375° F. Cream butter and sugar, add eggs, raisins, spices, and salt. Dissolve baking soda in the buttermilk and add alternately with the flour.

2. Drop by teaspoonfuls onto well-greased cookie sheets. Bake 10 to 15 minutes.

SHREWSBURY WAFERS *Makes about 60 small cookies.*

3 eggs
2 cups sugar
2 tablespoons butter, melted
¾ teaspoon vanilla

1 teaspoon salt
1 cup shredded coconut
2 cups uncooked quick-rolled oats

1. Preheat oven to 350° F. Beat eggs thoroughly. Gradually add sugar, beating constantly, and then butter, vanilla, and salt. Stir in coconut and oats.

2. Drop by ½ teaspoonfuls into shallow pans lined with waxed paper, 1 inch apart. Bake until light brown, about 8 minutes. Lift the sheets of waxed paper out of the pans, cool slightly, and remove the wafers.

CURLED WAFERS *Makes about 30 wafers.*

butter, at room temperature
3 egg whites
⅔ cup confectioners' sugar

½ cup flour
¼ cup toasted almonds, finely
  chopped

1. Spread 9-by-2-inch cookie sheets thickly with butter and place in the refrigerator. Preheat oven to 400° F.

2. Beat egg whites until stiff but still shiny; gradually add sugar and beat until stiff. Fold in the flour.

3. With the back of a spoon, spread the mixture as thin and smooth as possible over the buttered pans. Sprinkle lightly with the nuts. Bake for 5 to 8 minutes, until lightly browned.

4. With a sharp knife, cut into long strips, loosen each carefully with a spatula. Return to a hot oven for one minute just to soften, then roll each strip around the handle of a wooden spoon lengthwise and form into curls.

Kisses and Macaroons

KISSES

Meringue kisses can be quite versatile. The following cookies make good use of leftover egg whites, fresh or frozen. Remember that 8 whites equals about 1 cup. A free-standing electric mixer with a balloon whisk is useful to make meringues. Have whites at room temperature and be careful not to overbeat. They should be firm but not stiff. Use a spotlessly clean and dry bowl for best results.

FILLED MERINGUES   *Makes about 45 meringues.*

6 egg whites	1 teaspoon lemon juice
½ teaspoon salt	1 teaspoon vanilla
1½ cups granulated sugar	ice cream

1.   Preheat oven to 275° F. Beat the egg whites and salt until frothy. Gradually add ¾ cup of the sugar and beat until the whites hold soft peaks. Add lemon juice and vanilla and beat until stiff. Fold in the remaining sugar, 2 tablespoons at a time.

2.   Drop mixture from a tablespoon on a baking sheet lined with brown paper, to form rounds or ovals. Bake for 45 minutes. Cool on racks. To serve, cut off the top of each meringue, fill with ice cream, and replace top.

PRALINE KISSES   *Makes about 24 kisses.*

1 egg white	1 cup brown sugar, firmly packed
½ teaspoon salt	1 cup pecans, coarsely chopped

1.   Preheat oven to 250° F. Beat egg white until foamy, add salt and continue beating. Gradually beat in sugar until the egg white holds stiff peaks. Fold in the nuts.

2.   Drop batter from the tip of a spoon ½ inch apart on greased cookie sheets. Bake for 45 minutes. Let kisses cool slightly before removing from the pan.

CHOCOLATE KISSES   *Makes about 30 kisses.*

3 egg whites	2 ounces unsweetened chocolate,
½ cup sugar	finely chopped
½ teaspoon vanilla	

1.   Preheat oven to 250° F. Beat egg whites until foamy. Gradually beat in sugar until the egg whites hold stiff peaks. Add the vanilla and fold in the chocolate.

2.   Drop batter from the tip of a spoon ½ inch apart on greased cookie sheets. Bake for 45 minutes. Let kisses cool slightly before removing from the pan.

COCONUT KISSES   *Makes 24 to 30 kisses.*

2 egg whites   2 cups shredded coconut
1½ cups confectioners' sugar

   1.   Preheat oven to 250° F. Beat egg whites until foamy. Gradually beat in sugar until the egg whites hold stiff peaks. Fold in the coconut.
   2.   Drop batter from the tip of a spoon ½ inch apart on greased cookie sheets. Bake for 45 minutes. Let kisses cool slightly before removing from the pan.

DATE AND ALMOND KISSES   *Makes about 24 kisses.*

1 egg white   1 cup blanched almonds, chopped
1 cup confectioners' sugar   lengthwise
30 pitted dates, chopped

   1.   Preheat oven to 300° F. Beat egg white very stiff; gradually beat in the sugar. Fold in the dates and nuts.
   2.   Drop from a spoon onto greased cookie sheets and bake for 25 to 30 minutes.

MACAROONS

Good-quality nuts are the secret to good macaroons. Use whole nuts and blanch and peel them just before using rather than purchasing ground nuts. Ground nuts that have been on the shelf for an extended amount of time lose their flavor rather quickly.
   To remove skins from almonds, blanch quickly and remove skins while hot. They will slip out easily. For pisatchios and filberts, heat in a moderate oven for a few minutes. Turn out onto a clean dish towel, bring up corners and rub vigorously. The friction will peel stubborn skins right off. Let cool completely before using.

BASIC MACAROONS   *Makes about 24 macaroons.*

½ pound almond paste (page 445)   4 egg whites
1 cup sugar

(continued)

1.   Preheat oven to 375° F. Blend almond paste and sugar. Gradually add the unbeaten egg whites and beat until smooth.

2.   Drop by teaspoonfuls, 1 inch apart, onto cookie sheets lined with parchment paper and bake for 15 to 20 minutes. To remove the cookies, cool slightly, moisten the back of the paper, and peel off.

ALMOND MACAROONS   *Makes about 24 macaroons.*

4 egg whites   ½ pound almonds, finely chopped
1 cup confectioners' sugar

1.   Preheat oven to 300° F. Combine egg whites and sugar in the top of a double boiler and cook for 10 minutes, stirring occasionally. Remove from heat, add nuts and mix thoroughly.

2.   Drop by teaspoonfuls onto greased cookie sheets and bake until crisp, about 30 minutes. Remove from pans immediately.

FILBERT MACAROONS   *Makes 18 to 24 macaroons.*

1½ cup filberts, coarsely chopped   2 egg whites
⅛ teaspoon cinnamon   ⅔ cup sugar
½ teaspoon finely grated lemon rind   2 tablespoons lemon juice

1.   Preheat oven to 275° F. Combine nuts with cinnamon and lemon rind. Beat egg whites until very stiff. Fold in sugar, lemon juice, and the nut mixture.

2.   Drop by teaspoonfuls, 1 inch apart, onto greased cookie sheets and bake for 30 minutes. Cool slightly before removing from pans.

BROWN SUGAR MACAROONS   *Makes about 12 macaroons.*

 1 cup light brown sugar, firmly   1 egg white
     packed
¼ cup pecans, finely ground

1.   Preheat oven to 300° F. Combine all ingredients and roll into balls the size of a hickory nut.

2.   Bake on greased cookie sheets, 2 inches apart, for 10 to 15 minutes.

CHOCOLATE MACAROONS   *Makes about 12 macaroons.*

¼ cup grated almonds
½ cup sugar
2 ounces unsweetened chocolate,
  finely chopped

¼ teaspoon vanilla
2 egg whites

1.   Preheat oven to 325° F. Combine almonds, sugar, chocolate, and vanilla. Beat egg whites until stiff and gently fold in the almond mixture.

2.   Drop by teaspoonfuls onto cookie sheets lined with greased paper. Bake for 15 to 20 minutes. Remove from paper while still warm.

PISTACHIO MACAROONS   *Makes about 24 macaroons.*

3 egg whites
1 cup sugar
¼ pound pistachio nuts, blanched
  and finely ground

¼ pound almonds, blanched and
  finely ground

1.   Preheat oven to 300° F. Beat egg whites until frothy, gradually add sugar and beat until stiff. Fold in nuts.

2.   Drop by teaspoonfuls onto greased cookie sheets. Bake until crisp, about 30 minutes.

CORNFLAKE MACAROONS   *Makes 18 to 24 macaroons.*

2 egg whites
¾ cup sugar
2 cups cornflakes

½ cup nuts, coarsely chopped
⅛ teaspoon salt
1 teaspoon vanilla

1.   Preheat oven to 300° F. Beat egg whites until frothy, gradually add sugar and beat until stiff. Fold in the remaining ingredients.

2.   Drop by teaspoonfuls onto cookie sheets lined with waxed paper. Bake 15 to 20 minutes. Remove from pan while still warm.

DATE MACAROONS   *Makes about 24 macaroons.*

4 egg whites
1 cup sugar

1 pound pitted dates, finely
  chopped
½ pound almonds, sliced lengthwise

(continued)

1. Preheat oven to 250° F. Beat egg whites until foamy, gradually add sugar and beat until stiff. Fold in dates and almonds and mix thoroughly.
2. Drop by teaspoonfuls ½ inch apart onto greased cookie sheets. Bake until dry, about 50 minutes. Cookies are done when they leave the pan readily.

FIG MACAROONS   *Makes 24 to 30 macaroons.*

1 cup boiling water
1 pound dried figs
4 egg whites

1 cup sugar
½ pound almonds, sliced lengthwise

1. Preheat oven to 250° F. Combine water and figs. Cover and let stand until cool. Drain and finely chop. Beat eggs until foamy, gradually add sugar and beat until stiff. Fold in figs and almonds and mix thoroughly.
2. Drop by teaspoonfuls ½ inch apart onto greased cookie sheets. Bake until dry, about 50 minutes. Cookies are done when they leave the pan readily.

Bar Cookies

Bar cookies are baked in a single sheet and cut up after baking. Brownies and similar cake-like cookies are baked in this manner, as are some of the shortbread type.

BLACK WALNUT AND COCONUT BARS   *Makes 9 to 12 bars.*

½ cup butter
½ cup brown sugar, firmly packed
1 cup flour, sifted

Topping
2 tablespoons flour
½ teaspoon baking powder

¼ teaspoon salt
½ cup shredded coconut
1 cup black walnuts, chopped
2 eggs, well beaten
1 cup brown sugar, firmly packed
1 teaspoon vanilla

1. Preheat oven to 375° F. Cream butter and sugar well. Blend in flour and spread mixture in a greased 9-inch square pan. Bake for 20 to 25 minutes.
2. Meanwhile, make topping by sifting together flour, baking powder, and salt. Mix with coconut and nuts. Beat eggs, add sugar and vanilla, and continue beating until fluffy. Combine the two mixtures and pour over the baked crust.
3. Bake for 20 minutes longer. Cool slightly and cut into oblong bars.

BISHOP'S BREAD

1 cup raisins
1 cup almonds, chopped, plus more
   for sprinkling
1¼ cups flour

2 teaspoons baking powder
salt
3 eggs
1 cup sugar plus more for
   sprinkling

1. Preheat oven to 350° F. Toss raisins and nuts with ¼ cup of the flour. Sift together the remaining flour with the baking powder and salt. Combine eggs and sugar and beat until light. Add the sifted ingredients and mix well. Fold in the nuts and raisins.

2. Spread in a greased 8-by-8-inch pan and bake for 12 to 15 minutes. Cut into rectangles while still warm. Sprinkle with additional sugar and finely chopped nuts.

BROWNIES   *Makes 12 to 15 brownies.*

2 ounces unsweetened chocolate, or
   6 tablespoons cocoa
2 tablespoons butter
2 eggs, lightly beaten
1 cup sugar

1 teaspoon baking powder
1 cup flour
½ cup chopped walnuts
1 teaspoon vanilla
¼ teaspoon salt

1. Preheat oven to 350° F. Melt chocolate and butter in the top of a double boiler. Beat eggs and sugar until light. Stir in the melted butter and chocolate and beat thoroughly. Add the remaining ingredients.

2. Bake in a greased 8-inch square pan for 35 minutes. Cut into squares and remove from pan while hot.

Variation: Add 1 cup coarsely chopped walnuts or pecans if desired. Fold in just before pouring batter into pan.

CHEWY BROWNIES   *Makes 12 to 15 brownies.*

½ cup butter
1 cup sugar
2 eggs
½ teaspoon vanilla

2 ounces unsweetened chocolate,
   melted, or 6 tablespoons cocoa
½ cup flour
1 cup chopped walnuts
¼ teaspoon salt

1. Preheat oven to 350° F. Cream butter and sugar well. Beat in eggs one at a time. Add remaining ingredients.

2. Bake in a greased 8-inch square pan for 20 to 30 minutes. Cut into squares when cool.

CARAMEL SQUARES   *Makes about 12 squares.*

1 cup brown sugar, firmly packed	1 teaspoon baking powder
¼ cup butter	¼ teaspoon salt
1 egg	¼ cup chopped nuts
1 cup flour	½ teaspoon vanilla

1. Preheat oven to 350° F. In a saucepan, combine sugar and butter and stir constantly over low heat until sugar is completely dissolved. Do not boil. Remove from heat and let cool. Add egg and beat well. Stir in flour, baking powder, salt, nuts, and vanilla.

2. Spread in a greased 9-inch square pan and bake for 20 minutes. Cut into squares and cool in pan.

CARD GINGERBREAD   *Makes 12 to 15 squares.*

⅓ cup butter	2 cups less 2 tablespoons flour
1 cup sugar, plus more for sprinkling	1 tablespoon baking powder
1 egg, well beaten	1 teaspoon ginger
1 teaspoon salt	1½ cups milk

1. Preheat oven to 350° F. Cream butter and sugar; add the egg. Sift together the dry ingredients and add them alternately with the milk. Mix well.

2. Spread in a greased 9-by-13-inch pan. Bake for 15 minutes. Sprinkle with sugar and cut into squares before removing from the pan.

CHOCOLATE TOFFEE BARS   *Makes about 30 bars.*

2 cups flour	1 teaspoon vanilla
¼ teaspoon salt	1 egg, well beaten
1 cup butter	¼ pound milk chocolate, melted
1 cup brown sugar, firmly packed	½ cup ground nut meats

1. Preheat oven to 350° F. Sift together flour and salt. Cream butter and sugar until light and fluffy. Add vanilla, egg, and sifted ingredients. Mix well.

2. Spread in a greased 9-by-13-inch pan. Bake about 25 minutes. Remove from oven, cover with melted chocolate, sprinkle with nuts, and cut into bars.

DATE BARS   *Makes about 30 bars.*

½ cup butter, melted
1 cup sugar
2 eggs, well beaten
¾ cup flour
¼ teaspoon baking powder

⅛ teaspoon salt
1 cup nut meats, finely chopped
1 cup dates, finely chopped
confectioners' sugar

1. Preheat oven to 350° F. Combine the first 8 ingredients in the order given.

2. Spread in a greased 9-by-13-inch pan. Bake about 20 minutes. Cut into bars and sprinkle with confectioner's sugar while still warm.

DATE-FILLED OATMEAL SQUARES   *Makes about 30 squares.*

1½ cups rolled oats
1¾ cups flour
½ teaspoon baking soda
½ teaspoon salt
1 cup chopped walnuts (optional)

1 cup brown sugar, firmly packed
1 teaspoon cinnamon
1 cup butter, melted
1 recipe Date Filling (below)

1. Preheat oven to 325° F. Combine all ingredients in the order given, except for filling, and mix well.

2. Pat half of the dough on the bottom of a greased 9-by-13-inch pan. Spread with Date Filling. Pat the remaining dough over the filling.

3. Bake for 30 minutes. Cut into bars while still warm. Dust with confectioners' sugar or top with Confectioners' Sugar Glaze (page 597).

DATE FILLING

1 pound pitted dates, finely chopped
1 cup sugar
½ cup water

1 teaspoon grated lemon rind
1 tablespoon grated orange rind

In a saucepan, combine dates, sugar, and water and boil until smooth. Stir in citrus rinds and cool.

DATE AND NUT STICKS   *Makes about 15 bars.*

2 eggs
1 cup sugar
2 cups chopped pecans
2 cups chopped dates

¼ pound candied cherries, coarsely
   chopped
1 teaspoon vanilla
½ cup flour
1 teaspoon baking powder

1. Preheat oven to 350° F. Beat eggs and sugar well, add nuts, dates, cherries, and vanilla. Stir in flour mixed with baking powder.
2. Spread in 2 greased 8-inch pans. Bake about 25 minutes. Cut into bars while still warm.

HONEY BARS   *Makes about 30 bars.*

⅔ cup strained honey
2 cups confectioners' sugar
½ pound blanched almonds, cut in
   half lengthwise
2 cups flour
1 ounce citron, very finely chopped

⅛ teaspoon grated nutmeg
⅛ teaspoon ground cloves
¼ cup lemon juice
1 recipe Confectioners' Sugar Glaze
   (page 597)

1. In a saucepan, boil honey and sugar, add almonds and stir thoroughly. Add the remaining ingredients, except for glaze. Turn dough out onto a well-floured board and knead well. Wrap in waxed paper and chill overnight.
2. Preheat oven to 375° F. Pat dough out ½-inch thick and bake in a greased 9-by-13-inch pan for 20 minutes. Frost with Confectioners' Sugar Glaze and cut into 1-by-2-inch bars.

MAPLE MERINGUE SQUARES   *Makes 30 to 45 squares.*

1¼ cups cake flour
1 teaspoon baking powder
pinch of salt
½ cup butter
1 cup sugar

2 eggs, separated
⅛ teaspoon almond extract
½ cup nuts, finely chopped
2 cups brown sugar, firmly packed

1. Preheat oven to 350° F. Sift together flour, baking powder, and salt. Cream butter and sugar, add egg yolks one at a time, then the sifted ingredients and the almond extract. Mix well.
2. Spread dough ¼-inch thick on well-greased cookie sheets and sprinkle with chopped nuts. Beat egg whites until frothy, beat in brown sugar and spread over the nuts. Bake for 30 minutes. Cut into squares when cool.

HURRY-UP BUTTER COOKIES   *Makes about 15 cookies.*

1 cup butter
1 cup sugar
1 egg, separated
1 teaspoon lemon juice

½ teaspoon grated lemon rind
2 cups flour, sifted
½ cup chopped nuts

1. Preheat oven to 300° F. Cream butter and sugar well, add egg yolk and continue beating. Add lemon juice, lemon rind, and flour and continue beating until well blended.

2. Pat dough out ¼ inch thick in a greased and floured 9-inch square pan. Brush with slightly beaten egg and sprinkle with nuts. Bake for 20 to 30 minutes. Cut while hot into squares or 1½-inch strips.

HURRY-UP CINNAMON COOKIES   *Makes about 15 cookies.*

1 cup butter
1 cup sugar
1 egg, separated

1 tablespoon ground cinnamon
2 cups flour, sifted
½ cup chopped nuts

1. Preheat oven to 300° F. Cream butter and sugar well, add egg yolk and continue beating. Add the cinnamon and flour and continue beating until well blended.

2. Pat dough out ¼ inch thick in a greased and floured 9-inch square pan. Brush with slightly beaten egg white and sprinkle with nuts. Bake for 20 to 30 minutes. Cut while hot into squares or 1½-inch strips.

HURRY-UP CHOCOLATE COOKIES   *Makes about 15 cookies.*

1 cup butter
1 cup sugar
1 egg, separated

1 ounce unsweetened chocolate, melted
2 cups flour, sifted
½ cup chopped nuts

1. Preheat oven to 300° F. Cream butter and sugar well, add egg yolk and continue beating. Add the chocolate and flour and continue beating until well blended.

2. Pat dough out ¼ inch thick in a greased and floured 9-inch square pan. Brush with slightly beaten egg white and sprinkle with nuts. Bake for 20 to 30 minutes. Cut while hot into squares or 1½-inch strips.

SCOTCH SHORTBREAD

1 cup butter   4 cups flour
½ cup sugar

1. Preheat oven to 350° F. Cream butter and sugar well. Gradually stir in the flour. Turn dough out onto a well-floured board and knead until smooth.

2. Line 2 9-inch pie pans with waxed paper; pat dough ½ inch thick into the bottom of the pans. Flute the edges; prick dough with a fork. Score in narrow wedges.

3. Bake for 25 to 30 minutes. Break into pieces following scores while still warm.

WALNUT STICKS   *Makes about 15 sticks.*

2 eggs   1 cup chopped walnuts
1 cup brown sugar, firmly packed   pinch of salt
½ cup flour

1. Preheat oven to 350° F. Beat eggs and sugar well; add flour, walnuts, and a pinch of salt.

2. Bake in a greased 8-inch pan for 15 to 20 minutes. Cut into finger-length strips.

PASTRIES, PIES, TARTS, FRUIT KUCHEN, AND STRUDEL

Pastry Shells

TO MIX

All ingredients should be well chilled before beginning. Measure flour and salt into a chilled bowl. Work in the shortening quickly and lightly, rubbing it in with the fingertips, or cutting it in with a pastry blender, fork, or two knives held in the same hand, until the particles are the size of peas. Sprinkle with ice water, 1 tablespoon at a time, stirring it in with a fork, just until the particles are moistened and stick together. Wrap the dough in plastic and chill for 30 minutes or longer before rolling.

TO MIX IN A FOOD PROCESSOR

Follow the instructions above: chill ingredients, measure carefully and have workbowl and blade cold. Process dry ingredients to blend, then cut in butter with several quick pulses and add liquid. Process just until dough forms a ball around blade. Do not overwork. Wrap and chill for 30 minutes before rolling out.

TO ROLL PIE PASTRY

Dust a pastry board lightly with flour. Special boards covered with stockinet may be used, or a marble or Formica countertop, or the dough may be rolled out between two sheets of waxed paper. Flatten the dough lightly. Roll it ⅛ to ¼ inch thick, from center to edges, with a lightly floured rolling pin, using short strokes, to make a round 1 inch larger than the pie pan.

Turn the dough often to keep it round. Do not turn it over, but lift from board occasionally. If the round splits at the edges, press together. Sprinkle board with flour as needed. To move a rolled piece from the board, carefully roll the dough partially around the rolling pin then unroll it onto the pie pan.

Two-Crust Pies

For a two-crust pie, divide the dough in two portions, one slightly larger than the other, and use the larger part for the bottom crust. Fit bottom crust loosely into an ungreased pie pan. Fill. Trim off overhanging dough. Moisten edges of dough with cold water or a little egg white. Fold top crust in half, adjust over filling, open out; slash or prick top crust. Trim extra pastry ½ inch beyond rim. Fold edge of top crust under edge of lower crust and press with fingertips or fork to seal. Press edges with finger on one hand and pinch the dough between thumb and forefinger of other hand to flute the rim.

One-Crust Pies

Fit bottom crust loosely into ungreased pie pan. Do not stretch the dough, but ease it into place to prevent shrinking. Trim edge ½ inch from pan. Fold edge under and flute rim, hooking at several points under pan edge to help hold shell in place during baking. Fill and bake as desired.

Prebaked Pie Shell

Proceed as for one-crust pie. Prick the shell well, line with waxed paper, and fill with dried beans, rice, or pastry weights to prevent puffing. Bake in very hot oven (450° F) 8 to 10 minutes. Remove weights, and cook for 2 to 3 more minutes. Cool and fill.

Lattice Top

Divide and roll out two rounds of pastry as for double-crust pie. Line pie plate with pastry, leaving 1 inch overhanging edge. Fill as desired. Take remaining pastry round and cut into ½-inch strips, using a pastry wheel to make an attractive edge. Lay half the strips across the pie, 1 inch apart. Weave the cross strips over and under these, beginning at the center. Trim the ends of the strips; moisten edge of pastry with water, and fold edge of bottom crust over strips. Press to seal.

SHORT PASTRY

This and the following recipes make two-crust pies. Halve if only a single crust is desired or make whole recipe, cut dough in half, and freeze the unused portion.

2 cups flour
1 teaspoon salt
½ cup shortening

¼ cup butter
ice water

 Follow the guidelines at the beginning of the chapter. Have all materials ice cold. Sift together flour and salt. Blend the shortening and butter into the flour. Add enough ice water, a little at a time, to hold dough together. Wrap and chill half an hour or more. Roll ¼ to ⅛ inch thick and line pie plate.

Note: If using a food processor, combine dry ingredients in the workbowl fitted with the metal blade. Pulse quickly to blend. Cut in chilled shortening and butter with several quick pulses. Add liquid a little at a time and process just until dough forms a ball. Wrap, chill, and roll out as for above.

FLAKY PASTRY

2 cups flour
1½ teaspoons salt

1 cup shortening
ice water

 Follow the same procedures as for Short Pastry.

QUICK PASTRY

 ½ cup shortening
¼ cup cold water
1½ cups flour

⅛ teaspoon baking powder
½ teaspoon salt

Melt shortening, add water, and mix with remaining ingredients to a smooth dough. Wrap and chill before rolling.

CREAM CHEESE PASTRY

3 ounces cream cheese
½ cup butter

1 cup flour

 Combine all to make a smooth dough. Chill. When ready to use, roll into desired shape for appetizers, tarts, or one-crust pies.

FLOUR-PASTE PIECRUST

2 cups flour	¼ cup ice water
½ teaspoon salt	⅔ cup shortening

 Sift together flour and salt. Make paste of ⅓ cup of the flour and the water. Blend shortening into the remaining flour. Add paste. Stir well. Wrap, chill, and roll out as with other pastries.

COOKIE DOUGH FOR OPEN PIES

2 cups flour	2 tablespoons butter
1 teaspoon baking powder	1 egg, lightly beaten
½ cup sugar	½ cup milk

Mix dry ingredients and butter. Add beaten egg to milk and combine the two mixtures. Roll ¼ inch thick.

Note: Makes enough to line two pie plates or oblong pans. Use for open-faced fruit tarts or kuchen.

MUERBE TEIG (RICH EGG PASTRY)

1 cup butter	¼ cup cold water
3 cups flour	grated rind and juice of 1 lemon
2 egg yolks	¼ cup sugar

 Mix butter and flour. In a separate bowl, beat egg yolks and add the water. Combine the mixtures, adding grated rind and juice of lemon and sugar. Pat into pan ¼ inch thick. Wrap and chill. Bake with desired filling.

GOLDEN EGG PASTRY

5 yolks of hard-cooked eggs	1 cup sugar
1 raw egg	3 cups flour
1½ cups butter	3 tablespoons lemon juice

Rub the cooked yolks to a paste, add the raw egg. Cream butter and add sugar. Add egg mixture and flour alternately, then the lemon juice. Pat dough ¼ inch thick onto pie plates. Wrap and chill. Bake with desired filling.

HINTS FOR TENDER PASTRY

Light tender pastry requires an experienced hand, and the beginning cook should not be discouraged if first attempts are not ideal. Minimum handling, chilled ingredients, and as little liquid as possible are especially important.

PUFF PASTE (BLAETTER TEIG)

1 pound butter
4 cups cake flour

ice water

Chill all utensils and ingredients. Divide butter into 3 parts and roll each into a thin oblong pat. Wrap 2 of these in waxed paper and refrigerate. Work the other butter pat into the flour with a fork or pastry blender. Add ice water a little at a time, using as little as possible to make a smooth paste. Toss the paste on floured board and knead just enough to form a ball shape. Then pat and roll out to ¼-inch thickness, keeping paste a little wider than long and corners square. Lay 1 pat of the chilled butter on the paste, sprinkle top very lightly with flour, and fold over the paste so as to enclose the butter. Roll up like a jelly roll and then pat and roll out again to ¼ inch thick. Wrap paste and chill for 30 minutes. Add remaining butter pat, roll out and fold as before. Wrap and chill another 30 minutes. Before baking, preheat oven to 500° F and roll out paste 4 or 5 times, with gentle strokes from center out. Paste should be ice cold, and the oven extremely hot. Place on a rack in the oven and bake, turning the pan frequently so that puff paste may rise evenly. When well risen, reduce the heat gradually to 350° F and continue baking until lightly browned. Used for pies, patties, vol au vents, and tarts.

PUFF PASTE PATTY SHELLS

Roll Puff Paste, above, ⅓ inch thick. Cut into 3-inch rounds with a cookie cutter. With a smaller cutter, remove the centers from two thirds of the rounds, thus forming rings. Fit two of these rings on each solid round and press lightly. Chill well before baking. Preheat oven to 500° F. Line baking sheet with parchment paper. Bake shells for 10 minutes, until well puffed, and then reduce heat to 350° F and continue baking for about 15 minutes, until brown. Bake half the cutouts separately; these may be used as covers. The remaining cutouts may be rerolled with the other scraps from the cutting, and filled with preserves or savory mixtures to make small sweet or cocktail turnovers.

PUFF PASTE TART SHELLS

 Preheat oven to 500° F. Cut out rounds of Puff Paste, cover backs of muffin tins or custard cups, pleating edges to fit. Prick well and bake until well risen, then reduce heat to 350° F and continue until browned.

PUFF PASTE PIE SHELL

 Roll half of Puff Paste ⅓ inch thick, in a round large enough to fit over the back of a pie plate. Trim excess; pleat edges to fit and prick well. Bake like Puff Paste Tart Shells, above. Cool and fill.

Crumb Shells

ZWIEBACK OR GRAHAM CRACKER SHELL

  Blend 2 cups Zwieback or graham cracker crumbs with 4 tablespoons confectioners' sugar and ½ cup melted butter. Spread and press mixture on buttered sides and bottom of springform pan. Chill for several hours before filling. For 8- or 9-inch pie pan use 1 cup crumbs, 2 tablespoons sugar, and ¼ cup butter.

CHOCOLATE WAFER OR OTHER COOKIE CRUMB SHELLS

 Spread softened butter thickly on sides and bottom of springform pan and pat on 1½ cups fine cookie crumbs. Chill for several hours before filling. Reserve ¼ cup crumbs to sprinkle on the top of torte when filled.

CORNFLAKE SHELL

  Blend 2 cups crushed cornflakes, ½ cup melted butter, 1 teaspoon cinnamon, and 4 tablespoons sugar. Reserve ¼ cup of mixture to garnish the filled pie. Spread remainder on sides and bottom of buttered springform pan. Chill for several hours before filling.

MATZO PIE SHELL

2 matzos
1 tablespoon fat
¼ cup matzo meal

2 eggs
2 tablespoons sugar
⅛ teaspoon salt

Preheat oven to 350° F. Soak matzos in water and press dry. Heat fat, add the soaked matzos, and stir over low heat until dry. Add matzo meal, eggs, sugar, and salt. Mix well and pat evenly against bottom and sides of pie plate, ¼ inch thick. Fill with any desired fruit filling and bake 30 to 40 minutes.

MERINGUE PIE SHELL

3 egg whites
1¾ cups confectioners' sugar

1 tablespoon cornstarch

Preheat oven to 275° F. Beat egg whites until stiff. Add ¾ cup confectioners' sugar gradually, in small amounts, beating after each addition until mixture holds stiff peaks. Mix the cornstarch and remaining sugar and fold gently into the egg-white mixture. Lay 9-inch round of parchment paper on baking sheet. Cover with meringue, shaping hollow with back of spoon to make shell. Bake for 45 minutes. Cool, fill with fruit or any cream pie filling, cover with sweetened whipped cream.

Pie Toppings

MATZO PIE TOPPING

2 matzos
½ cup shortening
2 hard-cooked egg yolks
1 cup sugar
1 teaspoon salt

2 eggs, well beaten
grated rind of 1 lemon
¼ teaspoon nutmeg
1½ cups matzo meal

Soak the matzos in water for 10 minutes and squeeze dry. Preheat oven to 350° F. Cream shortening, add matzos and stir until thoroughly blended. Mash yolks of hard-cooked eggs with a fork, add to mixture, then add sugar, salt, and beaten eggs. Add grated rind, nutmeg, and finally the matzo meal, stirring the batter thoroughly as each ingredient is added. Use as topping for apple, prune, apricot, or other fruit pie. Drop spoonfuls of batter, not too close together, on top of filling. Bake 30 to 40 minutes.

MERINGUE TOPPING

8-Inch Pies

2 egg whites   4 tablespoons sugar
¼ teaspoon cream of tartar

9-Inch Pies

3 egg whites   6 tablespoons sugar
¼ teaspoon cream of tartar

Preheat oven to 375° F. Beat egg whites with cream of tartar until frothy. Beat sugar in gradually, a little at a time. Continue beating until mixture is stiff and glossy, and sugar is dissolved. Swirl the meringue over the pie filling with a spatula, touching crust all around; lift spatula to form peaks but don't make the tips too high, or they will burn. Bake for 8 to 10 minutes until light brown.

Note: Bake at 300° F for 15 to 20 minutes for a crisper meringue with less risk of "dew drops" of moisture forming on the meringue after it has cooled.

Fruit Pies

APPLE PIE

1 recipe Short Pastry (page 521)   2 tablespoons butter, cut into bits
6 to 8 apples   cinnamon, nutmeg, or lemon juice
½ cup sugar

Preheat oven to 425° F. Line a pie plate with pastry. Pare, core, and slice apples. Fill the pie shell with apples, sprinkle with sugar, bits of butter, and spices or lemon juice. Cover with upper crust, seal and crimp the edges, and slash the top so steam can escape. Bake from 45 minutes to 1 hour until crust is brown and fruit is soft.

APPLE MERINGUE PIE

2 eggs, separated   1 8-inch Rich Egg Pastry pie shell
¾ cup sugar   (page 522), unbaked
4 large apples, chopped   2 tablespoons butter, cut into bits
¼ pound almonds, chopped   Meringue Topping (page 526)
¼ cup raisins, seeded
Juice and grated rind of 1 lemon

Preheat oven to 400° F. Beat egg yolks with sugar, add apples, almonds, raisins, and lemon juice and rind; beat egg whites until stiff and fold into yolk mixture. Line a pie plate with Rich Egg Pastry. Place mixture on dough, dot with butter, and bake for 20 to 25 minutes until crust is brown. Cover with Meringue Topping and return to oven to brown lightly.

CARAMELIZED APPLE PIE

¼ cup butter, melted
½ cup brown sugar, firmly packed
1 teaspoon honey, heated

½ cup pecan meats, chopped
1 recipe Apple Pie filling (above)
1 recipe Quick Pastry (page 521)

Preheat oven to 400° F. Place butter, sugar, honey, and nuts in an unlined deep pie plate. Make pie crust, and divide into 2 parts. Roll out bottom crust and lay it over the sugar mixture and up the sides of the pie plate. Fill with apples as in Apple Pie Filling and cover with upper crust. Seal the edges and make slits so steam can escape. Bake for 15 minutes, then reduce heat to 325° F and bake 20 to 30 minutes longer, until apples are tender and crust is brown. Cool. One-half hour before serving time, return to a hot oven for a few moments to loosen caramel. Invert and serve caramel side up.

BERRY PIE

1 pound fresh berries
1½ tablespoons tapioca
⅔ cup sugar

1 tablespoon lemon juice (optional)
cinnamon to taste (optional)
1 recipe Quick Pastry (page 521)

Preheat oven to 450° F. Cook berries until they begin to give off liquid and drain, reserving the juice. Mix tapioca and sugar with ¾ cup of the juice. Cook about 15 minutes until thick and clear. Add drained fruit and cool. Add lemon juice and a little cinnamon for extra flavor, if desired. Line an 8-inch pie plate with pastry, add filling, and cover with top crust and slash. Bake for about 20 minutes, then reduce heat to 375° F and bake about 15 minutes longer, or until crust is brown.

CANNED CHERRY PIE

1 recipe favorite pie pastry	2 tablespoons cornstarch
1 can (16 ounces) tart red cherries, pitted	½ teaspoon salt
6 tablespoons sugar	1 tablespoon butter

Preheat oven to 475° F. Line an 8-inch pie plate with pastry. Drain cherries and place on unbaked crust. Sprinkle dry ingredients over fruit. Pour on cherry juice. Dot with butter. Cover with top crust, slashed or latticed. Bake for 12 minutes, then reduce heat to 425° F and bake about 40 minutes longer.

FRESH CHERRY PIE

1 recipe favorite pie pastry	1½ to 2 cups sugar
1 quart sour cherries, pitted	2 tablespoons cornstarch or flour

Preheat oven to 450° F. Line an 8-inch pie plate with pastry. Mix fruit with sugar and cornstarch. Fill crust. Cover with lattice crust. Bake for about 20 minutes, then reduce heat to 375° F and bake about 15 minutes longer, until crust is browned.

CRANBERRY RAISIN PIE

1 recipe favorite pie pastry	1 teaspoon butter, melted
1 cup cranberries, washed	¾ cup sugar
4 cups seeded raisins, coarsely chopped	1 tablespoon flour

Preheat oven to 350° F. Line a small pie pan with pastry. Cut cranberries in halves, raisins in pieces. Combine with remaining ingredients, fill crust, cover with top crust, and slash. Bake for about 40 minutes.

GOOSEBERRY PIE

1 recipe favorite pie pastry	1 cup less 2 tablespoons sugar
1 pint fresh gooseberries	water

Preheat oven to 450° F. Line an 8-inch pie plate with pastry. Remove stem endings from both ends of the berries. Put in saucepan with sugar and just enough water to prevent burning and cook until softened. Cool. Fill pie, cover with top crust. Slash and bake about 25 minutes, until browned.

MINCE PIE

1 recipe favorite pie pastry

Preheat oven to 425° F. Line pie plate with pastry, fill with Mincemeat (below), or with commercially prepared mincemeat. Cover with top crust, slash, and bake 30 to 35 minutes. Then reduce heat to 325° F and bake for 10 minutes more.

MINCEMEAT

3 pounds beef or venison, chopped
1½ pounds beef suet, chopped
6 pounds apples, chopped
3 pounds seedless raisins
2 pounds currants
1 pound citron, chopped
finely grated rind of ½ lemon and ½ orange
2 tablespoons ground cinnamon

1 tablespoon ground cloves
1 nutmeg, grated, or 1 tablespoon ground nutmeg
3 pounds brown sugar, firmly packed
1 quart boiled apple cider
1 quart molasses
salt to taste

Cook all the ingredients together slowly for 2 hours and seal in sterilizd glass jars.

RHUBARB PIE

1 recipe favorite pie pastry
3 cups rhubarb
2 tablespoons cornstarch

1 egg, slightly beaten
1½ cups sugar

Preheat oven to 425° F. Line a pie plate with pastry. Cut rhubarb into ¼-inch pieces; sprinkle with cornstarch. Add egg and sugar, mix well, turn into lined pie plate. Cover with lattice strips or top crust slashed to let steam escape. Bake for 30 minutes, then reduce heat to 325° F for 15 to 20 minutes.

Variation: Mix equal parts rhubarb and sliced, fresh strawberries for variety.

Cream and Custard Pies

BANANA CREAM PIE

½ cup sugar
4 tablespoons cornstarch
½ teaspoon salt
2 cups milk, scalded

3 egg yolks
1 teaspoon vanilla
3 sliced bananas
1 9-inch pie shell, prebaked

Mix sugar, cornstarch, and salt. Add milk slowly, stirring constantly. Cook in double boiler until cornstarch is clear and begins to thicken. Beat egg yolks slightly. Add gradually to mixture, careful not to curdle them. Cook about 2 minutes. Add vanilla. Cool. Put alternate layers of bananas and filling into baked pie shell. Cover with whipped cream.

Variation: Cover pie with Meringue Topping (page 526) and bake at 375° F, until top turns golden.

BUTTERSCOTCH MERINGUE PIE

1½ cups water
1½ cups brown sugar, firmly
  packed
3 tablespoons cornstarch
2 tablespoons flour
½ teaspoon salt
2 tablespoons sugar

¼ cup cold water
2 egg yolks
½ tablespoon butter
1 teaspoon vanilla
1 8-inch pie shell, prebaked
Meringue Topping (page 526)

Heat water and brown sugar in a double boiler. Mix cornstarch, flour, salt, and sugar; add water to make a smooth paste. Add to the sugar mixture, and then cook in a double boiler over boiling water 15 minutes or until thick. Beat egg yolks slightly, stir carefully into cooked mixture; cook 5 minutes. Add butter and vanilla. Fill shell, cover with Meringue Topping.

OLD-FASHIONED CHEESE PIE

Cookie Dough (page 522)
1½ cups dry cottage cheese
pinch of salt
2 tablespoons flour
2 tablespoons cream
3 eggs, separated
¾ cup sugar

1 tablespoon butter, melted
¼ cup currants or raisins
½ teaspoon vanilla
grated rind of 1 lemon
¼ pound blanched almonds, finely
   chopped

Preheat oven to 350° F. Line a pie plate with dough. Rub cheese through sieve, add pinch of salt, flour, and cream; mix well. Beat yolks slightly, add sugar and butter, stir well, and mix with the cheese mixture. Add currants, vanilla, and lemon rind. Beat the egg whites until soft peaks form and fold them in. Place mixture in the shell; top with nuts and bake 1 hour.

REFRIGERATOR CHEESE CAKE

mixture for Zwieback or Graham
   Cracker Shell (page 524)
2 envelopes unflavored gelatin
½ cup cold water
3 egg yolks, slightly beaten
1 cup sugar

pinch of salt
½ cup warm milk
1 pound dry cottage cheese, riced
juice and grated rind of 1 lemon
3 egg whites, stiffly beaten
1 cup heavy cream, whipped

Line a buttered springform pan with crumb mixture. Reserve ¼ cup for top. Soak gelatin in cold water 5 minutes. Cook yolks, sugar, salt, and milk in a double boiler, stirring constantly until mixture coats the spoon. Add gelatin, stir until dissolved. Cool. When mixture begins to set, beat in cheese and lemon juice and rind. Fold in beaten egg whites and whipped cream. Pour mixture into springform. Sprinkle with remaining crumbs. Chill for 4 to 5 hours.

Variation: 1 cup crushed pineapple, ¼ cup nut meats, or ¼ cup maraschino cherries may be added to filling.

SOUR CREAM CHEESECAKE

1 recipe Cookie Dough or Rich Egg
   Pastry (page 522)
1¼ pounds dry cottage cheese
4 tablespoons cornstarch
dash of salt

5 egg yolks
1 cup sugar
2 cups thick, sour cream
5 egg whites, stiffly beaten

(continued)

Preheat oven to 350° F. Line a springform pan with Cookie Dough or Rich Egg Pastry, patted ¼ inch thick. Put cheese through sieve or ricer and add cornstarch and a little salt. Stir in egg yolks, sugar, and sour cream; beat until smooth. Fold in the beaten whites. Fill springform; bake 1 hour or until well set and browned at bottom.

CREAM CHEESE CAKE

mixture for Zwieback or Graham Cracker Shell (page 524)	4 8-ounce packages cream cheese, softened
4 eggs	2 cups sour cream
1¼ cups sugar	1 teaspoon vanilla
1 tablespoon lemon juice	

Line a springform pan with the crumb mixture; reserve ¼ cup for topping. Preheat oven to 375° F. Beat eggs, 1 cup of the sugar, and lemon juice until light. Add the cream cheese and beat thoroughly. Pour filling into crust and bake for 20 minutes. Remove cake from oven; increase oven heat to 475° F. Top cake with sour cream mixed with vanilla and the remaining ¼ cup sugar. Sprinkle with the remaining crumbs and bake 10 minutes longer. Cool, and chill in refrigerator overnight before serving.

CHESS PIE

2 eggs	1 teaspoon vanilla
1½ tablespoons flour	1 cup heavy cream
⅔ cup brown sugar, firmly packed	½ cup seedless white raisins
½ teaspoon salt	1 9-inch pie shell, unbaked
1 cup pitted dates, coarsely chopped	
1 cup walnut meats, coarsely chopped	

Preheat oven to 350° F. Beat eggs until thick and light. Mix flour, sugar, and salt and add to eggs, beating constantly. Add dates and nuts, vanilla, cream, and raisins to the batter. Place in pie shell and bake for 50 to 60 minutes, or until a knife inserted near the center of the pie comes out clean.

CHOCOLATE CUSTARD PIE

2 ounces unsweetened chocolate
1 cup milk
salt
¼ cup cornstarch
1 tablespoon butter

3 eggs, separated
1 cup sugar
1 teaspoon vanilla
1 9-inch pie shell, lightly baked

Preheat oven to 300° F. Melt chocolate in double boiler, add milk, a speck of salt, and cornstarch mixed with a little cold water, and cook until smooth and thick, stirring constantly; add butter. Mix the yolks and sugar and pour the hot mixture over them, stirring well; put back in double boiler and cook, stirring constantly, until mixture is very thick. Cool, add vanilla. Beat egg whites until stiff and fold in. Fill shell with chocolate custard and bake for 30 minutes. Serve with whipped cream.

COCONUT CUSTARD PIE

3 eggs, separated, whites stiffly
    beaten
½ cup sugar
2 cups scalded milk

dash of salt
½ cup shredded coconut
1 8-inch pie shell, lightly baked

Preheat oven to 300° F. Beat egg yolks with the sugar, add milk gradually, salt, then the coconut and stiffly beaten whites. If desired, mix ½ tablespoon cornstarch with the sugar and use only 2 eggs. Fill shell and bake 30 minutes.

CUSTARD PIE

1 8-inch pie shell, unbaked
2 eggs
¼ cup sugar

a little grated nutmeg
speck of salt
1½ cups milk, scalded

Preheat oven to 450° F. Lightly bake pie shell for about 10 minutes. Meanwhile, beat the eggs, add the sugar, nutmeg, and salt. Stir in the scalded milk. Pour the mixture into the hot crust. Lower oven temperature to 300° F. Bake about 30 minutes longer until a knife inserted near the center of custard comes out clean. Remove pie from oven at once; cool at room temperature.

LEMON MERINGUE PIE

1 cup sugar
¼ cup flour or cornstarch
1 cup boiling water
1 tablespoon butter
3 egg yolks

grated rind of 1 lemon
¼ cup lemon juice
1 9-inch pie shell, prebaked
1 recipe Meringue Topping (page 526)

Preheat oven to 300° F. Mix sugar and flour, add the boiling water slowly and boil until clear, stirring constantly over low heat. Add butter and, gradually, the egg yolks, beaten lightly. Cook over boiling water until very thick, stirring constantly. Add lemon rind and juice. Cool. Fold in half of Meringue Topping and fill shell with this mixture. Cover with remaining Meringue Topping. Bake for 15 minutes. Cool to let filling set before serving.

PECAN PIE

1 8-inch pie shell, unbaked
1 cup pecan halves
3 eggs
½ cup sugar

1 cup dark corn syrup
¼ teaspoon salt
1 teaspoon vanilla
¼ cup butter, melted

Preheat oven to 450° F. Spread nuts over bottom of shell. Beat eggs; add sugar, syrup, salt, vanilla, and butter. Pour filling over pecans. Bake 10 minutes then reduce heat to 350° F and bake for 35 minutes longer.

PUMPKIN OR SQUASH PIE

⅔ cup brown sugar, firmly packed
½ teaspoon salt
1 teaspoon cinnamon
½ teaspoon ginger
½ teaspoon cloves
1½ cups canned, or cooked and pureed, pumpkin or squash

2 eggs, lightly beaten
½ teaspoon vanilla
grated lemon rind (optional)
½ cup milk
½ cup half-and-half
1 beaten egg white, for brushing
1 9-inch pie shell, unbaked

Preheat oven to 425° F. Mix sugar, salt, and spices; add pumpkin or squash, lightly beaten eggs, vanilla, and lemon rind, if desired. Add the milk and half-and-half gradually. If pumpkin is very moist, use less liquid. Brush shell with egg white. Add the filling, and bake for 20 minutes. Reduce heat to 275° F and bake 40 minutes longer or until knife inserted near edge of custard comes out clean. Cool at room temperature.

STRAWBERRY CREAM PIE

1 cup sugar
2 quarts strawberries
1 tablespoon cornstarch

2 tablespoons cold water
2 cups heavy cream, whipped
1 9-inch pie shell, prebaked

Add sugar to berries. Let stand 1 hour. Strain, reserving liquid. Return half of the berries to the reserved juice and to this add cornstarch dissolved in the cold water. Cook 15 minutes to thicken. Chill. Just before serving, spread whipped cream about ½ inch thick in baked pie shell. Put whole berries on top of cream and over this pour the thickened berries with juice. Decorate around edges with remaining cream.

STRAWBERRY MERINGUE PIE

1 9-inch pie shell, unbaked
breadcrumbs
1 quart strawberries
½ cup confectioners' sugar

2 egg yolks
½ cup granulated sugar
Meringue Topping (page 526)

Preheat oven to 425° F. Sprinkle pie shell with breadcrumbs. Mix berries with confectioners' sugar and fill pie shell. Cover with egg yolks, beaten well with granulated sugar. Bake for 20 minutes, until shell is brown. Cover with Meringue Topping and return to oven until meringue is lightly browned.

Chiffon Pies

CHOCOLATE CHIFFON PIE

1 envelope unflavored gelatin
¼ cup cold water
½ cup sugar
2 ounces unsweetened chocolate
½ cup milk
½ cup strong coffee

½ teaspoon salt
1 teaspoon vanilla
1 cup heavy cream, whipped
1 9-inch pie shell, prebaked
whipped cream for garnish

Soak gelatin in water 5 minutes. Heat the sugar, chocolate, milk, coffee, and salt in double boiler until well blended. Add the softened gelatin to this mixture, stirring thoroughly. Cool, add the vanilla. When the mixture begins to thicken, fold in the whipped cream. Fill shell. Chill. Before serving, garnish with additional whipped cream.

LEMON CHIFFON PIE

1 envelope unflavored gelatin
¼ cup cold water
4 eggs, separated
1 cup sugar
½ cup lemon juice

½ teaspoon salt
1 teaspoon grated lemon rind
1 9-inch pie shell, prebaked
whipped cream for garnish

Soak gelatin in cold water 5 minutes. Beat yolks and add ½ cup sugar, lemon juice, and salt. Cook in double boiler until mixture coats spoon. Add rind and softened gelatin. Stir well and set aside to cool. Meanwhile, beat egg whites stiff with remaining ½ cup sugar. When the egg-yolk mixture begins to thicken, fold in whites. Fill pie shell and chill. Top with a thin layer of whipped cream and serve.

Variation:

Orange Chiffon Pie: Follow recipe for Lemon Chiffon Pie, substituting ½ cup orange juice, 1 tablespoon grated orange rind, and 1 tablespoon lemon juice for the lemon rind and the ½ cup lemon juice.

STRAWBERRY CHIFFON PIE

1 envelope unflavored gelatin
¼ cup cold water
½ cup boiling water
1 cup sugar
1 cup strawberry pulp and juice
¼ teaspoon salt

½ cup heavy cream, whipped
2 egg whites
1 9-inch pie shell, prebaked
whipped cream for garnish
whole strawberries, for garnish

Soak gelatin in cold water 5 minutes. Combine the boiling water, ¾ cup sugar, strawberry pulp and juice, and salt. Add to softened gelatin and stir until dissolved. Cool. When gelatin mixture begins to thicken, fold in whipped cream. Beat egg whites until foamy. Add remaining ¼ cup sugar gradually, beating until stiff and glossy. Fold into strawberry mixture, pour into baked pie shell, and chill. Serve garnished with whipped cream and whole strawberries.

Variations:

Fruit Chiffon Pies: Pineapple, apricots, berries, or any fresh fruit pulp and juice may be substituted for strawberries.

Tarts

TART SHELLS

Preheat oven to 475° F. Roll out any pastry dough to about ¼ inch thick. Cut out rounds 4 inches in diameter; fit over the backs of inverted muffin pans or custard cups. Pinch the edges to fit. Prick bottom with a fork and bake on a baking sheet until browned, about 15 minutes. Or use individual tart pans, and fit the rounds in as you would for a large pie shell, pricking well and fluting the edges.

Cool the tart shells and remove from the pans.

FRESH FRUIT TARTS

Shape tart shells with Cookie Dough for Open Pies (page 522). When cool, fill ⅔ full of Cream Custard Filling (page 607). Arrange large strawberries or raspberries on filling, brush with melted currant jelly or Apricot Glaze (page 450). Add a second coat of glaze when the first has set. Decorate with sliced pistachio nuts, if desired.

ICE CREAM TARTS

 Fill baked tart shells with ice cream; cover with very thick layer of Meringue Topping (page 526); broil at 350° F until meringue is lightly browned, or bake at 400° F about 5 minutes.

BANBURY TARTS

1 cup nuts, chopped	1 egg
1 cup raisins, chopped	1 tablespoon butter, melted
1 cup sugar	1 tablespoon water
juice and grated rind of 1 lemon	6 to 8 unbaked tart shells

Preheat oven to 450° F. Mix the first seven ingredients together; fill tart shells and bake until crust is brown, about 15 minutes.

PASTRY MINIATURES

VIENNA TARTS

Preheat oven to 450° F. Make Cream Cheese Pastry (page 521). Chill, roll out, and cut into 3-inch squares. Put 1 teaspoon of preserves in center of each. Pick up corners, press together to form square turnovers. Bake until browned.

RUSSIAN TEA CAKES

4 eggs
1 cup sugar
1 cup sour cream
4 to 6 cups flour

1½ cups butter, softened
1 cup chopped almonds
sugar and cinnamon

1.   Mix eggs, sugar, and sour cream, and add enough flour to make a dough that can be handled. Roll out ¼ inch thick into a rectangle three times as long as wide. Spread half the butter thinly over the right-hand two thirds of the dough. Fold the left-hand third over the buttered dough, then the right-hand third over this.

2.   Roll out, wrap in plastic, and chill for 1 to 2 hours. Repeat with remaining butter. Chill again for 1 to 2 hours, wrapped.

3.   Preheat oven to 400° F. Divide dough into 4 parts. Roll each part into a rectangle, as thin as possible. Sprinkle with some of the chopped almonds, sugar and cinnamon, and roll. Cut in slices, sprinkle with the rest of the almonds, sugar, and cinnamon. Bake cut side down on a baking sheet until delicately browned.

APRICOT HORNS

Dough
1 pound butter
1 pound creamed cottage cheese
4 cups flour

Filling
1 pound dried apricots
2 cups sugar

Coating
1½ cups almonds, ground
1½ cups granulated sugar
2 egg whites, slightly beaten
confectioners' sugar

1. Blend dough ingredients. Roll dough in balls 1 inch in diameter. Chill thoroughly.

2. Meanwhile, make the filling by cooking apricots in water to cover until soft. Add sugar and force through a sieve. Set aside.

3. Prepare the coating by combining almonds and granulated sugar.

4. Preheat oven to 375° F. Roll or flatten each ball into a 3-inch round. Work with only a few balls of dough at a time so that the others will remain cold. Place a teaspoon of the apricot filling in center of each round. Roll up and bend ends to the shape of a crescent. Dip into egg white and roll in coating mixture. Bake on greased cookie sheet for 12 minutes, or until lightly browned. Sprinkle with confectioners' sugar while warm.

LINZER TARTS

Preheat oven to 450° F. Roll Linzer Torte pastry (page 580) ⅛ inch thick. Shape with a fluted, round cutter dipped in flour. With a smaller cutter remove centers from half the pieces, leaving rings ½ inch wide. Brush the circles with cold water near the edge; fit on rings and press lightly. Chill. Bake 15 minutes. Brush with egg yolk beaten with 1 teaspoon water. Cool and fill with jam.

JAM TURNOVERS (SOUR CREAM KIPFEL)

1 cup butter	jam
4 cups flour	2 tablespoons sugar
¾ cup sour cream	⅛ teaspoon cinnamon
2 eggs, separated	¼ pound almonds, chopped

Cut butter into flour, add sour cream and egg yolks and chill thoroughly. Preheat oven to 400° F. Roll out and fold as in Puff Paste recipe (page 523), repeating 4 times. Roll thin, cut into 2-inch squares. Put a teaspoon of jam on each square, fold over the corners, press edges together. Spread top with the lightly beaten egg whites; sprinkle with sugar, cinnamon and chopped almonds. Bake for 15 to 20 minutes until brown.

Fruit Kuchen

Fruit Kuchen are open-faced fruit pies that differ from ordinary pies in that they are made with raised Plain Kuchen Dough or with Rich Egg Pastry rather than with ordinary pie crust, and the fruit is covered with an egg custard mixture.

APPLE KUCHEN AND VARIATIONS

 Preheat oven to 425° F. Line a well-greased oblong pan with a very thin sheet of raised Plain Kuchen Dough (page 439) or Rich Egg Pastry (page 522). Core, pare, and cut 4 or 5 apples in eighths. Lay them in parallel rows on top of the dough and sprinkle with sugar and cinnamon. Beat the yolk of an egg with 3 tablespoons cream, and drip around apples. Bake 20 or 30 minutes until crust is well baked and apples are soft.

Variations:

Strawberries: 1 quart, 2 eggs, 1 cup sugar.
Blueberries: 1 quart, 2 eggs, 3 tablespoons cream, ½ cup sugar.
Plums: 1 quart pitted and cut in half, 3 eggs, 1½ cups sugar.
Cherries: 1 20-ounce can unsweetened, or 1½ pounds fresh cherries, pitted, 2 eggs, 1 cup sugar.
Peaches: 1 quart pared and sliced, 1 egg yolk, 1 cup sugar.
Seedless Grapes: 1½ pounds, ¾ cup sugar, 2 tablespoons flour, 2 egg yolks.

APRICOT KUCHEN

3 cups dried apricots	2 eggs, beaten
1½ cups sugar	2 tablespoons milk
1 recipe Golden Egg Pastry (page 522)	few drops almond extract

Cook apricots in water to cover until tender but not mushy; the liquid should be almost absorbed. Add 1 cup of the sugar when fruit is nearly done. Cool. Preheat oven to 375° F. Line pan with Golden Egg Pastry. Fill with apricots. Beat eggs, add remaining ½ cup sugar, milk, and almond extract; mix well together, drizzle over fruit. Bake for 20 minutes; reduce heat to 300°, and bake 30 minutes longer, until browned.

CHERRY KUCHEN

1 quart sour cherries, pitted
1 recipe Rich Egg Pastry (page 522)
breadcrumbs
½ cup sugar

cinnamon to taste
1 egg yolk
3 tablespoons cream

Preheat oven to 425° F. Pit the cherries, reserving any juice. Place thin layer of Rich Egg Pastry in shallow pan; sprinkle with breadcrumbs. Spread evenly with cherries. Sprinkle with sugar and cinnamon. Beat egg yolk well, add the cream and cherry juice and pour over cherries. Bake until crust is well browned.

Variation: Add 1 cup pecans with fruit, if desired.

BLUEBERRY KUCHEN

1 recipe Rich Egg Pastry (page 522)
2 16–ounce cans or 2 pounds fresh
　blueberries
¼ cup sugar

1 tablespoon cornstarch
1 teaspoon butter
1 egg, slightly beaten
1 tablespoon lemon juice

Preheat oven to 425° F. Line pan with Rich Egg Pastry. If using canned berries, drain them, saving juice. Mix sugar and cornstarch; gradually add 1 cup of reserved berry juice, butter, and egg. Cook in double boiler until mixture coats the spoon. Add lemon juice. Spread berries on pastry, cover with custard. Bake until crust is brown, about 20 minutes.

GRAPE KUCHEN

1 recipe Rich Egg Pastry (page 522)
1½ pounds seedless green grapes
1 cup sugar

2 tablespoons flour
2 eggs, separated
¼ cup water

Preheat oven to 325° F. Line pan with Rich Egg Pastry. Toss grapes with ¾ cup of the sugar and flour; fill crust. Beat egg yolks with water, drizzle over fruit. Bake for 45 minutes. Beat egg whites until stiff, beat in remaining ¼ cup sugar, and continue beating until meringue is stiff. Spread over fruit and return to oven to brown lightly.

CANNED PEACH OR PEAR KUCHEN

1 recipe Rich Egg Pastry (page 522)
1 quart canned peaches or pears
3 eggs

½ cup sugar
½ cup cream or fruit juice
Almond Brittle (page 667)

Preheat oven to 400° F. Line bottom and sides of a greased 9-inch springform pan with Rich Egg Pastry. Drain fruit, reserving juice, and place on pastry. Make custard by beating eggs well with sugar; add cream or fruit juice. Pour custard over fruit and bake for 10 minutes. Reduce heat to 350° F and bake until custard is set. Cool, sprinkle with Ground Almond Brittle. Serve with whipped cream.

PRUNE KUCHEN

1½ pounds prunes
½ cup sugar
1 tablespoon cocoa
vanilla to taste

3 egg yolks
1 recipe Rich Egg Pastry (page 522)
Meringue Topping (page 526)

Cook prunes until soft, stone, rub through sieve, mix well with sugar, cocoa, vanilla, and egg yolks. Preheat oven to 425° F. Fill pie plate lined with Rich Egg Pastry. Bake until crust is brown. Cover with Meringue Topping. Return to oven and bake until lightly browned.

Strudels

STRUDEL DOUGH

¼ teaspoon salt
1½ cups flour
1 egg, slightly beaten

⅛ cup warm water
½ cup butter, melted

1. Mix salt, flour, and egg. Add the water, mix dough quickly with a knife, then knead on board, stretching it up and down to make it elastic, until it leaves the board clean. Toss on a small, well-floured board. Cover with a hot bowl and keep it warm ½ hour or longer.
2. Before stretching the dough, make sure that the room is free from drafts. Have fillings ready before stretching dough. Work quickly. Lay dough in center of a well-floured tablecloth on table about 30 by 48 inches. Flour dough. Roll into a long oval with rolling pin. Brush dough with ¼ cup of the melted butter.

With hands under dough, palms down, pull and stretch the dough gradually all around the table, toward the edges, until it hangs over the table and is as thin as paper. Cut off dough that hangs over edge and drip ¼ cup more butter over surface of dough.

3. To fill the dough, sprinkle desired filling over ¾ of the greased, stretched dough, fold a little of the dough at one end over the filling. Hold the cloth at that end high with both hands and the Strudel will roll itself over and over like a large jelly roll. Trim edges again. Twist roll into greased 11-by-16-inch pan or cut into 3 strands and lay them side by side in pan.

4. Preheat oven to 400° F. Brush top with more melted butter. Bake ½ hour; reduce heat to 350° F and bake ½ hour longer, or until brown and crisp, brushing well with butter from time to time during baking, using altogether about 1 cup melted butter for the strudel with its fillings.

APPLE STRUDEL FILLING

2 quarts cooking apples, finely chopped

1 cup seeded raisins

½ cup currants

¼ pound almonds, blanched and chopped

1 cup sugar mixed with 1 teaspoon cinnamon

½ cup butter, melted

Combine all ingredients except butter. As rapidly as possible, spread apple filling evenly over ¾ of the stretched, buttered Strudel Dough. Drip half of the melted butter over filling. Roll up, trim edges, then place in pan. Brush with rest of the butter from time to time while baking. Serve slightly warm.

ALMOND STRUDEL FILLING

4 egg yolks

½ cup sugar mixed with ¼ teaspoon cinnamon

rind of 1 lemon

1 tablespoon lemon juice

½ pound almonds, blanched, dried, and ground

½ cup butter, melted

Beat eggs, sugar, and cinnamon until light, add lemon rind, juice, and almonds. Spread evenly over ¾ of the buttered, stretched dough. Drip half of the melted butter over the filling. Roll, trim, and bake, brushing top with the remaining butter from time to time while baking.

CHEESE STRUDEL FILLING

2 pounds cottage cheese
4 egg yolks, beaten
2 tablespoons sour cream
salt

sugar
2 egg whites, stiffly beaten
½ cup butter, melted

Rice the cheese, add egg yolks, cream, salt, and sugar to taste. Fold in egg whites. Spread mixture over ¾ of the stretched buttered dough. Over this, drip ¼ cup melted butter. Roll, trim, and bake, brushing top with remaining melted butter from time to time while baking.

Variation:

Cheese, Nut, and Raisin Strudel: To the above ingredients add ¾ cup sugar, 1 cup ground almonds, and ½ cup seeded raisins.

CHERRY STRUDEL FILLING

½ cup bread, cracker or sponge
  cake crumbs
2 quarts sour cherries, fresh or
  canned

1½ cups sugar
½ cup butter, melted

Sprinkle crumbs over ¾ of the stretched dough, then the cherries, pitted and drained. Sprinkle with sugar and half of the melted butter, roll, trim, and bake, brushing with the remaining butter from time to time while baking.

COCONUT, RAISIN, AND MARASCHINO CHERRY STRUDEL FILLING

1 egg white
⅓ pound shredded coconut
¼ cup cracker crumbs
⅓ pound walnuts, ground
⅓ pound seedless raisins
juice of 1 orange
juice of 1 lemon

¾ cup sugar
½ cup preserves, drained, or ½ cup
  citron, chopped
½ cup maraschino cherries, finely
  chopped
½ cup butter, melted

 Stir egg white with coconut. Mix together the cracker crumbs, nuts, raisins, and juices. Over ¾ of the stretched and buttered dough, sprinkle the coconut mixture, the raisin and nut mixture, the sugar, preserves, and maraschino cherries. Drip ¼ cup melted butter over all. Roll up quickly, trim, and bake, brushing top with remaining melted butter from time to time while baking.

PRUNE AND APRICOT STRUDEL FILLING

1 cup stewed prunes, stoned	1 cup seeded raisins
1 cup stewed dried apricots	½ cup butter, melted
½ cup graham cracker crumbs	juice and rind of 1 lemon
1½ cups sugar	

 Drain prunes and apricots and finely chop. Mix together with the crumbs, sugar, raisins, and lemon juice and rind. Spread filling over ¾ of the stretched and buttered Strudel Dough. Drip ¼ cup melted butter over all. Roll, trim, and bake, basting with remaining butter from time to time while baking.

SOUR CREAM STRUDEL (RAHM STRUDEL) FILLING

1 quart thick sour cream	1 cup raisins
1 cup breadcrumbs	1 teaspoon cinnamon
2 cups granulated sugar	½ cup butter, melted
1 cup chopped almonds	

Spread ¾ of the stretched and buttered Strudel Dough with sour cream, sprinkle with breadcrumbs and remaining ingredients. Drip half of the butter over all. Roll, trim, and bake, brushing with remaining melted butter from time to time while baking.

CABBAGE STRUDEL

1 onion	1 quart cabbage, shredded and
¾ cup butter, melted	salted

Dice onion and sauté in ¼ cup of the butter until tender. Add salted cabbage, well drained, and cook ½ hour longer. Spread mixture over ¾ of the stretched and buttered Strudel Dough, and drip ¼ cup melted butter over all. Roll, trim, and bake, brushing with remaining ¼ cup melted butter from time to time while baking. Serve warm.

CAKES, SMALL CAKES, AND FROSTINGS

INGREDIENTS

All ingredients should be at room temperature for best results. Before starting to bake, assemble and measure all materials. Use a round-bottom mixing bowl large enough to hold all ingredients for the final beating and folding. Remember that all measurements in the following recipes are level.

Flour: All-purpose flour is meant unless cake flour is specified. If cake flour is called for, all-purpose flour may be substituted by removing 2 tablespoons from each cup of flour and adding 1½ tablespoons of cornstarch.

Baking Powder: One teaspoon "double-acting" baking powder equals 1½ teaspoons of tartrate baking powder.

Chocolate should be melted in a double boiler over hot water or in a micro-wave. Where chocolate is called for, always use unsweetened baking chocolate unless "sweet chocolate" is specified.

Granulated Sugar should be kept covered, away from heat.

Superfine Sugar dissolves easily and is handy for meringues and quick-cooking candies.

Confectioners' Sugar is a fine-powdered sugar used mostly for sprinkling. It is sometimes used in recipes when a quick dissolving is desired.

Brown Sugar must always be measured by packing solidly. To keep brown sugar soft, store in a closed container with a slice of apple or bread or in refrigerator.

MIXING CAKES

Cakes are mixed by using the following techniques:

To Stir

Let the spoon touch the sides and bottom of the bowl and move it around and around quickly.

To Beat

Tip the bowl to one side. Bring wire whisk, spoon, or fork quickly into the mixture and through it and turn it over and over, scraping the sides well each time it goes in. Beat hard and quickly, taking long strokes, folding in as much air as possible. Or use rotary or electric beater.

To Cut or Fold

To combine mixtures lightly, cut down through the base batter with a rubber spatula or side of a spoon. Fold it by lifting the mixture up from the bottom of the bowl and over the top of the batter. Turn bowl slightly after each stroke, folding as lightly as possible until blended.

To Cream Butter

Take butter or other shortening from refrigerator, let stand at room temperature until soft. With spoon, rub or work against sides of bowl until light and smooth.

To Add Sugar

Add sugar gradually to creamed butter, stirring well until light and fluffy.

To Add Whole Eggs

Drop into butter-sugar mixture one at a time and beat until well blended.

To Add Yolks

Beat with rotary beater until thick and lemon-colored. Pour into butter-sugar mixture, stirring until smooth.

To Beat Whites

Use a rotary beater or wire whisk and beat in a clean, dry mixing bowl until whites stand up in peaks but are still shiny. Do not overbeat.

To Combine Dry Ingredients

Sift flour and sugar once before measuring. Add baking powder, baking soda, spices, or cocoa if quantity is small, and sift again. Dry ingredients must be *dry*. Do not wash nuts or raisins. Blanch almonds the day before using and dry in oven. Nuts and raisins should be sprinkled with flour and added last.

To Add Milk or Other Liquids

Should be added a little at a time, alternately with the dry ingredients, and mixed only until blended.

To Alternate Flour and Milk

Flour and milk are added alternately to butter mixture, beginning and ending with the flour, which must be thoroughly incorporated. Then fold in beaten egg whites gently, until no whites show.

IMPORTANT NOTES

Using an Electric Beater

Cream butter and sugar together at medium speed. Add whole eggs or egg yolks, one at a time, still beating at medium speed. High speed may be used to beat this mixture until light and fluffy. Add flour and milk alternately in small amounts, combining at lowest beating speed and mixing only until blended. Overbeating after flour is added makes cakes dry, coarse, and prevents rising. Beat about ½ time required for hand beating. Scrape sides of bowl often with rubber spatula. *Fold in stiffly beaten egg whites by hand.*

Preparing Pans for Baking

Rub pan with shortening. Sprinkle lightly with flour, and shake pan to coat lightly, then tap upside down to shake out excess flour. For some cakes, pans should be lined with a round of parchment paper or aluminum foil, cut to fit the bottom of the pan. For cakes containing large amounts of fruit, the sides of the pan may be lined also. Angel food cakes and sponge cakes are baked in ungreased pans.

To Fill Cake Pans

Fill cake pans ⅔ full. For tube pans, bring batter well to the edges and tube, leaving a slight depression in center. Level sponge and angel food cakes with a spatula; butter cakes may be leveled by gently shaking the pan.

To Set the Oven

Accurate baking temperatures are important for success. Many ovens have an automatic thermostat to regulate heat. For ovens lacking automatic controls, an inexpensive oven thermometer can be very useful. Always preheat oven to indicated temperature *before* placing cake in oven. If baking in glass, bake at 15° F lower temperature than indicated in recipe.

Place cake in center of middle shelf for an even heat. Do not move or jar. Crowding the oven and allowing the pans to touch oven walls interferes with heat distribution and causes burning or uneven baking.

Description	Temperature
very slow	250° F
slow	300° F
moderately slow	325° F
moderate	350° F
moderately hot	375° F
hot	400° F
very hot	450° F
extremely hot	500° F

Test for Doneness

Cake is done when it rises and is brown, shrinks from the sides of the pan, and springs back when lightly pressed with a finger, or when a wire cake tester or a toothpick inserted in the center comes out dry.

To Remove Cake from Pans

When done, remove from oven, let stand 10 minutes. Loosen sides and invert on wire cake rack. Remove cake from pan and let stand until cool. Angel food and sponge cakes should be inverted in pan and allowed to hang on inverted funnel until cool. This stretches the cake and prevents settling.

CAKE RECIPE ADJUSTMENT GUIDE FOR HIGH ALTITUDES

Note: When two amounts are given, the smaller adjustment should be tried first; then if recipe still needs adjustment, the larger amount should be used the next time.

Adjustment	3,000 Feet	5,000 Feet	7,000 Feet
Baking Powder: reduce for each teaspoon in recipe	Less ⅛ teaspoon	Less ⅛ to ¼ teaspoon	Less ¼ teaspoon
Sugar: Decrease for each cup in recipe	Less 0 to 1 tablespoon	Less 0 to 2 tablespoons	Less 1 to 3 tablespoons
Liquid: Increase for each cup in recipe	Add 1 to 2 tablespoons	Add 1 to 2 tablespoons	Add 1 to 2 tablespoons

---

Butter Cakes

QUICK ONE-EGG CAKE

¾ cup sugar
1½ cups sifted flour
¼ teaspoon salt
2 teaspoons baking powder
¼ cup shortening, melted

1 egg, beaten
¾ cup milk
1 teaspoon flavoring (vanilla, lemon juice, almond extract, or liqueur)

Preheat oven to 375° F. Sift dry ingredients into mixing bowl. Stir egg into shortening, add milk and flavoring. Combine the two mixtures. Blend. Pour into a greased and floured 9-inch round or a shallow 9-inch square pan. Bake about 20 minutes.

QUICK TWO-EGG CAKE

1¾ cups flour
1 tablespoon baking powder
½ cup butter, softened
1 cup sugar

2 eggs
½ cup plus 1 tablespoon milk
¼ teaspoon salt
1 teaspoon vanilla

Preheat oven to 375° F. Sift together flour and baking powder, add remaining ingredients, and beat until light and smooth. Pour into two greased and floured 8-inch layer pans. Bake for 20 minutes.

QUICK ONE-BOWL DATE CAKE

⅓ cup butter, softened
1⅓ cups brown sugar, firmly
 packed
2 eggs
½ cup milk
1¾ cups flour

1 tablespoon baking powder
½ teaspoon cinnamon
½ teaspoon grated nutmeg
½ pound dates, figs, or raisins,
 finely chopped

Preheat oven to 325° F. Beat all ingredients together thoroughly for 3 or 4 minutes. Pour into a 9-inch pan lined with waxed paper. Bake for 35 to 40 minutes.

Leftover cake crumbs may be used as topping on coffee cake, or used to thicken fruit pies.

To freshen stale cake, sprinkle with water or wine, enclose in brown paper bag, and heat in 350° F oven. Or cover cake with applesauce or another fruit mixture and heat in 350° F oven. Serve warm as fruit pudding.

GOLD CAKE

½ cup butter
1 cup sugar
4 egg yolks, well beaten
1 teaspoon vanilla

2 cups cake flour
1 tablespoon baking powder
½ cup milk

Preheat oven to 350° F. Cream butter well, add sugar, continue beating. Then add yolks and vanilla; mix thoroughly. Sift together the flour and baking powder, then add alternately with the milk to the butter mixture. Beat, then pour in greased and floured 9-inch square pan or two 8-inch layer pans. Bake for 35 to 45 minutes.

MARBLE CAKE

¾ cup butter
2 cups sugar
4 eggs
3 cups cake flour
4 teaspoons baking powder
½ cup milk

¼ pound unsweetened chocolate,
grated
1 teaspoon cinnamon
½ teaspoon ground cloves
½ teaspoon vanilla

Preheat oven to 350° F. Cream butter, add sugar and stir well. Add eggs, one at a time, beating constantly. Sift together the flour and baking powder. Then add alternately with the milk to the butter mixture and stir until smooth. Put ⅓ of the dough in another bowl, mixing well with chocolate, spices, and vanilla. Pour layers of white and dark dough into a greased and floured 9-inch tube pan. Bake 45 minutes.

POUND CAKE

1 pound cake flour
1 pound butter
1 pound sugar

1 pound eggs in shell (9 or 10 eggs)
2 tablespoons vanilla or brandy

Preheat oven to 300° F. Sift flour twice, set aside. Cream butter well, add sugar gradually and beat until light and fluffy. Add eggs, two at a time, and beat well after each addition. Add vanilla or brandy. Add flour gradually and beat until smooth. Line three loaf pans with waxed paper. Pour mixture into pans and bake about 1 hour and 15 minutes.

BUTTERMILK CAKE

2 cups cake flour	½ cup shortening
⅔ teaspoon salt	1¼ cups sugar
2 teaspoons baking powder	2 eggs, separated
⅔ teaspoon baking soda	1½ teaspoons vanilla
1 cup buttermilk	

Preheat oven to 350° F. Sift flour. Add salt and baking powder and sift again. Add soda to buttermilk and allow to stand while cake is being mixed. Cream shortening, add sugar and beat until fluffy. Beat the yolks well, then add them and vanilla. Add the flour mixture alternately with the buttermilk, continue beating. Beat the egg whites stiffly. Carefully fold them into the batter. Pour into two greased and floured 9-inch layer cake pans. Bake about 30 minutes.

Note: This cake is especially good frosted with Caramel Frosting (page 605).

White Cakes

White cakes are butter cakes using only the egg whites; they differ from whole-egg cakes not only in color but also in texture; they are less rich and tend to be fluffy rather than moist and firm.

WHITE CAKE

½ cup butter	⅔ cup milk
1 cup sugar	½ teaspoon almond extract
2 cups cake flour	grated rind of 1 lemon
1 tablespoon baking powder	3 egg whites

Preheat oven to 350° F. Cream butter, add sugar and continue beating. Sift flour once, measure, sift with baking powder 3 times, add to the butter mixture alternately with the milk, beating thoroughly until smooth. Add almond extract and lemon rind. Beat the egg whites, stiff but not dry. Carefully fold into the batter. Pour into a greased and floured 12-by-8-inch pan. Bake about 1 hour.

Note: Or bake in two greased and floured 9-inch layer pans at 375° F, 25 to 30 minutes.

 Lady Baltimore Cake Bake White Cake (above) in two layers. Fill with Pecan Filling (page 609). Frost with Meringue Frosting (page 601).

Coconut Layer Cake   Bake White Cake (above) in two layers. Spread Seven-Minute Frosting (page 602) between layers and over top; sprinkle generously with grated coconut.

DELICATE COCONUT CAKE

1 cup sugar	1 tablespoon baking powder
¼ cup butter	⅔ cup milk
½ teaspoon almond extract	3 egg whites, stiffly beaten
½ teaspoon lemon extract	½ cup coconut
½ teaspoon salt	chopped almonds (optional)
2 cups cake flour	

Preheat oven to 350° F. Cream together the sugar and butter and add the almond and lemon flavorings. Sift together the dry ingredients and add them alternately with the milk to the butter mixture. Fold in the egg whites, add the coconut. Stir well. Pour into a greased and floured 9½-by-12-inch pan; sprinkle with additional shredded coconut and a few chopped almonds, if desired. Bake for 45 minutes.

Any type of cake may be frozen. It is best to freeze cakes *before* filling and frosting. For general directions on wrapping and freezing baked goods, see Chapter 26.

SILVER CAKE

3 cups cake flour	1½ cups sugar
3½ teaspoons baking powder	½ teaspoon vanilla
½ cup butter	4 egg whites, stiffly beaten
½ cup milk and ½ cup water, mixed	

Preheat oven to 375° F. Sift flour once, measure; add baking powder and sift together 3 times; cut butter into small pieces and blend with flour with pastry blender; add milk and water mixture, sugar, and vanilla and beat until smooth. Fold in egg whites and pour into greased and floured 9-by-13-inch pan. Bake 25 to 30 minutes.

Note: This cake is traditionally covered with whipped cream and shredded coconut.

Chocolate Cakes

QUICK ONE-BOWL COCOA CAKE

6 tablespoons cocoa
2 cups flour
1½ cups sugar
1 teaspoon baking soda
1 teaspoon baking powder

⅛ teaspoon salt
2 eggs
¾ cup butter, melted
1 cup cold water

Preheat oven to 350° F. Sift dry ingredients into mixing bowl. Add the other ingredients all at once. Beat well. Pour into two greased and floured 8-inch layer pans. Bake for 40 minutes.

CHOCOLATE CAKE

2 cups cake flour
2 cups sugar
⅛ teaspoon salt
½ cup butter
1¼ cups water

4 ounces unsweetened chocolate
3 eggs, well beaten
1 teaspoon vanilla
2 teaspoons baking powder

Sift flour, sugar, and salt, add butter, mixing with fingertips or pastry blender to the consistency of cornmeal. Boil water and chocolate. Cool and add to butter mixture. Beat very well. Chill thoroughly. Preheat oven to 325° F. Add eggs, well beaten, vanilla, and the baking powder last. Bake in two well-greased and floured 9-inch layer pans from 35 to 40 minutes.

OLD-FASHIONED DEVIL'S FOOD CAKE

2 ounces unsweetened chocolate
3 tablespoons water
1¼ cups sugar
½ cup butter

1 cup sour milk or buttermilk
1 teaspoon baking soda
1 egg yolk, beaten
2 scant cups flour

Preheat oven to 350° F. Melt the chocolate, water, and sugar in double boiler; when dissolved add the butter. Stir well. Set aside to cool. Mix sour milk or buttermilk, baking soda, and beaten yolk, add the melted chocolate mixture, and then the flour. Pour into two well-greased and floured 9-inch layer pans and bake for 25 minutes.

MOCHA DEVIL'S FOOD CAKE

¼ cup butter
1 cup sugar
2 eggs, well beaten
1½ cups flour
1½ teaspoons baking powder
½ teaspoon salt
½ cup thick, sour milk or
   buttermilk

½ cup boiling coffee
2 ounces unsweetened chocolate,
   melted, or 4 tablespoons cocoa
1 teaspoon baking soda
1 teaspoon vanilla

Preheat oven to 350° F. Cream butter, add sugar gradually, beat until very light. Add eggs. Beat thoroughly. Mix flour, baking powder, and salt. Add alternately with the sour milk or buttermilk, a small amount at a time. In a separate bowl pour boiling coffee over melted chocolate or cocoa and mix quickly. To this add the soda and stir until cool. Then add to cake batter. Add vanilla and mix thoroughly. Pour into two well-greased and floured 9-inch layer cake pans and bake for about 25 minutes.

FUDGE CAKE

1¾ cups cake flour
1 teaspoon baking powder
1 teaspoon baking soda
1 teaspoon salt
½ cup butter
1½ cups sugar

2 eggs
2½ tablespoons vinegar
1 cup milk
3 ounces unsweetened chocolate,
   melted

Preheat oven to 350° F. Sift together flour, baking powder, soda, and salt. Cream butter, add sugar gradually, and continue creaming. Add eggs one at a time and beat until fluffy. Add vinegar. Add the flour mixture alternately with the milk, and last the melted chocolate. Pour into two well-greased and floured 9-inch layer pans and bake for about 45 minutes.

Cakes with Fruit, Nuts, Spice

ALMOND OR FILBERT CAKE

½ cup butter
1 cup sugar
½ cup milk
1 teaspoon lemon or vanilla extract
2 egg yolks, well beaten
1½ cups flour
½ teaspoon baking powder

½ teaspoon cream of tartar
1 teaspoon salt
¼ cup finely ground nuts
½ teaspoon baking soda dissolved in
  2 teaspoons water
2 egg whites, beaten stiffly

Preheat oven to 350° F. Cream butter and sugar well. Add milk and flavoring to well-beaten yolks. Sift together dry ingredients. Add egg and flour mixtures alternately to the creamed mixture. Add nuts, then the soda, stirring well. Fold in egg whites. Pour into a greased and floured 8-inch square pan and bake about 50 minutes.

APPLESAUCE CAKE

½ cup butter
1 cup sugar
1 egg, well beaten
1 teaspoon vanilla
1 cup dates, finely sliced
1½ cups applesauce

1 cups nuts, coarsely chopped
1 cup raisins, chopped
½ teaspoon cinnamon
¼ teaspoon ground cloves
2 cups flour
2 teaspoons baking soda

Preheat oven to 350° F. Cream butter and sugar, add egg and the vanilla. Add the rest of the ingredients and blend. Bake in a greased medium-sized loaf pan for 1 hour.

BANANA CAKE

½ cup butter
1¼ cups sugar
2 eggs
1 teaspoon baking soda
4 tablespoons sour cream

1 cup banana pulp, mashed
1½ cups cake flour
¼ teaspoon salt
1 teaspoon vanilla

Preheat oven to 350° F. Cream butter and sugar, add eggs, very lightly beaten, and the soda, dissolved in the sour cream. Beat well, then add the bananas, flour, salt, and vanilla. Mix well. Pour into a greased and floured 8-inch square or 9-inch tube pan. Bake for 35 to 45 minutes.

CHERRY UPSIDE-DOWN CAKE

½ cup butter
1⅓ cups sugar
1 teaspoon vanilla
2 cups cake flour
¼ teaspoon salt
2 teaspoons baking powder

⅔ cup water
3 egg whites

Sauce
1 20-ounce can pitted sour cherries
1 cup sugar
1 teaspoon red food coloring

1.   Preheat oven to 350° F. Cream butter and sugar, add vanilla. Sift flour with salt and 1½ teaspoons baking powder and add alternately with the water to the butter mixture, beating well after each addition. Beat the remaining baking powder with the egg whites until stiff. Fold whites into mixture. Divide batter into two greased and floured 9-inch layer pans. Set aside.

2.   To make the sauce, drain cherries well, reserving ¾ cup of juice. Add water if needed to make up the difference. Combine juice, cherries, sugar, and coloring. Heat to the boiling point. Pour hot cherry sauce over cake batter.

3.   Bake for 35 minutes. Cool for 3 minutes. Turn upside down. Place layers so that sauce is both filling and topping. Serve with whipped cream.

DATE AND WALNUT LOAF CAKE

1 pound dates, pitted
1 pound English walnut meats
1 cup cake flour
½ teaspoon salt

4 teaspoons baking powder
1 cup sugar
4 eggs, separated
1 teaspoon vanilla

Preheat oven to 325° F. Leave dates and nuts whole; place in mixing bowl, sift the flour, salt, and baking powder over them. Mix carefully, add sugar and mix again. Beat yolks until light and thick. Add vanilla and stir into dry ingredients. Beat egg whites until stiff and fold in until well blended. Bake in a shallow loaf pan lined with buttered paper, for 1 hour.

GINGERBREAD

½ cup dried currants
3 cups flour
2 teaspoons baking soda
1 cup sour milk or buttermilk
1 cup molasses
2 teaspoons ginger

½ teaspoon cinnamon
½ teaspoon ground cloves
½ cup butter
1 cup sugar
1 egg

Preheat oven to 350° F. Toss the currants with ½ cup of the flour. Mix baking soda and sour milk or buttermilk and add to molasses. Sift remaining dry ingredients except sugar. Cream butter and sugar, add egg. Fold in the dry ingredients and the currants. Pour into greased and floured 8-by-12-inch pan and bake 30 to 45 minutes.

Note: Gingerbread is traditionally served with lightly sweetened whipped cream.

HICKORY NUT CAKE

½ cup butter
1 cup sugar
½ cup milk
1½ cups flour
3 egg whites, stiffly beaten

¾ cup chopped hickory nuts
1 teaspoon cream of tartar
½ teaspoon baking soda dissolved in
   1 teaspoon milk

Preheat oven to 350° F. Cream butter and sugar, add milk and flour, alternately; add egg whites and nuts and beat until smooth; add cream of tartar and the dissolved baking soda. Beat. Pour into greased and floured 9-inch square pan and bake for 45 minutes.

JAPANESE FRUIT CAKE

1 cup butter
2 cups sugar
4 eggs
1 teaspoon vanilla
3 cups flour
½ teaspoon salt
1 tablespoon baking powder
1 cup milk
1 teaspoon cinnamon
1 teaspoon allspice
1 teaspoon ground cloves
1 cup raisins (optional)

Filling
2 tablespoons flour
juice of 3 oranges
juice of 3 lemons
1 cup sugar
1 can (13½ ounces) crushed
   pineapple
1 cup grated coconut
1 cup chopped pecans (optional)

   1.   Preheat oven to 350° F. Cream butter and sugar until light. Beat eggs until light; add gradually to butter mixture, add vanilla and beat well. Combine flour, salt, and baking powder. Add alternately with the milk to the butter mixture. Put half of the batter into 2 greased and floured 8-inch layer cake pans.

(continued)

Add the spices and raisins, if using, to the remaining batter. Put this batter into 2 greased and floured 8-inch layer cake pans. Bake for 20 to 25 minutes.

2.   Meanwhile, prepare the filling. Mix flour with a little juice; add remaining ingredients. Boil slowly until mixture is thick. Cool. When cakes are cool, spread between layers of the cake, alternating the plain and spiced layers.

ORANGEADE CAKE

¾ cup butter
1½ cups sugar
2 eggs
2¼ cups flour
1 teaspoon baking powder
1 teaspoon baking soda

1 cup buttermilk or sour cream
½ cup seedless raisins (optional)
1 cup pecans, chopped
grated rind of 2 oranges
1 cup orange juice

Preheat oven to 350° F. Cream butter well, add 1 cup sugar gradually. Beat until light and fluffy. Add eggs one at a time, beating well. Sift together 2 cups flour, baking powder, and baking soda. Add alternately with buttermilk or sour cream to the butter mixture. Mix rest of flour with raisins, nuts, and grated rind, add to dough and stir until smooth. Pour into a greased and floured 9-inch tube pan. Bake 1 hour. Mix orange juice with remaining ½ cup sugar. Set aside. When cake is done, immediately pour juice mixture over it. Let stand in pan until cool.

PECAN CAKE

½ cup butter
1 cup medium brown sugar, firmly
   packed
2 eggs, separated
1½ cups cake flour

2 teaspoons baking powder
¼ teaspoon salt
¾ cup milk
1 teaspoon vanilla
¾ cup pecans, chopped

Preheat oven to 350° F. Cream butter and sugar until light and fluffy. Add yolks one at a time, beating well. Sift together flour, baking powder, and salt, and add alternately with the milk. Add vanilla and nuts. Stiffly beat egg whites and fold in. Pour into two greased and floured 9-inch layer pans and bake for 20 to 25 minutes.

PINEAPPLE UPSIDE-DOWN CAKE

Topping
½ cup butter
2 cups brown sugar, firmly packed
1 20-ounce can sliced pineapple
walnut meats, halved
candied cherries, halved

Cake
4 eggs, separated
1 cup sugar
1 cup flour
1 teaspoon baking powder

1.   Preheat oven to 350° F. To make the topping, melt butter in a heavy 10-inch oven-proof skillet. Remove from heat. Cover with brown sugar, spreading it evenly. Place 1 slice of pineapple in center on top of sugar; cut rest of the slices in half; arrange these in a circle around the center slice like the spokes of a wheel, rounded edges facing the same way. Fill spaces with walnut meats and candied cherries. Set aside.

2.   To make the cake batter, beat yolks and sugar until light; sift together flour and baking powder and fold into egg mixture ⅓ cup at a time. Beat the egg whites stiffly and fold into batter. Carefully pour over fruit in skillet. Bake about 30 minutes. Turn upside down. Serve with whipped cream, if desired.

Variations: Any canned fruit may be substituted for the pineapple.

Caramel Upside-Down Cake: Follow recipe above, using ½ cup additional nut meats, chopped, instead of fruit.

POPPY SEED CAKE

Cake
¾ cup poppy seeds
¾ cup warm milk
1½ cups sugar
¾ cup butter
3 cups flour
1 tablespoon baking powder
5 egg whites, stiffly beaten

Filling
2 tablespoons cornstarch
1½ tablespoons cold milk
4 egg yolks
½ cup sugar
1½ cups hot milk
vanilla
½ cup chopped nuts

1.   To make the cake, soak poppy seeds in warm milk for several hours. Preheat oven to 350° F. Cream sugar and butter thoroughly; add poppy seed

mixture and cream again; sift flour with baking powder and add. Then add egg whites. Pour into three greased and floured 9-inch layer cake pans and bake 25 minutes.

2. To make the filling, mix cornstarch in cold milk and cook in top of double boiler until smooth. Add yolks and sugar. Add hot milk gradually, and cook over hot water until custard coats the spoon, stirring constantly. When cool, add vanilla and nut meats. When cake is cool, fill layers and then frost with Chocolate Butter Frosting (page 599) or Caramel Frosting (page 605).

PRUNE CAKE

½ cup butter
1 cup sugar
2 eggs
¾ cup thick sour cream
1½ cups flour
1½ tablespoons cornstarch

2 teaspoons baking powder
1 teaspoon baking soda
1 teaspoon each cinnamon and
  ground cloves
2 tablespoons prune juice
1 cup stewed prune pulp

Preheat oven to 350° F. Cream butter and sugar well, add eggs and sour cream. Mix dry ingredients, combine the two mixtures, adding prune juice and pulp. Pour into two greased and floured 9-inch layer pans and bake for 25 minutes.

<u>Note:</u> This cake is best with Cream Cheese Frosting (page 600) between layers and over top.

FRUIT WEDDING CAKE

1 pound candied pineapple rings
1 pound each dates and figs
4 cups flour
1 teaspoon baking soda
2 teaspoons cinnamon
1 teaspoon ground cloves
1 teaspoon grated nutmeg
2 cups butter
2 cups brown sugar, firmly packed
12 eggs, separated and beaten
  separately
½ cup molasses

½ cup fruit juice, wine, rum, or
  brandy
2 pounds seeded raisins
1 pound sultana raisins
¼ pound each candied orange,
  lemon rind, and citron, finely
  chopped
1 pound candied cherries
½ pound almonds, blanched
½ pound pecans, unbroken
brandy

Preheat oven to 300° F. Cut each ring of pineapple in 2 slices, then in half crosswise. Remove stem end from figs, cut in half lengthwise. Stone and cut dates, and mix them with 1 cup of flour. Mix the rest of the flour with baking soda and spices. Cream butter, add sugar, then the well-beaten egg yolks and stir well. Add the flour mixture alternately with the molasses and fruit juice, wine, rum, or brandy. Gently fold in the beaten whites, then the dates and gradually the raisins. Line 4 greased loaf pans with waxed paper. Put in a layer of batter, add a layer of pineapple down the center, fill spaces and sides lightly with citron, orange, lemon rind, cherries, and nuts; another layer of batter, then a layer of figs, the rest of the fruit and nuts, and top with remaining batter. (Or cut up all fruit and mix through batter, adding beaten whites last.) Have pans ⅔ full. Set pans in oven, in a pan filled with 1 inch hot water. Bake ½ hour, cover with waxed paper, bake 2 hours longer, remove pans from water, and bake ½ hour more. Remove from pans. Remove paper. Wrap in cloth moistened with brandy. Store in tightly covered tin box.

Note: Cakes may be dry-baked in a very slow oven (from 200° F to 250° F) 4 to 5 hours.

SPICE CAKE

⅔ cup currants or raisins
½ cup walnut meats, chopped
2½ cups flour
½ cup butter
2 cups sugar

3 eggs
1 tablespoon baking powder
½ teaspoon each ground cloves,
   cinnamon, and ginger
1 cup cream

Preheat oven to 350° F. Mix the raisins and nuts with ½ cup of the flour. Cream the butter and sugar, add the eggs, one at a time. Mix remaining dry ingredients. Add cream and dry ingredients alternately to the butter mixture. Add raisins and nuts. Pour into two greased, floured 8-inch square pans and bake for 30 to 40 minutes.

Cream Cakes

BASIC CREAM CAKE

¾ cup sugar
1½ cups sifted flour
2 teaspoons baking powder

2 eggs
⅔ cup cream
1 teaspoon vanilla or other flavoring

Preheat oven to 350° F. Sift together dry ingredients. Add eggs, cream, and flavoring; beat well. Pour into greased and floured 8-inch square pan and bake for 45 minutes.

Note: If desired, split cake into layers, and fill and frost as desired.

WHIPPED CREAM CAKE

1 cup heavy cream
1 cup sugar
2 eggs
1 teaspoon vanilla

1½ cups cake flour
2 teaspoons baking powder
salt

Preheat oven to 375° F. Whip the cream until slightly thickened but not stiff enough to hold a peak. Fold in the sugar, then the beaten eggs, and the vanilla. Sift the flour with the baking powder and pinch of salt and add. Mix only until smooth. Pour into two greased and floured 8-inch layer cake pans and bake for 25 minutes.

SOUR CREAM CAKE

1 cup sugar
2 eggs
1 teaspoon lemon extract
½ teaspoon baking soda

1 cup sour cream
1¾ cups flour
½ teaspoon salt
1 teaspoon baking powder

Preheat oven to 350° F. Beat sugar and eggs until very light, add the flavoring. Stir baking soda into sour cream and add to the egg mixture alternately with the sifted together flour, salt, and baking powder. Pour into two greased, floured 8-inch layer pans and bake for 25 minutes.

SOUR CREAM COFFEE CAKE

½ cup shortening
¾ cup sugar
1 teaspoon vanilla
3 eggs
2 cups sifted flour
1 teaspoon baking powder

1 teaspoon baking soda
1 cup sour cream
6 tablespoons butter, softened
1 cup brown sugar, firmly packed
2 teaspoons cinnamon
1 cup chopped nuts

Preheat oven to 350° F. Grease a 10-inch tube pan or a 9-inch square pan. Cream shortening and sugar until light; add vanilla. Beat in eggs one at a time. Sift together flour, baking powder, and baking soda. Add to creamed shortening mixture alternately with the sour cream. Place half of batter in pan. Combine the softened butter with the brown sugar, cinnamon, and nuts. Sprinkle the batter with about half this mixture. Add the remaining batter and top with the rest of the brown sugar mixture. Bake 50 to 60 minutes. Cool cake in pan for about 10 minutes before removing it.

CHOCOLATE LAYER CAKE WITH SOUR CREAM

4 egg yolks
1⅓ cups sugar
2 ounces unsweetened chocolate
1 cup thick sour cream
1 teaspoon baking soda

pinch of salt
1½ cups flour
vanilla or other flavoring
3 egg whites, stiffly beaten

Preheat oven to 350° F. Beat the yolks and sugar until very light. In a double boiler melt the chocolate in part of the sour cream; cool and add it to the rest of the cream. Sift together the baking soda, salt, and flour and add alternately with the cream mixture to the yolks and sugar. Add desired flavoring and fold in the whites, beaten stiff but not dry. Put batter into two greased and floured 8-inch square layer pans. Bake for 30 minutes.

Note: This cake should be filled and iced with Meringue Frosting (page 601) or Chocolate Filling (page 607).

Sponge Cakes

Sponge cakes contain no butter or shortening, and are made light with the yolks and whites of eggs. Whole eggs, or egg yolks, are beaten well with the sugar. Sift the flour once, measure, and resift. Flour is folded in very lightly and carefully, and the egg whites, beaten stiff, are folded in last. Sponge cakes should be inverted and cooled completely in the pan before they are removed. They are usually baked in an ungreased tube pan, but may also be baked in layer pans lined with waxed or parchment paper.

FOUR-EGG SPONGE CAKE

1 tablespoon baking powder	1 cup sugar
1½ cups cake flour	1 teaspoon vanilla
4 eggs, separated, whites stiffly beaten	¾ cup water

Preheat oven to 325° F. Sift baking powder with ½ cup of the flour. Beat yolks until light and thick, add sugar gradually and continue beating. Add vanilla, the water, and the cup of flour alternately, then the baking powder mixture, and fold in the stiffly beaten egg whites last. Bake in ungreased 9-inch tube pan for 40 to 50 minutes. Invert pan; when cool, remove cake.

GOLDEN SPONGE CAKE

¼ teaspoon salt	½ cup boiling water
6 egg yolks	1½ cups cake flour
1 cup sugar	2 teaspoons baking powder
1 teaspoon lemon extract	

Preheat oven to 325° F. Add salt to egg yolks and beat until very light. Gradually add sugar to yolks, beating all the time. Add lemon extract. Stir in hot water. Sift flour and baking powder and fold into batter. Bake in 2 greased 9-inch layer cake pans for ½ hour.

Note: To complete the classic version of this cake, fill layers with Lemon Custard Filling (page 607), using 2 egg yolks, and spread Basic Butter Frosting (page 599) on top, adding 1 extra yolk to recipe.

Variation:

Coffee Sponge Cake: Substitute ½ cup strong coffee for water in Golden Sponge Cake, above, and use Chocolate Filling (page 607) flavored with 1 teaspoon instant coffee and Basic Butter Frosting (page 599). Proceed as above.

ORANGE PUFF CAKE

6 eggs, separated
2 cups sugar
½ cup orange juice
grated rind of 1 orange

½ cup boiling water
2 cups cake flour
2 teaspoons baking powder

Preheat oven to 325° F. Beat yolks well, add 1 cup sugar and beat until light. Add orange juice and rind, then water. Sift the flour with baking powder and add to the batter. Beat egg whites, gradually add the remaining 1 cup sugar, and beat until stiff, then add yolk mixture. Bake in a 10–inch ungreased tube pan for 20 minutes, then increase heat to 350° F. Bake 1¼ hours in all.

ORANGE SPONGE CAKE

Cake
8 eggs, separated
¼ teaspoon salt
1 teaspoon cream of tartar
1⅓ cups sugar
grated rind of 1 orange
¼ cup orange juice
1 cup and 2 level tablespoons cake
   flour

Filling
¾ cup sugar
juice and rind of 1 orange
3 tablespoons flour
1 egg
1 cup heavy cream

Frosting
4 tablespoons butter
1 egg yolk
2 cups confectioners' sugar
1 tablespoon heavy cream
2 tablespoons orange juice
⅓ cup pistachio nuts, chopped

1.   To make the cake, preheat oven to 325° F. Beat egg whites and salt until foamy. Add cream of tartar, beat until stiff, but not dry. Add ⅔ cup sugar gradually, beating well. Beat the yolks of the eggs very thick, add remaining sugar, orange rind, and juice. Fold the two mixtures together and fold in flour. Bake for 1 hour in an unbuttered 10–inch angel cake pan. Invert until cool. Split cake twice, making 3 layers.

2.   To make the filling, mix ingredients except cream and cook in a double boiler until custard coats the spoon, stirring constantly. Whip the cream until stiff and fold in. Fill the layers.

3.   To make the frosting, cream butter and egg yolk. Gradually add sugar and cream. Mix, add orange juice. Spread on top and sides of cake, sprinkle with nuts.

SUNSHINE CAKE

1 cup cake flour	grated rind of 1 lemon
6 eggs, separated	1 teaspoon vanilla
pinch of salt	⅓ teaspoon cream of tartar
1 cup sugar	

Preheat oven to 325° F. Sift flour, measure, then sift 4 times. Beat yolks and salt with rotary egg beater until light-colored and thick; gradually beat in half of the sugar and the lemon rind and vanilla. Beat whites until frothy, add cream of tartar. Beat until stiff but not dry. Beat in remaining sugar. Cut and fold some of the white mixture into yolk mixture; fold the flour and salt into yolk mixture, then the rest of the white mixture. Place in an ungreased 10-inch tube pan. Bake about 1 hour. Invert pan. When cool, remove cake.

Angel Food Cakes

Like sponge cakes, angel food cakes are made without shortening. They are made light with beaten egg whites, which must be beaten until stiff but not dry. The flour and sugar must be folded in very lightly, to avoid letting the air escape. Angel food cakes should be baked in a very clean, ungreased tube pan. To test for doneness, press top of cake with finger. If it springs back without leaving a dent, it is done. Invert over a rack until completely cold, about 1 hour. Loosen the sides of the cake with a spatula and remove. Cut angel food with a cake breaker or two forks, not with a knife.

ANGEL FOOD CAKE AND VARIATIONS

1½ cups egg whites (from 12 or 13 eggs)	1⅓ cups granulated sugar
1¼ teaspoons cream of tartar	1¼ teaspoons vanilla or other flavoring
½ teaspoon salt	1 cup plus 2 tablespoons cake flour

Preheat oven to 375° F. Beat egg whites. Add cream of tartar and salt when eggs are frothy. Beat until the egg whites are stiff but not dry. Sift 1 cup of the sugar twice and gradually beat it into the whites. Fold in the flavoring. Sift flour once before measuring, sift 3 times with remaining ⅓ cup sugar. Fold in flour gradually. Pour into ungreased 10-inch tube pan and bake 30 to 35 minutes. Test for doneness. Bake longer if necessary. Invert pan until cake is cold.

Variations:

Chocolate Angel Cake: Substitute ¼ cup of cocoa for ¼ cup of flour in Angel Food Cake, above.

Marble Angel Cake: Make ½ recipe Angel Food Cake and ½ recipe Chocolate Angel Cake, above. Put by tablespoons in pan, alternating chocolate and plain batters.

Fruit Angel Cake: Fold thin slices of fruit and nuts (cherries, pineapple, pistachio, walnuts, pecans) into the batter of Angel Food Cake.

Daffodil Cake: Mix stiffly beaten egg whites, cream of tartar, salt, and all the sugar of Angel Food Cake, above. Divide mixture in half. Add ¾ cup flour and 6 well-beaten yolks to one part, and ½ cup flour and flavoring to the other. Alternate batters when placing in pan.

Angel Cake Pieces: Bake an Angel Food Cake, above, or Sunshine Cake (page 568); pull the cake apart with a fork in irregular pieces about 2 inches in size; take each piece on a fork and dip in hot Chocolate Icing (page 598) and let cool on a platter.

Chiffon Cakes

Chiffon cakes are sponge-like cakes made with oil. The method of combining the ingredients is different from that of sponge cake and should be followed precisely.

GOLDEN CHIFFON CAKE

2 cups flour	7 eggs, separated
1½ cups sugar	¾ cup cold water
1 teaspoon salt	2 teaspoons vanilla
1 tablespoon baking powder	grated rind of 1 lemon
½ cup vegetable oil	½ teaspoon cream of tartar

Preheat oven to 325° F. Sift flour, sugar, salt, and baking powder. Add oil, egg yolks, water, vanilla, and lemon rind, and beat until smooth and light. Beat whites frothy, add cream of tartar, continue to beat until stiff but not dry. Fold yolk mixture into the whites only until blended. Pour into ungreased 10-inch tube pan; bake for 55 minutes. Increase heat to 350° F and bake for 10 minutes more. Invert pan until cake is cool.

Variation:

Banana Chiffon Cake: Substitute 1 cup of mashed bananas for the water and vanilla in Golden Chiffon Cake.

ORANGE CHIFFON CAKE

2¼ cups cake flour	5 egg yolks
1½ cups sugar	3 tablespoons grated orange rind
1 tablespoon baking powder	¾ cup orange juice
1 teaspoon salt	1 cup egg whites (8 or 9)
½ cup vegetable oil	½ teaspoon cream of tartar

Preheat oven to 325° F. Sift flour, sugar, baking powder, and salt. Add oil, egg yolks, rind, and juice and beat until smooth and thick. Beat whites and cream of tartar until stiff but not dry. Fold yolk mixture into the whites only until blended. Pour into ungreased 10-inch tube pan; bake for 55 minutes. Increase heat to 350° F and bake for 10 minutes. Invert pan until cake is cool.

Cake Rolls

Be careful not to overbake cake rolls. The paper on which the roll is baked is difficult to remove if cake is overbaked.

A cake roll is more easily rolled when warm. If it is not to be filled immediately, it should be rolled without filling and cooled. Unroll, fill with any desired filling or ice cream and reroll when ready to serve.

CLASSIC JELLY ROLL

¾ cup cake flour
¾ teaspoon baking powder
¼ teaspoon salt
4 eggs

¾ cup sifted sugar
1 teaspoon vanilla
confectioners' sugar
1 cup favorite jelly

Preheat oven to 400° F. Sift flour, baking powder, and salt. Beat eggs, place over bowl of hot water, and add sugar gradually to eggs, beating until thick and light. Remove bowl from hot water, fold in flour mixture and vanilla. Pour batter into 10-by-15-inch pan lined with greased or waxed paper. Bake for 10 minutes. Turn on towel dusted with the confectioners' sugar. Remove paper, cut off crusty edges, spread with jelly and roll. This roll may also be filled with any cake filling.

SPONGE JELLY ROLL

5 eggs, separated, whites stiffly
   beaten
1 cup sugar
grated rind of 1 lemon

2 tablespoons lemon juice
1 cup flour
confectioners' sugar
1 cup favorite jelly

Preheat oven to 375° F. Beat yolks well, add sugar, beat until thick; add lemon rind and juice. Then add alternately the stiffly beaten whites and flour. Pour batter, not more than ¼ inch deep, into 10-by-15-inch pan lined with greased or waxed paper. Bake 12 to 15 minutes. Turn on towel dusted with confectioners' sugar. Remove paper and trim off crusty edges. Beat jelly with fork and spread on cake. Roll while warm.

CHOCOLATE SPONGE ROLL

1¼ cups flour
2 teaspoons baking powder
¼ teaspoon salt
2 eggs
1 cup sugar
¼ cup hot water

1 teaspoon vanilla
2 tablespoons shortening, melted
2 ounces unsweetened chocolate,
   melted
confectioners' sugar

Preheat oven to 375° F. Sift flour, baking powder, and salt 3 times. Beat eggs and sugar until light, add hot water. Stir in vanilla, melted shortening, and melted chocolate. Fold in flour mixture as lightly as possible. Pour into a 10-by-15-inch pan lined with greased or waxed paper and bake 15 minutes. Turn out on towel dusted with confectioners' sugar, remove paper, trim edges, and roll. When cool, unroll and fill with Fluffy Chocolate Frosting (page 600).

WALNUT ROLL

6 eggs, separated, whites stiffly
  beaten
½ cup sugar
1 cup walnuts, chopped

confectioners' sugar
sweetened whipped cream or ice
  cream

Preheat oven to 350° F. Beat the yolks well with the sugar; add nuts and the stiffly beaten whites last. Grease a 10-by-15-inch shallow pan and line with waxed paper. Spread batter in pan and bake 15 to 20 minutes. Turn out on a towel sprinkled with confectioners' sugar, remove paper. Roll while hot. When cool, unroll, spread with sweetened whipped cream or ice cream. Roll again and serve with Caramel Sauce (page 648).

Passover Cakes

Cakes for Passover are made with special flours, and no leavening is used except eggs.

POTATO FLOUR CAKE

9 eggs
1¾ cups sugar

grated rind and juice of ½ lemon
1 scant cup potato flour

Preheat oven to 350° F. Separate the eggs. Beat the whites of 7 eggs stiff but not dry. Beat the remaining 2 whites and 9 yolks well, add the sugar and the lemon juice and rind. Beat thoroughly, add the potato flour, and beat again. Fold in beaten whites carefully, and bake in ungreased 10-inch tube pan, 40 to 50 minutes. Invert pan until cake is cool.

MATZO-LEMON SPONGE CAKE

8 eggs, separated, whites stiffly
  beaten
1½ cups sugar

pinch of salt
grated rind and juice of ½ lemon
1 cup sifted matzo cake meal

Preheat oven to 350° F. Beat yolks until light, add sugar and beat again; then add a pinch of salt, the lemon juice and rind, then the matzo cake meal. Fold in the beaten whites last. Bake in 10-inch ungreased springform pan 45 minutes. Invert pan until cake is cool. If desired, split in two layers. Serve with sweetened strawberries between the layers. Spread whipped cream, lemon-flavored and sweetened, over top and sides.

MATZO SPONGE CAKE

9 eggs, separated
1⅓ cups sugar

¾ cup matzo cake meal
1 teaspoon vanilla

Preheat oven to 350° F. Beat whites until stiff. Beat yolks and sugar until light. Fold beaten whites into the yolks, then fold in the cake meal and vanilla. Bake in ungreased 10-inch tube pan for 40 minutes. Invert pan until cake is cool.

MATZO SPICE SPONGE CAKE

12 eggs, separated, whites stiffly
  beaten
2 cups sugar
1½ teaspoons cinnamon

¼ teaspoon ground cloves
⅓ cup wine
1 cup chopped, blanched almonds
1½ cups matzo cake meal

Preheat oven to 325° F. Beat egg yolks and sugar until very light; add spices, wine, nuts, and cake meal. Fold in egg whites. Bake in large ungreased 10-inch tube pan about 1 hour. Invert pan until cake is cool.

MATZO SPONGE ROLL

4 eggs, separated
½ cup sugar

½ cup matzo cake meal

Preheat oven to 375° F. Beat yolks well, add sugar and sifted cake meal, and fold in the stiffly beaten whites. Spread on greased paper in a 10-by-15-inch shallow pan. Bake 10 minutes. Turn out on a sugared towel, remove the paper, spread with Lemon Custard Filling (page 607) or with jam. Roll.

Torten

Torten are cakes in which ground nuts or crumbs are usually used instead of flour. They generally contain no shortening.

Most of the following recipes are for 9-inch springform pans. The springform should be greased and sprinkled lightly with flour. Springforms are available with plain, tubed, and Mary Ann shell inverts.

For Frosting: Traditionally, nut tortes are spread with chilled whipped currant jelly and sprinkled with toasted, slivered almonds. They are also good with a dessert sauce or whipped cream alongside, or simply plain.

ALMOND TORTE

8 eggs, separated, whites stiffly
  beaten
1½ cups sugar
pinch of salt

grated rind of 1 lemon
2½ cups almonds, blanched and
  grated
¼ cup breadcrumbs

Preheat oven to 350° F. Beat yolks with sugar and salt; add lemon rind, fold in whites, the almonds, and the breadcrumbs last. Bake in greased and floured 9-inch springform pan for 45 minutes to 1 hour.

Note: This torte is great served with Quick Brandy Sauce (page 650).

ANGEL TORTE

2 cups almonds, blanched
½ pound whole dates
5 eggs, separated, whites stiffly
  beaten

¾ cup confectioners' sugar
2 teaspoons baking powder
heavy cream, whipped
sliced almonds for garnish

Preheat oven to 350° F. Finely grind the almonds. Stone dates, pour boiling water over them, drain, and mash to a smooth paste. Beat the yolks and gradually add the sugar and date pulp. Stir almonds lightly into the cake mixture. Fold the baking powder into the stiffly beaten whites and fold whites into the date mixture. Bake in a well-greased and floured 9-inch springform pan for about 45 minutes. When cool, cut in 2 layers and spread layers and top with whipped cream. Sprinkle with sliced almonds.

APRICOT MERINGUE TORTE

1 cup sifted flour
1 teaspoon sugar
½ cup butter, softened
1 egg yolk
1 12-ounce jar apricot jam

1 29-ounce can peeled apricot halves
4 egg whites
¼ cup blanched, sliced almonds

Preheat oven to 400° F. Mix flour and sugar; add gradually to the butter, stirring after each addition. Add egg yolk and mix well. Spread mixture on bottom of ungreased 9-inch springform pan. Bake for 18 to 20 minutes. Cool slightly in pan. Spread ½ of the jam over the baked layer. Drain apricots well. Place apricots on jam layer. Beat egg whites until stiff. Fold in remaining apricot preserves. Spread over apricot halves; sprinkle with almonds. Lower heat to 350° F and bake for 25 minutes or until meringue is lightly browned. Cool before removing sides of pan.

CARROT TORTE

1 pound carrots, peeled
8 eggs, separated, whites stiffly
  beaten
2 cups sugar
rind of 1 large orange, grated

1 tablespoon orange juice
1 pound almonds, blanched and
  grated
sweetened whipped cream

Preheat oven to 325° F. Cook the carrots until tender but slightly firm; chill and grate. Beat the yolks until light and thick. Add sugar gradually, then orange rind and juice, grated carrots, and nuts; mix well. Fold in the stiffly beaten whites. Bake in a greased and floured 9-inch springform pan for 45 to 50 minutes. Chill for several hours, cover with sweetened whipped cream, and serve.

CHEESE TORTE

1 cup butter
1 cup sugar
10 eggs, separated, whites stiffly
  beaten
½ pound dry cottage cheese, riced

½ pound almonds, blanched and
  grated
5 tablespoons breadcrumbs
juice and grated rind of 1 lemon

Preheat oven to 350° F. Cream butter, add sugar and continue creaming. Beat the egg yolks well and add, stirring constantly. Gradually add the cheese, the remaining ingredients, and the stiffly beaten egg whites last. Bake in a buttered 10-inch springform pan until well set, about 1 hour. Let stand in oven with door open until cool.

Note: This torte is usually served iced with Chocolate Butter Frosting (page 599).

CHERRY CREAM TORTE

Dough
1 recipe Rich Egg Pastry (page 522)

Almond Paste
½ pound shelled raw almonds
¾ cup sugar
grated rind of 1 lemon
4 egg whites

Cherry Filling
3 cups fresh or canned pitted cherries, well drained

Cream Custard
2 cups cream
3 tablespoons sugar
10 egg yolks, well beaten
10 egg whites, beaten stiff

    1.   Preheat oven to 350° F. Line a 10-inch springform pan with pastry dough.

    2.   To make the almond paste, finely grind the raw almonds and mix well with sugar and lemon rind. Fold in the stiffly beaten egg whites. Spread filling on dough.

    3.   Place cherry filling on top of almond paste.

    4.   To make the custard, heat the cream and the sugar in top of double boiler; when hot, pour very gradually onto the well-beaten yolks. Return to double boiler, cook slowly, stirring constantly until the mixture coats the spoon. Fold in the beaten egg whites and pour over the cherries. Bake for 1 hour.

CHESTNUT TORTE

1½ pounds chestnuts
milk
8 eggs, separated, whites stiffly beaten
½ cup sugar

1 teaspoon breadcrumbs
2 ounces grated almonds
1 tablespoon maraschino syrup or brandy

Preheat oven to 350° F. Shell chestnuts, then boil in a little milk until tender; put through ricer. Beat yolks and sugar until light, add chestnuts, crumbs, almonds, and the syrup or brandy. Fold in the beaten egg whites last. Bake in a greased and floured 9-inch springform pan for 45 minutes.

CHOCOLATE TORTE

9 eggs, separated, whites stiffly beaten
2 cups confectioners' sugar
1 teaspoon vanilla

½ pound sweet chocolate, melted
½ pound almonds, ground
¼ cup sliced, toasted almonds for decorating

Preheat oven to 325° F. Beat yolks, sugar, and vanilla until light; add melted chocolate and ground almonds, and fold in the whites. Bake in a greased and floured 9-inch springform pan for about 1 hour. Frost and then decorate with toasted almonds.

CHOCOLATE WALNUT TORTE

2 cups shelled walnuts or almonds
¼ cup grated unsweetened chocolate
9 eggs, separated, whites stiffly beaten

1 cup sugar
½ cup fine cracker crumbs

Preheat oven to 350° F. Chop the nuts, reserving ⅓ cup for decorating. Mix the nuts and chocolate. Beat the yolks and sugar until light. Then mix with the nuts, chocolate, and crumbs, and stir well. Add the stiffly beaten whites last. Bake in a greased and floured 9-inch springform pan for 45 minutes. Frost with Fudge Frosting (page 604) and sprinkle with remaining nuts.

COFFEE TORTE

8 eggs, separated, whites stiffly beaten
1 cup confectioners' sugar

½ pound blanched almonds, grated
2 tablespoons instant coffee
1 teaspoon vanilla

1. Preheat oven to 350° F. Beat yolks until thick. Add sugar and the remaining torte ingredients, the stiffly beaten whites last. Bake in 2 greased and floured 9-inch layer pans for about 30 minutes.

2. Cool, then fill and frost with Coffee Butter Frosting (page 599).

DATE TORTE

16 dates, pitted
2 tablespoons lemon juice, or ¼ cup wine or brandy
2 tablespoons almonds, chopped
2 tablespoons citron, finely chopped
9 eggs (2 whole, 7 separated)
1¾ cups sugar

¼ cup grated unsweetened chocolate
1 teaspoon cinnamon
1 teaspoon allspice
1¼ cups cracker crumbs
½ teaspoon baking powder

Preheat oven to 350° F. Mash the dates to a smooth paste with the lemon juice, wine, or brandy. Add almonds and citron. Beat together two whole eggs and seven yolks, add sugar, beat again. Stir in the dates, chocolate, spices, cracker crumbs, and baking powder. Beat the 7 whites stiffly and fold into the batter. Bake in a greased and floured 10-inch springform pan 40 to 60 minutes.

DATE AND WALNUT TORTE

2 eggs
1 cup sugar
2 tablespoons cream
2 tablespoons flour

1 teaspoon baking powder
1 cup walnuts, chopped
¼ teaspoon vanilla
1 cup dates, finely chopped

Preheat oven to 325° F. Beat eggs very light, add sugar and cream and continue beating. Add flour mixed with the baking powder, then the nuts, vanilla, and dates. Bake in a greased and floured 8-inch square pan for about 1 hour.

DOBOS TORTE (SEVEN-LAYER CAKE)

1 cup flour
¼ teaspoon salt
7 eggs, separated
1 cup confectioners' sugar

Filling
½ pound sweet chocolate
3 tablespoons cold water
3 eggs
1½ cups sugar
½ pound butter
1 teaspoon vanilla

1. Preheat oven to 375° F. Sift flour once, measure, add salt, sift four times. Beat egg yolks until thick, add sugar gradually, beat well. Fold in flour. Beat whites until stiff but not dry, and fold in lightly. Line bottoms of 4 shallow 8- or 9-inch cake tins, or dobos torte set, with heavy paper. Grease paper. Keep in mind that this batter must be divided into seven layers. Spread batter evenly into four pans for the first baking, reserving enough batter for the three remaining layers. Bake about 8 minutes. Remove at once from pans and strip off the paper. Prepare three pans again, fill with remaining batter and repeat. Let the layers cool completely.

2. Meanwhile make the filling. Melt chocolate with water in double boiler. Mix eggs and sugar, add to chocolate, cook until thick, stirring constantly. Remove from heat, add butter, stir until melted, and add vanilla. Beat until cool and stiff enough to spread. Spread between layers, over top and sides. To keep layers in place, put several toothpicks through top layers until filling sets. Chill for 24 hours.

FILBERT TORTE

8 eggs, separated, whites stiffly
  beaten
1½ cups confectioners' sugar
½ cup breadcrumbs

grated rind of 1 lemon
juice of ½ lemon
½ pound grated filberts or hazelnuts

Preheat oven to 325° F. Beat yolks and sugar until very light, add breadcrumbs and the rest of the ingredients in order, the beaten whites last. Bake in a greased and floured 9-inch springform pan for 40 to 45 minutes. Cover with Walnut Filling (page 610), substituting 1 pound filberts for walnuts. Decorate with additional nuts.

Variation: Bake in two layers; place fresh strawberries, or sweetened whipped cream, between layers and on top of cake.

HAZELNUT COFFEE TORTE

11 eggs, separated, whites stiffly
  beaten
2 cups confectioners' sugar, plus
  more for dusting

1 pound ground hazelnuts
1 teaspoon instant coffee

Preheat oven to 350° F. Beat yolks well, add sugar gradually, beating all the time. Then add the nuts, the coffee, and fold in the stiffly beaten whites last. Bake in a greased and floured 12-inch springform pan for 50 to 60 minutes. Dust with confectioners' sugar.

LADY FINGER TORTE

6 egg yolks
1½ cups sugar
1 cup lady finger crumbs
2 tablespoons brandy or 1
    tablespoon lemon juice

1 cup blanched, grated almonds
5 egg whites, stiffly beaten

Preheat oven to 325° F. Beat yolks and sugar until lemon-colored. Add the rest of the ingredients, folding in the whites last. Bake in two greased and floured 9-inch layer pans for 40 minutes.

Note: This torte is best spread with Pecan Filling (page 609) between layers.

LEMON TORTE

1 recipe Rich Egg Pastry (page 522)
½ pound butter
1 cup confectioners' sugar

grated rind of 1 lemon
juice of 2 lemons
6 eggs

Preheat oven to 400° F. Line bottom and sides of a greased 9-inch springform pan with pastry. Cream butter and sugar, add lemon rind and juice and stir well. Beat the eggs until thick and lemon-colored. Combine the mixtures lightly and place on dough. Place in oven immediately and bake ½ hour. Serve from bottom tin of springform.

LINZER TORTE

1 cup butter
1 cup sugar
3 eggs, separated, whites stiffly
    beaten
grated rind and juice of 1 lemon
1 tablespoon brandy

½ pound almonds, finely chopped
2 cups flour, sifted 3 times
1 teaspoon baking powder
12-ounce jar raspberry jam or
    preserves

Preheat oven to 350° F. Cream butter and sugar well. Add yolks, lemon rind and juice, brandy, and almonds. Add flour mixed with baking powder and fold in whites. Roll out or pat ⅔ of the dough in a greased and floured 9-inch springform having the dough a little thicker on the bottom than the sides. Fill with jam. Roll remaining dough, cut in strips and place crisscross on top. Bake for 40 minutes. Before serving, fill hollows on top with additional jam.

MACAROON TORTE

1 recipe Rich Egg Pastry (page 522)
14 egg whites
2 cups confectioners' sugar
1 teaspoon vanilla
1 pound blanched and grated
  almonds

Preheat oven to 325° F. Line sides and bottom of springform with Rich Egg Pastry. Beat egg whites very stiff, add sugar and beat again until stiff and dry, add vanilla and fold in the grated almonds. Place in the dough-lined springform and bake 1 hour.

MARZIPAN TORTE PASTRY

½ cup butter
2 cups flour
2 tablespoons sugar
2 egg yolks
2 tablespoons water

Filling
1 pound almonds, blanched and
  grated
2 cups confectioners' sugar
½ teaspoon salt
juice of 2 lemons
8 egg whites, stiffly beaten

1. Blend butter into flour and sugar, add egg yolks and water and mix well. Chill thoroughly, about 45 minutes. Roll out dough and line a greased 9-inch springform pan. Reserve a small quantity of dough for lattice strips for the top.
2. Preheat oven to 325° F. To make the filling, heat almonds, sugar, salt, and lemon juice in a double boiler, stirring until well blended. Cool. Add the whites. Put the mixture on the dough, weave strips of crust over the top. Bake 1 hour. Dust with confectioners' sugar and decorate with candied cherries, if desired.

MATZO MEAL ALMOND TORTE

5 eggs, separated, whites stiffly
  beaten
1 cup sugar
1 cup raw almonds, ground
½ cup matzo meal
1 teaspoon baking powder
1 teaspoon cinnamon
¼ teaspoon ground cloves
1 tablespoon lemon juice or brandy

Preheat oven to 350° F. Beat yolks and sugar until light; add the rest of the ingredients in order, the egg whites last. Bake in a greased and floured 8-inch springform pan for 1 hour.

MATZO MEAL APPLE TORTE

8 eggs, separated, yolks beaten
¼ teaspoon salt
¾ cup sugar
1 cup matzo meal
1 teaspoon cinnamon

1 tablespoon orange juice
¼ cup almonds or other nuts,
  chopped
8 apples, pared and grated

Preheat oven to 350° F. Beat egg whites with salt until very stiff; add sugar gradually, then beaten yolks. Mix together the matzo meal and cinnamon, add, then add orange juice, nuts, and apples last. Bake in greased and floured 9-inch springform pan 1 to 1¼ hours.

CHOCOLATE MATZO MEAL TORTE

4 eggs, separated, whites stiffly
  beaten
½ cup sugar
¼ pound almonds, blanched and
  grated
¼ pound raisins

⅓ cup matzo cake meal
¼ pound sweet chocolate, grated,
  or ½ cup cocoa
¼ cup white wine
juice of 1 orange

Preheat oven to 350° F. Beat yolks and sugar until very light, add grated almonds, raisins, matzo cake meal, chocolate, wine, orange juice, and fold in the stiffly beaten whites. Bake in a greased and floured 8-inch springform pan for 1 hour.

SCHAUM TORTE (MERINGUE TORTE)

6 egg whites
2 cups sugar

1 teaspoon vanilla
1 teaspoon vinegar

Preheat oven to 275° F. Beat whites until stiff enough to hold peaks; beat in 6 tablespoons sugar, 2 at a time, beating thoroughly after each addition. Add vanilla, vinegar, and the rest of the sugar, beating continuously. Grease and flour a 9-inch springform pan and fill with about ⅔ of the mixture. On a greased and floured baking sheet, form a circle of small kisses with the rest of the mixture. Bake all about 1 hour. Before serving, fill with whipped cream or ice cream and berries and decorate the top with the circle of kisses.

Note: High Temperature Method: Bake at 450° F for 7 minutes. Turn off heat and leave torte in oven for 3 hours.

Variation:

Coffee Schaum Torte: Follow recipe for Meringue Torte, above, but put all of the mixture into the springform. Cover baked meringue with mounds of coffee ice cream. Serve with sweetened whipped cream and toasted, sliced almonds.

ORANGE TORTE

8 eggs, separated, whites stiffly
  beaten
1 cup sugar
½ pound grated almonds

2 tablespoons breadcrumbs
grated rind and juice of 2 small
  oranges

Preheat oven to 350° F. Beat yolks and sugar until very light; add other ingredients, the stiffly beaten egg whites last. Bake in 2 greased and floured layer cake pans for ½ hour. When cold, spread favorite jelly between layers. Spread Orange Butter Frosting (page 599) over top of torte and decorate with orange sections.

MUSHKAZUNGE

7 egg whites
1 cup plus 2 tablespoons sugar
½ teaspoon cinnamon

grated rind of ½ lemon
½ pound unblanched almonds,
  grated

Preheat oven to 350° F. Beat whites until stiff enough to hold a soft peak. Gradually beat in sugar. Add cinnamon and lemon rind. Fold in grated nuts. Spread in a greased 9-by-13-inch shallow pan. Bake for 20 minutes.

POPPY SEED TORTE

1 recipe Rich Egg Pastry (page 522)
breadcrumbs
6 eggs, separated, whites stiffly
  beaten
¾ cup sugar
1 cup ground poppy seeds

grated rind of 1 lemon
2 tablespoons raisins, chopped
1 tablespoon citron, finely chopped
1 teaspoon vanilla
¼ cup ground almonds

Preheat oven to 350° F. Line a 9-inch springform pan with pastry, sprinkle with breadcrumbs. Beat yolks and sugar until light, add the rest of the ingredients, the stiffly beaten whites last. Fill the form and bake 1 hour or until well set.

CHOCOLATE POPPY SEED TORTE

1¼ cups ground poppy seeds
¾ pound grated almonds
1½ teaspoons cinnamon
1½ ounces grated sweet chocolate
1½ teaspoons baking powder

18 eggs, separated, whites stiffly
  beaten
1¼ cups sugar
¼ cup brandy
grated rind and juice of 1 lemon

Preheat oven to 350° F. Mix poppy seeds, almonds, cinnamon, chocolate, and baking powder. Beat yolks and sugar until very light. Add brandy, lemon rind and juice, and dry ingredients. Fold in stiffly beaten whites. Bake in a large greased and floured springform pan until well set, about 30 minutes.

PRUNE TORTE

1 recipe Rich Egg Pastry (page 522)
1 pound prunes
2 egg whites

¼ cup sugar
grated rind of 1 lemon
1 cup chopped nuts

Preheat oven to 400° F. Line bottom and sides of a greased 9-inch springform pan with pastry. Cook prunes, drain, stone, and finely chop. Beat the whites very stiff, add sugar, lemon rind, and fold in the prunes. Fill springform pan; sprinkle the chopped nuts on top. Bake 25 to 30 minutes.

RYE BREAD TORTE (BROD TORTE)

5 eggs, separated, whites stiffly
  beaten
1 cup sugar
1 cup rye or wheat bread crumbs

juice and grated rind of ½ lemon,
  or 2 tablespoons white wine
1 cup almonds, blanched and grated
1½ teaspoons baking powder

Preheat oven to 350° F. Beat the yolks and sugar until very light. Soak the crumbs in the lemon juice or wine; mix all ingredients, the stiffly beaten whites last. Bake in 2 greased and floured 9-inch layer pans for 45 minutes. Fill with Walnut Filling (page 610).

BRANDY RYE BREAD TORTE

6 eggs, separated, whites stiffly
    beaten
1 cup sugar
¾ cup rye bread crumbs
1 cup grated almonds

½ cup cooked, riced potatoes
¼ teaspoon cinnamon
¼ cup brandy or white wine

Preheat oven to 350° F. Beat yolks and sugar until very light. Add the rest of the ingredients, the egg whites last. Bake in a greased and floured 9-inch springform pan for 1 hour.

STRAWBERRY SHORTCAKE TORTE

9 egg whites
1½ cups sugar
1 teaspoon vanilla
¾ cup blanched and ground
    almonds

1 quart strawberries, cut and
    sugared
2 cups heavy cream, whipped

Preheat oven to 325° F. Beat whites stiff and dry. Add sugar gradually, beating constantly; add vanilla and fold in the nuts last. Spread evenly in 2 greased and floured cake pans with removable bottoms. Bake 25 to 30 minutes. When cool, put cut and sugared strawberries and whipped cream between layers and on top.

VIENNA TORTE

Torte
7 eggs, separated
1¼ cups sugar
1 cup flour
¼ cup cornstarch
2 teaspoons baking powder
pinch of salt

Filling
1½ cups milk
⅓ cup flour
⅓ cup sugar
1 cup butter, melted
1 teaspoon vanilla
1 cup confectioners' sugar
chopped nuts

1. Preheat oven to 350° F. Beat whites until frothy. Add ½ cup sugar gradually, beat until stiff. Beat yolks until thick, add rest of sugar gradually and

beat. Combine the two mixtures. Sift the flour with cornstarch, baking powder, and salt and fold in carefully. Pour into 4 greased and floured 8-inch layer cake pans. Bake about 20 minutes. Cool.

2. Meanwhile, make the filling. Heat 1¼ cups milk in double boiler. Mix together flour, sugar, and remaining ¼ cup cold milk. Add to heated milk and stir until thick, then cover and cook 15 minutes. When cool, add melted butter, mix well, then add vanilla and confectioners' sugar. Spread this between the cooked four layers and on top and sides. Cover well with chopped nuts.

WALNUT TORTE

6 eggs, separated, whites stiffly
   beaten
1 cup sugar
¼ pound grated walnuts

1¼ cups grated lady fingers
2 tablespoons flour
1 teaspoon baking powder
juice and grated rind of ½ lemon

Preheat oven to 350° F. Beat the yolks and sugar until light; add the other ingredients in the order given, mixing baking powder with flour and folding in the egg whites last. Bake in greased and floured 9-inch layer pans for 30 minutes.

Note: This torte is best with Cream Custard Filling (page 607) or Walnut Filling (page 610) between layers and Chocolate Butter Frosting (page 599) on top.

ZWIEBACK TORTE

6 eggs, separated, whites stiffly
   beaten
¾ cup sugar
¼ pound almonds, grated
juice and grated rind of ½ lemon
¼ pound zwieback, crushed

½ teaspoon cinnamon
½ teaspoon ground cloves
2 teaspoons baking powder
2 tablespoons brandy or maraschino
   cherry syrup

Preheat oven to 350° F. Beat yolks and sugar until very light. Add the remaining ingredients, except the brandy or syrup, adding the egg whites last. Bake in a greased and floured 9-inch springform pan for about 40 minutes. Sprinkle with brandy or syrup and bake 5 minutes longer.

Icebox Cakes and Other Cake Desserts

BASIC LADY FINGER SHELL

Line the bottom and sides of a large springform pan with split lady fingers (or fingers of sponge or angel food cake). You'll need about 2 to 3 dozen. Trim if necessary to fit, and arrange so that none of the pan is showing. Add a layer of prepared filling (see the following recipes), cover with lady fingers, and repeat to fill mold. The last layer should be lady fingers, arranged like the spokes of a wheel. Chill overnight, until very firm. Remove the sides from the pan and put the cake on the serving platter without removing the pan bottom. Garnish with sweetened, flavord whipped cream, and decorate with pistachio nuts or candied fruit if desired.

CHOCOLATE ICEBOX CAKE

2 ounces unsweetened chocolate	1 cup butter
½ cup granulated sugar	1 cup confectioners' sugar
¼ cup water	4 egg whites, stiffly beaten
4 egg yolks, well beaten	30 lady fingers, split

Cook chocolate, granulated sugar, and water in double boiler; when smooth gradually add the well-beaten yolks (see page 86); cook until thick and smooth, stirring constantly. Cool. Cream butter and confectioners' sugar well, add the egg mixture, stir well, and fold in the whites. Line cake form with lady fingers according to directions above and chill overnight.

LEMON-FILLED ICEBOX CAKE

3 eggs, separated	grated rind of ½ lemon
¼ cup granulated sugar	½ cup butter
1 tablespoon cornstarch	1 cup confectioners' sugar
¼ cup milk	3 dozen lady fingers, split
juice of 1 lemon	1 cup heavy cream, whipped

Beat yolks well and place in a double boiler with the granulated sugar and cornstarch mixed with the milk. Cook until thick and smooth, stirring constantly. Remove from heat, add lemon juice and rind, and cool. Cream butter and confectioners' sugar well, add to the egg mixture. Beat the egg whites stiffly and fold into the batter. Line springform with lady fingers according to directions on page 587 and chill overnight.

Variation:

Orange Icebox Cake: Follow recipe for Lemon-Filled Icebox Cake, substituting the juice of 1 orange for the lemon juice, and grated rind of 1 orange and 1 lemon.

MOCHA ICEBOX CAKE

1 cup hot milk
3 tablespoons instant coffee
3 eggs, separated, whites stiffly
  beaten
2 tablespoons cornstarch

⅛ teaspoon salt
½ cup sugar
1 teaspoon vanilla
30 lady fingers

Pour the hot milk over coffee and let it stand for 10 minutes. Beat the yolks well (see page 86). Mix cornstarch, salt, and sugar in double boiler, add the yolks, and stir in the coffee mixture. Cook slowly until thick and smooth; while still warm, add vanilla and fold in egg whites. Line bottom and sides of a springform pan with lady fingers according to the directions on page 587 and chill overnight.

ALMOND OR PECAN ICEBOX CAKE

18 lady fingers
30 macaroons
1 cup butter
1⅓ cups confectioners' sugar
3 whole eggs
3 eggs, separated, whites stiffly
  beaten

½ pound blanched, grated almonds
  or pecans
2 cups heavy cream
¼ cup confectioners' sugar
vanilla
candied cherries or chopped
  pistachio nuts

1. Cut ends off lady fingers. Split and place lady fingers close together on sides of 9-inch springform pan, the rounded side toward the pan. Lay half of the macaroons closely together on bottom, flat side down, and fill in the small spaces with the lady finger ends.

2. Cream butter and sugar, add 3 whole eggs, one at a time, and stir well (see page 86). Thoroughly beat and then add the yolks of the other 3 eggs, then

the nuts, and lastly fold in the 3 beaten whites. Cover the macaroons with half of mixture, add another layer of macaroons, then the rest of the mixture. Chill for 30 hours.

3. When ready to serve, remove rim of cake pan, leaving cake on pan bottom. Whip cream with powdered sugar and vanilla mixture; decorate with candied cherries or chopped pistachio nuts.

QUEEN OF TRIFLES

1 pound macaroons
2 cups sherry
30-40 lady fingers
½ cup sugar
2 tablespoons flour
1 egg, well beaten

2 cups hot milk
½ pound almonds, blanched and
   coarsely chopped
½ pound candied cherries, halved
4 cups heavy cream, whipped
whole candied cherries for garnish

Soak macaroons in the sherry. Line a large glass bowl with split lady fingers. Make a custard mixture by mixing sugar and flour with the egg, add gradually to the hot milk, and cook in double boiler until very thick, stirring constantly. Cool, add almonds, cherries, and ¾ of the whipped cream. Pour custard mixture over lady fingers; top with soaked macaroons. Cover with remaining whipped cream. Decorate with whole cherries.

CHOCOLATE CHARLOTTE RUSSE

2 envelopes unflavored gelatin
¼ cup cold water
2 ounces unsweetened chocolate,
   grated
2 cups milk

1 cup sugar
1 teaspoon vanilla
2 cups heavy cream
12 lady fingers, split
chopped candied cherries (optional)
chopped pistachio nuts (optional)

Soak gelatin in cold water 5 minutes. Melt chocolate in double boiler, add milk and sugar, cook 5 minutes or until smooth. Add gelatin and stir until dissolved. When cold, add vanilla. Beat cream until very stiff, gradually add the chocolate and gelatin mixture. Line a quart mold with split lady fingers, and fill with custard mixture. Chill for an hour or more. Unmold and serve with whipped cream and, if desired, sprinkle with bits of candied cherries, and pistachio nuts.

Variation:

Angel Charlotte Russe: Replace lady fingers in the above recipe with thin slices of Angel Food Cake (page 568).

ORANGE OR STRAWBERRY CHARLOTTE RUSSE

2 envelopes unflavored gelatin
⅓ cup cold water
⅓ cup boiling water
1 cup sugar
3 tablespoons lemon juice

1 cup fruit juice and pulp
3 egg whites, stiffly beaten
1 cup heavy cream, whipped
orange sections or whole
   strawberries

Soak the gelatin in cold water, then dissolve in boiling water. Add sugar, cool; add lemon juice, fruit juice, and pulp. When cold, beat until frothy; add whites (see page 86) and fold in cream. Line a mold with sections of orange or fresh, ripe strawberries. Pour in the mixture and chill until firm.

DESSERT IN CAKE SHELL
Carefully cut the top off a Golden Sponge or Angel Food Cake (page 566 or 568); scoop out the inside of the remaining cake, leaving a ¾ inch wall; fill with favorite icebox filling or thick pudding. Replace top of cake, cover with whipped cream, and garnish with candied cherries and blanched almonds. Chill until firm.

Small Cakes

The most elegant small cakes are made from a large sheet of plain cake; the large cake is cut into decorative shapes and each small cake is individually iced and decorated.

Other small cakes are made by dropping cake batter from a spoon to form a mound on a baking sheet; or by forcing the batter through a pastry tube; or by baking in special small pans.

PETITS FOURS

sheet cake
favorite jelly
Cooked Fondant (page 662)
pistachio nuts

candied cherries, candied orange
peel, candied lime peel, candied
pineapple, candied rose petals,
candied violets, candied mint
leaves.

Cut a sheet cake into small circles, diamonds, or squares about 1½ inches in diameter. Any sponge or butter cake or chiffon cake batter may be baked in a large, shallow pan for this purpose; a cake baked in a 13-by-9-by-2-inch pan will yield about 46 petits fours. Melt Fondant Icing of various colors and flavors over hot water, and keep it warm. To seal edges, brush cut sides of cake with jelly. Fix cakes on a fork and dip into icing; drain and invert on a rack over waxed paper to dry. Decorate each cake to taste with fruits and nuts. Pistachio nuts, cut lengthwise, can be used for leaves, and candied fruits for flowers. Or use candied flowers or leaves. Fix the decorations with a little warm Fondant, let harden. Put each cake in a little paper case, if desired.

Variation:

Filled Petits Fours: Cut out cake shapes, above, from any frosted cake before icing with fondant and decorating. Or hollow out the cakes, fill with whipped cream, almond paste, or a custard filling, and sandwich in pairs; ice and decorate to taste.

COCONUT SNOWBALLS

Make Angel Food Cake (page 568); bake in ungreased tube pan. Make Meringue Frosting (page 601). Cool cake, remove from pan, cut in 1½-inch cubes. Place on fork, dip into frosting, cover on all sides; roll in freshly grated coconut, place on waxed paper until set. Serve same day.

SMALL FROSTED CAKES

Bake Angel Food, Golden Sponge, or Sunshine Cake (page 566 or 568) in oblong pans 1½ inches deep. Cover with either of the two frostings here:

Chocolate Frosting
Frost cake with Chocolate Icing (page 598) and, while soft, cut into squares and place half a walnut on each.

Mocha Frosting
Let cake cool, cut into squares, cover with soft Coffee Icing (page 598). Sprinkle with finely chopped and blanched pistachio nuts, roasted almonds, or peanuts, or with dried and rolled macaroons.

NUT DROP CAKES

2 tablespoons butter	1 teaspoon baking powder
¼ cup sugar	¼ teaspoon salt
1 egg, well beaten	2 tablespoons milk
½ teaspoon lemon juice	½ cup chopped nuts
½ cup flour	

Preheat oven to 350° F. Cream butter and sugar, add egg and lemon juice. Beat well. Sift together dry ingredients, add alternately with the milk to first mixture; then add nuts. Drop on greased cookie sheet 1 inch apart. Bake 15 minutes.

LADY FINGERS

3 eggs, separated	½ cup flour
⅓ cup confectioners' sugar	¼ teaspoon salt
¼ teaspoon vanilla	1 teaspoon baking powder
3 tablespoons hot water	

Preheat oven to 350° F. Beat egg whites until foamy. Beat in sugar gradually and continue beating until stiff. Beat egg yolks until thick, and fold into whites. Add vanilla and hot water. Sift together dry ingredients and fold into batter. Put into lady finger tins, sprinkle with confectioners' sugar, and bake 8 to 10 minutes. Remove from tins while hot. Brush the flat surface of half the cakes with egg white and sandwich in pairs. Or, force batter through a pastry tube in 1-by-5-inch fingers onto a cookie sheet covered with waxed paper.

Variations:

Sponge Drops: Make Lady Fingers, above. Drop from teaspoon. Bake for 10 to 12 minutes in moderate oven. Put together with jelly.

Othellos: Force Lady Finger mixture, above, through a pastry tube onto a cookie sheet covered with brown paper, in inch rounds. When baked, spread the flat side of half of the cakes with Vanilla Custard Filling (page 606). Press together in pairs and dip in Chocolate Butter Frosting (page 599). Let dry on waxed paper.

CREAM PUFFS

½ cup butter   1 cup flour
1 cup water   4 eggs, unbeaten

Preheat oven to 450° F. Heat butter and water. When mixture is boiling, add flour all at once and stir vigorously until mixture no longer sticks to sides of pan. Remove from heat; cool slightly; add eggs one at a time, beating after each addition. Drop by heaping tablespoons onto a well-greased cookie sheet, 2 inches apart, and bake for 20 minutes. Reduce heat to 325°, and bake about 20 minutes longer. Remove from baking sheet and cool. When ready to serve, cut open on one side, and fill with whipped cream, custard, or any desired filling.

Variations:

Tiny Cream Puffs: Drop Cream Puff mixture, above, from teaspoon or force through pastry tube onto greased cookie sheets in 1- to 1½-inch mounds. They will take less time to bake, so watch carefully. When baked and cool, slit one side, fill with any custard filling. Ice tops with any of a variety of colored and flavored frostings.

Profiteroles: Fill Tiny Cream Puffs with ice cream and either freeze until serving time or serve at once with warm chocolate sauce.

Chocolate Eclairs: Force mixture for Cream Puffs, above, through pastry tube, in 4-by-1½-inch oblong shapes, 2 inches apart, onto greased cookie sheets. When baked and cool, fill with any custard filling; ice with Chocolate Icing (page 598).

Cupcakes

Any cake batter may be baked in greased cupcake pans, or in pans lined with paper baking cups designed especially for this purpose. Increase baking temperature to 375° F and reduce baking time to about 20 minutes, depending on the size of the cakes.

VANILLA CUPCAKES   *Makes 24 medium cupcakes.*

1 cup sugar
2 cups flour
¼ teaspoon salt
1 tablespoon baking powder

¼ cup shortening, melted
1 cup milk
1 egg, well beaten
1 teaspoon vanilla

Preheat oven to 375° F. Sift together dry ingredients; add melted shortening to the milk, egg, and vanilla and mix together. Combine two mixtures well. Bake in greased or lined muffin pans for 20 minutes.

COCOA CUPCAKES   *Makes 18 medium cupcakes.*

3 tablespoons shortening
1 cup sugar
1 egg, well beaten
1 teaspoon vanilla

1½ cups flour
1 tablespoon baking powder
⅓ cup cocoa
½ cup milk

Preheat oven to 375° F. Cream shortening and sugar; add egg and vanilla. Sift together dry ingredients and add alternately with the milk. Bake in greased or lined muffin pans for 20 minutes.

CHOCOLATE CUPCAKES   *Makes 18 medium cupcakes.*

½ cup shortening
1 cup brown sugar, firmly packed
1 egg
1 ounce unsweetened chocolate,
  melted

½ cup sour milk
1½ cups flour
1 teaspoon baking soda

Preheat oven to 350° F. Cream shortening and sugar; add egg and chocolate. Add milk alternately with the flour and soda mixed. Bake in greased or lined muffin pans for 20 to 25 minutes.

RAISIN CUPCAKES   *Makes 18 medium cupcakes.*

1 cup raisins
1½ cups flour
⅓ cup shortening
1 cup sugar

1 egg, well beaten
1 tablespoon baking powder
½ cup milk
½ teaspoon vanilla

Preheat oven to 350° F. Mix raisins with ¼ cup of the flour. Cream shortening and sugar; stir in egg. Sift together the remaining flour with the baking powder. Add milk and dry ingredients alternately. Mix well, add vanilla and floured raisins. Bake in greased or lined muffin pans about 20 minutes.

GINGER CUPCAKES *Makes 18 medium cupcakes.*

¼ cup butter
¼ cup brown sugar, firmly packed
1 egg
1½ cups flour
½ teaspoon cinnamon

¼ teaspoon ground cloves
1 tablespoon ginger
1 teaspoon baking soda
½ cup molasses
½ cup boiling water

Preheat oven to 350° F. Cream butter and add sugar gradually, then add the egg. Mix and sift dry ingredients and add alternately with molasses and hot water, mixed together. Bake in greased or lined muffin pans for about 20 minutes.

PECAN CUPCAKES *Makes 18 medium cupcakes.*

½ cup flour
⅛ teaspoon salt
½ teaspoon baking powder

1 cup brown sugar, firmly packed
2 eggs, slightly beaten
1 cup broken pecan meats

Preheat oven to 325° F. Mix and sift the first 3 ingredients. Add sugar to eggs, then the pecans sprinkled with flour, then the flour mixture. Bake in small greased or lined muffin pans for about 20 minutes.

Cake Frostings and Fillings

Frostings, icings, and fillings keep cakes moist, and add greatly to their flavor and appearance.

A cake should be cold and free from crumbs before it is frosted. Cover the cake plate with 2 strips of waxed paper to protect it from drippings. The paper may be withdrawn from each side after the cake is frosted. When frosting layer cake, invert one layer, spread filling evenly over flat surface, then place flat surface of second layer on top and frost by heaping frosting in center and with spatula, spreading over top and sides. Spatula may be dipped in hot water if the frosting thickens.

To prevent layers from slipping, insert several long toothpicks and remove when cake is frosted if desired. Frost the top of the cake last.

Try contrasting colors, flavorings, and textures when frosting and filling cakes. Following are some ideas for frostings and cakes that work together:

ANGEL FOOD CAKES
Sugar Glaze
Coffee Glaze
Lemon Icing
Fruit Juice Icing

FRUIT AND NUT CAKES
Rum- or Whisky-Flavored Icings
Lemon or Orange Icing

CHOCOLATE CAKES
Coffee Icing
Mocha Icing
Caramel Frosting
Butter Frosting

WHITE CAKES
Brown Butter Frosting
Fluffy Chocolate Frosting
Cream Cheese Chocolate Frosting

YELLOW CAKES
Coconut Frosting
Orange or Lemon Frosting
Fudge Frosting

FLAVORINGS FOR FROSTINGS AND CAKES

CARAMEL SYRUP

1 cup sugar   ½ cup boiling water

Melt sugar in heavy skillet, stirring occasionally until sugar becomes a light-brown liquid. Add water slowly. Simmer 5 to 10 minutes. Cool and bottle. Use to color and flavor cakes and frostings.

RUM FLAVORING

1 ounce medium-bodied New
England rum
1 ounce Jamaica rum

1 ounce arrack
1 ounce vanilla

Mix and bottle and use to flavor cakes or torten.

UNCOOKED ICINGS

The following icings are from days gone by when eggs were far from a health problem. We are including some that call for the addition of raw yolks or whites. We advise caution, however. The prudent reader might want to substitute a cooked icing or a recipe that doesn't list eggs as an ingredient.

Recipes containing 1 cup of confectioners' sugar will ice the top of one 8- to 9-inch cake. Double those recipes to make enough frosting for tops and sides.

CONFECTIONERS' SUGAR GLAZE

2 tablespoons hot water, milk, or
half-and-half
¼ teaspoon vanilla, lemon, or other
extracts, or 1 teaspoon lemon
juice or rum

1 cup confectioners' sugar

Stir some of the liquid and all of the flavoring into the sugar, adding more liquid, a few drops at a time, as needed. The icing is of the proper consistency when it coats a spoon.

CONFECTIONERS' SUGAR ICING

½ teaspoon butter
2 tablespoons hot milk

1½ cups confectioners' sugar
½ teaspoon vanilla

Add butter to hot milk; add sugar slowly to make right consistency to spread; add vanilla. Spread on top and sides of cake.

CHOCOLATE ICING

1 ounce chocolate, unsweetened, or	½ teaspoon vanilla extract
⅓ cup cocoa	1¾ cups confectioners' sugar
6 tablespoons boiling water	cinnamon to taste (optional)

Melt chocolate in top of double boiler or in microwave, add boiling water, and stir until smooth; or dissolve ⅓ cup cocoa in the boiling water. Add vanilla and the sugar; stir until mixture is smooth. A little cinnamon may be added, if desired.

COFFEE OR MOCHA ICING

3 tablespoons hot strong coffee	½ teaspoon vanilla
3 tablespoons dry cocoa	1⅓ cups confectioners' sugar

Add coffee to cocoa, stir until smooth, add vanilla and enough sugar to reach spreading consistency.

LEMON ICING

grated rind of ½ lemon	1 tablespoon boiling water
1 tablespoon lemon juice	1 cup confectioners' sugar

Add lemon rind to juice and water, stir into the sugar, a little at a time, until thick enough to spread.

FRUIT JUICE ICING

1 teaspoon lemon juice	1½ cups confectioners' sugar
2 tablespoons fresh fruit juice or	
fruit syrup	

Add lemon juice and strained fruit juice (strawberries, cherries, or grapes) to the sugar, a little at a time, until thin enough to spread.

GLACÉ

2 egg whites	1 teaspoon lemon juice
1½ cups confectioners' sugar	⅛ teaspoon cream of tartar

Beat whites until frothy. Add half the sugar gradually, beating until well blended. Add lemon juice, cream of tartar, then remaining sugar. Beat until thick. Spread on top and sides of cake.

UNCOOKED FROSTINGS

Frostings differ from icings in that they're richer and more substantial. They are usually made with butter, sometimes with cream cheese. Frostings may be used as a filling between cake layers, as well as to cover the top and sides of cakes.

BASIC BUTTER FROSTING

2 tablespoons butter
1 cup confectioners' sugar

2 tablespoons milk, cream, sherry, rum, or brandy
½ teaspoon vanilla

Cream butter and sugar well, add the flavoring and liquid until mixture spreads well.

CHOCOLATE BUTTER FROSTING

2 tablespoons butter
1 cup confectioners' sugar
½ teaspoon vanilla

1 ounce unsweetened chocolate melted over boiling water or in microwave, or ¼ cup cocoa

Proceed as for Basic Butter Frosting.

COFFEE BUTTER FROSTING

2 tablespoons butter
1 cup confectioners' sugar
2 tablespoons strong, hot coffee

1 teaspoon dry cocoa
½ teaspoon vanilla

Proceed as for Basic Butter Frosting.

ORANGE OR LEMON BUTTER FROSTING

2 tablespoons butter
1 cup confectioners' sugar
1 tablespoon milk or water

1 tablespoon orange or lemon juice and a little grated rind.

Proceed as for Basic Butter Frosting, above.

CARAMEL BUTTER FROSTING

½ cup butter
2 cups brown sugar, firmly packed

¼ teaspoon vanilla
heavy cream

Cream butter, add sugar gradually and mix very well, add vanilla and only enough cream to obtain desired consistency.

BROWN BUTTER FROSTING

¼ cup butter
2 cups confectioners' sugar

3 to 4 tablespoons milk
½ teaspoon vanilla

Melt butter until golden brown. Add to sugar, milk, and vanilla. Mix until desired consistency.

Variation:

Brown Butter Brandy Frosting: Replace the vanilla and 1 to 2 tablespoons of the milk with 2 tablespoons brandy in the recipe above.

FLUFFY CHOCOLATE FROSTING

2 cups confectioners' sugar
½ cup milk
2 eggs
¼ teaspoon salt

½ teaspoon vanilla
4 ounces unsweetened chocolate
6 tablespoons butter

Blend sugar, milk, eggs, salt, and vanilla in a bowl over ice water. Melt chocolate and butter together in top of a double boiler. Add while warm to first mixture and beat until desired consistency.

CREAM CHEESE FROSTING

3 ounces cream cheese
1 tablespoon warm milk

2½ cups confectioners' sugar
1 teaspoon vanilla

Mash cheese with milk. Add sugar gradually and then vanilla. Beat until creamy. Any other desired flavoring may be substituted for the vanilla.

TIPS FOR SUCCESSFUL CAKE FROSTING

1. Place strips of waxed paper under the edges of the cake; remove after cake has been frosted.

2. Cool cake and brush crumbs from it before frosting.

3. Fill layers and frost sides before flavoring top of cake.

MOCHA BUTTER FROSTING

1 cup butter
1 egg yolk, beaten
2½ cups confectioners' sugar

1 ounce unsweetened chocolate, melted
1 teaspoon instant coffee
1 teaspoon vanilla

Cream butter; stir in beaten yolk, sugar, chocolate, coffee, and vanilla. Mix well.

BROILED COCONUT FROSTING

3 tablespoons butter, melted
5 tablespoons brown sugar, firmly packed

2 tablespoons half-and-half
½ cup shredded dry coconut

Mix all ingredients. Spread on warm cake before removing cake from pan. Broil until sugar is melted and bubbles. This takes only a few minutes, and should be watched carefully, as it burns easily.

BOILED FROSTINGS

MERINGUE FROSTING

1 cup sugar
½ cup water

2 egg whites, stiffly beaten
½ teaspoon flavoring extract

Boil sugar and water over low heat until syrup spins a thread; pour very slowly onto whites and beat until smooth and stiff enough to spread. Add flavoring. Spread on cake.

(continued)

Variation:

Chocolate Meringue Frosting: Substitute firmly packed brown sugar for granulated in above recipe; add 1½ ounces grated unsweetened chocolate or ¼ cup cocoa, and proceed as above.

FOUR-MINUTE FROSTING

1 cup sugar
¼ teaspoon salt
3 tablespoons cold water

½ teaspoon cream of tartar
3 unbeaten egg whites
1 teaspoon vanilla

Put all ingredients in bowl. Set bowl over hot water and beat 4 minutes until fluffy. Any flavoring may be substituted for vanilla.

SEVEN-MINUTE FROSTING

1 egg white, unbeaten
3 tablespoons cold water
⅞ cup granulated sugar

¼ teaspoon cream of tartar
½ teaspoon vanilla

Place all ingredients except vanilla in top of double boiler. Beat with rotary beater until thoroughly mixed. Place over rapidly boiling water, beat constantly until frosting stands in peaks. Add vanilla. Put pan over cold water, beat until cool. Spread on top and sides of cake. For filling and frosting two 9-inch layers, double the quantities. For variety add 4 tablespoons flavored gelatin with sugar.

COCONUT FROSTING

Make Seven-Minute Frosting or Meringue Frosting and sprinkle shredded coconut thickly over the cake while the frosting is still soft.

TO FRESHEN COCONUT

To 1 cup dry shredded coconut add ¼ cup of milk. Cook in double boiler until milk is absorbed; let stand covered until ready to use.

MAPLE FROSTING

1 cup maple syrup	2 egg whites, stiffly beaten

Boil syrup until it spins a thread; add very slowly to whites of eggs, beating constantly until stiff enough to spread.

ORNAMENTAL FROSTING

Make Meringue Frosting and when stiff enough to spread, put over boiling water, stirring continually, until icing grates slightly on bottom of bowl. Spread some on cake, force rest through pastry tube to make decorative designs.

SEA FOAM FROSTING

2 egg whites	2 tablespoons water
¾ cup light brown sugar, firmly packed	¼ teaspoon cream of tartar
⅓ cup corn syrup	¼ teaspoon salt
	1 teaspoon vanilla

Cook all ingredients except vanilla in a double boiler, beating constantly, until mixture stands in peaks. Remove from heat, add vanilla, beat until thick enough to spread.

COOKED FUDGE FROSTINGS

BROWN BEAUTY FROSTING

2 cups brown sugar, firmly packed	1 ounce unsweetened chocolate
⅔ cup water	¾ cup butter

Boil sugar and water until it spins a thread. Melt chocolate with the butter, then mix it with the syrup. Beat until thick enough to spread.

CREAMY CHOCOLATE FROSTING

¼ cup water	1 ounce unsweetened chocolate, melted
¾ cup sugar	2 egg yolks, well beaten

Boil water and sugar to a thick syrup, add the chocolate, pour syrup over the beaten yolks, stirring constantly. Beat until thick enough to spread.

CHOCOLATE NUT FROSTING

1½ cups brown sugar, firmly
   packed
¾ cup half-and-half
½ cup butter

2 ounces unsweetened chocolate,
   melted
¾ cup chopped nut meats

Boil sugar, half-and-half, and butter until thick; stir until cool; then add melted chocolate and nuts; spread between cake layers.

CHOCOLATE CARAMEL FROSTING

1¼ cups brown sugar, firmly
   packed
3 ounces unsweetened chocolate,
   grated

½ cup milk
2 tablespoons butter
1 teaspoon vanilla

Cook sugar, chocolate and milk until smooth, add butter and vanilla; cool, spread between two layers of cake.

FUDGE FROSTING

2 ounces unsweetened chocolate
½ cup milk or half-and-half
1½ cups sugar

2 tablespoons butter
1 teaspoon vanilla

Melt chocolate over low heat, add milk and sugar and boil until a few drops form a soft ball in cold water. Add butter and vanilla. Let stand undisturbed a few minutes, then beat until thick enough to spread. If too thick, stir in a little more milk or half-and-half.

CHOCOLATE BRANDY FROSTING

3 cups confectioners' sugar
5 tablespoons butter
2 tablespoons half-and-half

3 tablespoons brandy
3 tablespoons strong coffee
½ cup grated, sweet chocolate

Combine all ingredients in double boiler and cook, stirring until well blended. If necessary, add half-and-half until thin enough to spread.

COOKED CARAMEL FROSTINGS

CARAMEL FROSTING

2 tablespoons granulated sugar	6 tablespoons half-and-half
6 tablespoons butter	1½ cups confectioners' sugar
¾ cup brown sugar, firmly packed	

Melt granulated sugar in heavy skillet, add butter and brown sugar; stir until dissolved; add half-and-half, a spoonful at a time, stirring well. Boil 1 minute. Remove from heat and add confectioners' sugar. Beat well until frosting has lost its gloss.

CARAMEL FUDGE FROSTING

1½ cups brown sugar, firmly packed	2 tablespoons butter
¾ cup half-and-half or milk	½ teaspoon vanilla

Cook sugar with half-and-half or milk until it forms a soft ball when dropped in cold water, add butter and vanilla, remove from heat and beat until stiff enough to spread.

SOUR CREAM CARAMEL FROSTING

1¼ cups brown sugar, firmly packed	¾ cup sour cream
¾ cup granulated sugar	1 teaspoon butter

Mix sugars and sour cream, let stand until dissolved, about ½ hour or longer. Add butter and boil 5 minutes or to the soft-ball stage. Beat and spread on cake.

UNCOOKED FILLINGS

WHIPPED CREAM FILLING

1 cup heavy cream	½ teaspoon vanilla
¼ cup confectioners' sugar	

Beat cream until it begins to thicken; add sugar and then gradually add vanilla; continue to beat until cream holds its shape when the beater is raised.

WHIPPED CREAM FILLING WITH NUT BRITTLE

1 recipe Almond or Peanut Brittle
  (page 667)

1 cup heavy cream, whipped
1 teaspoon vanilla

Make Peanut or Walnut Brittle. When cold, break in small pieces, put through grinder or food processor, and mix lightly with the whipped cream and flavoring.

COOKED FILLINGS

VANILLA CUSTARD FILLING

1 tablespoon cornstarch
½ cup sugar
1 cup scalded milk

2 egg yolks, slightly beaten
½ teaspoon vanilla

Mix cornstarch and sugar, add the hot milk, and pour gradually on the egg yolks. Cook in double boiler, stirring constantly until thickened. Cool and add vanilla.

Variations:

Almond Custard Filling: Prepare Vanilla Custard Filling and when cool add 1 cup blanched, chopped almonds.

Coffee Custard Filling: Prepare like Vanilla Custard Filling, substituting 1½ tablespoons instant coffee for the vanilla.

Chocolate Custard Filling: Add 2 ounces unsweetened chocolate, melted, to Vanilla Custard Filling, and blend well.

BUTTER CUSTARD FILLING

2½ cups milk
½ cup sugar
½ cup flour

¼ teaspoon salt
2 teaspoons vanilla
1 cup butter

Heat milk in double boiler. Mix together the sugar, flour, and salt and stir in hot milk gradually. Return to boiler, cook about 10 minutes, stirring constantly. Cool, add vanilla. Cream butter, add the custard gradually, stirring until smooth.

CARAMEL FILLING

1 cup sugar
1½ cups hot milk
⅓ cup flour

1 egg yolk, beaten
½ teaspoon vanilla

Melt ½ of the sugar in heavy skillet, stir in hot milk very gradually. Mix remaining sugar with flour, stir into hot mixture. Cook until mixture thickens, pour onto yolk, stirring constantly. Add vanilla and spread between layers.

CHOCOLATE FILLING

½ cup sugar
1 tablespoon cornstarch
2 ounces unsweetened chocolate,
   grated

½ cup milk
vanilla

Mix sugar, cornstarch, and chocolate, stir in the milk, cook in double boiler until thick, stirring constantly; when cool, add vanilla to taste.

CREAM CUSTARD FILLING

¾ cup sugar
⅓ cup flour
⅓ teaspoon salt

2 cups milk or half-and-half,
   scalded
2 eggs, slightly beaten
1 teaspoon vanilla

Mix dry ingredients, add the milk and pour gradually on the eggs. Cook in double boiler, stirring constantly until thickened; cool and add vanilla.

ORANGE CUSTARD FILLING

½ cup sugar
2 tablespoons flour
1 teaspoon grated orange rind
¼ cup orange juice

½ teaspoon lemon juice
1 teaspoon butter
1 egg, slightly beaten
speck of salt

Mix in order given, beat well, cook in double boiler about 15 minutes, stirring constantly until thick; when cool, spread between two 8-inch cake layers.

Variation:

Lemon Custard Filling: Use the grated rind of 2 lemons, ¼ cup lemon juice, and 1 cup sugar in place of the orange rind and juice, above.

LEMON CORNSTARCH FILLING

½ cup sugar
2 tablespoons cornstarch
¼ teaspoon salt
2 egg yolks, slightly beaten

¾ cup water
⅓ cup lemon juice
1 tablespoon butter
1 teaspoon grated lemon rind

Put sugar, cornstarch, and salt in double boiler. Mix egg yolks with water and lemon juice. Add to sugar mixture. Cook over boiling water about 15 minutes, stirring constantly. Add butter and lemon rind. Cool, then spread between cake layers.

SOUR CREAM FILLING

1 egg yolk
2 tablespoons sugar
1 tablespoon cornstarch

1 cup thick sour cream
½ teaspoon lemon or vanilla extract
1 cup chopped nuts (optional)

Beat yolk slightly, add sugar and cornstarch mixed, stir in the sour cream; cook in double boiler until mixture coats a spoon. Add flavoring and chopped nuts, if desired.

FRUIT AND NUT FILLINGS

APPLE LEMON FILLING

⅔ cup sugar
1 tablespoon flour
3 tablespoons lemon juice
1 tablespoon cold water

1 egg, beaten
speck of salt
1 apple, pared and grated

Mix sugar and flour in saucepan; add lemon juice, cold water, beaten egg, salt, and apple. Boil 2 minutes, stirring constantly. Cool before spreading.

FIG FILLING

¼ pound chopped figs
½ cup sugar
2 tablespoons cornstarch

½ cup boiling water
1½ tablespoons lemon juice
grated rind of ½ orange

Cook figs in small amount of water in double boiler until soft; set aside. Mix sugar and cornstarch in a double boiler, add the boiling water, stir until smooth and thick. Add the cooked figs, lemon juice, and orange rind.

FIG PASTE FILLING

1 pound figs, finely chopped	2 egg whites
1 cup sugar	¼ cup confectioners' sugar
½ cup water	vanilla to taste

Boil figs, sugar, and water slowly to a smooth paste, about 15 minutes. Set aside to cool. Beat whites until stiff, add confectioners' sugar and vanilla, and combine the two mixtures.

PECAN FILLING

1 tablespoon cornstarch	½ cup sugar
1 cup milk, heated	½ cup pecans, finely chopped
2 egg yolks	

Dissolve cornstarch in the milk and cook in double boiler until smooth; beat yolks and sugar until very light; pour hot milk mixture gradually over yolks; return to boiler and cook until mixture coats the spoon, stirring constantly; when cool, add nut meats.

PRUNE FILLING

1 cup cooked, stoned prunes	⅓ cups nuts, finely chopped
⅓ cup orange marmalade	1 teaspoon lemon juice

Chop prunes and mix with remaining ingredients; spread between layers of cake.

RAISIN FILLING

1 cup raisins, chopped	1 cup water
⅓ cup sugar	1 egg, slightly beaten
1 cup light corn syrup	½ teaspoon lemon extract

Cook raisins, sugar, syrup, and water until raisins are soft. Remove from heat, add egg, cook over water until thick, stirring constantly. Add lemon extract, cool, and spread.

STRAWBERRY CREAM FILLING

1 cup heavy cream
½ cup sugar

1 egg white, stiffly beaten
½ cup strawberries, mashed

Whip cream until stiff, fold in sugar, egg white, and the mashed strawberries.

WALNUT FILLING

2 egg yolks, beaten
½ cup sugar
¾ cup milk

½ teaspoon vanilla or rum flavoring
1 pound chopped walnuts

Mix eggs and sugar, add milk, cook in double boiler until thick. Cool, add vanilla or rum, and the nuts. Spread between layers of Walnut Torte (page 586).

DESSERTS AND DESSERT SAUCES

Grandmother's Hot Puddings

These old-fashioned puddings are treasured heirlooms that come down to us from days when hard physical labor and a need for thrift made a hearty, filling, hot dessert the best possible way to end a meal. Nowadays, we choose this kind of dessert to follow a light meal. Serve these warm, except where otherwise noted.

BAKED PUDDINGS

BREAD PUDDING

2 eggs
2 cups milk
½ cup sugar
nutmeg or cinnamon (optional)

4 cups dry bread or cake in cubes
¼ cup raisins
almonds

1. Beat the eggs, add milk, sugar, and nutmeg or cinnamon if desired. Pour liquid over the bread in a pudding dish and let stand until thoroughly soaked.
2. Preheat oven to 350° F. Add raisins and almonds, if desired. Bake for about 20 minutes or until firm. Serve with milk, jelly, or any pudding sauce.

BREAD PUDDING PUFFS

2 cups breadcrumbs
4 cups milk
4 eggs, separated, whites stiffly
    beaten

1 cup sugar
1 lemon rind, grated
¼ cup almonds, chopped
brown sugar

1. Soak breadcrumbs in milk ½ hour.
2. Preheat oven to 350° F. Beat yolks well with sugar, add soaked crumbs, lemon rind, almonds, and the beaten whites last. Place in individual molds generously greased with butter, and sprinkled with brown sugar. Bake about ½ hour or until firm. Remove to dessert plates and serve with Jelly Sauce (page 652) or Orange Sauce (page 651).

ENGLISH FRUIT PUDDING

7 or 8 slices of bread
2 tablespoons butter
1 quart blueberries, cooked

sugar to taste
¼ teaspoon salt

Remove the crusts from the bread and butter slices on one side. Grease a round-bottomed bowl and line with half of the bread buttered side up. Crush the berries with the sugar and salt and pour into the bowl. Cover with remaining bread, buttered side up. Weight well with a plate and chill for 24 hours. The bread will absorb the juice and the pudding may be unmolded. Serve with cream.

RICE FOR PUDDINGS

Processed rice, which will not disintegrate to make a cream, is unsuitable for these rice pudding recipes. Use regular, unconverted long grain rice. Serve puddings warm or chilled, as desired.

OLD-FASHIONED RICE PUDDING

½ cup uncooked rice
½ cup sugar

½ teaspoon salt
4 cups milk

Preheat oven to 325° F. Mix ingredients. Bake 2 hours in a buttered baking dish, covered, until the rice has softened. During the last few minutes, uncover to brown slightly. Serve with milk and sugar.

RAISIN RICE PUDDING

2 cups cooked rice
2 cups milk
⅛ teaspoon salt
⅓ cup sugar
1 tablespoon butter, softened

2 eggs, well beaten
rind of ½ lemon, grated
¼ cup raisins
½ cup breadcrumbs, optional

Preheat oven to 350° F. Mix ingredients well. Bake 20 minutes in buttered baking dish, with breadcrumbs on the top and bottom, if desired. If desired, fruit may be added to the rice in layers.

CHOCOLATE RICE PUDDING

4 cups milk
½ cup rice, uncooked
¼ teaspoon salt
5 tablespoons sugar

1 tablespoon butter
1 ounce unsweetened chocolate, grated
1 teaspoon vanilla

Heat milk in double boiler over hot water, add rice, salt, sugar, butter, chocolate, and vanilla. Cook 2 hours. Serve with whipped cream.

RICE PUDDING (KUGEL)

1 cup uncooked rice
4 cups boiling water
1 teaspoon salt
4 eggs, beaten

¼ cup sugar
¼ pound raisins
¼ cup fat (chicken, goose, or butter)

Cook the rice in the boiling water with the salt until nearly done, about 30 minutes. Preheat oven to 325° F. Mix drained rice with the rest of the ingredients, place in well-greased baking dish, and bake until quite brown, about 20 minutes.

CORNMEAL PUDDING (INDIAN PUDDING)

6 cups milk, scalded
1 cup yellow cornmeal
½ cup molasses
¼ cup sugar
1 teaspoon salt

1 teaspoon ginger or grated lemon rind
¼ teaspoon baking soda
2 eggs, slightly beaten

Preheat oven to 250° F. Pour milk slowly on the cornmeal, cook in double boiler 20 minutes, add other ingredients. Pour into buttered baking dish and bake 3 hours. Serve warm with cream.

NOODLE PUDDING

4 eggs, separated, whites stiffly beaten
1 cup confectioners' sugar

2 tablespoons grated almonds
½ pound fine noodles, cooked and drained

Preheat oven to 350° F. Beat yolks light with the sugar, add almonds and drained noodles and the whites last. Pour into a well-greased baking dish, set in a pan half filled with boiling water, and bake for 30 minutes.

NOODLE PUDDING WITH APPLES AND NUTS

½ pound broad noodles
2 tablespoons butter
3 eggs, separated, whites stiffly
   beaten
1 cup sugar

1 ½ teaspoons cinnamon
2 apples, sliced
¼ cup dried currants
½ cup chopped nuts

Preheat oven to 350° F. Boil noodles and drain. Heat butter in a skillet, add the noodles and cook just long enough to absorb the fat. Remove from heat, beat the yolks and add, then add sugar and rest of ingredients, the whites last. Place in well-greased baking dish and bake 30 minutes. Serve hot with any dessert sauce.

CHOCOLATE PUDDING CAKE

Cake
1 cup cake flour
2 teaspoons baking powder
½ teaspoon salt
⅔ cup sugar
½ cup milk
1 ounce unsweetened chocolate,
   grated
½ cup chopped nuts
2 tablespoons butter, melted
1 teaspoon vanilla

Topping
¼ cup white sugar
½ cup brown sugar, firmly packed
3 ounces unsweetened chocolate,
   grated, or 3 tablespoons cocoa
¼ teaspoon salt
1 teaspoon vanilla
1 cup boiling water

1.   Preheat oven to 350° F. To make cake, sift flour, baking powder, salt, and sugar into bowl. Add milk, chocolate, nuts, butter, and vanilla and blend well. Pour mixture into a greased baking dish. Set aside.

2.   To make topping, combine sugars, chocolate, salt, and vanilla and spread evenly over cake batter mixture. Pour the boiling water over this but do not stir. Bake for 1 hour, until the cake that rises to the top tests done. There will be a layer of fudge sauce beneath. Can be served warm or cold, with or without cream.

LEMON PUDDING CAKES

2 cups sugar
6 tablespoons flour
¼ teaspoon salt
¼ cup butter, melted
⅔ cup lemon juice

grated lemon rind
6 eggs, separated, whites stiffly
  beaten
3 cups milk

Preheat oven to 350° F. Blend sugar, flour, salt, butter, lemon juice, and rind. Beat yolks well, add milk and mix. Add flour mixture gradually, stirring well. Fold in whites last. Pour into 12 greased custard cups and place in shallow pan of hot water. Bake about 45 minutes. When baked each pudding will be part custard and part cake. Chill. Garnish with whipped cream.

COCONUT PUDDING

1 cup breadcrumbs
1 cup grated coconut
4 cups hot milk
2 tablespoons butter, melted

2 eggs, slightly beaten
4 tablespoons sugar
dash of salt
grated rind of ½ lemon

Soak the crumbs and the coconut in the hot milk for 1 hour. Preheat oven to 350° F. Mix all ingredients. Place in greased baking dish and bake until well set and brown, about 20 minutes.

COTTAGE PUDDING

½ cup butter
⅔ cup sugar
2 eggs, separated, whites stiffly
  beaten

2 cups flour
1 tablespoon baking powder
¼ teaspoon salt
1 cup milk

Preheat oven to 350° F. Cream butter and sugar; beat yolks until thick and add. Sift together flour, baking powder, and salt. Add to mixture alternately with milk. Fold in whites last. Bake in a greased and floured 8-by-12-inch pan for 30 to 45 minutes. Cut in squares and serve with Plain Hard Sauce (page 652) or Lemon Sauce (page 650).

CRANBERRY PUDDING

3 tablespoons shortening
1 cup sugar
1 egg, beaten
1 cup milk

2 cups flour
2 teaspoons baking powder
2 cups fresh cranberries

Preheat oven to 350° F. Cream shortening and sugar. Blend in egg and milk. Mix flour and baking powder and add to batter. Stir in cranberries. Bake in greased baking dish for 35 to 40 minutes. Serve warm with Custard Sauce (page 650).

STEAMED PUDDINGS

To Steam Puddings

A steamer is a covered kettle fitted with a rack on which molds can rest above boiling water. The food cooks in steam without touching the boiling water. As the water boils away, replenish it with boiling water so that you do not allow the boiling to stop.

Grease pudding mold and fill ⅔ full to allow for rising. Grease cover and adjust tightly. Or cover tightly with greased aluminum foil or waxed paper. Puddings may also be steamed in the top of a makeshift double boiler, over hot water. Set a colander in a large pot and pour in enough water to cover the bottom. Steam as directed, checking the water level frquently to prevent total evaporation.

STEAMED BREAD PUDDING

2 cups bread cubes
1 teaspoon baking soda
1 cup buttermilk
½ cup sugar
1 egg

1 teaspoon mixed spices (cinnamon, nutmeg, allspice, ground cloves, e.g.)
½ cup seedless raisins
1 tablespoon butter, softened

Sprinkle bread with soda; add buttermilk. Let stand until soaked. Mix well with rest of the ingredients. Put in greased mold and steam, as directed above, 1½ hours.

STEAMED CARAMEL ALMOND PUDDING

6 tablespoons sugar
1 cup hot milk
6 eggs, separated, whites stiffly
   beaten

¼ cup butter, melted
1 tablespoon flour
3 ounces ground almonds
sugar for sprinkling

Melt the sugar in a skillet until light brown. Add milk very gradually, stirring constantly. Cool. Beat yolks then add to milk mixture along with the butter, flour, almonds, and the whites last. Butter the mold and sprinkle with a little sugar. Add pudding. Steam, as directed above, 1 hour. Serve with whipped cream.

STEAMED CHOCOLATE PUDDING

1 egg
1 cup sugar
1 ounce unsweetened chocolate,
   melted, or 3 tablespoons cocoa
½ cup milk

2 tablespoons butter, melted
1 cup flour
4 teaspoons baking powder

Mix ingredients; put in greased mold and steam 1 hour. Serve with Vanilla Sauce (page 648) or Plain Hard Sauce (page 652).

CHOCOLATE ALMOND PUDDING

10 eggs, separated, whites stiffly
   beaten
1½ cups sugar
¾ cup grated unsweetened chocolate

2 teaspoons cinnamon
½ teaspoon cloves
¾ cup grated almonds
½ cup flour

Beat yolks until very light, add sugar, and beat again, add chocolate, spices, almonds, and flour; stir well and gradually fold in the stiffly beaten whites. Place in large buttered pudding mold, cover, and steam 2 hours. Serve hot with sweetened whipped cream flavored with vanilla.

STEAMED DATE PUDDING

1 pound stoned dates	1 cup flour
½ pound suet	1 teaspoon cinnamon
½ cup sugar	1 teaspoon ginger
1 scant teaspoon salt	1 cup soft breadcrumbs
½ cup milk	2 eggs, well beaten

Grind or chop dates and suet. Mix all ingredients well, adding the eggs last. Turn into well-buttered molds, and steam 2 hours, as directed above. Serve with Plain Hard Sauce (page 652).

Variations: Figs, raisins, currants, candied peel, prunes, or nuts, alone or in combination, may replace dates.

STEAMED OATMEAL DATE PUDDING

½ pound dates, chopped	⅔ cup water
1 cup rolled oats	½ teaspoon baking soda
2 eggs	¼ teaspoon salt
½ cup molasses	juice of ½ lemon

Mix all ingredients and steam in buttered mold 3 hours. Serve with any preferred pudding sauce.

STEAMED PRUNE WHIP

1 pound prunes	5 egg whites, stiffly beaten
¾ cup sugar	

Soak prunes 1 hour in water barely to cover. Boil until tender, stone and mash through a strainer. Add sugar to beaten egg whites. Blend with prunes. Pour into buttered mold. Cover and steam for 1 hour. Serve hot with whipped cream or Custard Sauce (page 650).

ENGLISH PLUM PUDDING

1 cup flour
1 pound seeded raisins
¼ pound each citron, candied
    orange peel, and candied lemon
    peel, finely cut
¼ pound seedless raisins
½ cup chopped almonds
1 cup dried breadcrumbs
½ cup sugar
1 teaspoon baking powder

1 teaspoon ground cinnamon
½ teaspoon ground allspice
½ teaspoon ground cloves
1 teaspoon salt
1 cup suet, finely chopped
3 eggs, beaten
1 cup molasses
1 cup pickled peach syrup or
    brandy

Sift flour over fruit, citrus peels, and nuts and mix well. Mix rest of dry ingredients, add suet, eggs, molasses, syrup or brandy and then the floured fruit. Pour into a couple of buttered molds ⅔ full; cover. Steam from 4 to 8 hours, according to the size of mold. Serve with Plain Hard Sauce (page 652) or Quick Brandy Sauce (page 650). Or pour rum or brandy over pudding just before serving, carefully ignite, and serve flaming.

Note: This pudding keeps well. To reheat, steam ½ hour or more.

STEAMED WHOLE WHEAT PUDDING

2 cups whole wheat flour
½ teaspoon baking soda
½ teaspoon salt
1 cup milk

½ cup molasses
1 cup stoned and chopped dates,
    raisins, or ripe berries

Mix ingredients in order given. Pour into a buttered mold and steam 2½ hours. Serve with whipped cream or any plain pudding sauce.

Variation: 1 cup of figs, stewed prunes, or chopped apples or raisins may be substituted for fruit, above.

Baked Fruit Desserts

Baked fruit desserts are as delicious as fruit pie, and they have advantages for the cook since they are much easier and quicker to prepare. Serve with a topping of sauce, ice cream, or whipped cream.

APPLE PANDOWDY (DIMPES DAMPES)

½ cup sugar
¼ teaspoon salt
2 cups flour

2 cups milk
1 cup butter, melted
1 quart apples, pared and sliced

Preheat oven to 350° F. Mix sugar, salt, and flour and gradually add the milk to make a smooth batter. Grease a 13-by-9-inch baking pan well with some of the butter, add the remaining butter and the apples to the batter. Mix and pour into pan. Bake for 30 to 45 minutes until brown.

APPLE SOUFFLÉ (AUF-LAUF)

Filling
½ cup brown sugar, firmly packed
4 apples

Batter
2 eggs, separated, whites stiffly beaten
¼ cup sugar
1½ tablespoons cold water
½ cup flour
½ teaspoon baking powder
½ teaspoon vanilla

1. To make the filling, preheat oven to 350° F. Butter baking dish. Sprinkle with brown sugar. Peel, core, and slice apples; place in bottom of pudding dish in layers, until dish is about ⅓ full. Bake until partially soft. Remove from oven.

2. To make the batter, beat yolks with sugar; add water alternately with flour mixed and sifted together with baking powder. Add vanilla and fold in whites last. Bake for 30 minutes or until brown.

Variation:

Macaroon Soufflé (Auf-Lauf): Preheat oven to 400° F. Line a buttered baking dish with macaroons or any stale cake. Cover this with fruit, pared and sliced, or raspberries, add sugar to taste. Cover with a sponge made of 6 yolks, 6 tablespoons sugar, 6 whites beaten stiff, and ¼ cup chopped almonds. Bake for 15 minutes.

APPLE CHARLOTTE

1 recipe Rich Egg Pastry (page 522)
2 quarts apples, diced
1 cup sugar
¼ cup almonds, blanched and
   chopped
1 teaspoon cinnamon

1 cup seeded raisins
½ cup currants
grated rind and juice of 1 lemon
¼ cup red or white wine

Preheat oven to 400° F. Line a well-greased baking dish with half of the Rich Egg Pastry, ¼ inch thick; mix rest of ingredients and fill dish. Cover with the remaining pastry, ¼ inch thick; bake 50 to 60 minutes.

APPLE STREUSEL

6 apples (2 pounds)
2 tablespoons granulated sugar
¼ teaspoon cinnamon

½ cup brown sugar, firmly packed
1 cup flour
½ cup butter, chilled

Preheat oven to 425° F. Butter bottom and sides of an 8-by-12-inch pan generously. Peel and core apples and cut into eighths. Place apples in pan in overlapping rows as closely together as possible; mix granulated sugar and cinnamon and sprinkle over the apples. Add brown sugar to flour, cut in butter, and rub with fingertips until in crumbs. Sprinkle over apples and pat to make a smooth surface. Bake for 30 minutes or until apples are tender.

<u>Variation:</u> Applesauce may be substituted for the sliced apples and sugar.

BROWN BETTY

2 tablespoons butter
2 cups soft breadcrumbs
½ cup sugar
¼ teaspoon cinnamon

¼ teaspoon nutmeg
rind and juice of 1 lemon
3 cups apples, chopped
¼ cup water

Preheat oven to 375° F. Melt the butter and add the crumbs. Mix together the sugar, spices, and grated lemon rind. Put one quarter of the crumbs in the bottom of a buttered baking dish. Cover with half the apples. Sprinkle with half the sugar mixture; then add another quarter of the crumbs, the remainder of the apples, and the rest of the sugar mixture. Add the lemon juice and the water, and put the rest of the crumbs over the top. Cover, bake 45 minutes, uncover and continue baking until brown.

SCALLOPED RHUBARB

2 tablespoons butter
2 cups soft breadcrumbs
1 cup sugar
grated rind of 1 orange
¼ teaspoon cinnamon

¼ teaspoon nutmeg
3 cups rhubarb, washed and cut
   into ½ inch slices
¼ cup water

Follow directions for Brown Betty, above. If rhubarb is old, strip off skin and just use the inside.

BLUEBERRY PUDDING

1 quart blueberries
¼ cup flour
4 cups hot milk
2 cups breadcrumbs (or graham
   cracker crumbs)

¼ cup sugar
few grains salt
2 tablespoons butter, cut into bits

Clean and drain berries, sprinkle with flour, let stand ½ hour. Preheat oven to 350° F. Pour milk over crumbs, add sugar, salt, and the berries. Put into greased baking dish, dot with butter, bake 45 minutes.

CHERRY PUDDING

4 cups milk
2 cups breadcrumbs
salt
3 tablespoons butter

4 eggs, slightly beaten
1½ cups sugar
1 quart sour cherries, pitted

Preheat oven to 350°. Scald milk and pour over the bread crumbs; add a pinch of salt and the rest of the ingredients. Bake 45 minutes, until set.

PRUNE PUDDING (PRUNE KUGEL)

5 whole wheat rolls
¾ pound suet, finely chopped
½ cup brown sugar, firmly packed
1 tablespoon molasses
1 teaspoon cinnamon

grated rind of 1 lemon
1 tablespoon water
salt
½ pound prunes, stoned and stewed

Preheat oven to 325° F. Soak rolls in water, squeeze dry. Mix remaining ingredients, except prunes, with the soaked bread to make a dough. Line a greased heavy casserole or baking dish with alternate layers of dough and prunes. Bake 2 hours, basting often with juices.

DRIED FRUIT PUDDING (HUTZLE, SNITZ, OR BIRNE KLOS)

1 loaf dry white bread
½ pound suet, finely chopped or
   ground
¾ cup brown sugar, firmly packed
2 eggs
grated peel of 1 lemon
½ teaspoon cinnamon
½ teaspoon cloves

½ teaspoon allspice
½ teaspoon salt
2 to 3 tablespoons flour
2 teaspoons baking powder
1 pound dried pears or other dried
   fruit, cooked and spiced with
   cinnamon, cloves, and allspice

Preheat oven to 350° F. Soak bread in water. Squeeze dry. Add to suet and work well with your hands. Add sugar, eggs, rind, and spices; then add flour mixed with the baking powder, to make a large ball. Place in center of a large kettle or greased roaster, on a layer of cooked, spiced dried fruit. Grease top of pudding and spoon remaining fruit and juice over it. Bake for 3 hours, adding more fruit juice if necessary.

GRANT THOMAS PUDDING

2 eggs, beaten
1 cup sugar
3 tablespoons flour

1 teaspoon baking powder
1 cup broken walnut meats
1 cup chopped figs

Preheat oven to 300° F. Beat eggs and sugar until very light, add flour, sifted 3 times with baking powder, and the remaining ingredients. Stir well and bake in greased, shallow pan 25 minutes.

Passover Desserts

The following desserts, which use matzos and matzo meal instead of leavened bread and wheat flour, are traditionally served during the Passover holiday. In many households they are favorite desserts throughout the year.

MATZO FRITTERS (CRIMSEL)

2 matzos
½ tablespoon salt
3 eggs

½ cup sugar
oil for deep-frying

Soak matzos in water and squeeze dry. Mix in the rest of the ingredients and stir well. Drop from teaspoon in hot, deep fat (about 375° F), and fry until browned. Serve warm with hot honey, stewed cherries, or stewed prunes.

MATZO FRUIT FRITTERS (FRUIT CRIMSEL)

3 matzos, soaked and squeezed dry
2 tablespoons seeded raisins, chopped
2 tablespoons chopped almonds
3 egg yolks

¾ cup sugar
grated rind of 1 lemon
1 tablespoon lemon juice
3 egg whites, stiffly beaten
oil for deep-frying

Mix in the order given and drop from tablespoon into deep, hot fat (about 375° F). Serve hot with stewed prunes flavored with orange juice.

FILLED MATZO FRITTERS

1½ matzos
1 tablespoon goose fat
¼ cup matzo meal, sifted
2 eggs
2 tablespoons sugar

½ teaspoon salt
strawberries, or stewed prunes, stoned
1 egg, beaten
oil for deep-frying

Soak the matzos in cold water and press dry; heat the fat, add matzos, matzo meal, eggs, sugar, and salt. Mix well and let stand 2 hours; form into oblong cakes. Place a prune or strawberry in the center of each cake and form into balls. Dip balls in beaten egg and fry in deep, hot fat (about 375° F) until brown. Serve hot with Jelly Sauce (page 652).

MATZO BATTER PUDDING

2 eggs
2 cups milk
1 cup matzo meal
⅔ cup brown sugar, firmly packed

4 tablespoons butter, melted
grated rind of 1 lemon
1 tablespoon rum

Preheat oven to 350° F. Make a batter of the eggs, milk, and matzo meal; add sugar, melted butter, and lemon rind; add rum. Pour into a greased baking dish and steam for 1 hour or bake for 1½ hours in oven.

MATZO APPLE PUDDING

4 eggs, separated, whites stiffly
   beaten
⅔ cup sugar
2 cups grated apples

grated rind of ½ lemon
½ cup matzo meal
4 tablespoons almonds, chopped

Preheat oven to 350° F. Beat the yolks, stir in sugar, add the apples, lemon rind, and matzo meal. Fold in beaten whites. Place in greased springform pan, sprinkle with almonds. Bake until brown, about 30 minutes.

MATZO CHARLOTTE

2 matzos
1 tablespoon goose fat or butter,
   melted
4 eggs, separated, whites beaten

pinch of salt
½ cup sugar
juice and grated rind of ½ lemon

Preheat oven to 350° F. Soak the matzos in cold water and squeeze dry. Stir matzos with the goose fat, add beaten yolks, salt, sugar, and lemon juice and rind. Fold in the beaten whites, pour into a well-greased baking dish. Bake about 30 minutes. Serve immediately with Jelly Sauce (page 652).

MATZO CHARLOTTE WITH APPLES

2 matzos
¼ pound suet, finely chopped
2 cups apples, sliced thin
¼ cup sugar
3 egg yolks, beaten

2 tablespoons raisins, seeded
1 tablespoon blanched and grated
   almonds
¼ teaspoon cinnamon
3 egg whites, stiffly beaten

Preheat oven to 350° F. Soak matzos in water and squeeze dry, add the rest of the ingredients, the beaten whites last. Bake in greased dish for about 1 hour.

POTATO PUDDING FOR PASSOVER

4 egg yolks, beaten
½ cup sugar
2 tablespoons almonds, blanched
   and grated
juice and rind of ½ lemon

¼ pound cold, boiled potatoes,
   riced
¼ teaspoon salt
4 egg whites, stiffly beaten

Preheat oven to 350° F. Mix in order given. Place in well-greased baking dish and set the dish in a pan half filled with boiling water. Bake for 30 minutes.

Dessert Soufflés

Soufflés are not difficult to make if a few rules are followed exactly. It is important that the egg whites be beaten until they are very stiff and glossy. (When the bowl is inverted they should not slip.) They should be folded into the soufflé base very gently, to retain all the air. To prepare the baking dish for the soufflé, butter generously, then sprinkle with sugar.

A soufflé is finished when it is well puffed and browned; some people prefer soufflés that are soft in the center, thus providing their own sauce. To make these French-style soufflés, bake in a hotter oven, 400° F. Soufflés begin to fall as soon as they are removed from the oven, and must be served at once.

CHOCOLATE SOUFFLÉ

1 tablespoon butter
2 tablespoons flour
½ cup milk
2 tablespoons water

3 tablespoons sugar
1 ounce unsweetened chocolate
2 eggs, separated

Preheat oven to 325° F. Heat the butter, add the flour, then the milk and cook until smooth. Add the water and sugar to the chocolate, stir until melted. Mix it with the milk mixture and cool. Beat the whites very stiff, then beat the yolks well. Into the base, stir in the yolks, fold in the whites. Bake in a greased baking dish set in a pan of hot water from 30 to 40 minutes until soufflé is puffed and well browned.

Variation:

Walnut Soufflé: Follow recipe for Sweet Chocolate Soufflé, but in place of the chocolate, use 1 cup finely ground walnut meats. Serve with any dessert sauce.

LEMON OR ORANGE SOUFFLÉ

6 eggs, separated
1 cup sugar

juice and rind of 1 large lemon or ⅓ cup orange juice and 1 tablespoon lemon juice

Follow soufflé directions above.

CHESTNUT SOUFFLÉ

1 cup chestnuts, shelled
½ cup sugar
2 tablespoons flour

½ cup milk
3 egg whites, stiffly beaten

Preheat oven to 300° F. Boil chestnuts, drain and rice or mash. Mix sugar and flour, add chestnuts and milk gradually, cook 5 minutes, stirring constantly; fold in whites. Fill buttered and sugared individual molds ¾ full. Set molds in a pan of hot water and bake until firm, about 30 minutes. Serve with Vanilla Sauce (page 648).

NUT SOUFFLÉ

3 egg yolks
3 tablespoons sugar
3 tablespoons flour
¼ teaspoon salt
1 cup milk

¾ cup pecans or hazelnuts, finely ground
3 tablespoons butter, melted
4 egg whites, stiffly beaten

Preheat oven to 325° F. Beat yolks until thick, add sugar and stir well; add flour and salt. Heat milk and nuts in double boiler. Add egg mixture and cook until thick, stirring constantly. Add the butter. Cool. Fold in the whites. Pour into well-buttered and sugared mold or casserole. Set in a pan of hot water and bake for 1 hour or until puffed and well browned. Serve at once with Caramel Sauce (page 648) or Quick Brandy Sauce (page 650)

APRICOT SOUFFLÉ

½ pound dried apricots	½ teaspoon baking powder
½ cup sugar	½ teaspoon lemon juice
5 egg whites	

Preheat oven to 275° F. Cook fruit in water until soft and rub through strainer. Add sugar and cook 5 minutes or until the consistency of marmalade. Cool. Beat whites stiffly with baking powder. Add cold fruit mixture and lemon juice gradually. Place in greased baking dish and bake 30 to 40 minutes. Serve cold with thin custard or cream. Prunes or dates may be substituted for the apricots.

Baked Biscuit Desserts

BASIC DOUGH FOR SHORTCAKE BISCUIT

2 cups flour	2 tablespoons sugar
4 teaspoons baking powder	½ cup shortening
½ teaspoon salt	¾ cup milk

 Preheat oven to 450° F. Mix dry ingredients, work in shortening with fork or pastry blender, add milk quickly. Toss on floured board. Pat, roll, cut with large biscuit cutter or roll to fit 2 8-inch round pans and bake 12 to 15 minutes. Split biscuits and serve warm, filled with cold sweetened fresh fruit and cream, plain or whipped.

STRAWBERRY SHORTCAKE

1 recipe Shortcake Biscuit dough, above	sugar to taste
	cream
1 to 1½ quarts strawberries	

Bake Shortcake Biscuits. Sweeten strawberries to taste. Crush slightly and put between and on top of shortcake. Serve with cream, plain or whipped.

Variations: Prepare as above, using sliced peaches, nectarines, berries, or bananas in place of strawberries.

BLACKBERRY ROLL

1 recipe Shortcake Biscuit dough, above
2 tablespoons butter, melted

1½ quarts blackberries
1 cup sugar
cinnamon

Preheat oven to 400° F. Roll dough ½ inch thick, spread with melted butter and ½ of the berries, cover with ½ of the sugar and cinnamon. Roll up like a jelly roll and put into well-greased pan, surround with the rest of the berries and sugar. Bake until crisp, about 20 minutes. Cut in slices and serve warm with sauce remaining in pan.

CHERRY COBBLER

1½ quarts cherries or 1 16-ounce can sour cherries, drained
1 cup water

1 cup sugar
1 recipe Shortcake Biscuit dough, above

Preheat oven to 400° F. Stone cherries if necessary and cook with the water and sugar. Roll dough ¼ inch thick and cut into small rounds. Place cherries in buttered baking dish, lay biscuits on top, bake until brown and bubbly, about 30 minutes. Serve with Lemon Sauce (page 650) or Vanilla Sauce (page 648) if desired.

RICH PEACH COBBLER

1 egg
⅔ cup sugar or to taste
2 cups sliced peaches or 1 16-ounce can, drained

2 tablespoons butter, cut into bits
1 recipe Shortcake Biscuit dough, above

Preheat oven to 400° F. Beat egg lightly, add sugar and peaches; pour this mixture into buttered baking dish, dot with butter, cover with dough rolled ½ inch thick, and bake until brown. Serve with Plain Hard Sauce (page 652).

COBBLERS

Cobblers are a wonderfully versatile dessert that make the most of seasonal fruit. Blueberries, peaches, blackberries, raspberries, plums, and apricots are good summer fruit choices. Apples, pears, and quince are best in the fall. Use ripe fruit or berries and learn how to adjust the amount of sugar desired. This will come naturally as you experiment.

BAKED APPLE DUMPLINGS

1 recipe Shortcake Biscuit dough (page 628)
6 apples, peeled and cored

1 cup sugar
6 teaspoons butter
1 cup water

Preheat oven to 400° F. Roll dough ¼-inch thick, cut into 6-inch squares. Fill each apple with 1 tablespoon sugar and 1 teaspoon butter. Place an apple on each dough square, bring up corners, twist and pinch together, and place in a well-greased baking pan. Make a syrup by boiling water and the remaining sugar for 10 minutes. Cover the apples with syrup. Bake for about 45 minutes. (Or omit syrup and bake until just crisp.) Serve hot with sauce in pan or with Quick Brandy Sauce (page 650).

APPLE ROLY POLY

Make Shortcake Biscuit dough (page 628) or any pie dough. Roll ½ inch thick. Preheat oven to 400° F. Spread with chopped apples or jam, raisins, sugar, and cinnamon; roll like jelly roll. Place in a baking dish, spread with melted butter. Make a syrup by boiling 2 cups of water and 2 cups of sugar for 10 minutes. Pour on top of roll. Bake about 1½ hours or until brown. Baste often with the sauce in the pan. Serve hot. Or cut in slices and bake cut side down.

DUTCH APPLE CAKE

2 cups flour
1 tablespoon baking powder
½ teaspoon salt
2 tablespoons sugar
½ cup butter, chilled

about ⅔ cup milk
1 egg, well beaten
4 sour apples
sugar and cinnamon

Preheat oven to 400° F. Mix and sift the dry ingredients, cut in butter, add milk with the well-beaten egg, and mix quickly. Spread dough in a shallow, greased 8-by-8-inch baking pan. Pare, core, and slice the apples; press apples into dough in parallel rows. Sprinkle with sugar and cinnamon. Bake 30 minutes. Serve hot with Lemon Sauce (page 650).

Tapioca Puddings

When tapioca is used to thicken a pudding, it results in an interesting texture because the tapioca swells and appears in tender, chewy droplets throughout the pudding. These recipes call for quick-cooking tapioca. When using the old-fashioned pearl tapioca, soak the tapioca for 1 hour in cold water before using. Tapioca is cooked when it is transparent.

TAPIOCA CREAM

⅓ cup quick-cooking tapioca
2 cups milk
2 eggs, separated, whites stiffly beaten

¼ teaspoon salt
⅓ cup sugar
1 teaspoon vanilla

Add tapioca to the milk and cook in double boiler until the tapioca is clear. Beat the yolks, add the salt, sugar, and the hot milk mixture and cook until it thickens. Remove from the heat, cool, fold in the whites. Add vanilla when cold. Or make meringue from egg whites, cover a casserole of pudding, and brown in oven a few minutes.

APPLE TAPIOCA

2½ cups boiling water
¼ teaspoon salt
⅓ cup quick-cooking tapioca
1½ pounds cooking apples

½ cup sugar
2 tablespoons butter, cut into bits

Preheat oven to 350° F. Add boiling water and salt to tapioca; cook in double boiler until clear. Core and pare apples, arrange whole in buttered baking dish, fill apples with sugar, add tapioca mixture, dot with butter, and bake until apples are soft. Serve with sugar and cream.

Variation: Use sliced apples instead of whole.

GOOSEBERRY TAPIOCA PUDDING

⅓ cup quick-cooking tapioca
2 cups boiling water
2 cups green gooseberries

1 cup sugar
1 tablespoon lemon juice

Cook tapioca in boiling water 15 minutes. Cook gooseberries and sugar until soft. Add lemon juice. Combine mixtures. Chill and serve with whipped cream.

Custards

Eggs should be beaten thoroughly when mixed with sugar and salt. Be careful to add the hot milk slowly stirring all the time. When custard is cooked in a double boiler, water in lower part should be kept below boiling point and should not touch upper part. When thickened, the custard coats a metal spoon. If custard curdles from overcooking, set in a pan of cold water and beat with a rotary beater until smooth. For baked custard, set the baking dish in a pan of hot water in the oven. Test for doneness by inserting a knife near, but not at, the center. The knife should come out clean. Custard continues to cook after it has been removed from the oven.

SOFT CUSTARD

3 egg yolks
¼ cup sugar
few grains of salt

2 cups hot milk
½ teaspoon vanilla

Beat eggs slightly. Add the sugar and salt. Stir in the milk gradually. Place in double boiler over hot water. Stir constantly until the mixture thickens and coats the spoon. Cool and add vanilla.

Variation:

Soft Chocolate Custard: Follow Soft Custard recipe, above, melting 1 ounce unsweetened chocolate with the milk.

STIRRED CUSTARD

4 tablespoons sugar
1 tablespoon cornstarch
¼ teaspoon salt

1 egg or 2 egg yolks, slightly
  beaten
2 cups milk, scalded
½ teaspoon desired flavoring

Mix sugar, cornstarch, and salt; add egg or egg yolks. Add scalded milk, stirring constantly. Cook in double boiler over hot water until custard thickens and coats the spoon. Cool and flavor.

BAKED CUSTARD

2 eggs
pinch of salt
4 tablespoons sugar
2 cups hot milk

¼ teaspoon nutmeg (optional)
½ teaspoon desired flavoring
  (optional)

Preheat oven to 325° F. Beat eggs slightly, add salt and sugar and stir until the sugar dissolves; pour milk gradually onto eggs, stirring constantly. If desired, add nutmeg or flavoring. Pour into buttered custard cups or a baking dish; place the cups in a pan of hot water. Bake 30 to 45 minutes until the custards are firm in the center.

Variation:

Caramel Crème: Melt ½ cup of granulated sugar in bottom of baking dish until brown, tilting dish until evenly coated, or use brown sugar. Then add custard mixture and bake as above.

COFFEE CUSTARD

2 tablespoons instant coffee
2 cups hot milk
3 eggs

4 tablespoons sugar
¼ teaspoon vanilla

Preheat oven to 325° F. Dissolve coffee in milk. Beat eggs with sugar; add milk mixture and vanilla and mix. Pour into small buttered custard cups, place cups in shallow pan of hot water. Bake until the custard is firm.

CARAMEL CUSTARD

½ cup sugar
4 cups scalded milk
5 eggs, slightly beaten

½ teaspoon salt
1 teaspoon vanilla

Preheat oven to 325° F. Heat sugar in a skillet on range, stir constantly until melted to a light brown syrup. Add 1 cup milk very gradually, stirring constantly, being careful that milk does not bubble up and over. As soon as sugar is dissolved add rest of milk; add mixture gradually to eggs; add salt and vanilla, then strain into buttered molds or custard cups. Place cups in a shallow pan of hot water. Bake 30 to 45 minutes or until firm. Chill and serve with Caramel Sauce (page 648).

COCONUT CUSTARD

2 cups milk
½ cup sugar
3 eggs, separated, yolks beaten until
    light

salt
½ cup cream
½ cup confectioners' sugar
¾ cup coconut

Preheat oven to 375° F. Heat milk with sugar, and stir into the egg yolks; add salt, cream, and cook until thick. Pour into a buttered baking dish. Beat the egg whites until frothy; beat in confectioners' sugar, beat stiff. Fold in coconut. Spread over the top of custard and brown lightly in the oven.

FLOATING ISLAND

4 cups milk
½ cup plus 2 tablespoons sugar
½ teaspoon salt
1 tablespoon constarch

3 eggs, separated
¼ teaspoon spice or ½ teaspoon
    flavoring

Heat the milk. Mix ½ cup of the sugar, salt, and cornstarch. Slightly beat the yolks and 1 egg white. Add sugar mixture, pour on the hot milk, and cook in a double boiler until it thickens, stirring constantly. When cool, stir in spice or flavoring. Cool completely then refrigerate for at least 2 hours. Beat the remaining 2 whites until frothy, beat in remaining 2 tablespoons sugar, and beat stiff. Drop by spoonfuls into a large pot of boiling water or milk. Cook two minutes on one side then turn and cook for two minutes on the other side. Drain well on paper towels. Pour custard into a large serving bowl. Float the meringues on top and serve immediately.

SEPARATING EGGS

To separate eggs easily, crack the egg smartly against the rim of a bowl. Pass the yolk from one half-shell to the other, letting the egg white drain into the bowl. Or break the whole egg into a funnel and the white will drain off.

MACAROON FRUIT PUDDING

1 pint raspberries or peaches
granulated sugar, to taste
6 eggs, separated

1 cup white wine
1 pound macaroons
6 tablespoons confectioners' sugar

Preheat oven to 375° F. Sweeten the fruit to taste and set aside. Beat the yolks until light, stir in the wine gradually. Cook in double boiler, stirring constantly, until mixture coats the spoon. Sweeten with additional sugar if desired. Cool. In a greased baking dish place layers of macaroons, fruit, and custard alternately. Beat egg whites frothy, beat in confectioners' sugar, and beat stiff. Spread this meringue on the pudding. Brown lightly in the oven.

Rennet

Rennet (also known as junket) is an extract that comes from the lining of a calf's stomach. While somewhat old-fashioned, it makes a pleasant, soothing dessert of unusual texture. Look for it in pharmacies or more rarely, in the pudding section of the supermarket.

CHOCOLATE RENNET CUSTARD

1 ounce unsweetened chocolate or 3
   tablespoons cocoa
2 cups milk

½ cup sugar
1 rennet tablet dissolved in 1
   tablespoon cold water

Melt chocolate or cocoa in ½ cup milk and boil 1 minute. Remove from heat, add rest of milk and the sugar. Heat until lukewarm and add the dissolved tablet. Stir quickly and pour into custard cups. Let stand at room temperature for 20 minutes or until firm. Chill.

RASPBERRY RENNET CUSTARD

2 cups milk	sweetened whipped cream
1 package raspberry rennet powder	fresh raspberries or raspberry jam

Heat milk only until lukewarm, add rennet powder, crush any lumps, stir 1 minute until dissolved. Pour into 4 to 6 sherbet glasses. Let stand at room temperature for 20 minutes until firm. Remove to cool place without jarring. Serve with sweetened whipped cream and top with fresh raspberries or raspberry jam.

Gelatin Cream Desserts

BAVARIAN CREAM

1 cup milk	1 envelope unflavored gelatin
2 eggs, separated, whites stiffly beaten	¼ cup cold water
½ cup sugar	½ teaspoon almond extract
¼ teaspoon salt	1 cup heavy cream, whipped

Heat milk in double boiler. Beat egg yolks, sugar, and salt well. Add milk gradually, stirring constantly. Return to double boiler. Cook until mixture thickens and coats the spoon. Soften gelatin in cold water and stir until dissolved. Add to custard. Cool. When mixture begins to thicken, add almond extract, whipped cream, and egg whites. Pour into mold rinsed in cold water. Chill.

Variation:

Butterscotch Bavarian: Make Bavarian Cream, above, omitting the sugar. Heat ¾ cup brown sugar and 2 tablespoons butter until well blended and add to hot custard. Proceed as above.

BAVARIAN CHARLOTTE RUSSE

1 envelope unflavored gelatin	½ cup hot milk
¼ cup cold water	2 teaspoons vanilla
5 egg yolks	1 cup heavy cream, whipped
½ cup sugar	12 lady fingers

Soften the gelatin in the water a few minutes. Beat yolks and sugar until very light; add milk and the softened gelatin. Cook in double boiler until gelatin is dissolved and the mixture coats the spoon, stirring constantly; cool, add vanilla and fold in the whipped cream. Pour into a mold lined with lady fingers. Chill until firm. Unmold and serve with fresh fruit or with Chocolate Sauce (page 649) or Caramel Sauce (page 648).

NESSELRODE PUDDING

5 eggs, separated, whites stiffly beaten
½ cup sugar
2 cups hot milk
2 envelopes unflavored gelatin
½ cup cold water

3 tablespoons blanched, chopped almonds
⅔ cup raisins
small piece of citron, finely chopped
salt
1 teaspoon vanilla

Beat egg yolks with sugar, stir in the hot milk. Cook in double boiler until custard coats the spoon, stirring constantly. Dissolve gelatin in the cold water. Add to hot milk mixture and stir until dissolved; then add the almonds, raisins, citron, and a little salt. Cool until the mixture is thick enough to mound on a spoon. Fold in the beaten whites and vanilla. Chill in a mold until firm. Unmold, serve with plain or whipped cream.

COFFEE CREAM

2 envelopes unflavored gelatin
¼ cup cold water
2 cups strong, hot coffee
1 cup sugar

2 cups heavy cream, whipped
½ teaspoon vanilla
chopped nuts

Soak gelatin in water 5 minutes, add coffee and sugar, and stir until gelatin is dissolved. Cool until mixture begins to thicken. Fold in 1 cup whipped cream and vanilla. Pour into a mold rinsed in cold water. Chill until firm. Unmold and serve with the rest of the whipped cream. Sprinkle with chopped nuts.

PRUNE CREAM

1 pound stewed prunes
2 envelopes unflavored gelatin
½ cup cold water
juice of 1 orange
juice of 1 lemon
rind of ½ orange, grated

rind of ½ lemon, grated
1 cup sugar
1 cup heavy cream, whipped
1 cup chopped almonds
whipped cream mixed with crushed
  macaroons

Stone prunes and drain, reserving hot juice. Soak gelatin in cold water, add enough boiling water to hot prune liquid to make 2 cups, add to gelatin. When dissolved, add the orange and lemon juice and rinds, sugar, and prunes; cool and when mixture begins to thicken, fold in the whipped cream and the almonds. Pour into mold and chill until firm. Serve with additional whipped cream mixed with crushed macaroons.

VANILLA CREAM PUDDING

1 envelope unflavored gelatin
¼ cup cold water
½ cup scalded milk

½ cup sugar
2 cups heavy cream, whipped
1 teaspoon vanilla

Soak gelatin in cold water 5 minutes and dissolve in hot milk; add sugar. Cool until mixture begins to thicken, add cream and vanilla. Turn into wet mold and chill. Serve covered with grated coconut and Butterscotch Sauce (page 649), or whole or crushed berries.

MACAROON CHOCOLATE PUDDING

1 envelope unflavored gelatin
2 tablespoons cold water
¼ cup boiling water

2 cups heavy cream, whipped
¼ pound sweet chocolate, grated
6 macaroons, broken

Dissolve gelatin in cold water, add the boiling water and stir until dissolved. When cold, add it to the whipped cream. Divide the cream in two parts and into one stir the grated chocolate, into the other the broken macaroons. Layer the two in a dish and chill until firm.

STRAWBERRY OR RASPBERRY CREAM

1 quart fresh strawberries or
    raspberries
½ to 1 cup sugar
2 envelopes unflavored gelatin

¼ cup cold water
¼ cup boiling water
2 cups heavy cream, whipped

Wash berries, reserving 12 or more for decoration. Sugar the rest of the fruit, let stand several hours, and crush. Soften the gelatin in cold water 5 minutes, add the boiling water, stir until dissolved; cool and add the crushed fruit. When mixture begins to jell, fold in the whipped cream. Place in wet mold. Chill for 2 or more hours. Unmold, decorate top with the whole berries.

Variation:

Pineapple Cream: Use 2 cups canned crushed pineapple and 1 tablespoon lemon juice, instead of the sugared fresh fruit

Ice Creams and Frozen Desserts

MAKING HOMEMADE ICE CREAMS

New appliances make the cumbersome process of churning a thing of the past. Fancy machines that produce creamy or icy concoctions of the finest taste and texture are popular in many modern kitchens. Simple, super-insulated devices require no more than placing the bowl in the freezer to achieve the same goodness of homemade ice cream or sherbet that the old-fashioned crank machines used to do. We find that the new machines do the following traditional recipes with utmost efficiency. Tradition is only made better by the convenience of modern equipment. Follow the manufacturer's directions for your particular appliance.

When making ice cream in a manually operated churn, scald and then chill can, cover, and dasher of freezer before using. Adjust can in tub, put in the thoroughly chilled mixture. Fill can not more than ¾ full. Adjust dasher; cover can. Pack with fine chopped ice and rock salt. *Use 3 parts ice to 1 part salt.* Pack freezer ⅓ full of ice before adding salt, then add the salt and remaining ice in alternate layers to above level of ice cream in can.

Turn crank slowly at first for about 5 minutes or until mixture begins to stiffen; then as quickly as possible until it is very difficult to turn. Add more ice and salt if necessary, using the same proportion. Pour off salt water. Do not let it flow over top of can. Push down ice and salt, wipe top with cloth. Uncover and remove dasher, scrape ice cream from it back into can. Place heavy paper over top of can, put on cover and place a cork in the hole. Repack the freezer in the ice and salt, put ice on top, cover with burlap or newspaper, and let stand several hours to ripen.

To Whip Cream for Ice Cream

Cream, bowl, and beater must be cold. Pour heavy cream into straight-sided mixing bowl with rounded bottom and beat with whisk, rotary, or electric beater until thick enough to mound softly on a spoon.

Cream doubles in bulk when whipped. It must not be beaten too long or it forms butter.

To Prepare Fruit for Ice Cream

Crush fruit, add sugar to taste; let stand until sugar is dissolved. Strain seedy fruits. Add to partially frozen cream and churn slowly for 1 minute to blend. Continue freezing until stiff.

FRENCH ICE CREAM

1 cup sugar	3 egg yolks
1 cup water	1 teaspoon vanilla
pinch of salt	2 cups heavy cream, whipped

Boil sugar and water slowly for 5 minutes to make a syrup. Add salt to eggs in top of double boiler, beat thoroughly, then gradually stir in the boiling syrup. Cook over boiling water 3 minutes, beating constantly. Place over cold water, beat until cold, add vanilla and cream, and freeze in churn freezer.

Variation:

Fruit Ice Cream: One quart mashed and sweetened fruit may be added to French Ice Cream when partially frozen. Finish freezing.

VANILLA ICE CREAM

 This recipe calls for uncooked egg whites to be added before freezing. This ingredient can be omitted to avoid possible contamination from a Salmonella infected egg, if desired.

2 tablespoons flour or cornstarch	2 eggs, separated, whites stiffly beaten
1 cup sugar	
⅛ teaspoon salt	1 quart half-and-half
2 cups hot milk	2 teaspoons vanilla

Mix flour or cornstarch, sugar and salt, and add the milk gradually. Cook over hot water 10 minutes, stirring occasionally. Beat the egg yolks well; stir in the hot milk mixture very gradually. Cook until the custard coats the spoon. Cool, add half-and-half, stiffly beaten egg whites, and vanilla. Strain and freeze in churn freezer or modern ice-cream maker.

Variations:

Orange Ice Cream: Proceed as for Vanilla Ice Cream, omitting the vanilla and substituting the grated rind of 2 oranges and of ½ lemon added while custard is hot. Cool the custard and add the juice of 4 oranges. Freeze as directed.

Caramel Ice Cream: Proceed as for Vanilla Ice Cream. While custard is hot, melt 1 scant cup sugar to a brown liquid in a heavy skillet, and pour gradually into hot custard. When cool, reduce the amount of vanilla added to ½ teaspoon, and omit egg whites.

Peach or Apricot Ice Cream: Add 4 cups sweetened peach or apricot pulp and 1 teaspoon almond extract to partially frozen Vanilla Ice Cream or New York Ice Cream. Finish freezing.

Banana Ice Cream: Add 2 cups mashed bananas, mixed with ½ cup lemon juice, to partially frozen Vanilla or French Ice Cream. Finish freezing.

Papaya Ice Cream: Add 4 cups mashed, ripe papayas to partially frozen Vanilla Ice Cream. Finish freezing.

PISTACHIO ICE CREAM

4 ounces pistachio nuts	½ teaspoon almond extract
few drops of rose water	1 recipe Vanilla Ice Cream, above
¼ cup sugar	green food coloring (optional)
¼ cup half-and-half	

Blanch and shell pistachio nuts. Grind and mix with a few drops of rose water, add sugar, half-and-half, and almond extract; stir to a fine paste. Add to Vanilla Ice Cream. Tint pale green with food coloring, if desired, and freeze in churn freezer, or modern ice-cream maker.

NEW YORK ICE CREAM

1 quart half-and-half
4 eggs, separated

1 cup sugar
2 teaspoons vanilla

Scald half the half-and-half in the top of a double boiler over hot water. Beat yolks until thick, add sugar and beat again. Beat whites stiff, add to yolks, mix well, turn back into double boiler. Stir constantly until the custard coats the spoon. Cool; add the rest of half-and-half and the flavoring, and freeze in churn freezer or modern ice-cream maker.

CHESTNUT ICE CREAM

3 cups chestnuts, shelled and peeled
1½ cups sugar
1½ cups water
6 egg yolks, well beaten

3 cups half-and-half
½ teaspoon vanilla
½ pound candied fruit, finely chopped

Boil and rice chestnuts. Cook sugar and water 5 minutes. Add chestnuts, bring to boil. Stir syrup and chestnuts gradually into egg yolks. Stir until cold, add half-and-half, vanilla, and candied fruit. Freeze in churn freezer or modern ice-cream maker.

OLD-FASHIONED CHOCOLATE ICE CREAM

1 cup sugar
1½ ounces unsweetened chocolate, melted, or ¼ cup cocoa

¼ cup hot water
1 quart half-and-half
1 tablespoon vanilla

Add sugar to chocolate or cocoa; add the hot water gradually, stir smooth. Cool, add half-and-half and vanilla, and freeze in churn freezer or modern ice-cream maker.

COFFEE ICE CREAM

4 egg yolks
1¼ cups sugar
¼ teaspoon salt

1 cup very strong coffee
1 quart half-and-half

Mix the slightly beaten yolks with the sugar and salt; stir in coffee and half the half-and-half. Cook in double boiler until thick. Cool, add remaining half-and-half and freeze in churn freezer or modern ice-cream maker.

MAPLE ICE CREAM

1 cup maple syrup
4 egg yolks, well beaten

2 cups heavy cream, whipped
1 egg white, stiffly beaten

Heat syrup to the boiling point and pour gradually on the well-beaten yolks. Cook in double boiler, stirring until custard coats spoon. Cool. Fold in whipped cream and egg white; freeze in churn freezer or modern ice-cream maker.

MOCHA ICE CREAM

½ pound sweet chocolate
1 quart half-and-half
¾ cup sugar

1 cup very strong coffee, or 3
teaspoons instant coffee
6 egg yolks

Melt chocolate in 1 cup of half-and-half in double boiler. Add sugar and coffee, stir well. Beat egg yolks with a little half-and-half and add to chocolate mixture. Cook until thick, stirring constantly. Cool. Add remaining half-and-half. Freeze in churn freezer or modern ice-cream maker.

Variation:

Rich Chocolate Ice Cream: Make Mocha Ice Cream, above, substituting for the coffee 1 cup hot milk and 1 teaspoon vanilla.

PEPPERMINT STICK ICE CREAM

1 cup sugar
½ pound peppermint stick candy,
  crushed

2 cups milk or half-and-half
2 cups heavy cream, whipped

Add sugar and crushed candy to milk or half-and-half. Let stand several hours to dissolve. Add the whipped cream, then freeze in churn freezer or modern ice-cream maker

Fruit Ices and Sherbets

The method for freezing fruit ices and sherbets in a manually operated churn freezer is the same as that for ice cream. Use fresh, seasonal fruit of exceptional quality for best results.

LEMON ICE

4 cups water
1½ cups sugar

1 egg white, stiffly beaten (optional)
¾ cup lemon juice

Boil water and sugar 5 minutes to make a syrup. Cool, fold in egg white, if desired, and add lemon juice. Freeze in churn freezer or modern ice-cream maker.

CRANBERRY FRAPPE

1 quart cranberries
4 cups water

2 cups sugar
½ cup lemon juice

Cook the berries in water 5 minutes or until they stop popping and strain. Add sugar and bring to the boiling point. Cool, add lemon juice; freeze in churn freezer or modern ice-cream maker.

FRESH FRUIT ICE

4 cups water
2 cups sugar
2 cups fruit juice or crushed fruit, strained

lemon juice to taste
1 egg white, stiffly beaten (optional)

Boil water and sugar for 5 minutes to make a syrup, cool, add fruit juice or crushed fruit and lemon juice. Fold in egg white, if desired, and freeze in churn freezer or modern ice-cream maker.

GRAPE FRAPPE

4 cups water
2 cups sugar
2 cups grape juice

¼ cup lemon juice
⅔ cup orange juice
1 egg white, stiffly beaten (optional)

Make a syrup by boiling water and sugar 5 minutes; cool; add grape, lemon, and orange juices; cool, add the egg white, if desired, and freeze in churn freezer or modern ice-cream maker.

STRAWBERRY OR RASPBERRY ICE

1½ cups sugar
4 cups water

2 cups strawberry or raspberry juice
1 tablespoon lemon juice

Boil sugar and water for 10 minutes and cool. Add berry juice and lemon juice. Strain and freeze in churn freezer or modern ice-cream maker.

PINEAPPLE ICE

1 cup sugar
2 cups water
1 cup fresh pineapple or 1 8-ounce
  can crushed pineapple

juice of 2 lemons
2 egg whites, stiffly beaten
  (optional)

Boil sugar with water 5 minutes to make a syrup. Cool, add pineapple and the lemon juice. Freeze until slightly thickened, then fold in whites, if desired, and finish freezing in churn freezer or modern ice-cream maker.

LEMON MILK SHERBET

1¾ cups sugar
grated rind of ½ lemon

½ cup lemon juice
1 quart milk or buttermilk

Mix in the order given and freeze in churn freezer or modern ice-cream maker.

BERRY MILK SHERBET

1 cup sugar
1 cup raspberry, strawberry, or
  loganberry juice

1 tablespoon lemon juice
1 quart milk

Mix sugar, berry juice, and lemon juice and set aside until sugar is dissolved. Add the milk and freeze in churn freezer or modern ice-cream machine.

Mousses

These desserts may be made in covered molds by burying in 4 parts ice to 1 of salt, or in molds or refrigerator trays in the home freezer. They are all made with heavy cream, whipped stiff, combined with a thick, flavored base, then frozen without stirring.

The dessert will be much smoother if the cream is whipped only until it mounds softly on a spoon.

Use only crushed fruits; whole fruit is apt to crystallize.

All ingredients should be about the same temperature when combined to prevent separation, especially when folding mixtures into whipped cream.

To Prepare Molds

Fill mold to top. If mold has a lid, cover the filling with waxed paper, bringing the paper down over the sides. Adjust the lid. If the mold is to be buried in salt and ice, apply a thin coat of shortening to the outside of the seam, to seal the closing and prevent water from seeping in. If the mold has no lid, cover mold with a double thickness of aluminum foil, bringing the foil well down the sides and tie securely with string.

To Unmold

Dip mold into hot water almost to top edge. Remove cover, run knife around edges of cream, and invert on serving dish. If frozen mixture does not slip out at once, put hot, damp cloth on top of inverted mold.

MACAROON AND FRUIT MOUSSE

¼ cup confectioners' sugar
¼ pound candied cherries
12 crushed macaroons

½ slice candied pineapple, finely
   chopped
vanilla or maraschino syrup to taste
2 cups heavy cream, whipped

Fold all ingredients into whipped cream. Freeze in refrigerator tray or mold.

PEANUT BRITTLE MOUSSE

1 pound peanut brittle   2 cups heavy cream, whipped
1 dozen macaroons

Chop the peanut brittle and macaroons together and mix with the whipped cream. Freeze in refrigerator trays or mold. Unmold onto platter, slice. Serve with whipped cream and candied cherries.

PRALINE MOUSSE

¾ cup almonds   ½ cup confectioners' sugar
1 cup granulated sugar   pinch of salt
2 cups heavy cream

Blanch almonds, toast them in a 300°F oven, and chop. Place granulated sugar in small skillet; stir until it melts to a light brown syrup. Place chopped nuts on greased inverted dripping pan, pour hot syrup over quickly, cool, then break into small pieces. Beat cream until stiff; add confectioners' sugar, salt, and the broken almond pieces. Freeze in refrigerator trays or mold.

STRAWBERRY MOUSSE

1 quart strawberries   1 teaspoon vanilla
1½ cups confectioners' sugar   2 cups heavy cream, whipped
¼ teaspoon salt

Wash and hull berries, add sugar, let stand 1 hour. Mash and strain. Add salt and vanilla to whipped cream. Fold into mashed strawberries. Freeze in two refrigerator trays or in a mold, without stirring. Other berries or fruits, mashed or cut in very small pieces, may be used.

CHESTNUT MOUSSE

1 pound chestnuts   2 cups heavy cream, whipped
2 cups sugar   1 tablespoon maraschino syrup or 1
1 cup water   teaspoon vanilla

Blanch, shell and completely cook fresh chestnuts. Boil sugar with water for 10 minutes. Add cooked chestnuts and boil for 5 minutes. Drain and rice chestnuts. Chill and serve with whipped cream flavored with maraschino syrup or vanilla.

Dessert Sauces

A well-chosen dessert sauce will transform the simplest dessert into a special treat. Choose a sauce, hot or cold, to complement and contrast with the dessert; a tart, fruit-based sauce with a creamy rice pudding; a fluffy whipped-cream sauce for plain cakes; a rich and nutty butterscotch sauce over warm spice cake; a butter or hard sauce for a steamed fruit pudding. A special group of sauces for ice cream is also included, to make even supermarket ice cream into a company dessert.

SAUCES FOR CAKES AND PUDDINGS

CARAMEL SAUCE

| 1 cup sugar | 1 cup boiling water |

Spread sugar evenly in heavy skillet, place over heat, stir gently with a spoon, moving sugar constantly to the hottest part of pan until melted to a smooth, light-brown syrup. Then very gradually add the boiling water and simmer for 5 to 10 minutes. The sugar may again become hard, but will melt in a few minutes. If too thick when cold, add a little hot water and boil again.

Variation:

Burnt Almond Sauce: Blanch ⅓ cup almonds. Place in pan in oven and roast until crisp and slightly browned. Chop fine and add to Caramel Sauce, above.

VANILLA SAUCE

2 tablespoons butter	2 tablespoons sugar
2 tablespoons flour	1 teaspoon vanilla
1 cup boiling water	

Melt the butter, add flour and stir until it bubbles; add the boiling water and sugar, stirring constantly. Cook until smooth and well blended. Add vanilla and serve hot or cold.

CLEAR BUTTERSCOTCH SAUCE

4 tablespoons butter
1 cup brown sugar, firmly packed
1 teaspoon cornstarch

½ tablespoon vinegar
¼ cup water

Combine and boil ingredients until of desired consistency. Serve hot.

BUTTERSCOTCH NUT SAUCE

1 cup brown sugar, firmly packed
½ cup butter

1 cup half-and-half
½ cup chopped nuts

Combine first 3 ingredients and cook in double boiler ½ hour. Add nut meats. Serve hot or cold.

BUTTERSCOTCH SAUCE

2 cups brown sugar, firmly packed
½ cup butter

½ cup half-and-half

Mix well. Boil rapidly, without stirring, for 5 minutes. Serve hot or cold.

CHOCOLATE SAUCE

1½ tablespoons cornstarch
2 cups cold milk
2 ounces unsweetened chocolate,
  grated

2 eggs, separated
⅔ cup confectioners' sugar
1 teaspoon vanilla

Mix cornstarch with a little of the cold milk, add to rest of milk, cook in double boiler until thick, add chocolate and cook until melted. Beat egg whites stiff, add sugar, then unbeaten yolks. Add to cooked mixture. Cook 1 minute, stirring, let cool, add vanilla. Serve hot or cold.

EASY CHOCOLATE SAUCE

1 cup boiling water
pinch of salt
1 ounce unsweetened chocolate

½ cup sugar
1 teaspoon vanilla

Cook first 4 ingredients slowly until desired consistency. Just before serving, add 1 teaspoon of vanilla. Serve hot or cold.

CUSTARD SAUCE

3 egg yolks
½ cup sugar
⅛ teaspoon salt

2 cups scalded milk
½ teaspoon vanilla or rum

Beat yolks slightly, add sugar and salt; stir constantly while adding the hot milk gradually. Cook in a double boiler until mixture thickens; chill and flavor.

MELBA SAUCE

¾ cup sugar
½ cup water

1 pint raspberries or strawberries, chilled and crushed

Boil sugar and water 10 minutes; cool and when ready to serve, add to chilled and crushed pulp and juice of berries.

LEMON SAUCE

1 cup sugar
2 tablespoons cornstarch
2 cups boiling water

rind and juice of 1 lemon
2 tablespoons butter

Mix the sugar and cornstarch, add boiling water gradually, stirring constantly. Cook 8 to 10 minutes, add lemon juice, rind, and butter. Serve hot or cold.

Variation:

Quick Brandy Sauce: Follow recipe above. Omit lemon and substitute brandy or kirsch to taste and add a sprinkling of nutmeg.

ORANGE SAUCE

2 tablespoons butter
2 egg yolks
3 tablespoons sugar

4 tablespoons half-and-half
¼ cup orange juice

Cream butter in top of double boiler. Stir in egg yolks, sugar, and half-and-half. Put over hot water, cook until thick. Add orange juice. Serve hot or cold.

WHIPPED CREAM SAUCES

CREAM FRUIT SAUCE

¾ cup fruit pulp
¾ cup heavy cream

sugar to taste

To make fruit pulp, mash fruit and drain, or rub fruit through sieve. Whip cream, fold in fruit pulp and sweeten to taste.

CREAM FRUIT JUICE SAUCE

2 teaspoons butter
2 teaspoons flour
1 cup fruit juice, hot

juice of ½ lemon
1 cup cream, whipped
sugar to taste

Melt butter in double boiler, add flour and blend; add fruit juice and lemon juice. Stir constantly until it thickens. Chill; fold in whipped cream sweetened to taste.

STRAWBERRY CREAM SAUCE

1 cup strawberry pulp
1 cup cream, whipped

1 tablespoon maraschino syrup
sugar to taste

To make strawberry pulp, mash and drain berries. Mix together all ingredients. Serve cold over any pudding or sponge cake.

HARD SAUCES

PLAIN HARD SAUCE

¼ cup butter
1 cup confectioners' sugar

1 tablespoon rum or 1 teaspoon
vanilla

Cream the butter, add sugar gradually, and flavoring, adding more sugar if necessary for desired consistency.

CREAM CHEESE HARD SAUCE

1 3-ounce package cream cheese
3 cups confectioners' sugar
3 tablespoons sherry

¼ teaspoon each cinnamon and
nutmeg
¼ teaspoon salt

Soften the cream cheese, combine with the other ingredients. Sauce will be stiff. Chill thoroughly. Serve on hot Mince Pie (page 529) or hot Prune Pudding (page 623).

STRAWBERRY HARD SAUCE

⅓ cup butter
1 cup confectioners' sugar

⅔ cup strawberries

Cream the butter, add the sugar gradually, add the strawberries and beat until berries are well mashed. Add more sugar if necessary for desired consistency.

JELLY SAUCES

JELLY SAUCE

¼ cup hot water
1 6-ounce jar tart jelly

1 tablespoon butter
1 tablespoon flour

Add hot water to jelly and melt very slowly. Heat butter in saucepan, add flour and gradually the hot jelly liquid. Cook until smooth and serve hot over any pudding. Or the jelly may be melted with just the hot water and served.

JAM OR MARMALADE SAUCE

 Heat ¼ cup jam or marmalade, the juice of 1 lemon, and ½ cup of water. Stir until dissolved and serve hot or cold.

SAUCES FOR ICE CREAM

CHOCOLATE SUNDAE SAUCE

2 cups sugar	pinch of salt
4 cups water	2 tablespoons cornstarch
4 ounces unsweetened chocolate	2 teaspoons vanilla

Boil sugar and water 5 minutes to make a syrup; add chocolate, salt, and cornstarch dissolved in a little cold water. Cook slowly and stir until chocolate is melted and mixture is smooth, 5 to 8 minutes. Cool; add vanilla. Keep in jar in refrigerator.

MILK CHOCOLATE FUDGE SAUCE

 ½ pound milk chocolate   ½ cup hot milk

Melt chocolate in top of double boiler, stirring constantly. When thoroughly dissolved, add milk gradually and stir until smooth. Serve warm.

MAPLE SUNDAE SAUCE

 2 cups maple syrup   ¼ cup butter

Boil syrup and butter until it forms a thread when dropped from spoon. Serve hot.

BUTTERSCOTCH SUNDAE SAUCE

1 cup light brown sugar, firmly packed	¼ cup milk or cream
	2 tablespoons butter
2 tablespoons corn syrup	

Cook sugar, syrup, and milk, stirring constantly, until it forms a soft ball in cold water. Add butter. Serve hot.

FRUIT SUNDAE SAUCE

 Cook 1 cup sugar and ¼ cup water 5 minutes. Pour over 1½ cups halved or sliced strawberries. Cool and serve over ice cream. Sauce may be kept a few days after making. Any berries—whole, sliced, or crushed—or peaches may be used.

STRAWBERRY WHIPPED CREAM SAUCE

 Sprinkle ½ cup sugar over 1 cup crushed strawberries. Let stand about 1 hour. Put through a sieve and fold in 1 cup whipped cream.

CANDIES AND CONFECTIONS

Use a smooth, round-bottomed pan with straight sides for candy cookery. If sugar crystals form on the side of the pan, wipe them off with a fork wrapped in a wet cloth. Watch carefully and test frequently, removing the pan from the heat for each testing. Use fresh cold water for each test.

TEMPERATURES AND TESTS FOR CANDY

Temperature	Cold Water Test	Texture
230° F–234° F	thread	Little syrup dropped from spoon forms flexible thread.
234° F–236° F	soft ball	Ball flattens but does not ooze out when
238° F–240° F		pressed between fingers.
242° F–248° F	firm ball	Ball firm, yet can be flattened a little.
250° F–265° F	hard ball	Ball very firm, yet plastic, holds its shape.
270° F–290° F	crack stage	Ball pressed flat will be brittle under water, bend out of water.
300° F–310° F	hard-crack stage	Ball pressed will be brittle in and out of water.

A thermometer makes candy making easier by indicating the exact temperature, and thus the concentration of the syrup. The concentration of the syrup determines whether the finished product is a soft and creamy fudge or a hard brittle. The thermometer should be immersed below the surface of the syrup, but it should not touch the bottom or sides of the pan. Hold the thermometer at eye level to read it accurately. Check the accuracy of thermometer by immersing it in boiling water—water boils at 212° F at sea level. At higher altitudes candy cooks faster.

Fudge

Do not stir fudge mixtures after the syrup has dissolved. Cool the fudge, without beating, to 110° F (warm to the touch). Then beat it until it is glossy and begins to harden. Most fudges are turned out at once into a buttered pan, allowed to harden, and cut into squares. Other are molded. Nuts and fruits should be added just before pouring. Store fudge in a tightly covered container.

CHOCOLATE FUDGE   *Makes about 1 pound.*

2 cups white, firmly packed brown, or maple sugar	½ teaspoon salt
2 teaspoons corn syrup	2 tablespoons butter
1 cup cream, milk, or water	1 teaspoon vanilla
2 ounces unsweetened chocolate or ⅔ cup cocoa	

Cook sugar, syrup, the cup of liquid, chocolate or cocoa, and salt over low heat; stir occasionally to prevent burning. Boil to a soft-ball stage, 234° F. Add butter and vanilla. Cool until lukewarm and beat until thick and creamy. Press into buttered pans. Mark into squares and cut.

Variation:

Nut Fudge: When fudge is thick and beaten until almost creamy, add 1 cup chopped nut meats and 1 tablespoon candied fruit, chopped. Form into balls, roll in chopped nut meats or grated bitter chocolate.

CREAM FUDGE   *Makes about 2 pounds.*

4 cups sugar	1½ cups undiluted evaporated milk
4 tablespoons light corn syrup	2 tablespoons butter
2 heaping teaspoons cornstarch	2 teaspoons vanilla

Cook sugar, syrup, cornstarch, and milk to soft-ball stage, 238° F, stirring constantly. Add butter and vanilla; do not stir. Cool to lukewarm, then beat until candy loses its sheen. When thick enough to handle, knead and shape into rolls. When set, cut in pieces.

MEXICAN FUDGE   *Makes about 1½ pounds.*

3 cups sugar	grated rind of 1 orange
¼ cup boiling water	4 tablespoons butter
1 cup undiluted evaporated milk	1 cup chopped nut meats
pinch of salt	

Put 1 cup sugar into heavy skillet and place over low heat, stirring constantly. When melted to a light brown add the boiling water. Boil until sugar is dissolved and syrup forms. Add remaining sugar, evaporated milk, and salt and cook until it reaches firm-ball stage, 242° F. Add orange rind and remove from heat. Do not stir after removing from stove. Drop the butter on the candy and let stand until cool. Beat until the mixture starts to lose its sheen. Add the nuts. Knead and form into rolls. Cut into 1-inch pieces.

PENUCHE   *Makes about 1 pound.*

2 cups firmly packed brown or
   maple sugar
¾ cup milk

2 tablespoons butter
1 teaspoon vanilla
2 cups chopped nuts

Boil sugar and milk to the soft-ball stage, 236° F. Remove from heat; add butter, vanilla, and nuts. Cool to lukewarm. Beat till creamy and thickened; press into a greased pan, and when firm, cut into squares.

QUICK FUDGE   *Makes about 1½ pounds.*

4 ounces unsweetened chocolate
½ cup butter
1 egg, slightly beaten

2 cups confectioners' sugar
¼ cup sweetened condensed milk
1 teaspoon vanilla

Melt chocolate and butter in top of double boiler. Mix together egg and sugar; add milk, and stir in the chocolate-butter mixture. Add vanilla. Turn into buttered pan, chill, and cut into squares.

NEW ORLEANS PRALINES   *Makes about 1 pound.*

2 cups confectioners' sugar
1 cup maple syrup

½ cup cream
2 cups pecan halves

Boil sugar, syrup, and cream to the soft-ball stage, 236° F. Then beat until mixture begins to crystallize. While still warm, add nuts and drop on waxed paper into 2-inch patties.

COCONUT CANDY   *Makes about 1 pound.*

2 teaspoons butter
1½ cups sugar
½ cup milk

⅓ cup shredded sweetened coconut
½ teaspoon vanilla or lemon extract

Melt butter in saucepan; add sugar and milk and stir until sugar is dissolved. Boil 12 minutes or to soft-ball stage, 238° F; remove from heat, add coconut and vanilla, and beat until creamy and mixture begins to crystallize slightly. Pour at once into a buttered pan and mark into squares.

SEA FOAM   *Makes about 1½ pounds.*

2 cups sugar
½ cup light corn syrup
½ cup water
2 egg whites, stiffly beaten

1 teaspoon vanilla
1 cup walnut meats, broken in large
    pieces

Boil sugar, syrup, and water to very hard ball stage, 265° F. Pour slowly onto beaten egg whites, beating constantly. When very thick and creamy, add vanilla and nuts. Drop from spoon onto waxed paper.

Variation:

Turkish Candy: Follow recipe for Sea Foam, and when stiff and creamy, add nuts, and place in small, deep, well-buttered pan. Cover with 2 ounces melted unsweetened chocolate. When cold, cut into slices or squares.

Caramels

CLASSIC CARAMELS   *Makes about 1 pound.*

2 cups sugar
2 tablespoons butter
1 cup milk

1 teaspoon vanilla
chopped nuts or candied cherries
    (optional)

Boil sugar, butter, and milk to firm-ball stage, 245° F. Do not stir after sugar is dissolved. Pour on buttered platter, cool, beat until creamy. Add vanilla and chopped nuts or cherries if desired. Press into buttered pans; when firm, cut into squares. Wrap in waxed paper.

CHOCOLATE CARAMELS   *Makes about 1½ pounds.*

2 cups white sugar
1 cup brown sugar, firmly packed
1 cup dark corn syrup
½ cup cream
½ cup butter

3 ounces unsweetened chocolate
⅛ teaspoon salt
1 teaspoon vanilla
1 cup chopped nuts (optional)

Place all ingredients except vanilla in a heavy saucepan. Cover and boil for 5 minutes. Uncover, boil to firm-ball stage, 247° F. Remove from heat, add vanilla; add nuts if desired. Pour into buttered 10-by-6-inch pan. When cold, cut into 1-inch squares. Wrap in waxed paper.

VANILLA CREAM CARAMELS   *Makes about 2 pounds.*

3 cups cream, heated
2 cups sugar
2 cups light corn syrup

1 cup walnuts, coarsely chopped
1 teaspoon vanilla

Boil 1 cup cream with sugar and syrup to soft-ball stage, 238° F. Heat 1 cup cream and add; boil again to soft-ball stage. Heat remaining cup cream, add, and boil again to soft-ball stage. Remove from heat, stir in nuts and vanilla, and pour into well-buttered pans. When cold, cut into squares. Wrap in waxed paper.

Pulled Candies and Toffees

WHITE TAFFY   *Makes about 1 pound.*

2 cups sugar
⅔ cup water
4 tablespoons butter

2 teaspoons cream of tartar
½ teaspoon desired flavoring

Combine ingredients and boil to crack stage, 272° F, stirring as needed to prevent scorching. Add any flavoring desired. Pour into well-buttered pan and when cool enough to handle, pull quickly and lightly with oiled fingertips. It should become porous. Stretch out on board to harden; cut into pieces.

SALT-WATER TAFFY   *Makes about 1 pound.*

1¼ cups corn syrup
1 cup sugar
1 tablespoon water

1 teaspoon butter
1 tablespoon vinegar
½ teaspoon vanilla

Mix all ingredients. Boil until syrup reaches the crack stage, 272° F, stirring as needed to prevent scorching. Pour into buttered pan. As soon as it is cool enough to handle, pull until candy is light and porous. When cold, chop into pieces.

Variation:

Cinnamon Balls: Add ½ teaspoon essence of cinnamon to Salt-Water Taffy before it is pulled. Let it cool and roll into balls.

MOLASSES CANDY   *Makes about 1½ pounds.*

1 teaspoon butter
1 cup dark molasses
1 tablespoon water

½ cup sugar
¼ teaspoon baking soda

Melt the butter in a heavy skillet, add molasses, water, and sugar, and stir until sugar is dissolved. Stir occasionally until nearly done, and then constantly. Boil until the spoon leaves a track in the bottom of pan while stirring, to hard-ball stage, 255° F. Stir well, add the soda, stir thoroughly, and pour in a very well greased pan. When cool enough to handle, pull until light-colored and porous. Work candy with fingertips and thumbs; do not squeeze in the hands. When it begins to harden, stretch to the desired thickness, cut in small pieces with large shears. Cool on buttered plates.

ENGLISH TOFFEE   *Makes about 1 pound.*

1¾ cups sugar
⅛ teaspoon cream of tartar
1 cup cream

½ cup butter
1 teaspoon rum or fruit extract

Place sugar with cream of tartar in a deep saucepan, rounded at the bottom; add cream, boil a few minutes, stirring with wooden spoon. Add butter, boil to crack stage, 290° F, stirring all the time. Add 1 teaspoon rum or fruit extract. Pour into buttered pan. Cut into squares while still warm.

Variation:

Almond Toffee: Make English Toffee, omitting rum. Add 6 tablespoons chopped almonds. Pour at once into greased pan.

SUGAR CRYSTALS

To prevent sugar crystals from forming on sides of pan, stir sugar and liquid over slow heat until sugar is dissolved; cover pan for the first 2 or 3 minutes of boiling.

CLASSIC STICK CANDY   *Makes about 1 pound.*

2 cups sugar   ½ cup water
½ cup light corn syrup   juice and rind of 1 lemon

Boil all ingredients without stirring to crack stage, 285° F. Remove from heat. Flavor with either of the variations below, or experiment with your own flavors.

For Lemon Sticks

Add 1 teaspoon lemon extract. Pour on a buttered platter. When cool enough, pull and roll into sticks and cut.

For Peppermint Sticks

Add 1 teaspoon peppermint extract. Divide candy into two parts. To one part add a little red vegetable coloring. Pour on buttered platters; when cool enough, pull each and roll separately, then twist one around other; form into canes or sticks.

SOFT BUTTERSCOTCH   *Makes about 1 pound.*

2 cups brown sugar, firmly packed   ½ cup water
¼ cup butter

Put sugar, butter, and water in skillet; boil and stir until the spoon leaves a track in bottom of pan, or to hard-ball stage, 252° F. Pour ¼ inch deep in buttered pans. When cool, cut into squares.

HARD BUTTERSCOTCH   *Makes about 1½ pounds.*

1 cup corn syrup
2 cups brown sugar, firmly packed
½ cup butter

¼ cup water
1 tablespoon vinegar
1 teaspoon vanilla

Boil until syrup dropped into cold water separates into hard thin cords (288° to 290° F). Pour into buttered pan. When hard, break into pieces.

Fondant and Dipped Candies

Fondant, sometimes called "Stock Dough for Candy," is the base for many candies. It may be flavored and colored to taste, and shaped as desired; or used to coat fruits, nuts, other candies or small cakes; or mixed with chopped nuts or dried or candied fruits, or used as centers for chocolate-covered bonbons. Fondant should be allowed to ripen at least 1 hour before it is used to make candies. It improves with ripening overnight or longer.

COOKED FONDANT   *Makes about 1 pound.*

2 cups sugar
⅔ cup cold water

⅛ teaspoon cream of tartar

Bring sugar and water to a boil, stirring only until sugar is completely dissolved. Add cream of tartar. Continue to boil until syrup reaches the soft-ball stage, 238° F. If any crystals form on sides of pan, wash off with damp cloth wrapped around fork. Pour onto a buttered marble slab or large platter to cool. When mixture is lukewarm and still on the slab, use a spatula or wooden spoon to lift and beat fondant until it is white and creamy. Knead on slab until smooth. Cover with a damp towel and let rest for 1 hour. Knead again and store in an airtight jar in the refrigerator.

UNCOOKED CREAM FONDANT   *Makes about ½ pound.*

This recipe contains a raw egg white. Use a cooked one if Salmonella contamination is a problem.

1 cup confectioners' sugar
1 teaspoon vanilla

3 tablespoons cream
1 egg white

Mix ingredients and knead thoroughly. Mold to shape.

UNCOOKED BUTTER FONDANT   *Makes about ½ pound.*

This recipe contains a raw egg white. Use a cooked one if Salmonella contamination is a problem.

1 egg white	1 teaspoon flavoring
4 tablespoons butter, creamed	1 teaspoon cream of tartar
¼ cup cold water	1¼ cups confectioners' sugar

Mix ingredients in order, knead thoroughly, and mold to shape.

PEPPERMINT, WINTERGREEN, OR FRUIT PATTIES

Put desired fondant in top of double boiler, soften over hot water. Flavor with a few drops of peppermint, wintergreen, or fruit flavors. Add coloring. Drop from tip of spoon onto waxed paper.

NUT CREAMS

Add enough cream to a cup of desired fondant to make it thin enough to beat. Beat until consistency of whipped cream; add a little flavoring and ½ cup nuts. Press flat on a buttered baking sheet and cut into squares.

FONDANT DIP

To dip bonbons, melt cooked fondant in a saucepan over hot water. Add coloring and flavor as desired. Stir as little as possible; add a little boiling water if mixture seems too thick, confectioners' sugar if too thin. Remove pan from heat while dipping. A second saucepan of fondant may be melting in the hot water, to use alternately. Put centers—nuts, candied fruit, fondant shapes, or other candies—on a dipping fork (pronged or with a loop at the end), lower into fondant, lift out, drain off excess fondant, and invert candy on waxed paper over rack to cool. Stir the fondant as necessary between dippings to prevent crust from forming.

CHOCOLATE DIP

Melt 1 pound semisweet or milk chocolate over boiling water. Let stand until it feels cool (85°). Add a little butter or cocoa butter if chocolate is too thick. Proceed as for Fondant Dip, above.

DIPPED FRESH STRAWBERRIES   *Makes about 20 strawberries.*

1 quart fresh strawberries   1 cup desired Fondant (page 662)

Do not hull berries. Dip berries, one at a time, halfway into fondant or chocolate, softened over hot water holding the berry by the stem. Lift the berry out quickly, turning it round and round in the air a moment, tip upward, to dry; then invert berry, stand on tip on waxed paper. Place each berry in a paper bonbon cup. Serve within an hour, because these cannot be stored.

CHOCOLATE CREAM DIP   *Makes about 1 pound.*

1 recipe desired Fondant (page 662)   4 ounces bitter, sweet or milk
                                             chocolate, melted

Make cone-shaped forms of Fondant. Place on waxed paper to harden. Dip, one at a time, into Chocolate Dip (above) and cover all sides. Set on waxed paper to harden. Drizzle over melted chocolate for decoration.

CHOCOLATE-DIPPED CHERRIES

fresh pitted or maraschino cherries   Chocolate Dip (above)
Fondant (pages 662)

Drain the cherries, but not too dry. Melt Fondant in double boilder, and dip the cherries one at a time; drop on waxed paper and let stand in cool place just long enough to harden. Then dip into Chocolate Dip.

CHOCOLATE-COATED FUDGE

Follow recipe for any Fudge (pages 655–657), dip squares into Chocolate Dip (page 664), let harden on waxed paper.

DATE, FIG, OR MARSHMALLOW CHOCOLATES

 Remove stones from dates or cut figs in half lengthwise. Press into uniform shape and coat with Chocolate Dip. Marshmallows are also great dipped.

MINT JELLIES   *Makes about 1 pound.*

2 envelopes unflavored gelatin	2 tablespoons lemon juice
1½ cups water	green food coloring
2 cups sugar	few drops peppermint oil

Soak gelatin in ⅔ cup cold water 5 minutes. Place sugar and rest of water in a saucepan, and bring to a boil. Add dissolved gelatin, bring to the boiling point and boil slowly but steadily 20 minutes. Remove from heat, add rest of the ingredients. Pour the mixture into a shallow pan to about 1-inch thickness, let stand for about 12 hours or until firm. Remove to board, cut in cubes, roll in confectioners' sugar.

Variations:

Fruit Jellies: Different varieties can be made by using fruit juices instead of water and different coloring, also by adding ½ cup chopped nut meats or candied fruits.

MARSHMALLOWS   *Makes about 1 pound.*

2 envelopes unflavored gelatin	peppermint or wintergreen oil
1¼ cups water	green or red food coloring
2 cups sugar	confectioners' sugar
speck of salt	

Soak gelatin in ½ cup cold water 5 minutes. Cook sugar and remaining ¾ cup water in saucepan until it threads (230° F), pour onto dissolved gelatin, let stand until partially cooled. Add salt and, if desired, a few drops of oil of peppermint or wintergreen, and a little green or red coloring. Beat until light and thick. Pour into a pan that is thickly dusted with confectioners' sugar, and put in a cool place to set. Turn out, cut into squares and roll in more confectioners' sugar.

Nuts and Brittles

PREPARING NUTS

To Blanch Nuts: Pour boiling water over shelled nuts, let stand 5 minutes, or longer. Strain, put into cold water; slip off skins. Dry in oven before storing.

To Chop: Use special nut chopper or chopping knife and bowl.

To Grind: Use special nut grinder, electric blender, or food processor.

To Slice: Use very sharp, thin-bladed knife to avoid breaking nuts.

To Roast: Spread nuts in one flat layer on a cookie sheet or jelly-roll pan. Cook for 5 to 10 minutes in a preheated 350° F oven. Watch carefully—some nuts roast faster than others.

BURNT ALMONDS

2 cups sugar
½ cup water
1 pound raw almonds

1 teaspoon cinnamon
red food coloring

Boil sugar and water until thick and clear. Add almonds, stir with a wooden spoon until the nuts crackle. Reduce heat, stir until dry. Remove nuts, add just enough water to sugar in skillet to moisten. Add cinnamon and red coloring and boil until syrup spins a thread, 230° F. Add sugared nuts and stir until thoroughly coated and separated.

COFFEE CANDIED NUTS

1½ cups sugar
1 tablespoon corn syrup
½ cup strong coffee

2 ½ cups unbroken halves of nut meats

Cook sugar, syrup, and coffee to soft-ball stage, 240° F. Remove from heat and add nuts. Stir gently until creamy. Spread on greased cookie sheet; separate with fork and cool.

Variation:

Orange Candied Nuts: Substitute ½ cup orange juice for coffee in Coffee Candied Nuts. Add ¼ teaspoon ground cinnamon with the nut meats.

ALMOND OR PECAN BRITTLE

 1 cup sugar

1 cup blanched almonds or pecans, coarsely chopped

Melt sugar in skillet to a light-brown syrup. Add nuts. Cook a few minutes, stirring constantly. Spread on a greased pan, cool, break into pieces.

PEANUT BRITTLE

 2 cups sugar

½ to 1 cup shelled skinned peanuts, coarsely chopped

Heat sugar in a heavy skillet until it becomes a thin, light-brown syrup, stirring constantly. Pour over peanuts; spread on a buttered pan in a single layer. Mark into squares while still warm. When cool, break in pieces.

Variations: Brazil, pecan, or walnut meats, puffed rice, or puffed wheat may be used in place of the peanuts.

CREAMY NUT BRITTLE

1 cup sugar
⅓ cup water
⅛ teaspoon cream of tartar
1 tablespoon cream

1 tablespoon molasses
½ cup chopped nuts
¼ teaspoon baking soda

Cook sugar, water, and cream of tartar to 280° F, crack stage. Then add the cream and molasses and cook to 300° F, hard-crack stage. Add nut meats and soda, mixing quickly. Spread thin on well-buttered cookie sheet. When cool, break into pieces.

BUTTER CRUNCH   *Makes about 1 pound.*

1 ½ cups butter
2 cups sugar

3 ounces milk chocolate, melted
½ cup chopped, toasted almonds

Cook butter and sugar slowly in a deep saucepan, rounded at the botom, to the hard-crack stage, 300° F. Pour into large buttered pan. Cool. Brush with melted chocolate, then sprinkle with almonds. Chill. Lift from pan, brush other side with melted chocolate and sprinkle with almonds. Cool until chocolate hardens. Break into pieces.

To Caramelize Sugar: Put sugar into a heavy skillet; heat in moderate oven or on range over low heat until melted. Turn into lightly buttered pan. When cold, break into pieces.

To Crush Sugar: Put pieces of caramelized sugar through meat grinder, roll with rolling pin, or use food processor.

Glacéed and Candied Confections

GLACÉED NUTS OR FRUITS

2 cups sugar
1 cup boiling water

⅛ teaspoon cream of tartar

Heat ingredients in a saucepan, stirring until sugar is dissolved. Then heat to the boiling point and let boil, without stirring, to hard-crack stage, 300° F. Place over pan of hot water to keep syrup from hardening. Then quickly dip fruits and nuts, a few at a time, in the hot syrup and remove them with fork or wire spoon to waxed paper. Glacéed fruits should only be attempted in cold, clear, dry weather. Oranges and tangerines should be separated into sections and allowed to dry a few hours or overnight before dipping.

Variation:

Glacéed Prunes: Remove stones from prunes, fill cavity with nut meats. Follow recipe for Glacéed Nuts and Fruits.

MARRONS GLACÉS   *Makes about 1 pound.*

2 cups whole chestnuts   1 cup water
2 cups sugar   ¼ vanilla bean

Boil chestnuts for 20 minutes, peel the chestnuts whole, cover with fresh boiling water and a little sugar, and cook until tender but not broken; drain. Boil sugar, water, and vanilla bean, without stirring, until syrup reaches hard-crack stage, 300° F; add chestnuts at once. Leave them in 5 minutes. Take out carefully with silver fork, place on warm sieve in warm place. The next day heat syrup, repeat dipping and drying processes. Place in tiny paper cases or, lifting carefully with a fork so they do not break, put them in a sterilized bottle or jar and cover with boiling syrup. Seal and store.

CANDIED CHERRIES

2 cups sugar   1 pound fresh cherries, pitted
1 cup water

Boil sugar and water until the syrup spins a thread, 232° F. Add cherries, let come to a boil; cool. Lift cherries with perforated spoon to platter. Boil syrup 5 minutes longer, pour over cherries. Cover with glass or cheesecloth, set in sun for several hours. Allow cherries to dry by turning onto a clean cloth spread over wire cake rack. Store in glass jars.

CANDIED ORANGE PEEL   *Makes about ¼ pound.*

peel of 1 orange
½ cup sugar

¼ cup hot water

Wipe orange, remove peel in quarters and cut in narrow strips. Place peel in saucepan, cover with cold water, let boil up once and drain. Repeat five times. Heat the sugar with the hot water, and when dissolved, add orange peel. Cook slowly until syrup is nearly evaporated, drain and roll the strips in granulated sugar.

Variation:

Candied Grapefruit Peel: Peel grapefruit, cut peel into sticks. Measure the peel. Proceed as for Candied Orange Peel, using an equal amount of sugar and half as much water.

CHOCOLATE-DIPPED CANDIED PEEL

Melt 2 ounces of unsweetened chocolate in double boiler and keep over hot water. Prepare Candied Orange or Grapefruit Peel. Dip each in melted chocolate. Remove to waxed paper and let stand until dry.

GINGER-AND-NUT-STUFFED DATES

Remove the stones from dates. Chop together equal measures of preserved ginger and blanched nuts (use hickory nuts, pecans, or almonds). Mix with desired Fondant (page 662) or a paste of confectioners' sugar and ginger syrup. Use only enough to hold the ingredients together. Fill the dates with this mixture and roll in granulated sugar.

STUFFED GLAZED FIGS

½ pound large dried figs
½ cup orange juice
2 tablespoons sugar
1 teaspoon lemon juice

maraschino cherries, halved
pecan meats, broken
granulated or confectioners' sugar

Cook figs very slowly in sauce of orange juice, sugar, and lemon juice, turning and basting until tender. Drain, cool. Open and stuff each fig with maraschino cherries and pecan meats. Close, press into shape, and roll in granulated or confectioners' sugar.

STUFFED PRUNES

Steam 1 pound of large prunes until plump. Cool. Remove stones. Fill cavity with desired Fondant (page 662) and half a pecan or walnut. Let stand until partially dry. Roll in granulated sugar.

DATE AND WALNUT BONBONS

½ pound shelled walnuts	1 egg white
½ pound pitted dates	2 tablespoons sugar

Finely mince nuts and dates, knead and form into date-shaped bonbons. Chill overnight. Preheat oven to 300° F. Beat egg white slightly, add sugar, dip bonbons in mixture. Place on greased baking sheet, bake until crisp.

SPANISH SWEETS   *Makes about 2 pounds.*

¼ pound candied cherries	½ pound English walnut meats
¼ pound seedless raisins	¼ pound hickory nut or pecan
¼ pound figs	meats
¼ pound dates, pitted	confectioners' sugar
¼ pound almonds	

Mix together everything except sugar and finely grind or chop. Sprinkle board with confectioners' sugar, toss on the mixture, knead well. Cut into small squares. Will keep packed in layers between sheets of waxed paper.

CANDIED FRUIT AND NUT SLICES *Makes about 1½ pounds.*

½ pound mixed candied fruit, chopped
¼ pound seedless raisins, chopped
¼ pound dates, pitted and chopped

1 cup pecan meats, coarsely chopped
2 tablespoons brandy
½ cup chocolate sprinkles

Mix the fruits, nuts, and brandy together and knead. Form into a roll and cover with chocolate sprinkles. Cut into slices.

CARAMEL APPLES *Makes 5.*

5 medium apples
1 cup sugar
¾ cup dark corn syrup
1 cup cream

2 tablespoons butter
1 teaspoon vanilla
coarsely chopped nuts (optional)

Wash apples, remove stems, and stick skewers into stem ends of apples. Cook sugar, syrup, cream, butter, and vanilla to firm-ball stage, 245° F. Do not stir. Remove from heat. Dip apples into syrup; spoon syrup over apples to cover completely. Remove apples; hold skewer between palms of hands and spin for a moment to cool caramel. If desired, roll in coarsely chopped nuts. Place apples upright on waxed paper.

POPCORN *Makes about 1 quart.*

Heat 2 teaspoons oil in corn popper or in skillet with cover. Add ⅓ cup popcorn kernels, cover tightly. Shake over heat until kernels pop. Melt 2 tablespoons butter, pour over popcorn, sprinkle with salt, toss well, and serve.

CARAMELIZED POPCORN BALLS *Makes about 24.*

3 quarts Popcorn (above)
1 cup molasses
½ cup sugar

1 tablespoon butter
½ teaspoon salt

Place popcorn in a large bowl. Cook molasses, sugar, butter, and salt to crack stage, 270° F. Pour over Popcorn and stir. Dip hands in water or oil and roll lightly into balls.

CHOCOLATE BALLS

½ pound sweet chocolate
1 egg
2 tablespoons butter

chocolate sprinkles, chopped roasted
almonds, or pistachio nuts

Melt chocolate in double boiler, add egg, stir until smooth, then stir in butter. When cool, form into balls, roll quickly in chocolate sprinkles or chopped roasted almonds or pistachio nuts.

NUT BARS   *Makes about 1 pound.*

½ pound semisweet chocolate
¼ teaspoon salt

⅔ cup seeded raisins, finely chopped
⅔ cup chopped peanuts

Melt chocolate over hot water. Stir until smooth and nearly cool, then add salt, chopped raisins, and nuts. Mix well, spread in buttered shallow pan to ¼ inch depth. When set, cut into strips.

RUM OR BOURBON BALLS   *Makes about 1 pound.*

½ pound vanilla wafers
1 cup pecans, finely chopped
2 teaspoons cocoa

½ cup light corn syrup
¼ cup rum or bourbon
confectioners' sugar

Crush wafers very fine. Add nuts, cocoa, syrup, and rum. Stir until well blended. Dust hands with confectioners' sugar and roll mixture into balls the size of a walnut. Let stand for about 1 hour to dry partially. Then roll in confectioners' sugar.

PRESERVES, JAMS, MARMALADES, AND CONSERVES

Preserves, jams, marmalades, and conserves are made by cooking fruits—and sometimes vegetables—with anywhere from ¾ to their full weight in sugar. They retain their best flavor and bright color if not more than 2 to 4 cups are cooked at a time. Jams made with pectin require less boiling. They require extra sugar but produce more jam and jelly. Some fruits are naturally more sweet than others. Riper fruit requires less addition of sugar than young "green" fruit. Always select the most perfect fruit possible for best results.

Special glass jars are best for preserving. Follow manufacturer's instructions. These jars come with rubber gaskets and screw-band lids with separate metal disks. They should be scrubbed clean with hot, soapy water then rinsed well and sterilized before filling. All equipment used in the processing process must be clean. Seals must be secure and tight fitting to prevent danger of spoilage.

Virtually all of the recipes in this chapter are heirloom. We find that the strength of the book comes from time-honored recipes like the ones found within. We've kept them intact because they are still so appealing.

Preserving seasonal offerings to be enjoyed at a time when such foods were not available reflects the traditional, frugal approach of The Settlement Cookbook. The jams, marmalades, conserves, pickles, relishes, and condiments featured here are still useful in today's busy kitchen.

Using Less Sugar in Preserves, Jams, and Marmalades

In any recipe, up to ⅓ of the granulated sugar may be replaced with corn syrup. Up to ½ of the granulated sugar may be replaced with honey. This requires longer cooking. Substitutions should be made with care, since the sugar is a preservative as well as a sweetening agent.

Packing Preserves

Pour hot preserves into hot, sterilized jars. Seal at once, with a thin layer of melted paraffin, or a sheet of flexible plastic wrap cut to cover the surface, or a special jar cover. In warm climates, or if storage conditions are poor, process 10 to 20 minutes in a water bath, at simmering point, before sealing.

Preserves

STRAWBERRY PRESERVES

1 quart strawberries   1½–2 cups sugar

1. Wash, drain, and hull berries carefully.
2. In a preserving kettle, arrange berries and sugar in layers of 1 cup strawberries and 1 cup sugar. Let stand overnight.
3. Bring to a boil and boil rapidly 10 to 12 minutes, or until juice is clear. Cover and let stand overnight.
4. Before packing, reheat to boiling and pack in hot sterilized jelly glasses or jars and seal while hot.

SUNSHINE STRAWBERRIES

1 quart strawberries   4 cups sugar

Put alternate layers of berries and sugar in the preserving kettle. Heat slowly to the boiling point. Skim carefully. Boil rapidly for 10 minutes. Pour on platters, cover with glass propped up about ¼ inch from platter. Let stand in full sunshine 2 or 3 days, until syrup has formed a jelly. After each day's sunning, turn the berries. Take in house at night. Without reheating, pack jelled preserves in hot, sterilized jars and seal.

Variation:

Sunshine Currants or Cherries: Select large, firm red or white fruit, remove the stems, and proceed as for Sunshine Strawberries, above. Stone the cherries before measuring them.

GINGER APPLE PRESERVES

1 quart tart apples
2 cups water
2 cups brown sugar, firmly packed

juice and grated rind of 1 lemon
6 1-inch pieces gingerroot

Wipe, pare, quarter, core, and cut the apples into small cubes. Boil water, sugar, and lemon juice 5 minutes or until clear. Add apples, lemon rind and gingerroot and cook slowly 2 or more hours until thick and brown. Pour into hot, sterilized jars and seal.

BEET PRESERVES

4 pounds beets
6 cups sugar
2 ounces fresh or dried gingerroot,
    blanched and thinly sliced

rind and juice of 3 lemons
¼ pound blanched almonds, finely
    ground

Wash and peel young beets, grind or slice very thin. Cover with water and cook until tender. Add sugar, gingerroot, lemon rind and juice. Cook gently until thick and clear, about 1 hour. When nearly done, add almonds. Pour into hot, sterilized glasses and seal.

CHERRY OR RASPBERRY PRESERVES

5 pounds cherries or raspberries   10 cups sugar

Wash raspberries, or wash and stone the cherries. Place alternate layers of sugar and fruit in kettle; let stand overnight. Bring slowly to a boil and boil rapidly until thick and clear. Pour into hot sterilized glasses and seal.

GRAPE PRESERVES

4 pounds Concord grapes   8 cups sugar
½ cup water

Wash, drain and remove stems from grapes. Heat grapes and water to the boiling point and cook until the seeds are free. Rub through a fine sieve or food mill. Discard seeds and skins. For each cup of fruit add 1 cup of sugar. Simmer for 30 minutes, stirring occasionally to prevent burning. Pour into hot sterilized glasses and seal.

WHOLE PRESERVED KUMQUATS

1 quart kumquats	1½ cups water
1½ cups sugar	

Wash kumquats thoroughly, cut two slight gashes at right angles across blossom end. Make a syrup of sugar and water. Cool, add kumquats, cover the kettle and cook gently 1 hour or until clear. Do not remove cover until the fruit is cold. Put into sterilized jars, cover with syrup and seal.

GINGER PEAR PRESERVES

5 pounds pears	4 lemons, rind cut into long thin
8 cups sugar	strips and juice reserved
¼ pound conserved ginger, finely chopped	

Pare, quarter, core, and remove the stems of the pears and cut into small slices. Add sugar, ginger, lemon rind and juice. Mix all together and let stand overnight. Cook slowly for 3 hours, or until thick and clear. Pour into hot, sterilized jars and seal.

QUINCE PRESERVES

4 pounds quinces	sugar

Wash, peel, core and cut quinces in ½-inch cubes. Add cold water to cover, boil until tender. Drain juice and reserve. For each cup of fruit use 1 cup of sugar. Boil juice and sugar 5 minutes, add fruit. Boil until fruit is clear and deep red. Pour into hot sterilized jars and seal.

RUSSIAN-STYLE RADISH PRESERVES

1 quart black radishes	1 ounce gingerroot, diced
1 quart strained honey	

Cut radishes into thin slices ¼ inch by 1 inch, or grate coarsely. Cook in boiling water 3 or 4 minutes. Drain and dry. Add honey and gingerroot and cook until mixture sheets from the side of a spoon (see page 687). Pour into hot sterilized jelly glasses and seal. Served mixed with sliced almonds.

RHUBARB AND FIG PRESERVES

½ pound figs

5 cups sugar

2 pounds rhubarb

juice and grated rind of 2 lemons

Wash figs and rhubarb and cut into small pieces. Add sugar, lemon juice, and grated rind and stir until juice is formed. Cook gently for 45 minutes, until thick and clear. Pour into hot sterilized glasses and seal.

GREEN TOMATO PRESERVES

1 quart sliced green tomatoes

grated rind and pulp of 1 lemon

1 quart sugar

1 stick cinnamon

Place tomatoes in a skillet. Add sugar, lemon rind and pulp, and cinnamon. Let stand for several hours to draw juice. Cook until tomatoes are thick and clear. Pour into hot, sterilized glasses and seal.

TOMATO PRESERVES

1 pound yellow pear tomatoes or
  red tomatoes

1 cup water

2 ounces conserved ginger

2 cups sugar

grated rind and juice of 1 lemon

If using yellow tomatoes slice them. If red tomatoes are used, scald and peel them. Make a syrup with sugar and water. Cover tomatoes with syrup and let stand overnight. Drain the syrup into preserving kettle and boil until thick; skim. Add ginger, grated rind and juice of lemon, and tomato pulp. Cook until preserve is clear. Pour into hot sterilized glasses and seal.

1-2-3 PRESERVE

1 pineapple, peeled, cored, and cut
  into thin wedges

3 quarts strawberries, washed and
  hulled

2 oranges, sliced very thin

8 cups sugar

In a preserving kettle mix fruit with sugar until the sugar is dissolved. Boil for 1 hour and 15 minutes. Pour into hot sterilized glasses and seal with paraffin.

BAKED CRABAPPLE PRESERVES

2½ pounds crabapples	4 cups sugar
¼ cup water	

Preheat oven to 250° F. Wash, dry and remove the blossom ends of large red crabapples. Pour water into bottom of a large casserole or covered baking dish. Add apples and sugar in alternate layers, the sugar on top. Cover and bake 2 to 3 hours, basting 3 or 4 times with the hot syrup. Pack in sterilized glasses and seal.

Variations:

Baked Seckel Pear Preserves: Prepare like Baked Crabapple Preserves. Flavor with ginger or lemon juice, if desired.

Baked Quince Preserves: Quinces may be wiped, cored and quartered, and baked like Baked Crabapple Preserves, in a slow oven, 250° F, 3 or more hours until translucent.

APPLE BUTTER

1 peck apples	3 pounds sugar
4 quarts water	3 teaspoons cinnamon
2 quarts sweet cider	1½ teaspoons cloves

Wash the apples and cut into small pieces. Add the water; boil until the apples are soft; rub apples through a sieve or food mill, discard the skin and seeds. Boil cider until it is reduced by half; add hot apple pulp, sugar, and spices, and cook until thick enough to spread. Stir constantly to prevent scorching. Pour into hot, sterilized jars and seal.

Jams

APRICOT JAM

4 pounds pitted apricots, pits reserved

8 cups sugar

1. Combine sugar and fruit and let stand overnight.
2. Crack apricot pits, remove nut, blanch and slice.
3. In a large preserving kettle, cook fruit and sugar until thickened, about 20 to 25 minutes.
4. Add some of the sliced nuts before pouring into hot, sterilized glasses. Seal.

DRIED APRICOT JAM

1 pound dried apricots
1 orange, cut into small pieces

1 cup seedless raisins
1½ cups sugar

1. Wash apricots and cover with cold water to soak for 1 hour.
2. Drain apricots and reserve ¾ cup of the soaking liquid.
3. In a preserving kettle, combine apricots, orange pieces, raisins, sugar, and reserved saoking liquid. Cook slowly until thick, about 1 hour.
4. Pour into hot sterilized glasses and seal.

BLUEBERRY AND CRABAPPLE JAM

3 quarts crabapples
1 quart blueberries

10–12 cups sugar

Cut crabapples into quarters, core but do not peel, and coarsely chop. In a large preserving kettle, combine the chopped crabapples with enough water to almost cover and cook for 10 minutes. Add berries and sugar, cook until clear. Pour into hot sterilized glasses, cool and seal.

PEACH JAM

5 pounds peaches, peeled, pitted, and sliced, pits reserved

7 cups sugar

In a large preserving kettle, combine the sliced peaches with the sugar and a few of the peach pits. Slowly bring to a boil, stirring until the sugar is dissolved. Then cook rapidly for 30 minutes. Remove the pits. When the mixture jells, pour into hot sterilized glasses and seal.

STRAWBERRY-RHUBARB JAM

3 cups rhubarb
3 cups strawberries

4 cups sugar

Use tender, red rhubarb. Trim off hard ends, wash, and without skinning, cut into small pieces. Mix strawberries with rhubarb and sugar; let stand for several hours. Cook gently until thick and clear. Pour into hot sterilized jars and seal.

Marmalades

CARROT MARMALADE

3 pounds peeled and grated, raw carrots
6 cups sugar

grated rind and juice of 6 lemons
¼ pound grated almonds

1. In a large saucepan, cover grated carrots with water and cook until tender. Press through a strainer.
2. In a large preserving kettle, combine carrots with sugar, lemon rind, and juice and cook gently about ½ hour, or until thick and clear. When nearly done, add almonds. Put into sterilized glasses and seal.

CITRUS MARMALADE

2 whole grapefruit
2 oranges cut into small pieces

2 lemons cut into small pieces
sugar

(continued)

1.   Wash fruit. Peel the rind off the grapefruit and cut into fine strips. Discard the thick white pith. Remove core and seeds of grapefruit.

2.   In a large preserving kettle, mix oranges, lemons, grapefruit pulp, and grapefruit rind. Add three times as much water as fruit and let stand overnight.

3.   Boil for 10 minutes. Remove from heat, cover and let stand for 24 hours. Repeat process.

4.   On the third day, measure an equal amount of sugar, and boil 1 hour, or until thick. Pour into sterilized glasses and seal.

ORANGE MARMALADE

4 oranges	cold water
1 lemon	sugar

1.   Wash fruit, cut in half, remove seeds and stem end. Slice very thin or finely grind. For every cup of fruit add 1½ cups cold water. Let stand overnight.

2.   Pour into a preserving kettle, cook slowly from 1 to 2 hours or until tender; again let stand overnight.

3.   Measure fruit and for each cup add 1 cup of sugar and cook 20 minutes or until mixture sheets from the side of a spoon (see page 687). Pour into hot sterilized glasses and seal.

GOLDEN CHIP MARMALADE

6 pounds pumpkin, peeled, seeded, and cut into cubes	4 lemons, thinly sliced
2 ounces fresh gingerroot	1 quart water
	6 cups sugar

1.   In a large preserving kettle, combine pumpkin, ginger, lemons, and water. Let stand overnight.

2.   Simmer until tender, add sugar and cook until mixture sheets from the side of a spoon (see page 687). Pour into hot sterilized glasses and seal.

PINEAPPLE-GRAPEFRUIT MARMALADE

1 pineapple, peeled, cored, and shredded	1 unpeeled lemon, cut into quarters, then into thin slices
1 unpeeled grapefruit, cut into quarters, then into thin slices	sugar

1. Measure fruit and cover with water, 3 pints water to 1 pint fruit. Let stand overnight.

2. Boil 3 or more hours until the rind is very tender. Let stand overnight.

3. Measure and add an equal amount of sugar. Boil until a drop jells on a cold plate. Pour into sterilized glasses and seal.

Conserves

CHERRY CONSERVES

5 pounds ripe cherries, washed, stemmed, and pitted
1½ pounds seedless raisins, washed

10 cups sugar
juice of 4 oranges
juice of 2 lemons

In a large preserving kettle, mix all the ingredients and let stand overnight. Boil slowly and steadily for several hours, or until thick and clear. Pour into hot sterilized jars and seal.

CRANBERRY CONSERVE

1 quart cranberries, washed and picked over
1½ cups water
¼ pound raisins

1 orange, coarsely chopped
3 cups sugar
½ pound walnuts, chopped

Boil cranberries with half the water until they burst. Add the remaining ingredients and boil 25 minutes. Pour into hot sterilized jars and seal.

GOOSEBERRY CONSERVE

3 large oranges
3 pounds gooseberries, washed and stemmed

6 cups sugar
1 pound seedless raisins

Grate the rind of the oranges and chop the pulp. In a large preserving kettle, mix all the ingredients and slowly cook until thick. Pour into hot sterilized jars and seal.

GRAPE CONSERVE

8 pounds Concord grapes, washed
and stemmed
3 or 4 oranges, finely chopped
2 lemons, finely chopped

1 pound seeded raisins or thinly
sliced figs
sugar

1.   In a large preserving kettle, combine the grapes with a little water and simmer until the seeds are free. Press the pulp through a sieve, discarding seeds and stems.

2.   Mix the grape pulp with the remaining fruit and measure. For each cup of fruit add a cup of sugar and boil until thick.

3.   Pour into hot sterilized jelly glasses and seal.

FOUR FRUIT CONSERVE

1 quart sour cherries, washed,
stemmed, and pitted
1 quart currants, cleaned and
stemmed

1 quart raspberries
1 quart gooseberries, cleaned and
stemmed
sugar

Combine the fruits and measure. For each cup add 1 scant cup of sugar. In a large preserving kettle, cook fruit for 20 minutes, stirring often to prevent burning. Add sugar and cook 5 to 10 minutes longer. Pour into hot sterilized jars and seal.

PEAR CONSERVE

1 peck pears, peeled, cored, and
sliced into large pieces crosswise
8 cups sugar
1 pound seedless raisins

1½ pounds broken walnut meats
juice of 3 lemons
juice of 3 oranges

Combine pears and sugar and let stand overnight. Drain the liquid into a kettle and boil to a syrup, about 12 minutes. Add pears and ingredients to the syrup and cook slowly until thick and clear, about 1 hour. Pour into hot sterilized jars and seal.

PEAR AND APPLE CONSERVE

9 hard pears, peeled, quartered, and cored

6 tart apples, peeled, cored, and cut into ½-inch slices

2 ounces preserved ginger, cut into small pieces

sugar

rind and juice of 1½ lemons

1 cup water

Combine pears, apples, and ginger and measure. For each cup of fruit use 1 cup of sugar. In a large preserving kettle, add the remaining ingredients and boil ¾ of an hour or until thick and clear. Pour into hot sterilized jars and seal.

PLUM CONSERVE

3 pounds blue plums, washed, pitted, and cut into small pieces

1 pound seedless raisins

3 oranges cut into small pieces

juice of 2 lemons

6 cups sugar

In a large preserving kettle, combine all ingredients and cook until the fruit is thick and clear. Pour into hot sterilized jars and seal.

QUINCE CONSERVE

4 medium quinces, peeled and thinly sliced

3 large tart apples, peeled, cored, and coarsely chopped

½ cup maraschino cherries, finely chopped

1 cup seedless raisins

¼ pound pitted prunes

¼ pound dried figs, coarsely chopped

1 quart water

4 cups sugar

In a large preserving kettle, combine all ingredients except for the sugar and cook slowly until the quinces are tender. Add sugar and slowly bring to a boil. Cook until thick and clear. Pour into hot sterilized jars and seal.

RHUBARB CONSERVE

3 cups rhubarb, coarsely chopped
3 cups sugar
juice and finely grated rind of 3
  oranges

juice and finely grated rind of 1
  lemon
½ pound coarsely chopped almonds

In a large preserving kettle, combine rhubarb, sugar, and juice and rind of the oranges and lemon. Cook slowly for 30 minutes. Add almonds and cook 5 minutes longer. Pour into hot sterilized jars and seal.

Jelly

A good jelly is clear and bright in color. It should be tender and quivery, but firm enough to hold its shape.

Preparing the Fruit

Use small quantities: 2 pounds or 4 cups of prepared fruit will make about 2 cups juice; 2 cups fruit juice mixed with 1½ cups sugar makes about 2 cups jelly.

Larger fruit should be washed, stemmed, and cut into quarters. Add water to cover and cook, covered, until tender. Berries, currants, grapes, and other juicy fruits should be mashed with a spoon or masher. They need very little water, as mashing releases their own juices.

Extracting the Juice

Put cooked fruit into a jelly bag (see below) and let it drip for several hours or overnight. Do not squeeze the bag if a clear jelly is wanted. It is possible to make a second extraction, for a less clear jelly, after the first clear juice has been taken off. Add a small amount of water to the pulp remaining in the bag, reheat the mixture, return it to the bag and squeeze it through.

Cooking Jelly

Cook in an enamel preserving kettle or pan. Measure the fruit juice. Allow ¾ to 1 cup sugar for each cup of juice according to the amount of natural pectin in the fruit. (See Pectin, page 688.) Fruit with less pectin requires more sugar. Boil the juice rapidly for 5 minutes to reduce it slightly, add the sugar and boil rapidly until the mixture reaches the jelly point (see below). Skim the froth from the jelly, pour at once into hot sterilized glasses and seal (see below).

Substitutions for Sugar in Jelly

Substitutions must be made with care, since the sugar is a preservative as well as a sweetening agent. Up to half the sugar called for may be replaced with an equal measure of honey, or up to one fourth the sugar with an equal measure of corn syrup. Adding these liquids instead of sugar increases the cooking time.

Testing for "Jelly Point"

A thermometer is the most reliable way to judge when the mixture has reached the jelly point, the point at which it will stiffen when it is cold. The thermometer should hang down the inside of the kettle with the bulb completely covered with jelly, but it should not touch the bottom of the kettle.

The "jelly point" is reached at 8° F above the boiling point of water in a given area; that is, at 220° F in localities where water boils at 212° F.

"Jelly point" tests that can be used when a thermometer is not available include the "sheet test": When a spoon filled with jelly is tilted, two drops poured from the side of the spoon flow together and fall as one. Or, a few drops of jelly may be spooned onto a cold plate and quickly chilled. When a spoon drawn through this jelly leaves a track, it indicates that the rest will stiffen sufficiently when it is cold.

Making a Jelly Bag

Make a bag of cotton cloth or several thicknesses of cheesecloth. Place the cooked fruit in the bag and hang it over a bowl to catch juice as it drips. Or place the bag in a colander set inside a bowl. Pour the fruit into the bag, gather the top ends of the bag and tie securely. Then lift the bag from the colander and hang it over a bowl.

Filling and Sealing Jelly Glasses

Wash glasses thoroughly, place in cold water, bring to boiling point gradually and boil 5 minutes. Keep hot. When ready to use, drain without handling the inside. Set glasses on a board or on hot, wet cloth and fill. To prevent cracking glasses, place sterilized spoon in glass. Pour in jelly at once, filling to ½ inch from top. Pour a tablespoon of melted paraffin over the surface. (To melt paraffin, break into small pieces and place over very low heat.) When jelly is cool and the paraffin is set, wipe off any jelly splashes around top and fill with melted paraffin. Protect the paraffin with a cover of metal or paper. Label the glasses.

Suitable Fruits for Jelly

Fruit should be fresh, just ripe or a little underripe. Juicy fruits, currants, and raspberries should not be gathered after a rain. Currants, sour apples, crabapples, underripe grapes, quinces, wild cherries, and green gooseberries contain ample amounts of natural pectin and make the best jellies.

Wild Fruits for Jelly

Wild raspberries, blackberries, barberries, grapes, and beach plums all make good jellies. Failure in making these occurs because the fruit is not fresh, or because it is overripe.

Pectin

Pectin is the natural substance in some fruit that, when heated and combined with fruit acid and sugar, causes the mixture to congeal or jell. All fruits do not contain this substance. The acid and pectin may be supplied by the addition of the juice of apples, plums, quince, etc., or homemade apple or commercial pectin. To use commercial pectin, either liquid or powdered, follow the manufacturer's directions accurately for the best results.

HOMEMADE APPLE PECTIN

4 pounds apples, skins and cores   9 cups water

1. Select hard, tart apples. Remove any bruised spots. Cut into thin slices.
2. In a large enamel kettle, combine apples and water and bring quickly to the boiling point. Cover and let boil rapidly for 20 minutes.
3. Remove from heat and strain apple pulp through a jelly bag, or let drip through 4 thicknesses of cheesecloth. When juice stops dripping, press pulp lightly with a spoon, but do not squeeze bag. Set juice aside.
4. Remove pulp from the bag and weigh or measure it. Add to it an equal amount of water. Boil again for 20 minutes and strain again as above.
5. Pour the 2 extractions into a large, shallow pan so that liquid is not more than 2 inches deep. Boil rapidly 30 to 45 minutes, or until liquid is reduced to 1½ pints (or about ½ inch deep in the pan).
6. If not to be used immediately, pour at once into hot, sterilized 4-ounce jars and seal.

APPLE JELLY

4 pounds apples, washed and cut   water
     into pieces (include peels, cores,   sugar
     and seeds)

1. In a large enamel kettle, combine the apples with enough cold water to cover and cook until very soft.
2. Remove from heat and strain pulp through a jelly bag.
3. Measure strained juice and combine with an equal amount of sugar. Bring to a boil and cook to the jelly point (page 687). Flavor with vanilla or other extracts, if desired.
4. Pour hot jelly into hot sterilized glasses and seal.

CRABAPPLE JELLY

8 quarts underripe crabapples,
washed and cut in half (include
peels and seeds)

4 quarts water
sugar
rose geranium leaves (optional)

1. In a large enamel kettle, boil apples in water until soft.
2. Remove from heat. Mash and strain through a jelly bag.
3. Measure juice and use an equal amount of sugar. Add a few rose geranium leaves, if desired. Boil juice 5 minutes, add sugar and continue to boil to the jelly point (page 687).
4. Skim and pour hot jelly into hot sterilized glasses and seal.

Note: Crabapple sauce may be made by straining the pulp after the juice has dripped through. Add sugar and cinnamon or lemon juice to taste, and heat only long enough to dissolve the sugar.

BERRY JELLY WITH PECTIN

2 quarts blackberries, boysenberries,
or dewberries
½ cup water

lemon juice as needed
1 box powdered pectin
5 cups sugar

1. In a large enamel kettle, mash the berries. Add water and slowly bring to the boiling point. Boil rapidly for a few minutes until the berries are soft.
2. Remove from heat and strain fruit through a jelly bag.
3. If berries are quite ripe and mild in flavor, add 1 teaspoon lemon juice to each cup of berry juice. Mix juice with pectin and stir over high heat until the mixture boils hard. Immediately stir in the sugar. Bring to a full rolling boil, then boil hard for 1 minute, stirring constantly.
4. Remove from heat and skim off foam with a metal spoon. Pour hot jelly into hot sterilized jars and seal.

CHERRY JELLY TIPS

Unless cherries are very tart and underripe they will not make stiff jelly. Combine them with other fruits, such as currants or underripe gooseberries, or add pectin and proceed according to the manufacturer's directions.

CRANBERRY JELLY

Make Cranberry Sauce (page 414). Pour hot jelly into hot sterilized jars and seal.

CURRANT-RASPBERRY JELLY

4 quarts currants, washed, stems intact

4 pints raspberries
sugar

1. In a large enamel kettle, mash the fruit and cook slowly until the currants are nearly white.
2. Remove from heat and strain through a jelly bag.
3. Measure juice and stir in an equal amount of sugar. Boil over high heat to the jelly point (page 687).
4. Skim and pour hot jelly into hot sterilized jars and seal.

BAR-LE-DUC (CURRANT JELLY)

1 pound large currants, washed and stemmed

1½ cups sugar

1. In a large enamel kettle, combine currants and sugar and let stand over-night.
2. Bring slowly to a boil, stirring until the sugar dissolves. Cook rapidly to the jelly point (page 687). Stir occasionally to prevent sticking.
3. Skim. Pour hot jelly into hot, sterilized jars and seal.

Black Currant Jelly: Substitute black currants for the currants in Currant Jelly. Proceed as for above.

ELDERBERRY JELLY

2 quarts elderberries
2 quarts apples, cut into small chunks (include peels, core, stem, and seeds)

sugar

(continued)

1.   In a large enamel kettle, combine fruit with enough cold water to cover and boil until soft.

2.   Remove from heat. Mash fruit and strain through a jelly bag.

3.   Measure juice and use an equal amount of sugar. Boil juice, skim and add sugar. Boil to the jelly point (page 687).

4.   Pour hot jelly into hot sterilized jars and seal.

GRAPE JELLY

4 pounds tart, underripe grapes, washed and stemmed

4 cups tart apples, diced (include peels, cores, stems, and seeds)
sugar

1.   In a large enamel kettle, combine grapes and apples and boil until the seeds are free.

2.   Remove from heat. Press fruit through a colander, then strain through a jelly bag.

3.   Measure juice and to every 1 cup juice use ¾ cup of sugar. Bring juice to a boil, add sugar and cook to the jelly point (page 687).

SPICED GRAPE JELLY

8 quarts wild grapes or 12 pounds Concord grapes
1 quart vinegar

¼ cup whole cloves
6 sticks cinnamon
12 cups sugar

1.   In a large enamel kettle, combine the grapes, vinegar, and spices and cook until the grapes are soft.

2.   Remove from heat and strain through a jelly bag.

3.   Boil the strained juice for 20 minutes, add sugar and boil to the jelly point (page 687), about 5 minutes.

4.   Pour hot jelly into hot, sterilized jelly jars and seal.

Note: This jelly is especially good with venison and other game.

GUAVA JELLY

1 quart green guavas (if guavas are   sugar
ripe, add a little lime or lemon
juice), blossoms and stems
removed and thinly sliced

1. In a large enamel kettle, combine the guava slices with enough cold water to cover and boil slowly until fruit is very soft.
2. Remove from heat and strain fruit through a jelly bag.
3. Measure juice and use an equal amount of sugar. Boil juice 10 minutes, add sugar and boil to the jelly point (page 687).
4. Pour hot jelly into hot, sterilized jars and seal.

MINT JELLY

 4 quarts mild, sweet apples (Golden   sugar
Delicious or Rome Beauty),   ½ cup fresh mint leaves
washed, ends removed, and cut   2 tablespoons lemon juice
into quarters

1. In a large enamel kettle, combine apples with enough cold water to cover. Cover and cook slowly until apples are soft.
2. Remove from heat. Mash fruit and strain through a jelly bag.
3. Measure juice and use an equal amount of sugar. Boil juice for 5 minutes, add sugar and boil for 2 minutes. Add mint leaves and boil to the jelly point (page 687). Stir in lemon juice.
4. Strain hot jelly into hot, sterilized jars and seal.

PLUM JELLY

4 quarts underripe, tart plums,   sugar
washed and stems removed

1. In a large enamel kettle, combine fruit with enough cold water to cover and simmer until the plums are very soft.
2. Remove from heat and strain fruit through a jelly bag.
3. Measure juice and use an equal amount of sugar. Boil juice for 5 minutes, add sugar and boil to the jelly point (page 687).
4. Pour hot jelly into hot sterilized jars and seal.

PEACH JELLY

The skins from peaches used for home canning may be used to make juice for jelly. Cover the skins with water, boil hard and strain. Reduce to 2 cups.

2 cups peach juice
2 cups apple juice

juice of ½ lemon
3 cups sugar

In a large enamel kettle, combine peach, apple, and lemon juice. Bring to a boil, add sugar and boil rapidly to the jelly point (page 687). Remove from heat. Skim and pour hot jelly into hot, sterilized jars and seal.

QUINCE JELLY

Use the peels, cores (toss out the seeds), and the imperfect parts of the quince for this jelly. Reserve the nicer pieces of the fruit in a bowl half full of cold water and can them or use them to make preserves.

4 quarts quince, washed, blossom
    ends removed, and finely
    chopped

sugar

In a large enamel kettle, combine the peels, cores, and finely chopped pieces of quince. Add a cup of water for every 2 cups of fruit and cook gently for 2 hours. Remove from heat. Strain and finish as for Apple Jelly (page 689).

RASPBERRY-APPLE JELLY

2 quarts apples, washed and
    quartered
5 pints red raspberries

sugar

1. In a large enamel kettle combine the apples and berries with enough cold water to cover and cook until the apples are very soft.
2. Remove from heat and strain fruit through a jelly bag.
3. Measure juice and use an equal amount of sugar. Boil juice for 5 minutes, add sugar and boil to the jelly point (page 687).
4. Skim and pour hot jelly into hot sterilized jars and seal.

BLACK RASPBERRY JELLY

If a firm jelly is desired add 1 unpeeled tart apple, sliced thin, for every quart of berries.

4 quarts black raspberries   sugar
1 cup water

1. In a large enamel kettle, combine berries and water and heat slowly to the boiling point.
2. Remove from heat and strain fruit through a jelly bag.
3. Measure juice and use an equal amount of sugar. Boil juice for 5 minutes, add sugar and boil to the jelly point (page 687).
4. Pour hot jelly into hot, sterilized jelly jars and seal.

Variation:

Blackberry Jelly: Follow directions for Black Raspberry Jelly, above.

Pickles and Relishes

Cucumbers for pickling must be fresh when picked, not over 24 hours old. Kirbys are always a good choice, especially when young and tender. Dill is best when seeds are full grown, but not so ripe that the seeds fall off the stalk. Do not use iodized salt. Use kosher salt or sea salt. Use a good, clear pickling vinegar (4 to 6 percent acid).

Pickles will spoil if not kept completely under the brine. Use half as much brine as measure of cucumbers. To hasten dissolving of salt, mix with small amount of water, then add rest of the water.

Notes: Follow manufacturer's instructions for sterilizing jars.

These quantities may often seem too large. Simply reduce to desired amount, maintaining proportions listed.

Brine

A salt brine is a solution of 1 cup salt to 5 cups water. A weak brine, 1 cup salt to 9 cups water, will cause quicker fermentation, but pickles kept in this brine will spoil in a few weeks, unless the scum that rises to top of jars is constantly skimmed off and the brine is kept clear.

It is best, when all fermentation stops and the pickles are done, to remove them to jars, cover them with their own brine, or add fresh-cooled brine, and seal.

Pickles will shrivel if too much sugar or salt is added or if the vinegar is too strong. Pickles that are cured (salt or dill pickles) may be made into sweet, sour, or mixed pickles and will not shrivel.

DO'S AND DON'TS FOR PICKLING
- Soak pickles in pottery crock, glass, or enamel container, *never in metal*.
- Cook in enamel-lined kettle, not in metal.
- Avoid corrosion by storing in glass jars with glass tops.

Salting Cucumbers for Future Use

Cucumbers picked fresh from the vines every day may be preserved in strong salt brine for storing until they are made into sweet, sour, or mixed pickles. Leave from ¼-inch to ½-inch stems on cucumbers, wash carefully without removing the prickles; put them, as they are gathered, into a large stone crock. Make brine (see below) to half fill the crock, which will completely cover the pickles. When ready to use, first soak the pickles in cold water until freshened.

SUMMER DILL PICKLES

100 large cucumbers	*Brine*
dill blossoms	1 cup salt
bay leaves	6 quarts water
1 ounce black peppercorns	1 cup vinegar (optional)
grape or cherry leaves	

1. Soak cucumbers in cold water overnight or 12 hours. Drain and dry.
2. Fill a crock with alternate double layers of cucumbers, then 3 or 4 blossom ends of dill, a bay leaf and a teaspoon of whole black pepper; repeat, covering top layer with dill and adding some cherry or grape leaves.
3. To make the brine, boil salt and water, cool and pour over the pickles to cover. Cover the surface with cloth. Weight well with a plate to keep pickles under brine. Let stand in a warm place to ferment for a week. Add 1 cup of vinegar if desired. Rinse off scum that rises and settles on the cloth, every day in warm weather and once or twice a week when cooler.

WINTER DILL PICKLES

100 cucumbers, 4 inches long
mustard seed
horseradish root
garlic (optional)
dill blossoms

Brine
6 quarts water
1 pint cider vinegar
¾ cups salt

1. Soak cucumbers overnight in cold water. Drain, wash, and dry.
2. Place 1 tablespoon mustard seed, a small piece of horseradish root, and, if desired, a clove of garlic in each 2-quart sterilized jar, add cucumbers and dill blossoms alternately until jar is filled.
3. To make brine, boil water, vinegar, and salt and pour over pickles to cover. Seal jars at once. If after a few days brine oozes out, wait until fermentation ceases, then open jars, add fresh brine to cover, and seal again.

SWEET PICKLES

100 large cucumbers
6 quarts water
1 cup salt
1 large bunch fresh sprigs dill

onion slices
8 cups sugar
4 cups cider vinegar

1. Wash and drain cucumbers. Place in a large crock.
2. Boil water with salt and pour over the cucumbers, add dill and let stand overnight. Drain and dry.
3. Cut cucumbers into slices. Place in jars, adding 2 onion slices to each jar.
4. Boil sugar and vinegar to make a syrup. Cool, pour over pickles and seal.

CRISP DILL PICKLES

100 cucumbers, 4 inches long,
   scrubbed
1 large bunch dill
1 small horseradish root, diced

Brine
10 quarts water
1 cup salt
¾ cup vinegar
alum (optional)
fresh sprigs dill

1. Soak cucumbers in salt water overnight (1 cup salt to 4 quarts water). Drain and wipe dry.

2. Place in 2-quart sterilized jars with layers of dill and small pieces horseradish.

3. To make brine, boil water, salt, and vinegar and pour over pickles. Add a small piece of alum to each jar if desired. Seal at once.

RIPE CUCUMBER PICKLES

12 large ripe cucumbers, peeled,
   seeded, and cut into chunks
1 cup salt
8 cups water
1 quart small white onions
6 stalks fresh dill
horseradish root, sliced
¼ cup mixed pickling spices

Brine
vinegar
1 tablespoon dry mustard
½ cup mustard seeds, inside a
   square of cheesecloth, tied
   securely

1. Peel onions, sprinkle with salt and let stand in a bowl overnight. In another large bowl, combine cucumbers with 1 cup salt and 8 cups water. Let stand 5 hours or more. Drain.

2. In a crock place alternate layers of cucumbers, onions, dill, a few slices of horseradish root, and mixed spices.

3. To make the brine, combine equal amounts of vinegar and water, mixed with dry mustard, and pour over pickles to cover. Place the bag filled with mustard seeds on top and let stand in a warm place for 3 days. Place cover on crock and let stand in a cool, dry place.

DILL BEANS

8 quarts wax beans, strings
    removed
½ ounce black peppercorns
2 large stalks fresh dill
6 bay leaves

6 grape or cherry leaves
4 quarts water
1 cup salt
1 cup vinegar (optional)

1. Cook beans in boiling salted water 5 to 7 minutes, allowing 1 teaspoon salt to each quart of water. Drain.

2. Pack layers of beans in a crock, adding a few peppercorns, a little dill, and some pieces of bay leaf. Repeat, covering top layer well with dill and adding the grape or cherry leaves.

3. Combine water and salt and bring to a boil. Cool and pour over beans to cover. Cover surface with a cloth. Weight well with a plate, to keep beans under brine. Let stand in a warm place to ferment for a week. Add 1 cup vinegar if desired. Rinse off scum that rises and settles on the cloth, every day in warm weather and once or twice a week when cooler.

PICKLED BEANS

Use as a salad or sweet and sour vegetable.

8 quarts wax beans, strings
    removed and cut into 1-inch
    pieces

1 cup vinegar
½ cup sugar

1. In a large pot of boiling, salted water blanch the beans until tender but still crisp. Drain and reserve 2 quarts of the cooking liquid.

2. Combine the reserved cooking liquid with the vinegar and sugar and bring to a simmer. Add the beans and bring to a boil.

3. Pour at once into sterilized jars and seal.

SWEET PICKLED BEANS

8 quarts green beans, washed,
    strings removed, and cut into 1-
    inch pieces
1 quart vinegar
1 quart water

2 cups sugar
1 tablespoon cloves
1 stick cinnamon, broken

(continued)

1. In a large pot of boiling salted water, cook the beans until tender but still crisp. Drain, dry, and pack into sterilized jars.

2. Combine the remaining ingredients and boil for 15 minutes. Cool, pour the liquid into the jars and seal.

PICKLED BEETS

1 quart cold cooked beets, peeled and sliced	1 teaspoon brown sugar
1 teaspoon salt	1 teaspoon caraway seeds
⅛ teaspoon pepper	1 pint vinegar

In a crock, layer the beets with salt, pepper, sugar, and caraway seeds. Cover with vinegar. Pour into sterilized jars and seal.

SWEEET PICKLED BEETS

3 cups beet cooking liquid	mace
1 cup sugar	2 quarts cold cooked beets, peeled and sliced
2 cups vinegar	
cloves	2 teaspoons pickling spice

1. Combine beet cooking liquid with the sugar, vinegar, a few cloves, and a little mace. Boil to a syrup, add beets and heat thoroughly.

2. Put 1 teaspoon pickling spice into each sterilized quart jar; fill with pickled beets to overflowing, and seal.

PICKLED CARROTS

2 pounds carrots, washed and peeled, cut in half lengthwise, then crosswise in 2-inch pieces	1 pint vinegar
	4 cups sugar
	¼ cup mixed pickling spices

1. In a large pot of boiling, salted water, cook carrots until tender but not broken. Drain. Reserve 2 cups of the cooking liquid.

2. Combine reserved cooking liquid with vinegar, sugar, and spices. Boil to a syrup, add carrots and simmer for several hours, until carrots are clear.

3. While still very hot, pack in hot, sterilized jars and seal.

PICKLED CABBAGE

Delicious served cold, or hot as a vegetable in place of sauerkraut. Keeps a long time.

4 teaspoons salt
4 quarts thinly sliced cabbage, red or white
½ teaspoon pepper
¼ cup mustard seed

1 cup sugar
¼ cup mixed pickling spices, tied in a square of cheesecloth
2 quarts vinegar, not too strong

1. Sprinkle salt over cabbage, mix thoroughly and let stand overnight.
2. Drain cabbage slightly, add pepper and mustard seed, mix and place in a crock.
3. Add sugar and pickling spices to the vinegar. Boil in a heavy, nonreactive pan for 1 to 2 minutes. Pour over cabbage. Cover and keep cool.

PICKLED ONIONS

4 quarts small white onions
1 cup salt
¼ cup mixed pickling spices, tied inside a square of cheesecloth

2 cups sugar
2 quarts vinegar

1. Pour boiling water over unpeeled onions to cover, let stand 2 minutes, drain, rinse with cold water, and peel.
2. Cover peeled onions with cold water, add salt and let stand overnight. Rinse and drain.
3. Combine spice bag and sugar with the vinegar and boil to a syrup. Remove spice bag, add onions and return to a boil.
4. While still hot, fill hot, sterilized jars and seal.

PICKLED RED PEPPERS

These make a great garnish for salads.

8 quarts red peppers, washed, stemmed, and seeded

2 cups sugar
1 quart vinegar

1. Cover peppers with boiling water, let stand for 2 minutes and drain. Place in ice water, let stand for another 10 minutes, drain well and pack solidly in sterilized pint jars.
2. Boil the sugar and vinegar, pour over the peppers to cover and seal.

GREEN DILL TOMATOES

50 small firm, green tomatoes
   (depending on size)
dill blossoms
bay leaves
1 ounce black peppercorns
grape or cherry leaves

Brine
1 cup salt
6 quarts water
1 cup vinegar (optional)

1. Soak tomatoes in cold water overnight or 12 hours. Drain and dry.

2. Fill a crock with alternate double layers of tomatoes, then 3 or 4 blossom ends of dill, a bay leaf, and a teaspoon of whole black pepper; repeat, covering top layer with dill and adding some cherry or grape leaves.

3. To make brine, boil salt and water, cool and pour brine over the tomatoes to cover. Cover the surface with cloth. Weight well with a plate to keep tomatoes under brine. Let stand in a warm place to ferment for a week. Add 1 cup of vinegar if desired. Rinse off scum that rises and settles on the cloth, every day in warm weather and once or twice a week when cooler.

CHOW-CHOW

1 quart very small cucumbers
1 quart large cucumbers, cut in
   cubes
1 quart green tomatoes, sliced
1 quart large onions, sliced
1 quart small onions
1 quart cauliflower

4 green peppers, seeded and
   chopped
1 cup flour
1½ cups sugar
6 tablespoons dry mustard
1 teaspoon powdered turmeric
3 pints vinegar

1. Combine the vegetables and cover with salt water, using 1 cup of salt to every 4 quarts water, and let stand for 24 hours.

2. The next day, slowly bring the vegetables to a boil, cook for 5 minutes and drain.

3. Mix the flour, sugar, mustard, and turmeric to a smooth paste with 1 pint of the vinegar. Heat remaining vinegar in a double boiler, add flour paste gradually and cook until thick, being careful not to boil.

4. Add paste to the hot vegetables. Pack in sterilized jars and seal.

Sauerkraut

OLD FASHIONED SAUERKRAUT

15 heads large, heavy cabbages
3–4 cups salt

24 tart apples, peeled and finely
chopped (optional)

1.   Remove and reserve the outer leaves of the cabbages. Cut the heads into quarters, core and shred.

2.   Into a large nonreactive pan, place about ¼ of the cabbage with ¼ cup salt. Mix thoroughly and pack into a crock. If desired, add a cup of finely chopped apples.

3.   Pound and stamp down the cabbage with a wooden stamper until the brine flows and covers the cabbage. Mix another ¼ of cabbage with ¼ cup salt and pack into the same crock, cover with apples and pound as before. Continue until all the cabbage is used, using as much salt as is required per each quarter of cabbage. Cover with reserved cabbage leaves and a fitted square of cloth. Weight down with a board and stone to keep the contents under the brine. Leave enough space in the crock for the cabbage to swell without overflowing. Put in a warm place to ferment and let stand for 2 weeks.

4.   Remove the stone and board and carefully lift off the cloth, picking it up at the corners to catch all the scum. Wash cloth, stone, board and sides of the crock; cover again with cloth, stone and board and remove to a cool place. Sauerkraut is now ready to use. Remove scum and wash cloth board and stone weekly as long as kraut lasts.

Note: The fermented kraut may be also packed in jars. Cover with brine, heat thoroughly in a hot-water bath, and seal. If there is not enough brine add ¼ cup salt mixed with 1 quart of water.

Relishes

SWEET BEET AND CABBAGE RELISH

2 quarts boiled beets, peeled and
chopped
2 quarts cabbage, chopped
1 cup grated horseradish

2 cups sugar
2 teaspoons salt
freshly ground black pepper to taste
cold vinegar

Combine beets, cabbage, horseradish, sugar, salt, and pepper in a gallon jar. Add vinegar to cover and store in a cool place.

BEET RELISH

3 cups chopped cold boiled beets
½ cup grated horseradish root
¼ teaspoon pepper

1 teaspoon salt
2 tablespoons sugar
¾ cup vinegar

Mix beets and horseradish, season with pepper, salt, and sugar. Add as much vinegar as the beets and horseradish will absorb. Store in the refrigerator in a covered jar.

ENGLISH CHUTNEY

1 pound apples, peeled, cored, and chopped
¾ pound seedless raisins, chopped
1 dozen ripe tomatoes, chopped
2 red peppers, seeded and chopped
6 small onions, peeled and chopped

¼ cup mint leaves, chopped
1 ounce white mustard seed
¼ cup salt
2 cups brown sugar, firmly packed
1 quart vinegar, boiled and cooled

Combine all ingredients and cook slowly until thick and clear. Fill small sterilized jars and seal.

CORN RELISH

1 quart raw corn, cut from the cob
3 cups chopped cabbage
1 cup chopped celery
2 red peppers, seeded
2 green peppers, seeded

1 onion, peeled
1 cup sugar
2 tablespoons salt
3 cups vinegar

1. Grind or chop together the corn, cabbage, celery, peppers, and onion.
2. Combine chopped vegetables with the remaining ingredients and cook until the corn is tender, about 15 minutes.
3. Bottle in sterilized jars and seal.

CUCUMBER RELISH

2 green cucumbers, peeled, seeded, and chopped
2 cups finely chopped celery
1 tablespoon salt
1 cup vinegar
¼ cup sugar

dash of cayenne pepper
2 tablespoons horseradish
1 tablespoon chopped onion
1 tablespoon chopped green pepper
1 teaspoon black pepper

1. Combine cucumbers and celery, sprinkle with salt and drain overnight in a cheesecloth bag. Rinse well and drain.

2. Mix with remaining ingredients and serve immediately or pack into sterilized jars and seal.

PEPPER RELISH

12 large red peppers, seeded and chopped
12 large green peppers, seeded and chopped
15 small onions, peeled and chopped
vinegar

3 tablespoons salt
3 cups sugar
3 tablespoons mustard seed

1. Combine peppers and onions, cover with boiling water, let stand for 5 minutes and drain.

2. Make a solution of 1 part vinegar and 2 parts water, add peppers and onions, and bring to a boil. Remove from heat, let stand 10 minutes and drain.

3. Cover with 1 pint vinegar, salt, sugar, and mustard seed, boil for 2 minutes; bottle and seal.

SPANISH PICKLE (PICCALILLI)

4 quarts green tomatoes, chopped
12 red peppers, seeded and chopped
12 green peppers, seeded and chopped
1 medium head cabbage, cored and chopped
10 large onions, peeled and chopped

3 tablespoons salt
3 cups sugar
3 cups vinegar
3 tablespoons mustard seed
1 teaspoon turmeric

(continued)

1. Combine the tomatoes, peppers, cabbage, and onions with the salt. Mix well and let stand overnight. Drain.

2. In a large kettle, combine the vegetables with the sugar, vinegar, mustard seed, and turmeric. Boil for 20 minutes. Pour into hot sterilized jars while hot and seal.

SPICED GREEN TOMATO RELISH

Use as a relish or as a filling for a pie.

1 peck green tomatoes, chopped into small pieces	1 tablespoon cinnamon
1 tablespoon salt	½ tablespoon ground cloves
8 cups sugar	finely grated rind and juice of 2 oranges
1 pound seedless raisins	finely grated rind and juice of 2 lemons
1 pound dried currants	
1 cup vinegar	

1. Place the chopped tomatoes in a colander and pour boiling water over them 3 times, draining well each time.

2. Remove tomatoes to a preserving kettle, add salt, sugar, raisins, and currants and boil slowly until tender. Add vinegar and remaining ingredients and heat to the boiling point. Bottle while hot in sterilized jars and seal.

GREEN TOMATO RELISH

1 peck green tomatoes, sliced	½ gallon cider vinegar
¾ cup salt	4 cups brown sugar, firmly packed
2 quarts onions, peeled and sliced	4 red peppers, seeded and chopped
1 tablespoon white mustard seed, 2 sticks cinnamon, 2 tablespoons cloves, heads removed, tied in a square of cheesecloth	2 stalks celery, trimmed and chopped

1. In separate bowls, mix tomatoes with ½ cup salt and the onions with ¼ cup salt. Let stand overnight and drain.

2. In a large kettle, place the spice bag with the vinegar and sugar. Bring to a boil, add the tomatoes, onions, peppers, and celery and simmer slowly for 20 minutes. Remove the spice bag. Pack hot into hot sterilized jars and seal.

PREPARED HORSERADISH

1 pound horseradish root, washed,
    peeled, and grated
3 tablespoons sugar

white vinegar

Combine grated horseradish and sugar with enough white vinegar to cover. Mix well. Pack into sterilized jars and seal.

Pickled, Spiced, and Brandied Fruit

PICKLED CHERRIES

2 quarts sour cherries, pitted
vinegar

sugar

1. Place cherries in a crock, add enough vinegar to cover and let stand for 24 hours, stirring occasionally. Drain off vinegar.

2. Measure cherries and use an equal amount of sugar. In a clear crock, alternate layers of cherries and sugar, ending with the sugar. Stir each day for 3 days until the sugar is dissolved. Seal in sterilized jars.

PICKLED CRABAPPLES

9 pounds crabapples, stems and
    peels intact
12 cups sugar
1½ quarts vinegar

1½ pints water
¼ cup broken cinnamon sticks and
    cloves, mixed, tied in a square of
    cheesecloth

1. In a crock, combine the crabapples with the sugar, vinegar, and water. Cover and let stand overnight. Drain the juices from the crabapples and reserve.

2. Add the spice bag to the reserved juices and heat slowly. When clear, add the crabapples and boil just until tender.

3. Using a skimmer, transfer the apples to sterilized jars and cover to keep warm. Reduce juices to a medium syrup, remove spice bag, and pour boiling syrup over fruit. Seal at once.

PICKLED APPLES

9 pounds apples, peeled, quartered
   and cored
12 cups sugar
1½ quarts vinegar

1½ pints water
¼ cup broken cinnamon sticks and
   cloves, mixed, tied in a square of
   cheesecloth

1. In a crock, combine the apples with the sugar, vinegar, and water. Cover and let stand overnight. Drain the juices from the apples and reserve.

2. Add the spice bag to the reserved juices and heat slowly. When clear, add the apples and boil just until tender.

3. Using a skimmer, transfer the apples to sterilized jars and cover to keep warm. Reduce juices to a medium syrup, remove spice bag and pour boiling syrup over fruit to overflowing. Seal at once.

SPICED GOOSEBERRIES

2 cups vinegar
8 cups sugar
1 tablespoon ground cinnamon
½ tablespoon ground allspice

½ tablespoon ground cloves
5 pounds underripe gooseberries,
   washed and stemmed

In a large kettle, bring vinegar, sugar, and spices to a boil. Add berries and boil slowly for 20 minutes. Pack to overflowing in hot, sterilized jars and seal at once.

PICKLED PEACHES

6 pounds large clingstone peaches
6 cups sugar
1 pint cider vinegar

2 tablespoons cloves, heads
   removed, and 2 sticks cinnamon,
   broken, tied in a square of
   cheesecloth

1. Scald peaches in boiling water and slip off their skins.

2. Boil sugar, vinegar, and spice bag until clear, about 12 minutes. Add just enough peaches to fill one jar at a time and cook until tender.

3. Using a skimmer, transfer peaches to sterilized jars and cover to keep warm. When all the jars are full, reduce cooking liquid to a medium syrup, remove spice bag, and pour boiling syrup over the peaches to overflowing. Seal at once.

PICKLED PEARS

10 pounds Seckel pears, peeled with
  stems intact
9-10 cups sugar
1 cup water

3 cups vinegar
¼ cup broken stick cinnamon and
  cloves, mixed, tied in a square of
  cheesecloth

1. In a stone crock, alternate layers of pears and sugar and cover with water and vinegar. Cover and let stand overnight. Drain and reserve liquid.

2. In a large kettle, add the spice bag to the reserved liquid and heat slowly until the syrup is clear. Add the pears, a few at a time, and boil until tender but not soft. Place pears in sterilized jars and cover to keep warm. When all jars are full, remove the spice bag and pour boiling syrup over pears. Seal at once.

SWEET PICKLED WATERMELON RIND

7 pounds watermelon rind
water
½ teaspoon salt
½ teaspoon alum
5 cups granulated sugar
4 cups light brown sugar, firmly
  packed

1 quart vinegar
1 pint water
6 sticks cinnamon and 1 tablespoon
  cloves, tied in a square of
  cheesecloth
2 lemons, sliced

1. Pare green from rind and discard. Cut white into strips.

2. In a large kettle, cover rind with water, add salt and alum and boil until tender and clear. Drain. Chill in ice water, drain and dry.

3. Boil sugar, vinegar, and 2 cups water to a light syrup. Add spice bag, melon rind, and lemon slices and boil until clear. Remove spice bag and pack rind and syrup in hot sterilized jars. Seal at once. Let stand 4 weeks before using.

BRANDIED DRIED FRUITS

dates, figs, apricots, prunes, or any
  dried fruit

strained honey
brandy

Fill jars with any combiantion of dried fruit and cover with a mix of 2 parts honey to one part brandy. Seal jars and let stand 4 weeks before using.

BRANDIED CHERRIES

5 cups sugar	5 pounds bing cherries
2 cups water	2 cups brandy

1. Combine sugar and water and boil to a clear syrup, about 8 minutes. Pour syrup over cherries and let stand overnight. Drain cherries and reserve syrup.

2. Bring the reserved syrup slowly to the boiling point, add cherries and boil about 8 minutes.

3. With a skimmer, remove the cherries to hot, sterilized jars and cover to keep warm. Reduce the cooking liquid to a thick syrup. Add brandy and pour boiling syrup over cherries. Seal at once.

BRANDIED PEACHES OR PEARS

9 pounds large clingstone peaches, or pears, peeled	2 sticks cinnamon, 2 tablespoons cloves, heads removed, tied in a square of cheesecloth
9 pounds sugar	
1 quart water	3 pints brandy

1. Weigh peeled fruit and adjust sugar to an equal amount.

2. In a large kettle, boil sugar and water with the spice bag until clear. Add fruit, a few at a time, and boil until tender but not soft. Be careful to keep fruit whole. Place cooked fruit on a platter to drain. Repeat until all the fruit is cooked.

3. Reduce cooking liquid to a thick syrup. Remove spice bag and cool. Add brandy and stir well. Place fruit in sterilized jars, cover with syrup, and seal at once.

PRESERVES AND THE MICROWAVE

The microwave oven can be useful for cooking the fruit and sugar that goes into preserves. While the kettle of long-simmering bubbling richness evokes memories of days past and of good things to come, the efficiency of time and the lack of heat generated in the kitchen make this an attractive idea. Many of the heirloom recipes included here can be done in the microwave with a little adaptation. Since there is still a great deal of variation in the ovens on the market, we suggest that you follow manufacturer's instructions for your specific appliance. Some general tips to consider are as follows:

1. Sterilizing bottles should be done conventionally, in boiling water. The microwave is not useful for this important procedure.

2. Be sure to stop and stir often to distribute heat and to dissolve sugar.

3. If paraffin is used to seal preserves, melt slowly in a double boiler. It will not melt in the microwave.

4. When preparing preserves, either conventionally or in the microwave, try heating the sugar for 2 or 3 minutes before combining with the fruit. It will make blending and dissolving quicker and more efficent.

5. Use pot holders and heavy kitchen towels when handling preserves prepared in the microwave. The sugar mixtures tend to be deceptively hot and can cause burns. Turn the lid away from you when removing to avoid dangerous steam burns. The same precautions should be taken when removing plastic wrap.

6. Always use small amounts and cook on high power.

MAKING YOUR KITCHEN WORK FOR YOU

Menu Planning

Planning meals that are satisfying, nutritious, and economical has been one of the main purposes of The Settlement Cookbook *since it first appeared in 1901.*

A carefully thought-out menu is an excellent way to orchestrate a meal. It guides the cook through all the stages from marketing to serving. It helps organize thoughts so that a smooth and orderly progression of events is almost guaranteed. Planning a menu is as useful for everyday family meals as it is for elaborate dinner parties.

Common sense dictates some facets of the process. For example, don't offer a fish appetizer only to be followed by a fish course. Serve a light fruit sherbet rather than an egg custard dessert after a main course of pasta. Don't include a cream soup as a first course in a menu that features a main course with a creamy sauce. Begin a meal with tomato soup only when the main course that follows doesn't feature a tomato sauce.

This kind of logic is obvious. Some more subtle considerations include color, texture, and the ideas of contrasting and complementing flavors for balance. Vary foods in the menu to provide an interesting array of choices. Use foods with lots of color for visual appeal. Serve bright orange carrots and vibrant green beans to dress up a grayish piece of roast beef, for example. Serve zucchini rather than yellow squash with corn. Don't serve cauliflower with potatoes. In a similar way, consider texture, too. Crisp potatoes are a nice contrast to poached fish. A soft puree of vegetables goes well with the crackling skin of a roast bird. And finally, choose flavors that complement and blend in rather than oppose and compete. Combinations like chicken and rice, roast beef and potatoes, tomatoes and cucumbers, carrots and peas, and sweet beets with chopped onion are popular because they are traditionally good matches. Let your palate guide you to achieve this kind of balance. Experience is the best guide for skillfully matching elements when putting together a menu, but you'll certainly enjoy experimenting as well.

Use the following suggestions as a basic guide to planning meals for all sorts of occasions. Expand on the menus listed below using your imagination to create meals that fit your specific needs.

ECONOMICAL MENUS

White Bean Soup with Tomato and Thyme   (page 65)
Milwaukee Rye Bread   (page 458)
Mixed Salad
Orange Puff Cake   (page 567)

Cucumber Salad (page 111) with Vinaigrette Sauce   (page 129)
Braised Curried Chicken Legs   (page 238)
Rice Pilaf   (page 177)
French Bread   (page 455)
Baked Apples   (page 412)

Dressed Green Beans   (page 367)
Macaroni and Cheese   (page 152)
Banana Cake   (page 557)

Braised Short Ribs of Beef   (page 288)
Baked Sweet Potatoes   (page 389)
Mixed Greens Salad
Baking Powder Biscuits   (page 475)
Fresh Fruit Salad (page 124) with Honey Dressing   (page 134)

Fried Catfish   (page 202)
Grilled Tomatoes   (page 358)
Cole Slaw   (page 111)
Quick One-Bowl Cake and Sliced Strawberries   (page 555)

FAMILY MEALS

Roast Beef with Pan Gravy   (page 257, 277)
Scalloped Potatoes   (page 389)
Winter Vegetable Stew   (page 397)
Chocolate Almond Cookies (page 487) with Vanilla Ice Cream   (page 641)

Pasta with Lamb and Eggplant   (page 158)
Seasonal Green Salad
Fresh Strawberries with Ginger Wafers   (page 487)

Lemon Herb Broiled Mackerel   (page 191)
Boiled Potatoes in Jackets   (page 385)
Chopped Spinach   (page 391)
Parker House Rolls   (page 465)
Apple Pie   (page 526)

Basic Sautéed Chicken Breast   (page 239)
Lemon Carrots   (page 371)
Green Rice Ring   (page 174)
Chocolate Cake   (page 555)

Braised Pork Chops with Red Cabbage   (page 315)
Applesauce   (page 413)
Cauliflower Au Gratin   (page 372)
Pumpkin or Squash Pie   (page 346)

SINGLE DISH MENUS

(serve with good bread, fresh salad, and favorite light dessert)
Winter Vegetable Stew   (page 397)
Lasagne with Sausage and Peppers   (page 161)
Beef Stew   (page 284)
Braised Lamb Shanks with White Beans   (page 326)
Chicken Pot Pie   (page 245)
Quick Shrimp Curry with Rice   (page 218)
Baked Beans   (page 183)

INFORMAL DINNER PARTIES

Sauerbraten   (page 291)
Potato Cakes   (page 388)
Cabbage and Apples   (page 370)
Gingered Figs (page 415) and Butter Cookies   (page 485)

Tomato Soup   (page 68)
Filet of Beef with Pan Juices   (page 275, 277)
Puffy Corn Fritters   (page 375)
Sautéed Zucchini   (page 392)
Praline Mousse   (page 647)

Fresh Asparagus (page 367) with Vinaigrette Sauce   (page 129)
Oven-Braised Chicken with Lemon and Fennel   (page 236)
Rice Pilaf   (page 177)
Mixed Greens Salad
Vanilla Ice Cream (page 641) with Burnt Almond Sauce   (page 648)

Endive, Beets, and Walnuts Salad   (page 110)
Dilled Butter Salmon Steaks   (page 191)

(continued)

Cucumber and Mint Salad   (page 112)
Lemon Torte   (page 580)

Winter Squash and Leek Soup   (page 85)
Sherry-Glazed Pork   (page 307)
Potato Croquettes   (page 387)
Brussels Sprouts   (page 368)
Pears in Red Wine   (page 417)

MEATLESS MENUS

Black Bean Soup   (page 66)
Corn Bread   (page 470)
Spinach Salad   (page 114)
Brown Betty (page 621) with Vanilla Ice Cream   (page 641)

Pasta with White Beans, Tomatoes, and Herbs   (page 159)
Mixed Greens Salad
French Bread   (page 455)
Fresh Fruit Tarts   (page 537)

Ratatouille   (page 396)
Fresh Goat Cheese with Cracked Black Pepper   (page 104)
Caraway Potato Wafers   (page 78)
Lemon Ice with Ginger Cookies   (page 644)

Tabbouli   (page 124)
Grilled Pepper Salad   (page 113)
Homemade Yogurt Cheese with Fresh Herbs   (page 104)
Chilled Halves of Melon with Berry Milk Sherbet   (page 645)

Cracked Wheat Pilaf   (page 169)
Baked Onions   (page 381)
Chopped Turnip Greens or Kale   (page 378)
Cherry Cobbler   (page 629)

LOW-CALORIE MENUS

Grilled Flank Steak   (page 349)
Green Beans   (page 367)
Grilled Tomato   (page 358)
Orange and Grapefruit Salad with Zests   (page 125)

716 • THE NEW SETTLEMENT COOKBOOK

Broiled Swordfish Steaks with Soy and Ginger (page 192)
Baked Acorn Squash (page 392)
Mixed Greens Salad
Exotic Fruit Salad with Lemon Dressing (page 125)

Cucumber and Mint Salad (page 112)
Panfried Loin Chops (trimmed of fat) with Tomato and Garlic (page 324)
Spinach (page 391)
Fresh Fruit Ice (reduce sugar if desired) (page 644)

Cold Stewed Artichokes (page 366)
Turkey and Mushroom Meat Loaf (page 257)
Lemon Carrots (page 371)
Chilled Melon Slices with Chopped Fresh Mint

Chicken Breasts in Citrus Marinade (page 345), Grilled (page 352)
Grilled New Potatoes (page 357)
Mixed Greens Salad with Commercial Low-Calorie Dressing
Baked Bananas (page 415)

BRUNCH MENUS

Platter of Fresh Fruit and Assorted Yogurts
Pork Sausages
Apple Fritters (page 437)

Fresh Fruit Salad (page 124) with Banana Fruit Salad Dressing (page 135)
Buckwheat Cakes with Maple Syrup (page 423)
Crisp Bacon

Berries in Season
Platter of Chicken Livers (page 244)
Ham, and Crisp Bacon surrounding Scrambled Eggs (page 91)
Hashed Brown Potatoes (page 388)
Cinnamon Toast (page 468)

Cheese Soufflé (page 100)
Baked Ham Slices (page 309)
Banana Bread (page 473)

Gingered Figs (page 415)
Fishcakes (page 203)
Grits (page 170)
Scrambled Eggs (page 91)
Blueberry Muffins (page 481)

Gingerbread Waffles with Cream Cheese   (page 430)
Exotic Fruit Salad   (page 125)
Viennese Coffee   (page 19)

HOLIDAY MENUS

Saint Valentine's Day

Tomato Soup (page 68) with Heart Shaped Croutons   (page 77)
Grilled Lamb Chops   (page 351)
Mashed Potatoes   (page 386)
Mixed Greens Salad with Herb Vinaigrette Sauce   (page 129)
Strawberries or Cherries Dipped in Chocolate   (page 664)

Easter

Classic Baked Ham   (page 309)
Scalloped Potatoes   (page 389)
Brussels Sprouts and Chestnuts   (page 369)
Salad of Spring Greens
Hot Cross Buns   (page 441)
Rhubarb Pie   (page 529)

Passover

Salted Almonds
Wine
Matzos
Soup with Matzo Balls   (page 79)
Roast Leg of Lamb (page 320) or Basic Roast Chicken   (page 230)
Boiled New Potatoes with Chopped Parsley   (page 386)
Fresh Asparagus   (page 367)
Boiled Carrots   (page 371)
Potato Pudding for Passover   (page 626)
Stuffed Prunes   (page 671)
Nuts and Raisins

Thanksgiving

Oyster Stew   (page 73)

Roast Turkey (page 254) with Corn Bread Stuffing   (page 248)

Scalloped Sweet Potatoes with Green Apples   (page 390)

Baked Acorn Squash   (page 392)

Brussels Sprouts   (page 368)

Fresh Cranberry Relish   (page 414)

Pumpkin Pie   (page 534)

Pecan Pie   (page 534)

Christmas Dinner

Consommé (page 61) with Wafers   (page 78)

Roast Goose (page 260) with Prune and Apple Stuffing   (page 249)

Mashed Potatoes   (page 386)

Cauliflower Polonnaise   (page 372)

Braised Celery   (page 373)

Fresh Cranberry Relish   (page 414)

English Plum Pudding (page 619) with Hard Sauce   (page 652)

Mince Pie with Whipped Cream   (page 529)

Fourth of July

Barbecued Spare Ribs   (page 351)

Cole Slaw   (page 111)

Deviled Eggs   (page 88)

Potato Salad   (page 113)

Relishes and Pickles

Chocolate Brownies   (page 513)

Chilled Watermelon Chunks

BUFFET ENTERTAINING

Buffalo Chicken Wings   (page 243)
Cold Ratatouille   (page 396)
Hot German Potato Salad   (page 114)
Green Salad with Herb Vinaigrette Sauce   (page 129)
Bread Twists   (page 466)
Peach Cobbler   (page 629)

Cold Boiled Shrimp (page 216) with Cucumber Cream Sauce   (page 408)
Grilled Pepper Salad   (page 113)
Tabbouli   (page 124)
Toasted Triangles of Pita Bread
Angel Food Cake (page 568) with Fresh Fruit Salad   (page 124)

COCKTAIL PARTIES

Crudités with Herb Dip   (page 51)
Corn Chips and Crackers with Salsa   (page 48)
Canapés with Goat Cheese Spread   (page 45)
Assortment of Olives and Nuts
Stuffed Celery Stalks   (page 38)

Cocktail Party for 8

Tapenade   (page 45)
Eggplant Caviar   (page 50)
Sliced Cold Lamb with Spanish Chili Sauce   (page 406)
Assorted Cheeses
Breads, Crackers, and Rolls

Cocktail Party for 12

Chicken Liver and Mushroom Canapés   (page 42)
Chutney and Cheese Canapés   (page 43)
Smoked Fish Spread on Toasts   (page 44)
Spicy Glazed Nuts   (page 47)
Stuffed Olives

Cocktail Party for 20

Efficient Marketing

In order to get the best value for your money and to provide excellent meals at the same time, it pays to develop special skills in shopping for food. Modern markets provide a broad selection of products for the modern consumer. Moreover, farmer's markets are increasingly popular and offer locally grown, seasonal goods at relatively inexpensive prices. Health-food and specialty stores are good sources for organically grown fruits, vegetables, and whole grains that are important to include in today's diet. As with planning a menu, organization is the key to efficient shopping.

Here are five basic rules to remember while marketing:

1. Plan meals in advance and buy accordingly. Planning menus over a few days or a week makes shopping easier, saves time, and allows for good use of items bought in bulk.
2. Keep menus flexible to allow for taking advantage of special prices in the marketplace.
3. Make an effort to buy in season. While modern means of farming and transportation have provided us with fruits and vegetables that are available year-round, respecting the forces of mother nature results in fresher and less-expensive produce.

4. Keep an eye on basic food supplies. Check the vegetable bin, refrigerator, cupboards, and freezer before shopping. See that the kitchen is well stocked and that the provisions for impromptu meals and snacks are on hand.

5. Read the labels of foods that you select. Ingredients are listed in order of importance along with descriptions of the product and information on use. Most shoppers are health conscious and are reminded to avoid foods high in saturated fats, high in sodium content, and loaded with sugar. Labels are required by law to provide the consumer with accurate descriptions of contents and should be closely inspected when purchasing an unfamiliar product.

EMPTYING THE MARKET BASKET

Unpack purchases promptly upon arriving home. Sort frozen foods to go directly into the freezer: meats and poultry should be unwrapped, then covered loosely for storage in refrigerator or prepared and rewrapped for freezing. Separate dairy products and assemble so that they may be carried easily to refrigerator and stored. Packaged goods should be grouped for storage in pantries and cupboards.

Work with items that require freezing or refrigeration first. Save sacks and bags for reuse rather than simply throwing them out. Recycle as much as possible and think of creative ways to avoid wear and tear on our already fragile environment.

Remember also that foods tend to lose moisture or take on other flavors in the refrigerator. Wrap foods for storage in sealed plastic containers or other wrappings. Plastic wrap and bags can be used and reused to prevent waste. Store vegetables in a closed container or crisper. Save reusable glass containers for holding small amounts of leftovers.

The internal temperature of a refrigerator should be a constant 38° to 42° F. Most new refrigerators are "frost-free" and require little maintenance. If this is not the case, defrost as often as necessary to prevent an accumulation of frost on the freezing coils that can dangerously raise the temperature. Pay special attention to the interior temperature during warm weather or when the refrigerator is being opened frequently.

Housekeeping Tips

The following information comes from the earliest editions of *The Settlement Cookbook*. While the modern homemaker might find some of this out of date, it seems a shame to let go of such a fine heritage. In the move toward less dependence on gadgets, and household gimickry, the idea of a good, old-fashioned sweeping is comforting. Times may change but necessary household tasks never seem to go out of style.

Sweeping a Room

Before begining to sweep, see that no food is left uncovered in the room and that all movable articles and furniture are removed or raised above the floor. Sweep from the edges of the room toward the center. Sweep with short strokes, keeping the broom close to the floor. Turn it edgewise to clean cracks. Always sweep a floor before washing or scrubbing it.

Dusting a Room

Begin at one corner and take each article in turn as you come to it. Dust from the highest things to the lowest, taking up the dust in the cloth.

Dust the woodwork, furniture and movable articles with a soft, cotton cloth. Shake it frequently out of the windows.

Airing a Room

Lower the upper sash of a window to let out the foul air that always rises to the top. Raise the lower sash of an opposite window, of same or an adjoining room, to admit fresh air. This will create a draft that will thoroughly air the room. Bedroom windows should always be open from the top at night.

Removing Stains

When possible remove all stains while they are fresh, as they are less obstinate before dried into the cloth.

If a stain is of unknown origin, but seems nongreasy, soak it in cold water, then wash in warm suds. If it seems greasy, sponge with carbon tetrachloride or a similar dry-cleaning solvent and then wash.

General laundering directions apply to spot stain removal as well. Wool, rayon, and many synthetics cannot be washed in hot water or bleached with some types of household bleach. Combinations of fibers should be treated according to the most delicate fiber in the combination.

REMOVAL OF COMMON STAINS

Stains	Pre-treatment	Treatment	If Stains Persist
Adhesive Tape	Sponge with kerosense	Wash in hot suds	
Alcoholic Beverages	Soak or sponge with cool water	Wash in warm suds	Soak in weak solution of household bleach and wash again
Ballpoint Ink	Sponge with carbon tetrachloride	Wash in warm suds	
Blood	Sponge or soak in cold water	Wash in warm, not hot suds	Soak in weak solution of household bleach and wash again
Candle Wax	Scrape off excess wax, place fabric between white blotters and press with a hot iron	Wash in warm suds	Rub with cold turpentine, wash again in warm suds
Cheese	Scrape off excess, sponge with cool water	Wash in hot suds	
Chocolate or Cocoa	Wash in hot suds	Soak in weak solution of household bleach or hydrogen peroxide, wash again	
Cod-Liver Oil	Sponge with glycerine or carbon tetrachloride, rinse in warm water	Wash in warm suds	Old stains are almost impossible to remove
Coffee and Tea	Stretch fabric taut over a bowl, pour boiling water through stain from a height of 3 or 4 feet	Wash in hot suds	
Egg	Scrape off excess, soak in cool water	Wash in warm suds	

Stains	Pre-treatment	Treatment	If Stains Persist
Fruits: Peach, pear, cherry and plum	Sponge with cool water and rub lightly with glycerine, let stand a few hours. Apply a few drops of vinegar, rinse	Wash in warm suds	
Berries, other fruits	Stretch fabric taut over a bowl, pour boiling water through stain from a height of 3 or 4 feet	Wash as usual	
Ink, washable		Wash in hot suds	
Ink, oil-based	Rub with glycerine	Wash in hot suds	
Lipstick	Rub with glycerine	Wash in hot suds	
Mayonnaise	Sponge with cold water, then sponge with warm suds	Wash as usual	
Meat Juices	Soak in cool water	Wash in hot suds	
Mildew	Wash in warm suds, dry in sun	Rub with lemon juice and salt, dry in sun. Wash again	
Milk or Cream	Sponge or soak with cool water	Wash in hot suds	
Mustard	Sponge with cool water, rub with warm glycerine	Wash in hot suds	
Paint	If fresh, wash in hot suds. If dry, sponge with turpentine or kerosene	Wash in hot suds	
Scorch		Wash in hot suds	Bleach in the sun, or dampen with hydrogen peroxide, dry in sun, then launder in hot suds
Shoe Polish White liquid	Sponge with cool water	Wash as usual	
Wax Types	Sponge thoroughly with suds	Wash as usual	Soak in household bleach, then launder again

Stains	Pre-treatment	Treatment	If Stains Persist
Soft Drinks Fresh	Sponge with cool water or with a solution of equal parts of alcohol and water	Wash in hot suds	
Dry	Rub glycerine into the stain, let stand half an hour	Rinse with warm water. Wash in hot suds	
Stamping Ink	Soak in weak solution of household bleach	Wash in hot suds	
Tomato and Tomato Catsup	Sponge with cool water. Rub with glycerine, let stand half an hour	Wash in hot suds	

To Make Soap

5 pounds lukewarm melted fat
1 1-pound can lye
1 quart cold water
3 teaspoons borax

1 teaspoon salt
2 tablespoons sugar
½ cup cold water
¼ cup ammonia

Fats that are not fit for food may be made into soap. Melt fat and strain through cheesecloth. Dissolve the lye in cold water and let stand until cool, then add the fat slowly, stirring constantly. Mix the other ingredients together and add to the first mixture. Stir the whole until thick and light-colored. Pour into a pan lined with cloth. Mark into pieces of desired size before the soap becomes hard. When hard, break pieces apart and pile in such a way that soap may dry out well.

To Start a Wood and Coal Fire

Plan to build the fire on a surface where air can circulate. To improvise a firesite outdoors, dig a shallow hole in the ground, then make a base through which air can circulate by piling uneven rocks loosely. On a loose mound of twisted paper or twigs or bits of wood and bark, pile larger pieces of wood in a cone shape, or scatter with fine coal or charcoal. In a stove with a firebox or in a fireplce with a grate, have all drafts open. Ignite the paper, and as wood or coal settles down, add more gradually. In using a firebox, add coal until the firebox is filled. When the blue flame of coal disappears, close the dampers, and open the dampers again when more coal is added. When the coal is red it is nearly burned out. To keep a fire several hours, shake out the ashes, fill with coal, close the dampers and partially open the slide above the fire. For continual use it is better to add a little fuel at a time, but not in the midst of baking. For soft coal, keep the chimney damper partially open to allow the soot and smoke to escape. Remove ashes every day.

A charcoal or wood fire is hottest when flames die down and gray ash shows.

Kitchen Equipment

When purchasing pots and pans and utensils choose individual pieces according to how they will be used rather than selecting a matched set of many different sizes. The following materials are readily available in all sorts of items and are useful for different purposes because of their basic qualities:

Aluminum Pans: Good-quality aluminum heats evenly, and is satisfactory for general-purpose cooking. Look for heavy, thick, treated brands for best results. Aluminum reacts with some acids in foods. This results in either a bitter metallic aftertaste or in discoloration of foods. Avoid cooking wine, lemon juice, vinegar, or eggs in untreated aluminum cookware.

Cast-Iron Pans: Heavy, even heat for browning or cooking in fat. Good for use over high heat and can go into the oven if necessary. Like aluminum, they are reactive.

Tin-Lined Copper Pans: Excellent distribution of heat, will not react with acidic foods, and heavy enough to prevent scorching. Need polishing after use.

Copper-Clad or Copper-Interlined Stainless-Steel Pans: As with copper pans, these conduct heat quickly yet evenly. Excellent for sauce making, sautéeing, braising.

Earthenware: Versatile enough to use on top of the range or in the oven. Cracks and chips easily and must be used over relatively low heat and guarded against sudden changes of temperature.

Glass or Ceramic Materials: Heat quickly, excellent for boiling and braising, only satisfactory for frying and baking. Temperatures should generally be slightly reduced to compensate for faster heating. Some are made for top-of-range cooking, conventional ovens, and microwave ovens.

Nonstick Coated Pans: Finished so that foods may be cooked without fat or liquid, without sticking. Lower temperature must be used for these and wooden or plastic spatulas are recommended for stirring to prevent scratching the nonstick surface.

Stainless Steel: Expensive but extremely durable, stainless steel pots and pans distribute heat evenly, will not discolor foods, or give off unusual flavors.

BASIC KITCHEN INVENTORY

Pots and Kettles and Pans

3 heavy skillets, 6-, 8- and 12-inch sizes (preferably heavy-duty, nonstick)

1 large kettle or pot, 6 to 8 quarts

double boiler, 1½-quart size

3 saucepans, 2-cup, 1- and 3-quart sizes (at least one tin-lined copper saucepan is recommended)

1 large Dutch oven or similar ovenproof pot with a cover

1 coffee pot

1 tea kettle

1 roasting pan (about 15 inches long) with rack and cover

2 oven-to-table-style casseroles, 1½- and 2-quart size

1 pie plate, 9 inches

1 muffin tin, 12 cups, about 3 inches in diameter

2 layer pans, 8 inches

1 square or round casserole or pan, 9 inches

1 tube pan with removable bottom, 9 inches

1 loaf pan, 9 inches by 5 inches

1 springform pan

1 shallow-sided baking sheet

2 baking sheets for cookies

Electrical Appliances

Blender

Electric Mixer

Food Processor

Microwave Oven

Toaster

Waffle Iron

Kitchen Tools

can opener

colander

pastry blender

pastry brush

cookie cutters
cutting boards
food mill
garlic press
grater
juicer
kitchen and poultry shears
knives: paring knife, bread knife,
   butcher knives, and large chopping knives (choose either carbon
   knives that keep a sharper edge
   but require attention due to their
   tendency to rust or easier-to-
   maintain stainless steel)
ladle
measuring spoons
mixing bowls (4 to 5 in varying
   sizes)

rolling pin
scales
spatulas (rubber and metal)
stainless-steel strainer
timer
whisk
wire racks for cooling
wooden spoons
vegetable peeler
vegetable scrub brush

Entertaining Guests

A successful party depends as much upon a relaxed and charming host or hostess as it does on the food served. A simple meal of a few courses, with the guests seated comfortably and unaware of the hostess's work, can often be as impressive and enjoyable as an elegant "formal" and often ceremonial dinner.

Although entertaining today is primarily of an informal nature, there are certain traditions and conventions about serving that are important to know. These rules can and should be adapted to take into account the number of guests to be invited, the space available for entertaining, budget limitations, and whether auxiliary help is available. The type of meal and service style will depend upon these factors.

PLANNING AHEAD

Planning ahead will insure entertaining success. Here are a few good rules to remember:

1. Simple, carefully prepared and familiar dishes are preferable to experimentation. Be wary of recipes never before attempted.

2. Dishes that can be cooked ahead of time and either frozen or refrigerated until needed are a great convenience.

3. Well in advance, write out the menu and marketing lists. Check the pantry for necessary staples.

4. Start the marketing at least one day ahead to accommodate last-minute changes, should certain foods not be available.

5. Plan linen, china, silver, and serving pieces to be used; see that all are clean and silver polished ahead of time.

6. Plan menus that do not complicate either use of oven or refrigerator storage. Ideally foods to be cooked in the oven should require the same or similar oven temperatures. There should be ample space in the refrigerator to accommodate all cold dishes. Otherwise, change the menu to avoid such problems.

7. Do as much as possible in advance: set table, prepare raw vegetables and salad in the morning; bake and cook component parts of dishes to assemble later. This is particularly helpful where the host or hostess must do all the planning, preparing, cooking, and serving without assistance.

8. Make a timetable to determine the order that foods should be cooked. Start with dish that takes the longest cooking time, then the next longest, and so on. Such a timetable will help all elements of the meal to be ready to serve properly cooked at the proper time.

9. If cocktails are planned, serve appetizers with them that do not have to be prepared at the last minute.

10. Meat and rolls can be kept hot in a slow oven (125° F). Other foods can be warmed in a double boiler.

TYPE OF SERVICE

Most entertaining today falls into two general classifications: the "sit-down" meal, which is served by help or by the host or hostess, and the buffet meal, at which guests serve themselves and are then seated either at the dining table or at small tables scattered through the living-dining area. The advantages of each are obvious. With fewer guests and ample space, the sit-down meal at the table is most convenient and comfortable. Where there are many guests, and possibly limited space, the more informal buffet is preferable. The buffet has also become extremely popular for small groups since it generates a more relaxed and convivial atmosphere.

TABLE SETTINGS

Linens

Cover the table with table pads or a silence cloth of felt or flannel. Over this spread a tablecloth, the middle crease up, dividing the table exactly in half and the edges hanging evenly all around the table. Lace tablecloths require no silence cloths, but would need trivets under hot dishes.

For breakfast, luncheon, supper, or any dinner except the most formal kind, placemats—or heat-resistant mats for hot plates—may be used instead of a cloth.

Decorations

The center decoration should not obstruct the view between guests. Fruit, vegetables, or flowers are all desirable. For formal occasions, two candelabra or four candlesticks are placed at each side of the centerpiece. Compote dishes, filled with nuts and candies, may be placed toward the ends of the table. Use your imagination to create a suitable mood or theme on the tabletop.

For luncheons no candles are used. Small ornaments of glass or china are substituted if desired.

Place everything on the table as neatly and attractively as possible, and avoid crowding.

Individual Covers

A cover consists of plates, glasses, silver, and napkin to be used by one person. The covers should be one inch from the edge of the table, allowing about twenty-five inches between plates.

The actual settings and their variations are best shown and clearly explained in the diagrams that follow.

Heat and china and silver dishes in which hot food is served by placing in warm oven, protected by pad, or by rinsing in hot water. Chill dishes for salads and ices.

Silver or Stainless

Place at each side of the plate in the order in which it is used, commencing from the outside and continuing toward the plate, at right angles to the edge of the table.

Knives Place at the right, sharp edges toward the plate.

Forks Tines are turned up and placed to the left of the plate.

Spoons Bowls are turned up and placed to the right of the knives. The cocktail spoon or fork is placed at the extreme right end. Other spoons are brought in with their respective courses.

Silver for the dessert course is not put on with the other silver at a formal dinner nor are more than three forks laid. Additional silver is brought in with the dessert and coffee, either on the plate or placed, from a napkin or tray, at the right of the plate.

Water Glass

Place at the right, at or near the point of the knife. It should be only three fourths full.

Wine Glass

Place below and to the right of the water glass. It should be only three fourths full. If both red and white wine glasses are included, the smaller one should go to the left of the larger one.

Service Plate

On the service plate is placed the plate containing the cocktail glass for fruit or shellfish, the appetizer, the bouillon cup or soup plate and the entree.

Bread-and-Butter Plate

Place directly above the forks, with the spreader straight across the top of the plate, handle to the right. At formal dinners no spreader is used and sometimes the bread and butter service is omitted entirely.

Individual Salt and Pepper

Where used, these may be placed above each plate or between each two covers.

Napkin

Place to the left of the forks with the fold at the top, the hemmed edges parallel with the forks and the table edge. At formal dinners, the napkins may be placed on service plate.

Finger Bowls

Usually the finger bowl is half filled with tepid water, containing a thin slice of lemon or a few flower petals. It is brought in before the dessert course on a plate on which is first placed a doily and the dessert silver. It is set before each person, who removes the doily and finger bowl to the left, and the silver to the right.

Serving Table or Sideboard

Use to hold all silver for serving and all extras that may be needed during a meal.

BASIC SETTINGS FOR INFORMAL LUNCH OR DINNER

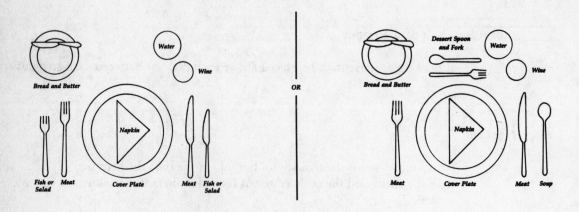

FORMAL SETTING

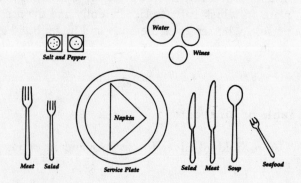

DIRECTIONS FOR SERVING

When There Is No Maid

All the food belonging to one course is placed on the table in platters or suitable dishes before the person who is to serve or on a nearby teacart or small table. The number of plates necessary may be in a pile directly in front of the server, or the plates may be passed by each individual in rotation. Salad plates may be placed at the left or right of the cover for informal service.

SETTING WHERE HOSTESS SERVES

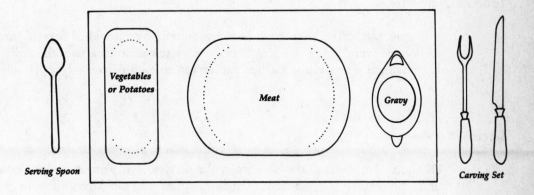

Serving Spoon   Vegetables or Potatoes   Meat   Gravy   Carving Set

At Table Service When There Is a Maid

The table is set with a plate and silver for each person. The platter or dish containing the main course is placed before the host, who serves the first portion on the plate before him. While the host is carving, the waiter or waitress holds an empty plate in his or her left hand and stands to the left of the server. She removes the filled plate, places the empty plate before the server, and passes the plate with the food to the first person to be served, at the same time taking the empty plate from this place. He or she brings this empty plate back to the server, removes the second filled plate, replacing it with the empty plate, and continues in the same manner until everyone is served. The last empty plate is then set aside.

Platter Service

By this method everything pertaining to a complete course is served from large platters.

Any number of guests may be served in this manner provided a proportionate amount of help is supplied in the kitchen and dining room. One waiter or waitress can easily serve from six to eight persons.

Individual Service

A simple way of serving large seated groups is by individual service. Small portions of everything belonging to one complete course are artistically arranged on individual plates in the kitchen and served to each person.

Formal Service

The host and hostess take no part in the service. No platters are put on the table. All serving is done from the pantry or serving table by waiters or waitresses. Four to six guests are assigned to one waiter or waitress. Each plate may be brought to the table with a portion of the main dish of the course, or the plates are set down empty and the food is served from platters from which the person helps himself. The waiter or waitess removes one plate with the right hand and places the plate for the next course with the left hand, the table never being without plates. Before serving the dessert, everything but the decorations is cleared away, then crumbs are removed from the cloth. After-dinner coffee may be served at the table or poured by the host or hostess in the living room.

Order of Service

The host sits at the head of the table, the hostess directly opposite. The guest of honor, if a man, is seated at the right of the hostess; if a woman, at the right of the host. Serve the lady guest of honor first and continue toward the right. The next course should be served toward the left, that no side be always served last. At a formal dinner two waiters or waitresses serve, one from the hostess to the right, the other from the host to the right.

Buffet Table Service Suggestions

A long narrow table, placed against one wall and covered with an appropriate cloth, is particularly convenient for buffet service, although a round or square or oblong table can also be used. The principle to observe is to have plates available at one end, and then the main dish and accompaniments in the order in which you wish guests to serve themselves. The traffic should move in one direction only.

A TYPICAL BUFFET SETTING

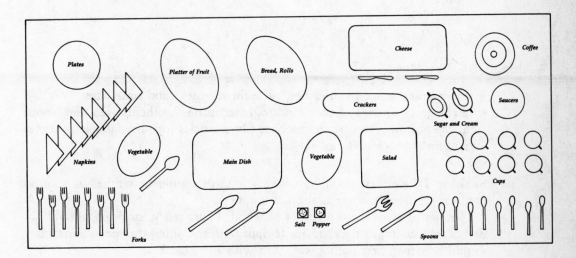

With the availability of electrical hot plates, chafing dishes and hot trays, the dishes you serve can be kept properly hot whether simple or elaborate. It is customary to avoid food that requires the use of a knife, although poultry, ham, and other meats are often served and carved at the buffet in small, thin slices. Dessert and coffee can be served from a sideboard, or from a rolling cart.

Clearing the Table

- When the main course is finished, remove all dishes containing food first: the platters, vegetable dishes, and smaller serving dishes, not taking the silver from them; next the individual cover, consisting of the larger plates and the butter plates, then the sauce dishes, if any, and last of all the clean plates and silver not used.
- Do not remove cutlery or silver from dishes at the table.
- Do not pile dishes one upon the other.
- Before serving the dessert, remove salts and peppers, relishes, and all other dishes. Remove all crumbs with a folded napkin, brushing them on a plate or crumb tray.
- After the meal is over and the family or guests have left the dining room, the table should be cleared of the last course.
- Brush the crumbs from the cloth and remove it. Brush the crumbs from the floor.

Washing Dishes by Hand

- First scrape waste from dishes, rinse them; empty and rinse cups.
- Arrange all articles of each kind together: plates by themselves, the largest at the bottom; cups by themselves; silver articles together, and steel knives and forks by themselves.

Soaking Dishes: If possible, cooking utensils should be washed as soon as used, or filled with water as soon as emptied.

Handles of knives and forks, if of wood, bone, ivory, or pearl, should not be put into water, as they are apt to split. After washing the metal parts, they should be wiped first with a wet, then with a dry cloth.

Cold water should be used for soaking dishes that have been used for milk, eggs, fish, and starchy foods; hot water, for dishes used for sugar substances and for sticky, gummy substances like gelatin. Greasy dishes of all kinds, including knives, are more easily cleaned if first wiped with soft paper.

To Wash Dishes: Order: (1) glassware; (2) silver; (3) cups and saucers; (4) plates; (5) platters, vegetable dishes, etc.; (6) cooking utensils.

Have a pan half filled with hot water containing soap or detergent. Slip glasses and fine china in sideways, that the hot water will touch outside and inside at the same time, and thus avoid danger of cracking. If dishes are very greasy, add a little washing soda, or ammonia. Rinse all dishes in clean hot water, drain, wipe with clean, dry towels if necessary. If water is sufficiently hot, dishes will not require wiping.

Draining Dishes: As the dishes are washed and rinsed, place them in a dish drainer. For fine dishes and glassware, do not use drainer, but place on a folded dish cloth to avoid nicking.

Care of Silver

Use silver often; sterling improves with use, and frequent use prevents the formation of tarnish. Polish silver periodically with good silver polish, following the manufacturer's directions, and wash in hot soapy water before drying and putting away. Tarnish-retarding storage chests for silver flatware are available. Less frequently used pieces may be tightly covered with plastic wrap to retard tarnishing. "Dip and shine" polishes, which direct that silver be soaked in liquid, are not recommended for finely engraved silver. The darker pattern areas in silver of this type are part of the design, and should not be removed.

Salt and eggs darken silver. When these foods are served in silver holders, empty vessels as soon as possible and clean silver in usual way at once. It is best to protect silver salt-dishes with glass liners.

Silver serving dishes may be heated in hot water. When used over direct heat, as in silver chafing dishes, they blacken and require thorough polishing.

FREEZING AND DRYING FOODS

Freezing

GENERAL FREEZING TIPS

Freezing has revolutionized the modern kitchen. Storage of precooked foods as well as the ever-increasing availability of store-bought frozen products has made life easier for the home cook. While some argue that flavor and texture is often lost in the process, most of us agree that the convenience makes up for any loss.

1. Frozen foods must be stored at 0° F or lower.
2. Select foods of best quality. Freezing does not improve food but will only retain the original quality and flavor.
3. Prepare, package, and freeze food immediately after picking or purchasing.
4. Food expands when frozen. Allow ½ inch head space in all containers.
5. Moisture- and vapor-proof packaging is essential.
6. Materials to be frozen should be placed along bottom of shelf or along side walls of freezer. Stack packages only when frozen solid.
7. Label and date all packages clearly. Use older packages first.
8. Do not refreeze foods that have been thawed.
9. In case of power failure, keep freezer doors closed. Fully loaded freezer will hold temperature for 2 days. If failure lasts longer, add dry ice on racks above food—25 pounds per 10 cubic feet.

FREEZING FRUITS

Packaging Materials for Fruits

Use cartons, wide-mouthed jars, and plastic containers especially designed for freezing. Plastic bags with secure zipper-like closures are useful, too.

Preparing Fruits for Freezing

Three methods are used to prepare fresh fruits for freezing. They may be packed covered in cold syrup of the designated strength; or with dry sugar, or without sweetening. Ascorbic acid is usually added to fruits that tend to darken after cutting, to retain light color; it may be dissolved in the syrup, or mixed with the sugar, or dissolved in water. Use ¼ teaspoon ascorbic acid for each quart of syrup, unless otherwise noted; or ¼ teaspoon per quart of fruit; or ¼ teaspoon per cup of sugar. Peel and slice fruit for best results.

Sugar Syrup for Frozen Fruits
(Sugar listed is amount to be used per quart of water.)

Syrup	Sugar	Yield of Syrup
Light 30%	2 cups	5 cups
Medium Light 40%	3 cups	5½ cups
Medium Heavy 50%	4¾ cups	6½ cups
Heavy 60%	7 cups	7¾ cups

In any of the above syrups white corn syrup may be substituted for one quarter of the sugar.

Bring sugar and water to a boil over moderately high heat, stirring and washing down crystals that form on side of pan. Remove after 1 to 2 minutes of steady boiling.

Storing Frozen Fruits

Most fruits maintain high quality at 0° F for 8 to 12 months. Citrus fruits and citrus juices should be used within 4 to 6 months. Unsweetened fruits lose quality faster than those packed in sugar or syrup.

Thawing Fruits

Leave fruit in sealed container to thaw. Frozen dessert fruits are best when slightly frosty. A 1-pound package will thaw in 6 to 8 hours in the refrigerator or in 2 to 4 hours at room temperature.

FREEZING VEGETABLES

TIPS FOR FREEZING VEGETABLES

1. Process not more than 1 pound of vegetables at a time.
2. Place prepared vegetables in colander or wire basket.
3. Immerse colander or basket in large quantity of rapidly boiling water.
4. Cover kettle to bring water back to boil as quickly as possible.
5. As soon as water returns to boil, begin to time blanching. Time accurately.
6. After blanching, plunge immediately into cold running water or ice water to cool. It takes about as long to cool foods as to heat them.
7. Drain well and dry.
8. Pack and freeze immediately, allowing ½ inch head space.

Packaging Materials for Vegetables

Use plastic bags, cartons, wide-mouthed jars, and plastic containers especially designed for freezing.

Preparing Vegetables for Freezing

Certain vegetables, among them mushrooms, pumpkins, sweet potatoes, and winter squash, may be steamed instead of blanched. Put a rack in a kettle or saucepan fitted with a tight lid. Put an inch or two of water in the bottom of the kettle; bring to a boil. Put vegetables in a colander or steaming basket in a single layer and cook covered, in the steam, for the designated time.

Storing Frozen Vegetables

All vegetables except asparagus, corn, and green beans maintain high quality for 8 to 12 months. Asparagus should be used within 6 months; corn and green beans within 8 months.

Cooking Frozen Vegetables *(Except corn on the cob and greens.)*

Put the frozen vegetables into a small amount of rapidly boiling, salted water. Separate vegetables with fork to insure uniform cooking. Cook until tender.

Corn on the Cob: Thaw, cook in rapidly boiling salted water.

Greens: Thaw partially before cooking in rapidly boiling, salted water.

FREEZING MEAT

Any high-quality meat can be frozen satisfactorily. All meats should be cut into size and quantity convenient for family needs. If more than one cut is placed in packages, such as a number of chops or steaks, place two sheets of moisture- and vapor-proof paper between the layers for easy separation.

Freezing meat must be done correctly. Wrap package tightly and seal. If package is uneven, protect wrapping by covering package with stockinette. Label and date package clearly. Freeze immediately after purchasing. Do not season uncooked meats before freezing. Pat dry with paper towels but do not rinse.

Packaging Materials for Meats

Heavy aluminum foil
Heavy-weight freezer paper
Freezer-weight plastic wrap
Polyethylene bags
Stockinette
Freezer tape

Cooking Frozen Meats

Roasts: Thaw in wrapping in refrigerator. Roast immediately. Or roast frozen—allow 1½ times cooking time used for unfrozen meat.

Steaks, Chops, and Hamburger Patties: Broil 4 inches below heating unit; if still frozen increase prescribed broiling time by half.

Ground Beef and Variety Meats: Thaw completely in the refrigerator and cook as fresh meat.

FREEZING POULTRY

Packaging Materials

Use the same methods as for meat.

Preparing Poultry for Freezing

Any poultry can be frozen satisfactorily. Poultry may be frozen whole or cut up. Separate pieces with two sheets of moisture- and vapor-proof paper. Pack giblets in moisture- and vapor-proof paper. They may be replaced, wrapped, in the cavity, if poultry is to be used within 3 months, or packed separately. It is advantageous to pack livers separately, for special uses. Wrap tightly; seal. Label and date. Do not stuff poultry before freezing.

Cooking Frozen Poultry

Thaw completely in the refrigerator and use like fresh poultry. Poultry may be stewed or braised without thawing.

FREEZING FISH

Packaging Materials

Use the same as those for meat and poultry.

Preparing Fish for Freezing

Fish, freshly caught, should be cleaned, scaled, and frozen as rapidly as possible. Leave fish whole or cut into steaks or fillets. Immerse lean fish in salt solution, ½ cup salt to 2 quarts of water, for 30 seconds. Do not immerse fatty fish such as salmon or mackerel. Wrap in moisture- and vapor-proof materials. Seal, label, and date.

Preparing Shellfish

Oysters, Clams, and Scallops: Shell and wash in brine, 1 tablespoon salt to 1 quart of water. Drain, pack in moisture- and vapor-proof plastic containers. Label, date, freeze immediately.

Shrimp: Clean, package, and freeze. Or cook, shell, package and freeze.

Cooking Frozen Fish

Thaw in the refrigerator and prepare like fresh fish. Or, broil frozen.

RECOMMENDED STORAGE PERIODS

The recommended storage periods for home-frozen meats and fish held at 0° F are given below. For best quality, use the shorter storage time.

Product	Storage Period (months)
Beef	
Ground Meat	2 to 3
Roasts	8 to 12
Steaks	8 to 12
Lamb	
Chops	3 to 4
Ground Meat	2 to 3
Roasts	8 to 12
Poultry	
Game Birds	8
Chickens	6
Turkeys, Ducks, Geese	6
Giblets	3
Shellfish	
Oysters	1
Clams	3
Shrimp	4
Pork, cured	
Bacon	less than 1 month
Ham	1 to 2
Pork, fresh	
Chops	3 to 4
Roasts	4 to 8
Sausage	1 to 2
Veal	
Cutlets, Chops	3 to 4
Ground Meat	2 to 3
Roasts	4 to 8

FREEZING EGGS

Eggs should be frozen without shells, yolks and whites mixed together, or yolks only, or whites only. Package small quantities of eggs. Pack in one package only the amount that can be used at one time.

Whites, yolks, or yolks and whites mixed together can be frozen for 8 to 12 months.

Packaging Materials

Use the same as those for fruits and vegetables.

Preparing Eggs for Freezing

Whites need no treatment other than packaging and labeling.

Prepare yolks by adding 1 teaspoon salt to 1 cup of yolks. Stir, but do not beat. If eggs are to be used for baking, substitute 1 tablespoon sugar or white corn syrup for salt. Package and label, noting on label whether sugar or salt has been added.

Prepare whole eggs by adding 1 teaspoon salt to 1 cup of eggs. If eggs are to be used for baking, substitute 1 tablespoon sugar or white corn syrup for salt. Stir thoroughly but do not beat. Package and label, noting on label whether sugar or salt has been added.

Cooking Frozen Eggs

Thaw in refrigerator. Use as you would fresh eggs.
1½ tablespoons white equals 1 egg white.
1 tablespoon yolk equals 1 egg yolk.
2½ tablespoons whole egg equals 1 egg.

FREEZING BAKED GOODS

Packaging Materials

Use any moisture- and vapor-proof materials, plus boxes to protect the cake or pie.

Pies

TIPS FOR FREEZING PIES

1. Freeze unbaked. Use disposable foil or paper pie plates.
2. Fruit and mincemeat pies freeze successfully.
3. Chiffon pies freeze well. Defrost in the refrigerator for 1½ hours.
4. Do not freeze custard pies.
5. Unbaked pie shells or pie dough may be frozen.

Baking Frozen Pies

Remove wrapping. Bake like freshly made pie, at prescribed temperature. Slit crust when sufficiently thawed. Allow 10 to 12 minutes additional baking time at high control heat.

Freezing Cakes

Any type of cake may be baked and frozen. It is best to fill and frost cakes when ready to serve. Wrap cakes carefully and label. Thaw cakes in wrapping in the refrigerator.

Baked Rolls, Cookies, Muffins, and Bread

Wrap in moisture- and vapor-proof material, seal, and label. May be thawed at room temperature, or placed in moderate oven or microwave to thaw.

STORAGE PERIODS FOR BAKED GOODS

Bread, Rolls, Cakes	3 months
Cup Cakes	2 to 4 months
Pies, Unbaked	8 months
Biscuits, Muffins, Cookies	2 to 3 months

Freezing Sandwiches

Meat, fish, poultry, and peanut butter fillings freeze well. Spread bread generously with butter or margarine to edge of bread. Package sandwiches individually in moisture- and vapor-proof wrapping. Seal, label, and freeze immediately. Keep only 2 to 3 weeks. Sandwiches will thaw in 5 to 6 hours in the refrigerator, 2 to 3 hours at room temperature.

Sandwich Fillings That Do Not Freeze Well

Raw vegetables
Salad greens
Whites of hard-cooked eggs
Cheese, unless combined with other foods
Jellies
Mayonnaise

Freezing Canapés or Hors d'Oeuvres

Fancy party sandwiches and hors d'oeuvres can also be frozen. Although the fillings and spreads will be different from those used in lunch sandwiches, the rules for making, packaging, and storing are the same. Freeze in a single layer on baking sheets. Package in moisture- and vapor-proof materials, placing two pieces of paper between layers. Canapés that are to be broiled or toasted may be transferred from the freezer to the broiler or oven. Sandwiches, canapés, and hors d'oeuvres should be stored no longer than 1 month.

FREEZING COOKED FOODS

Cooked foods, either leftovers or foods cooked especially for the purpose, may be frozen for future use. They should be used within 2 to 3 months. They may be wrapped in the containers in which they are to be heated and served, or in plastic freeze containers, cartons, or jars especially designed for freezing. It is economical of time and effort to make double or triple recipes of certain dishes, in order to freeze some for later use. The following dishes are particularly suitable:

Baked Beans	Candied Sweet Potatoes
Stews	French Fried Potatoes
Spaghetti Sauce and Meat Balls	French Toast
Chili	Waffles
Soups and Stocks	Meat Pies and Turnovers
Chicken à la King	Stuffed Peppers
Fried Chicken	

Generally speaking, most cooked foods freeze well, with the following exceptions:

Cheese and crumb toppings for casseroles should not be added until just before reheating.

Mixtures containing hard-cooked egg white or potatoes—the egg whites get rubbery in consistency, and the potatoes become mushy.

TIPS FOR FREEZING COOKED FOODS

1. Foods cooked especially for freezing should be slightly undercooked, since they cook during the reheating process. This is especially true of combinations containing vegetables, pasta, or rice.
2. Cool the food to be frozen as quickly as possible by setting the pan of hot food in a pan of ice and water. Package and freeze, allowing ample head space.
3. Casseroles may be left temporarily frozen in the dish in which they were cooked, then turned out of the dish, and wrapped in moisture) and vapor-proof paper. At serving time, they can be refitted into the same dish, and heated in it.
4. Do not allow food to thaw before reheating.
5. Stews, creamed mixtures, and the like are most easily heated in a double boiler over boiling water.
6. Casseroles should be heated in the oven, allowing ample time for them to heat thoroughly.
7. Fried foods may be heated in a moderately hot oven (400° F) in a single layer, without a cover, to restore crispness.
8. Frozen waffles and sliced bread may be heated in a toaster.
9. Cooked foods remain at top quality for 2 to 3 months, and up to 6 months under ideal conditions (perfect wrapping, uniform 0° storage). After 6 months storage, the quality may decline, although the food is still safe.

FRUITS FOR FREEZING

Most of these directions call for added sugar. This may be omitted but a small amount will improve flavor and texture.

Fruit	Preparation	Sugar or Syrup
Apples for Dessert	Peel and slice directly into syrup with ascorbic acid.	Pack in 40% syrup with ½ teaspoon ascorbic acid per quart.
Apples for Pie	Peel and slice directly into cold water with 1 teaspoon ascorbic acid for each quart of water. Steam in single layer 1½ to 2 minutes. Cool in cold water, drain.	Add ½ cup sugar for each quart of apple slices, stir.
Apricots for Dessert	Dip into boiling water, remove skins, cut in half and discard pits.	Pack in 40% syrup, with ¾ teaspoon ascorbic acid per quart.
Apricots for Pie	Peel and pit as above; sprinkle each quart fruit with solution of ¼ teaspoon ascorbic acid to ¼ cup cold water.	Add ½ cup sugar for each quart fruit; stir until dissolved.
Avocados	Peel and mash. Add ⅛ teaspoon ascorbic acid to each quart fruit.	Use no sugar.
Blackberries, Boysenberries, Dewberries, Loganberries		
FOR DESSERT	Wash and sort. Handle as little as possible.	pack in 40–50% syrup.
FOR PIES	Wash and sort. Handle as little as possible.	Use ¾ cup sugar for each quart berries.
Blueberries, Elderberries, Huckleberries		
DRY PACK	Sort and wipe clean.	Freeze in single layer, then pack.
FOR DESSERT	Wash and sort.	Pack in 40% syrup, or use ¾ cup sugar for each quart berries.
Cherries, sour		
FOR DESSERT	Sort, stem, and wash. Drain and pit.	Pack in 60–65% syrup.
FOR PIES	Sort, stem, and wash. Drain and pit.	Use ¾ cup sugar for each quart cherries.

Fruit	Preparation	Sugar or Syrup
Cherries, sweet	Prepare very quickly! Sort, stem, wash and drain. Remove pits.	Pack in 40% syrup, with ½ teaspoon ascorbic acid per quart.
Cranberries, whole		
UNSWEETENED	Stem and wash. Dry, pack into containers, seal and freeze.	Use no sugar
SWEETENED	Stem and wash	Pack in 50% syrup.
Currants, whole		
UNSWEETENED	Stem and wash. Dry. Pack into containers, seal and freeze.	Use no sugar.
SWEETENED	Stem and wash.	Pack in 50% syrup, or use ¾ cup sugar for each quart.
Figs	Sort, wash, cut off stems. Peel if desired, slice or leave whole.	Pack in 35% syrup with ¾ teaspoon ascorbic acid for each quart.
	Or, prepare as above, pack into containers. Cover with water with ¾ teaspoon ascorbic acid for each quart.	Use no sugar.
Gooseberries		
FOR DESSERT	Sort, stem, and wash.	Pack in 50% syrup.
FOR PIES OR PRESERVES	Sort, stem, and wash, and pack into containers.	Use no sugar.
Grapefruit	Wash and peel, divide into sections, removing all membranes and seeds.	Pack in 40% syrup with ½ teaspoon ascorbic acid per quart.
Grapes	Wash and stem. Leave seedless grapes whole, cut other grapes in half, remove seeds.	Pack in 40% syrup.
Melon	Cut melon flesh into cubes, balls, or slices.	Pack in 30% syrup.
Nectarines	Sort, wash, and pit fruit. Peel and cut up, if desired, and drop directly into container of syrup with ascorbic acid.	Pack in 40% syrup with ½ teaspoon ascorbic acid for each quart.

Fruit	Preparation	Sugar or Syrup
Oranges, see Grapefruit		
Peaches, halves and slices	Sort, wash, pit, and peel. For best results, peel peaches without blanching.	Pack in 40% syrup with ½ teaspoon ascorbic acid for each quart. or Dissolve ¼ teaspoon ascorbic acid in ¼ cup cold water, sprinkle peaches. Pack with ⅔ cup sugar for each quart of fruit.
Pears	Wash, peel, cut in halves or quarters.	Heat pears in boiling 40% syrup for 1 to 2 minutes. Drain and cool. Pack with cold 40% syrup with ¾ teaspoon ascorbic acid for each quart.
Pineapple	Pare, remove core and eyes. Slice, dice, crush, or cut into wedges. Pack tightly. Seal and freeze without sugar, or in syrup pack.	Pack in 30% syrup made with pineapple juice if available.
Plums, Prunes	Wash, cut in halves or quarters.	Pack in 40–50% syrup with ½ teaspoon ascorbic acid for each quart syrup.
Raspberries	Select fully ripe, juicy berries. Sort, wash and dry. Freeze in a single layer and drypack.	Use ¾ cup sugar for each quart berries; or pack in 40% syrup.
Rhubarb	Choose firm, tender, well-colored stalks with few fibers. Wash, trim, cut into 1- to 2-inch pieces. Heat in boiling water for 1 minute, plunge into cold water.	Pack in 40% syrup.
Strawberries		
WHOLE, DRY PACK	Sort. Wipe clean. Do not hull.	Freeze in single layer; pack without sugar.
WHOLE, WATER PACK	Choose firm ripe berries. Sort, wash, and hull. Pack into containers.	Cover with water with 1 teaspoon ascorbic acid for each quart.
WHOLE, SWEETENED	Sort, wash and hull.	Use ¾ cup sugar for each quart of berries or pack in 50% syrup.
SLICED, SWEETENED	Sort, wash, hull, and slice.	use ¾ cup sugar for each quart of berries.

VEGETABLES FOR FREEZING

Vegetable	Preparation	Blanching Time in Boiling Water
Asparagus	Sort according to thickness of stalk. Wash, snap off tough ends.	Small stalks: 2 minutes. Medium stalks: 3 minutes. Large stalks: 4 minutes.
Beans		
Limas, shell	Shell and blanch: sort according to size, or blanch in pods, shell after cooling.	Small beans or pods: 2 minutes. Medium beans or pods: 3 minutes. Large beans or pods: 4 minutes.
Snap, green or wax	Pick over stringless beans. Wash, remove ends. Cut in 1- to 2-inch lengths or in julienne strips.	3 minutes.
Soybeans	Select, wash. Blanch in pods, cool, squeeze beans out of pods.	5 minutes, in pods.
Beets	Select beets not more than 3 inches across. Wash and sort according to size. Trim, leaving ½-inch stems. Cook until tender. Cool. Peel and cut into slices or cubes, pack and freeze.	Blanching time for small beets: 25–30 minutes. Medium beets: 45–50 minutes.
Broccoli	Select tight dark heads with tender stalks. Wash, peel stalks, and trim. If necessary to remove insects, soak for ½ hour in solution of 4 teaspoons salt to 1 gallon cold water. Split into florets.	3 minutes or steam 5 minutes.
Brussels Sprouts	Trim, remove coarse outer leaves. Wash thoroughly. Sort for size.	Small heads: 3 minutes. Medium heads: 4 minutes. Large heads: 5 minutes.
Carrots	Wash and peel. Leave small carrots whole. Cut others into ¾ inch cubes, thin slices or lengthwise strips.	Whole small: 5 minutes. Diced or sliced: 2 minutes. Strips: 2 minutes.
Cauliflower	Break or cut into 1-inch pieces. If necessary to remove insects, soak for 30 minutes in a solution of salt and water—4 teaspoons salt to 1 gallon of water.	Blanch in salted water (4 teaspoons salt to each gallon of water) for 3 minutes.
Celery	Select crisp stalks, free from coarse strings. Wash thoroughly, trim and cut into 1-inch lengths.	3 minutes.

Vegetable	Preparation	Blanching Time in Boiling Water
Corn: whole kernel, or cream style	Husk, remove silk, and wash. For whole kernel—cut kernels from cob at ⅔ the depth of the kernels. For cream style—cut kernels from cob at center of kernels. Scrape cob to remove juice and heart of kernel. Pack and freeze.	Blanch corn on cob as below. Then cut from cob.
Corn on the Cob	Husk, remove silk, wash and sort ears according to size.	Small ears (1 to 1¼ inches in diam.): 7 minutes. Medium ears (1¼–1½ inches in diam.): 9 minutes. Large ears (over 1½ inches): 11 minutes.
Greens: Beet Greens, Chard, Collards, Kale, Mustard, Spinach, Turnip	Select tender, young leaves. Wash thoroughly. Remove tough stems and imperfect leaves.	Beet greens, kale, chard, mustard, turnip greens: 2 minutes. Collards: 3 minutes. Spinach: 2 minutes. (very young, tender leaves: 1½ minutes.)
Kohlrabi	Select small to medium, young kohlrabi. Cut off tops and roots. Wash, peel, and leave whole or dice in ½-inch cubes.	Whole: 3 minutes. Cubes: 1 minute.
Mushrooms	Sort according to size. Wash in cold water, trim off ends of stems. If larger than 1 inch in diameter, quarter and slice. Dip for 5 minutes in solution of 1 teaspoon lemon juice or 1½ teaspoons citric acid for each pint of water.	Steam whole: 5 minutes. Caps or quarters: 3½ minutes. Slices: 3 minutes.
Okra	Select young, tender green pods. Cut off stems, but do not open pods. Leave whole or slice crosswise.	Small pods: 3 minutes. Large pods: 4 minutes.
Parsnips	Choose small to medium parsnips. Remove tops, wash and peel. Cut into ½-inch cubes or slices.	2 minutes.
Peas, field (black-eyed)	Shell, and pick over, discarding hard peas.	2 minutes.
Peas, green	Shell. Discard hard peas.	1½ minutes.
Peppers, Green	Wash, cut out stems, cut in half, remove seeds. If desired, dice or cut in strips or rings. If peppers are to be used in salads, do not blanch.	Halves: 3 minutes. Strips: 2 minutes.
Peppers, hot	Wash and stem. Pack into small containers, leaving no head space.	No blanching.

Vegetable	Preparation	Blanching Time in Boiling Water
Pimientos	To peel, first roast until skin begins to blacken in a hot oven (400° F) 3 to 4 minutes. Rinse off charred skins in cold water. Drain and pack.	No blanching.
Pumpkin	Select mature pumpkin with fine texture, not stringy. Wash, remove seeds and fibers; dice.	Cook until soft in boiling water, steam, or cook until tender in a pressure cooker, or in the oven. Remove pulp from rind, puree, cool, and pack.
Rutabagas	Cut off tops, wash and peel, cut into ½-inch cubes	2 minutes.
Squash, Summer	Wash, cut into ½-inch slices.	3 minutes.
Squash, Winter, mashed	Prepare like pumpkin.	
Sweet Potatoes	Peel, dip into solution of 1 tablespoon citric acid to each quart of water.	Cook until tender; drain. Roll in sugar if desired.
Sweet Potatoes, mashed	Cook as above; mash.	
Turnips	Wash, peel, dice.	2 minutes.

Food and Health

LOW-FAT AND LOW-CHOLESTEROL DIETS

It is generally agreed that most of us benefit from a fat-restricted diet. Excess calories are stored in the body as fat, which now accounts for 40 percent of the calories in the diet of many Americans. Doctors recommend a general lowering to about 25 to 30 percent. Fats have more than twice as many calories per gram as do proteins and carbohydrates. In addition to fats such as butter and margarine, oil and shortening, there are fats in the tissues of meats and poultry, and in foods such as egg yolks, milk, and nuts, as well as in baked goods, sauces, and other dishes.

Most nutritionists believe that a low-cholesterol high fiber diet is a healthy way to live. Here a distinction is made between fats of different types: saturated fats, which are generally solid at room temperature and are primarily of animal origin, and polyunsaturated fats, which are generally vegetable in origin and are liquid at room temperature.

When an excess of cholesterol in the body is revealed, doctors often recommend reducing or eliminating saturated fats from the diet, and substituting polyunsaturated fats for cooking and table use.

Foods low or lacking in saturated fat content

Chicken, without skin
Cottage cheese (low-fat plain, not creamed)
Egg whites
Farmer cheese
Fish
Fruits

Grains and cereals (barley, cornmeal, farina, oatmeal, rice, wheat flour)
Oils (canola, corn, cottonseed, olive, safflower, sunflower)
Nuts (except Brazil nuts and coconut)
Vegetables
Low or Nonfat Yogurt

Foods high in saturated fat content

Butter
Butterscotch
Cakes and pastries
Caramels
Cheese (except skim milk, low-fat cheese)
Chicken fat
Chocolate candies
Coconut and coconut oil
Egg yolks
Frankfurters and sausages

Fried foods (in solid fats)
Goose fat
Gravies and sauces
Ice cream
Lard
Margarine (ordinary kinds)
Meats
Milk (whole)
Potato chips
Shortenings (hydrogenated)
Soups (creamed types)

For readers who would like to lower their cholesterol, calorie intake, or both, some easy substitutions are available:

- For heavy cream (as an ingredient, not for thinning), use equal amounts of undiluted evaporated milk.
- For light cream, use equal amounts of undiluted evaporated skim milk.
- For butter, use equal amounts of corn oil or safflower margarine. This type of margarine has the same number of calories but the amount of cholesterol is nil.
- For butter, use olive or canola oil. Again, these oils have the same number of calories but no cholesterol.
- Yogurt can be substituted for sour cream. However, yogurt will separate at high temperatures. Make this substitution with only cold preparations.
- Use Yogurt Cheese (page 104) in place of cream cheese.
- Frozen concentrate of apple juice can be used in place of sugar.

Calorie Table*

The Calorie Table is organized into sections by food group to make it easier to compare similar types of foods. Sections for foods that are combinations of several food groups—mixed main dishes and fast-food entrees; soups; and desserts, snack foods, and candy—are also included.

All calorie values in the table were rounded to the nearest 5 calories. The portion sizes listed in the table are in common household units or in pieces of a specified size. All portion sizes are for level measures. If you choose larger or smaller portions than listed, increase or decrease the calorie counts accordingly. The calorie value for a food item does not include calories from any added fat, sugars, sauce, or dressing unless listed with the item.

BREADS, CEREALS, AND OTHER GRAIN PRODUCTS

	Calories		Calories
BREADS		**ROLLS**	
Bagel, plain, 3-inch diameter, one	165	**Croissant,** 4½ × 4 × 1¾ inches, plain,	
Cracked-wheat, 18-slices-per-pound		one	230
loaf, one slice	65	**Dinner,** 2½-inch diameter, one	85
French, 18-slices-per-pound loaf, one		**Frankfurter or hamburger,** one	130
slice	70	**Hard,** medium, one	155
Italian, 18-slices-per-pound loaf, one		**Submarine,** medium, one-half	145
slice	70		
Pita, 5¼-inch diameter, one		**QUICK BREADS, BISCUITS,**	
white	125	**MUFFINS, AND BREAKFAST**	
whole-wheat	115	**PASTRIES**	
Pumpernickel, 18 slices-per-pound		**Baking powder biscuit,** 2-inch diame-	
loaf, one slice	60	ter, one	
Raisin, 18-slices-per-pound loaf, one		from home recipe	115
slice	70	from mix	105
Rye, 18-slices-per-pound loaf, one slice	65	from refrigerated dough	55
Vienna, 18-slices per pound loaf, one		**English muffin,** plain, one	130
slice	70	**Muffin,** 2⅝-inch diameter, one	
White		blueberry or corn	165
regular-slice, 18-slices-per-pound loaf,		bran	125
one slice	65	**Pancake,** plain, 5-inch diameter, one	90
thin-slice, 22-slices-per-pound loaf,		**Toaster pastry,** 4¼ × 3 × ⅜ inches, one	210
one slice	55	**Waffle**	
Whole-wheat, 18-slices-per-pound		from mix, 7-inch diameter (about 2¾	
loaf, one slice	60	ounces), one	205

*Information provided by the USDA in "Eating Right: The Dietary Guidelines Way," USDA's ongoing nutrition education program to help consumers put the Dietary Guidelines into practice.

	Calories
Waffle (*cont.*)	
from frozen (about 1½ ounces), one square	100

BREAKFAST CEREALS

	Calories
All-Bran®, 1 ounce (about ½ cup)	70
Bran flakes (40% bran), 1 ounce (about ⅔ cup)	90
Cheerios®, 1 ounce (about 1 cup)	110
Corn Flakes, 1 ounce (about 1 cup)	110
Corn (hominy) grits	
regular or quick, cooked, ¾ cup	100
instant, plain, prepared, 1 packet	80
Corn Pops®, 1 ounce (about 1 cup)	105
Cream of Wheat®	
regular or quick, cooked, ¾ cup	100
instant, cooked, ¾ cup	130
Mix'n Eat, plain, prepared, 1 packet	100
Frosted Flakes®, 1 ounce (about ¾ cup)	110
Frosted Mini-Wheats®, 1 ounce (about ½ cup)	100
Grape-Nut Flakes®, 1 ounce (about ¾ cup)	100
Honey Smacks®, 1 ounce (about ¾ cup)	105
Nature Valley® Granola, 1 ounce (about ¼ cup)	130
Oatmeal or rolled oats	
regular, quick, or instant, cooked, ¾ cup	110
instant, prepared, 1 packet	
plain	105

	Calories
flavored	150
Raisin bran, 1 ounce (about ½ cup)	85
Rice Chex®, 1 ounce (about ¾ cup)	110
Rice Krispies®, 1 ounce (about 1 cup)	110
Shredded wheat, plain	
spoon size, 1 ounce (about ½ cup)	100
large biscuit (about ¾ ounce), one	85
Special K®, 1 ounce (about 1¼ cups)	110
Total®, 1 ounce (about ¾ cup)	100
Wheaties®, 1 ounce (about 1 cup)	100

PASTA AND RICE

	Calories
Macaroni, cooked, plain, ½ cup	75
Noodles, cooked, plain, ½ cup	100
Rice, cooked, plain, ½ cup	
brown	115
instant	90
white	110
Spaghetti, cooked, plain, ½ cup	75

CRACKERS

	Calories
Cheese, plain, 1-inch square, 10	50
Graham, plain, 2½-inch square, two	55
Matzo, 6-inch square, one	120
Oyster, 10	45
Rye wafers, whole-grain, 1⅞ × 3½ inches, two	50
Saltines, 1⅞-inch square, two	25
Sandwich-type, peanut butter or cheese filled, two	80
Snack-type, round, about 2-inch diameter, two	30
Whole-wheat, 1⅞ × 1⅝ inches, two	30

FRUITS

(Calories in cooked and canned fruit include both fruit and liquid.)

FRUITS

Apples, raw, medium, one	80
Applesauce, canned, ½ cup	
unsweetened	50
sweetened	95
Apricots	
raw (about 12 per pound), three	50
canned, halves, ½ cup	
in juice	60
in heavy syrup	105
dried halves, cooked, unsweetened, ½ cup	105

Avocados	
California varieties, 8 ounces each, one-half	140
Florida varieties, 16 ounces each, one-half	245
Bananas, medium, one	105
Blueberries, ½ cup	
raw	40
frozen	
unsweetened	40
sweetened	95
Cantaloup, raw	

	Calories
medium melon, one-fourth	60
cubed, ½ cup	25
Cherries, ½ cup	
raw	
sour	40
sweet	50
canned, sweet	
in juice	70
in heavy syrup	105
Cranberry sauce, ¼ cup	105
Dates, dried, pitted, whole, five	115
Fruit cocktail, canned, ½ cup	
in juice	55
in heavy syrup	90
Grapefruit	
raw, white, pink, or red	
medium, one-half	40
sections, ½ cup	35
canned, ½ cup	
in juice	45
in light syrup	75
Grapes, raw, adherent skin (thompson, red flame, tokay, and emperor), ½ cup	55
Honeydew melon, raw	
6- to 7-inch melon, one-eighth	55
cubed, ½ cup	30
Kiwifruit, raw, medium, one	45
Nectarines, raw, medium, one	65
Oranges, raw, medium, one	60
Peaches	
raw	
whole, medium, one	40
sliced, ½ cup	35
canned, ½ cup	
in juice	55
in light syrup	70
in heavy syrup	95
dried halves, cooked, unsweetened, ½ cup	100
frozen, sliced, sweetened, ½ cup	120
Pears	
raw, medium, one	100
canned, ½ cup	
in juice	60
in heavy syrup	100
Pineapple	
raw, diced, ½ cup	40

	Calories
canned	
crushed, tidbits, or chunks, ½ cup	
in juice	75
in heavy syrup	100
slices, two	
in juice	55
in heavy syrup	75
Plantains, sliced, cooked, ½ cup	110
Plums	
raw, medium, one	35
canned, ½ cup	
in juice	75
in heavy syrup	115
Prunes	
dried, cooked, unpitted, ½ cup	
unsweetened	130
sweetened	150
dried, uncooked, five	85
Raisins, 1 snack pack, ½ ounce (1½ tablespoons)	40
Raspberries, ½ cup	
raw	30
frozen, sweetened	130
Rhubarb, cooked, sweetened, ½ cup	140
Strawberries, ½ cup	
raw, sliced	25
frozen, sweetened, sliced	110
Tangerines, raw, medium, one	35
Watermelon, raw	
wedge or slice (about 1¼-pound piece), one	90
diced, ½ cup	25

FRUIT JUICES
(A 6-fluid-ounce serving is ¾ cup)

	Calories
Apple juice or cider, canned or bottled, 6 fluid ounces	85
Apricot nectar, canned, 6 fluid ounces	105
Cranberry juice cocktail, bottled, sweetened, 6 fluid ounces	110
Grape, 6 fluid ounces	
canned or bottled	115
frozen concentrate, sweetened, reconstituted	95
Grapefruit, 6 fluid ounces	
fresh	70
canned	
unsweetened	70

	Calories		Calories
Grapefruit (*cont.*)		**Orange,** unsweetened, 6 fluid ounces	
sweetened	85	fresh or frozen concentrate, reconsti-	
frozen concentrate, unsweetened, re-		tuted	85
constituted	75	canned	80
Lemon, fresh, canned, or bottled, 1		**Pineapple,** canned, unsweetened, 6	
tablespoon	5	fluid ounces	105
Lime, fresh, canned, or bottled, 1 ta-		**Prune,** canned or bottled, 6 fluid	
blespoon	5	ounces	135

VEGETABLES

(Calories are for cooked vegetables prepared from raw, canned, or frozen.)

VEGETABLES			
Alfalfa sprouts, raw, ½ cup	5	**Celery**	
Artichoke, globe or french, cooked,		raw, stalk 7½ × 1¼ inches, one	5
one medium	55	cooked, diced, ½ cup	10
Asparagus, cooked		**Chives,** chopped, raw, 1 tablespoon	**Trace**
cuts and tips, ½ cup	20	**Collards,** chopped, cooked, ½ cup	10
medium spears, four	15	**Corn,** cooked	
Beans, cooked, ½ cup		on cob, 5-inch ear, one	80
lima (baby or Fordhook)	110	kernels, ½ cup	90
snap (green or yellow)	25	cream-style, ½ cup	90
Bean sprouts, mung, ½ cup		**Cucumbers,** raw, six to eight slices	10
raw	15	**Eggplant,** cubed, cooked, ½ cup	15
cooked	30	**Endive,** pieces for salad, raw, 1 cup	5
Beets, diced or sliced, cooked, ½ cup	25	**Kale,** chopped, cooked, ½ cup	20
Beet greens, chopped, cooked, ½ cup	20	**Lettuce,** raw	
Broccoli		head (iceberg)	
raw, flowerets, three	10	pieces for salad, 1 cup	5
cooked		wedge, ⅙ of 6-inch head	10
chopped, ½ cup	25	looseleaf, pieces for salad, 1 cup	5
5-inch spears, three	30	**Mushrooms**	
Brussels sprouts, cooked		raw	
medium sprouts, four	35	one medium	5
½ cup	30	pieces, ½ cup	10
Cabbage, ½ cup		cooked, pieces, ½ cup	20
raw		**Mustard greens,** chopped, cooked, ½	
plain, shredded or sliced	10	cup	10
coleslaw	70	**Okra**	
cooked, shredded	15	3-inch pods, fried, eight	115
Carrots		cooked, sliced, ½ cup	30
raw		**Onions**	
7½ × 1⅛ inches, one	30	raw, chopped, 2 tablespoons	
shredded, ½ cup	25	young green	5
cooked, sliced, ½ cup	35	mature	5
Cauliflower, flowerets		cooked, mature, whole or sliced, ½ cup	30
raw, four	10	**Onion rings,** breaded, frozen, pre-	
cooked, ½ cup	20	pared, 2- to 3-inch diameter	
		rings, two	80

	Calories
Peas, green, cooked, ½ cup	65
Peppers, sweet, green or red	
raw	
chopped, ½ cup	20
ring, 3-inch diameter, ¼-inch thick, one	Trace
cooked, medium, one	20
Potatoes	
au gratin, home-prepared, ½ cup	175
baked, 4¾ × 2⅓ inches, flesh and skin, one	220
boiled without skin	
2½-inch diameter, one	105
diced or sliced, ½ cup	65
french-fried (from frozen), 2- to 3½-inch strips, 10	
fried	160
oven-heated	110
hashed brown (from frozen), ½ cup	155
mashed, ½ cup	
from home recipe	
milk added	80
milk and fat added	115
from dehydrated flakes, milk and fat added	110
puffs, oven-heated, 10	175
salad, home prepared, ½ cup	130
scalloped, home-prepared, ½ cup	120
Pumpkin, canned, ½ cup	30
Radishes, raw, medium, four	5
Sauerkraut, heated, ½ cup	15

	Calories
Spinach	
raw, pieces for salad, 1 cup	5
cooked, chopped, ½ cup	20
Squash, ½ cup	
summer, sliced	
raw	10
cooked	20
winter	
baked, cubed	40
boiled, mashed	45
Sweet potatoes	
baked, 5 × 2 inches, peeled, one	115
candied, piece 2½ × 2 inches, one	145
canned, vacuum or syrup pack, ½ cup	
pieces	90
mashed	115
Tomatoes	
raw, medium, one	25
cooked, ½ cup	25
Tomato sauce, ½ cup	35
Turnips, cubed, ½ cup	
raw	20
cooked	15
Turnip greens, chopped, cooked, ½ cup	15

VEGETABLE JUICES
(A 6-fluid-ounce serving is ¾ cup.)

	Calories
Tomato juice, 6 fluid ounces	30
Vegetable juice cocktail, 6 fluid ounces	35

MEAT, POULTRY, FISH, AND ALTERNATES

(Serving sizes are cooked, edible part.)

BEEF

	Calories
Corned beef, canned, 3 ounces (two slices 4½ × 2½ × ¼ inches)	210
Ground beef, broiled, 3 ounces	
regular	245
lean	230
extra lean	215
Oven-cooked roast, 3 ounces (two slices 4½ × 2½ × ¼ inches)	
relatively fat cuts, such as rib	
lean and fat	225
lean only	165
relatively lean cuts, such as eye of round	

	Calories
lean and fat	205
lean only	155
Pot roast, braised or simmered, 3 ounces (two slices 4½ × 2½ × ¼ inches)	
relatively fat cuts, such as chuck blade	
lean and fat	330
lean only	235
relatively lean cuts, such as bottom round	
lean and fat	225
lean only	190
Steak, sirloin, broiled, 3 ounces (one piece 4½ × 2½ × ½ inches)	

	Calories
Steak, sirloin (*cont.*)	
lean and fat	240
lean only	180
Veal cutlet, broiled or braised, 3 ounces (one piece 4½ × 2½ × ½ inches)	185

LAMB
Ground lamb, broiled, 3 ounces	305
Leg, roasted, 3 ounces (two slices 4½ × 2½ × ¼ inches)	
lean and fat	235
lean only	160
Shoulder chop, broiled, 3 ounces of meat	
lean and fat (from about a 5-ounce chop, as purchased)	285
lean only (from about a 7-ounce chop, as purchased)	175

PORK
Cured
Ham, canned, heated, lean and fat, 3 ounces (two slices 4½ × 2½ × ¼ inches)	160
Ham, cured, roasted, 3 ounces (two slices 4½ × 2½ × ¼ inches)	
lean and fat	205
lean only	135

Fresh
Loin, roasted, 3 ounces (two slices 4½ × 2½ × ¼ inches)	
lean and fat	270
lean only	205
Loin chop, broiled, 3 ounces of meat	
lean and fat (from about a 5-ounce chop, as purchased)	290
lean only (from about a 7-ounce chop, as purchased)	215
Shoulder (picnic), braised, 3 ounces (two slices 4½ × 2½ × ¼ inches)	
lean and fat	295
lean only	210

SAUSAGE AND LUNCHEON MEATS
Bacon, cooked, slices, three (20 slices per pound uncooked)	140

	Calories
Bologna, 2 ounces (two slices 4½ × ⅛ inches)	
beef and pork	180
chicken or turkey	115
Braunschweiger, 2 ounces (two slices 2½ × ⅜ inches)	205
Canadian bacon, cooked, two slices (2 ounces uncooked)	85
Chicken roll, light meat, 2 ounces (two slices 4½ × ⅛ inches)	90
Frankfurter, heated, one (10 per pound unheated)	
beef and pork	150
chicken or turkey	110
Ham, chopped, 2 ounces (two slices 4 × 4 inches)	140
Ham, boiled, 2 ounces (two slices 6¼ × 4 inches)	
regular	90
extra lean	75
Pork sausage	
bulk, cooked, one patty (about 2 ounces uncooked)	100
link, cooked, two links 4 × ⅞ inches (2 ounces uncooked)	95
Salami, 2 ounces (two slices 4½ × ⅛ inches)	140
Vienna sausage, canned, sausages 2 × ⅞ inches, three (about 1¾ ounces)	135

ORGAN MEATS
Beef liver, fried, 3 ounces (one piece 6½ × 2⅜ × ⅜ inches)	185
Chicken liver, cooked	
one liver	45
3 ounces (about four livers)	195

POULTRY
Chicken
fried	
breast half, one medium	
meat only	160
flour-coated, meat and skin	215
batter-dipped or breaded, meat and skin	365
drumstick, one medium	
meat only	80
flour-coated, meat and skin	120

	Calories
batter-dipped or breaded, meat and skin	195
thigh, one medium	
meat only	110
flour-coated, meat and skin	160
batter-dipped or breaded, meat and skin	235
roasted	
breast half, one medium	
meat only	140
meat and skin	190
drumstick, one medium	
meat only	75
meat and skin	110
Turkey, roasted, 3 ounces (three slices 3 × 2 × ¼ inches)	
light meat only	135
light meat and skin	165
dark meat only	160
dark meat and skin	185

FISH AND SHELLFISH

	Calories
Clams, canned, drained, 3 ounces (about five to nine medium)	80
Crabmeat, canned or cooked, 3 ounces (about ⅔ cup)	85
Cod, breaded, fried, 3 ounces	180
Fish, battered, fried, 3 ounces	185
Fish sticks, frozen, reheated, three	175
Flounder, baked or broiled, 3 ounces	115
Haddock, baked or broiled, 3 ounces	110
Ocean perch, breaded, fried, 3 ounces	190
Oysters, breaded, fried, large, three	155
Salmon, 3 ounces	
baked or broiled, red (piece 3 × 1¾ × 1 inches)	145
canned, drained (about ½ cup)	125
Sardines, Atlantic, canned in oil, drained, 3 ounces (about seven medium)	175
Shrimp, 3 ounces	
canned (about 27 medium)	100
french-fried, five large or eight medium	210
Tuna, chunk light, drained, 3 ounces (about ½ cup)	
canned in oil	170
canned in water	110

EGGS

	Calories
Deviled, one large	125
Fried, one large	95
Hard or soft cooked, one large	80
Omelet, plain, one large egg, milk and fat added	105
Poached, one large	80
Scrambled in fat, one large, milk added	105

DRY BEANS AND PEAS

	Calories
Baked beans, canned, ½ cup	
with pork and tomato sauce	155
with pork and sweet sauce	140
Black-eyed peas, cooked, drained, ½ cup	95
Chickpeas (garbanzos), cooked, drained, ½ cup	150
Lima, cooked, drained, ½ cup	105
Pinto, cooked, drained, ½ cup	95
Red kidney, canned with liquid, ½ cup	110
White (Navy (pea), Great Northern), cooked, drained, ½ cup	120

NUTS AND SEEDS

	Calories
Almonds, 1 ounce (about 22)	165
Cashews, dry-roasted or oil-roasted, 1 ounce (about 18)	160
Coconut, dried, sweetened, flaked, 2 tablespoons	45
Mixed nuts, with peanuts, 1 ounce (about 20 assorted)	
dry-roasted	165
oil-roasted	175
Peanuts, dry-roasted or oil-roasted, 1 ounce (about 28 whole)	165
Peanut butter, 2 tablespoons	190
Pecans, 1 ounce (about 20 halves)	185
Pistachio nuts, dry-roasted, 1 ounce (about 47)	170
Sesame seeds, 1 tablespoon	50
Sunflower seeds, roasted, hulled, 2 tablespoons	105
Walnuts	
black, chopped, 1 ounce (about ¼ cup)	170
English, 1 ounce (about 14 halves)	180

MILK, YOGURT, AND CHEESE

FLUID MILK

	Calories
Buttermilk, 1 cup	100
Lowfat, no milk solids added, 1 cup	
1% fat	105
2% fat	120
Skim, no milk solids added, 1 cup	85
Whole, 1 cup	150

CANNED MILK

	Calories
Condensed, sweetened, undiluted, ½ cup	490
Evaporated, undiluted, ½ cup	
whole	170
skim	100

MILK BEVERAGES

	Calories
Chocolate milk, 1 cup	
2% fat	180
whole	210
Eggnog, plain, commercial, 1 cup	345
Malted milk, prepared from powder with whole milk, 1 cup	
natural	210
chocolate-flavored	200
Thick shake, commercially prepared, 10 fluid ounces	
chocolate	360
vanilla	355

YOGURT

	Calories
Made from lowfat milk, with added nonfat milk solids	
8-ounce container	
plain	145
flavored	195
fruit varieties	230
6-ounce container	
flavored	145
fruit varieties	175
Made from skim milk, with added nonfat milk solids, plain, 8-ounce container	125
Made from whole milk	
8-ounce container	
plain	140
flavored	230
fruit varieties	270

	Calories
6-ounce container	
flavored	170
fruit varieties	200

CHEESE

	Calories
American	
process	
1-ounce slice	105
1-inch cube	65
shredded, ½ cup (2 ounces)	210
process cheese food	
1-ounce slice	90
1-inch cube	55
1 tablespoon	50
process cheese spread, 1 tablespoon	45
Blue, crumbled, ¼ cup	120
Brick	
1-ounce slice	105
1-inch cube	65
Cheddar	
1 ounce	115
1-inch cube	70
shredded, ½ cup (2 ounces)	225
Colby	
1-ounce slice	110
1-inch cube	70
Cottage cheese, ½ cup	
creamed (4% fat)	110
lowfat (2% fat)	100
dry curd (less than ½% fat)	60
Cream cheese	
1 ounce	100
1-inch cube	55
1 tablespoon	50
Edam or Gouda	
1 ounce	100
1-inch cube	60
Feta, crumbled, ¼ cup	90
Mozzarella, made with whole milk or part skim milk (low moisture)	
1 ounce	80
1-inch cube	50
shredded, ½ cup (2 ounces)	160
Muenster	
1 ounce	105
1-inch cube	65

	Calories		Calories
Parmesan, grated, 1 tablespoon	25	1-inch cube	55
Provolone		shredded, ½ cup (2 ounces)	210
1-ounce slice	100	**Swiss**, process	
1-inch cube	60	1-ounce slice	95
Swiss, natural		1-inch cube	60
1-ounce slice	105	shredded, ½ cup (2 ounces)	185

MIXED DISHES AND FAST FOOD ENTREES

MIXED DISHES

	Calories
Bean salad, sweet-sour dressing, ½ cup	70
Beef and vegetable stew, 1 cup	175
Chili with beans, 1 cup	305
Egg roll, with meat, one	120
Fried rice, with meat, 1 cup	290
Lasagna, piece 2½ × 4 inches, ⅙ of 8-inch square	330
Macaroni and cheese, 1 cup	515
Potpie, frozen, baked, 8 ounces	
beef	540
chicken	495
Quiche Lorraine, ⅛ of 8-inch quiche	470
Spaghetti in tomato sauce with cheese, 1 cup	155
Spaghetti with meat sauce or meat balls and tomato sauce, 1 cup	310

FAST FOOD ENTREES

	Calories
Breakfast sandwich (egg, cheese, Canadian bacon, english muffin), one	385
Cheeseburger, with catsup, mustard, lettuce, tomatoes, pickles, and/or onions	
2-ounce patty (before cooking)	360
4-ounce patty (before cooking)	565
Pizza, ⅛ of 15-inch-diameter pizza	
cheese	255
pepperoni	325
Roast beef sandwich, 2½ ounces meat, without condiments	345
Taco, meat, one	
small	370
large	570

SOUPS

CANNED SOUPS

(Canned, condensed, prepared with equal volume of water unless otherwise stated.)

	Calories
Bean with bacon, 1 cup	170
Beef bouillon, broth, or consommé, 1 cup	15
Beef noodle, 1 cup	85
Chicken broth, 1 cup	40
Chicken noodle, 1 cup	75
Chicken rice, 1 cup	60
Clam chowder, 1 cup	
Manhattan-style	80
New-England-style	
prepared with water	95
prepared with skim milk	130
prepared with whole milk	165
Cream of broccoli, 1 cup	235

	Calories
Cream of chicken, 1 cup	
prepared with water	115
prepared with skim milk	160
prepared with whole milk	190
Cream of mushroom, 1 cup	
prepared with water	130
prepared with skim milk	170
prepared with whole milk	205
Minestrone, 1 cup	80
Pea, 1 cup	
green	165
split, with ham	195
Tomato, 1 cup	
prepared with water	85

	Calories		Calories
Tomato (*cont.*)		**DEHYDRATED SOUPS**	
prepared with skim milk	130	*(One packet, prepared with 6 fluid ounces*	
prepared with whole milk	160	*of water.)*	
Vegetable, 1 cup		**Chicken noodle**	35
with beef, chicken or turkey	80	**Onion**	25
vegetarian	70	**Tomato vegetable**	55

DESSERTS, SNACK FOODS, AND CANDY

CAKES

	Calories
Angelfood cake, without frosting, 1/16 of 10-inch tube cake	145
Boston cream pie, 1/12 of 8-inch round cake	225
Carrot cake, with cream cheese frosting, 1/16 of tube cake	340
Cheesecake, 1/12 of 9-inch round cake	405
Devil's-food or chocolate cake, with chocolate frosting, 1/16 of 8- or 9-inch round 2-layer cake	285
Fruitcake, dark, 1/32 of 7-inch round cake	165
Gingerbread, 1/9 of 8-inch square cake	240
Pound cake, without frosting, 1/16 of loaf 9 × 5 × 3 inches	220
Cupcakes, with frosting, 2¾-inch diameter	
chocolate	155
not chocolate	170
Sponge cake, without frosting, 1/16 of 10-inch tube cake	145
Yellow cake	
without frosting, 1/16 of bundt or tube cake	190
with chocolate frosting, 1/16 of 8- or 9-inch round 2-layer cake	290

COOKIES AND BARS

	Calories
Brownie, with nuts, 2-inch square, one	
without frosting	130
with frosting	175
Chocolate chip cookie, 2-inch diameter, one	50
Fig bar, 1½-inch square, one	55
Oatmeal cookie, with raisins, 2⅝-inch diameter, one	60
Peanut butter cookie, 2⅝-inch diameter, one	80

	Calories
Sandwich cookie, chocolate or vanilla, 1½-inch diameter, one	55
Shortbread cookie, 2-inch diameter, one	75
Sugar cookie, 2½-inch diameter, one	70
Vanilla wafer, 1¾-inch diameter, one	20

PIES

	Calories
One-crust pies, 1/8 of 9-inch pie	
Chocolate cream	405
Custard	285
Lemon meringue	340
Pecan	485
Pumpkin	330
Strawberry	385
Two-crust pies, 1/8 of 9-inch pie	
Apple	455
Blueberry	410
Cherry or peach	405
Fried pies	
Apple	310
Cherry	285

MILK-BASED DESSERTS

	Calories
Custard, baked, ½ cup	130
Ice cream, ½ cup	
regular (about 10% fat)	135
rich (about 16% fat)	175
Ice milk, ½ cup	
hardened	95
soft serve	115
Puddings, ½ cup	
(Prepared from mix with whole milk; puddings prepared with skim milk are about 30 calories less per ½-cup serving.)	
chocolate	
instant	160
regular	160
chocolate mousse	190

	Calories
rice	160
tapioca	130
vanilla	
instant	150
regular	140
Sherbet, ½ cup	135
Yogurt, frozen, ½ cup	105

OTHER DESSERTS

	Calories
Fruit juice bars, frozen, 2½ fluid ounces	70
Gelatin dessert, prepared, plain, ½ cup	70
Popsicle, 3–fluid-ounce size	70

SNACK FOODS

	Calories
Cheese curls or puffs	
10 pieces	85
1-ounce package	160
Corn chips	
10 chips	95
1-ounce package	150
Crackers (see Crackers, page 758)	
Nuts (see Nuts and Seeds, page 763)	
Popcorn, 1 cup	
air-popped	30
popped in vegetable oil	65
Pork rinds, deep-fried, 1 ounce (about 1 cup)	150
Potato chips, regular	
10 chips	105
1-ounce package	145
Pretzels	
Dutch, twisted, 2¾ × 2⅝ inches, one	60
Soft, twisted, one	190
Stick, 2½ inches long, 10	20
Thin, twisted, 3¼ × 2¼ × ¼ inches, five	115

CANDY

	Calories
Caramels, 1 ounce (about three pieces)	

	Calories
chocolate	85
plain	110
tootsie roll, 1¼-ounce roll	140
Chocolate, sweetened	
candy-coated, 10 pieces	
plain	35
with peanut butter	35
with nuts	100
milk (about 1½-ounce bar)	
plain	245
with almonds	235
with rice cereal	215
with peanuts (1¾-ounce bar)	280
semisweet chips, ¼ cup	215
Fondant, 10 pieces	
uncoated	
candy corn	35
mints, pastel (about ⅝-inch square)	75
chocolate-coated	
miniature mints	95
Fruit leather, 1 ounce	80
Fudge, vanilla or chocolate, 1 ounce	
plain	110
with nuts	120
Granola bar (about 1½ ounces), one	
oats, raisins, coconut	195
oats, peanuts, wheat germ	205
Gum drops, 1 ounce (about 8 pieces)	95
Hard candy, 1 ounce (about 5 pieces or 2 lollipops)	105
Jelly beans, 1 ounce (10 pieces about ¾ × ½ inch)	95
Licorice	
bite size, ¼ cup	170
stick, 6½ inches long, one	40
shoestring, 43 inches long, one	70
Marshmallows, 1 ounce (about 1⅛-inch diameter), about four	90

BEVERAGES

(Milk beverages are in the Milk, Yogurt, and Cheese section.
Juices are in the Vegetable and Fruit sections.)

FRUIT DRINKS

	Calories
Fruit-flavored drink, prepared from powder, 8 fluid ounces	
presweetened	
regular	120

	Calories
low calorie	5
sugar added	90
Fruit drinks, canned, 8 fluid ounces	
fruit punch	115
grape or orange	125

	Calories
Lemonade or limeade, frozen concentrate, sweetened, reconstituted, 8 fluid ounces	100

CARBONATED BEVERAGES

	Calories
Club soda, 12-ounce can	0
Cola-type, 12-ounce can	
regular	150
diet	5
Fruit-flavored, 12-ounce can	
regular	150
diet	0
Ginger ale, 12-ounce can	
regular	125
diet	0
Root Beer, 12-ounce can	
regular	150
diet	0

COFFEE AND TEA

	Calories
Coffee and tea, brewed or instant, unsweetened, 6-fluid-ounce cup	Trace
Tea, instant, presweetened mix, 8 fluid ounces	
regular	25
low calorie	5

ALCOHOLIC BEVERAGES

Beer, 12-ounce can or bottle	
regular	150
light	100
Gin, rum, vodka, scotch, or bourbon, 1½-fluid-ounce jigger	105
Wines	
table, red or white, 5-fluid-ounce glass	100
dessert, 3½-fluid-ounce glass	155
coolers, 8-fluid-ounce glass	120

SUGARS, SYRUPS, JAMS, AND JELLIES

Chocolate syrup, 1 tablespoon	
thin type	40
fudge type	70
Honey, 1 tablespoon	65
Jams and preserves, 1 tablespoon	55
Jellies, 1 tablespoon	50
Sugar, granulated or brown, 1 tablespoon	50
Table syrup, 1 tablespoon	55

FATS, OILS, AND CREAMS

FATS AND OILS

Butter or stick margarine	
1 teaspoon or 1 pat	35
1 tablespoon	100
Margarine, soft, 1 teaspoon	
regular	35
diet	15
Table spread, 1 teaspoon	25
Oil, 1 tablespoon	120
Salad dressings, commercial, 1 tablespoon	
regular	
blue or Roquefort cheese	75
buttermilk	55
creamy-type	70
french	65
italian	70
mayonnaise	100
mayonnaise-type	55
russian	75
thousand island	60
low-calorie	
french	20
italian	15
mayonnaise	35
mayonnaise-type	35
thousand island	25

CREAM

Half-and-half (milk and cream), 1 tablespoon	20
Light, coffee or table, 1 tablespoon	30
Sour, 1 tablespoon	30
Whipped, pressurized, 2 tablespoons	20
Whipping, heavy	
unwhipped, 1 tablespoon	50
whipped, 2 tablespoons	50

	Calories			Calories

IMITATION CREAM PRODUCTS
(Made with vegetable fat.)
Creamers

	Calories
liquid, 1 tablespoon	20
powdered, 1 teaspoon	10

Sour dressing (nonbutterfat sour cream), 1 tablespoon — 25

Whipped dessert topping, 2 tablespoons

	Calories
frozen	30
powdered, made with whole milk	20
pressurized	25

CONDIMENTS

	Calories
Barbecue sauce, 1 tablespoon	10
Catsup, 1 tablespoon	20
Gravy, 2 tablespoons	
meat or poultry	20
mushroom	10
Horseradish, 1 tablespoon	5
Mustard, prepared, yellow, 1 teaspoon	5
Olives, canned	
green, stuffed or with pits, four small or three large	15

	Calories
ripe, mission, pitted, three medium or two extra large	15
Pickles	
dill, 3¾ inches long, one	5
sweet gherkin, about 2½ inches long, one	20
Relish, sweet, finely chopped, 1 tablespoon	20
Soy sauce, 1 tablespoon	10
Steak sauce, 1 tablespoon	10
Tartar sauce, 1 tablespoon	75

METRIC CONVERSION CHART

LIQUID AND DRY MEASURE EQUIVALENCIES

Customary	Metric
¼ teaspoon	1.25 milliliters
½ teaspoon	2.5 milliliters
1 teaspoon	5 milliliters
1 tablespoon	15 milliliters
1 fluid ounce	30 milliliters
¼ cup	60 milliliters
⅓ cup	80 milliliters
½ cup	120 milliliters
1 cup	240 milliliters
1 pint (2 cups)	480 milliliters
1 quart (4 cups, 32 ounces)	960 milliliters (.96 liter)
1 gallon (4 quarts)	3.84 liters
1 ounce (by weight)	28 grams
¼ pound (4 ounces)	114 grams
1 pound (16 ounces)	454 grams
2.2 pounds	1 kilogram (1000 grams)

OVEN TEMPERATURE EQUIVALENCIES

Description	°Fahrenheit	°Celsius
Cool	200	90
Very slow	250	120
Slow	300–325	150–160
Moderately slow	325–350	160–180
Moderate	350–375	180–190
Moderately hot	375–400	190–200
Hot	400–450	200–230
Very hot	450–500	230–260

The authors wish to acknowledge the following agencies for their co-operation with *The Settlement Cookbook*:

National Coffee Association of U.S.A., Inc.
U.S.D.A.
National Broiler Council
National Turkey Federation
American Egg Board
Cornell Cooperative Extension Service
Wheat Foods Council
Rice Council of America
National Livestock and Meat Board
U.S.D.A. Human Nutrition Information Service

BIBLIOGRAPHY

Bugialli, Giuliano, *Bugialli on Pasta,* New York, Simon and Schuster, 1988.
Burum, Linda, *Asian Pasta,* Berkeley, Aris Press, 1975.
Child, Julia and Simone Beck, *Mastering the Art of French Cooking,* New York, Alfred A. Knopf, 1979.
Clayton, Bernard, *The Complete Book of Pastry,* New York, Simon and Schuster, 1981.
Cone, Marcia and Thelma Snyder, *Mastering Microwave Cookery,* New York, Simon and Schuster, 1986.
Courtine, Robert J., *Larousse Gastronomique,* Paris, Librarie Larousse, 1984.
Cunningham, Marion, *The Fannie Farmer Cookbook,* New York, Alfred A. Knopf, 13 ed., 1990.
Jaffrey, Madhur, *An Invitation to Indian Cookery,* New York, Vintage Books, 1975.
Johnson, Hugh, *Modern Encyclopedia of Wine,* New York, Simon and Schuster, 1987.
Johnston, Mireille, *The French Family Cookbook,* New York, Simon and Schuster, 1988.
Kafka, Barbara, *Microwave Gourmet,* New York, William Morrow and Co., 1987.
Lang, Jenifer, *Tastings,* New York, Crown Publishers, 1986.
Lin, Florence, *Chinese Regional Cookbook,* New York, Hawthorn Books Inc., 1975.
McClane, A. J., *The Encyclopedia of Fish,* New York, Holt, Rinehart and Winston, 1977.
Olney, Richard, *Time-Life Series,* "The Good Cook", New York, 1982.
Rombauer, Irma S. and Marion Rombauer Becker, *Joy of Cooking,* Indianapolis/New York, The Bobs-Merril Company, Inc., 22 ed., 1981.
Willan, Anne, *French Regional Cooking,* New York, William Morrow and Co., 1981.

INDEX